TRANSPARENCY GAMES

TRANSPARENCY GAMES

HOW BANKERS RIG THE WORLD OF FINANCE

RICHARD FIELD

Published by
Institute for Financial Transparency, LLC

Transparency Games **by Richard Field**

ISBN - 978-0-9903968-0-2 (hardcover)
ISBN - 978-0-9903968-1-9 (paperback)
10 9 8 7 6 5 4 3 2 1
Colophon
Type Fonts:
Adobe Caslon Pro
Frontmatter Titles, Part Titles, Chapter Titles

To my sons and parents who encouraged and supported me over the years as I was experiencing first hand how Wall Street plays the Transparency Games.

CONTENTS

SECTION 4
How Wall Street exploits the fatal flaw in the original FDR Framework

SECTION 5
Original FDR Framework failure: Evidence from the financial crisis

SECTION 6
Opacity made policy response to 2007 financial crisis possible

SECTION 7
The Transparency Label Initiative™ and fixing the global financial system

PREFACE

Introduction

HOW WALL STREET CONQUERED THE WORLD WITHOUT FIRING A SINGLE SHOT

There are events, such as the Space Shuttle Challenger exploding or terrorists flying jets into the World Trade Center, where you remember exactly what you were doing and where you were. For me, one of those events occurred on September 23, 2008, when the United States, the world's only superpower, surrendered to Wall Street without a single shot being fired.

Shortly thereafter, England and the European Union also surrendered.

Why did governments around the world surrender to Wall Street and England's version, The City of London? How could governments around the world allow the bankers to continue rigging the global financial markets and looting Main Street without any resistance?

What happened on September 23, 2008?

On that day, U.S. Treasury Secretary Hank Paulson, accompanied by then Chairman of the Federal Reserve Ben Bernanke, requested from the U.S. Congress an initial payment to Wall Street of $700 billion dollars to buy toxic assets from the largest commercial and investment banks.

In making this request, Secretary Paulson demonstrated the salesmanship and political shrewdness that saw him reach the top of one of the largest investment banks, Goldman Sachs, before becoming Treasury Secretary.

He laid out the case that the U.S. economy and particularly Main Street was facing serious problems if the banks weren't bailed out.

It was not what Mr. Paulson said that gave his argument credibility, but rather Fed Chair Bernanke and his reputation.

Before joining the Federal Reserve Board, Mr. Bernanke had been a Princeton economics professor who prided himself on his studies of the Great Depression. In fact, he called himself a "Great Depression buff".[1] In 2000, he

1 Bernanke, Ben S. (2000), Essays on the Great Depression, Princeton, New Jersey: Princeton University Press, page vii.

published a book, *Essays on the Great Depression*, which included nine articles he coauthored over a period of two decades. He felt these articles presented a "largely coherent view of the causes and propagation of the Depression."[2]

For Secretary Paulson's argument to carry any weight, he needed Fed Chair Bernanke's agreement with his analysis that without using taxpayer funds to bail out the banks, Main Street was facing a second Great Depression. After all, Fed Chair Bernanke had access to the same information as Secretary Paulson, and it was assumed if there was anyone who should be able to assess if this was necessary and the U.S. was potentially heading into a second Great Depression, it was Fed Chair Bernanke.

As Fed Chair Bernanke sat there with his ashen, panic-stricken face, there could be no doubt he truly believed we were headed into a second Great Depression. His visual appearance and testimony sealed the deal.

Congress did not immediately give Mr. Paulson what he wanted. Instead, they waited for over a week before surrendering.

While watching Secretary Paulson's virtuoso performance, a single thought kept recurring to me: What am I missing? Why was the need to surrender to Wall Street for fear of a second Great Depression not credible?

It wasn't credible because in redesigning and rebuilding the financial and banking systems during the Great Depression, the FDR Administration and Congress, seeing the damage caused by an opacity driven financial crisis, took steps to insure the banking system could survive another opacity driven crisis without being explicitly bailed out.

The FDR Administration and Congress actually went further than just redesigning and rebuilding the financial and banking systems. They demonstrated how to use the new financial and banking systems to end an opacity driven crisis and restrain Wall Street.

Why did I know there was no need to surrender to Wall Street, but nobody in the Congressional hearing on that day seemed aware of this fact or was willing to mention it?

At this point, allow me to introduce myself. *Boston Magazine* referred to me as the "Man who would save the economy."[3]

During my career, I worked at the Federal Reserve in the area that developed the monetary policies that ended inflation in the early 1980s, and at a Too Big to Fail bank in its Asset/Liability Management and Capital Management areas. Subsequently, I designed, developed, and patented an information system to bring valuation transparency to structured finance securities.

---

2 ibid, page viii.

3 Kix, Paul (2008, February), The Man Who Would Save the Economy, Boston Magazine, http://www.bostonmagazine.com/2008/01/the-man-who-would-save-the-economy

In short, I have exactly the background you would expect of someone who publicly said before the financial crisis that we have an opacity problem in the global financial system. The only proven solution for an opacity problem is valuation transparency. Why is this the only proven solution? It is only with valuation transparency that market participants can throw off the shackles of fear caused by opacity in the financial system. Market participants need the information provided by valuation transparency so they can know what they own or are thinking of buying. Market participants need the information so they can adjust the size of their investments so they do not have a greater exposure than they can afford to lose. Knowing what you own is the source of confidence in the financial system. It involves independently assessing risk and reward before and after making an investment decision. By definition, an investment provides valuation transparency if market participants have access in an appropriately, timely manner to all the useful, relevant information needed so this independent assessment can be made.

As I described it in a *Bloomberg* article[4] in late 2007, the problem at the heart of the global financial system was investors could not independently assess the risk of or value opaque, toxic subprime mortgage-backed securities. Why could they not independently assess the risk of or value these securities? It was the equivalent of trying to assess the risk of or value the contents of a brown paper bag. The solution was and still is to eliminate the opacity of these securities by providing valuation transparency so these deals can be assessed and valued as if the contents were in a clear plastic bag.

By September 2008, the recognized opacity problem in the global financial system had expanded. Investors now realized that assessing the risk of and valuing a bank or broker-dealer was the equivalent of trying to assess the risk of or value the contents of a black box. Just like with the mortgage-backed securities, the solution was and still is to eliminate opacity so the banks and broker-dealers can be assessed and valued as if the contents were in a clear glass box.

By September 2008, the broader solution for moderating and ending our current financial crisis was, and still is, to eliminate opacity in all the opaque areas of the financial system, so these areas can be assessed and valued as if the contents were in a clear container.

In late 2008, I observed until valuation transparency was brought to all the opaque corners of the global financial system, the global economy, absent ongoing fiscal and monetary stimulus, would remain in a downward spiral. Years later, nothing of substance has been done to bring valuation transparency to any

---

4 Salas, Caroline (2007, December 4), Subprime Seizure Solution May Be in Hospital Bills, Bloomberg, http://www.bloomberg.com/apps/news?pid=newsarchive&sid=a_gBF9OjtfQI

of the opaque corners of the financial system. As a result, not surprisingly, we are still relying on ongoing fiscal and monetary stimulus to prevent the global economy sliding into a deep recession.

I am writing this book in the hope that we will recognize there was, and still is, no need to surrender to Wall Street. Every day our nation's policymakers have to choose to continue to surrender to Wall Street and put the welfare of the bankers ahead of the welfare of its other citizens. Policymakers could make the choice today, tomorrow, or Tuesday of next week, to put Main Street ahead of Wall Street. In making this choice the crisis could be ended.

Every day our policymakers choose to continue to surrender to Wall Street, and follow policies to protect Wall Street, the same negative results occur. The real economy is further hollowed out, the growth in inequality between the rich and poor increases, our social contract is further eroded, and our nation is fundamentally weakened.

Every day our policymakers have the option to remove Wall Street's shackles from the real economy. By doing this they can restrain Wall Street so that it engages primarily in activities that support the real economy.

Every day our policymakers could choose to bring valuation transparency to all the opaque corners of the financial system. By choosing valuation transparency, our policymakers would be choosing an eloquent, proven solution for ending the global financial crisis. By choosing valuation transparency, our policymakers would also address many of the problems including Too Big to Fail, banker misbehavior, and regulatory capture that confront us today.

Fortunately, we don't have to wait any longer for our policymakers to choose Main Street over Wall Street. I will present a solution in this book whereby Main Street can bring valuation transparency to all the opaque corners of the financial system.

In writing this book, I hope to answer a number of still unanswered questions about the financial crisis. In the process, I hope to explain what valuation transparency is capable of doing, and what it cannot do.

- Why did the financial crisis happen? Does an analysis of the root causes of the global financial crisis show there was one primary cause that expressed itself through a host of related symptoms or were there several underlying causes?
- Are the financial reforms and regulations introduced since the beginning of the financial crisis likely to be effective at preventing another financial crisis?
- What will it take to restore trust and confidence in the financial system?
- What will it take to end the current global financial crisis?

- Why have fiscal stimulus and extraordinary monetary policy measures not restored a self-sustaining recovery or confidence in the financial system?
- What policy responses were, and still are, available to the politicians and financial regulators to respond to our financial crisis? There are two basic policy responses: the Japanese Model, and the Swedish Model. The Japanese Model favors Wall Street over Main Street. The Swedish Model favors Main Street over Wall Street.
- Why was the Japanese Model chosen as the policy response to the financial crisis? The Japanese Model is known to have two fundamental flaws. First, nowhere it has been tried has it ever succeeded in ending a financial crisis, and then started a self-sustaining economic recovery. Second, it maximizes both the short- and long-term negative impacts of a financial crisis on the real economy and its citizens.
- Why has the Swedish Model still not been pursued? The Swedish Model has a long record of successfully ending financial crises while minimizing the negative impact on the real economy and taxpayers. It was first used by the FDR Administration, and succeeded in ending the worst of the Great Depression.
- What will it take to return to a global economy where we are no longer confronted with what Professor Paul Krugman calls a choice between unsustainable bubbles or endless depression?

To explain why restoring transparency to all the opaque corners of the global financial system will achieve more than all the complex regulations and regulatory oversight adopted since the beginning of the financial crisis, *Transparency Games* is broken down into seven sections.

The First Section

The First Section provides an overview of how our financial system and the tools to address a financial crisis have evolved since 1900. There were two financial crises, the Panic of 1907 and the Great Depression, which resulted in the creation of tools for responding to a financial crisis. These tools included the creation of both a lender of last resort and a safety valve in the financial system to protect the real economy from excess debt in the financial system. Together, these tools dramatically changed how policymakers could respond to a financial crisis compared to the 1800s. Specifically, these tools allowed policymakers to protect Main Street and the real economy should a financial crisis occur. Subsequently, there were several smaller crises, like the Less Developed Country Debt crisis and the collapse of Continental Illinois, which allowed Wall Street and the City to capture these tools. By the time our financial crisis hit, it would be Wall Street and the City that were protected by these tools and not, as originally intended, Main Street and the real economy.

The Second Section

The Second Section looks at how our financial and banking systems are designed to work under the FDR Framework. The FDR Framework was put in place in response to the stock market crash at the beginning of the Great Depression. It builds upon the Federal Reserve's lender of last resort role and added a safety valve in the financial system to the policymakers' toolkit for handling a financial crisis. More importantly, the FDR Framework also addressed the issue of preventing a financial crisis in the first place. It did this by adding both a regulatory infrastructure and the philosophy of disclosure to the principle of *caveat emptor* (buyer beware) based financial and banking systems.

Under the original FDR Framework, the government was responsible for implementing the philosophy of disclosure and ensuring market participants have access to valuation transparency for every publicly traded security. Valuation transparency has two vital roles. First, it is the necessary and sufficient condition for the invisible hand of the market to operate properly. Without it, one or both parties to a transaction are blindly gambling and, as a result, there is no reason to think the result of the transaction is the efficient allocation of resources. Second, valuation transparency is necessary for market discipline. Under the FDR Framework, *caveat emptor* gives market participants the incentive to use the information disclosed under valuation transparency to assess the risk of each of their exposures and practice self-discipline to limit the size of each exposure to what they can afford to lose. The ongoing adjustment by investors of the amount of exposure based on changes in the risk of each exposure results in market discipline. Market discipline is the primary means of restraining bank risk taking.

Under the FDR Framework, it is recognized that regulatory discipline is a complement to, but never an adequate substitute for, market discipline. There were several reasons why regulatory discipline complements market discipline including regulators are always susceptible to political pushback that weakens the enforcement of regulations.

The original FDR Framework relied on regulators to ensure valuation transparency. As shown by the major financial crises since the Great Depression, the framework's dependence on regulators to ensure valuation transparency was a fatal flaw. To update the FDR Framework for the 21st century and beyond, I introduce the solution for permanently fixing this flaw.

The Third Section

The Third Section looks at the seeds of our current financial crisis. By looking at previous financial crises, we can see how the fatal flaw of a reliance on financial regulators to ensure valuation transparency undermined the original FDR Framework, particularly as it was applied to the Too Big to Fail banks.

One crisis in particular, the collapse of banking giant Continental Illinois, represented the culmination of banks becoming opaque. It also highlighted how regulators react to each financial crisis by substituting additional complex regulations and regulatory oversight for valuation transparency and market discipline. The Continental Illinois crisis is special because it represented a preview of our current crisis right down to the adoption of the Too Big to Fail policy.

The Fourth Section

The Fourth Section looks at how Wall Street and the City bankers were able to reintroduce opacity into the global financial system for both themselves and the products they sell. They did this by taking advantage of the original FDR Framework's reliance on regulators to ensure investors have access to valuation transparency. The section also clears up all the misperceptions that surround valuation transparency. Wall Street's Opacity Protection Team created these misperceptions, like investors are stupid and lazy, to justify opacity.".

The Fifth Section

The Fifth Section reviews the findings of international investigations conducted in Ireland, the UK, and the U.S., into the causes of the financial crisis that began on August 9, 2007. These investigations confirmed the reliance on regulators to ensure valuation transparency both for banks, and the financial products they sold was the fatal flaw in the original FDR Framework.

These investigations also showed why regulatory discipline was always, and everywhere, an inadequate substitute for market discipline.

When regulatory discipline is the first line of defense, it leaves us prone to a financial crisis that the regulators, who failed to prevent the financial crisis, will make the taxpayer pay for.

The Sixth Section

The Sixth Section looks at how opacity made possible the policy choice between the Japanese and Swedish Models for responding to our current financial crisis. Under the Japanese Model, policies are adopted that favor Wall Street over Main Street. The goal of the Japanese Model is the preservation of the existing banks.

It assumes saving these banks also saves the real economy. Under the Swedish Model, policies are adopted that favor Main Street over Wall Street. The goal of the Swedish Model is the protection of the real economy. It assumes that saving the real economy also saves as much of the banking system as is necessary to support the real economy. This section shows the global financial system is designed to support pursuing the Swedish Model. It also shows why pursuing the Swedish Model is needed if we are to end our financial crisis.

The Seventh Section

The Seventh Section looks at how the investor led Transparency Label Initiative™ would fix the global financial system. In addition, it would also prevent opacity driven financial crises for the 21st century and beyond.

This section contains three case studies and shows how the presence of valuation transparency would have prevented all three:

- Anglo Irish Bank: Bankers cynically bankrupting Ireland
- JPMorgan's "London Whale" trade: Regulators missed it
- Libor interest rate: Bankers manipulating the price of money for their own benefit

Before going on, I want to make an observation. The global financial crisis that began on August 9, 2007, and the subsequent policy response ended trust in the financial markets, the banks, the regulators, the politicians, and the economists.

My goal in writing this story is to focus on what needs to be done to restore trust, particularly in the financial markets and the global banking system.

There are two primary benefits of restoring trust in the financial markets and the global banking system. First, it starts a self-sustaining recovery in the real economy. Second, it ends the need for both extraordinary monetary policy and fiscal stimulus on an ongoing basis.

SECTION 1

RIGGING THE GLOBAL FINANCIAL MARKETS AND LOOTING MAIN STREET

Chapter 1

A CENTURY OF FINANCIAL CRISES AND THE EVOLUTION OF THE GLOBAL FINANCIAL SYSTEM

The global financial crisis began on August 9, 2007, when BNP Paribas suspended three funds because it couldn't value the opaque subprime mortgage-backed securities the funds had invested in. Since then, policymakers have faced the choice of two well-worn playbooks for how to respond.

The first playbook is the Japanese Model under which policies are adopted that favor Wall Street over Main Street. The goal of the Japanese Model is the preservation of the existing banks. It assumes saving these banks also saves the real economy. Policymakers protect the banks in a number of ways, including by injecting taxpayer funds into the banks and by not requiring them to recognize their existing losses. This allows the banks to report income at a time when they should be recognizing losses on their existing exposures. Naturally, so long as the banks report income, banker bonuses are also protected and paid out.

However, as Sheila Bair, the former head of the FDIC, observed,

> "I think the bailouts saved the [huge financial institutions from Citigroup to Goldman Sachs]. We didn't save the economy."[5]

The second playbook is the Swedish Model under which policies are adopted that favor Main Street over Wall Street. The goal of the Swedish Model is the protection of the real economy. It assumes that saving the real economy also saves as much of the banking system as is necessary to support the real economy. One way policymakers protect the real economy is by eliminating the excess debt in the financial system as quickly as possible. This minimizes the damage to the real economy caused by this debt.

---

5 St. Anthony, Neal (2014, April 14), Bair says bailouts saved banks, not the economy, *Star Tribune*, http://www.startribune.com/business/254991831.html

To date, policymakers have chosen the Japanese Model playbook. This choice was made despite the fact that throughout history policies that put Wall Street ahead of Main Street have never worked to end a financial crisis and simply undermine trust in the financial markets and the banks. There is no reason to think protecting banker bonuses is good for anyone other than the bankers. There is no reason to believe that this time it will be different.

On the other hand, responding to a financial crisis with policies that put Main Street before Wall Street has consistently been shown to work to end a financial crisis, restore trust in the financial markets and the banks, as well as prevent another crisis from occurring. There is reason to think requiring banks to recognize their losses on the excess debt in the global financial system benefits everyone except the bankers. As Jens Weidmann, the head of Germany's central bank, observed,

> Moreover, looking at the experiences with debt crises in Scandinavia and Japan in the 1990s, there is much to be said for not putting off the balance sheet repair process.[6]

Why were policymakers able to choose to pursue the Japanese Model? Given the subsequent struggles of the real economy and the fact they are not locked into continuing to pursue the Japanese Model, why haven't policymakers changed to the Swedish Model? Opacity.

Opacity has been the major factor throughout history in every financial crisis and the response to the crisis. We can see this by looking at the major financial crises since 1907 that shaped our current global financial system. The following table lists both the relevant crises and the policy response.

---

6 Weidmann, Jens (2014, April 7), Stable banks for a Stable Europe, speech at the 20th German Banking Congress, Berlin, BIS. http://www.bis.org/review/r140415b.htm?utm_content=buffer8af00&utm_medium=social&utm_source=twitter.com&utm_campaign=buffer

Table 1: The crises that shaped our global financial system

Crisis	Policy Response
The Panic of 1907	Creation of the Federal Reserve
The Great Depression	Adoption of the philosophy of disclosure Passage of deposit insurance
1937 Recession	Dependence on bank supervision as banks exempted from disclosing risks
Continental Illinois in 1984	Adoption of the Too Big to Fail policy Acceptance of Policy of Deceit
Less Developed Country Debt Crisis 1982-1987	Adoption of Policy of Secrecy Cures All
US Savings & Loan Crisis 1980s — early 1990s	Acceptance of Terribly Rotten Accounting Principles (TRAP)
Financial Crisis of 2007 - Anglo Irish Bank - JPMorgan's London Whale trade - Libor Interest Rate	Implementation of Japanese Model

The presence of opacity in all these financial crises is not surprising, as opacity is the necessary condition for a financial crisis to occur.

Why is opacity the necessary condition?

With valuation transparency, investors have the information they or third party experts they trust need to evaluate their investments' risks and value. Based on this evaluation, investors can adjust the amount of their investments to what they can afford to lose or how much they want to risk. Valuation transparency gives investors the information they need to make informed decisions.

However, with opacity investors have to trust without being able to independently verify what they have been told by supposedly credible sources like financial regulators or credit rating firms. As a result, the adjustment happens all at once when investors discover the investment is much riskier or less valuable than what they had been led to believe.

A financial crisis occurs when this abrupt adjustment happens across a large part of the financial system. Depositors and other short-term creditors begin withdrawing their money from their banks, which can lead to bank failures. If the crisis is severe enough credit is tightened and economic growth is affected because companies can't borrow. A financial crisis continues until valuation transparency is brought to all the opaque corners of the financial system. Only then can investors assess and adjust the amount of their investments to what they can afford to lose given their risk/reward assessment.

The Panic of 1907: A turning point in how financial crises are handled

While there were a number of major financial crises before the Panic of 1907, this crisis is notable for two reasons.

First, it was a classic financial panic. Investors lost trust in both opaque trust companies and then their banks. As a result, short-term creditors began withdrawing all their money, and the opaque trust companies failed.

Behind this classic financial panic there was an immediately identifiable trigger. Specifically, it was concentrated in the opaque trust companies that in 1907 performed most of the functions of banks, but were allowed to invest in riskier assets and hold much less cash to meet client requests for funds. Once doubt was raised about the trust companies' solvency, panic spread as opacity hid the facts and prevented anyone from assessing the on-going viability of the trust companies. The panic didn't end until valuation transparency replaced opacity so banks could evaluate the trust companies' collateral, and lend sufficient funds to end the panic.

Second, it was the last major crisis without a lender of last resort. While valuation transparency limited the withdrawal of funds at the large New York City banks, the Panic of 1907 showed there was also a need for a lender of last resort to provide funds to healthy financial institutions during periods of panic. The creation of the Federal Reserve in 1913 provided a lender of last resort that could, and would, lend the healthy financial institutions the funds they needed to meet investor withdrawals. The creation of the Federal Reserve represented a fundamental change in how a financial crisis could be responded to that lessens the impact of a crisis on the real economy.

The Great Depression: Banishing Opacity

The next major financial crisis was the Great Depression. In addressing this crisis, the FDR Administration established a balance between self-discipline, market discipline, and regulatory discipline. This created a financial system that over the next seven decades was not only efficient in how it allocated resources, but was also stable and resilient to unexpected surprises. The Great Depression was notable for several reasons.

First, it too began in an opaque part of the financial system. In this case, it was the stock market where the lack of disclosure left investors blindly gambling.

While blindly gambling tends to work out well for Wall Street, it doesn't tend to work out too well for investors. On the other hand, when investors have the information they need to make a fully informed investment decision, it tends to work out well for investors, and Wall Street still makes money.

Philosophy of Disclosure

Providing investors with the information they needed was achieved with the adoption of the philosophy of disclosure. Under this principle, the government was responsible for ensuring investors had access to all the useful, relevant information in an appropriate, timely manner so they could independently assess this information and make a fully informed decision. The cost of disclosure was paid by the issuer of the security, as they were the one's who benefited from selling risk to the investors.

The philosophy of disclosure is the foundation for our current global financial system. Using information made available through disclosure, investors are able to know what they own and willingly accept responsibility for all gains and losses on their investments. With a clear plastic bag view of the contents of each investment, investors can independently assess the risk and value of each investment. Knowing the risk/reward tradeoff, investors can engage in self-discipline, and limit the amount of their exposure to any investment to what they can afford to lose based on their perception of the investment's risk.

Market discipline is the result of investors engaging in self-discipline, and over time making decisions to adjust their investment exposures based on changes in how they assess each investment's risk and reward. Specifically, as the risk of an investment increases, investors both demand a higher return and reduce the size of their exposure to keep the exposure within what they can afford to lose given the level of risk. Management responds to the higher cost and reduced availability of funds by restraining its risk taking.

Second, the role of banks was fundamentally altered with the decision to provide deposit insurance. Specifically, it allowed viable banks suffering temporary financial problems to survive. A viable bank is one with a sustainable business model that allows it to generate more in interest income and fees than it spends in interest and operating expenses. Before the government deposit guarantee, even viable banks suffering temporary financial problems went out of business as depositors removed their funds. With deposit insurance, depositors no longer removed their funds. As a result, so long as a bank is viable, it can continue in operation and support the real economy. Recovering banks can provide the new credit the real economy needs to grow.

This ability of banks to recover from even major credit or investment losses represented a fundamental change in both the response to a financial crisis, and its impact on the real economy. By default, it made bank capital accounts the safety valve to protect the real economy from the damage excess debt in the financial system can cause. Banks protect the real economy and minimize any potential damage to it by recognizing upfront the losses on the excess debt.

The ability of banks to act as a safety valve contrasts sharply with the experience from centuries of previous financial crises. In these crises, it took years for the real economy to recover and work through the initial set back and subsequent harmful effects caused by the overhang of excess debt. Concentrating the excess debt's destruction on the banks' book capital levels was appropriate since it was the bankers who benefited by creating this excess debt in the first place, and their shareholders who failed to restrain them. The ability of banks to recover from even major losses also eliminated the need for a taxpayer funded bank bailout. After recognizing the losses, banks could use their power of recovery to rebuild their book capital accounts over time.

Third, regulatory discipline was recognized as always a complement to, and never a replacement for market discipline. Market discipline is the "cop on the beat"[7] restraining risk taking at each firm and regulatory discipline is the "fire warden"[8] making sure the whole system doesn't burn down. While regulatory oversight and complex regulations can provide the illusion of safety, they are at best a safety net in case market discipline fails.

There are several reasons why regulations are at best a safety net. This includes the fact that the writer and enforcer of these regulations, the regulators, report to politicians, and will always be susceptible to political pushback. Because of the fear of political pushback, regulators will not restrain bank risk taking when everything is going well. Investors, on the other hand, are not worried about political pushback. They are worried about the risk of their investment. As a result, it is market discipline driven by each investor's self-discipline that operates to limit risk taking by bank management when everything appears to be going well.

In addition, by not substituting regulatory discipline for market discipline, regulators are kept out of the business of allocating capital across the real economy. The allocation of capital, both its price and quantity, is left to the investors and reflects what the investors are willing to lose money on. Included in these investors are the banks themselves. The banks are responsible for the losses on their investments in risky assets like loans or securities. If the banks lose

---

7 McGrane, Victoria (2014, November 21), N.Y. Fed President Dudley: I'm More of a Fire Warden, Not a Cop on the Beat, Wall Street Journal, http://blogs.wsj.com/economics/2014/11/21/n-y-fed-president-dudley-im-more-of-a-fire-warden-not-a-cop-on-the-beat/

8 ibid

money, this affects the investors in the banks. As a result, investors in the banks have an incentive to exert market discipline to restrain the banks' risk-taking by limiting their exposure to the banks to what the investors can afford to lose.

Finally, attempting to restrain bank risk-taking using regulations requires hundreds of complex regulations. These regulations must cover everything from restricting how much risk a bank can take on from a single borrower, to how much in easily resold assets a bank must hold so it can meet an unexpected demand for funds. Each of these regulations represents a technocratic solution for restricting a type of risk that the banks face.

There is a great deal of uncertainty about the analytical underpinnings of these regulations, and as a result, they are prone to failure. This tendency for complex regulations to fail is best illustrated by the failure of the Irish banking system at the beginning of our current financial crisis. The Irish bank regulators relied on complex capital requirements that linked the amount of risk each bank took to what the regulators thought was each bank's ability to absorb losses. It turned out the size of the losses greatly exceeded what the complex regulation assumed was possible. For all these reasons and more, the choice was made by the FDR Administration to emphasize ensuring banks provided valuation transparency, rather than relying on regulatory oversight and complex regulations.

Seven decades of regulatory failure to restrain opacity

The policy responses to each major financial crisis since the Great Depression have all worked to undermine the philosophy of disclosure based financial and banking systems that emerged from the Great Depression. Each of these financial crises occurred because opacity crept back into some corner of the financial system. Yet, the response was not to replace the brown paper bags of opacity that caused the crisis with the clear plastic bags of valuation transparency. Rather, each response left the brown paper bags of opacity untouched, and focused on giving financial regulators yet another chance to use ever more regulatory oversight and complex, failure prone regulations to prevent the next financial crisis. The ongoing series of financial crises showed the response of more regulatory oversight and increasingly complex, failure prone regulations didn't work. It didn't work for the reasons already discussed and that everyone knew of in advance.

The response of more regulatory oversight and complex, failure prone regulations had three additional negative consequences. First, the cost of each financial crisis escalated dramatically from the preceding crisis. Second, it completely undermined the philosophy of disclosure based financial systems with its collective assessment of risk, and replaced it with a financial system dependent on the regulators and their risk assessment. The dependence on only the regulators' risk assessment distorted both self-discipline and market discipline in ways that made both the financial and banking systems far more prone to a crisis. Third, it prevented bank capital accounts from being used as a safety valve when the current financial crisis hit and from protecting the real economy from the fallout of the excess debt in the financial system. As a result, the real economy bore the pain of our current financial crisis, and not the banks and bankers.

The first step in moving towards a dependence on regulators and complex failure prone regulations was the 1937 Recession. Despite the fact it was not caused by banks providing transparency into their current exposure details, the Federal Reserve insisted the banks be granted relief from this on-going disclosure requirement.

The Collapse of Continental Illinois

The collapse of Continental Illinois National Bank and Trust Company in 1984 represented a preview of our current financial crisis. A Congressional hearing into the collapse and subsequent bailout of the bank raised several issues, including the need to ensure banks provided valuation transparency. Had the financial regulators addressed these issues, or at a minimum, just gotten one issue addressed and required the banks to provide valuation transparency, it would have prevented our current financial crisis.

Before its collapse, Continental Illinois had a reputation as a conservatively run, well-managed bank. This reputation survived its decision to grow into one of the largest banks in the world. To do so, meant increasing its risk by growing its loan portfolio and funding this growth with uninsured deposits. There are two ways for a bank to grow a loan portfolio: let it grow at the rate total loans in the economy are growing, which wouldn't achieve Continental Illinois' goal, and/or try to steal market share. When a loan portfolio grows at the growth rate of total loans in the economy, its risk characteristics tend to be fairly stable. When a loan portfolio grows faster than the growth rate of loans in general, its risk characteristics tend to change, and it tends to become much riskier, since it's easier to gain market share by making more high-risk loans. This is what Continental Illinois did.

By the time Continental Illinois engaged in the strategy of becoming one of the largest banks in the world, banks were no longer providing valuation transparency or disclosing their current exposure details. Rather, Continental Illinois and the other banks disclosed a summary of their current exposure details that allowed them to hide the true amount of risk they were taking. Without current exposure details, investors could not assess the risk of its loans or exert market discipline on it to restrain its risk taking. As a result, the only restraint on Continental Illinois' risk-taking was regulatory discipline. Because the bank was doing so well, regulatory discipline was weakly enforced. However, even if it had been strongly enforced, there is no reason to believe regulatory discipline by itself would have prevented the bank's collapse.

The exact same story played out with our largest banks in the run-up to our current financial crisis. Opacity prevented investors from exerting market discipline to restrain risk taking, and weakly enforced regulatory discipline was inadequate to prevent their failure.

Continental Illinois also highlighted the risk of funding an opaque bank with funds from uninsured short-term creditors. Banks are susceptible to the uninsured sources of funding engaging in a classic financial panic and asking for their money back *en masse*. Because of the run on Continental Illinois, financial regulators were aware of the need for requiring banks to provide valuation transparency. Financial regulators put it on their to do list, but failed to do anything about it.

Too Big to Fail

The response by the financial regulators to the collapse of Continental Illinois was to adopt the policy of Too Big to Fail. They put the taxpayers at risk by guaranteeing the uninsured short-term creditors out of concern over financial contagion, and the potential for the fire sale of assets. Financial contagion is the domino effect when the collapse of one bank triggers the collapse of other banks that have too much exposure to the first bank. Financial contagion occurs when there is opacity. Banks cannot assess the risk of each bank they do business with, and as a result cannot engage in self-discipline to limit their exposure to what they can afford to lose. In justifying the use of taxpayer funds, the financial regulators cited the possibility the failure of this $44 billion bank would cause a very significant national, or even international, financial crisis. In our current financial crisis, financial regulators used the same type of argument for why taxpayer funds were needed to guarantee the uninsured investors, and bailout the Too Big to Fail banks. This time the financial regulators argued it was to save us from a second Great Depression. After Continental Illinois, financial regulators were aware of the need to end the policy of Too Big to Fail, but again they failed to do so.

Finally, because the veil of opacity hid Continental Illinois' true financial condition, the financial regulators faced a choice: implement a policy of deceit or restore valuation transparency. The financial regulators chose the policy of deceit over requiring the bank to provide valuation transparency.

As a precursor to the stress tests claims the financial regulators have made throughout our current financial crisis, they issued a press release hoping to convince market participants the health of Continental Illinois was better than it actually was. Naturally, the press release didn't work for two predictable reasons: market participants didn't have the information they needed to verify what the government said, and the lack of disclosure of the needed information was a red flag waving saying something was being hidden. Like the stress tests, all the press release succeeded in doing was creating moral hazard and the obligation to protect the uninsured investors from loss using taxpayer funds. Financial regulators were aware they were promoting an investment in Continental Illinois, and that this both created a moral hazard and undermined their credibility. The financial regulators put ending the promotion of an investment in a bank on their to do list and again didn't do anything.

The Less Developed Country Debt Crisis

It is not surprising that in response to the collapse of Continental Illinois the financial regulators did not require the banks to provide valuation transparency. They convinced themselves that secrecy cures all by their handling of the Less Developed Country Debt crisis.

As its name suggests, the Less Developed Country Debt crisis involved bank loans made to less developed countries. The loans were made under the assumption that, unlike individuals, countries never go broke. Of course, they do. As a result of extending too much credit, all of the Too Big to Fail U.S. banks faced significant losses. Recognizing these losses upfront would have caused the banks to report little or even negative book capital levels. The question the bank regulators faced was do they exercise regulatory forbearance and preserve the banks' book capital levels by letting the banks continue to carry the debt at book value or do they require the banks to write-down the debt to its true value, and subsequently rebuild their book capital levels. The regulators opted for forbearance and let the banks carry the debt at book value. Several years later, the banks finally recognized their losses and saw their stock price increase in response. The bank regulators erroneously took this as a sign that secrecy cures all works.

It was not secrecy that cured all, but rather the fact that the precise amount of the losses and not their approximate size was the only thing market participants did not know about each bank's losses on its less developed country debt. Before the crisis began, the banks had disclosed their gross exposure to each country. Throughout the crisis, market participants could access the price at which loans to each country traded. As a result, market participants could estimate the likely size of the loss for each bank. Market participants did this by taking a bank's pre-crisis exposure to each country and adjusting it for the current market price loans for each country traded at. Market participants then adjusted each bank's financial statements for this estimated loss.

What the bank regulators thought was hidden was in fact well known, and already factored into the pricing of each bank's debt and equity securities. Also factored in was the fact that market participants understood that viable banks with a sustainable business model could recover from major credit or investment losses. As shown by Security Pacific bank, this was true even if fully recognizing its losses upfront would have temporarily caused the bank to have a negative book capital level. The rise in each bank's stock price reflected relief that the cost of regulatory forbearance was over, and higher earnings would now flow through to the bank's bottom line.

It was also not surprising that in response to the collapse of Continental Illinois, the financial regulators did not require the banks to provide valuation transparency. With their handling of the U.S. Savings and Loan crisis, they expanded the notion of regulatory discretion to include manipulation of bank financial statements.

In the early 1980s, the Federal Reserve pursued a policy of high interest rates to break the back of inflation. These high interest rates also destroyed the savings and loans' business model, which involved investing in long-term fixed rate mortgages, and funding these investments with short-term deposits. As a result, when interest rates increased, so too did the savings and loans' cost of funds. In fact, because of the Federal Reserve raising interest rates, interest expense at the savings and loans greatly exceeded interest income.

Once again, bank regulators faced a decision: acknowledge the problem or try to hide the problem. The bank regulators opted to be inventive about how they tried to hide the problem. In a precursor to suspension of mark-to-market accounting in our current financial crisis, the bank regulators' inventiveness included relaxing adherence to accounting principles to such an extent that the guiding principles for putting together a savings and loan's financial statement were known as Terribly Rotten Accounting Principles ("TRAP").

Of course, market participants knew the savings and loans had losses. The only thing market participants didn't know was the exact size of the losses at each savings and loan.

In addition, by not requiring valuation transparency while regulatory forbearance was being granted, there was no way for market participants to exert market discipline and restrain risk taking by management of the savings and loans. Naturally, management took on much more risk by making new loans and buying risky securities in a gamble on redemption. The lack of valuation transparency also made it easier for management to loot the savings and loans through bonuses on briefly higher earnings before the losses on the new high-risk loans and securities were realized.

Wall Street reintroduces rigged markets

For bankers, the financial regulators' response to the collapse of Continental Illinois, the Less Developed Country Debt crisis, and the U.S. Savings and Loan crisis, was an open invitation to engage in bad behavior. The banks' veil of opacity meant sunlight could not act as the best disinfectant, and the bankers could secretly engage in wrongdoing.

The Libor interest rate manipulation scandal vividly illustrates the type of activities bankers engaged in that would not have been possible if there had been valuation transparency. The Libor interest rate is effectively the price of money. However, according to an email from Mr. del Missier, then Barclays' chief operating officer, the secret behind this price of money was that these were all fantasy rates.[9]

Why was the price of money using the Libor interest rate a fantasy? The Libor interest rate was set every business day using an opaque process controlled by the banks. Banks, including Barclays, submitted the interest rate at which they may or may not have been able to borrow large amounts of unsecured money. Naturally, bankers used this process to move the Libor interest rate up or down to turn trades they had made that were losers into winners. They also used this process to misrepresent their financial condition during the early stages of our current financial crisis. If banks were required to provide valuation transparency, the Libor interest rate would have been based off what it actually cost the banks to borrow on an unsecured basis. The bankers' ability to manipulate the Libor interest rate would have been eliminated.

For bankers, the financial regulators' response to the collapse of Continental Illinois, the Less Developed Country Debt crisis, and the U.S. Savings and Loan crisis, was also an open invitation to loot the banks in the run-up to our current crisis and to loot the taxpayers when the crisis hit. The bankers knew before our current financial crisis the financial regulators would not require the banks to provide valuation transparency or be subjected to market discipline that would restrain their risk taking. This allowed the bankers to loot the banks through bonuses on briefly higher earnings before the losses became apparent. The bankers also knew when the inevitable crisis hit the lack of transparency gave the bankers a huge advantage in shaping how policymakers and the financial regulators reacted to the financial crisis. Opacity allowed the bankers to sell a self serving agenda under which the financial regulators would use the taxpayers to bail out the banks, rather than use the banks' capital accounts to protect the real economy and absorb the losses. This bailout allowed the bankers to loot the

9 Chellel, Kit (2014, March 21), Del Missier Called Libor Rates a 'Fantasy' in E-Mail to Diamond, Bloomberg, http://www.bloomberg.com/news/print/2014-03-21/del-missier-called-libor-rates-a-fantasy-in-e-mail-to-diamond.html

taxpayers as the bankers continued to receive bonuses that would otherwise have been used to rebuild the bank capital levels.

Fed blindly gambles in its lender of last resort role

The Federal Reserve showed in a period of eight days why a financial system dependent on the regulators for anything more than ensuring valuation transparency is always prone to financial crises.

- In its March 10, 2008 discussion over extending its lender of last resort function to firms like Goldman Sachs, the members of the Federal Open Market Committee (FOMC) examined the risk inherent to being an investor and relying on the primary supervisors for their risk assessment.
- In its March 18, 2008 discussion about the need to exercise great care when its members made public comments about the solvency of the banks, the FOMC members explained why the primary supervisors always understate risk.

When the primary supervisors understate risk and investors use those statements as the basis for both market discipline and self-discipline, the result is banks take on too much risk and investors have more exposure than they can afford to lose. This condition is only possible when there is opacity and is the very definition of a financial system prone to systemic financial crises.

On its March 10, conference call on extending its lender of last resort function to broker-dealers, the Federal Reserve found itself facing a problem.

> **VICE CHAIRMAN GEITHNER:** I agree with the concerns expressed about giving access to liquidity when we haven't done it before without a full capacity to affect the supervisory constraints these guys operate under. We are not doing this for them, though. We are doing it because we think it is necessary to help improve market functioning more generally. We do not have the capacity in these circumstances to redesign the regulatory framework to give us, as a condition of access to something that we are doing for market functioning, the ability to affect and constrain the risk-taking behavior of those institutions. All primary dealers, except for one, I believe, are subject to consolidated supervision in some form. Those primary supervisors, with which we have a very close-running relationship, often subject those institutions to a set of constraints, including in the investment banks a consolidated capital regime and a set of other constraints on liquidity.
>
> We will, of course, be in very close contact, as we have been with those primary supervisors, about the evolving financial conditions of those institutions. If we have evidence, directly or through the supervisors, of some

material erosion in the financial business of those institutions from a solvency perspective, that will cause us to reflect on what we do with those institutions going forward. I wish it were the case that we could condition this step on a change in the regulatory regime that would give us that capacity. But we just don't have that ability now. Are we protecting ourselves carefully against that risk? We are protecting ourselves carefully, but not perfectly, against that risk. [10]

MR. EVANS: This discussion stimulated a question that I didn't anticipate. If we decide that there is a broker — dealer that we can't allow to enter into this program and then it ends up not doing very well and going under, is there some type of risk that we are taking on by hastening that in making that determination? Do we have the right information to take that action?

VICE CHAIRMAN GEITHNER: As many of us have learned over the past six to nine months, even the primary supervisors of these institutions have limits around their capacity to understand in real time what is actually happening. So we face that vulnerability — I agree with you — and that will limit, realistically, how much protection we are going to be able to take for ourselves in this context.[11]

As described by Tim Geithner, then the president of the New York Federal Reserve Bank and subsequently the U.S. Treasury Secretary, the Federal Reserve was prevented from both assessing the risk and value of the broker-dealers or exerting market discipline and restraining the risk these firms could take. Why could the Federal Reserve not independently assess the solvency of the broker-dealers it was extending its lender of last resort function to?

The answer is opacity!

Opacity meant that when it came to broker-dealers, the Federal Reserve did not have the information it needed to assess the risk and value of the broker-dealers. This lack of information the Federal Reserve was experiencing was a subset of the larger problem that no financial institution provided valuation transparency. As a result, outside of the primary supervisors, no market participant could assess the risk and value of any financial institution. Mr. Geithner acknowledged the Federal Reserve didn't have the correct information in order to take action or exert market discipline.

What did the Federal Reserve and every other market participant do to work around the lack of valuation transparency?

---

10 FOMC (2008, March 10), Transcripts and Other Historical Materials: March 10, 2008 FOMC conference call, Federal Reserve, http://www.federalreserve.gov/monetarypolicy/fomchistorical2008.htm, page 17

11 ibid, page 19

The Federal Reserve relied on financial regulators to both properly assess and communicate the risk and value of the financial institutions. In this case, the Federal Reserve was blindly gambling because it was dependent on the broker-dealers' primary supervisors if it wanted to exercise self-discipline, and limit its exposures to what it could afford to lose.

What is the problem with relying on the primary supervisors?

Our financial system is designed so everyone can independently assess the risk and value of each firm. It is the collective assessment of risk operating through each investor's self-discipline that results in market discipline on banks and broker-dealers. When the only market participant assessing risk is the primary supervisor, the stability of the financial system is dependent on them to both accurately assess and communicate the current level of risk. If the primary supervisor does not accurately assess and communicate the current level of risk, the financial system is prone to a crisis.

As Mr. Geithner acknowledged, primary supervisors, including the Federal Reserve, have limits on their real time ability to understand what is actually happening at the financial institutions they supervise. This is a very big problem. If the primary supervisors don't understand what is going on, there is little chance they accurately assess the current level of risk of a financial institution. If there is little chance the current level of risk is accurately assessed, it would only be by pure luck that investors, including the Federal Reserve, would be able to limit their exposure to what the investors can afford to lose. If self-discipline doesn't properly reflect risk/reward, then market discipline of financial institutions doesn't work properly either.

The $6.2 billion loss JPMorgan recognized on trades made by the "London Whale" vividly illustrated in 2012 primary regulators still did not understand what was happening at the financial institutions they supervised. The trades were suppose to reduce the bank's overall risk, but were in reality simply a bet. If the regulators don't *understand* the difference between what reduces or increases a bank's risk, what chance is there they can accurately *assess* the bank's risk?

Just over a week later, at its March 18, meeting, Mr. Geithner reminded the other members of the Federal Reserve's Open Market Committee why bank regulators needed to take great care when they talked about the risk of each individual bank and the banking system as a whole less their statements spook the market. In offering this reminder, he showed that even if the primary supervisors accurately assess the risk of each financial institution and the financial system, they systematically understate the current level of risk to other market participants. By understating the current level of risk, the primary supervisors guarantee market participants who rely on their assessment have too much exposure and do not exert sufficient market discipline. Too little market discipline results in financial institutions taking on too much risk and increasing the chances of a financial crisis. Too much exposure results in concerns about financial contagion when a financial crisis does occur.

> **VICE CHAIRMAN GEITHNER:** There is nothing more dangerous in what we're facing now than for people who are knowledgeable about this stuff to feed these broad concerns about our credibility and about the basic core strength of the financial system. So, I just want to underscore the importance of exceptional care in how we talk about those things, even in private. A lot of people out there who should know better — none of us is guilty of this — are casting broad aspersions about solvency that are very dangerous in this context. May we get to the point where those concerns are justified? Of course, we may get to that point. If we systematically mismanage policy, we may get to that point. But please be careful in that context.[12]

Mr. Geithner's statement captured the complete breakdown of the philosophy of disclosure based financial and banking systems that emerged from the Great Depression, and their replacement with a system dependent on financial regulators. Why should Mr. Geithner and the other members of the Federal Reserve's Open Market Committee, be so concerned about the impact of their statements on bank solvency?

Opacity!

Everyone involved in that meeting knew the Federal Reserve, through its examiners, had access to information about the banks that wasn't available to any other market participant. Due to opacity, the other market participants were not in a position to independently assess the banks' risk and value. As a result, the other market participants relied on, and were very sensitive to, what members of the Federal Reserve Open Market Committee had to say. If someone at the Federal Reserve hinted there were solvency problems, it might trigger a classic financial panic in which the uninsured investors would withdraw their funds from the banking system *en masse*.

If the primary supervisors, the Federal Reserve in the case of banks, are concerned about possibly triggering a classic financial panic, there is no chance they properly communicate the banks' risk level. If there is no chance they accurately communicate the risk level, there is no chance investors who rely on the primary supervisors' statement will be able to limit their exposure to what they can afford to lose. If the investors' don't limit their exposures to what they can afford to lose, then market discipline on banks is too weak and banks take on too much risk.

---

12 FOMC (2008, March 18), Transcripts and Other Historical Materials: March 18, 2008 FOMC meeting. Federal Reserve, http://www.federalreserve.gov/monetarypolicy/fomchistorical2008.htm, page 75

Just like Continental Illinois, the facts of each bank and broker-dealer were hidden behind a veil of opacity. This left market participants with carefully worded statements about the current level of risk in both the financial system and each financial institution by primary regulators who had a limited ability to understand what was happening in real time, and an incentive to downplay the level of risk they found. Just like Continental Illinois, opacity set up the situation where investors would want to rapidly decrease their exposure once more was known about the actual level of risk being taken.

Think of how dramatically different these discussions and the course of the financial crisis would have been had the banks and broker-dealers provided valuation transparency to the other market participants. At a minimum, investors would not have been dependent on primary supervisors who have a limited ability to understand what is happening in real time, and an incentive to understate any risk they find. Instead, investors, including the Federal Reserve, could have independently assessed the risk level and each banks' and broker-dealers' value. Then investors could have exercised self-discipline to limit their exposure to each bank and broker-dealer to what they could afford to lose. This would have subjected the banks and broker-dealers to market discipline. This would also have eliminated the need for taxpayer-funded bailouts, since the risk of financial contagion would have gone away.

When investors limit their exposure to what they can afford to lose, it becomes possible to have the investors absorb the losses on the non-viable banks and broker-dealers. In addition, comments made by members of the Federal Reserve Open Market Committee would not risk triggering a financial panic. In fact, their comments would be seen as simply a reminder to continue to monitor the risk of the financial institutions, and exert market discipline to restrain their risk-taking.

In his statement, Mr. Geithner took on individuals, such as myself, who were saying the banks and the financial system were facing a problem. He tried to marginalize us by saying we were dangerous for saying the problem existed. However, in making this statement he missed two simple facts. First, the problem of opacity existed. It had not gone away. It continued to prevent investors from independently valuing banks and structured finance securities. Second, not only was I saying opacity was the problem, but I was also saying providing valuation transparency was, and still is, the only proven solution to the opacity problem. It is only valuation transparency and not monetary or fiscal policy that was/is the solution for ending an opacity-driven financial crisis.

International Investigations

There have been several international investigations into the causes of our current global financial crisis. In Ireland, the Nyberg Commission investigated the causes of the Irish banking system collapse. In the UK, the Financial Services Authority looked into why RBS failed. In the U.S., the Senate Permanent Subcommittee on Investigations looked into the role of the rating firms, and their failure to accurately assess the risk of subprime mortgage-backed securities. In the U.S., the Financial Crisis Inquiry Commission investigated the causes of the U.S. financial crisis. There was one common thread that linked the findings of each of these investigations: the absence of valuation transparency and the presence of opacity was the necessary condition for our current global financial crisis.

The global investigations confirmed my diagnosis of the cause of our current financial crisis. As Paul Tucker, a former member of the BoE's Financial Policy Committee, observed:

> But the standard is not what banks have been publishing to date; it's what is needed to provide reassurance and much greater transparency around the complex web of exposures.... the worst possible outcome would be a crisis of confidence that was more severe than it needed to be because of insufficient transparency about the resilience of banks.... [banks need to] be transparent about their exposures so there isn't an unnecessary threat to confidence if banks have got a good story to tell.
>
> And of course going forward, if it's understood that banks should be more transparent about their exposures, then in the generality of things banks will be more careful about the exposures that they take on.[13]

It is time we use the classic prescription for ending the financial crisis, and bring valuation transparency to all the opaque corners of the global financial system.

Opacity made the current financial crisis inevitable. The presence of opacity meant the banks were not subject to market discipline, and were only restrained in their risk-taking by regulators who had limits on both their ability to understand in real time what was actually happening at the banks they supervised, and their ability to restrain risk-taking when a bank appeared to be doing well. Even worse, not only was the Federal Reserve not accurately communicating the level of risk at each bank, it was turning a blind eye to bad behavior, such as manipulating the Libor interest rate. Instead, the Federal Reserve was promoting overconfidence by leading the cheers for financial innovation, claiming it reduced the banks' risk. Opacity allowed the situation to develop where there would be an abrupt adjustment by investors when the current level of risk and the inability to value opaque securities was discovered.

---

13 Bank of England (2011, June), Financial Stability Report Press Conference Transcript, Bank of England, http://www.bankofengland.co.uk/publications/Pages/fsr/2011/fsr29.aspx, page 10

August 9, 2007: Start of perhaps the biggest financial crisis ever

In the presence of opacity, all that is required for a financial crisis is a trigger, and on August 9, 2007, BNP Paribas provided that trigger when it said it couldn't value opaque subprime mortgage-backed securities. From there, the financial crisis spread along the opacity fault line. Next to go were the opaque entities set up by the banks to hold those opaque securities. Last in line were the opaque banks that held both opaque securities, and had financial commitments to fund the opaque entities.

Former Fed Chair Bernanke described to the Financial Crisis Inquiry Commission what happens when there is opacity and market participants do not know who holds the losses, and how bad the losses are.

> As a scholar of the Great Depression, I honestly believe that September and October of 2008 was the worst financial crisis in global history, including the Great Depression. If you look at the firms that came under pressure in that period…only one…was not at serious risk of failure…. So, out of maybe the 12, 13 of the most important financial institutions in the United States, 12 were at risk of failure within a period of a week or two.[14]

Because of opacity, investors did not know who was holding losses, and therefore could not tell which, if any, firm or firms were no longer viable. As a result, investors didn't distinguish between the banks, but rather tried to reduce their exposure to them *en masse*.

The financial regulators responded by putting the banking system on life support. As Fed Chair Bernanke described it:

> In the face of this instability, in 2008 and 2009 policymakers had taken a range of extraordinary measures: The Federal Reserve supplied liquidity to banks and other financial institutions, helping to calm the panic and begin the process of restoring the flow of credit to households and businesses; the Treasury Department guaranteed money market funds and injected capital into banks under the Troubled Asset Relief Program; the Congress expanded deposit insurance under the Federal Deposit Insurance Corporation (FDIC); and the FDIC guaranteed banks' issuance of long-term debt.[15]

---

14 Financial Crisis Inquiry Report (2011, January), Final Report of the National Commission on the Causes of the Financial and Economic Crisis in the United States, http://fcic.law.stanford.edu/report, page 354.

15 Bernanke, Ben S. (2013, April 8), Stress Testing Banks: What Have We Learned, Federal Reserve, http://www.federalreserve.gov/newsevents/speech/bernanke20130408a.htm

The one activity the policymakers did not engage in to defuse the situation was to provide valuation transparency. It wasn't as if the financial regulators were blind to the ability of valuation transparency to restore confidence and answer the questions about how bad the losses were, and where they were held. Just like Continental Illinois, the financial regulators had a problem. They faced a choice between providing valuation transparency or engaging in a policy of deceit. Just like Continental Illinois, the financial regulators chose deceit. As Fed Chair Bernanke described it:

> In retrospect, the SCAP [Supervisory Capital Assessment Program, also known as the stress tests,] stands out for me as one of the critical turning points in the financial crisis. It provided anxious investors with something they craved: credible information about prospective losses at banks.[16]

Investors wanted to know how bad it really was. They knew the banks had losses. They knew the banks had exposures to structured finance securities, and other opaque securities that couldn't be valued. Investors wanted to see the exposure details so they could determine for themselves the risk and value of each financial institution. They wanted the facts so they could make an informed decision about the level of exposure they had to each financial institution.

In early 2009, the U.S. financial regulators tried to harness the virtues of valuation transparency. They ran stress tests on the banks and claimed the faux transparency provided by the tests should have the same benefits as valuation transparency. As Mr. Geithner said when the stress tests results were released,

> Greater disclosure will help improve confidence. Today's results should make it easier for investors to evaluate risk and to differentiate across institutions. The stress test will help replace the cloud of uncertainty hanging over our banking system with an unprecedented level of transparency and clarity. This is important, as markets work best when they have full access to the information on which to make informed investment decisions.[17]

However, the stress tests did not provide the market with full access to the information by which investors could make informed investment decisions. Specifically, the stress tests did not provide the current exposure level data former Fed Chair Bernanke said in 2013 was needed by the Fed or anyone else,

---

16 ibid

17 US Treasury (2009, May 7), Statement from Treasury Secretary Tim Geithner Regarding the Treasury Capital Assistance Program and the Supervisory Capital Assessment Program, US Treasury. http://www.treasury.gov/press-center/press-releases/Pages/tg123.aspx

including investors and banking competitors, to independently assess the current level of risk and a bank's value.

> We have also improved our tools for estimating projected bank losses, revenues, and capital under alternative scenarios. The original SCAP was supervisors' first attempt to produce comprehensive and simultaneous estimates of the financial conditions of the nation's largest banking firms, and the required data and analytical methods were developed under great time pressure. Of necessity, when projecting losses and revenues under alternative SCAP scenarios, supervisors relied on the firms' own estimates as a starting point. Although we scrutinized and questioned the firms' estimates and made significant adjustments based on our own analysis, for that inaugural round of stress tests, it was not possible to produce completely independent estimates.
>
> However, over the past four years, considerable progress has been made in data collection and in the development of independent supervisory models. For our most recent supervisory stress tests, we collected and analyzed loan- and account-level data on more than two-thirds of the $4.2 trillion in accrual loans and leases projected to be held by the 18 firms we evaluated this year. Those detailed data include borrower, loan, and collateral information on more than 350 million domestic retail loans, including credit cards and mortgages, and more than 200,000 commercial loans.... These ongoing efforts are bringing us close to the point at which we will be able to estimate, in a fully independent way, how each firm's loss, revenue, and capital ratio would likely respond in any specified scenario.[18]

Without valuation transparency, which Fed Chair Bernanke said the Fed was in the process of obtaining, market participants could not trust, but verify, the results of the stress tests. They also could not independently assess each bank's risk and value. Without valuation transparency, regulators couldn't, and still can't, accurately perform the stress tests. This was recently confirmed when Bank of America announced an adjustment to its regulatory capital levels due to the mispricing of structured notes[19] and then when RBS announced it had overstated its capital ratio as part of the ECB's stress test.[20]

---

18 Bernanke, Ben S. (2013, April 8), Stress Testing Banks: What Have We Learned, Federal Reserve, http://www.federalreserve.gov/newsevents/speech/bernanke20130408a.htm

19 Bank of America (2014, April 28), press release: Bank of America Announces Adjustment to Estimated Regulatory Capital Ratios, Bank of America, http://newsroom.bankofamerica.com/press-releases/corporate-and-financial-news/bank-america-announces-adjustment-estimated-regulatory-c

20 Leighton-Jones, Phillipa (2014, November 21), RBS on what went wrong in the European Stress Tests, Wall Street Journal, http://blogs.wsj.com/moneybeat/2014/11/21/rbs-admits-mistake-in-european-stress-tests/

Former Fed Chair Bernanke acknowledged at the time the first stress tests results were released, that there was information that would remain hidden from the market.

> These examinations were not tests of solvency; we knew already that all these institutions meet regulatory capital standards.[21]

The information that would remain hidden from the market was the actual financial condition of the banks the investors were interested in finding out. Fed Chair Bernanke's statement was quite ironic given Secretary Geithner's justification for the stress tests:

> ...this meritocratic form of triage would be brutal to the shareholders of the institutions that most deserved brutality, while avoiding the panic-inducing consequences of nationalization or liquidation. "I don't see why you want to portray this as so generous to the banks," ... "They're going to be diluted in proportion to their sins."[22]

How could shareholders face dilution in proportion to the sins of the bank when, according to Fed Chair Bernanke, the stress tests specifically did not try to answer the question of whether or not a bank was solvent, and the market value of its assets was greater than the book value of its liabilities? The stress tests also didn't try to tell investors anything about the size of the losses being hidden, on and off each bank's balance sheets. This was done with the regulators' blessings.

Please note Fed Chair Bernanke left several things off his list of extraordinary measures. First, was the fact the regulators helped the banks hide their losses by allowing them to treat their bad debt as good debt. Then, the regulators also allowed the banks to treat their investments as if they were worth what they paid for them, rather than what they could actually sell them for. This was left off because as shown by the Less Developed Country Debt crisis, and the U.S. Savings and Loan crisis, helping banks hide their losses was standard operating procedure for bank regulators. If the stress tests weren't going to answer questions about the current financial condition of the banks, what would the stress tests show?

---

21 Bernanke, Ben S. (2009, May 7), Statement Regarding the Supervisory Capital Assessment Program, Federal Reserve, http://www.federalreserve.gov/newsevents/press/bcreg/bernankescap20090507.htm

22 DeLong, Brad (2014, May 15), From Tim Geithner: Stress Test: Thursday Focus: May 15, 2014, http://equitablegrowth.org/2014/05/15/tim-geithner-stress-test-thursday-focus-may-15-2014/

> Rather, the assessment program was a forward-looking, "what-if" exercise intended to help supervisors gauge the extent of the additional capital buffer necessary to keep these institutions strongly capitalized and lending, even if the economy performs worse than expected between now and the end of next year.[23]

Why would investors care about prospective losses when the investors knew the regulators were helping the banks hide their existing losses? The answer was, the investors didn't care.

> The results released today should provide considerable comfort to investors and the public. The examiners found that nearly all the banks that were evaluated have enough Tier 1 capital to absorb the higher losses envisioned under the hypothetical adverse scenario.[24]

Where was the comfort to be taken from the financial regulators effectively saying they didn't think investors could handle the truth about the banks' current financial condition? It wasn't lost on investors the stress tests didn't provide them with information on each bank's current financial condition or information they needed to independently confirm the test results. Investors derived no comfort from the stress tests.

So, what was the real purpose of the stress tests? They were simply an exercise in the government promoting, and implicitly guaranteeing, an investment in a private security. In this case, the private security was the banks' unsecured debt and common equity. The implicit guarantee was the investors wouldn't lose their investment due to any solvency problems at the banks. After all, the government had just come out and said the banks didn't have solvency problems, even if the economy performed worse than expected.

> Roughly half the firms, though, need to enhance their capital structure to put greater emphasis on common equity, which provides institutions the best protection during periods of stress. Many of the institutions have already taken actions to bolster their capital buffers and are well positioned to raise capital from private sources over the next six months.
>
> However, our government, through the Treasury Department, stands ready to **provide whatever additional capital may be necessary to ensure that our banking system is able to navigate a challenging economic downturn.** (emphasis added)[25]

---

23 Bernanke, Ben S. (2009, May 7), Statement Regarding the Supervisory Capital Assessment Program, Federal Reserve, http://www.federalreserve.gov/newsevents/press/bcreg/bernankescap20090507.htm

24 ibid

25 ibid

The 2009 stress tests were a significant event in the financial crisis. This wasn't because they provided investors with credible information about the viability and solvency of the banks or their ability to absorb losses as on-going viable operating entities. It was a significant event because in certifying the banks' solvency, it included the Geithner Guarantee. This Guarantee was a pledge by the U.S. Treasury Department to provide whatever additional capital might be necessary so investors in the banks' unsecured debt and equity wouldn't lose their money due to solvency issues. Just like with Continental Illinois, the financial regulators put the taxpayers at risk by guaranteeing to cover any losses the banks had. Just like with the U.S. Savings and Loans, the financial regulators were using the taxpayers to buy time, hoping the banks would recover.

The financial regulators were right that the stress tests did make it easier to assess a bank's risk, and make a decision whether or not to invest. To assess a bank's risk, all investors had to do was look at the sovereign's credit quality. The financial regulators refused to make each bank provide valuation transparency or impose losses on investors. Instead, they offered an explicit taxpayer backed guarantee. With this explicit guarantee, the U.S. financial regulators turned an opacity driven financial crisis from one confined to the financial system, and in particular the banks, to a global sovereign debt crisis, too. Oops.

Of course, not everyone disapproved of the stress tests and their results. Wall Street was unanimous in its approval, as there were high-fives all around. After all, from the bankers' perspective what was there not to like about the policymakers choosing to pursue the Japanese Model? The bankers had their bonuses guaranteed by the taxpayers, and they were free to continue placing bets.

Policymakers turn to bankers for how to end financial crisis

The presence of opacity also allowed bankers to have an outsized influence over the global policy response to the financial crisis. As illustrated by Anglo Irish Bank, bankers argued for a policy response that was beneficial for the bankers, even while it was bad for the taxpayers and the real economy. The Anglo Irish bankers used the "end of the world" argument to successfully argue for being bailed out with a €7 billion loan to address what the bankers called a liquidity problem.

The "end of the world" argument goes as follows: if policymakers don't do what the bankers ask, then the banking system will collapse and bring down the real economy with it. In reality, the size of the loan the Anglo Irish Bankers asked for was pulled from a banker's "arse," with the intention the government would agree, and become committed to subsequent rounds of financial support for the bank.

The bankers knew opacity prevented other market participants from showing the bank's problems stemmed from the fact the bank was no longer viable. This lack of viability meant the bankers' self serving solution to help it out of a liquidity problem should not have been adopted. Rather, the bank should have wound down.

Had the bankers' solution not been adopted, the Irish taxpayers would have saved a lot of money. There was no reason to believe that similar one-sided conversations did not occur between bankers in other countries and their governments, with the result being favorable to the bankers, and very expensive for the taxpayers.

When the Irish government hired Merrill Lynch, it provided an excellent example of the one-sided banker friendly nature of the advice bankers offered to global policymakers. The Irish government had already guaranteed all the bank liabilities by the time Merrill Lynch had been hired.

Merrill Lynch's November 18, 2008, presentation framed three banker friendly alternatives for how to handle the Irish banks going forward:

1. Recapitalization
2. Setting up a bad bank to hold the bad debt currently on the banks' balance sheets
3. Strategic mergers

This framing eliminated discussing a number of relevant issues, and took any solutions that might have been bad for bankers and their bonuses off the table.

First, since bank liabilities were guaranteed, why would the banks need the government to inject capital so they could show a high capital ratio in 2008? Why couldn't banks recognize their losses and then over the next several years retain all pre-banker bonus earnings until book capital levels had been rebuilt? After all, banks didn't, and still don't, need to be bailed out since their ability to make loans is not constrained by their ability to hold the loans on their balance sheet. The banks just have to sell the loans to third parties, like insurers or pension funds, until banks have rebuilt their balance sheets. By framing the issue the way Merrill Lynch did, it was assumed that bailing out the banks was necessary.

Second, framing the issue the way Merrill Lynch did assumed away whether or not the banks were actually viable and capable of rebuilding their book capital levels after recognizing their losses. If a bank was viable, there was no need either for a national "bad bank" to take on its losses or for a bailout. If a bank wasn't viable, there was also no reason for Irish taxpayers to take on the losses on its bad loans through a "bad bank" or to bailout the bank.

Third, framing the issue the way Merrill Lynch did assumed it was important to recapitalize the banks. Why? Given the guarantee, the only potential beneficiary from the banks being recapitalized by the taxpayers were the bankers, as it allowed them to continue collecting their bonuses without any interruption from having blown up the banks. Instead of addressing these issues, the presentation focused on how other countries were recapitalizing their banks, and what were the alternatives facing Ireland.

Before a decision could be made to inject capital into the banks, the issue of how much capital was needed had to be addressed. Nowhere in its presentation to the Irish government did Merrill Lynch discuss if each bank was viable. Nowhere in its presentation was a simple chart showing the total size of each bank's loan portfolio, and saying if X amount of this portfolio was no good, then the bank shouldn't be bailed out. Instead, Merrill Lynch used a complex, jargon filled analysis that hid the fact that due to opacity nobody knew the true condition of the banks. This complex analysis allowed Merrill Lynch to assume the banker friendly conclusion that the banks should be bailed out either directly or their losses transferred to the "bad bank" where they could be picked up by the taxpayers.

Merrill Lynch hid the existence of opacity and the fact that no one knew the true condition of the Irish banks by building its argument for bailing out the banks on numbers plucked from thin air. First, as disclosed in the presentation's footnotes, it used the average estimated loan loss provision from several sell-side brokerage research reports to anchor expectations about the size of the losses hiding on each bank's balance sheets. Of course, these research reports came from the financial market participants with the most to gain by understating the size of the problem with the banks.

Then, Merrill Lynch layered a sensitivity analysis on top of its own series of assumptions about the credit quality of the individual banks. For example, Merrill Lynch assumed for its worse case that 5.5% of Anglo Irish Bank's loans would turn out to be bad.[26] As a result, Anglo Irish would need a €5.63 billion capital injection to both cover the losses on these bad loans, and to build up its core Tier 1 capital ratio from 6.1% to 8.5%. By making this capital injection, the government would end up owning 87% of the bank.

Finally, Merrill Lynch totaled the estimated amount of capital needed for each individual bank to estimate the "maximum" amount of capital Ireland would have to inject into its banks at €16.4 billion.[27] This was a level of capital injection within the capacity of the Irish government to finance that wouldn't result in the banks being fully nationalized or banker bonuses being curtailed. In reality, the Irish taxpayer would have saved a considerable amount of money by not

---

26 Merrill Lynch (2008, November 18), Presentation to the Irish Department of Finance Discussion Materials, Merrill Lynch, https://docs.google.com/file/d/0B_p5wXj7Q88MZnpSUG1pQy1lR28/edit, page 9.

27 ibid, page 4.

bailing out the banks, because the Irish banking system required four times more capital than estimated in the report, with Anglo Irish alone needing €30+ billion. Apparently, Merrill Lynch's estimate of the "maximum" amount of capital needed was a little low.

The one-sided advice provided by bankers was well received by policymakers and regulators who on the one hand wanted to escape blame for allowing the financial crisis to occur, and on the other hand saw an opportunity to increase their role in the financial system. Secretary Geithner vividly illustrated the desire to escape any blame for the financial crisis with his observation:

> Financial crises cannot be reliably predicted, so they cannot be reliably prevented. They're kind of like earthquakes that way, or they would be if earthquakes were triggered by manias and fears and human interactions. We know some of the warning signs, most notably credit booms, substantial and sustained increases in private borrowings relative to income. But we can't outlaw stupidity or irrational exuberance or herd behavior, and we can't anticipate with any confidence exactly when manias will turn into panics. We can't count on fallible central bankers or regulators to stop financial booms before they become dangerous, because by the time the danger is clear, it's often too late to defuse the problem.[28]

He wanted us to know that central bankers and regulators could not prevent a financial crisis, because there was no way to reliably predict a financial crisis. Under his logic, if you cannot predict an event, there is no reason to think you could prevent the event from occurring. Therefore, he argued, you could not blame the central bankers and regulators, because the financial crisis happened. However, this ignores the fact that the regulators were not responsible for predicting a financial crisis, but rather for ensuring valuation transparency that would prevent a financial crisis, and limit its fallout.

The choice: Save the banks or protect Main Street

Next, Secretary Geithner wanted us to trust these same central bankers and regulators who didn't do their job and ensure valuation transparency in the run-up to the financial crisis.

> Still, governments can do a lot to reduce the damage of financial disasters, just as they can with natural disasters. In the same way building codes can require sturdier construction in fault zones or elevated structures in floodplains,

[28] Geithner, Tim (2014), *Stress Test: Reflections on Financial Crises*, New York, NY: Crown Publishers, page 318

> strong financial regulations can limit the severity of future crises. Even though governments can't eradicate crises, they can reduce the system's vulnerability to crises, as well as the risk that crises will spiral out of control.[29]

Mr. Geithner wanted us to believe that these same central bankers and regulators could do some good by pursuing a save the banks, save the world policy, and significantly increasing the amount of financial regulations in an effort to limit the damage caused by a future crisis. The centerpiece of these new regulations is the idea banks should have more book capital to absorb losses. Of course, this ignores the fact that none of the global bank regulators required the banks they oversee to use their existing book capital to absorb losses on the excess debt in our financial system during our current financial crisis. Hence, there is absolutely no reason to believe they would or could do so in the future.

However, by focusing on saving the banks and limiting the damage caused by a future financial crisis, he ignored and didn't address the damage our current crisis is causing to the real economy because of the existing excess debt in the financial system. For example, this excess debt blunted the positive impact of central banks printing money and using low interest rates to encourage businesses to invest.

Businesses are unwilling to invest if there is no demand for their products. This lack of demand is caused by the diversion of resources from the real economy to debt service payments.

Secretary Geithner also ignored the need to restore confidence in the financial system, and that the only way to do this was by restoring valuation transparency. Stress tests do not restore confidence, since in the absence of valuation transparency investors have no way to Trust, but Verify, what the regulators said was true.

It was the presence of opacity that forced the global policymakers and financial regulators from August 9, 2007 to September 23, 2008 to pursue the Japanese Model, rather than the Swedish Model, for responding to our current financial crisis. Using the well-known Japanese Model playbook, they protected bank capital levels at all costs. This was done under the assumption that protecting the banks from recognizing the losses already on and off their balance sheets would reduce the damage from the financial disaster. Protecting bank capital levels also protected the bankers' bonuses. These bonuses become an explicit part of the budget for how the banks' earnings are used. Earnings are used first to pay bonuses, then to pay dividends, then retained to build book capital levels to reduce the vulnerability of the system to a future financial crisis, and then finally to absorb the losses currently hidden on and off the banks' balance sheets.

---

[29] ibid, page 318

After September 23, 2008, protecting bank capital levels also included bailing out the banks. This inflamed public opinion. It was apparent to all that for the Too Big to Fail banks, it was heads the bankers win, and tails the bankers win. When things went well, the bankers got their bonuses from private profits. When things went badly, the bankers got their bonuses from the taxpayers.

In pursuing the Japanese Model playbook, policymakers justify to themselves policies that benefit Wall Street over Main Street by saying these distasteful policies are necessary as they prevent Main Street from being hurt by any number of potential problems ranging from a lack of credit availability to financial contagion. Then, the policymakers wonder why and express anger when Main Street doesn't accept the policymakers' rationalizations. Main Street's failure to appreciate the policies pursued under the Japanese Model is not a perception problem, but rather an acknowledgement that Main Street knows the politicians and financial regulators are screwing Main Street.

Since September 23, 2008 when the taxpayers were asked to backstop the financial system, Main Street has known that the current set of banks need the host country taxpayers for their continued existence. Main Street also knows it doesn't need the current set of banks. New banks could replace the existing banks and provide all the necessary credit. This fact holds true for all financial institutions across all countries. In short, Goldman Sachs and JPMorgan need the U.S.; the U.S. doesn't need Goldman Sachs or JPMorgan.

In addition, Main Street knows implementing the Japanese Model and its policies has never been successful in promoting recovery from a financial crisis. Instead, it condemns Main Street and the real economy to a long-term economic malaise punctuated by the occasional bubble. For example, just look at Japan still struggling to recover from its financial crisis 2+ decades ago.

The reason pursuing the Japanese Model doesn't successfully promote recovery is it directly hurts the economy in two ways. First, it puts the burden of the excess debt on the real economy. This acts like a tax on the real economy and diverts capital needed for reinvestment, growth and social programs Main Street counts on to debt service. Second, it keeps uncertainty in the real economy. Everyone knows there were losses associated with the excess debt in the financial system at the beginning of the financial crisis. Everyone also knows the losses have not been realized. What nobody knows is when the losses will be realized or the extent to which hiding the losses is distorting the price of assets in the real economy. This creates uncertainty. Uncertainty undermines confidence and that in turn negatively affects everything from current consumption to how savings are invested. No amount of fiscal stimulus, extraordinary monetary policies or financial regulators declaring everything is okay will restore confidence. The only way to restore confidence is by eliminating uncertainty. This can only be done by providing credible information to investors by bringing valuation transparency to all the currently opaque corners of the financial system so all questions about the losses can be answered.

In addition, Main Street understands and the economists at the Bank for International Settlements have confirmed that monetary policy is not the right tool for spurring a recovery from a financial crisis. Their research shows what accelerates recovery from a financial crisis is private sector deleveraging (i.e., recognition of the losses on the excess debt in the financial system).[30] Central bank policymakers also understand this.

> Monetary policy — and this is something I would like to be quite clear about — cannot resolve these structural problems in the financial sector, for we have neither the tools nor the mandate to do so.
>
> Being a central bank we cannot rectify the solvency problems of distressed institutions. But what we can do is combat temporary liquidity shortages.[31]

In fact, while monetary policy can help to prevent a financial crisis from escalating in the very short run,

> when interest rates stay very low for a very long time, we may experience unwanted side-effects.[32]

Furthermore, banks were redesigned in the 1930s with the introduction of deposit insurance to facilitate the use of the well-known Swedish Model playbook. This playbook calls for both requiring banks to absorb upfront their losses on the excess debt in the financial system so this debt can be restructured and valuation transparency to confirm that fact. It was first used successfully by the FDR Administration to end the worse of the Great Depression.

Under the Swedish Model, it is banker bonuses that are suppose to take the hit from the losses on the excess debt in the financial system and not Main Street's social programs. These annual bonuses are substantial. According to the Institute for Policy Studies, the $26.7 billion in bonuses paid by Wall Street in

---

30 Bech, Morten L., Gambacorta, Leonardo, Kharroubil, Enisse (2014), Monetary Policy in a Downturn: Are Financial Crises Special? In *International Finance,* Volume 17, Issue 1, pages 99-119, DOI: 10.1111/infi.12040 http://onlinelibrary.wiley.com/doi/10.1111/infi.12040/abstract

31 Weidmann, Jens (2014, April 7), Stable banks for a Stable Europe, speech at the 20th German Banking Congress, Berlin, BIS. http://www.bis.org/review/r140415b.htm?utm_content=buffer8af00&utm_medium=social&utm_source=twitter.com&utm_campaign=buffer

32 Dombret, Andreas (2014, April 15), speech to the Federal Reserve Bank of Dallas, The State of Europe: End of the Crisis or Crisis without End?, BIS, http://www.bis.org/review/r140417c.htm

2013 was over $11.5 billion more than the total amount made by all 1,085,000 full time workers in the U.S. who received the federal minimum wage in 2012.[33]

If these annual bonuses were not paid out, banks could have easily rebuilt their book capital levels over time after recognizing their losses and protecting the real economy. If the Swedish Model was adopted today to protect the real economy from further harm from the losses on the excess debt in the financial system, these bonuses could be used to rapidly rebuild book capital levels.

Main Street recognizes even though most of the crisis era programs have been ended the banks are still effectively on life support that began on September 23, 2008. Main Street understands that while the financial system is still on life support is a good time to adopt the Swedish Model and restore valuation transparency to all the opaque corners of the financial system. At the same time market participants are using valuation transparency to confirm the losses on the excess debt in the global financial system have been realized, they can also adjust their exposures to what they can afford to lose. As a result, going forward viable banks would be subjected to market discipline while they recover from recognition of their losses.

The choice of the Japanese Model and bank stress tests created a number of long lasting problems. One problem is how to end Too Big to Fail. No one believes that large, global financial institutions will ever be allowed to fail. This lack of belief is not based on the international regulators failing to agree on a resolution mechanism so the banks can be international in death. Rather, this lack of belief is based on the fact that due to a lack of valuation transparency, market participants are unable to assess the risk of the Too Big to Fail banks and limit their exposure to what they can afford to lose. As a result, no one knows what the impact on the global financial system of this failure would be and nobody thinks the regulators would run the risk of triggering a global financial crisis. Reinforcement for the notion regulators won't run the risk was provided by the U.S. Justice Department and its policy of Too Big to Jail. The Justice Department didn't pursue legal action against the individuals at the Too Big to Fail banks for fear of triggering a global financial crisis. The only way to restore confidence that a Too Big to Fail bank can actually fail and that bankers will be subject to the rule of law is to require valuation transparency. With this information, market participants could assess the risk of the banks and exert self-discipline knowing the bank could fail.

Another problem is how to end the policy of deceit. We now have a situation where everyone knows the banks' financial statements do not reflect

33 Anderson, Sarah (2014, March 12), Wall Street Bonuses and the Minimum Wage, Institute for Policy Studies, http://www.ips-dc.org/reports/wall_street_bonuses_and_the_minimum_wage

their underlying economic reality. In addition, there is an implicit guarantee to protect investors in the unsecured debt and common equity of the tested banks from any losses due to insolvency. The implicit guarantee exists because in 2009 the government explicitly encouraged investors to rely on the government's statement about the tested banks in making their investment decision. The only way to end both the policy of deceit and the implicit guarantee is to require the banks to provide valuation transparency.

It's not too late to protect Main Street and end Wall Street's looting

Opacity made the financial crisis inevitable. From August 9, 2007 to September 23, 2008, opacity limited policymakers to pursuing policies that clearly benefitted Wall Street over Main Street. However, this limitation ended on September 23, 2008 when Secretary Paulson and Fed Chair Bernanke asked Congress to put the financial system on taxpayer backed life support. Once this occurred, the choice to pursue policies under the Swedish Model that favored Main Street over Wall Street became possible.

Since September 23, 2008, Main Street has waited patiently for policymakers to choose the Swedish Model. This hasn't occurred. Why? It cannot be because policymakers do not know it is the right thing to do. As former Bank of Japan Governor Masaaki Shirakawa observed

> The lesson that Japan can offer ... is to recognize the economy's fundamental problems and tackle them earnestly. The most important regret I have is that the initial root of Japan's problems – non-performing loans (NPLs) – was not addressed more swiftly in the early 1990s.[34]

Then why hasn't the Swedish Model been adopted? Because at the urging of Secretary Paulson and Fed Chair Bernanke, policymakers did more than agree to put the financial system on taxpayer backed life support. At the urging of Secretary Paulson and Fed Chair Bernanke they also surrendered to Wall Street and the City.

In surrendering, they accepted the one-sided, banker bonus friendly idea the banks needed and still need to be bailed out. This idea was then and still is today patently absurd. Once they were on implicit taxpayer backed life support, the banks effectively had and still have unlimited equity as all of their losses are socialized. There was and is no reason to explicitly put taxpayer funds into the

---

34 Goldman Sachs Global Investment Research (2014, November 13), Top of Mind, Goldman Sachs, https://360.gs.com/research/portal//?st=1&action=action.binary&d=18294469&fn=/document.pdf&a=ed623b89e3bd44e9a68a532d060125b2, page 4.

banks and hide the banks' losses as these funds would not change the perception the banks were protected from closure by the taxpayer. The only beneficiary from explicitly funding the banks and hiding their losses was and is the bankers. They saw their bonuses continue virtually without interruption despite their blowing up the global financial system. The loser from explicitly recapitalizing the banks and hiding their losses is Main Street. Main Street suffers because the real economy has to cope with the burden of continuing to deal with the unrecognized losses on the excess debt the banks were designed to absorb.

Fortunately, Main Street has the ability to force adoption of the Swedish Model, recognition of the losses on the excess debt and end our current financial crisis. Main Street can do this because it has the ability as market participants to exert market discipline and force recognition of the losses on the excess debt in the global financial system. However, to do this requires valuation transparency so market participants know who is holding the losses.

Given the existing opacity in the global financial system and the refusal by policymakers to address it, how can Main Street restore valuation transparency?

In the next section of this book, I will answer this question and provide a specific solution to remove the existing opacity and prevent the return of opacity in the future. Implementing this solution doesn't rely on the policymakers who have surrendered for new legislation or regulations. It relies solely on Main Street insisting on its right to have valuation transparency and where valuation transparency is not available being unwilling to blindly gamble with its investments.

Before presenting the solution, the first step is to look in depth at how our financial and banking systems are designed. This allows us to identify the flaw in the global financial system's design that allowed the current financial crisis and the policy response favoring Wall Street over Main Street to occur. It also allows us to understand what needs to be done to fix this flaw and ensure a policy response favoring Main Street over Wall Street always occurs beginning with our current financial crisis and in the future.

We begin by establishing the intellectual underpinnings of valuation transparency as the necessary condition for the invisible hand of the market to operate properly and allocate resources efficiently. For those of you who are into economics and investment theory, I encourage you to read the next section. For those of you who would rather skip the theory and get straight to the solution, I would ask that you familiarize yourself with the theory by simply looking at the diagrams in the next section and resume reading with "The FDR Framework".

SECTION 2

THE FDR FRAMEWORK AND THE DESIGN OF OUR FINANCIAL SYSTEM

Chapter 2

KNOW WHAT YOU OWN

I have great faith in the capacity of people to make good financial decisions — when they have good information. No one makes great decisions — consumers or businesses — if the relevant information is hidden from view.

— Senator Elizabeth Warren[35]

Since the 1930s, valuation transparency has been the foundation on which our economic and financial systems are based. On the surface, this doesn't sound like a very profound statement. However, this simple statement explains why our current financial crisis happened and what needs to be done to fix the financial system. This simple statement also explains why

> The crisis has also laid bare the latent inadequacies of economic models with unique stationary equilibria and rational expectations. These models have failed to make sense of the sorts of extreme macro-economic events, such as crises, recessions and depressions, which matter most to society. The expectations of agents, when push came to shove, proved to be anything but rational, instead driven by the fear of the herd or the unknown.
>
> In this light, it is time to rethink some of the basic building blocks of economics.[36]

The invisible hand of the market needs valuation transparency to work

Like most building foundations, valuation transparency is hidden from view. In any introductory economics textbook, you will find something like the following boilerplate text about Adam Smith, the concept of the invisible hand of the

35 Puzzanghera, Jim (2010, October 26), Q&A with Elizabeth Warren: 'the changes are starting now', Los Angeles Times, http://articles.latimes.com/2010/oct/26/business/la-fi-elizabeth-warren-20101027

36 Haldane, Andrew (2014), Forward: Post-Crash Economics Society at the University of Manchester, Economics, Education and Unlearning, http://www.scribd.com/doc/220136144/Economics-Education-and-Unlearning, page 4

market he introduced in the 1776 classic, *Wealth of Nations*, and the conditions that must exist for the invisible hand to work properly.

> The political economist Adam Smith had a truly profound insight. The free operation of forces in decentralized markets would lead not to chaos but to order: resources would tend to be allocated to produce goods that society valued most. He likened the operation of these forces to the workings of an invisible hand.
>
> Smith argued that market mechanisms coordinate the actions of companies and households — all serving their own self-interest — to produce things that people want in the right quantities. It was as if some giant benevolent, but invisible hand were guiding and coordinating the millions of economic decisions made each day.
>
> But market outcomes would only be efficient under certain circumstances: when agents understand the nature of the goods that are being offered for sale; when those agents behave rationally; when goods are produced under competitive conditions (i.e. no monopolies); and when all commodities that have value are offered for sale (i.e. when markets are 'complete').
>
> Efficiency here has a special, and unusual, meaning. The allocation of resources is efficient if a reallocation of resources (perhaps as a result of government intervention) is unable to make anyone better off without making someone worse off. We call such a situation **Pareto efficient**, named after the Italian economist Vilfredo Pareto (1848-1923).
>
> The idea that market forces encourage the efficient use of resources is immensely powerful. There is also a simple intuition behind it: free markets tend to be efficient in this sense, because if they were not, then profitable opportunities would not be exploited. However, the conditions required to operate this invisible hand efficiently are demanding.[37]

The first condition for the invisible hand to operate properly, "when agents understand the nature of the goods that are being offered for sale", says buyers and sellers need to know what they are buying and selling. Left unsaid is the only way buyers and sellers can know what they are buying and selling is if there is valuation transparency.

Valuation transparency exists when both buyer and seller have access to all the useful, relevant information in an appropriate, timely manner so they or a third party expert they trust can independently assess this information and then, using this assessment, the buyer and seller can make a fully informed decision.

It is only when there is valuation transparency and the buyer knows what he is buying and the seller knows what he owns and is selling that the invisible hand of the market can work through prices to encourage the efficient use of resources.

---

37 email from David Miles with text from Miles, David, Scott, Andrew (2012), Macroeconomics: Understanding the Wealth of Nations, London, England: Wiley

Opacity is anything preventing either the buyer knowing what he is buying or the seller knowing what he owns and is selling. Opacity occurs in many different forms including a lack of disclosure where both buyer and seller don't have access to all the useful, relevant information or information asymmetry where either the buyer or seller has access to all the useful, relevant information, but the other party does not. By definition, opacity is the ultimate market imperfection.

The clear corollary to the statement valuation transparency is necessary for the invisible hand to work through prices to encourage the efficient use of resources is any form of opacity interferes with the ability of the invisible hand to work through prices and results in the inefficient use of resources. If the invisible hand is not properly setting prices because opacity prevents both parties to the transaction from having the necessary information, then the resulting price just reflects blindly gambling and the only beneficiary is the third party who gets paid a commission for getting the two parties to the deal to engage in blindly gambling on the asset being sold. If the invisible hand is not properly setting prices because opacity prevents one party to the transaction from having the necessary information, then the resulting prices must favor either the buyer or the seller.

The effect of opacity on prices has not been lost on Wall Street or the City. They understood how to use opacity to hijack the invisible hand and make it work for their benefit. A recent example of Wall Street and the City using opacity and the resulting mispricing for its benefit was the manipulation of Libor, a benchmark interest rate on which the pricing of hundreds of trillions of dollars of financial instruments is based.

This was not the first or only time Wall Street or the City used opacity to its advantage. During the Great Depression, the Pecora Commission documented how Wall Street used opacity and the fact investors didn't know what they were buying and selling for its benefit. The Republican controlled Senate established the bipartisan commission. Its findings highlighted the fact the need for valuation transparency so the invisible hand of the market works properly is politically blind. In the U.S., it is not a Democratic or Republican party issue. In the UK, it is not a Conservative, Labour or Liberal Democrat party issue. In China, it is possible even with government run by the communist party. Where valuation transparency is a political football is between the Wall Street Party, which doesn't want valuation transparency, and the Main Street Party, that wants valuation transparency. This is sometimes referred to as the "Financial Services Party" versus the "Reform Party."[38]

---

[38] O'Donnell, Paul (2014, January 28), How Wall Street Is Redefining Bipartisanship, Washingtonian Capital Comment, http://www.washingtonian.com/blogs/

The Philosophy of Disclosure

In the run-up to the Great Depression, the global financial system was based on the principle of *caveat emptor* (buyer beware). Under this principle, buyers were responsible for all losses on their investments whether the investment was a bank savings account or a financial product sold by Wall Street.

The principle of caveat emptor gave rise to the idea the marketplace is best regulated by market discipline that results from the self-discipline of cautious individual investors. Underlying this doctrine was the assumption that buyers would protect themselves from losses by demanding all the useful, relevant information before making an investment. The Roaring 20s showed this assumption to be false as Wall Street rolled out and sold increasingly opaque products whose primary beneficiary was Wall Street.

To prevent this from happening again, the FDR Administration and Congress redesigned the financial system and put in place through legislation, specifically, the Securities Acts of the 1930s, the philosophy of disclosure.

As the Congressional Oversight Panel's January 2009 Special Report on Regulatory Reform states:

> From the time they were introduced at the federal level in the early 1930s, disclosure and reporting requirements have constituted a defining feature of American securities regulation (and of American/global financial regulation more generally).
>
> President Franklin Roosevelt himself explained in April 1933 that although the federal government should never be seen as endorsing or promoting a private security, there was — 'an obligation upon us to insist that every issue of new securities to be sold in interstate commerce be accompanied by full publicity and information and that no essentially important element attending the issue shall be concealed from the buying public.'[39]

FDR's description of the philosophy of disclosure is very important for what he includes and what he excludes.

What he includes is the idea investors should know what they are buying or know what they own and are selling. This is the bedrock principle for both protecting investors and ensuring unrigged financial markets. As FDR said, the buying public should have access to "full information" in an appropriate, timely

---

capitalcomment/the-hill/how-wall-street-is-redefining-bipartisanship.php#.UufnF_PF0L4.twitter

39 Congressional Oversight Panel (2009, January), Special Report on Regulatory Reform, http://cybercemetery.unt.edu/archive/cop/20110402010517/http://cop.senate.gov/documents/cop-012909-report-regulatoryreform.pdf, page 13.

manner so they can independently assess this information and make a fully informed investment decision.

FDR's statement is clear that the intention is to error on disclosing more rather than less. He sets a very high standard for "full information". This standard is "no essentially important element ... shall be concealed from the buying public".

What makes this standard for disclosure so high is to meet it requires the experts in the buying public have access to what they consider all the essentially important information. Disclosure is based on what the most demanding expert considers an important piece of information and not what the non-expert, unsophisticated investor (basically everyone other than a professional money manager[40]) thinks is important.

FDR's statement acknowledges the experts are able to handle additional complexity even if the unsophisticated investor cannot. Therefore this difference in ability to use the disclosed information should not place limits on the information disclosed.

While insisting on full disclosure, FDR's statement acknowledges the fact investors are not required to invest in or have any exposure to an investment where they cannot make a fully informed investment decision. It was understood in FDR's time unsophisticated investors have two choices. First, they don't have to invest where they cannot make use by themselves of the disclosed information. Second, they can rely on their trusted advisors and experts who can use the disclosed information for help in making an investment.

FDR's statement recognizes while disclosure is for all investors, it should not be constrained by the notion of one-size fits all. Hence, disclosure is effective only when it is timely, easily accessible for analytics and, from the most demanding expert's perspective, complete.

This definition of effective disclosure recognizes that it is impossible to know all the ways different investors will choose to use the information disclosed to value an investment or exert market discipline. For example, what a shareholder might find they need could and does differ from what a counterparty to a trade might need. By focusing on full disclosure, this definition of effective disclosure also eliminates the ability of issuers and Wall Street to gain a foothold to argue against more disclosure.

It is only the investors and their trusted third party experts who have the relevant say on what needs to be disclosed and not Wall Street or the issuers of the securities.

---

40 My definition of an unsophisticated investor is different from the SEC's. It defines a sophisticated investor based on their net worth or earnings over the last three years. I would argue your salary or net worth doesn't equate to your degree of sophistication when it comes to investing.

FDR's statement ended the argument over the paradox of transparency. This paradox can be stated as the more information disclosed, the greater the complexity in assessing this information. The opponents of transparency say this paradox is a flaw rather than a feature of transparency. They argue that if there is too much transparency market participants will be overwhelmed and unable to make use of the disclosed information. This statement is the same as saying the individuals at JPMorgan would not be able to assess the risk of Bank of America if these individuals had access to the same level of granular information they see internally about JPMorgan every day (and visa versa). FDR ended the paradox of transparency argument with the focus on investors making a fully informed decision. If even the experts cannot use the information to assess the disclosing firm then, since no one can make a fully informed investment decision, the disclosing firm is too complex and needs to be restructured. If in our example the opponent's argument is true, this suggests both JPMorgan and Bank of America need to be reduced in size and complexity until the individuals in these firms can assess both their own and each other's risk.

Please note FDR's statement included a very specific prohibition. Governments are prohibited from endorsing or promoting a private security. This prohibition exists for two reasons. First, violating the prohibition creates a moral obligation on the part of the government to protect the investors in the security from loss. This moral obligation is created because it can be reasonably assumed investors relied on the government's endorsement in making the decision to invest. Second, the prohibition reinforces the obligation to provide "full information". Governments might be tempted to endorse an investment if they are in possession of information that is not available to investors. Rather than provide an endorsement, governments are responsible for ensuring "full information" and making sure the information they are in possession of is disclosed.

Specifically excluded from FDR's statement is the notion there should be a cost/benefit analysis performed to justify disclosure requirements for each individual financial product Wall Street creates. The goal in adopting the philosophy of disclosure was to prevent opaque financial securities causing another financial crisis. Avoiding another financial crisis was a benefit that far outweighed the costs of requiring disclosure.

If the cost of providing full information so that no essentially important element is concealed is so high that it makes a security unattractive for the issuer to offer, the intent is the security should not be offered.

With this description of the philosophy of disclosure, FDR drew a solid bold line between the state and investors, including the financial sector. The state is responsible for disclosure. Investors are responsible for risk-taking and the results of this risk-taking.

Going forward, opacity became not just a market failure, but also a government failure.

The "What" of disclosure

By making the philosophy of disclosure the centerpiece of the financial system, the FDR Administration recognized the invisible hand of the market sets prices properly only if investors know what they are buying or selling.

The FDR Administration placed on government the responsibility for ensuring investors could know what they are buying or selling. Specifically, the government was made responsible for ensuring investors have access to all the useful, relevant information about an investment in an appropriate, timely manner so they can make a fully informed decision.

But "what" information should be disclosed so that buyers and sellers have valuation transparency?

Answering this question for each investment requires choosing between two different models of disclosure: the "pure information" model and the "intermediary depiction" model.[41]

To understand the difference between these two disclosure models it is easiest to think of a piece of paper with three boxes drawn on it as shown in Figure 1. One box is labeled "reality". Another box is labeled "intermediary". The last box is labeled "investors". There are two ways to get the information in the box labeled "reality" to the box labeled "investors": directly, which would be the "pure information" model or indirectly, by going through the box labeled "intermediary" first.

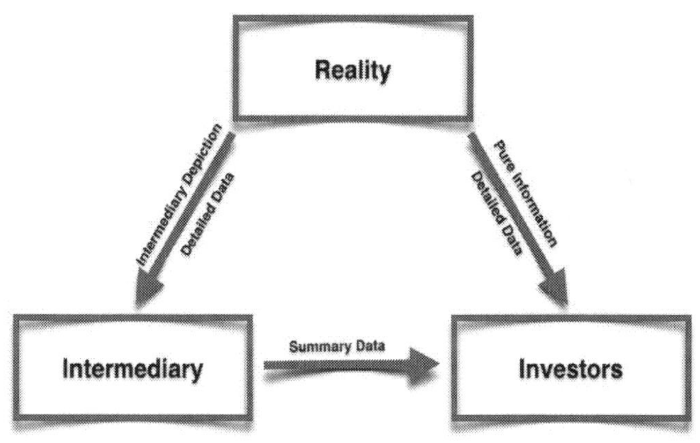

Figure 1: Flow of information Under Pure Versus Intermediary Depiction Disclosure Models

---

[41] Hu, Henry (2012, May 30), Too Complex to Depict? Innovation, 'Pure Information,' and the SEC Disclosure Paradigm, Texas Law Review, Volume 90, Number 7, 2012, http://papers.ssrn.com/sol3/papers.cfm?abstract_id=2083708

Each of these disclosure models has circumstances under which it works best. The pure information model works best for entities like banks and structured finance securities where a summary of their exposure details would result in concealing useful, relevant information. The intermediary depiction model works best for manufacturers where a summary by the intermediary of the reality they face can still contain all the useful, relevant information.

The government initially answered and currently answers the question of what to disclose using only the intermediary depiction model. Given the state of information technology in the 1930s, the choice of the intermediary depiction disclosure model made sense. The information technology to fully support the pure information model did not exist. It only really became possible to fully support the pure information model for banks and structured finance securities with the information technology revolution that began in the 1970s and 1980s.

In the early 1990s, I designed, developed and patented an information infrastructure for one of Wall Street's financial innovations: opaque, asset-backed securities. These structured finance securities were created by the financial engineering technique known as securitization. As shown in Figure 2, my information infrastructure was probably the first application of the pure information disclosure model using 21st century information technology. It was designed to end the opacity of these opaque, structured finance securities by providing valuation transparency.

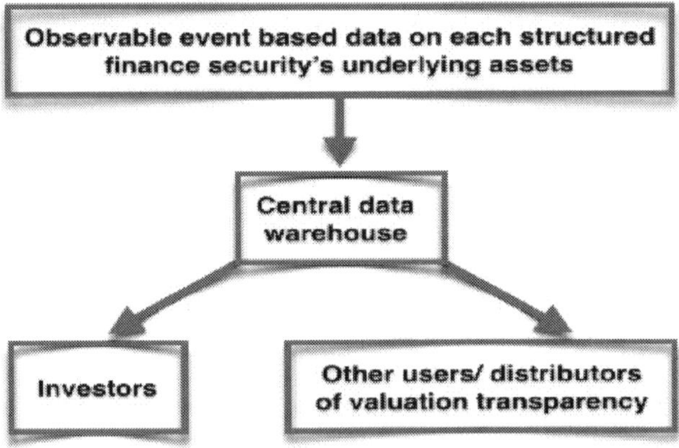

Figure 2: Overview of the flow of observable event based data on each structured finance security's underlying assets needed to provide valuation transparency

While designed explicitly to support the financing of health care account receivables using a commercial paper conduit, the information infrastructure could also handle any other type of asset, like mortgages, credit cards or auto loans, used as collateral to back an asset-backed security. The information infrastructure also supported asset-backed securities ranging in complexity from simple mortgage-backed securities to more complicated asset-backed commercial paper conduits to the most complex financially engineered securities like collateralized debt obligations.

The information infrastructure was designed to give investors the ability to know what they owned. They could see the current performance of the assets backing a specific security they owned in the context of the terms of the deal.

Since access to this information wasn't restricted to current investors, the information infrastructure also supported ongoing liquidity in the secondary market for these securities. The information infrastructure made available to prospective investors the information they needed to assess a security they had an interest in buying.

The reason I created the first practical use of the pure information disclosure model was to deal with the legacy of fraud that Towers Financial cast upon the financing of health care accounts receivable as collateral for an asset-backed security. I understood by capturing the receivable data in a standardized, auditable manner investors would trust the data and use it as the basis for their assessment of the risk and value of these securities. Trusting in their analysis, the investors would resume buying health care receivable backed securities.

Almost two decades have passed since I first demonstrated the need for and viability of the pure information disclosure model based on 21st century information technology. On April 14, 2008, I authored a Learning Curve column, Implementing Transparency, in the leading securitization industry trade publication, Total Securitization. I laid out the gold standard for bringing valuation transparency to structured finance securities. This involved using a central data warehouse to collect, standardize and distribute asset-level data on an observable event based basis.

Meanwhile, the government is still using the intermediary depiction model and talking about if it should adopt the pure information disclosure model so investors can know what they own when it comes to asset-backed securities and financial institutions.

While the choice between the pure information and the intermediary depiction disclosure models is important, the most important element of disclosure is "when."

The gold standard for the "When" of disclosure: Paper or Plastic?

Why is "when" the most important element of disclosure? The timing of "when" disclosure is made is what separates disclosing stale, useless data from providing transparency so buyers and sellers have access to all the fresh, current, useful, relevant information in an appropriate, timely manner so they can fully assess this information and make a fully informed decision.

The intuition behind "when" disclosure should be made so it results in transparency is shown in Figure 3 and goes as follows: paper or plastic?

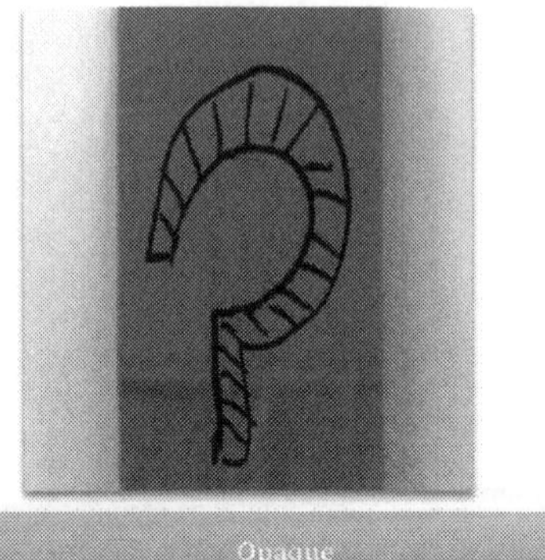

Figure 3: If you cannot open the bag, which bag's contents would you rather value?

Which is easier to value, the contents of a clear plastic bag you can see or the contents of a brown paper bag you cannot see?

If you are like me, you answered the contents of a clear plastic bag.

The same logic applies to securities. You need disclosure that provides the same degree of transparency as a clear plastic bag so you can know what you are buying or know what you own and are selling. After all, if you don't know what is in the bag currently, there is no reason to think you can value what can come out of the bag or security in the future.

To show how the paper or plastic model works, let's apply it to an asset-backed security. To create an asset-backed security, loans or receivables are placed into a trust for the benefit of the investors. Among its other duties, the trustee provides reports to the investors on the performance of the underlying loans or receivables. Under existing global securitization disclosure practices, these reports are provided on a once-per-month or less frequent basis.

The "when" of disclosure addresses the question of how frequently the trustee should provide reports on the performance of the underlying loans or receivables.

A brown paper bag is the physical model that best represents these asset-backed securities. Investors know what loans or receivables went into the bag, but under current reporting practices they do not know what is currently in the bag, i.e. how the loans are currently performing.

This raises the interesting question of "what is the value of the contents of the brown paper bag today?"

Based on the once-per-month report, current and potential investors do not know what is in the brown paper bag right now. With the old stale data in the trustee reports they can only guess at what is a knowable historical fact. Once-per-month or less frequent reporting blocks investors from knowing the current performance of the loans or receivables backing the security. Regardless of how sophisticated the investor's modeling capabilities are, this frequency of reporting limits each investor's valuation of the security to an exercise of blindly betting. If the investor guesses incorrectly, the investor loses money.

However, if we change the frequency when the trustee issues its reports, we can achieve the equivalent of putting the loans or receivables into a clear plastic bag. Doing this requires having the trustee report on an observable event basis. Observable event based reporting involves reporting to investors before the next business day whenever an activity, like a payment or delinquency, occurs involving the underlying loans or receivables.

With observable event based reporting, investors have fresh current information on the performance of the underlying loans and receivables so they know what they own or what they are buying. As a result of addressing "when" disclosure is made, investors don't have to guess about knowable historic facts, but rather have all the knowable historic facts and can make fully informed buy, hold and sell decisions with respect to an asset-backed security.

The paper or plastic bag model can also be applied to a bank.

What would an investor like to know in order to assess the risk and value of a bank? According to the Financial Stability Board's Enhanced Disclosure Task Force:

The seven fundamental principles for enhanced risk disclosures are:

Disclosures should be clear, balanced and understandable.

Disclosures should be comprehensive and include all of the bank's key activities and risks.

Disclosures should present relevant information.

Disclosures should reflect how the bank manages its risks.

Disclosures should be consistent over time.

Disclosures should be comparable among banks.

Disclosures should be provided on a timely basis.[42]

---

42 Report of the Financial Stability Board Enhanced Disclosure Task Force (2012, October 29), Enhancing the Risk Disclosures of Banks, Financial Stability Board, http://www.financialstabilityboard.org/publications/r_121029.pdf, page 6.

In short, an investor would like to know each bank's current exposure details. The investor would like to be able to use modern information technology to drill-down from standardized summary reports to each bank's current exposure details of interest. These standardized details include the current performance of the loans on the bank's balance sheet as well as the current investments the bank has made that are both on its balance sheet, like bonds, or off its balance sheet, like derivatives. With this information, an investor can trust what management has to say about the risk of the bank and independently verify the statements are accurate.

If this is the information an investor would like to have to assess the risk and value of a bank, is it provided under current disclosure practices? No.

Currently, financial institutions issue financial statements under the intermediary depiction disclosure model. In theory, these financial statements reflect the underlying reality of how the loans and investments on and off the financial institution's balance sheet are performing. In reality, these financial statements don't reflect the underlying reality. As the Bank of England's chief economist and former executive director for financial stability Andrew Haldane observed,

> A lot more can and probably should be done to shed a little light on both sides of the balance sheet ... Globally, banking remains too much of a black box which is why, for many investors today, banks are scarcely an investible proposition.[43]

Moving financial institutions to disclosing on a pure information model is the equivalent of putting their information into a clear plastic bag. Under a pure information model, financial institutions would disclose on an ongoing basis at the end of the business day their current global asset, liability and off-balance sheet exposure details.

The combination of "what" is disclosed with the appropriate "when" it is disclosed results in transparency. Specifically, it results in what is known as "valuation transparency". Valuation transparency is the principle focus of the philosophy of disclosure.

Having established what valuation transparency is under the philosophy of disclosure, we turn to how the invisible hand of the market uses valuation transparency to set prices that efficiently allocate resources.

---

[43] MacLellan, Kylie (2011, November 14), Bank's Haldane says banks still too much of a black box, Reuters, http://uk.reuters.com/article/2011/11/14/uk-banks-haldane-idUKTRE7AD29D20111114

The distinction between investing and gambling

You'll look up and down streets. Look 'em over with care.
About some you will say, "I don't choose to go there."
With your head full of brains and your shoes full of feet,
you're too smart to go down any not-so-good street.

— *Dr. Seuss*[44]

Adopting the philosophy of disclosure made possible the distinction between investing and gambling. The distinction is investing involves going through the cyclical three-step process shown in Figure 4.

The Investment Process

The first step in the investment process is to independently assess the risk and value of an investment. This requires access to all the useful, relevant information in an appropriate, timely manner or more simply, valuation transparency. With valuation transparency, the buyer can analyze the investment so they know what could cause the investment to lose money, how likely this is to happen, and how much could be lost if this occurs in addition to knowing what could cause the investment to increase in value. As a result of the first step in the investment process, a potential buyer would know what they were thinking of buying or a seller would know what they owned.

The second step in the investment process is to solicit the price Wall Street is willing to buy and/or sell an investment at.

The third and final step in the investment process is to compare the independently determined value with the prices from Wall Street to make a buy, hold or sell decision.

By comparison, gambling involves simply buying or selling based on the price shown by Wall Street. Rather than using the information disclosed through valuation transparency, gambling instead uses price transparency and the last price that a financial instrument traded at. As everyone knows, price is not an indicator of value. The last price can reflect either what the best investor or biggest fool paid.

---

44 Dr. Seuss (1960), Oh, the Places You'll Go!, New York, NY: Random House Children's Books

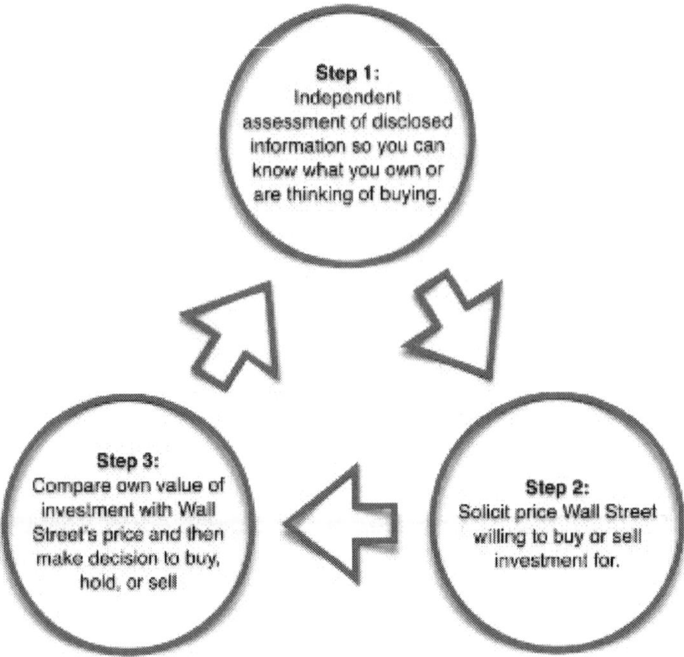

Figure 4: The Investment Process

Besides providing the conditions necessary so the invisible hand can set prices that efficiently allocate resources, the philosophy of disclosure and the investment process has other benefits.

Trust, but Verify key to confidence in the financial system

As shown in Figure 5, trust and confidence in the financial system comes from valuation transparency and the ability to implement the investment process. Investors use the information disclosed by valuation transparency in their own independent assessment. Investors trust this assessment.

Why does this matter?

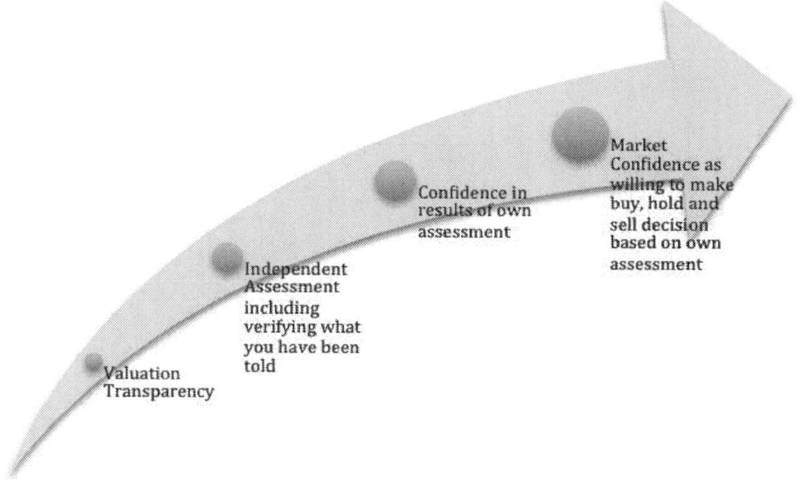

Figure 5: The Investment Process with the Ability to Trust, but Verify Leads to Market Confidence

Confidence is the result of being able to Trust, but Verify.

Investors have confidence when their independent assessment confirms what the investors are being told. However, without valuation transparency, it is virtually impossible to restore trust and confidence in the financial system. Investors have no way of verifying what they have been told is true.

For example, since the beginning of the current financial crisis, governments have run stress tests on the banks and said because the banks passed the tests they are adequately capitalized. Subsequently, banks in several EU countries that passed the tests have been nationalized within a couple months of passing the test. In addition, banks in the U.S. have had another stress test indicating they need to raise more capital. If banks were adequately capitalized, then why were they subsequently nationalized? If banks were adequately capitalized, then why did subsequent tests find they needed to raise more capital? More importantly, if the banks were adequately capitalized, why didn't the regulators require the banks to provide valuation transparency so investors could confirm the fact?

The lack of valuation transparency is a huge red flag waving that reminds market participants something important is being hidden.

Disclosure key to Market Discipline

If I finance a bank and I know if the bank will get in trouble, I will be hit and I will lose money, I will put a price on that.
—*Jeroen Dijsselbloem*[45]

With the introduction of the philosophy of disclosure, the principle of *caveat emptor* was reinforced as now investors had access to the information they needed to assess the risk of an investment and limit their exposure to what they could afford to lose. With valuation transparency, it is possible for investors to do their homework before making an investment and while the investors hold the investment. This applies whether they are investing in bank deposits, AAA-rated securities, junk bonds or equities.

While the principle of *caveat emptor* gives investors a strong incentive for doing their own homework or hiring trusted third parties to do the assessment for them, investors are not required to do their homework. They can blindly gamble if they want.

However, the benefit investors get from independently assessing the risk and value of an investment is they know what they own and can exercise self-discipline by adjusting how much they own of an investment to what they can afford to lose given the investment's risk.

As shown in Figure 6, the driving force behind market discipline is self-discipline and the adjustment of the size of the investors' exposures to what they can afford to lose based on an investment's risk. As the risk of an investment increases, the rate of return investors require also increases. At the same time, the amount of funds investors are willing to put at risk to the investment decreases. The result is a natural restraint on risk taking.

The combination of the philosophy of disclosure and principle of *caveat emptor* also makes the financial system anti-fragile. Because investors can exercise self-discipline and limit the size of their exposures to what they can afford to lose, losses can be recognized as they occur without causing the financial system to collapse.

Compare and contrast this with an opaque financial system like we currently have. The opaque financial system is inherently prone to bubbles and crashes as investment decisions are not restrained by facts, but rather based on emotions. The lack of valuation transparency means investors cannot independently assess the risk of an investment and, even if there is the principle of *caveat emptor*,

---

45 Spiegel, Peter (2015, March 25), Cyprus rescue signals new line on bailouts, Financial Times, http://www.ft.com/intl/cms/s/0/68c9c18e-955e-11e2-a151-00144feabdc0.html?siteedition=intl#axzz35anudA8Y

investors can acquire more exposure to any investment than the investors can afford to lose given the underlying risk of the investment. As a result, an opaque financial system is prone to systemic collapse due to financial contagion as a loss by one investor on one investment can trigger a domino effect that drags down other investors too. If the only benefits a financial system based on the philosophy of disclosure and the principle of caveat emptor provided were investors knowing what they owned, market discipline and financial market stability, it would be enough. However, there are other significant benefits.

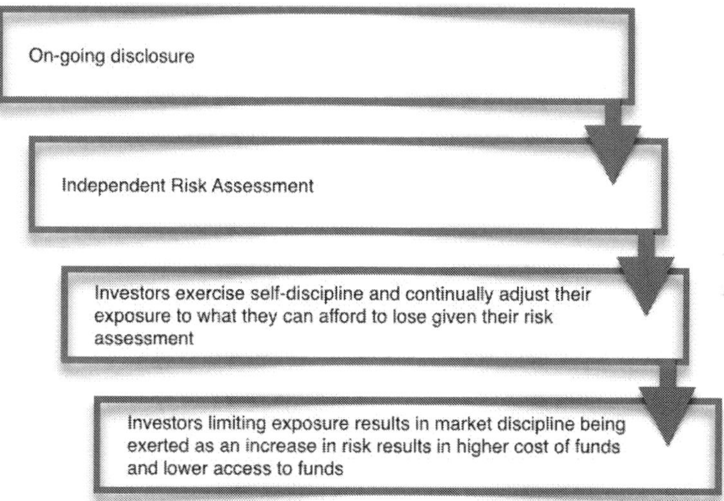
On-going disclosure
Independent Risk Assessment
Investors exercise self-discipline and continually adjust their exposure to what they can afford to lose given their risk assessment
Investors limiting exposure results in market discipline being exerted as an increase in risk results in higher cost of funds and lower access to funds

Figure 6: Process by which on-going Disclosure results in Market Discipline

Recall governments are prohibited from offering opinions about or endorsing specific investments.

Why is this important?

Even with access to valuation transparency, it is understood the investors who do their homework and exercise self-discipline might still lose money on an investment. Investors accept this risk because, with the exception of a bank deposit guarantee, there are no guarantees in investing. Since they accept this risk when they have valuation transparency, investors do not look to be bailed-out of their losses.

This is very important so it bears repeating: because investors are able to know what they are buying and own, investors are willing to accept losses. This willingness to accept losses limits the damage to the real economy caused by capitalism's inherent instability due to disruptive innovations.

When investors do not have valuation transparency so they cannot know what they own, there are several possible outcomes: investors know they are gambling and accept any losses; or investors don't know they are gambling and respond to any rumor of potential losses by trying to get their money back or by looking to be bailed-out of their losses. A 1930s style "run on the bank" is the classic example of investors not knowing they are gambling and responding to any rumor of potential losses by trying to get their money back.

The FDR Framework

> The securities laws of the 1930s are a model for today's solution. They required transparency about stocks and the other investment vehicles of the time. These reforms played perhaps the central role in restoring trust in financial markets. The rules for disclosure need to be updated for modern financial instruments. A proper role for government is to require better disclosure of information.[46]

In redesigning the financial system, the FDR Administration chose to focus on the provision of valuation transparency so the invisible hand of the market could work properly and, where necessary, the market could exert discipline. The FDR Administration understood the need for valuation transparency so investors can know what they own or are buying is applicable to every aspect of the global financial system. Valuation transparency is necessary whether investing in publicly traded or privately placed securities. Valuation transparency is necessary whether these securities are stocks, bonds, fund shares or derivatives. Valuation transparency is necessary whether investing with and through mutual fund or alternative investment asset managers. Valuation transparency is necessary in the setting of benchmark financial prices otherwise like Libor interest rates, foreign exchange rates and commodity prices they can and will be manipulated for the benefit of the banks.

In creating an institutional infrastructure for implementing the combination of disclosure and *caveat emptor*, the focus was not on creating lots and lots of complex regulations requiring regulatory oversight, but rather it was on providing valuation transparency. Specifically, the institutional infrastructure gave the SEC the primary responsibility for ensuring valuation transparency. As the regulator

---

46 Crovitz, Gordon L. (2008, October 28), Credit Panic: Stages of Grief, Wall Street Journal, http://online.wsj.com/news/articles/SB122506810764970701

responsible for preventing opacity, it is the SEC that ensures market participants can access all the useful, relevant information in an appropriate, timely manner.

It is this package of institutional infrastructure and the combination of the philosophy of disclosure plus the principle of *caveat emptor* that I refer to as the FDR Framework. It was the FDR Framework the U.S. exported to the world after World War II. It was the FDR Framework that allowed the U.S. to brag about having the most transparent, liquid capital markets.

The fatal flaw in the original FDR Framework

The FDR Framework was appropriate for the U.S. financial markets in the 1930s. In fact, the FDR Framework continued to work successfully during our current financial crisis for large areas of the financial system that exist today much as they did in the 1930s. However, the financial markets themselves did not remain as they were in the mid-1930s.

Since the 1930s, we have had the information technology revolution. For example, it takes investors just a few computer keystrokes to run a simple analysis to identify all companies with a stock price less than the cash on their balance sheet or a more complex analysis such as an Altman Z-score that models the probability of bankruptcy for a company within a 2 year period to compare dozens of companies within an industry.

For a number of reasons that will be covered in this book, the original FDR Framework with its reliance on regulators, particularly the SEC, proved to be static in its implementation of disclosure. It was unable to adapt to either changes in information processing technology or to keep pace with Wall Street's financial innovations. This meant large opaque areas like banks and structured finance securities developed and created the condition for our current financial crisis.

The Bank of England's Financial Policy Committee documented the failure of the original FDR Framework to prevent our darkest hour since the Great Depression when it described our current opacity driven financial crisis.

> Information frictions were at the heart of the breakdown of trading and the associated evaporation of liquidity in many markets during the crisis. In periods of stress, investors with imperfect information over the quality of assets reduce their buying prices, while holders of 'good' assets are unwilling to sell at prevailing market prices. The collapse of securitization markets in the recent crisis was one manifestation of this problem. The greater the opacity of instruments, the greater the risk to market functioning.[47]

---

47 Bank of England (2011, June), Financial Stability Report, Bank of England, http://www.bankofengland.co.uk/publications/Pages/fsr/2011/fsr29.aspx, page 14.

Because of its failure to prevent opacity from occurring across large areas of the financial system, the original FDR Framework is no longer the appropriate method for implementing the combination of disclosure and *caveat emptor* in the 21st century and beyond. A new FDR framework built on and addressing the points of failure in the original FDR Framework is needed.

This new FDR framework must recognize that one of the greatest strengths of our financial system is it is a dynamic, adaptive system. It evolves to meet the changing needs of the economy it supports. One of the greatest weaknesses of our financial system is also one of the primary drivers of change in the system. It is Wall Street's incentive to reintroduce opacity so it can profit from the mispricing of securities by investors.

This new FDR Framework must also recognize the fatal flaw in the original FDR Framework was its reliance on regulators to ensure valuation transparency. This reliance left the original FDR Framework vulnerable to Wall Street's outsized influence over the process by which the disclosure legislation and regulations are created. Since Wall Street receives a significant benefit in terms of increased profitability from opacity, it has a financial incentive to organize and use its considerable resources to lobby aggressively during the process.

> There are more than 2,000 lobbyists for financial firms and trade groups and many are spreading money around Washington, enlisting like-minded members of Congress to write letters, propose legislation, hold hearings and threaten agency budgets as they pressure regulators to ease up on banks.
>
> Regulators say they try to treat input from lawmakers like that from anyone else.
>
> However, "there are all these other factors, like the budget, like the fact that they can call you up to testify, and they can make your life pretty miserable," said the former head of one regulatory agency who asked not to be identified, as did many of those contacted for this story.
>
> The campaign is working.
>
> While Hensarling's committee can't move legislation on its own — the Senate Banking Committee supports Dodd-Frank — the House panel can work its will in other ways. And it has. Almost four years after Dodd-Frank became law, community banks face lower capital standards than originally proposed and are therefore more likely to fail; fewer derivatives traders have to register with regulators and they face lower hurdles in booking trades than they otherwise would have, partly undermining the law's aim to make this corner of the financial system more transparent; and big banks may soon have a green light to keep investing in potentially risky securities that regulators tried to limit.
>
> In the current election cycle, employees and political action committees of financial companies have donated nearly $149 million to congressional candidates, more than any other industry, according to data compiled by the

> Center for Responsive Politics. That's more than two-and-a-half times the $57 million donated by the health care sector, the second-most-generous industry.
>
> "It's an exceedingly rich industry with a lot at stake," said Brad Miller, a member of the House financial committee from 2003 until he left office in 2013 and currently a lawyer with the firm Grais & Ellsworth. With lawmakers under constant pressure to raise money, Miller said, deep-pocketed lobbyists "don't have to worry about having access to members, because all you have to do is wait for the phone to ring — and you don't have to wait very long."[48]

By lobbying, Wall Street effectively blocks valuation transparency through either reform legislation or regulation.

In contrast, because of the sheer number of investors compared to Wall Street firms and the fact investors can choose not to invest where there isn't valuation transparency, investors are not well organized to lobby for valuation transparency. While investors need valuation transparency in order to know what they are buying or know what they own, they don't commit the same level of resources as Wall Street to lobbying. As a result, even though the investors are as important as Wall Street to the functioning of the global financial markets, their views do not carry at least equal weight during the process by which disclosure legislation and regulation is created.

What is needed to both keep our financial system's greatest strength and minimize its greatest weakness is a 21st century version of the FDR Framework that adds a dynamic element to the existing infrastructure. This dynamic element must create pressure on issuers and regulators to bring valuation transparency to all the currently opaque corners of the global financial system. It must address the classic problem of concentrated benefit to Wall Street and diffuse harm to investors. It must bypass Wall Street's control over the legislative and regulatory process to ensure implementation of the combination of disclosure and *caveat emptor* doesn't fail again and result in another opacity driven financial crisis.

The original FDR Framework Fix: The Transparency Label Initiative™

What is this dynamic element? As shown in Figure 7, it is a global investor led initiative that determines whether or not a security or a benchmark financial price, like the Libor interest rate, qualifies for a label indicating it provides valuation transparency. Regardless of what the SEC's disclosure regulations say

---

48 Wagner, Daniel, Fitzgerald, Alison (2014), The Center for Public Integrity Meet the Banking Caucus, Wall Street's Secret Weapon in Washington, http://www.publicintegrity.org/2014/04/24/14595/meet-banking-caucus-wall-streets-secret-weapon-washington?utm_source=email&utm_campaign=watchdog&utm_medium=publici-email

is needed for compliance, securities without the label from this initiative are by definition opaque and investors are blindly betting when they buy and sell these securities. Regardless of what the financial regulators say, benchmark financial prices without the label are by definition set through an opaque process that Wall Street can use to rig the market against the investors.

With the Transparency Labeling Initiative™ (TLI), a clear dividing line between investing and gambling is created. Where there is a label, investors can know what they own or what they are buying. Where there is no label, investors, regardless of how fancy their models, are blindly gambling. Where there is a label, markets are fair and unrigged. Where there is no label, markets are rigged.

By using a simple label to make a clear distinction between investing and blindly gambling, the Transparency Label Initiative™ brings C.A.L.M. to the global financial system.

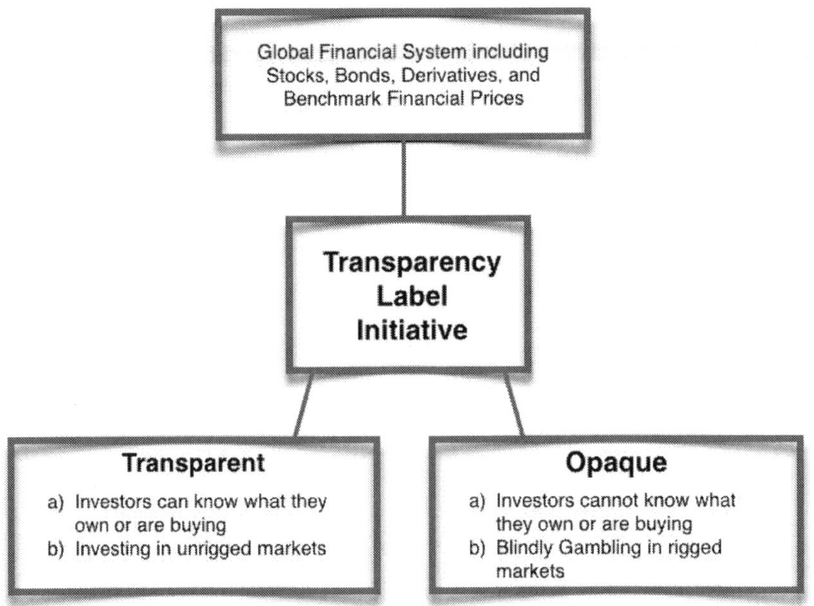

Figure 7: Transparency Label Initiative™ Creates Bright Distinction Between Transparent and Opaque Parts of Global Financial System

- "C" stands for the confidence market participants exhibit as a result of using the clarity provided by valuation transparency to Trust, but Verify.
- "A" stands for the application of discipline on the buy-side so that it enforces disclosure that results in valuation transparency.

- "L" stands for the losses on investments investors' accept rather than expecting a bailout. Investors' know where there is valuation transparency they can independently assess the disclosed information and know what they own or are thinking of buying.
- "M" stands for the market discipline that prevents financial crises and results from investors exercising self-discipline and limiting the size of their individual investments to what they can afford to lose given the risk of each investment.

Where the label is present, investors have access to the information they need so they can independently assess the risk and value of an investment and know what they own or are thinking of buying. Where the label is present, the return on an investment is not rigged. Where the label is present, benchmark financial prices are set in a transparent manner.

Where the label is not present, investors are blindly gambling. Regardless of how sophisticated the investor might be or how much money they oversee, where the label is not present there is not access to the information needed to independently assess the risk and value of an investment. Hence, the purchase or sale of these securities whether they are publicly traded or privately placed is simply blindly gambling on the contents of a brown paper bag. Where the label is not present, a private placement is likely to be rigged against the investor. Where the label is not present, the market, particularly benchmark financial prices, is likely to be rigged against the investor.

Given the label's division of the global financial system between investing and blindly gambling, the label can be used in a number of different ways.

It could be built into the rules for eligible investments for public pension funds, foundations or endowments, since there is no reason they should be blindly gambling.

Bank regulators could use the label in capital regulations and require banks to hold 100% equity against any position where the banks are blindly betting on a security without a label.

The public sector could use the label to restrict its use of financial products sold by Wall Street since there is no reason taxpayer money should be put at risk by civil servants blindly gambling[49].

---

[49] Armitage, Jim (2014, July 17), *How London bankers at Goldman Sachs and Nomura made millions from taxpayers*, The Independent, http://www.independent.co.uk/news/business/analysis-and-features/exclusive-blinded-by-science-the-goldman-deal-that-went-off-the-rails-9613719.html

The following is the calculation of the interest rate a small EU public utility agreed to pay. The complexity of the interest rate calculations makes it

The labeling initiative would be the permanent visible embodiment of the investors demanding valuation transparency. It is needed because the process used by the SEC to craft disclosure regulations does not always result in valuation transparency. For example, the information disclosed by opaque, toxic subprime mortgage-backed securities is in compliance with the disclosure regulation, but it does not provide valuation transparency. The absence of a label is the investors' way of effectively vetoing inadequate disclosure regulations.

---

virtually impossible to know what you own or are buying from the public utility's perspective and it would not receive a transparency label.

Interest: PayIndex[1]+PayIndex[2]+PayIndex[3]

PayIndex[1]: If Index 1 is less than or equal to 7.75%, 1.665%+Radial [1,n], subject to a maximum of AverageCap [1,n]

Otherwise,

7.75%+Radial[1,n], subject to a maximum of AverageCap[1,n]

PayIndex[2}: Radial[2,n]subject to a maximum of AverageCap[2,n]

PayIndex[3]: Radial[3,n], subject to a maximum of AverageCap[3,n]

Index1: Max (12m Euribor, 12m USD Libor), Reset in Arrears

Index2: 10 year EURSwap Rate - 2 year EUR Swap Rate, Reset in Arrears

Index3: 10 year GBP Swap Rate - 10 year EUR Swap Rate, Reset in Arrears

12m Euribor: EUR-EURIBOR-Reuters, with a Designated Maturity of 12 months as published on Reuters page [EURIBOR01]

12m USD Libor: USD-LIBOR-BBA, with a Designated Maturity of 12 months as published on Reuters page [LIBOR01}

10 year EUR Swap Rate: 10 year EUR Interest Rate Swap Rate

Source: Reuters Page ISDAFIX2, 11am London Time Fixing

2 year EUR Swap Rate: 2 year EUR Interest Rate Swap Rate

Source: Reuters Page ISDAFIX2, 11am London time fixing

10 year GBP Swap Rate: 10 year GBP Interest Rate Swap Rate

Source: Reuters Page ISDAFIX3, 11am London time Fixing

Radial[1,n]: Max (Radial[1,n-1]+Index1-7.75%,0),Radial[1,0]=0

Radial[2,n]: Max (Radial[2,n-1]-0.30%-Index2, 0), Radial[2,0]=0

Radial[3,n]: Max (Radial[3,n-1]-0.45%-Index3, 0), Radial[3,0]=0

n: Number of the Interest Calculation Period, n=1,...,80

For the avoidance of doubt, n=1 corresponds to the Interest Calculation Period from 15feb08 to 15May08

AverageCap[i,n]: {SumDCF[n]x6.33%-SumCpn[i,n-1]}/DCF[n], Where i=1,2,3

SumCpn[i,n] = SumCpn[i,n-1]+Cpn[i,n], SumCpn[i.0]=0, Where i=1,2,3

Cpn[i,n]:PayIndex[i]xDCF[n], Where i=1,2,3

DCF[n]: Daycount Fraction of Interest Calculation Period n, according to 30/360, adjusted modified following convention

SumDCF[n]: Daycount Fraction from the Effective Date to the Interest Payment Date of Interest Calculation Period n, according to 30/360, adjusted modified following convention.

The global securities commissions should embrace the TLI. Where the commissions require disclosure that results in valuation transparency, the TLI confirms this with a label. However, if the disclosure requirements are inadequate, and our current financial crisis shows the commissions are capable of adopting inadequate requirements, the lack of a label provides the commissions with instant feedback to change the requirements without subjecting the global economy to another financial crisis.

The TLI is needed because the process used by financial regulators to oversee the setting of benchmark prices does not always produce prices set using valuation transparency. For example, regulators permitted banks to operate an opaque process for setting the benchmark interest rate for the price of money that allowed the banks to manipulate the interest rate for their own gain.

The global financial regulators should embrace the TLI. Where the financial regulators require global benchmark financial prices using valuation transparency, the TLI confirms this with a label. However, if the global benchmark financial prices continue to be subject to manipulation by the bankers behind a veil of opacity, the lack of a label provides the regulators with instant feedback to change how the global benchmark financial prices are set.

The TLI is needed to limit Wall Street's ability to sell opaque products. It does not prevent Wall Street from selling opaque products. After all, there are always going to be asset managers and investors who think they have a unique ability to analyze the risk of and value an opaque product. Rather, the TLI confines the sale of these products to only those investors willing to accept the risks associated with buying the investment return generated by the unknown contents of a brown paper bag.

With the TLI, asset managers would have to disclose in their prospectus if the manager is restricted to only purchasing investments with a label or whether the manager can engage in blindly betting with the investor's money. This disclosure would allow investors to make an informed decision on which asset managers they use and how much, if any, of their money they want to gamble with on opaque investments. The likely outcome is investors would put the bulk of their money in investments with a label either directly or through asset managers who are restricted to only investing where there is a label.

The TLI allows the investors to directly exert discipline on the issuers so they provide valuation transparency. It doesn't need either congressional action or regulatory approval to set-up and operate. It allows the investors to by-pass Wall Street's influence over the politicians and regulators. It allows investors who are effectively outsiders to have the final say over Washington DC or London or Frankfurt or Tokyo insiders.

If Wall Street wants a valuation transparency label on a security it is selling, it can present to the labeling initiative its case for how the security's disclosure results in valuation transparency. As shown in Figure 8, the security will be put through the labeling initiative's process for determining if a label indicating the security provides valuation transparency is warranted.

The process begins by independently assessing what disclosure is actually needed for the security to provide valuation transparency. If Wall Street's proposed disclosure and the independently assessed disclosure match, the security is awarded a label indicating it provides valuation transparency.

Monitoring the securities that have a valuation transparency label is also an important task for the labeling initiative. Monitoring exerts discipline on the issuers of the securities to ensure they continue to provide valuation transparency where the data is standardized and available for free to all market participants.

The Transparency Label Initiative™ must be free from all conflicts that could call into question the quality or integrity of its labels. Every aspect of its ownership and day-to-day operation must be looked at through the prism of does the potential exist for any type of conflict that would jeopardize the quality or integrity of its labels. Where there is any doubt, the working assumption must be a conflict exists.

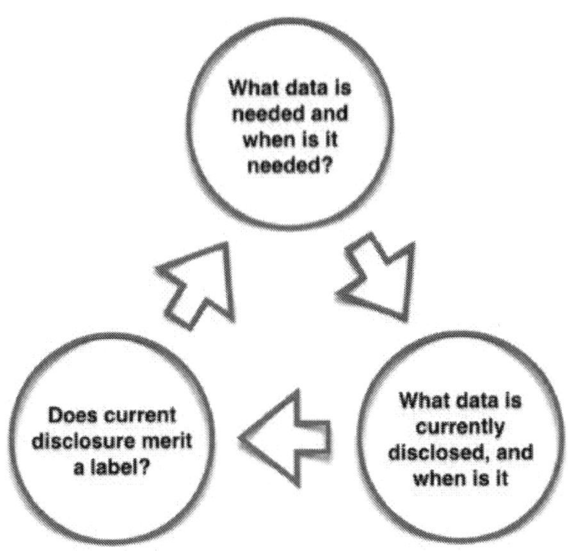

Figure 8: Process for Awarding a Valuation Transparency Label

The primary and only business the Initiative should be in is performing the analytical work that results in the awarding of a label. This eliminates any potential conflicts with other business lines.

The Initiative should exclude from involvement in its ownership or day-to-day operation any individual or firm with a direct conflict of interest. This would include firms like:

- An investment bank that underwrites securities; or
- A financial market self-regulatory entity that is Wall Street's self-funded regulator; or
- A firm that is paid to rate securities; or
- An accounting firm that audits security issuers; or
- A financial information service provider selling pricing data and indexes where it has proprietary access to the underlying information.

The Initiative should exclude from involvement in its ownership or day-to-day operation any individual or firm with an indirect conflict of interest. This includes firms like an asset manager that sells a service that values opaque securities.

Finally, to ensure the integrity of its label, the Transparency Label Initiative™ should avoid the conflict of interest that would exist if it were paid for by issuers. Funding for the Transparency Label Initiative™ should be provided by the institutional part of the buy-side. This would allow individual investors to benefit from and access label related information for free.

Who specifically should fund the initiative? Investors who should fund the initiative include, but are not limited to, wealthy individuals, pension funds, sovereign wealth funds, endowments and insurers. Other market participants who should fund the initiative include asset managers who focus on investing in assets where they can know what they own or what they are selling. Finally, each country's central bank should help to fund this initiative. As a lender, they don't want to blindly gamble with taxpayer money on the contents of a brown paper bag. Instead, central banks want the market to be able to determine the value of any collateral the central banks would receive when making a loan as the lender of last resort.

The Bank of Japan showed how a central bank can lose taxpayer money when there isn't valuation transparency and a central bank is called on to gamble as the lender of last resort.

> In my experience, the most illuminating example of this role of the central bank was the Bank of Japan's decision to provide an unlimited amount of liquidity to Yamaichi Securities after massive off-balance sheet losses were revealed at the brokerage in the fall of 1997. Yamaichi, which had assets of 3.7 trillion yen or 30 billion U.S. dollars at that time, could be regarded as the Japanese equivalent to Lehman Brothers in 2008. Yamaichi also had a sizeable presence internationally, especially in European capital markets. At the time,

> Japan did not have a bankruptcy law that enabled an orderly resolution of securities companies. Given such circumstances, the Bank of Japan decided to provide an unlimited amount of liquidity to the firm. This measure essentially enabled an orderly resolution by effectively replacing all exposures of domestic and overseas market participants against Yamaichi with exposures against the Bank of Japan. The materialization of systemic risk was thus prevented.
>
> The decision to provide unlimited liquidity to Yamaichi was truly a tough one for the Bank of Japan. It was made without knowing whether the institution was solvent or insolvent. While the Bank of Japan eventually suffered some losses.[50]

Finally, the TLI is the investors' contribution to financial stability. Investors know they are responsible for any losses on their exposures whether they have a valuation transparency label on them or not. As a result, they have an incentive to concentrate their investments where there is a transparency label. While the label does not guarantee the investments will make money, at a minimum the investor can know what they are buying and own. Investors can assess the disclosed information and restrict their exposure to what they can afford to lose. By limiting their exposure to what they can afford to lose, investors end the fear of financial contagion and also exert market discipline on management to restrain its risk taking. In addition, TLI makes it possible for investors to exert discipline on the financial regulators to do their job. This includes forcing policymakers to respond to a financial crisis using the Swedish Model that puts Main Street ahead of Wall Street rather than the Japanese Model that puts Wall Street ahead of Main Street.

The TLI is needed because investors and taxpayers cannot afford the SEC or its peers in other countries failing again and having another opacity driven global financial crisis. Having said this, the burden is on me in the remainder of this book to show that we had an opacity driven financial crisis and that the Transparency Label Initiative™ is therefore needed. However, before doing that, it is necessary to understand how along with its adoption of the FDR Framework, the FDR Administration also redesigned the banking system to reduce bank runs and make the banking system capable of protecting the real economy from excess debt in the financial system. For readers who are into economics and investment theory, they should read the following pages on how our banking system is designed. For readers who would rather skip the theory and get straight to how the Transparency Label Initiative™ would have prevented our current financial crisis and the policy response to it, you can skip ahead to Section 3 and the financial crises that undid the FDR Framework and planted the seeds for our current financial crisis.

---

50 Shirakawa, Masaaki, My Intellectual Journey in Central Banking, BIS Papers No. 77, page 61. https://www.bis.org/publ/bppdf/bispap77e.pdf.

Chapter 3

ENDING BANK RUNS WITHOUT ENDING MARKET DISCIPLINE ON BANKS

The worst thing you can do is try to manipulate or control perceptions. It's impossible, and when you are found out the result is disastrous. Better to be transparent and play well with others so that when bad things happen you have a reservoir of good will to bank on.

—*John Gerzema*[51]

The core business of a bank is to support the real economy. One of the ways a bank does this is through financial maturity transformation. On the one hand, banks take in short-term deposits. On the other hand, they invest the money in long-term assets like government securities, bonds, mortgages, and consumer and commercial loans. These investments are used in the real economy to fund the purchase of goods and services.

As a result of investing in long-term assets to support activity in the real economy, banks do not keep 100% of the depositors' money in a safe. Rather, banks retain enough cash to handle the normal needs of its depositors plus a cushion for unexpected fluctuations.

Prior to the creation of central banks, banks had one choice for raising additional cash should the amount of cash depositors needed exceed what the bank has immediately available. They could sell their investments beginning with government securities. The limit to a bank's ability to sell its investments to meet the demand for cash is the lack of a market for its security investments and loans. If these had to be sold quickly, they could only be sold at prices below their real value. These fire sale prices guaranteed the depositors could not get all of their money back.

Critical to the willingness of depositors to keep their money in the bank is the belief that they can get their money back. The cause of bank runs is this belief is undermined.

---

51 Schwabel, Dan (2013, April 16), John Gersema: How Women Will Rule the Future of Work, Forbes, http://www.forbes.com/sites/danschawbel/2013/04/16/john-gerzema-how-women-will-rule-the-future-of-work/

Depositors know banks invest most of their deposits and have only a limited amount of cash available. If the depositors think the bank is no longer capable of returning their money as a result of losses on its loans and investments, they know the depositors at the end of the line asking for their money back won't get all of their money back. Hence, they have an incentive to race to the bank to be at the front of the line. This race is why this phenomenon is referred to as a "run on the bank". Typically, a bank run confirms the depositors' loss of confidence, as the bank is unable to raise through the fire sale of its assets enough to repay the depositors.

"It's a Wonderful Life"

The important point to remember about bank runs is they are triggered by a change in the belief of either retail or wholesale depositors on whether or not they can get all of their money back. This change in belief can be triggered by a simple rumor or excessive losses on the bank's investments.

Can rumor driven bank runs be stopped? Yes.

The character George Bailey demonstrated how a banker could stop a rumor driven bank run in the 1946 movie *It's a Wonderful Life*. The depositors in his bank, the Bailey Building and Loan Association, formed an angry mob and demanded their money back. Mr. Bailey responded by giving a guided tour of where the money was and why the bank didn't have it in its vaults.

> Your money's in Joe's house…and in the Kennedy house, and Mrs. Macklin's house, and a hundred others…We've got to stick together …. to have faith in each other."[52]

As the character George Bailey demonstrated, the only way to effectively stop rumor driven bank runs is by making information available that would allow a depositor to answer the question "can my bank repay me?"

If all of a bank's current exposure data were available, depositors could determine for themselves or rely on independent third party experts to determine for them if their bank had the ability to absorb its losses, continue operating and payoff its depositors when they ask for their money back. In the case of the depositors at the Bailey Building and Loan Association, the townsfolk knew each other and trusted each other to repay their loans.

Knowing the bank has the ability to absorb its losses and continue operating allows depositors to ignore rumors to the contrary and stops the need for the depositors to run to get their deposits back.

---

52 Bailey, George (1946), It's a Wonderful Life, http://thepioneerwoman.com/entertainment/2011/11/the-five-things-i-learned-from-george-bailey/

Naturally, as George Bailey demonstrated, disclosure was the solution of choice by banks to show they could stand on their own two feet

Disclosure is the antidote to bank runs

Transparency is not about restoring trust in institutions.
Transparency is the politics of managing mistrust.

— *Ivan Krastev*[53]

Banks have a long history of using disclosure to prevent bank runs and show they are well run. How did banks do this? By hanging up a brightly lit sign saying "we have nothing to hide and can stand on our own two feet."

All the accounts fit to print

So how does a bank hang up this sign?

If you were J.M. Nichols, president of First National Bank of Englewood, in 1931 you took out a two-page advertisement in the South Town Economist of Chicago and publish a detailed statement of all of your bank's exposure details showing down to the last five cents, just where the bank's money was invested.[54]

This detailed bank statement showed

> every bond ... the price ... carried at on the books ... and ... value at the market; ... a complete list of the commercial paper holdings ... it details its customers' loans ... without mentioning names[55]

Why did J.M. Nichols publish this detailed bank statement?

> Nichols believes, every bank, no matter how large or how small, owes [it] to its depositors.[56]

53 Krastev, Ivan (2013, February), The Transparency Delusion, Eurozine, http://www.eurozine.com/articles/2013-02-01-krastev-en.html

54 First National Bank of Englewood (1931), South Town Economist of Chicago, http://www.newspapers.com/newspage/3955863/

55 American Banker (1931, February), Bank Sets Precedent by Detailing Every Asset, http://www.americanbanker.com/175/index.html?page=28

56 First National Bank of Englewood (1931), South Town Economist of Chicago, http://www.newspapers.com/newspage/3955863/

Mr. Nichols understood disclosing the bank's exposure details would prevent rumor driven bank runs as depositors could assess the solvency of the bank. In addition, Mr. Nichols understood the best way to manage the bank's reputational risk was disclosing the bank's exposure details. Disclosure boxes in bankers' animal spirits because it subjects bank management to the Tabloid Test. This test asks the simple question of would bank management be proud to have all of their business affairs appear in the paper. Mr. Nichols understood this test is why sunshine is the best disinfectant for bad bank behavior. With transparency, bankers would restrain their own behavior for fear of market discipline.

Providing a detailed bank statement also enhanced trust in the bank that went beyond the credibility a bank achieved by honoring its commitments. Disclosure built confidence in the bank, as market participants could trust the bank was capable of continuing as a going concern and verify its financial health. This increased the bank's brand equity.

In addition, it was exactly this type of detailed disclosure that was needed if the central banks were to fulfill what Walter Bagehot called their lender of last resort role. Mr. Bagehot, the father of modern central banking, realized that sometimes rumor driven bank runs could occur on healthy banks that provided detailed disclosure. In the case of a healthy bank experiencing a rumor driven bank run, Mr. Bagehot said central banks should lend freely against good collateral at high rates.

However, in FDR's day, the problem wasn't just rumor driven bank runs.

FDR ends retail bank runs

While admirers of capitalism, we also to a certain extent believe it has limitations that require government intervention in markets to make them work.

—*Janet Yellen*[57]

By the time FDR was inaugurated in March 1933, the U.S. banking system was on the verge of collapse as trust in the banks and bankers had completely evaporated. A week later, he announced a bank holiday and shut the banks.

57 Mitchell, Russ (2012, Fall), A Force at the Fed, BerkeleyHass, http://www.haas.berkeley.edu/groups/pubs/berkeleyhaas/fall2012/feature01.html

The FDR Administration attempts to end bank runs

With the banks shut, FDR and his administration set about restoring confidence. In his first fireside chat on March 12, 1933, he explained the cause of the problem.

> We have had a bad banking situation. Some of our bankers have shown themselves either incompetent or dishonest in their handling of the people's funds. They had used some money entrusted to them in speculation and unwise loans.[58]

He then discussed why the government was stepping in and assuming responsibility for cleaning up the banking system.

> This was of course not true in the vast majority of our banks but it was true in enough of them to shock the people of the United States for a time into a sense of insecurity and to put them in a frame of mind where they did not differentiate but seemed to assume that an act of a comparative few had tainted them all. And so it became the government's job to straighten out this situation and to do it as quickly as possible and that job is being performed.
>
> I do not promise you that every bank will be reopened or that individual losses will not be suffered, but there will be no losses that possibly could be avoided; and there would have been more and greater losses had we continued to drift. I can even promise you salvation for some at least of the sorely pressed banks. We shall be engaged not merely in reopening sound banks but in the creation of sound banks through reorganization.[59]

Left unanswered was the question of how the government was going to determine if a bank was sound. Rather, FDR said a bank was sound if the government let it reopen.

By itself, this review by the government may or may not have restored the depositors' trust in the banking system. It would only have been effective at restoring trust if depositors and other third parties could confirm by assessing the reopened banks' current exposure details the banks were healthy.

FDR cut off the need for this review with the second part of his message: the explicit guarantee of all deposits in the banks that the government allowed to reopen after the bank holiday.

When FDR explicitly prohibited government from endorsing or promoting an investment in a "private" security, he was speaking from his experience with the banks. He understood the moral obligation he had created to bailout any

---

58 Roosevelt, Franklin D. (1933, March 12), First Fireside Chat, http://www.berfrois.com/2012/11/fireside/

59 ibid

investor in bank deposits. This moral obligation resulted in the government's guarantee of each investor' deposits below a certain total amount in each bank.

For many individual depositors, this meant that the government protected all of their deposits. This eliminated their need to worry about could their bank absorb all of its losses and continue operating.

> It is possible that when the banks resume a very few people who have not recovered from their fear may again begin withdrawals. Let me make it clear that the banks will take care of all needs—and it is my belief that hoarding during the past week has become an exceedingly unfashionable pastime. It needs no prophet to tell you that when the people find that they can get their money— that they can get it when they want it for all legitimate purposes—the phantom of fear will soon be laid. People will again be glad to have their money where it will be safely taken care of and where they can use it conveniently at any time. I can assure you that it is safer to keep your money in a reopened bank than under the mattress.
>
> The success of our whole great national program depends, of course, upon the cooperation of the public—on its intelligent support and use of a reliable system.
>
> Remember that the essential accomplishment of the new legislation is that it makes it possible for banks more readily to convert their assets into cash than was the case before. More liberal provision has been made for banks to borrow on these assets at the Reserve Banks and more liberal provision has also been made for issuing currency on the security of these good assets. This currency is not fiat currency. It is issued only on adequate security, and every good bank has an abundance of such security.[60]

The commitment by the Federal Reserve to provide the banks with the currency they needed by lending freely against the banks' assets meant depositors could access their cash even if the bank was insolvent.

> Confirmation of the turnaround in expectations came in two parts: the Dow Jones Industrial Average rose by a statistically significant 15.34 percent on March 15, 1933 (taking into account the two-week trading halt during the Bank Holiday), and by the end of the month, the public had returned to the banks two-thirds of the currency hoarded since the onset of the panic.[61]

The combination of deposit insurance and access to central bank funding stopped the retail depositor bank runs and ended the depositors' concern over the solvency or insolvency of their bank.

---

60 ibid

61 Silber, William L. (2009, July), Why Did FDR's Bank Holiday Succeed, Federal Reserve Bank of New York Economic Policy Review, Volume 15, Number 1, pages 19-30, http://www.newyorkfed.org/research/epr/2009/EPRvol15n1.pdf, page 20

The banks and their shareholders were not bailed out. Each bank was still responsible for the losses on its loans and securities. This was intentional. Market participants, like the bank's unsecured debt and equity investors, knew their investments in the bank would continue to be the first used to absorb losses so they had an incentive to exert discipline on the bankers.

Market discipline versus failure prone regulations to restrain bank risk taking

> *Market participants usually have strong incentives to monitor and control the risks they assume in choosing to deal with particular counterparties. In essence, prudential regulation is supplied by the market through counterparty evaluation and monitoring rather than by authorities. Such private prudential regulation can be impaired—indeed, even displaced—if some counterparties assume that government regulations obviate private prudence. We regulators are often perceived as constraining excessive risk-taking more effectively than is demonstrably possible in practice. Except where market discipline is undermined by moral hazard, for example, because of federal guarantees of private debt, private regulation generally has proved far better at constraining excessive risk-taking than has government regulation.*
>
> *—Alan Greenspan, former chairman of the Federal Reserve*[62]

In redesigning the banking system to stop bank runs by retail depositors and the harm they do to the economy, the FDR Administration drew a very bright line between the state and the banks. This line was consistent with the line FDR drew using the philosophy of disclosure between the state and investors.

An eloquent solution for preventing or ending a financial crisis

Even though the state was taking on the role of an investor through the deposit guarantee, the state did not take on the role of promoting investments in the banks. Like every other investor, the regulators used information disclosed by the banks. In the case of the regulators, they were given the power to examine the banks, including their current exposure details.

Like every other investor, the regulators had an incentive to restrain risk taking by the banks. In the regulators' case, the goal was to limit losses incurred by the deposit insurance fund and ultimately the taxpayers. One of the ways regulators

62 Greenspan, Alan (2005, May 5), *Risk transfer and financial stability*, Federal Reserve Board, http://www.federalreserve.gov/Boarddocs/Speeches/2005/20050505/

did this was through enforcement of regulations. Think of these regulations as the equivalent of covenants in debt securities. For example, a regulation might say a bank has to have a minimum level of book capital to its total assets.

The FDR Administration also made sure the unsecured debt investors and shareholders understood they would absorb losses before the state if a bank failed. To put teeth into unsecured debt investors and shareholders taking losses first and exerting self-discipline driven market discipline, the FDR Administration gave the regulators the authority over when the regulator would step in to takeover a failing bank.

Because of the FDR Administration's redesign, the banks were subject to two different mutually reinforcing types of restraint on their risk taking. The first is market discipline. In the presence of valuation transparency, it is always on and as the risk at each bank increases market discipline ratchets up. The second is regulatory discipline. When everything is going well, it is the less binding form of discipline. It becomes more binding as a financial institution approaches failure.

The redesign of the banking system reflected the FDR Administration's choice on whether to emphasize market discipline, regulatory restraint or both. The following European Commission graphic shows the financial reform puzzle the global policymakers' and financial regulators' are trying to solve in 2014. This puzzle focuses on complex regulations and regulatory enforcement while minimizing the role of valuation transparency and market discipline in restraining bank risk taking.

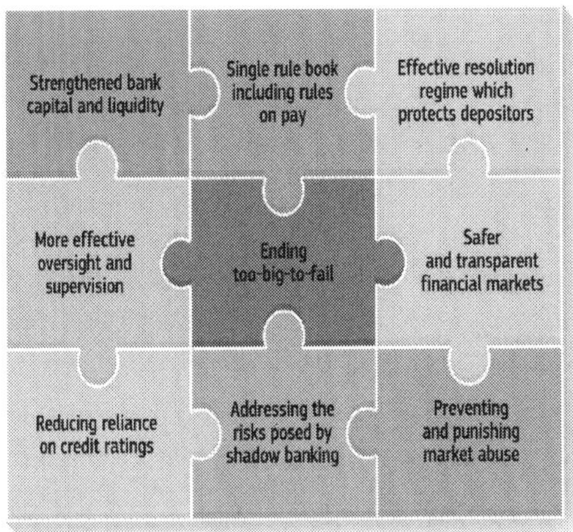

Figure 9. Key pieces of the EU-wide financial reform puzzle.[63]

---

63 Barnier, Intmarser, Comdoc, European Commission (2014, April), Banking Union: restoring financial stability in the Eurozone, http://europa.eu/rapid/press-release_MEMO-14-294_en.htm

Faced with the same opportunity to put in place regulatory micro-management with hundreds of complex regulations to restrain the banks like global policymakers and financial regulators are doing today, the FDR Administration's redesign of the banking system explicitly traded off retaining and ensuring the provision of valuation transparency for fewer regulations. Why? First, the FDR Administration understood that regulators should focus on what they could reasonably be expected to control, namely ensuring valuation transparency, and not what they could not be expected to control, namely the financial performance of the banks. There was and still is no reason to think the regulators can do a better job of assessing the riskiness of a loan or security than the banks and the rest of the financial market participants. As economists at the New York Federal Reserve Bank recently observed "there may be limits to what regulation can achieve."[64] Second, the FDR Administration understood it would be the taxpayer who bore the cost if all the complex regulations failed rather than the investors in the banks. Third, the FDR Administration recognized fully informed market participants practicing self-discipline because their money was on the line would do a better job as the cop on the beat of restraining risk-taking than regulators. Market participants have an incentive to restrict leverage in the financial system, promote liquidity in the banks and moderate interconnectedness between the banks as each of these contributes to the overall risk of an investment in a bank.

The primary restraint on risk taking by the banks is market discipline exerted by unsecured debt holders and equity investors. Knowing their investment can and would be used to absorb losses, these investors lean against the inherent dangers in the credit cycle and box in the bankers' animal spirits. The exposure to losses gives them an incentive to monitor the level of risk and to exert restraint on risk taking. Market discipline from these investors is not limited to simply restraining risk taking by linking it to an increase in the cost of the bank's funding. These investors also control the primary determinants of the total amount of risk taken on by each bank. They elect the board of directors that is responsible for setting the bank's strategy and hiring and firing the managers running the bank.

Market discipline as exerted by unsecured depositors retains the element of the threat of a run on the bank. As a result, banks have an incentive to retain the same high level of liquidity and low risk of their assets as they did before the introduction of deposit insurance when there was the risk of retail depositors engaging in a bank run. This limits the balance sheet capacity of the banks to

---

64 Antill, Samuel, Hou, David, Sarkar, Asani (2014, March), The Growth of Murky Finance, Liberty Street Economics, http://libertystreeteconomics.newyorkfed.org/2014/03/the-growth-of-murky-finance.html#.U0lYWFe73jc

hold loans, but does not limit the total amount of credit in the economy because banks can originate loans for other investors to fund.

The secondary restraint on bank risk taking is regulatory discipline. Restraint by bank regulators is designed to complement and not replace the market discipline provided by investors. While regulatory oversight and complex regulations offer the illusion of safety, they are at best a safety net if market discipline fails. A safety net that can be expanded with more rules, but a safety net that will not prevent a financial crisis in the first place.

By design, restraint by bank regulators is indirect and its ultimate effectiveness is dependent on enforcement. The choice facing bank regulators is between regulating by principle, bright yellow lines banks must stay within, or by rule, rigorous guardrails of what is and is not permissible. Regardless of which choice is made, the regulations are never going to be perfect nor do they guarantee individual banks will not fail or that the banks as a whole will not lose a lot of money. Restraint on risk taking and loss of money is through market discipline. Whether the choice on how to regulate is by principle or by rule, the resulting regulation is the first step in regulatory restraint.

Equally important and the second step in regulatory restraint is how the rules are enforced. When it comes to enforcement of a rule, there is no escaping the role of regulatory judgment. Regulatory judgment affects everything from how a rule will be interpreted to how it will be implemented to how aggressively a rule will be enforced. Starting with their ability to monitor, bank regulators have a number of enforcement tools ranging from the light touch approach of calling attention when they find something they don't like to requesting corrective actions be taken to the heavy handed approach of consent orders if the bank doesn't correct the problem.

Regulatory oversight and complex regulations are at best a safety net. The fact is bank regulators are dependent on the banks and trust the bankers. This dependency includes everything from reliance on the expertise possessed by the bankers as the regulators try to stay on top of the rapidly evolving financial markets to the revolving door (former regulators getting hired by the banks). As a result, the bank regulators are not in a position using a technocratic solution to restrain risk taking or improve on bankers' risk management the same way other market participants like unsecured creditors can. For example, if unsecured creditors think the bank is taking on too much risk, they respond by increasing the bank's cost to borrow money. This reduces the profitability of the bank and is a less than subtle hint to reduce risk. By contrast, bank regulators try asking bankers to restrain their risk taking, but jawboning is simply not very effective when the bankers see there is money to be made.

Charles Partee, a former Federal Reserve Governor who focused on bank supervision and regulation, provided an additional reason for why regulatory restraint is a complement to and not a replacement for market discipline. He observed that financial regulators are political entities.

> To impose prudential restraints is meddlesome and it restricts profits. If the banking system is expanding rapidly, if they can show they're making good money by the new business, for us to try to be too tough with them, to hold them back, is just not going to be acceptable.[65]

In short, because regulators are political entities there is an element of "political will" in the exercise of regulatory restraint. Politicians appoint and oversee the leadership of banking regulators in charge of supervision and regulation. At the same time, banks lobby these politicians. This creates the situation where risk can be building in the financial system, but as Governor Partee observed, it just isn't acceptable to the politicians being too tough on the banks. After all, how does the political appointee explain when everything appears to be going well putting the clamps on bank risk taking is prudent and necessary?

The relationship between politicians and bank regulators creates an asymmetry in how the regulators respond to increased risk taking by the banks. When everything appears to be going well and the banks are taking on more risk, bank regulators do not respond for fear of triggering significant pushback from politicians. Even when things are not going well, as Senator Dick Durbin observed, "And the banks -- hard to believe in a time when we're facing a banking crisis that many of the banks created -- are still the most powerful lobby on Capitol Hill. And they frankly own the place."[66] Wall Street's ownership of Congress can be easily seen when at the urging of Wall Street, bipartisan legislation was introduced to restrain the U.S. Commodity Futures Trading Commission's efforts to reign in Wall Street's ability to place bets using derivatives.

> Despite its formal name, H.R. 1256 should really be called the "Intimidate a Financial Regulator Act."[67]

---

65 Grieder, William (1987), Secrets of the Temple: How the Federal Reserve Runs the Country, New York, NY: Simon & Schuster, Inc., page 525.

66 Durbin, Dick (2009, April), The Banks own the place, interview on WJJG 1530 AM's "Mornings with Ray Hanania. https://www.youtube.com/watch?v=CZbC_IqWEJY

67 Goldstein, Alexis (2013, June), The 'Intimidate the CTFC Act', Washington Post opinion column, http://www.washingtonpost.com/opinions/alexis-goldstein-the-intimidate-the-ctfc-act/2013/06/12/18451f48-d374-11e2-a73e-826d299ff459_story.html

Regulators are aware politicians will pushback. For a bank regulator like the Federal Reserve, this is a major concern. The Federal Reserve places a much higher value on its "political independence" particularly as it applies to the conduct of monetary policy than it does on being tough with the banks when everything appears to be going well. While the Federal Reserve knows it is not truly politically independent, any political pushback raises the prospect of losing what independence it has as politicians can simply change the laws covering the Federal Reserve.

The bottom line is the same for bank regulators everywhere. Due to the prospect of political pushback, they will not exert discipline to restrain bank risk taking when everything appears to be going well. This lack of restraint on bank risk taking when everything appears to be going well is particularly pronounced where the bank regulator is part of a larger organization that also conducts monetary policy.

This lack of regulatory restraint is why market discipline is the primary means for restraining bank risk taking. Market discipline also applies to bank regulators. Market discipline holds bank regulators accountable. In the absence of market discipline, bank regulatory restraint is rigged in the banks favor as enforcement of the regulations doesn't occur when everything is or isn't going well for banks.

By design, bank regulators were given the power to close a bank and are required to choose the strategy for closing a bank that will minimize the cost to the deposit insurance fund and ultimately, the taxpayers. As a result, regulators can take over a bank, restructure a bank, force a write-off of its equity and a write-down of its uninsured liabilities, liquidate its assets or sell it as a whole or in pieces.

Bank regulators were given discretion as to "when" to step in and close a bank. The bank regulators' control over when a bank is closed provides an incentive for the other market participants whose exposures could be used to absorb losses to focus on exerting market discipline to restrain risk taking.

Like regulatory restraint on risk taking, the ability of the regulators to close a bank is also restrained by political will. Bank regulators have to explain to politicians why they closed a bank. As a result, bank regulators are heavily influenced by political will in how they respond to a financial crisis. Specifically, it influences how quickly the bank regulators step in to close banks that are facing large losses on their exposures.

Because the bank regulators are not required to step in and close a bank just because it is insolvent (the market value of its assets is less than the book value of its liabilities), they can allow a bank to stay open and see if it can return to solvency. This is a very important feature of the redesigned financial system.

Banks become special

Like all other investors under the FDR Framework, banks were still held responsible for all losses on their investment exposures. This includes losses on loans they make or securities they buy.

What made banks special was they were now redesigned so they could absorb losses in excess of their book capital levels and so long as they are viable and had a sustainable business model they could continue operating and supporting the real economy.

Banks are able to do this because of the combination of the deposit guarantee and access to central bank funding. The deposit guarantee effectively makes the taxpayers the banks' silent equity partner when the banks have low or negative book capital levels. Access to central bank funding means that banks have funds to meet any depositor requests for withdrawals.

Bank insolvency is no longer permanent

By definition, at any moment in time a bank is solvent if the market value of its assets exceeds the book value of its liabilities. Similarly, at any moment in time, a bank is insolvent if the market value of its assets is less than the book value of its liabilities.

With the addition of the deposit guarantee, a predictable benefit of the redesign of the banks was it made it possible for a viable bank with a sustainable business model to transition from solvent to insolvent and back again as the market value of its assets changes between greater than to less than to greater than the book value of its liabilities.

Without the deposit guarantee, a bank that became insolvent would shortly thereafter be put out of business by the bank run triggered by its insolvency. With the deposit guarantee, the regulators were given responsibility for determining when a bank should be closed.

This is a very important point. Once it became the responsibility of the regulators to determine when a bank would be closed, regulators could make use of the deposit guarantee to allow banks to transition from solvent to insolvent and back to solvent again.

The Bank of England's Andrew Haldane confirmed global bank regulators allow the banks to transition from solvent to insolvent and back to solvent. In a speech, Accounting for bank uncertainty, Mr. Haldane presented the following chart demonstrating this fact. The chart compared aggregate book capital levels to an estimate of the aggregate decline in the market value of major UK bank loan books. The estimate is based on the weekly moving average price of similar traded instruments.

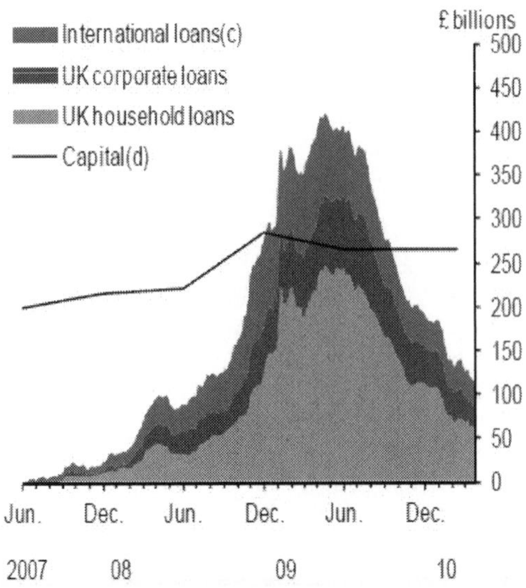

Chart 2: Market value discount to face value of major UK banks' loan books(a)(b)

Sources: Bank of England, Bloomberg, published accounts, UBS Delta, Merrill Lynch, JPMorgan Chase and Bank calculations.

(a) Based on weekly moving average prices of traded instruments as proxies for market value of similar banking book exposures.
(b) Group comprises of Barclays, HSBC, Lloyds Banking Group, Nationwide, Northern Rock, Royal Bank of Scotland and Banco Santander, with aggregate banking book exposures of £2.2 trillion.
(c) International exposures include United States and Europe only.
(d) Held fixed from last reported data at end-2009 H1.[68]

Figure 10: UK banks transitioning between solvent and insolvent

Figure 10 begins in 2007 with the banks being solvent as their book capital level exceeds the decline in the market value of their loan books. By October 2008, the banks are insolvent as the decline in the market value of their loan books exceeds their book capital level. By October 2009, the banks are solvent again as their book capital levels once again exceed the decline in the market value of their loan books. As Mr. Haldane observed,

---

68 Haldane, Andrew (2012), Accounting for bank uncertainty, Bank of England speech, http://www.bankofengland.co.uk/publications/Pages/speeches/2012/540.aspx, page 9

> Had their loan books been marked to market during the crisis, UK banks would have had significantly negative net worth for a protracted period.... Most global banks would have been in a similar position.[69]

Had the regulators not allowed the banks to continue operating and supporting the real economy while they were insolvent, the chart would have ended in 2008 when the decline in the value of the banks' loan portfolios made them insolvent.

The deposit guarantee also lifted Walter Bagehot's restriction on central banks only lending to solvent banks. Central banks could now lend to insolvent banks in the event of a bank run. As a result, illiquidity no longer kills insolvent banks.

The deposit guarantee also changed the length of time a central bank could lend money to a viable bank. It could lend money for periods of time considerably longer than the brief period a panic might last. This put a premium on the central bank charging a higher rate of interest so as to encourage the bank to find alternative sources of funding as soon as possible.

The deposit guarantee did not change the restriction on central banks lending against good collateral at market rates or higher because there was still the possibility that the borrowing bank would not be able to repay its loan.

The deposit guarantee changed the resolution hierarchy for apportioning the pain of restoring an insolvent bank to solvency or absorbing the losses if the regulators determine the bank has failed. The resolution hierarchy became:

1. Future earnings generated by the bank and repayment of bonuses earned through fraud;
2. Common stock holders;
3. Preferred stock holders;
4. Junior unsecured bondholders;
5. Senior bondholders;
6. Uninsured depositors;
7. Host country taxpayers through the deposit guarantee;
8. Foreign taxpayers.

If a bank becomes insolvent under this hierarchy, it should retain 100% of pre-banker bonus earnings with the expectation that it can earn its way out of insolvency. As the bank retains earnings, it reduces the amount of its insolvency. If enough earnings are retained, the book value of the liabilities drops below the market value of the assets and the bank becomes solvent again.

---

69 ibid, page 6.

This only works for banks that have a viable franchise and can continue operating as a going concern. If after recognizing all its losses on its bad debt exposures the bank's income from fees and interest exceeds its interest expense and operating costs, the bank can generate the earnings to restore its solvency and rebuild its book capital levels. A bank that has a viable franchise doesn't go past Step 1 in the hierarchy.

If after recognizing all its losses on its bad debt exposure the bank's income from fees and interest, is less than the bank's interest expense and operating costs, the bank should be resolved. This bank is not viable and should not be bailed out under any circumstances. As part of resolving (closing) this bank, its losses are distributed starting with common stock holders and working down the hierarchy.

Naturally, bankers fight against this hierarchy. The reason they fight is it puts the pain for the losses directly on the bankers. Specifically, while a bank is generating earnings to absorb the losses, banker pay is likely to be highly restricted. Compare and contrast this to the current situation where taxpayers are absorbing the losses and bankers are paying themselves near record levels of pay.

Of course, from the standpoint of everyone lower down in the hierarchy, including taxpayers, they prefer to maximize the amount of future earnings generated by the bank that are used to absorb the losses.

How quickly do banks need to be recapitalized?

This preference for maximizing the use of past, present and future earnings to absorb losses highlights a critical question "how quickly do banks need to be recapitalized after they become insolvent?"

As redesigned by the FDR Administration, banks do not need to be immediately recapitalized. Instead, banks can rebuild their book capital levels over several years by retaining 100% of their pre-banker bonus earnings.

Global policymakers and financial regulators have recognized there is no need for immediate recapitalization on numerous occasions in their handling of insolvent financial institutions. The UK's Financial Services Authority observed

> Adequate liquidity helps a bank survive long enough for a perceived lack of confidence to correct itself or for the bank to implement changes to boost confidence in its credit-worthiness.
>
> If genuine solvency issues exist, adequate liquidity gives the bank more time to try to improve its position sufficiently to restore confidence in it.[70]

---

70 U.K. Financial Services Authority (2011, December), The failure of the Royal Bank of Scotland, FSA, http://www.fsa.gov.uk/pubs/other/rbs.pdf, page 94

Examples of gradually recapitalizing insolvent banks over several years include two earlier crises: the U.S. Savings and Loans crisis and the Less Developed Countries Debt crisis.

This preference for maximizing the use of past, present and future earnings to absorb losses also highlights the expectation banks will absorb losses on their bad loans and investments. By making the bankers responsible for the losses, it restrains their risk taking. If bankers are not responsible for the losses, then they are free to gamble with the result being they privatize any gains and socialize any losses.

In addition to absorbing the losses, the banks also restructure their bad loans to the greater of what the borrowers can afford to repay or to what an independent third party would pay for the collateral securing the loan.

Safety valve between excesses in financial system and real economy

There was one more predictable benefit of redesigning the banking system with the addition of a deposit guarantee. The ability of a bank to withstand an economic shock was no longer limited to its existing book capital. The ability of a bank to withstand an economic shock now also included its ability to generate future earnings after it had absorbed the losses caused by the economic shock.

Because banks could continue to support the real economy even when they have negative book capital levels, banks could now act as a safety valve between the excess debt in the financial system and the real economy. Banks could do this by absorbing the losses on the excess debt upfront. This confines the damage caused by excess debt in the financial system to the banks' book capital levels.

The banks' role as a safety valve can be easily shown. A bank might lend more to a borrower than the borrower is capable of repaying. This loan would have two parts: the portion of the loan the borrower could afford to repay and the portion of the loan in excess of the borrower's capacity to repay.

The portion of the loan in excess of the borrower's capacity to repay is part of the excess debt in the financial system. Since the borrower cannot repay this portion of the debt, the bank should recognize the loss on this portion of the debt as part of restructuring the loan to reflect the borrower's capacity to repay. In recognizing the loss, the bank's book capital level declines.

This decline in book capital acts as a safety valve between the excess debt in the financial system and the real economy and confines the damage. The bank takes the loss and the borrower repays what they can afford. If the bank doesn't take the loss, the real economy has to divert funds that were otherwise being used for reinvestment and growth to debt service on the excess debt.

The ability of banks to act as a safety valve also meant that deleveraging when the financial system contains too much debt could involve a quick cleanup of the excess debt without any need for asset fire sales. This is preferable to the alternative of a long drawn out process where credit is misallocated, as new loans to creditworthy borrowers are not funded in hopes that by rolling over the bad debt it will recover.

To recognize all the benefits of the redesigned banking system, banks had to continue providing valuation transparency and disclose their current exposure details. In the absence of the Transparency Label Initiative™ and the resulting pressure from the buy-side on the banks to disclose their current exposure details, this did not happen.

The ability of banks to act as a safety value is also consistent with the accepted theory on how money is created and how central banks engage in monetary policy. Money is created when a bank makes a loan. At the moment a loan is created, a bank increases both the asset side of its balance sheet, the loan, and the liability side of its balance sheet, a deposit. This deposit, also known as fountain pen money, represents over 97% of the money, broadly defined, currently in circulation.[71] The demand for money comes from borrowers. The supply of new money is limited by the interest rate on the loans and this rate is influenced by central banks. Please note that in creating money the amount of book capital a bank has plays no role. This is a very important point. Using book capital to absorb the losses on the excess debt in the financial system and protect the real economy doesn't cause a contraction in the money supply. When a bank recognizes a loss on a loan, it reduces both the asset side of its balance sheet, the loan, and its book equity. Deposits and therefore the money supply are unchanged. This is a second very important point. Because banks recognizing losses doesn't change the amount of money outstanding, it actually complements both the ongoing creation of money and the implementation of monetary policy. Protecting bank book capital by not recognizing losses actually impairs the creation of money and implementation of monetary policy. It impairs the creation of money by making it harder for borrowers to get a loan by creating uncertainty in the value of their collateral.

---

71 McLeay, Michael, Radia, Amar, Thomas, Ryland (2014), *Money Creation in the Modern Economy*, Bank of England Quarterly Bulletin 2014 Q1, http://www.bankofengland.co.uk/publications/documents/quarterlybulletin/2014/qb14q1prereleasemoneycreation.pdf, page 2

SECTION 3

POST GREAT DEPRESSION FINANCIAL CRISES REVEAL FATAL FLAW IN ORIGINAL FDR FRAMEWORK

In Washington in 2008, the G20 committed to fundamental reform of the global financial system. The objectives were to correct the fault lines that led to the global crisis and to build safer, more resilient sources of finance to serve better the needs of the real economy. … the job of agreeing measures to fix the fault lines that caused the crisis is now substantially complete.[72]

— *Mark Carney, Chairman Financial Stability Board and Governor of the Bank of England*

72 Carney, Mark (2014, November 7), Financial Reforms: Completing the Job and Looking Ahead, Financial Stability Board, http://www.financialstabilityboard.org/wp-content/uploads/FSB-Chair's-Letter-to-G20-Leaders-on-Financial-Reforms-Completing-the-Job-and-Looking-Ahead.pdf, page 1

Chapter 4

THE 1937 RECESSION: BANKS ESCAPE MARKET DISCIPLINE

If institutions had been required to recognize their exposures promptly and value them appropriately, they would have been likely to curtail the worst risks.[73]
— Lloyd Blankfein, CEO Goldman Sachs

The introduction of deposit insurance and increased regulatory oversight did not change the fact that disclosure of all the accounts fit to print was still the sign of a bank that could stand on its own two feet. J.M. Nichols understood this. He also saw a need for banks to be subject to market discipline made possible by this level of disclosure. He was concerned deposit insurance had the potential to reduce market discipline. As he said when describing why he resisted joining the other banks in accepting deposit insurance,

> [S]hould a banker worry about the kind of loans he makes if he knows that if he gets into difficulties the government will make good his losses?[74]

J.M. Nichols was right. Deposit insurance would reduce market discipline on the banks. However, while deposit insurance would reduce market discipline, it could not totally eliminate market discipline on banks by itself. Competitors as well as equity and uninsured debt investors could still exert market discipline so long as banks continued to disclose their current exposure details.

There was a fatal flaw in the FDR Administration's solution for ending retail depositor bank runs. It guaranteed the bank regulators had access to each bank's current exposure details, but it did not guarantee that other market participants had access to each bank's current exposure details. Rather, it was left to the SEC

---

73 Blankfein, Lloyd (2009, October 12), To avoid crises, we need more transparency, Financial Times editorial, http://www.ft.com/intl/cms/s/0/94c6ab6c-b763-11de-9812-00144feab49a.html#axzz2pdbqQ2K2

74 First National Bank of Englewood (1931), South Town Economist of Chicago, http://www.newspapers.com/newspage/3955863/

to require banks to continue with the banks' then current practice of disclosing their current exposure details to the other market participants.

Unfortunately, the SEC adopted the intermediary depiction disclosure model. This meant banks weren't required to continue disclosing their current exposure details. When banks stopped disclosing their current exposure details, they ceased to be clear plastic bags that could be assessed. Instead, they became black boxes. While they were clear plastic bags, the banks and their regulators were subject to market discipline by competitors, unsecured debt investors and equity investors. When they became black boxes, the bankers and their regulators were no longer subject to market discipline. They were no longer subject to market discipline because it is impossible to exert market discipline on a bank or its regulator when the market has no idea of the risks being taken by the bank. When the banks became black boxes, they eliminated the primary restraint on both their risk taking and how the bank regulators performed their responsibilities.

When banks stopped disclosing their current exposure details, it created an information gap between the bank regulators and every other market participant. In theory, the bank regulators knew what was happening inside the black box. Every other market participant did not.

This information gap led to several predictable results. First, bank regulators would exercise discretion as to the timing of banks recognizing their losses. Second, the inability to see inside the black box meant unsecured debt holders like wholesale depositors at the largest banks would engage in the same old fashion bank runs as retail depositors.

Bank financial statements gamed

It didn't take the banks long to stop disclosing their current exposure details. Historically, banks provided disclosure of their current exposure details to prevent rumor driven bank runs by retail depositors. With deposit guarantees effectively ending these bank runs and the SEC not requiring current exposure detail disclosure, the banks limited this disclosure to the bank regulators.

By ending the practice of disclosing current exposure details to all the other market participants, a gap was created between the information available to bank regulators and to the other market participants. No place is this gap better shown than in the use of amortized cost accounting rather than fair value accounting for presenting a bank's financial statements.

Under fair value accounting, the bank's assets are marked-to-market. Lloyd Blankfein, the chief executive of Goldman Sachs, saw this as the key to risk management by banks as well as enforcement of market discipline by other market participants.

> If institutions had been required to recognize their exposures promptly and value them appropriately, they would have been likely to curtail the worst risks.[75]

Under amortized cost accounting, the bank's assets reflect their historical purchase price and not their current market value. When asset values are declining, this effectively hides the true condition of the banks from the other market participants.

When banks were disclosing to all market participants their current exposure details, whether the banks prepared their financial statements on a fair value or amortized cost basis made no difference.

This is a very important point.

With access to a bank's current exposure details, investors could adjust the financial statements prepared on an amortized cost basis to show what they would look like under fair value accounting principles. J.M. Nichols had the First National Bank of Englewood list every bond it held, the price it carried the bond on its books for and the market price of the bond to make this adjustment easy to do.

The perfect complement to bank financial reporting is access to each bank's current exposure details because it eliminates pro-cyclicality. When banks are required to disclose their current asset, liability and off-balance sheet exposure details, it is impossible for them to hide losses on the downswing, thus eliminating the fog of forbearance, and harder for them to be aggressive in booking mark-to-market gains on the upswing.

However, when banks stopped disclosing their current exposure details to anyone other than the bank regulators, it made two substantial differences if the financial statements were prepared on an amortized cost basis.

First, under amortized cost accounting only the regulators know the true financial condition of the banks. J.M. Nichols understood banks could hide their losses when preparing their financial statements using amortized cost accounting and this is why he felt it was an obligation of the banks to disclose their current exposure details so depositors and investors could know the bank's true financial condition.

Second, under amortized cost accounting banks are no longer subjected to market discipline. If the other market participants do not know what is on and off the bank's balance sheet, it is impossible for them to independently assess the risk of the bank. Without this independent assessment of risk, it is impossible for the other market participants to link both the amount and price of their

---

75 Blankfein, Lloyd (2009, October 12), To avoid crises, we need more transparency, Financial Times editorial, http://www.ft.com/intl/cms/s/0/94c6ab6c-b763-11de-9812-00144feab49a.html#axzz2pdbqQ2K2

exposure to the banks to the risk the banks are taking. Without this link, there is no market discipline.

So when did market discipline on U.S. banks end?

According to the Bank of England's Andrew Haldane, it officially ended on June 26, 1938. The Federal Reserve led the charge and was the entity responsible for putting an end to market discipline for the banks or their regulators.

A little background is necessary to understand why the Federal Reserve ended market discipline on U.S. banks. Prior to 1933 and the creation of deposit insurance, banks disclosed their current exposure details. Consistent with this level of disclosure, bank financial statements were prepared on fair value principles where

> securities were carried at market values and their fixed assets at "appraised values".[76]

However, by 1938, on the heels of the 1937 Recession caused by the Federal Reserve tightening monetary policy, the opportunity to end market discipline on banks had arrived. Of course, the banks disclosing their current exposure details and using fair value accounting to prepare their financial statements had nothing to do with the 1937 Recession. Proof of this can be seen by the fact banks had been disclosing their current exposure details and using fair value accounting to prepare their financial statements during the early part of the recovery that began in 1933 after the bank holiday.

On the other hand, bankers had a reason to hate market discipline. Since the beginning of the Great Depression, 10,000 banks had closed. Those banks that remained open saw their profits fall. Naturally, the bankers wanted opacity back to boost their profits and their pay.

The fear of a slowdown in the U.S. recovery in 1938 provided a convenient excuse as the banks, their regulators, primarily the Federal Reserve, and politicians pushed to end fair value accounting.

> At the Fed's prompting, Franklin D Roosevelt called a convention comprising the U.S. Treasury, the Federal Reserve Board, the Comptroller of the Currency and the Federal Deposit Insurance Corporation (FDIC). Its purpose was to determine what should be done with prudential standards to safeguard recovery.
>
> This was no ordinary regulatory convention. Marriner S Eccles, Chairman of the Federal Reserve, called it "guerrilla warfare".

---

76 Haldane, Andrew G. (2010, March), Fair value in foul weather, Bank of England speech, http://www.bankofengland.co.uk/archive/Documents/historicpubs/speeches/2010/speech427.pdf, page 4.

> In one corner were the regulators, the Comptroller of the Currency and FDIC. Scarred by their regulatory experience, and fearing further bank failures, the Comptroller and FDIC pushed for high prudential standards, including preservation of fair values for banks' assets.
>
> In the other corner was the Fed. Scarred by their monetary policy experience, and fearing a further collapse in lending, the Fed argued for laxer prudential standards and the abandonment of fair values. Battle commenced.[77]

It is not clear how hard the Comptroller of the Currency pushed for retention of fair values for banks' assets. Preston Delano, U.S. Comptroller of the Currency in 1938 said

> "...the soundness of the banking system depends upon the soundness of the country's business and industrial enterprises, and should not be measured by the precarious yardstick of current market quotations which often reflect speculative and not true appraisals of intrinsic worth."[78]

Only the FDIC recognized banks disclosing their current exposure details and preparing their financial statements using fair value principles resulted in fewer banks failing.

> The tussle lasted two months, often played out in public through the *New York Times*. In the end, the Fed prevailed.
>
> On 26 June 1938, Franklin D Roosevelt announced (without so much as a hint of irony) the Uniform Agreement on Bank Supervisory Procedures. Banks' investment grade assets were to be valued not at market values but at amortized cost. And banks' sub-investment grade assets were to be valued at a long-run average of market prices.
>
> In the teeth of crisis, and in the interests of macroeconomic stability, the first phase of fair value had ended.[79]

> This was regulatory forbearance on a system-wide scale. And a suspension of fair value accounting rules lay at its heart.[80]

For suspension of fair value accounting rules to provide regulatory forbearance on a system-wide scale in 1938, many banks must have already stopped disclosing their current exposure details to all the other market participants. If market participants had the current exposure details, they would

---

77 ibid, page 5.

78 Ibid, page 3.

79 Ibid, page 5

80 ibid, page 2.

have known the extent of the losses each bank was facing and there would have been nothing gained by switching from fair value accounting to amortized cost accounting.

More importantly, the financial regulators now actively supported banks not providing their current exposure details and ending the ability of the other market participants, like investors, to exert discipline on the banks. Going forward, the justification for continuing to pursue this regulatory policy and preventing the banks from being subject to market discipline was 1938 saw the end of the 1937 Recession and an economic rebound. Of course, there were a variety of other factors contributing to macroeconomic stability and the recovery, including the Federal Reserve easing monetary policy.

What did using accounting to grant system-wide regulatory forbearance and create fog around and uncertainty about the banks' current financial condition achieve?

In 1933, the FDR Administration proved the banking system had two capabilities. First, the combination of deposit insurance and access to central bank funding was sufficient to end bank runs even on banks disclosing their exposure details so everyone knew they were insolvent. Second, these insolvent banks continued to invest in assets, like making loans, to support the real economy.

Why did the Federal Reserve support ending both the banks' tradition of disclosing their current exposure details and market discipline on the banks? The Federal Reserve had to know a lack of disclosure hides a plethora of sins and that it is disclosure that prevents sins from being committed in the first place. The Federal Reserve had to know the part of the Fed responsible for setting monetary policy distains subject matter experts in the part of the Fed responsible for bank supervision. The Federal Reserve had to know the part of the Fed responsible for setting monetary policy prefers to operate off of assumptions and feels no need to defer to the part of the Fed responsible for bank supervision with its focus on details.

What did the Federal Reserve and the other bank regulators think was the benefit of ending market discipline given how bank supervision is thought of and treated at the Federal Reserve as well as how the examination process is practiced?

Everyone dependent on bank supervision

A number of people believe that supervisors paid excessive deference to banks and as a result they were less aggressive in finding issues or in following up on them in a forceful way. Information asymmetry subtly influences the relationship between supervisors and the supervised. Banks have superior information about their business and are the primary gateway to information the supervisor needs. Banks inherently have an information advantage over the supervisors. To understand a bank's exposures and risks the supervisor must request information and often explanations of what the information means. Getting good, timely information is therefore dependent on the willingness and enthusiasm of bank staff in providing that information. Supervisors need good working relationships with their firm, and they believe that a non-confrontational style will enhance that process. Large information requests, lengthy exams, and frequent meetings with management can be a source of friction with the bank.*

**"Within three weeks on the job, I saw the capture set in,"*[81]

As I was taking the Federal Reserve's bank examination classes, the frequently repeated mantra was "Trust, but Verify". Trust what bank management says, but do your homework on all the available useful, relevant information to verify what bank management says is an accurate representation of the facts.

The mechanics of bank supervision

The key to understanding how Trust, but Verify works for bank examiners is to realize they act just like any other investor, albeit a very large investor. They are there to assess the risk of each bank. However, they perform this task with the goal of protecting the deposit insurance fund. Since it would be expecting the impossible, bank examiners are not there to prevent all the bad things bankers might do or all the dumb decisions bankers might make. By assuring the safety and soundness of each financial institution, they act like fire wardens trying to ensure that the failure of any one bank does not bring down the entire banking system. Despite what politically appointed bank regulators claim, bank examiners do not do their job as the "cop on the beat" with the goal of restraining risk taking so that unsecured creditors and equity holders cannot lose all of their investment. It is up to these investors to exert market discipline to restrain risk taking that can result in a bank failing.

---

81 Beim, David (2009, August 18), *Report on Systemic Risk and Bank Supervision*, Prepared for the NY Federal Reserve, http://s3.documentcloud.org/documents/1303305/2009-08-18-frbny-report-on-systemic-risk-and.pdf,

The current bank examination model, as practiced by regulators like the Bank of England's Prudential Regulation Authority and the Federal Reserve, involves an analytical component and a box-ticking component.

- The analytical component involves sending out small numbers of examiners to look through the banks' books, demanding lots of detailed information for their internal review and asking the banks to run stress tests on assumptions the regulators provide.
- The box-ticking component involves confirming the bank complies with all of the various rules and follows industry standard best practices. Typically, this means asking the banks if they comply with the different rules and then double-checking the banks' work. It also means checking to see if the banks are following industry standard best practices. For example, examiners check to see if the banks are following best practices for managing a loan portfolio and maximizing the amount of recovery by tracking the current performance of their loans and promptly following up the next day on missed payments.

A key feature of this model is that no detailed information is shared with other market participants even if these market participants, like the bank's competitors, are experts in assessing the riskiness of a bank. In fact, bank regulators have an obligation to keep bank supervisory records secret. Bank regulators argue that this obligation outweighs the public's right to know and exempts supervisory records from Freedom of Information Act requests. Because of this secrecy, the bankers get to weigh in on how the examiners interpret what is happening inside their bank, but other market participants do not get to express an opinion.

If banks provided valuation transparency and disclosed their current exposure details, keeping the supervisory records secret would not be a problem. However, in the absence of valuation transparency, the secrecy of supervisory records has expanded. The Federal Reserve expanded it to cover all of the programs it used to support the banks during our current financial crisis.

Each year, the bank regulators prepare a Report of Examination that tells the bank's board of directors what they found. This report and the examination itself are organized around the CAMELS rating system. The rating is on a scale of 1 to 5, in which 1 signifies a safe and sound bank with no cause for supervisory concern and 5 signifies an unsafe and unsound bank with severe supervisory concerns. This rating summarizes a bank's overall condition by looking at the areas of capital adequacy (C), asset quality (A), management (M), earnings (E), liquidity (L) and sensitivity to market risk (S). Significantly, the rating does not include a measure of a bank's transparency or opacity. It does not reward banks for disclosing their current exposure details and it does not punish banks for creating opacity through opaque corporate structures with thousands of subsidiaries.

The Report of Examination and a bank's CAMELS rating represents the bank supervisors speaking with one voice on the financial condition of the bank. It is produced only after a large bureaucracy has reviewed and accepted or rejected the findings of the bank examiners.

Bank examiners in the field report their findings to their superiors in the area of Supervision and Regulation. As the findings move through the bank regulator to the political appointee at the top, the findings are reviewed at every level. Each level has the right to dispute the findings based on what that person knows about the situation including conversations that person has with senior management of the bank.

Talking about the need for the bank regulator to achieve consensus on the Report of Examination,

> "Interviewees noted the tension involved in getting buy-in from various stakeholders who need to sign off on a decision. In most cases this is a healthy goal that brings different viewpoints to the table and results in support of better decisions and next steps. Indeed exam findings and supervisory ratings need to be subjected to vigorous debate.
>
> But achieving consensus has costs. One of them is delay - "ideas get vetted to death". The structure within supervision at the System level, with Board staff and other Reserve Banks at the table, requires consensus. While different approaches have been tried over the years, there appears to be no real method for forcing decisions when they can be appealed to many different levels within the System, or stymied by those opposed to particular initiatives. Consensus leadership is seen by some as a way to deflect accountability for certain policies or approaches, in that no one feels personal responsibility for particular outcomes.
>
> An allied issue is that building consensus can result in a whittling down of issues or a smoothing of exam findings. Supervisory judgments can be smoothed over so that only the most black-and-white issues will be taken forward as concerns with the bank. Compromise often results in less forceful language and demands on the banks involved."[82]

The focus of bank supervision

At the heart of the bank examination process and the CAMELS rating, is answering the question: does the bank have enough book capital to absorb its estimated losses.

---

[82] ibid, page 9

To answer this question, bank examiners attempt to estimate how much the bank might lose on each of their loans, securities and derivative exposures and what is the probability this loss will occur. They then compare the total of their estimate of losses to the total of the loan loss reserve plus book capital level to see if the bank can absorb the expected losses.

This seems like a lot of work when one considers that it would be a lot easier to insure the banks had adequate book capital to absorb their losses if the bank supervisors approved or disapproved of every exposure (loan, security or derivative) taken on by the bank.

There are several very important reasons why this easier approach is not taken and bank supervisors never have, currently do not and never will approve or disapprove of individual bank loan, security or derivative exposures.

- If the bank supervisors approved or disapproved of every exposure, they rather than the invisible hand operating through the bankers would be the ones determining where capital flows in our financial system and the real economy.
- Bank supervisors cannot do a better job of assessing risk or valuing exposures than the market. The market has more resources and expertise and as a result is better at assessing risk or valuing an individual exposure than bank supervisors.
- If the bank supervisors approved or disapproved of every individual exposure, it would create moral hazard and put the government on the hook for bailing out investors should a bank ever have losses.

Given the fact that bank supervisors globally don't approve or disapprove of individual exposures taken on by banks, it was interesting to see JPMorgan's executives saying the bank regulators had been notified of the London Whale's credit default swap trades.

> [T]hose positions are fully transparent to the regulators ... the bank's regulators get the information on those positions on a regular and recurring basis as part of our normalized reporting.[83]

Because the bank supervisors knew of the trades doesn't mean they approved of the trades. It is not their role to approve or disapprove of any exposure taken by a bank.

---

83 Weil, Jonathan (2013, January 17), Jamie Dimon offers the illusion of transparency, BloombergView, http://www.bloombergview.com/articles/2013-01-17/jpmorgan-s-jamie-dimon-offers-illusion-of-transparency

The statement also implied that the bank supervisors were comfortable with the risk of the trades and the level of losses that had occurred.

Bank supervisors' comfort with losses

How do bank supervisors react when losses actually occur? What level of losses are they willing to tolerate? When do they step in when losses are occurring? What do they do, if anything, to stop the losses from continuing?

Based on my experience in the late 1980s, the answer to these questions is it depends on the situation.

I worked at a Too Big to Fail bank that purchased a multi-billion dollar portfolio of 30-year U.S. Treasury bonds for its trading account. The bank could do so because it was free from any market discipline because it did not report its current exposure details. Naturally, the Federal Reserve and its examiners said nothing when the bonds were purchased.

When the end of the quarter arrived, the bank's financial statements showed an increase in the trading account. Financial market analysts noticed the increase and wanted to know what the trading position or positions were behind the increase. The Federal Reserve and its examiners didn't need to ask questions as they knew the specific securities that had been added to the trading account.

The value of 30-year bonds is highly sensitive to movements in interest rates. During the next quarter, interest rates increased and the value of the bonds decreased. The loss on the bonds climbed to $200 million. The Federal Reserve and its examiners said nothing about the losses.

On the other hand, the financial market analysts saw interest rates increasing and began asking what the impact of the interest rate increase would be on the positions in the trading account and therefore on the bank and its income statement. The bank's response was to end fair value accounting for the bonds and move the bonds into its investment account where amortized cost accounting was used and the bonds would no longer be subject to mark-to-market accounting. Moving the bonds into the investment account didn't stop the market value of the bonds from changing. It just meant that the value of the bonds reported in the bank's financial statements would no longer change.

The Federal Reserve and its examiners said nothing about the change in how the bonds would be accounted for even though the change was done to deliberately hide the market value losses from rising interest rates. The bank regulator saying nothing was not an indication it approved of hiding the losses from the market. Rather, it was an indication of the bank regulator's belief in and comfort with the use of opacity to promote the safety and soundness of the financial system.

Interest rates continued to increase and the market value of the bonds continued to decline. The loss in the market value of the bonds climbed past $500 million. The financial market analysts continued to express concern as they suspected the bank was incurring an economic loss of value, but the Federal Reserve and its examiners said nothing.

Interest rates continued to increase and the value of the bonds continued to decline. The loss in the market value of the bonds climbed to $650 million or more than half of the bank's book equity. This triggered a meeting at the Federal Reserve where the bank's management was instructed to stop the losses, but was not told specifically how to do this.

The U.S. Treasury bond bet had a number of lessons.

- It confirmed without valuation transparency banks were not subjected to market discipline. Management would never have put on an interest rate bet of this size had it been required to provide current exposure details as the result of either regulation or pressure from the buy-side to meet the requirements for receiving a Transparency Label Initiative™ label. With valuation transparency, the market would have known exactly what was going on and at a minimum would have hammered the bank's stock price so that it reflected the increased risk represented by the interest rate bet. Declining stock prices tend to get management's attention.
- It confirmed the Federal Reserve and its examiners do not restrain a bank from entering into a trade or booking a loan. This would have violated the principle of letting the invisible hand of the market allocate capital. As the losses began piling up, they also did not exert any discipline on the bank to suggest it should cut back its position. This included saying nothing when the accounting treatment of the trade was changed to hide the losses. Rather, they waited until the market value of the losses reached a level where there might be a threat to the ongoing viability of the bank.

Sometimes in the presence of opacity, like in the case of the bond bet, the regulators' corrective action order arrives in time to prevent the need for further regulatory responses. Other times, as shown by Continental Illinois, corrective action is not taken soon enough and the regulators think a much bigger response is needed.

Chapter 5

CONTINENTAL ILLINOIS: A WARNING THAT SHOULD HAVE PREVENTED OUR CURRENT CRISIS

The strongest bank in the United States will last only so long as the people will have sufficient confidence in it to keep their money there.

— *Carter G. Woodson*[84]

In 1984, Continental Illinois National Bank and Trust became the first Too Big to Fail U.S. bank to be bailed out. Its failure revealed the instability at the heart of the global financial system caused by the lack of valuation transparency and the resulting lack of market discipline on the large, global banks. It also showed:

- Bank regulators using supervision and regulation could not prevent the failure of the large, global, interconnected banks.
- Without valuation transparency, a permanent feature of the banking system was Too Big to Fail banks were subject to old fashion rumor driven bank runs by large depositors not covered by the deposit guarantee. [spacing between bullet points]
- The financial system is very unstable when it is dependent on bank regulators. Bank regulators are there to enhance market discipline and not to replace it.
- Without valuation transparency, the regulatory response to the failure of a large, global bank will always be to bail it out for fear of financial contagion.

---

84 Woodson, Carter Godwin (2000), The Mis-education of the Negro, USA: African American Images, pages 83-84

Continental Illinois: A preview of 2008 bank bailouts

Continental Illinois' failure and the regulatory response to containing the bank run set the precedent for many of the policies adopted to deal with our current financial crisis.

Continental Illinois was a Chicago based bank with a reputation for conservative lending practices. In the early 1970s, management adopted a policy of growth with the intention of becoming one of the largest banks in the world. This growth was fueled in part by acquiring loans from other banks. At its peak, Continental Illinois had $44 billion in assets and over $30 billion in uninsured purchased funding.

One of the banks Continental Illinois was a larger buyer of loans from was Penn Square. Penn Square was an originator of billions of dollars of especially risky loans to the energy industry. When it failed in 1982, its shoddy lending practices were exposed. When the market discovered Continental Illinois had credit problems with its Penn Square loans, it cast doubt on Continental Illinois' solvency. This doubt resulted in a 40% drop in domestic purchased funding as some domestic investors were unwilling to rollover their investments. This debt was replaced with foreign funding which made the bank even more susceptible to a rumor driven bank run.

By 1984, rumors about further deterioration in the health of Continental Illinois began to surface. These rumors quickly turned into a liquidity problem as banks in Tokyo with money to lend refused to lend Continental Illinois money in the unsecured interbank lending market for fear of not being repaid and suffering losses on their investment.

Why did the Tokyo banks engage in an old fashion rumor driven bank run when they feared they wouldn't be repaid? The banks did this because the lack of disclosure by Continental Illinois of its current exposure details meant the banks could not independently assess the solvency of Continental Illinois. Simply put, there were no fact based independent assessments to counter the rumors of insolvency.

As the Continental Illinois' liquidity problems worsened and its access to funds in the unsecured interbank lending market dried up, financial regulators became concerned not just for the bank, but also for the entire global financial system. In an effort to restore trust and confidence to both the bank and the global financial system, the U.S. Office of the Comptroller of the Currency issued a press release on May 10, 1984 saying

> A number of recent rumors concerning Continental Illinois National Bank and Trust Company have caused some concern in the financial markets. The Comptroller's Office is not aware of any significant changes in the bank's

operations, as reflected in its published financial statements, that would serve as the basis for these rumors.[85]

Translation, the Comptroller's Office was saying to the market 1) trust us because we have access to Continental Illinois' current exposure details and 2) you don't have to fear any losses because the bank is still solvent. It didn't work.

There is no surprise the press release failed to stop the bank run occurring in the unsecured interbank lending market. Trust and confidence in the financial markets are the result of valuation transparency. It is only when market participants can independently assess all the useful, relevant information that trust and confidence is restored. Trust and confidence is restored because market participants trust their own assessments and use valuation transparency to verify what is happening with their investment exposures.

A press release from the Comptroller's Office is simply not a credible substitute for valuation transparency. Market participants see the press release as waving a red flag. They wonder if there is nothing to hide, why offer a press release rather than valuation transparency.

When the press release didn't work, the U.S. financial regulators rolled out a series of additional measures to halt the bank run. These measures included guaranteeing repayment of the uninsured depositors and creditors in the bank and ultimately, bailing out the bank. This stopped the bank run. Taken together, all of the actions by the bank regulators set the precedent for how they responded to our current financial crisis.

While the bank run on Continental Illinois was stopped, it didn't restore market confidence in the bank. Market confidence is the result of market participants independently assessing all the useful, relevant information. It is not restored by desperate actions like the government issuing a statement.

Continental Illinois was the first global bank to experience a rumor driven bank run by institutional investors who were not covered by deposit insurance. In the absence of valuation transparency, these investors responded to rumors about the bank's solvency just like the retail depositors had in the 1930s. Absent valuation transparency, there was no evidence to rationally restrain their emotion to run and get their money back.

---

85 Inquiry into Continental Illinois Corp. and Continental Illinois National Bank, Hearings before the Subcommittee on Financial Institution Supervision, Regulation and Insurance of the Committee on Banking, Finance and Urban Affairs, House of Representatives, Ninety-eighth Congress, September 18, 19 and October 4, 1984, Washington, DC: U.S. Government Printing Office, http://fraser.stlouisfed.org/docs/historical/house/house_cinb1984.pdf, page 290.

Lessons from the Continental Illinois bank run

During the fall of 1984, the U.S. House of Representative's Committee on Banking, Finance and Urban Affairs investigated the collapse of Continental Illinois. The investigation reveals the extent history, as in the specifics of Continental Illinois, doesn't repeat itself, but it does, as shown by our current financial crisis, rhyme.

The investigation showed how skeptical Congress was about what the bank regulators claimed was a successful response to the bank's failure and what this response meant for the future. The regulators defined success as restoring stability to the financial system. Congress noticed this stability came at the taxpayer expense. Foreshadowing our current financial crisis, Congress wanted to know how a future call on the taxpayer would be prevented.

Lesson 1: History in banking rhymes

In his opening remarks, Chairman Fernand J. St. Germain highlighted why when it comes to Too Big to Fail banks, history does rhyme.

> This morning we open hearings into the problems of Continental Illinois National Bank, an institution that failed to survive without massive, record breaking, infusions of Federal moneys and credit.
>
> Déjà vu….
>
> In 1977 and 1978, we battled uphill against the combined bank and regulatory lobby to enact an entire set of new and improved supervisory powers—to make certain that no one in the Federal supervisory bureaucracy could claim they lacked the tools.
>
> Yet, today, we return to this forum faced with what is, for all practical purposes, the granddaddy of bank failures, a $44 billion money center bank that rolled into the ditch uncontrolled by its $500,000-a-year chairman and the rest of the megabucks management team—or the Federal bank supervisory system.[86]

Sound familiar? Did anyone in the Federal supervisory bureaucracy claim since the beginning of the financial crisis on August 9, 2007 they lacked the necessary tools? [Hint: this claim was made numerous time and used to explain why the regulators stood aside and let Lehman Brothers file for bankruptcy and as justification for why a global bank could not be taken over and resolved.]

To paraphrase Rep. St. Germain: today, for all practical purposes, we have the granddaddy of bank failures, global banks with assets in the hundreds of billions, if not trillions, of dollars have rolled into the ditch uncontrolled by

[86] ibid, page 2.

their multi-million dollar-a-year chairmen and the rest of their megabucks management teams-or the global bank supervisory system.

He then identified the reason this occurs. Specifically, he looked at why a financial system built on valuation transparency has opacity when it comes to its banks. The bank regulators want opacity.

> In the world of the regulators, secrecy cures all. In my opinion, regulatory secrecy dupes the innocent, the unsophisticated, and doesn't fool, for long, the wise men of international finance....[87]

When I was working at the Fed, I experienced first hand how a bank regulator justified regulatory secrecy. Fed officials justified secrecy about which banks borrowed at the discount window by saying it carried a stigma. Specifically, there was the perception banks that borrowed from the discount window had problems. Had the banks provided valuation transparency, market participants would have known why a bank borrowed from the discount window. Market participants would have known if the bank happened to be short on reserves or if it actually was experiencing financial difficulty.

There is an irony in Rep. St. Germain's observation "in the world of the regulators, secrecy cures all". It is not secrecy that cures the banks, but time. Time bank regulators try to obtain through secrecy, but time market participants would willingly give if there were valuation transparency. Banks are remarkably resilient in their ability over time to recover from their financial difficulties. Market participants are capable of assessing if a bank can do this or not. If it can, market participants grant the time. If not, market participants push for the bank's resolution.

Rep. St. Germain then laid out the Holy Grail for bank regulation.

> We must have a banking system and a regulatory system for all seasons—for good times and bad times.[88]

The only way to achieve a banking and regulatory system for all seasons is if there is valuation transparency. It is only with valuation transparency that the problems with the current system of bank regulation and supervision exposed by Continental Illinois and our current financial crisis are fixed. It is only with valuation transparency that both bankers and regulators are subjected to market discipline.

---

87 ibid, page 2

88 ibid, page 2

Rep. St. Germain doubted five dozen bank examiners are up to the task of really understanding what is happening at a large, global bank with $44 billion in assets let alone one of the behemoths that exist today that have over $1 trillion in assets.

> The size of these institutions make it impossible for examiners to walk through all the loan documents—as might be possible in a smaller institution—and thus much of the regulatory process hinges on the integrity of internal audits, review and control processes. When internal review is faulty, the burden on the examiners increases dramatically.[89]

His doubt is one of the reasons why valuation transparency is needed. With valuation transparency, market participants are able to use 21st century information technology to really understand what is happening at a global bank.

For example, IBM's Watson is designed to be able to look through all the loan documents and highlight where there might be problems.

> The ability to consume vast amounts of information to identify patterns and make informed hypotheses naturally make Watson an excellent solution to help make informed decisions about investment choices, trading patterns and risk management.[90]

Finally, Rep. St. Germain looked at the precedent set by bailing out Continental Illinois. He identified both the potential size of future bailouts and the funding subsidy that big banks receive when their unsecured creditors know they are protected from loss.

> With Continental, we add a new ingredient—the safety and soundness of the U.S. Treasury. For it is the Federal Government, the American taxpayer and bank customers across the land who will bear much of the burden for the mistakes at Continental.
>
> The bailout—the nationalization, assistance package, whatever name fits one's philosophical viewpoint—is enormous by any standard....
>
> And the estimates [of the cost of the bailout of Continental Illinois] may well be only the tip of the iceberg if the FDIC and the Federal Reserve have created—without congressional approval—a brand new entitlement program for money center banks. If Continental is a precedent, the big bank fail-safe security program may, someday, rival defense outlays.

---

89 ibid, page 10

90 IBM (2014), Watson Solutions, http://www-03.ibm.com/innovation/us/watson/watson_in_finance.shtml

> For the banking industry, the bailout presents some significant policy questions. If the bailout program is to proceed on the basis on bank size, there may be a substantial impact on the small and medium size institutions across the Nation that have not enjoyed the automatic bailout features incorporated in the Continental case. The fail-safe banks—with the Continental style 100 percent plus insurance of everything—will clearly have a big let up in the market in the competition for funds and investors.[91]

The implications of the bailout were not lost on the banking industry. In the U.S., the number of banks deemed Too Big to Fail increased from 11 at the time of the Continental Illinois bailout to 19 for our current financial crisis. The bankers also learned the rewards for taking on risk were privatized while the losses would be socialized.

Lesson 2: By design, bank regulators are not a replacement for market discipline

In his prepared remarks, C.Todd Conover, the Comptroller of the Currency said the number one role of bank regulators is to maintain the systemic safety and soundness of the nation's banking system. Bank regulators do this using the combination of regulation and supervision to minimize bank failures while allowing the banks to take on the risk needed to support economic growth.

There are a couple of ways to limit the number of bank failures while permitting the banks to take on risk. One way is enhancing the effectiveness of valuation transparency and market discipline with the combination of regulation and regulatory oversight. This was the system originally designed by the FDR Administration that restored confidence in the banking system in 1933. Another way, which is our current system, is to only use complex regulations and regulatory oversight. At the bank regulators' insistence, this system replaced the system designed by the FDR Administration in 1938.

With the system designed by the FDR Administration, market participants don't prevent banks from taking risk and carrying out their role as financial intermediaries in fueling economic growth. Rather market participants use valuation transparency to simply link each bank's cost of funds to the amount of risk they take. This link between risk and cost of funds makes possible market

---

91 Inquiry into Continental Illinois Corp. and Continental Illinois National Bank, Hearings before the Subcommittee on Financial Institution Supervision, Regulation and Insurance of the Committee on Banking, Finance and Urban Affairs, House of Representatives, Ninety-eighth Congress, September 18, 19 and October 4, 1984, Washington, DC: U.S. Government Printing Office, http://fraser.stlouisfed.org/docs/historical/house/house_cinb1984.pdf, page 10

discipline. Market discipline restrains the total amount of risk taking by each bank by increasing its cost of funds to reflect its level of risk. It is this restraint that prevents bank failures. Regulation and supervision is then used to reinforce market discipline.

With our current system, opacity prevents the constant presence of market discipline. Our current system is solely dependent on complex regulation and regulatory oversight to indirectly control the bankers' risk taking. Regulators do this by issuing regulations that shape the overall industry and limit the scope of business activities. In some cases, bank regulations are very detailed like the Basel III bank capital rules or the Volcker Rule.

Mr. Conover asserted a tradeoff exists between economic growth and the prevention of bank failures using regulations and supervision. To prevent the failure of the Too Big to Fail banks using regulation and supervision would also prevent economic growth, as it would have to be so stifling it would prevent these and the other banks from supporting the real economy.

Mr. Conover's observation about the tradeoff raises an important question: under the current system where we are dependent on complex regulations and regulatory oversight, how do we know that we have achieved the right amount of economic growth to compensate for these bank failures, particularly when bank failures require the taxpayers to bailout the banks? When valuation transparency and market discipline are present, at least we experience the amount of economic growth consistent with market participants' willingness to fund the banks and absorb any losses on these exposures.

Mr. Conover described what bank regulators don't do.

> We do not take over and manage institutions; we cannot substitute for private management in making lending or any other decisions. The primary responsibility for any bank's performance rests with its management and board of directors.[92]
>
> It is not the proper function of regulators to decide what business strategy an individual bank should undertake.[93]

What the bank regulators are not is the cop on the beat. They do not do the jobs of the other market participants in exerting market discipline. Shareholders have direct responsibility for the bank's performance because they choose the board of directors who determine the business strategy for the bank, as well as hire and oversee management. Unsecured creditors have responsibility to exert discipline on bank investment and lending decisions. If a bank makes risky

92 ibid, page 175

93 ibid, page 190

investments or underprices the risk of its loans, the unsecured creditors can and should respond to the increased risk of the bank by decreasing the availability of funds to the bank and charging more for these funds.

However, in the absence of valuation transparency, the ability of the other market participants to do their job is compromised. Unsecured creditors cannot exert discipline to restrain risk taking because they don't know how much risk the bank is taking. Investors in the bank's shares recognize the bank is a black box. They know buying the shares is not an investment but rather a gamble. As a result, they don't elect directors with a dual mandate including a restraint on risk taking, but rather they elect directors with a single mandate to maximize return on equity.

Mr. Conover described what bank regulators do.

> However, as supervisors we do monitor risk exposure, work to see that policies and controls are appropriate to that level of risk, and enforce compliance with the law.[94]
>
> The regulator's role is to see that whichever business strategy a bank chooses, it has the mechanisms in place to implement that strategy in a safe and sound manner....[95]

Bank supervisors act as fire wardens. None of their activities directly limits risk before the bank runs into trouble. Rather, their activities are directed at either trying to make sure a bank is well run by asking questions about sources of risk like loan concentrations or, if the bank fails, trying to make sure its failure doesn't threaten the rest of the financial system.

> It is our responsibility to identify and point out concentrations to the bank. We criticize them if we think there is a problem in the way they are dealing with the loans they are making and if their policies and practices need strengthening. We have to be careful in the concentration area, however, because some concentrations are inevitable. For example, in some parts of the country, you almost can't avoid having a concentration in agricultural loans, auto-industry-related loans or forest product loans.
>
> We don't want to be in the business of allocating credit. If we do choose to criticize a concentration, we ask management and the board to reconfirm their policy or change it. If they decide to change it, we ask them to develop a strategy and a timetable for reducing their concentration.[96]

---

94 ibid, page 175

95 ibid, page 190

96 ibid, Page 298

Not only don't regulators want to be in the business of allocating credit, but also history shows they are not very good at it when they do allocate credit. The closest bank regulators come to allocating capital is with Basel risk-weighted capital requirements. These requirements gave banks an outsized incentive to hold the highly rated, opaque subprime mortgage-backed securities and government debt securities that lost value at the beginning of our current financial crisis.

What happens when a problem like losing over one half of the bank's capital on a bond bet occurs?

> When we identify major weaknesses, we institute corrective measures, and follow up on their implementation. This results in significant improvement in the vast majority of institutions that we identify as having problems.
>
> For some institutions, even prompt and stringent corrective measures are unsuccessful.[97]

The issue here is the timing of when major weaknesses are identified and corrective measures instituted. Unlike the other market participants who are in a position and incented to limit the amount of risk ***before*** it is taken, the regulators do not limit the amount of risk beforehand. They can only hope their corrective measures are adequate to deal with the problem in a timely manner or contain it ***after*** the problem has emerged.

> The safety and soundness of the banking system also requires allowing such poorly managed, financially weak institutions to disappear from the system in an orderly manner.[98]

This is also true when banks provide valuation transparency and are subject to market discipline. There are some bankers who despite regulatory and market discipline will blow up their banks.

> In an important sense, this is what has happened to Continental. The doors are still open, but the officers who allowed the bank's deterioration are no longer part of Continental. Moreover, those that bear responsibility for approving management policies have paid a price. The shareholders face substantial if not total loss, and the directors and former management face potential legal liability.[99]

---

97 ibid, page 175

98 ibid, page 175

99 ibid, Page 175

In our current financial crisis, bank management and shareholders came out much better because of the taxpayer-funded bailout. This shows the bankers learned a lesson on how to dictate better bailout terms. Bank management kept both their jobs and bonuses. Shareholders were protected from losses.

If bank regulators don't help set the business strategy of the banks and don't approve or disapprove of any exposures the banks take on, how do bank regulators restrain risk and prevent bank failure? Regulations. Specifically, bank capital regulations.

Think of the combination of supervision and regulation as a two-pronged approach to limiting bank failures. The goal of supervision is to monitor the banks and hopefully to intervene before a bank fails. The goal of regulation is to require the bank to have enough book capital to absorb all the losses should the bank fail.

The problem is supervision and regulation does not directly restrain the bankers' choice of their loan and investment exposures. What gives rise to risk at a bank are the very exposures the bank regulators do not approve or disapprove of so as not to be in business of credit allocation. It is the responsibility of the other market participants, particularly the investors, to approve or disapprove of these exposures. However, the other market participants cannot exercise market discipline because they lack valuation transparency.

Lesson 3: Bank capital gone before regulators can intervene

If the other market participants, particularly the investors, cannot exercise market discipline, this creates a problem. The problem is who is left to tell management of a global bank to stop implementing a strategy that while it has been working successfully in the past is creating so much risk for the bank that the strategy threatens the bank's viability. Only the regulators and the regulators won't take on the bankers at a global bank.

Mr. Conover described the timidity of the regulators in dealing with a successful bank until it is too late.

> Continental's management strategy of rapid growth with a specialty in energy was quite successful for several years. During the late 1970's, Continental outperformed its peers in growth, earnings, and market perception, and its loan loss record was excellent. In 1978, "Dun's Review" described Continental as one of the five best-managed companies in America.
>
> In 1981, the very strategy that generated praise began to turn against the bank....[100]

[100] Ibid, Pg 173

> With the benefit of hindsight, it is clear that our generally favorable assessment of Continental ... was overly influenced by the bank's outstanding performance during the years 1974 through 1981....[101]
>
> However, the loans that crippled Continental were already on the books.[102]

If the bank regulators cannot step in and say that even a successful strategy is creating too much risk, when can the bank regulators step in? During his testimony, Mr. Conover observed.

> Mr. CONOVER. SO I would say, first of all, that we have the tools to get the information that we need.
>
> Do we need any new enforcement powers or tools of that nature? I honestly don't think so. I will engage in all kinds of conversations with you to get different points of view on the subject, but we have cease and desist powers, civil money penalty powers, authority to remove officers.
>
> Somebody asked me the other day if we shouldn't have a system where we don't have to wait until the bank fails or almost fails to take some action, where we could go in much, much earlier. That sounds good except when you start defining what that trigger point would be. You could say that when you get to 3 percent capital, the regulators can go in and seize the bank. We are seizing private property if we do that. When classified loans get to a particular level do you then, through some emergency power granted to the regulators, automatically let us go in and do something we couldn't otherwise do? Those are possibilities. But they would have to be thought through very carefully.[103]

In short, the bank regulators can only step in when the bank is already experiencing financial difficulty that makes its failure likely.

Rep. Charles Schumer noticed this problem with how bank supervision and regulation works.

> Mr. SCHUMER. In effect, what you have said is, there was no reason to suspect anything was wrong with Continental before 1982, and nothing could have been done about it after 1982. You have made a very persuasive argument that your whole operation of bank examination is useless.[104]

Mr. Conover's argument shows why bank examination is a backstop to market discipline and why bank supervision and regulations is a fundamentally flawed replacement for market discipline.

---

101 ibid, Pg 174

102 Ibid, Pg 174

103 Ibid, Pg 338

104 Ibid, Pg. 343

Mr. CONOVER. No, I don't think so. I think you are overstating the case rather dramatically.

Mr. SCHUMER. That is because I think you did when you said those two things.

Mr. CONOVER. Well, all right. I have outlined in the testimony what our role is as bank supervisor. I have also indicated precisely what the causes of this particular situation were, noted that there were some weaknesses in the way we handled it, and identified the improvements that we have made in our process for the future.

Now, I don't think you can take the particular case at hand and extend it logically to a conclusion that you ought not to have a Comptroller's Office or a bank regulatory function, or whatever because it can't get the job done. I think that before even entertaining such a judgment you have to consider the condition of the rest of the banking system and the timely corrective actions that have been taken by the regulators vis-à-vis any number of other problem banks that have restored them to health.

Mr. SCHUMER. Can you give me an example?

Mr. CONOVER. I will not give you an example.

Mr. SCHUMER. That is the problem.

Mr. CONOVER. Let me finish what I was going to say. I will not give you an example of a specific bank because I don't want to name a bank that is open today, and by definition, we are talking about a bank that is open today. I will, however, provide you with the following information.

As of 1980, when Penn Square became a 3-rated bank [where a 3 refers to its CAMELS score] originally, there were some 250 banks that were also rated three at that particular time. We have gone through and traced exactly what has happened to those banks since then, and I will provide this to you in writing. Now, recognize that you could do this for banks that were rated 3 or 4, or whatever, at any point in time. The data for that particular group of banks indicates that some 65 percent of them have been returned to health and are now rated 1 or 2. Another very large number of them remains rated 3 today but has not deteriorated from that status. A much smaller percentage has declined to 4 or 5 or has failed.

Mr. SCHUMER. HOW many have been money center banks or extremely large banks? You never let us see the details so we are sort of groping in the dark here too, but it is my hunch that you do a much better job in examining little banks than big banks.

I mean, the people here yesterday didn't even know what was going on in the oil and gas division of midcontinental division of Continental Illinois until it was in their words "too late."

How many were large banks? How many of those banks were in the top 50 banks of this country?[105]

---

105 Ibid, page 343

The problem with relying solely on the regulators to restrain the banks is, unlike the market, the regulators can only step in when things are going poorly. It is virtually impossible for the regulators to step in and say stop to a bank when everything is going well. Market participants who are responsible for losses do not have this constraint. They can speak very loudly about the level of risk a bank is taking by simply reducing their exposure with the result of lowering the bank's stock price and increasing the bank's cost of purchased funds.

Lesson 4: Banks regulators' early warning systems don't work

Rep. St. Germain expressed considerable concern over whether the bank regulators were really up to the task not of preventing the failure of a global bank, but of recognizing a global bank was failing early enough so that it would not require a taxpayer bailout. He asked Mr. Conover whether it was really possible given their size to have an early warning system for the large global banks. Mr. Conover responded,

> I think we get a sufficient amount of information. The information we get and the analysis we do, don't enable us to reach a conclusion, per se, about the situation in the bank, but they do raise red flags. They help identify areas that ought to be looked at in greater depth.[106]

The FDR Framework has a built in early warning system. Market participants monitor each bank's risk and adjust their exposure level based on their perception of the bank's risk and their willingness to absorb losses given this risk. As a result, the cost of each bank's funding increases as the risk of each bank increases. An increase in a bank's cost of funds relative to its peers serves as an early warning.

However, since 1938, the link between a bank's cost of purchased funds and its risk has been weakened as market participants have not had the current exposure details they need to accurately assess the risk the banks are taking. The regulators are the only market participants left to try to determine when the red flag on the level of risk at a bank should be raised. Clearly, the regulators are not going to tell the other market participants a red flag has been raised for fear of spooking the market with the result being a run on the bank as participants dramatically reduce their exposure to the bank. Instead, the regulators are hoping the red flag goes up while there is still time for the bank to address its problems without needing a taxpayer-funded bailout.

106 Ibid, page 279

Continental Illinois showed the regulators' red flags don't work for a global bank. These banks can look healthy and well managed one day and the next day look unhealthy and poorly managed. Our current financial crisis confirmed the regulators' warning system doesn't work as it failed in the run-up to the crisis.

Lesson 5: Markets need more information than is currently provided

Mr. Conover was fully aware of the market's need for more information about each bank's financial condition. He observed,

> The market's evaluation of the banking system depends, in large part, on the information that is publicly available. To enhance the credibility of bank financial statements and reduce the likelihood that the market will overreact to incomplete information, the OCC is considering requiring increased disclosure of information about banks.[107]

The question according to Mr. Conover was what information should the banks disclose to reduce the likelihood that market participants will overreact to incomplete information. Every banker in the 1930s knew the answer to this question was and still is a bank's current exposure details.

> Finally, we are continuing to work with other federal banking agencies and the Securities and Exchange Commission to review additional means of improving bank disclosure.[108]

So long as only the SEC is involved and insists on using the intermediary depiction model for disclosure, banks will be opaque, black boxes. In the absence of the Transparency Label Initiative™, it is only when the SEC adopts the pure information model for disclosure that banks will have the transparency of a clear plastic bag. With the Transparency Label Initiative™ the banks will be under pressure to obtain a label by providing the transparency of a clear plastic bag even if the SEC continues to use the intermediary depiction.

Mr. Conover understood Continental Illinois experienced an old fashion rumor driven bank run and that the only way to stop a rumor driven bank run is with disclosure. As shown by our current financial crisis, the additional disclosures approved by the banking agencies and the SEC in the aftermath of the bailout of Continental Illinois were insufficient to prevent a bank run by the same sources of funding that ran from Continental Illinois.

---

107 Ibid, page 221

108 Ibid, page 222

Lesson 6: Absent valuation transparency, imprudent to rely on uninsured short-term funding

In his prepared remarks, Mr. Conover talks about how the market did not provide Continental Illinois with the time it needed to recover. This is interesting because it is the regulators who decide when a bank has failed and is unable to recover. Following Walter Bagehot's dictum, if the regulators thought Continental Illinois was both solvent and viable as Mr. Conover argues it was the Fed should have lent the bank all the money it needed to pay off the investors who wanted their money back.

> Market confidence is an unpredictable but crucial element in the stability of individual banks and the banking system as a whole. Whether a bank survives adverse circumstances is often a matter of whether the market allows it the needed time to work out problems. In the case of Continental, the market didn't provide this needed time....[109]
>
> Although Continental was weakened by asset deterioration, its losses never exceeded capital, and thus it never reached book insolvency.
>
> Rather, funding problems triggered its near-collapse. Beginning in the second half of 1982, the bank was forced to rely increasingly on foreign funding, as federal funds and certificates of deposit rapidly eroded. For almost two years, the overseas funding provided Continental with relatively stable, much needed liquidity. It also made the bank vulnerable to the liquidity problems that occurred in May 1984 when uncertainty about Continental's condition caused the overseas markets to close completely.
>
> Clearly Continental's reliance on uninsured, short-term funds meant that it was particularly vulnerable to a loss of confidence. However, Continental's earlier decision to become a major corporate lender made the wholesale market a natural funding source. The wholesale market was practically a necessity given the restrictive branching statutes in Illinois that made establishment of a broad retail customer base difficult.
>
> Although reliance on uninsured, short-term funds makes a bank sensitive to market perceptions, it is not by itself an imprudent banking practice. If a bank maintains sufficient liquidity and asset quality, periodic shortfalls in funding can be readily accommodated.[110]
>
> Even an extremely conservative liquidity position would not have protected Continental from the major funding crisis it experienced last spring.[111]
>
> Market confidence had begun to turn against the bank in July 1982 when its Penn Square loan problems surfaced publicly. Despite nearly constant OCC

---

109 Ibid, page 199

110 Ibid, page 206

111 Ibid, page 207

supervision and presence in the bank over the next two years, and the efforts by bank management and the board of directors, Continental was unable to fully regain market confidence. In May of this year, the market reacted adversely to rumors of further problems at Continental, and large depositors began withdrawing funds. The bank was unable to stem the run, and federal intervention was required to prevent the bank's collapse.[112]

The imprudent banking practice was to rely on uninsured, unsecured short-term funds while not disclosing the bank's current exposure details. When the Penn Square loan problems surfaced, had Continental Illinois' current exposure details been disclosed market participants could have independently confirmed the impact on the bank and seen the bank was still both viable and solvent. This would have prevented the subsequent rumor driven bank run.

In our current financial crisis, the large, global banks used the same imprudent banking practice of funding their assets with uninsured, unsecured short-term funding and not disclosing their current exposure details. This made them susceptible to the bank run when the interbank lending market froze, lenders refused to extend repurchase agreement based financing and wholesale depositors didn't rollover their maturing unsecured funding.

Lesson 7: Markets trust disclosure, not government statements

Rep. St. Germain and Mr. Conover turned to the effort by the Comptroller of the Currency to use a statement rather than disclosure of the bank's current exposure details to end the rumor driven bank run.

> Mr. CONOVER. Let me clarify what I said in the release on May 10, because I think there has been a significant amount of misunderstanding.
>
> I did not say that the bank was just fine, thank you. What I did say was that the Comptroller's Office was not aware of any significant changes in the bank's operations that would serve as a basis for the rumors that were being circulated. The release also denied a report that had been carried by a Japanese news service that our office had discussed the bank with or requested aid for Continental from any Japanese bank or securities firm.
>
> Obviously, the condition of the bank, as was reported in its financial statements, was well known to the banking industry and to the public at large.[113]

Actually, absent disclosure of the bank's current exposure details, the true financial condition of the bank was not well known. The reason rumors were able to gain traction is the market participants knew the bank had problems, but

---

112 Ibid, page 208
113 Ibid, page 279

did not know or have any ability to independently assess its true condition and exactly how bad its problems were.

This same inability to assess the banks also occurred in our current financial crisis.

> We were not denying that the condition of the bank was poor or shaky. We were simply saying that we knew of no change in its condition, the condition that everybody knew about, that could have served as the basis for those rumors that were flying around all over the place.
>
> Chairman ST GERMAIN. Excuse me. Are you telling me that John and Jane Q depositor, who were constituents of Mr. Annunzio in Illinois—this is the little old man and the little old lady who have worked hard all their lives, and as a result of very penurious living, they happened to have, instead of $100,000, they have $150,000 in Continental Illinois.
>
> Now do we expect that these unsophisticated day laborers read the financial reports in such a manner as to be able to reassure themselves of the fact that Continental did have problems? Because as Comptroller of the Currency, you issued a statement. I know how to make these statements, too. You can make a statement that really is designed to do one thing, but you have got yourself covered so that if the implications that are derived therefrom are what you want them to be, but yet are not accurate, then you can say, well, here is what I said exactly.
>
> Mr. Comptroller, in fact, word went out to the effect that you, the Comptroller, said that there were no big problems that people should be concerned about at Continental. That was the interpretation of your statement. That was on May 10, 1984. Now if you or one of your successors should make that type of statement in the future, how much credence do you think will be given to it?
>
> That is my concern in this instance. Again, where were the red flags?
>
> Mr. CONOVER. The words in the statement were carefully chosen to have only the meaning that they had.
>
> Chairman ST GERMAIN. OK, how about
>
> Mr. CONOVER. There was no intent on our part to give any other meaning to any potential reader of that statement as to the condition of Continental Illinois.
>
> Chairman ST GERMAIN. Was this before or after, help me out here, the statement by Bill Isaac stating all accounts would be covered?
>
> Mr. CONOVER. Oh, this was before.
>
> Chairman ST GERMAIN. Before.
>
> Mr. CONOVER. That statement was not made until the temporary assistance package had been put together, around May 7.
>
> Chairman ST GERMAIN. The purpose of this, then, obviously, was to attempt to stem the outflow of funds, right?

Mr. CONOVER. It was to indicate that there were rumors that clearly were bashing Continental and that in our view those rumors were unjustified. We didn't know what the basis of them was.

Chairman ST GERMAIN. Excuse me, Mr. Conover. My question is, wasn't it the purpose of this to stem the outflow of funds that were occurring at that time in a very dramatic way?

Mr. CONOVER. It was intended to say, again, that we knew of no basis for the rumors so that the run, if you like, that was the result of those rumors, would stop.

Chairman ST GERMAIN. YOU were attempting to stop the run on the bank?

Mr. CONOVER. We were attempting to provide accurate information to the marketplace so that any run that was based on misinformation would stop.

Chairman ST GERMAIN. And you feel that this was accurate information? It is a cute statement. It says there haven't been any significant changes; right, essentially it says this.

Mr. CONOVER. That is what it says.

Chairman ST GERMAIN. NO significant changes. It doesn't say, however, that there should be some significant changes so that there wouldn't be a reason for a run.

Mr. CONOVER. Of course it doesn't say that. That wasn't the situation we were in.

Chairman ST GERMAIN. It wasn't?

Mr. CONOVER. NO; the point, Mr. Chairman

Chairman ST GERMAIN. Well, if that is the case why did we put new management in? Why did we get rid of Mr. Taylor and all those wonderful things?

Mr. CONOVER. The point was that the bank was having funding difficulties as a result of rumors and that we had no knowledge of any reason that those rumors were circulating.

Chairman ST GERMAIN. Mr. Conover, I have got

Mr. CONOVER. The alternative was not to issue the statement.

Chairman ST GERMAIN. That's right. But, remember, the rumors that gave rise to funding difficulties came about as a result of actual factual information that international money managers and domestic money managers were aware of. Is that not the case?

Mr. CONOVER. I wouldn't put it that way, sir. I would say that the rumors had the effect they did because the bank was in fact extremely vulnerable to rumors due to its financial condition, due to the known weaknesses in its loan portfolio, and due to its funding strategy. Where the rumors started from and why they started, I don't know to this day.

Chairman ST GERMAIN. But the rumors were not inaccurate?

Mr. CONOVER. Sure they were. There were rumors that were circulating and had circulated in the previous several days, for example, that the bank was going to declare bankruptcy. That got a little coverage in the press. Anybody who knew anything about how

Chairman ST GERMAIN. Why would that type of rumor arise?

Mr. CONOVER. Mr. Chairman, I don't know how the rumor arose.

Chairman ST GERMAIN. Because some financial analysts in New York a year previously had said they wouldn't even analyze that stock any further and they wouldn't recommend its purchase by anyone. Isn't it things like that that led to this eventually?

Mr. CONOVER. Well, we can speculate as to what the cause and source of the rumors were. But I don't know to this day what they were.[114]

Rumors that there was no way to disprove because of the lack of valuation transparency.

Continental Illinois was seen by the bank regulators as having enough capital to absorb the losses on its nonperforming loans, but due to a lack of valuation transparency the market didn't know how bad the situation was and as a result responded to rumors.

Lesson 8: Regulators prefer Policy of Deceit over Disclosure

Rep. St. Germain and Mr. Conover continued their exchange over the statement issued by the Comptroller. Having already said he thought the statement was designed to deceive market participants about the true status of Continental Illinois' health, Rep. St. Germain now looks at the proverb fool me once, shame on you; fool me twice, shame on me.

Chairman ST GERMAIN. All right. Now, I agree with Chalmers that you do have a duty to try to maintain confidence in the system, as well as in individual institutions. And it is for that reason that I am concerned about this particular statement, its timing, the fact that 7 days later a letter that is—it is not a usual letter. It is an unusual letter because it served to trigger one of the biggest bailouts—the first nationalization in many, many years of a bank in the United States of America.

My concern is that in the future, when the Comptroller, as I stated earlier, either yourself or one of your successors, attempts to make this type of statement, the marketplace, and this is very important as you are dealing in big numbers, is going to say:

Aha, is this another carefully worded pronouncement that can give no more credence to than we should have given to that one of May 10, 1984 with respect to Continental Illinois? Is it a repeat?

That is my concern.

---

[114] Ibid, page 281

> Mr. CONOVER. I share your concern about any decision to make a similar statement in the future and how the marketplace might react to that statement. I just want to make it absolutely clear that in issuing the statement we did, we acted with the full knowledge of the facts that were available to us at the time. And there was never any intent to mislead anybody as to the condition of Continental Illinois.[115]

Please recall FDR's prohibition on government endorsing or promoting an investment in a "private" security. Here were the bank regulators with access to the bank's current exposure details. This was information the market did not have. Giving the bank regulators the benefit of the doubt, they thought this information would make investors willing to fund the bank. The bank regulators had two choices: offer an endorsement or have the bank disclose its current exposure details. The bank regulators offered a qualified endorsement.

The endorsement was qualified because the bank regulators didn't want to be on record as having overstated the condition of the bank. Mr. Conover acknowledged the problem with bank regulators having issued an intentionally deceitful statement. They have reduced their credibility to other market participants to nothing.

The statement issued by the Comptroller marks the adoption of a policy of deceit by financial regulators. The justification for this policy was it was okay to try to deceive market participants to protect the safety and soundness of the financial system. Why was the safety and soundness of the system threatened? Continental Illinois experienced an old fashion rumor-driven bank run. Why did this old fashion rumor driven bank run occur? Market participants could not debunk the rumor because they did not have access to the bank's current exposure details so they could independently assess the risk and solvency of the bank.

Faced with the choice between deceit and disclosure, the bank regulators opted for deceit. Had the bank regulators embraced disclosure they would not have had to issue a statement at all.

In our current financial crisis, bank regulators have also pursued this policy of deceit. One example is the annual stress tests. In the EU, banks had to be nationalized within weeks of passing these stress tests.

Lesson 9: Financial contagion is foundation for Too Big to Fail doctrine

As Mr. Conover's testimony continued, he began taking questions from Rep. Frank Annunzio and Rep. Carroll Hubbard about the bailout ranging from the

---

115 ibid, page 284

specifics of the bailout to why the bailout was necessary. In response to what would have happened if Continental Illinois failed and why the bailout was necessary, Mr. Conover unveiled the Too Big to Fail doctrine.

> Mr. CONOVER. We debated at some length how to handle the Continental situation—whether it ought to be done on an open bank or a closed bank basis, what the consequences of a payoff might be, and so forth. Participating in those debates were the directors of the FDIC, the Chairman of the Federal Reserve Board, and the Secretary of the Treasury.
>
> In our collective judgment, had Continental failed and been treated in a way in which depositors and creditors were not made whole, we could very well have seen a national, if not an international, financial crisis the dimensions of which were difficult to imagine. None of us wanted to find out.[116]
>
> Mr. HUBBARD. Could the depositors be paid off on liquidation?
>
> Mr. CONOVER. There were roughly $3 billion of insured deposits in the bank. That means that there were roughly $37 billion of uninsured deposits in the bank. That leads rather quickly to the conclusion that you couldn't pay off the bank. You could pay off the $3 billion. Then you would be in the position of liquidating $37 billion worth of assets. And, as I indicated earlier, that would have had a tremendous effect on a large number of other banks and borrowers and on the national financial system, if not the world's. Nobody wanted to find out what the full effect was.[117]
>
> Mr. Conover. The Continental situation and how we dealt with it was obviously influenced by our judgment as to the impact of failure on the Nation's, if not the world's, financial system.[118]

Thus was born the doctrine of Too Big to Fail. It applied to every large global bank.

The key assumption behind the doctrine was financial contagion. Should one of these large banks fail, it would trigger a domino effect of failures across the global financial system as well as the companies that used the banking system.

As Mr. Conover said, Too Big to Fail banks would always be bailed out, as no regulator would be willing to risk the resulting impact on the global financial system.

> Mr. ANNUNZIO. Mr. Conover, what you are telling the committee is that without action, there would have been sweeping repercussions in the entire economy of the country and in the banking system of this country....

---

116 Ibid, page. 288

117 ibid, page 301

118 Ibid, page 304

Mr. CONOVER. Let me try to provide some perspective in response to your question. In the case of the 66 banks that I referred to that had more than 100 percent of their equity deposited in Continental, their total assets were approximately $4.8 billion. In the case of the 113 banks that had between 50 and 100 percent of their equity on deposit in Continental, their total assets were $12.3 billion, I don't know what portion of the $12.3 billion to count, nor do I have a way of assessing the impact of lost jobs in those institutions or in businesses that were customers of those institutions.[119]

The regulators, working together, put this package together over a period of several months. I think that the American public, the banking community, and the international financial community ought to take some solace from the fact that the U.S. Government has stood behind its banking system, that the regulators have worked together effectively to accomplish this goal.

The package is not without some weaknesses, however, and we can discuss those later, if you like. But I think the important thing is that the overall goal of maintaining the financial stability of the Nation's banking system has been achieved.[120]

Mr. Conover describes the financial contagion that would result from the failure of Continental Illinois without discussing it was the opacity of the bank that gave rise to financial contagion in the first place. If the bank was not opaque, then market participants knowing they were responsible for losses would engage in self-discipline and limit their exposure to what they can afford to lose. By definition, this eliminates the concern over financial contagion.

Mr. Conover would like some praise for the regulators maintaining financial stability. It is hard to give the regulators credit for stability when it was not the U.S. government that stood behind the U.S. banking system, but rather the U.S. taxpayer.

Our current financial crisis shows Continental Illinois was not a fluke, but rather large opaque global banks are prone to failure.

Lesson 10: Rumor driven bank runs are a feature of our opaque banking system

Rep. Annunzio, Rep. Doug Barnard and Mr. Conover searched for how to end the rumors that fuel old fashion bank runs.

Mr. ANNUNZIO. We have to find some way to end rumors, which destroy confidence.

Mr. CONOVER. I agree with that.

---

119 ibid, page 288

120 Ibid, page 289

Mr. ANNUNZIO. Confidence is the one thing that the people have always had in the banking system of this country. What makes banks institutions that are respected by people is the amount of confidence that they have.

We cannot destroy confidence in the banking system. What the regulators tried to do is save that confidence.[121]

Mr. BARNARD. You know, I want to draw a scenario. Here is a bank that is a good bank, a survivable bank. All of a sudden a rumor begins. It starts to rumbling. This is a big bank. All of a sudden, the international press grabs hold of this. Here is a bank that is subject to bankruptcy. Here is a bank subject to insolvency. Here is a bank that is going to be taken over by a foreign government. And it hits the press. East, west, across the Pacific, into Japan, across to China. Here we go. Aleutian Islands, Alaska, and Australia.

But here we go, all across the world that this bank is failing. What is your remedy? Is there a remedy in law, especially when the information is false?

Mr. CONOVER. When the information is false, you get into the dilemma that I found myself in.

Mr. BARNARD. But you don't have a remedy in law, do you?

Mr. CONOVER. NO, I don't believe we do.

Mr. BARNARD. There are some State laws which say that anyone who starts rumors that cause failure of a bank can be prosecuted, isn't that true?

Mr. CONOVER. I understand that that is true in several States. It is, as I understand it, not a Federal law.

Mr. BARNARD. Isn't it just as serious in this instance?

Mr. CONOVER. Absolutely.

Mr. BARNARD. As crying "fire" in a crowded theater?

Mr. CONOVER. It is. You may not solve that problem, however, by simply passing a law that says if you yell the equivalent of "fire" in a movie house or a church, that becomes a crime because it is virtually impossible to trace the source of rumors and how they get started, just as it is virtually impossible to find a leak that originate in your agency.

Mr. BARNARD. Are you telling us that in this instance, though, there had to be unusual steps taken because of this singular situation with Continental?

Mr. CONOVER. Oh, absolutely.

Mr. BARNARD. Although Continental had been rumored previously not to have been in the greatest of condition, on the other hand, the rumors you feel like were tantamount to causing a run on the bank?

Mr. CONOVER. The condition of Continental was well known. It had not only been reported in the business press but had been reported in the popular press, in newspapers and magazines throughout the country.[122]

---

121 Ibid, page 290

122 Ibid, page 306

The remedy to stop the rumors that destroy confidence is with disclosure of each bank's current exposure details. This can be seen in the following exchange between Rep. Chalmers Wylie and Mr. Conover. The exchange confirms how important it is that market participants be able to perform their own independent assessment of the useful, relevant data (in this case, Continental Illinois' current exposure details).

> Mr. Wylie. But the point there is, and you make in your statement, that although Continental was weakened by asset deteriorations, its losses never exceeded capital and thus it never reached book insolvency.
>
> Rather, its near collapse was triggered by funding problems. Would you like to expand on that?
>
> Mr. CONOVER. That is correct. At the time that the final package was put together, Continental's losses had still not wiped out its capital. We were confident of that because the 1984 examination was done jointly by the Comptroller's Office, the FDIC, and the Fed.[123]

Mr. Conover dismissed the rumors as false. What is his basis for dismissing the rumors as false? The regulators' independent assessment of Continental Illinois' current exposure details showed it was solvent. Mr. Conover had access to this independent assessment. Other market participants did not have access to current exposure details and therefore could not do their own independent assessment.

Banks have known disclosing their current exposure details was necessary to stop rumor driven bank runs since well before 1907. Despite Mr. Conover's claim the condition of Continental was well known, the specifics of its true financial condition were not well known. It was this lack of specifics that allowed rumors to trigger an old fashion bank run.

Lesson 11: Bailing out banks is inherently unfair

Rep. St. Germain pushed back against the doctrine of Too Big to Fail by highlighting the unfairness of the doctrine.

> Chairman ST GERMAIN. …did you ever stop to estimate how much grief and how many lost jobs occurred when W.C. Grant went down the tube?
>
> How many banks were affected? How many developers and shopping centers went into dire difficulty and how many actually failed? How about WPPSS?
>
> How many senior citizens who put their life's savings into WPPSS have been destroyed? How about Baldwin-United? We could have gone in and saved

[123] Ibid, page 291

> all those people. And Penn Square. How many people ended up with no money and, therefore, couldn't buy the groceries, like you said in your answer? …[124]

Lesson 12: Impossible to stop Too Big to Fail policy without valuation transparency

Finally, Rep. St Germain and the other representatives turn their sights on the simple fact the doctrine of Too Big to Fail is impossible to end when the a country has large, opaque global banks.

> But the big question is, what do we do with the next big bank that ends up in this situation? Do we have to come in and do the same thing all over again? How do we say no in the future?[125]
>
> Ever see the fellow who is painting himself into that corner? He doesn't realize there is no door back there. And there is less floor for him to walk over. I got news for you. You are painting yourself in a corner because my question now is: Can you foresee, in view of all the reverberations internationally that you described, had Continental Illinois been allowed to fail, and all those people put out of work and all those corporations out of money and all those other banks that would have failed, in view of that, can you ever foresee one of the 11 multinational money center banks failing? Can we ever afford to let any one of them fail?
>
> Mr. CONOVER. The answer to that, Mr. Chairman, is that we have got to find a way to.[126]
>
> The fact of the matter is, as a practical matter, neither you nor your successors are ever going to let a big bank the size of Continental Illinois fail.
>
> Mr. CONOVER. Mr. Chairman, it isn't whether the bank fails or not. It is how it is handled subsequent to its failure that matters. And we have to find a way. I admit that we don't have a way right now. And so, since we don't have a way, your premise appears to be correct at the moment.[127]

Mr. Conover's observation is spot on. Given our current system of opaque global banks, the bank regulators have no way to abandon the policy of bailing out each Too Big to Fail bank after it fails. Regulators will always be concerned about the potential for financial contagion. This was shown with our current financial crisis.

Mr. Conover is also right what matters isn't whether the bank fails or not, but how it is handled subsequent to its failure. How it is handled is dramatically

---

124 ibid, page 290

125 ibid, page 291

126 Ibid, page 304

127 Ibid, page 300

different when the bank is opaque versus when it is transparent and discloses its current exposure details.

> Chairman ST GERMAIN. That is one of the prime reasons for these hearings. We have quite a few, but one of our principal reasons is we have to make a decision. Do we allow, ever, a large bank to fail?[128]
>
> Mr. [STEWART] MCKINNEY. With all due respect, I think seriously, we have a new kind of bank. ... Mr. Chairman, let us not bandy words. We have a new kind of bank. It is called too big to fail. TBTF, and it is a wonderful bank....[129]

Too Big to Fail is a wonderful bank for the bankers. They keep the profits from their risk taking. It is a terrible bank from the taxpayers' perspective as the taxpayers end up with the losses.

> Mr. [BILL] PATMAN. What, in your judgment, would warrant doing the same thing for another institution?
>
> Mr. CONOVER. Under the present set of laws and the present deposit insurance scheme, I think if we found a situation similar in characteristics to this one, in which we could find no buyer, and the only alternative was to provide direct Federal assistance through the FDIC and the Fed or pay off the bank and run the risk of jeopardizing in a very serious way the Nation's entire banking and financial system, we might
>
> Mr. PATMAN. If any of the banks got themselves in the same predicament as Continental Illinois, you would anticipate we would do the same thing for them, wouldn't you?
>
> Mr. CONOVER. I didn't say it precisely that way.
>
> Mr. PATMAN. IS there any one of them that you would not do it for?
>
> Mr. CONOVER. I certainly wouldn't answer by identifying one. If conditions existed as in this case, since I think this was a good, sensible solution to the problem at hand, it would make sense to deal with it in the same way.
>
> Mr. PATMAN. For any of the other large money center banks?
>
> Mr. CONOVER. For any whose failure might have the same impact on the Nation's financial system as we thought this one could have.
>
> Mr. PATMAN. TO your way of thinking, wouldn't you say that any of the others, upon failing, would have the same impact?
>
> Mr. CONOVER. That is probably true.[130]

---

128 ibid, page 305

129 Ibid, page 305

130 Ibid, page 379

By definition, the failure of any opaque global bank will have a large impact. The question is how can the system be designed so these banks don't have to be bailed out if they fail.

> Mr. CONOVER. I agree with you if we can design such a system and put it in place so that everybody knows in advance. I am not sure exactly how you do that, but you say starting January 1, 1986, we are putting you all on notice that it is going to be like this from now on. Of course, nobody will believe you until the first one is really done that way.
>
> You have touched on the fact that the deposit insurance system needs to be reevaluated and perhaps revamped. We think so, too. The approach that we tried as an experiment in 1984—the so-called modified payout system—was an attempt to provide some market discipline on the part of large depositors by letting them know in advance that they were going to be subject to some loss in the event that a bank failed.[131]

In the absence of valuation transparency, all a policy of telling the large depositors in advance they are going to be subject to some loss in the event a bank fails is to increase the probability of bank runs by making the large depositors more responsive to rumors about each bank's solvency.

In the absence of valuation transparency, large depositors cannot exert market discipline because they do not have the current exposure details necessary to link a bank's cost of funds to its level of risk.

> There has been a lot of hue and cry about that particular practice. And, as I say, I haven't seen the final report on the evaluation of it. But it was an attempt to try something different, to see if we couldn't get large depositors to pay more attention to where they were putting their funds and thereby provide leverage on the management of those institutions to keep their house in order and run their affairs in a prudent way.
>
> I think that is still a fundamentally sound principle. Whether the modified payout practice is the one that ends up being adopted, I am not prepared to say. But we need something like that, and we need to implement it carefully over time, in a way that does not provide a tremendous shock to the system and does not have people screaming, "Gee, we didn't know."[132]

The solution for ending the doctrine of Too Big to Fail is to require these banks to disclose their current exposure details. With this disclosure, market participants know they will be held responsible for losses and can adjust their

---

131 Ibid, page 308

132 Ibid, page 314

exposure to each bank to what they can afford to lose. This brings market discipline to the banks and ends the reason for bailing out the banks.

Continental Illinois previewed what has happened since 2007

In 1984, Continental Illinois was the first Too Big to Fail bank to actually fail. Its failure influenced subsequent regulatory reforms.

> These [reforms] included attempts to increase market discipline of large banks by creditors and uninsured depositors, to strengthen capital adequacy, and to reduce regulatory discretion to forbear.[133]

Notice how the response to the failure of Continental Illinois did not include making the Too Big to Fail banks disclose their current exposure details so that market discipline could restrain risk taking. Instead, the response was to substitute more complex rules and regulatory oversight for valuation transparency and market discipline.

This is exactly the same response as has occurred during our current financial crisis with the passage of the Dodd-Frank Act and the adoption of the Basel Committee capital and liquidity requirements.

The collapse of Continental Illinois was the result of opacity that hid from the market what a combination of irresponsible lending, hot money and lack of restraint by the bank regulators allowed to be done to a global bank that because of existing disclosure requirements was a "black box" and therefore not subject to any market discipline.

By the mid-1980s, Too Big to Fail had become the policy of the Federal Reserve and other bank regulators. So too had the idea that as long as banks were making money they could take any risk they wanted and the regulators would make sure that depositors and creditors were saved from any losses.

Imagine valuation transparency

Imagine the impact on our current financial crisis had the response to the collapse of Continental Illinois been recognition banks as well as structured finance securities need to disclose on the pure information model. Imagine if all banks had been required to provide valuation transparency and disclose on an ongoing basis their current exposure details. Imagine if all structured

---

133 Herring, Richard J. (1993), The Collapse of Continental Illinois National Bank and Trust Company: The Implications for Risk Management and Regulation, University of Pennsylvania, The Wharton School Financial Institutions Center, http://fic.wharton.upenn.edu/fic/case%20studies/continental%20full.pdf

finance securities had been required to provide valuation transparency and disclose any activity involving the underlying collateral on an observable event basis so all market participants had current information. Or imagine as a result of the collapse of Continental Illinois the Transparency Label Initiative™ had been set-up and the buy-side had pressured banks into disclosing their current exposure details or the absence of a label would have been a warning sign to stay away from subprime mortgage-backed securities.

J.M. Nichols, the president of the First National Bank of Englewood, provided the template for banks when he disclosed all of his bank's positions in detail. Of course, this template would have had to be updated. It would need links to observable event based performance data for the collateral underlying any structured finance security the bank invested in.

One possible impact of requiring valuation transparency is our current financial crisis might never have happened. With valuation transparency, market participants would have exerted discipline on the banks to restrain their risk taking. With valuation transparency, buyers and sellers of mortgage-backed securities would have known what they were buying and what they were selling. With valuation transparency, market participants could have limited their exposures to what they could afford to lose. In short, with valuation transparency, our current financial crisis would, if not have been entirely prevented, have been greatly reduced in severity.

However, pursuing valuation transparency or setting up the Transparency Label Initiative™ with the resulting pressure from the buy-side effectively forcing issuers to provide valuation transparency was not the response to the collapse of Continental Illinois. Instead of valuation transparency, we continued to have opacity. Opacity that assured when our current financial crisis started market participants including investors and regulators would be asking questions that could not be answered because

> modern finance was plagued by a data fog.... [I]nvestors could find timely information about equities ... [L]imited transparency about other areas ... because banks had a commercial interest in maintaining that fog.[134]

Instead, the response to the collapse of Continental Illinois was more complex regulations and regulatory oversight as well as adoption of the policy of Too Big to Fail. A policy whose justification the financial regulators could and would use repeatedly to justify any number of non-transparent actions. After all, the failure of one of these opaque global banks could trigger an international financial crisis the dimensions of which could not be imagined.

---

134 Tett, Gillian (2012, March 8), Guiding light need to cut through data fog, Financial Times, http://www.ft.com/intl/cms/s/0/31f4e2e6-692d-11e1-956a-00144feabdc0.html

Chapter 6

BANK REGULATORS HIDE FROM INVESTORS ECONOMIC REALITY BANKS FACE

Handcuffing regulators to GAAP or distorting GAAP to always fit the needs of regulators is inconsistent with the different purposes of financial reporting and prudential regulation.

Regulators should have the authority and appropriate flexibility they need to effectively regulate the banking system. And, conversely, in instances in which the needs of regulators deviate from the informational requirements of investors, the reporting to investors should not be subordinated to the needs of regulators. To do so could degrade the financial information available to investors and reduce public trust and confidence in the capital markets.
—Robert Herz, chairman of the Financial Accounting Standards Board[135]

The Less Developed Country Debt crisis was the next step on the evolution of the concept of Too Big to Fail banks. This crisis was very important because it cemented into the regulatory culture the notion that if the regulators and the Too Big to Fail banks "hid" the true extent of the losses at these banks, the market would go on as if the losses did not exist.

The Less Developed Country Debt Crisis: Secrecy Cures All

A little background is necessary to understand this crisis.

Walter Wriston, a former chairman and CEO of Citicorp, famously observed that "people go bankrupt, but countries don't". Based on this observation, the large U.S. banks plunged into lending to less developed countries.

Of course, Mr. Wriston was wrong. Countries do go bankrupt and this point had become obvious by the mid-1980s.

---

135 Herz, Robert H. (2009, December 8), Remarks of Robert H. Herz, Chairman, Financial Accounting Standards Board, AICPA National Conference on Current SEC and PCAOB Developments, http://goo.gl/44EmXd, page 6.

Unfortunately, by the time this point was obvious, the exposure of the largest U.S. banks to the less developed countries was multiples of their book capital levels. A fact that was well known to market participants as banks disclosed the total amount of their exposures to each less developed country prior to the loans running into trouble.

In fact, the market knew the general magnitude of the losses on these loans. Predecessors to Bloomberg terminals reported the prices at which the loans to less developed countries traded. When a less developed country's loans traded at fifty cents on the dollar, it was a pretty safe bet that the value of its loans held by the banks was also fifty cents on the dollar.

So the question that the Fed as the lead regulator for the Too Big to Fail banks faced was "do we require the banks to write down their loans to less developed countries upfront to reflect current market valuations or do we engage in regulatory forbearance and let the banks engage in extend and pretend and bring the losses slowly through their income statement as they generate earnings?"

The Fed chose regulatory forbearance and the idea of "hiding" the actual magnitude of the losses from the market. This was the first wholesale implementation of the strategy of "delay and pray". Under delay and pray, recognition of losses is delayed in the hope that banks can build up their book capital levels through earnings retention and equity issuance so recognition of the losses doesn't result in negative book capital levels. Naturally, the market doesn't think the Fed relies solely on prayer to help build up the book capital levels, but instead engages in non-transparent acts to boost the banks' earnings. Non-transparent activities could include cutting interest rates or providing banks with below market rate financing. It was rumored during the Less Developed Country Debt crisis that to boost the earnings of the banks, the Fed cut interest rates so the banks could realize sizable gains on their holdings of long-term U.S. Treasury securities.

Please note, the market had a very good idea of the size of the losses, it just did not know the exact amount of the losses at each bank.

When John Reed at Citicorp eventually "recognized" the losses on the less developed country loans, the market responded by bidding up Citicorp's stock price. The write-off confirmed the market's conclusion about the size of the losses Citicorp faced.

The Fed mistakenly believed the fact the financial market had not collapsed when it became obvious initially the banks were insolvent and effectively had little or even negative book capital levels and the subsequent positive reaction by the stock market was an endorsement of its policy choice to hide the banks' insolvency.

In fact, the market didn't collapse because there was sufficient transparency into each of the Too Big to Fail banks to determine a) the general magnitude of its loss and b) each bank appeared viable as it reported it had sufficient interest and fee income, net of the interest income on its loans to the less developed countries, to cover its interest and ongoing operating expenses.

For example, it was well known that writing-down Security Pacific's loans to less developed countries to their true market value would result in the bank having negative book capital. However, Security Pacific reported ample earnings from other sources with which to rebuild its book capital so the financial markets didn't care. In fact, while Security Pacific was insolvent due to its exposures to less developed countries, it was allowed to complete a major merger with Washington based Rainier Bank.

The Fed's policy response to the Less Developed Country Debt crisis showed the bank regulators were willing to allow the banks to maintain an accounting fiction. The loans to less developed countries didn't stop falling in value just because the regulators granted forbearance and didn't require reserves to be set aside or the losses to be realized. When market participants look at a bank's financial statements, they want to know how much its assets are really worth. The Fed's policy response helped the banks to make their financial statements look better, but at the same time it confirmed the financial statements a Too Big to Fail bank files with the SEC are worthless. As former Federal Reserve Governor Kevin Warsh observed during our current financial crisis:

> Investors can't truly understand the nature and quality of the assets and liabilities.... disclosure obfuscates more than it informs... government is not just permitting it but seems to be encouraging it."[136]

The Fed's policy response to the Less Developed Country Debt crisis set the precedent it was okay for bank regulators to hide the condition of the Too Big to Fail banks.

Regulators choose to hide condition of insolvent banks

> "The often repeated — but never substantiated — argument is that revealing information could cause depositors and other liability holders to 'run' on the bank, remove their funds, and potentially cause a failure. The primary reason for non-disclosure is that banks do not want to be disciplined by the market and manipulate regulators to help them keep information private." Professor Ross Levine[137]

---

136 Eisinger, Jesse, Partnoy, Frank (2013, January/February), What's Inside America's Banks?, The Atlantic, http://www.theatlantic.com/magazine/archive/2013/01/whats-inside-americas-banks/309196/

137 Schwartzkopff, Frances (2014, July 30), *Bank risks hidden from investors to be disclosed in Sweden*, Bloomberg, http://www.bloomberg.com/news/2014-07-30/sweden-set-to-disclose-bank-risks-most-investors-can-t-discern.html

Bank regulators understood it was only with the pure information model for disclosure that market participants could assess the actual condition of the banks. Bank regulators knew the intermediary depiction model for disclosure being used by the SEC did not provide market participants with an accurate representation of the condition of the banks. This left bank regulators with discretion over whether or not to hide the condition of the insolvent banks.

How can bank regulators hide the condition of an insolvent bank?

Under the intermediary depiction model, the deterioration in a bank's asset quality is not immediately visible. Assets held in the bank's trading account or designated as available for sale recognize gains or losses as their current market value changes. Assets held in the bank's banking book or designated as held to maturity recognize losses only after there has been demonstrated credit quality deterioration, like a delinquency, or when it is reasonable to expect an event demonstrating deterioration in the credit quality to occur. There is discretion in determining when it is reasonable to expect an event demonstrating deterioration in the credit quality to occur and therefore recognize a loss. In our current financial crisis, losses on investments in subprime mortgage-backed securities preceded bank recognition of lending losses.

Let me use an example to show how bank regulator discretion works. I will start with a solvent bank. The traditional definition of a solvent bank is the market value of its assets is greater than the book value of its liabilities. In this example, the market value of the bank's assets is 100 and the book value of its liabilities is 90.

Figure 10. Solvent Bank where financial statements accurately reflect underlying economic reality

Assets		Liabilities & Equity	
Cash	5	Funds from Central Bank	0
Bonds:		Deposits:	
Government	10	Core Deposits	70
AAA-rated	15	Hot Money Deposits	20
Total Bonds	25	Total Deposits	90
Loans:		Total Liabilities	90
Performing	70		
Non-performing	0		
Total Loans	70	Equity	10
Total Assets	100	Total Liabilities & Equity	100

Not only is this bank solvent, but it has terrific capital ratios. It shows a simple equity to asset ratio of 10% (equity/assets = 10/100 = 10%). Its Basel I, II or III risk-weighted capital ratios are even better.

Unfortunately, it turns out that this bank was heavily exposed to subprime mortgages, commercial real estate and other areas of the financial system that collapsed at the beginning of our financial crisis. The effects on this bank of marking all of its assets to market and using fair value accounting are shown below. Its AAA-rated bonds suffer a loss of 10. Its loans suffer a loss of 10. Its equity absorbs the total loss on the bonds and loans and declines by 20.

Figure 11. Insolvent bank where financial statements accurately reflect underlying economic reality

Assets		Liabilities & Equity	
Cash	5	Funds from Central Bank	0
Bonds:		Deposits:	
Government	10	Core Deposits	70
AAA-rated	5	Hot Money Deposits	20
Total Bonds	15	Total Deposits	90
Loans:		Total Liabilities	90
Performing	45		
Non-performing	15		
Total Loans	60	Equity	(10)
Total Assets	80	Total Liabilities & Equity	80

Clearly, this bank is insolvent as the market value of its assets (80) is less than the book value of its liabilities (90). This is the view of the bank that market participants should have and would have if the bank disclosed under the pure information model.

However, this bank also happens to be opaque because it provides only the required intermediary model disclosures. Disclosures that result in this bank being like all the other banks, a 'black box'.

Naturally, this opacity is very important as it gives policymakers and financial regulators a choice: make the bank publicly acknowledge and absorb its losses upfront or allow the bank to hide the true extent of its losses and slowly absorb them into earnings over the course of time. Please note that regardless of which choice is made the bank is still by definition insolvent.

What the choice comes down to is when do the bank's financial statements reflect its true condition: now or at some point in time in the distant future.

If the financial regulators want to hide the true extent of the bank's losses, they use amortized cost accounting for the banks' financial statements. This lets the bank regulators suspend mark to market accounting and adopt mark to model accounting for its securities. The bank regulators can also engage in regulatory forbearance and let banks practice 'extend and pretend' to turn non-performing loans into 'zombie' loans. Global policymakers and bank regulators did both of these in response to our current financial crisis.

The impact of these actions is shown below for our now insolvent, opaque bank. The suspension of mark to market accounting and adoption of mark to model accounting holds the losses on the AAA-rated bonds to only 1. Regulatory forbearance allows the bank to practice extend and pretend and reduce its losses on its loans to only 1 and its increase in non-performing loans to 4. As a result of the regulators' policy choices, the value of the bank's book equity only declines by 2.

Figure 12. Insolvent Bank where as a result of bank regulators hiding losses the financial statements do not accurately reflect the underlying economic reality

Assets		Liabilities & Equity	
Cash	5	Funds from Central Bank	0
Bonds:		Deposits:	
Government	10	Core Deposits	70
AAA-rated	14	Hot Money Deposits	20
Total Bonds	24	Total Deposits	90
Loans:		Total Liabilities	90
Performing	65		
Non-performing	4		
Total Loans	69	Equity	8
Total Assets	98	Total Liabilities & Equity	98

Market participants cannot assess the risk of this bank. In the absence of valuation transparency, market participants do not have the information they need to tell the percentage of the bank's performing loans that are actually 'zombie' loans or how much of the bank's bond portfolio is really junk.

In addition, the bank's book capital, which is an accounting construct, no longer reflects the true condition of the bank (it shows +8 when the bank's true condition is -10). Because of measurement errors introduced by the bank regulators, this bank's capital is deceptive. It does not present an accurate picture of the bank's risk or solvency.

Before going on, let me summarize three key points:

- First, the bank is insolvent under the traditional definition of solvency regardless of what its financial statements show.
- Second, by fiddling with the accounting, policymakers and bank regulators are explicitly saying a bank can operate and support the real economy even when it is insolvent under the traditional definition.
- Third, by fiddling with the accounting, policymakers and bank regulators are explicitly saying a bank that is currently insolvent under the traditional definition can generate and retain enough earnings or its assets can increase enough in value so that it becomes solvent again.

So, why do global policymakers and financial regulators engage in hiding bank insolvency or insist that banks must be recapitalized quickly?

Perhaps they believe a bank that shows low or negative book capital levels is prone to bank runs or it is hampered in its ability to support the real economy.

Let me address bank runs first.

Why should this bank be any more susceptible to bank runs after it reveals the true extent of its losses than it is when the losses are being hidden? Do global policymakers and financial regulators think market participants missed the implosion of subprime securities, commercial real estate and other areas of the financial system that made this bank insolvent?

What market participants don't know is the exact extent of the losses suffered by each bank. Market participants are keenly aware of the fact each bank suffered extensive losses. Losses that if fully recognized may in fact have left the bank with substantial negative book capital levels.

So why aren't depositors fleeing the banks? Deposit guarantees and access to central bank funding.

I break depositors into two groups: core and hot money.

Core depositors like individuals and small and medium size enterprises have a long-term relationship with their bank. They trust that even highly indebted governments will honor their explicit and implicit deposit guarantees and protect them from any losses due to bank insolvency. As Cyprus showed, hurting the small and medium size enterprises devastates the economy so policymakers and financial regulators have a strong incentive not to do this.

Because they trust their governments, core depositors don't care and probably couldn't tell you what the book capital level for their bank was at the end of last quarter (to know if you are a core depositor, simply ask yourself if you know how much book capital your bank had at the end of last quarter). Core depositors are with their bank for the long haul.

This is a key point because it is these depositors that are the key to the viability of the banking franchise. Their business allows a bank to generate and retain the earnings that rebuild its book capital level and restore it to solvency over many years.

Hot money depositors are, as their name implies, only dealing with the bank as an investor. At the first sign of problems and clearly this bank has problems; they are gone as soon as they can get their money out.

This group is in fact already engaged in a bank run. A run that is slowed down to a jog by having their money tied up in time deposits.

So what does the bank look like after all of its hot money depositors have left if all the bank's assets are marked to market?

Figure 13. Insolvent bank after hot money depositors have withdrawn their funds

Assets		Liabilities & Equity	
Cash	5	Funds from Central Bank	20
Bonds:		Deposits:	
Government	10	Core Deposits	70
AAA-rated	5	Hot Money Deposits	0
Total Bonds	15	Total Deposits	70
Loans:		Total Liabilities	90
Performing	45		
Non-performing	15		
Total Loans	60	Equity	(10)
Total Assets	80	Total Liabilities & Equity	80

Please note that under Walter Bagehot's principle for central banks acting as lender of last resort, central banks are suppose to lend freely against good collateral only to solvent banks. However, in the presence of a deposit guarantee, the restriction on lending only to solvent banks is lifted as the guarantee effectively makes the loan a secured loan to the government.

In this example, good collateral at 60 (bonds of 15 plus performing loans of 45) is 3 times greater than the size of the loan from the central bank. Therefore, a bank run by hot money depositors does not cause the bank to sell assets at distressed prices nor does it cause the central bank to take on undue risk of loss on its loan to the insolvent bank.

Let me now address the issue of recognizing the losses would hurt the banks' ability to support the real economy.

Why would it hurt the banks' ability to support the real economy?

As shown in the example, there is no reduction in the bank's ability to fund new loans after it absorbs its losses. Cash didn't change.

However, if banks have low or negative book capital levels, how can they support the real economy by lending?

A distinction must be made between a bank's ability to originate a loan and its ability to fund the loan over time on its balance sheet.

Banks can always originate loans. When they are rebuilding their book capital levels, they are restricted in their ability to fund the loan on their balance sheets. This is okay because banks can always sell the loan to investors including insurance companies, pension funds, hedge funds and other banks that have the balance sheet capacity and desire to hold the loan.

U.S. Savings & Loan Crisis: Terribly Rotten Accounting Practices

The involvement of bank regulators in distorting bank balance sheets really took off with the U.S. Savings & Loan crisis.

In the early 1980s, Paul Volcker and the Federal Reserve broke the back of inflation in the U.S. by raising interest rates. Unfortunately, the savings and loans were a casualty of this policy. Savings and loans were a form of limited banking. They were restricted to primarily making mortgage loans. As a result, when interest rates increased, the savings and loans became insolvent as the market value of their fixed rate mortgage assets fell and became less than the book value of their liabilities. By mid-1982, the savings and loan industry was insolvent by almost $100 billion or an amount equal to 15% of its liabilities.[138]

To deal with this insolvency, the savings and loan regulator, the Federal Home Loan Bank Board, engaged in a number of accounting activities that violated generally accepted accounting principles. For example, the FHLBB granted a one-time boost to equity to offset losses realized by the savings and loans. At the time, I was working as a consultant to a large savings and loan and its Chief Financial Officer referred to these gimmicks as "the Federal regulators' Terribly Rotten Accounting Practices".

Why would bank regulators engage in TRAP?

Bank regulators recognize bank solvency and insolvency are temporary conditions. If a bank can continue operating while insolvent, it can potentially

138 Ely, Bert (2008), Savings and Loan Crisis, The Concise Encyclopedia of Economics, http://www.econlib.org/library/Enc/SavingsandLoanCrisis.html

retain enough earnings or have the market value of its assets increase by enough so the bank can return to solvency.

Why can banks continue to operate while they are insolvent?

Because of deposit insurance the taxpayers effectively become the banks' silent equity partner.

As shown by the Less Developed Country Debt crisis, when banks are viable they are able to operate for years while insolvent and earn their way back to solvency. As shown by the savings and loans, when banks are not viable, allowing them to continue to operate simply drives up the cost to the taxpayer when they are ultimately closed.

The savings and loans also demonstrated why banks must provide valuation transparency while they are insolvent as someone needs to restrain their risk taking otherwise they take on a significant amount of risk in a gamble for redemption. Regulators allowed management of the savings and loans to gamble by making high-risk investments that were classified as loans. Specifically, they could make acquisition, development and construction loans to support real estate development. Unfortunately, the result of too many savings and loans making these types of loans was too much real estate development and a collapse in real estate prices. In gambling on redemption, the management of the savings and loans increased the losses at these firms. Management was able to gamble on redemption because, like the banks, the savings and loans were opaque black boxes. As a result, market participants were prevented from exerting discipline to prevent gambling on redemption.

Congress responded to and tried to put a stop to both this gambling on redemption and regulators manipulating bank balance sheets. In 1991, it passed the Federal Deposit Insurance Corporation Improvement Act. Under this Act, regulators must pursue the doctrine of prompt corrective action (PCA). In an effort to stop the deterioration of a bank's financial condition, PCA provides incentives for banks to address their bad debt exposures and mandates the FDIC must put in new management, technically known as appointing a conservator or receiver, for a financial institution if its tangible equity falls to or below 2% of total assets.

This 2% tangible equity rule is at the heart of the conflict between prudential regulation and financial reporting. Tangible equity is an easily manipulated accounting construct calculated from a bank's financial statements. It is calculated by subtracting goodwill and the regulators' make believe capital from the book value of a bank's common equity. When a bank recognizes its losses, the losses flow through its income statement and then the bank's common equity accounts. If as a result of recognizing its losses its tangible equity falls below 2% of total assets, the bank must be put into receivership.

Bank regulators would prefer not to takeover the banks and this can be easily achieved by manipulating tangible equity by not making the banks recognize their losses. Unfortunately, a consequence of not requiring the banks to recognize their losses is the banks' financial statements no longer reflect the economic reality faced by the banks.

At first blush, this Act appears to prevent regulators pursuing the Swedish Model to end a financial crisis and using the banking system as it is designed to absorb the losses on the excess debt in the financial system. In fact, the Act appears to create what British economist Charles Goodhart called the "regulatory paradox".

> Imagine you arrive at an unknown railway station late at night and there is exactly one taxi at the station's taxi rank, which you wish to take to your hotel. The taxi driver tells you that he is sorry but he cannot take you because the city authorities demand that there must always be at least one taxi waiting in front of the station.
>
> Metaphorically speaking, the traditional minimum requirements guarantee that there is exactly one taxi at the taxi rank. However, this capital cannot be used to absorb losses, as hard-hitting supervisory sanctions would be imposed if capital falls below requirements.[139]

However, this is not the case. Bank regulators were given an out for Too Big to Fail firms. They didn't have to appoint a conservator or receiver if the bank is determined to be systemically important.

When Sec. Paulson and Fed Chair Bernanke went before Congress asking for $700 billion for the Trouble Asset Relief Program (TARP), they could instead have asked Congress to pass legislation to remove two potential impediments to the banks protecting the real economy by absorbing the losses on the excess debt in the financial system. First, the legislation could have waived the 2% tangible equity requirement. After all, it is not as if the 1991 Act was biblical and carved in stone. Had they done so, the banks would have been unquestionably freed up to absorb the losses on the excess debt rather than impose the losses on the real economy. Second, the legislation could have overturned the *Nobelman v American Savings Bank* decision that made it difficult, if not impossible, for a borrower to retain their property and get relief from a mortgage in bankruptcy. If borrowers had the threat of this relief, banks would

139 Weidmann, Jens (2014, April 7), Stable banks for a Stable Europe, speech at the 20th German Banking Congress, Berlin, BIS, http://www.bis.org/review/r140415b.htm?utm_content=buffer8af00&utm_medium =social&utm_sourch=twitter.com&utm_campaign= buffer

have had an incentive to recognize their losses and work out a modification with the borrowers.

Japan and Zombie banks

In late 1989, Japan's credit bubble burst. Taking a page from the U.S. bank regulators' Too Big to Fail playbook, Japan's bank regulators set about propping up its insolvent banks.

The market nickname for these insolvent banks was borrowed from the US. They were called zombie banks. A zombie bank is a bank where the market value of its assets is less than the book value of its liabilities. There are two primary reasons these banks can continue to exist. First, deposit insurance prevents a bank run by retail deposits. Second, bank regulators are allowing it to continue to operate because it is capable of generating sufficient revenue to cover its expenses.

The zombie banks highlight the thin line between bank regulators helping to hide losses and bank regulators actually telling a bank to misrepresent its condition. This thin line exists solely because the disclosures required under the intermediary depiction model are inadequate.

Just like the individual exposures taken on by the banks, the bank regulators do not approve or disapprove of each bank's disclosures to other market participants. By design, the SEC is responsible for ensuring disclosure of all useful, relevant information. However, due to the inadequacy of this disclosure, regulators have been more than willing to exercise discretion in requiring banks to acknowledge their true condition to all market participants.

Under the FDR Framework and the FDR Administration's redesign of the banks, bank regulators were not given the discretion to engage in nontransparent acts to save the banks. Bank regulators were given discretion on when to close a bank, but not on hiding the true condition of the bank. By hiding the true condition of the banks, bank regulators exempt the banks from market discipline.

Zombie banks demonstrate this regulatory discretion. The lack of disclosure of their current exposure details means market participants cannot assess the magnitude of the losses on and off the zombie banks' balance sheets. Bank regulators recognize this fact and engage in nontransparent actions like regulatory forbearance under which the zombie banks engage in 'extend and pretend' with their non-performing loans. By not requiring recognition of their losses, bank regulators help to hide the magnitude of the zombie banks' losses from other market participants.

Under the FDR Framework, market participants have every right to rely on the adequacy of each bank's disclosures. Clearly, market participants cannot do so when the SEC requires disclosures under the intermediary depiction model and the financial regulators work with the financial institutions they supervise through the use of regulatory forbearance, for example, to keep relevant information from market participants.

What is needed so all market participants have adequate information to assess a bank is either the SEC adopts the pure information model under which banks are required to disclose their current global asset, liability and off-balance sheet exposures or the Transparency Label Initiative™ which uses market discipline from the buy-side to force the banks to disclose their current global exposures.

SECTION 4

HOW WALL STREET EXPLOITS THE FATAL FLAW IN THE ORIGINAL FDR FRAMEWORK

If you like what Wall Street did for the housing market, you'll love what Wall Street is doing for commodities. Some of the same people who brought us the synthetic mortgage-backed security – and with it, the term "toxic asset" and the recent financial crisis – now dominate the commodities futures markets....

Bank involvement with physical commodities also raises concerns about unfair trading. In some cases, banks have been implicated in outright market manipulation...

Activities involving physical commodities also give Wall Street banks access to valuable nonpublic information with which they can profit in physical and financial commodity markets at the expense of other market participants. The banks and their regulator, the Federal Reserve, acknowledge as much.

-- *Senator Carl Levin*[140]

140 Levin, Carl (2014, November 20), Wall Street Bank Involvement with Physical Commodities, Opening Statement for Permanent Subcommittee on Investigations, http://www.levin.senate.gov/newsroom/speeches/speech/levin-opening-statement-permanent-subcommittee-on-investigations-hearing-wall-street-bank-involvement-with-physical-commodities

CHAPTER 7

THE SEC: UNFIT FOR PURPOSE

"When the SEC was created, its purpose was to serve as an independent regulator of the unbridled profit-seeking activity of self-interested individuals and firms in the securities markets. It was not, however, to supplant the market or directly participate in it…."

— Christopher Cox, former SEC chairman[141]

If bank supervisors don't approve or disapprove of any bank exposure and effectively don't exert any restraints on risk taking until the deposit insurance fund is threatened, then who restrains the bank's choice of exposures?

Under the FDR Framework, it is the other market participants, principally investors in each bank's securities, who restrain the riskiness of each bank's choice of exposures. These market participants also push each bank to recognize its economic losses upfront through their exercise of market discipline.

Please recall that the FDR Administration's solution to bank runs complemented, but did not substitute for the FDR Framework. Both were initially implemented when the industry standard was for banks to disclose all of their current exposure details.

The FDR Administration intended a "belt and suspenders" approach to restrain risk taking and ensure the long-term solvency of banks. By providing valuation transparency through the disclosure of their current exposure details, banks would be subject to market discipline. At the same time, they would also have regulatory discipline.

Under the original FDR Framework, the SEC was given the responsibility for implementing the philosophy of disclosure and ensuring market participants had access to all the useful, relevant information so they could exercise self-discipline and in doing so enforce market discipline.

141 Cox, Christopher (2008, December 4), Address to Joint Meeting of the Exchequer Club and Women in Housing and Finance, SEC, http://www.sec.gov/news/speech/2008/spch120408cc.htm

The SEC

The SEC was founded on June 6, 1934. As described by former SEC chairman Christopher Cox,

> The creation of the Securities and Exchange Commission in 1934 marked a deliberate effort to clearly define and separate the role of the national government, on the one hand, and the capital markets, on the other. Henceforth, fraud and unfair dealing in the stock and bond markets would be subjected to external discipline by the federal government. Minimum standards would be enforced, such as requiring that every investor be told the essential details about the security in which he or she was investing. Registration of securities, and licensing of broker-dealers, would be required. It was, in short, arms-length regulation of an unabashedly private market, rather than nationalization….
>
> The original premise of the securities laws, which was that government is an auxiliary to the market, not a substitute for it or a participant in it. Virtually every aspect of the 1933 and 1934 Acts, and the regulations implementing them, follows from the notion that markets should be efficient, competitive, transparent, and free of fraud.
>
> The normative judgment implicit in this legislative and regulatory scheme is that markets are good. So long as they are in fact operating efficiently, competitively, openly, and honestly, they are good for consumers, investors, producers, and our entire economy.[142]

To ensure every investor has access to the essential details about the security they are investing in, the SEC adopted the intermediary depiction model for disclosure. This model works well for non-financial firms without large finance subsidiaries.

At the time the intermediary depiction model was adopted, it didn't appear to be a problem for banks. First, banks had a tradition of disclosing all of their current exposure details. Second, the bank regulators had separate legal authority that granted them access to the banks' current asset, liability and off-balance sheet exposure details 24 hours a day, 7 days a week, 365 days a year. Between tradition and the bank regulators' authority, it did not appear necessary to require the banks to provide disclosure under the pure information model to other market participants.

Please note the SEC did not prevent banks from continuing to disclose under the pure information model. It just said that this additional disclosure was optional by setting a minimum level of required disclosure. Naturally, over time, in the absence of a Transparency Label Initiative™ and the resulting pressure to continue providing valuation transparency, fewer banks exercised this option.

---

[142] ibid

By making the pure information model optional, the SEC effectively replaced it as the industry standard with the intermediary depiction model that left banks resembling black boxes.

This meant that going forward the regulators would be the only brakes on bank risk taking as gone were the current exposure details that investors needed to assess the risk of the banks and exert market discipline. With banks no longer subject to market discipline, the march to the financial crisis became inevitable.

The use of the intermediary depiction model for disclosure created two significant problems.

Bank regulators violate principle on endorsing investment

Ending investors' access to the current exposure details they needed to assess the risk of an individual bank made the investors dependent on the bank regulators correctly assessing the risk of each bank and communicating this risk to the market.

Why did investors rely on what the bank regulators said?

Investors *knew* bank regulators had an information monopoly on the current exposure details needed to assess the risk of each bank and an incentive to minimize the losses on the deposit insurance fund. Investors *assumed* that bank regulators would restrain bank risk taking to minimize the risk of losses on the deposit insurance fund.

Despite FDR's explicit prohibition against government directly endorsing an investment, bank regulators were now in the business of making endorsements. Unfortunately, due to concerns about the safety and soundness of the banking system, bank regulators had an incentive to understate the risk of the banks.

Given the absence of data, what investor was going to question the bank regulators when they said in the run-up to the financial crisis that the risk of the banking system had been reduced by financial innovation?

With the government proclaiming the banks to be low risk, investors, particularly other banks, took on far more exposure than they could afford to lose given the true risk of each bank.

With the government proclaiming the banks to be low risk, the government also took on the moral obligation to protect investors from losses. Investors could legitimately argue they relied on the government's representations about the banks when making their investment decision.

SEC's Intermediary depiction model doesn't handle structured finance

The second significant problem the SEC's intermediary depiction model for disclosure caused is this model made it impossible to provide valuation transparency into structured finance securities.

Structured finance securities are just like banks in that both require a pure information model approach to achieve the necessary level of disclosure so that investors have a clear plastic bag view and access to all the relevant, useful information in an appropriate, timely manner.

For structured finance securities, this means the securities disclose on an observable event basis all activities, like a payment or delinquency, involving the underlying assets to market participants before the beginning of the next business day. By having information on the collateral's current performance, investors have the valuation transparency they need to know what they own.

In an April 19, 2010 Fortune.com article, *How Goldman Exploited the Information Gap*[143], I looked at how Wall Street firms benefitted from their ownership of companies that made and collected subprime mortgages. This ownership gave the Wall Street firms the equivalent of tomorrow's news today and, without any insider trading restrictions, the Wall Street firms used this news to trade for their benefit. These firms gave Wall Street a clear plastic bag view into the subprime mortgage-backed securities. At the same time, investors were limited to guessing as their brown paper bag view under the intermediary depiction model hid what was actually happening with the underlying mortgages.

Over four years later, the U.S. government confirmed my analysis in its legal motion in the *Federal Housing Finance Agency v Goldman, Sachs & Co.* case.

> Only one red flag appears to have gotten Goldman's attention—but not so Goldman could fulfill its duty to verify "the soundness of the security and the correctness of the registration statement and prospectus."…
>
> Starting in 2005, Goldman partially owned two subprime originators, Lownhome and Senderra, from which it gathered intelligence about the mortgage market. In December 2006, Senderra reported that "credit quality has risen to become the major crisis in the non-prime industry. *We are seeing unprecedented defaults and fraud in the market* …. [including] inflated appraisals, inflated income and occupancy fraud."
>
> Rather than conduct additional diligence or modify existing diligence processes, the Goldman employees who saw this confidential report focused on developing and implementing a strategy for Goldman Sachs to "take advantage" of the "even greater distress" it knew was occurring. Goldman Sachs promptly established massive and lucrative short positions in mortgage-related securities, while continuing to sell such securities to investors without disclosing

---

143 Field, Richard (2010, April 19), *How Goldman Exploited the Information Gap*, Fortune.com, http://money.cnn.com/2010/04/19/news/companies/goldman_sachs_gap.fortune/?postversion=2010041914

its true assessment of the underlying loans, as later confirmed by the Senate's Permanent Subcommittee on Investigations[144].

By trying to use the intermediary depiction model as the basis for structured finance security disclosure, the SEC was destined to fail.

And fail it did.

The failure resulted in the sale of almost $2 trillion of the now infamous opaque, toxic mortgage-backed securities.

Using the wrong disclosure model wasn't the only reason the SEC failed.

Undone by the revolving door and the process of creating regulations

The SEC was also primed to fail by the revolving door through which its staff traveled. As described by Jim Kidney, a former trial attorney at the SEC,

> The revolving door is a very serious problem. I have had bosses, and bosses of my bosses, whose names we all know, who made little secret that they were here to punch their ticket. They mouthed serious regard for the mission of the Commission, but their actions were tentative and fearful in many instances. You can get back to Wall Street by acting tough, by using the SEC publicity apparatus to promote yourself as tough, and maybe even on a few occasions being tough, if you pick your targets carefully. But don't appear to fail. Don't take risks where risk would count. That is not the intended message from the ticket punchers, of course, but it is the one I got on the occasions when I was involved in a high profile case or two. The revolving door doesn't push the agency's enforcement envelope very often or very far.
>
> The attitude trickles down the ranks. Combined with the negative views of the civil service promoted by politicians and the beatings we take from the public, it is no surprise that we lose our best and brightest as they see no place to go in the agency and eventually decide they are just going to get their own ticket to a law firm or corporate job punched. They see an agency that polices the broken windows on the street level and rarely goes to the penthouse floors. On the rare occasions when Enforcement does go to the penthouse, good manners are paramount. Tough enforcement — risky enforcement — is subject to extensive negotiation and weakening.
>
> For the powerful, we are at most a tollbooth on the bankster turnpike. We are a cost, not a serious expense.[145]

---

144 *Federal Housing Finance Agency v Goldman, Sachs & Co.* (2014, July 8), *Plantiff's memorandum of law in support of its motion for partial summary judgment on Defendents' due diligence and reasonable care defenses, Case 1:11-cv-06198-DLC, Document 769, page 3*

145 Kidney, Jim (2014, March), *Retirement Remarks*, SEC Union, http://www.secunion.org/files/RetirementRemarks.pdf, page 5

In addition, the SEC was also primed to fail by its use of lawyers not just to document disclosure requirements, but in the process for determining what the disclosure requirements should be under the pure information model.

For example, as part of the SEC's effort after the current financial crisis began to rewrite the disclosure regulations covering structured finance securities, the SEC engaged in a multi-year effort to try to determine the exact data fields that should be disclosed. Recall that FDR set the bar for disclosure very high. He set it at the level of what the most demanding expert would want disclosed and not what Joe-Six Pack might want. Why focus on a minutia driven exercise like specifying the exact data fields to disclose? This is what lawyers are trained to engage in.

The fact is there is a simpler, better alternative that ensures the most demanding expert always has access to the data fields they want. Given the originators and servicers who do the billing and collecting of the underlying collateral are experts, it is safe to assume that any data field they track they think is relevant for valuing or monitoring the underlying collateral. By simply requiring all the data fields the originators and servicers track be disclosed while protecting borrower privacy, the SEC assures the most demanding expert is satisfied that all the useful, relevant information is made available.

It is okay if the originators and servicers don't track all of the same data fields. There is information in knowing both the data fields they do track and the fact they don't track data fields other originators and servicers consider important enough to track.

A lack of understanding of 21st century information technology also had a significant impact on how the SEC staff determined what is timely disclosure for structured finance securities. By not understanding 21st century information technology, they didn't realize the databases used by originators and servicers only operate on an observable event basis. It is the observable event involving the underlying collateral that causes the databases to update. 21st century information technology is designed to support "plastic" in the form of observable event based reporting as the choice in the "paper or plastic" model for the timing of when disclosure should be made.

Credit cards provide an excellent example of how the databases used by originators and servicers operate using observable event based reporting. Anyone with a credit card can use the Internet to access the details of all the transactions involving their credit card. This includes all the observable events like charges or payments made today.

Since the performance data for all assets underlying structured finance is already available on an observable event basis and 21st century information technology makes it easy for market participants to access this data, why not make the data available to market participants this way?

Why not make the data available to market participants so they have valuation transparency, because it would reduce Wall Street's profitability.

Chapter 8

SECRECY IS WALL STREET'S GUIDING PRINCIPLE

"The most valuable commodity I know of is information."
— Gordon Gekko, Wall Street[146]

The financial system will kick back against transparency…
Those working in markets see information as power and money,
so they depend on a lack of transparency for success.
—Joseph Stiglitz[147]

Since the Pecora Commission in the 1930s, it has been well known that Wall Street's profitability is driven by information. Specifically, information that Wall Street has but investors do not.

Wall Street has five sources of information it uses in its trading. It has information based on "whom" it knows. It has information it uncovers through due diligence of publicly available information. It has information from its advisory assignments. It has information from its position as a market maker between buyers and sellers. Finally, it has proprietary information as the result of information asymmetry created by the opacity of the financial products it designs and sells.

Wall Street profits from SEC's choice of intermediary depiction model

If it wasn't complicated, it wouldn't be allowed to happen. The
complexity disguises what is happening. If it's so complicated
you can't understand it, then you can't question it.
— Michael Lewis[148]

---

146 Gekko, Gordon (1987), Wall Street, http://spinnakr.com/blog/data-2/2013/03/44-more-of-the-best-data-quotes/

147 Kennedy, Simon, Benjamin, Matthew (2009, January 26), Darkness at Davos might hide Secrecy from Transparency Spotlight, Bloomberg, http://www.bloomberg.com/apps/news?pid=newsarchive&sid=aawQ9NWNUsQw

148 Kroft, Steve (2014, March 30), Is the U.S. Stock Market Rigged?, CBS News, http://www.cbsnews.com/news/is-the-us-stock-market-rigged/

Holders of the credit-linked notes requested information ... They were told that the deal was designed to include a "blind pool" of obligations, and that the bank "is not obliged to disclose, and has not disclosed, the identities of the reference entities relating to the reference obligations," the notice said.

It can't be good to hear you don't have a right to know what you're invested in at a time when it suddenly matters.[149]

Wall Street uses opacity to create information asymmetry and give itself proprietary information about the value of a security the buyer or seller of the security does not have, but could and should have if there was adequate disclosure. By design, these financial products result in Wall Street valuing the contents of a clear plastic bag and the other market participants guessing at the value of the contents of a brown paper bag. Under the original FDR Framework, it is the responsibility of the SEC to eliminate Wall Street's opacity based informational advantage and make sure for all financial products sold by Wall Street all market participants are valuing the contents of a clear plastic bag.

There is another type of information that Wall Street has: inside information. While it is illegal to use a company's inside information to trade its securities, the Chinese walls erected by Wall Street still allow the bird's eye view of the real health and vulnerabilities of different industries gained from advisory assignments to pass through to trading.

Naturally, proprietary information from opacity is very valuable as it puts Wall Street at a significant advantage when it buys or sells a security. With this advantage from opacity comes increased profitability that in turn leads to increased compensation. Thus, Wall Street has a tremendous incentive to innovate and create opaque financial products.

As Gary Gensler, the former chairman of the U.S. CFTC observed

> I think markets work best when they're transparent, [but I] benefited from darkness in [my] Wall Street career.[150]

Financial consultant Henry Kaufman also noted

---

149 Harrington, Shannon D. (2014, August 5), *Banco Espirito Santo loan mystery confronts derivatives buyers*, Bloomberg, http://www.bloomberg.com/news/2014-08-05/banco-espirito-santo-loan-mystery-confronts-derivatives-buyers.html

150 Gensler, Gary (2013, November), quote, Zero Hedge, http://www.zerohedge.com/news/2013-11-14/quote-day-gary-batman-gensler

> Leading financial institutions actively "pushed legal structures that made many aspects of the financial markets opaque."[151]

There are two basic ways for Wall Street to create opacity. First, design the product so that it doesn't disclose all the useful, relevant information in an appropriate, timely manner. Second, design the product so that it is complex and hides its risk.

The first place Wall Street increased its profitability from opacity was with itself. Wall Street knew it required the pure information model and disclosure of each banks' current exposure details to independently assess the risks each bank was taking. However with the SEC's adoption of the intermediary depiction model and the use of summaries to depict the reality a company is facing, Wall Street had a choice: it could either point out to the SEC the need for disclosure of current exposure details or it could use these summaries to hide the additional risk it was taking. Naturally, Wall Street elected to game the intermediary depiction model and increase its risk. Wall Street's profits increased as the market did not increase its cost of funds to reflect its increased risk.

Gaming the intermediary depiction model had another very important benefit for Wall Street. This gaming meant Wall Street could sell the bank regulators on the fear of financial contagion should a financial crisis occur. Nobody could assess the risk of any bank so who could argue against the idea there was a strong likelihood the banks had more exposure to each other than they could afford to lose.

Second, Wall Street created the aptly named "shadow" banking system. Here, I am referring not to money market mutual funds, but rather to the $15+ trillion in structured finance securities and $700+ trillion in derivatives. Securities in these markets primarily trade over-the-counter despite a recent push by regulators to create central clearing platforms. The choice of over-the-counter trading reflected Wall Street's ability to structure these markets in ways that were most profitable for Wall Street and that maximized Wall Street's leverage over the buy-side. In over-the-counter markets, investors are dependent on Wall Street to create a market if they ever want to sell a security. The reliance on Wall Street means investors in these markets have little to no leverage to demand valuation transparency as doing so hurts the investor's ability to buy or sell these securities by undermining the investor's "goodwill" with Wall Street.

---

[151] Congressional Oversight Panel (2009, January), Special Report on Regulatory Reform, Modernizing the American Financial Regulatory System: Recommendations for Improving Oversight, Protecting Consumers and Ensuring Stability, http://cybercemetery.unt.edu/archive/cop/20110402010517/http://cop.senate.gov/documents/cop-012909-report-regulatoryreform.pdf, page 14.

Wall Street understood that the SEC was using the intermediary depiction disclosure model for providing valuation transparency. The shortcomings of this model were not lost on Wall Street. In fact, Wall Street designed structured finance securities to take advantage of these shortcomings.

The subprime mortgage-backed securities at the heart of the current financial crisis are the classic example of the financial products Wall Street has an incentive to create. This product could have been created as either a transparent, low margin product that provided observable event based reporting or as an opaque, high margin product that provided once-per-month or less frequent reporting. Naturally, Wall Street went for opaque, high margin.

Wall Street's opacity driven business model as it applies to financial assets like mortgages and, by extension commodities, can be summarized as follows:

> So the banks made loans to third-party mortgage originators and they got paid for warehouse lines from those. One distinct business opportunity. They took the mortgages they received. They pooled them, they packaged them, and they securitized them. They sold them to investors. Second distinct line of business. Then they were able to trade them in a secondary market on behalf of those customers. Third income stream. They also were able to trade them on a prop basis. Fourth income stream. They had servicing businesses that they owned and were able to glean information advantage both in advance of their customers, it turns out, and also for the income streams provided by that servicing."[152]

Because it originated and serviced the underlying collateral, Wall Street had valuation transparency into these securities on a pure information disclosure model basis. This proprietary information allowed Wall Street to value these securities as if they were looking at the contents of a clear plastic bag. The other market participants, because of the SEC's use of the intermediary depiction model, had useless stale data disclosed on a once-per-month or less frequent basis. They were left to guess the value of the contents of a brown paper bag.

Due to the fact structured finance securities are designed to have no insiders, this proprietary information also allowed Wall Street to trade with the benefit of inside information without breaking any insider trading laws. Think of how

---

152 Josh Rosner (2014, April 16), Managing Director, Graham Fisher & Co. testimony before U.S. Seanate, Committee on Banking, Housing and Urban Affairs, Subcommittee on Financial institutions and Consumer Protection, Sherrod Brown, Elizabeth Warren urge Fed to address risks associated with bank ownership of physical commodities, http://www.brown.senate.gov/newsroom/press/release/brown-warren-urge-fed-to-address-risks-associated-with-bank-ownership-of-physical-commodities, footnote 41, page 7.

much easier having inside information under the pure information model made it to select subprime mortgage-backed securities that would fail to put into deals so Wall Street could profit by shorting these securities.

What did Wall Street know and when did they know it when selling CDOs?

Mortgage-backed securities are constructed to delay the public's access to data and give Wall Street a permanent information advantage. By design, the predominant frequency of reporting in U.S. securitizations is once-per-month. Once-per-month reporting is permitted in the U.S. under the Securities and Exchange Commission Regulation AB, 17 C.F.R. §§ 229.1100-1123.

There is a process built into most securitization transactions to generate a once-per-month report. At the beginning of the month, the servicer or sub-servicer performing the daily billing and collecting function transmits to the trustee, at a minimum, a monthly servicer report that reflects the daily data for the prior month. The trustee then forwards the monthly servicer report to other market participants. These reports come out from 5 to 10 business days after the month ends.

What did Wall Street know and when did Wall Street know it as it relates to the construction and sale of subprime mortgage-backed securities and collateralized debt obligations (CDOs)? Wall Street had the equivalent of "tomorrow's new today".

The press has reported on how some Wall Street firms used their ownership of subprime mortgage origination and servicing platforms and the resulting information asymmetry to their benefit.

On November 9, 2007, the Wall Street Journal's Heard on the Street column documented how Morgan Stanley used its access to current subprime loan performance data from its ownership of a subprime mortgage company. According to the column, Morgan Stanley used such loan performance data to profitably short the securitization market. Morgan Stanley's reported use of this information suggests that there is no legal or Chinese wall between Wall Street's access to observable event based performance data and its trading and/or underwriting businesses.[153]

Morgan Stanley was not the only firm that used its superior access to current loan performance data to profitably trade in the securitization market. On January 21, 2010, the Wall Street Journal discussed Goldman Sachs' acquisition of a subprime mortgage lender. Goldman invested in the subprime lender when it was launched in 2005 and bought the firm in 2007. According to the article,

---

153 Smith, Randall (2007, November 9), How a Good Subprime Call Came to Hurt Morgan Stanley, Wall Street Journal, http://online.wsj.com/news/articles/SB119456736420887284

"mortgage experts say the acquisition likely gave Goldman a clearer view of the market as other parts of the company made bets on home loans." These bets generated nearly $4 billion in profits for Goldman.[154]

HSBC took a different approach in order to profit from its access to current loan performance data. On March 18, 2010, the Financial Times reported on Project Opaque, an initiative at HSBC to reduce its exposure to Wall Street because of its concerns about the health of Wall Street companies. HSBC was worried about "overly optimistic assumptions about ...the value of asset-backed securities."[155] With its ownership of HSBC Finance Corp., and its resulting access to current data regarding loans backing ABS, HSBC was in a position where it could compare Wall Street's assumptions with actual performance and therefore could manage the risk of its exposure better.

Whether they bought the mortgages from a third party or originated the mortgages themselves, the Wall Street firms knew just how quickly the quality of the underwriting of the mortgages was deteriorating and used this information for their benefit. This has been confirmed by lawsuits brought by both states and the U.S. government.

From their servicing of the mortgages, Wall Street had access to material nonpublic information that showed how these subprime mortgages were performing. The Commonwealth of Virginia confirmed this fact when it observed in its complaint alleging securities fraud against twelve of the largest Wall Street firms:

> Merrill Lynch gained additional knowledge of the failures to meet underwriting standards when it acquired loan originator, First Franklin in December 2006. This acquisition vertically integrated every significant aspect of Merrill Lynch's RMBS business, from origination through securitization. Additionally, this integration gave Merrill Lynch greater visibility into First Franklin's loan origination practices.[156]

Wall Street's underwriting and trading areas could see the poorly underwritten mortgages were defaulting at a faster rate than the models used by the rating firms

---

154 Lucchetti, Aaron (2010, January 21), Goldman Subprime Fallout hits Home in South Carolina, Wall Street Journal, http://online.wsj.com/news/articles/SB1000142405274870340570457501548236691946 8

155 Sender, Henry (2010, March 18), HSBC drew up exit plans amid liquidity fears, Financial Times, http://www.ft.com/intl/cms/s/0/572c9c3a-32ba-11df-a767-00144feabdc0.html#axzz2n1XHTzHB

156 The Commonwealth of Virginia's Complaint-In-Intervention Case No. CL14-399 (2014, September 16), http://www.oag.state.va.us/Media%20and%20News%20Releases/News_Releases/Herring/Complaint%20-%20FINAL%20(9.16.14).pdf, page 266.

or investors to value subprime mortgage-backed securities had predicted. The Commonwealth of Virginia confirmed this fact when it observed in its complaint:

> A vice president in Morgan Stanley's due diligence department stated in an interview with the FCIC that Morgan Stanley routinely rejected Clayton's findings with respect to sampled loans. He further admitted that the Morgan Stanley traders responsible for the RMBS deals had information concerning the inferior quality of the loans they were securitizing, and that significant aspects of the due diligence process, including which loans were to be sampled, were dictated by Morgan Stanley traders in New York.[157]

Of course, Wall Street used this information to its advantage. The Commonwealth of Virginia confirmed this fact when it observed in its complaint:

> Not content with simply misrepresenting its RMBS to unsuspecting investors, Goldman Sachs concocted a variety of schemes to further profit off its non-public insider knowledge of originators' shoddy practices in what one industry expert analogized, in testimony before Congressional investigators, to "buying fire insurance on someone else's house and then committing arson."[158]

It certainly helps when participating in the process for selecting the assets to short in a CDO if you have material information regarding their performance that the other side of the deal does not have. Perhaps more importantly, the other side cannot get this material information unless it too happens to have a subprime mortgage origination and servicing platform.

A motion filed in the case of the *Federal Housing Finance Agency v Goldman, Sachs & Co.* shed more light on how Wall Street used the opacity of subprime mortgage-backed securities to its advantage.

> 2. Goldman's Own Originators Informed It Of The Sub-Prime Crisis In December 2006, But Goldman's Only Response Was To Begin Shorting The Market
>
> Beginning in 2005, Goldman took an ownership stake in two subprime originators, Lownhome and Senderra, with Goldman fully acquiring Senderra in 2007. Goldman used these originators to gather intelligence about the state of the market, "what loans competitors were willing to purchase," and to see those competitors' underwriting standards.[159]

---

157 ibid, page 277

158 ibid, page 254

159 *Federal Housing Finance Agency v Goldman, Sachs & Co.*, (2014, July 8), Plantiff's memorandum of law in support of its motion for partial summary judgment on

Goldman had the equivalent of tomorrow's news today. Unless you also owned one of these firms, you didn't know the current state of the market. Unlike Goldman, you had to wait to find out what was happening with the mortgages.

How big was the time gap between when Goldman got the news about the current state of the market and when investors would know the same facts? This time gap is measured in months beginning from when a borrower applied for a mortgage and extending all the way until an investor finally received a report describing the performance of the mortgage. As described in the motion, a mortgage could be on the books of the originator for a "few" months[160] until purchased by Goldman and then on Goldman's books for an additional 1 to 6 months or longer[161] until sold as one of the mortgages backing a specific security.

> On December 10, 2006, Senderra's CEO, Brad Bradley, sent an email to Kevin Gasvoda that highlighted "the dramatic shifts and disruption in the" subprime mortgage industry. Bradley informed Gasvoda that "credit quality has risen to become the major crisis in the non-prime industry. *We are seeing unprecedented defaults and fraud in the market*....[including] inflated appraisals, inflated income and occupancy fraud." (emphasis added). Bradley wrote that "[a] ll in all, it is a perfect storm, the wrong way, for the origination market right now." Mr. Gasvoda forwarded this report to several Goldman executives and traders, including Daniel Sparks and Michelle Gill, informing them that this proprietary report was "INTERNAL ONLY." (capitalization in original).
>
> Four days later, another Senderra senior executive delivered a follow-up email to underscore what Mr. Bradley had written regarding the state of the subprime mortgage market. Senderra informed Mr. Gasvoda that "[w]e know that many of our competitors have not taken the necessary credit measures and will pay the price for this. Less production = less fees .... To add insult to injury we now are faced with irrational competitors chasing volume to stay in business, thus they have decreased rates on any loan which smells of quality." A day later, Mr. Gasvoda forwarded this email to the same Goldman executives and traders, this time informing them "do not distribute" but that the email was "[v]ery telling."... [162]

The news Senderra sent to Goldman was the existing mortgages were failing at a faster rate than currently expected and the quality of new mortgages was rapidly declining. So did Goldman understand this news?

Defendents' due diligence and reasonable care defenses, Case 1:11-cv-06198-DLC, Document 769, page 36

160 ibid, page 12

161 ibid, page 8

162 ibid, page 37

Yes!

> But on December 14, 2006, four days after Mr. Sparks was forwarded Senderra's alert of "unprecedented defaults and fraud in the market", Mr. Sparks met with Goldman Sachs's senior executives—including David Viniar, Goldman Sachs's CFO— to begin discussing how Goldman could "[r]educe exposure" in the subprime market and "*be in [a] position to take advantage*" of the "even greater distress" he and the executives knew was occurring. (emphasis added). On that same day, Mr. Gasvoda instructed his staff to begin selling Goldman's RMBS inventory "even if you have to take a small loss" because "[t]here will be big opportunities the next several months."...
>
> Mr. Sparks "c[ould not] over state the importance to the business of selling [Goldman's] positions and new issues," such that by March 2007 Goldman had "effectively halt[ed] new purchases of sub-prime loan pools".
>
> Goldman did not stop securitizing subprime loans, however; to the contrary, it continued selling Certificates to the GSEs from seven subprime Securitizations.
>
> By September 2007, Goldman was publicly bragging that any "[s]ignificant losses on non-prime loans and securities were more than offset by gains on short mortgage positions."[163]

The benefit of having tomorrow's news today for Goldman was it was able to not only unload its portfolio of subprime mortgage-backed securities, but it was also able to short the market before the market finally received the news that subprime mortgages were not very valuable. This short position was immensely profitable for Goldman.

Not only did Goldman unload its portfolio of subprime mortgage-backed securities, but it also continued selling the subprime mortgages that it had purchased.

G. Goldman Knew The Information In The Prospectus Supplements Was False And Deliberately Concealed The Truth

> Another independent reason to grant FHFA's motion is Goldman's undisputed failure to disclose to investors its belief that much of the information in the Prospectus Supplements was inaccurate. This was especially egregious with respect to Goldman's knowledge that the LTV ratios stated

[163] ibid, page 38

> in the Prospectus Supplements were based on inaccurate appraisal values. An underwriter cannot meet its due diligence defense when it "had access to all information that was available and deliberately chose to conceal the truth."[164]

Goldman was not alone in selling subprime mortgage-backed securities where it knew the quality of the mortgages backing the securities was not what it represented in the prospectus describing the deal. Citigroup also engaged in this activity. In Citigroup's Statement of Facts associated with its $7 billion settlement for misleading investors about the quality of the mortgages included in these securities,

> a trader at Citigroup wrote an internal email that indicated that he had reviewed a due diligence report summarizing loans that the due diligence vendor had graded as EV3s and had noted that "a lot" of these rejected loans had unreasonable income and values below the original appraisal, which resulted in combined loan- to-value in excess of 100 percent. The trader stated that he "went thru the Diligence Reports and think that we should start praying... I would not be surprised if half of these loans went down. There are a lot of loans that have unreasonable incomes, values below the original appraisals (CLTV would be >100), etc. It's amazing that some of these loans were closed at all."[165]

In short, in the absence of valuation transparency which provides the ability to trust, but verify, you simply cannot trust Wall Street and firms like Goldman or Citigroup. Rather, you should assume they are selling you a brown paper bag filled with horse manure at a very high price.

Opaque structured finance products allow the City to 'swizz' UK market participants

Wall Street was not alone in creating opacity through its innovations. The "City" in London, the UK's version of Wall Street, also pursued opaque innovations. Opaque structured finance products are not limited to mortgage-backed securities. Many of the products sold by Wall Street and the City are opaque including complex products like structured bonds.

Structured bonds appeal to investors chasing yield. In return for the higher yield on the bonds, the investor takes on risk related to the performance of

---

164 ibid, page 56

165 US Department of Justice (2014, July 14), Global Settlement with Citigroup for Misleading Investors about Securities Containing Toxic Mortgages, *Statement of Facts*, US Department of Justice, http://www.justice.gov/iso/opa/resources/558201471413645397758.pdf, page 8.

the stock market. If the stock market stays above a specified level, the investor receives both the higher return and their money back. If the stock market falls below the specified level, the investor loses some or all of their money.

The complexity of these products hides just how difficult it is for an investor to assess the risk of or value the security.

This was experienced first hand by the personal private secretary to the UK's George Osborne. He was offered a structured bond that despite his having eight years of experience working in derivatives he was unable to value.

> He said the complicated nature of the product revealed that banks still had a long way to go to make their offers transparent and suitable for investors.[166]

He called the product a "swizz" and wondered why financial regulators would allow it. As defined in the Oxford Dictionary, a swizz is something that represents a mild swindle.

This question of why the financial regulators would allow it applies to every opaque product created by the City or Wall Street.

The problem currently is and has been since well before the beginning of the financial crisis that enforcement of the FDR Framework and ensuring valuation transparency has been and still is inadequate. That is why the Transparency Label Initiatve™ is needed.

2007: bringing valuation transparency to structured finance

On December 4, 2007, my patented information system for bringing valuation transparency to structured finance securities was featured in a Bloomberg article. Speaking on the need for valuation transparency in structured finance securities, Arthur Levitt, the former chairman of the SEC, observed

> For Wall Street, the choices are either working with people like Field to come up with a solution or having one forced on them by regulators…[167]

At the heart of my solution is a single database that collects on an observable event basis, standardizes and disseminates the current performance information for the underlying assets. Market participants could access this information for

---

166 Ahmed, Kamal (2011, October 8), Greg Hands levies 'swizz' jibe at Barclays, Telegraph, http://www.telegraph.co.uk/finance/newsbysector/banksandfinance/8815439/Greg-Hands-levies-swizz-jibe-at-Barclays.html

167 Salas, Caroline (2007, December 4), Subprime Seizure Solution May Be in Hospital Bills, Bloomberg, http://www.bloomberg.com/apps/news?pid=newsarchive&sid=a_gBF9OjtfQI

free and use it in the cash flow models of their choice to assess the risk of and value any structured finance security. As a result, market participants could know what they own or know what they are buying.

On the surface, you wouldn't think there would be anything controversial about proposing that investors receive observable event based data for all structured finance securities. After all, the SEC's Enforcement Division recognized the need for this type of information.

> Information about the delinquency status of mortgage loans that provide collateral for an RMBS offering was important to investors. The mortgage loans that provide the collateral in an RMBS transaction are the primary source of funds by which investors potentially can recover and profit from their investments. The presence and extent of current and historical delinquencies is important information to investors because it helps enable them to assess the likelihood that borrowers will be able to repay their mortgage loans and, as a result, whether investors will suffer losses on, or will recover and profit from, their investments.[168]

Not only did the SEC's Enforcement Division recognize the need for this type of information, but it also acted on it. For example, on July 24, 2014, the SEC and Morgan Stanley enter into an agreement under which Morgan Stanley paid a fine for misleading investors in the sale of residential mortgage-backed securities. In the press release announcing the agreement, the chief of the SEC Enforcement Division's Complex Financial Instruments Unit said,

> Morgan Stanley understated the number of delinquent loans behind these securitizations during a critical juncture of the financial crisis and denied investors the full extent of the facts necessary to make informed investment decisions.[169]

According to the SEC's order,

> The transactions, which were the last subprime RMBS Morgan Stanley sponsored, issued, and underwrote, came against a backdrop of rising borrower delinquencies and unprecedented distress in the subprime market. In the midst of these adverse market conditions, Morgan Stanley misrepresented in the

168 SEC Administrative Proceeding File No. 3-15982 (2014, July 24), *SEC v Morgan Stanley and Co., LLC,* SEC, http://www.sec.gov/litigation/admin/2014/33-9617.pdf, page 8

169 SEC press release (2014, July 24), *Morgan Stanley to Pay $275 Million for Misleading Investors in Subprime RMBS Offerings,* SEC, http://www.sec.gov/News/PressRelease/Detail/PressRelease/1370542355594#.U9E6K2NgC7Z

> offering documents the current or historical delinquency status of certain loans collateralizing the transactions.[170]
>
> Information about current and historical delinquent loans was information that investors would have considered important in deciding whether to invest in the NC4 and HE7 transactions. Morgan Stanley knew or should have known that the disclosures concerning current and historical delinquencies were materially inaccurate and would mislead purchasers in the NC4 and HE7 securities offerings.[171]

It was not as if observable event based data didn't exist. It existed and was used by Wall Street for its benefit.

> Although the offering documents for the transactions stated the number of delinquent loans as of the cut-off date, Collateral Analysis received updated remittance data between the cut-off and closing dates, which the Finance Group used to finalize the loan pool.[172]
>
> In determining the delinquency information disclosed in the HE7 prospectus supplement, Morgan Stanley used data that included payments as of September 20 (not the September 1 cut-off date) to determine which months the loans were paid thru. By using payment information that included payments made after the cut-off date, Morgan Stanley counted 46 loans as current that otherwise would have been delinquent as of the cut-off date. As a result, Morgan Stanley underreported the number of loans that were more than 30 days delinquent as of the cut-off date and the percentage of such loans in the trust.[173]

The fact Wall Street had and used observable event based information to its advantage meant my proposal was actually quite controversial.

Part of the reason it was controversial is Wall Street knows it doesn't have to work with people like myself who would bring valuation transparency to structured finance securities or to the banks themselves. It already knows the regulators will not require valuation transparency. The SEC is still using the intermediary depiction model that is incapable of handling structured finance securities or banks. Both of these need the pure information model for disclosure if they are to provide valuation transparency.

---

170 SEC Administrative Proceeding File No. 3-15982 (2014, July 24), *SEC v Morgan Stanley and Co., LLC,* SEC, http://www.sec.gov/litigation/admin/2014/33-9617.pdf , page 2

171 ibid, page 3

172 ibid, page 4

173 ibid, page 8

Wall Street also knows it can create its own companies to manage the single database and perpetuate opacity in structured finance. These companies perpetuate opacity by offering performance data reported on a once per month basis and/or by offering a subset of the data fields actually tracked by the firms engaged in billing and collecting. Current examples of these companies include the EU Data Warehouse and the Common Securitization Solutions LLC being created by Fannie Mae and Freddie Mac.

The major reason my proposal was controversial is that valuation transparency threatens the profits Wall Street makes from opacity.

Chapter 9

WALL STREET'S OPACITY PROTECTION TEAM

I have been told that if you say anything in Washington often enough, it is eventually treated as fact — regardless of whether it is true or false. While making baseless claims might be shrewd tactics for those who want to undermine . . . , they are flatly wrong.
— *Senator Elizabeth Warren*[174]

Not only do structured finance securities not have valuation transparency, they also don't have price transparency. However, price transparency in the absence of valuation transparency is essentially meaningless. All price transparency shows is the last price paid. Either the smartest investor or biggest fool could have paid this price. Without an independent valuation of the security made possible by valuation transparency, investors don't have a comparison to know if the last price paid was by the smartest investor or biggest fool.

With price transparency and not valuation transparency, the gamblers in the market can see the latest wager.

However, when there is valuation transparency, price transparency is very valuable. For most corporate bonds where the SEC's intermediary depiction model for disclosure is appropriate and there is valuation transparency, a study on price transparency showed that after its introduction, investors experienced

> A reduction of approximately 50% in trade execution costs for bonds eligible for TRACE transaction reporting.[175]

---

174 Protess, Ben (2011, May 24), Warren and Republicans Spar Over Bureau's Power, NY Times Dealbook, http://dealbook.nytimes.com/2011/05/24/warren-and-g-o-p-lawmakers-spar-over-bureaus-power/?_php=true&_type=blogs&_r=0

175 Bessembinder, Hendrik, Maxwell, William, Venkataraman, Kumar (2005, October), Market Transparency, Liquidity Externalities, and Institutional Trading Costs in Corporate Bonds, Journal of Financial Economics, forthcoming, http://finance.eller.arizona.edu/documents/facultypublications/wmaxwell.jfe_transparency.pdf

When the introduction of price transparency can reduce per trade revenue by this much, naturally Wall Street and the City are going to fight to protect the billions of dollars of profits they make from opacity.

Wall Street's Opacity Protection Team

Wall Street and the City know they will continue to profit even if there is valuation transparency. However, with opacity the profits are much higher on a per transaction basis. With valuation transparency, the profits are lower on a per transaction basis, but the number of transactions is much higher.

Wall Street and the City know the current high level of total profits from opacity. The great unknown for any financial product like structured finance securities is whether Wall Street and the City's total profits will be higher with opacity or with valuation transparency.

Whenever their profits from opacity are threatened by valuation or price transparency, the Opacity Protection Team springs into action. The Opacity Protection Team includes Wall Street and the City firms, their lobbyists and industry trade groups they control, Wall Street and the City's legal advisors, think-tanks funded and therefore controlled by Wall Street and the City, and economists who rent out the reputation of the university they work for. The Opacity Protection Team's reach is extensive. From Wall Street and the City to Washington, Frankfurt and elsewhere.

Its mission is simple: protect the profits the banks make from opacity at all cost. Of course, if the Opacity Protection Team is successful, valuation transparency, trust and integrity are never restored in the financial system. If the Opacity Protection Team is successful, the invisible hand of the market does not work and resources are not properly allocated. Instead, we are left with a financial system that operates for the benefit of the banks at the expense of society.

Retaining opacity in structured finance securities is the number one focus of the Opacity Protection Team. The reason it is the number one focus is once it has been shown that banks can provide observable event based reporting to bring valuation transparency to structured finance it is only a small step to banks having to disclose their current exposure details on the same basis.

The point bears repeating. The same 21st century information technology banks currently use that would support valuation transparency for structured finance securities would also support valuation transparency for the banks themselves. This makes the fight to prevent valuation transparency in structured finance securities into a fight over preventing market discipline of the bankers themselves.

To fend off market discipline, the Opacity Protection Team has created a dense fog by raising numerous objections to bringing both valuation and price transparency to structured finance and financial institutions. These objections take two forms: general or specific. General objections are a knee-jerk response by the Opacity Protection Team at the mention of transparency. Specific objections are an indicator the Opacity Protection Team is concerned and has worked to get its messaging down.

The Opacity Protection Team understands

> "We are all well aware ... that ideas universally believed are not necessarily true. We are also aware that it is only after the untruth of such ideas has been exposed that it becomes apparent how pervasive and insidious their influence have been."[176]

As a result, the Opacity Protection Team's strategy is to keep throwing these objections out hoping that one of them will work to prevent adoption of valuation transparency.

What I have found is in the absence of someone like myself to blow away the fog by debunking all the false claims, the Opacity Protection Team's strategy works because the individuals involved in reporting on or implementing valuation transparency either do not have the ability to evaluate the objections or have a perceived career risk in questioning the objections.

I first published a list of these objections and showed they had as much substance as the emperor's new clothes on December 20, 2010. In Appendix I, Debunking Wall Street's myths and misrepresentations about valuation transparency, there is an expanded update of that list with sixty plus claims grouped into categories so that readers can listen to what the members of the Opacity Protection Team have to say and then easily look up why it isn't true.

---

176 Jacobs, Jane (1969), *The Economy of Cities*, Random House: New York, page 1.

Table 2: Categories of false claims made by the Opacity Protection Team

Category	Example of False Claims
Don't need valuation transparency	Investors don't need to know what they own. They can rely on the combination of complex regulations, financial regulators and credit rating firms.
Valuation transparency is too hard to use.	Most investors cannot use the data that would be disclosed and it will only confuse them.
Valuation transparency will hurt (fill in the blank).	It will hurt the economy because banks won't be able to make new loans It will hurt liquidity because banks won't be able to buy securities
Valuation transparency will not (fill in the blank)	It will not make the banks safer It will not make the investors do their homework.
Valuation transparency costs too much	The benefits to be gained from disclosure do not outweigh the cost of providing the data.
Valuation transparency makes it harder to recover from a financial crisis	Financial regulators won't be able to pursue the Japanese Model and the banks will stop lending if they have low levels of book capital.
That's proprietary information you are talking about	If banks have to disclose this information, then the competition will know how we price credit risk
Generic objections to valuation transparency	Requiring valuation transparency creates an unlevel playing field. More data is not the same as better data.
Valuation transparency will require ending borrower privacy	If banks have to disclose this information, everyone will have access to all of the borrower's financial information

Each objection the Opacity Protection Team makes takes the form of a false claim that wraps a fiction around a kernel of truth.

Like everyone else, the Opacity Protection Team led with its best reason not to provide transparency first. To deal with the threat of valuation transparency being brought to asset-backed securities, the Opacity Protection Team trotted out the false claim that valuation transparency could be bad because it could have harmful effects on liquidity and volatility of valuations.

It is true that valuation transparency has an impact on both how many buyers there are for a security, liquidity, and the how widely the price of the security changes between trades, the volatility of valuation. However, it is not true that valuation transparency makes a security less liquid or that it increases the volatility of valuations. This is an example of falsely claiming valuation transparency could create the same bad outcomes as opacity.

It is easy to demonstrate with the clear plastic bag and the brown paper bag why the Opacity Protection Team's claim isn't true. For example, I ask what you would offer to pay me for the contents of a clear plastic bag holding $60 dollars. Your response is likely to be $60 or slightly below. However, what would you offer me for the contents of a brown paper bag containing some money? $10? $20? $60? By using the clear plastic and brown paper bags, I have shown

- Where there is valuation transparency and we are valuing the contents of a clear plastic bag, there is both little volatility in valuation as everyone can know what they are buying and lots of liquidity as everyone is willing to buy at approximately the same price; and
- Where there is opacity and we are valuing the contents of a brown paper bag, there is lots of volatility in valuation as nobody knows what they are buying and illiquidity as they are susceptible to not being willing to buy at any price.

Looking at what happened to the opaque, toxic subprime mortgage-backed securities market in September 2008 confirms the findings of my plastic and paper bag valuation transparency model. The subprime mortgage-backed securities market effectively froze and prices dropped from 70 one day to 10 to 20 the next. Further confirmation is found in the interbank lending market which froze at the beginning of the financial crisis because no one could figure out which opaque bank was solvent or not.

Appendix I has many other examples of the Opacity Protection Team making false claims about valuation transparency in an attempt to retain opacity.

Opacity protection as practiced in the executive suite

"There is no reason why we cannot be fully transparent."
Douglas Flint, Group Chairman, HSBC Holdings,
— United Kingdom Davos 2014[177]

Wall Street and the City know the claims made by the Opacity Protection Team are all false. The claims are not made to convince individuals like myself who would debunk them or to convince individuals who might be skeptical. Rather, the claims are made to provide cover for members of the Wall Street Party so they can justify their actions in opposing transparency in financial reform legislation or the global financial regulators so they can justify their action in not requiring transparency in their regulations. The claims are simply used to buy time so Wall Street and the City can continue to profit from opacity. Wall Street and the City know the laws necessary for the global financial regulators to require valuation transparency have already been passed. As a result, it is only a question of "when" do the financial regulators enforce valuation transparency for any given product like structured finance securities or the banks themselves.

At the 2014 Davos panel discussion on *Are Markets Safer Now*, HSBC Holdings Plc. Chairman Douglas Flint demonstrated Wall Street and the City know the claims are false and the Opacity Protection Team will continue to engage in tactics to delay implementation of valuation transparency when he responded to the charge banks are opaque.

> I take the point on opaque and lack of transparency, but surely, we can fix that. I mean the Financial Stability Board did a study last year along with the industry and indeed the buy-side on enhanced disclosure. We need to keep enhancing disclosure so that the points that Paul made that it is too opaque and we don't understand it recede into history.
>
> There is no reason that we cannot be fully transparent.
>
> We should never have as an excuse "we don't understand the risks on your balance sheet". I can tell you we understand the risks on our balance sheet. Our regulators understand the risk on our balance sheet and if we need to do more to let the analysts and the public understand the risks on the balance sheet then tell us how to do it.[178]

---

177 Flint, Douglas (2014), Are Markets Safer Now, Davos 2014, http://www.weforum.org/sessions/summary/forum-debate-are-markets-safer-now

178 ibid

Mr. Flint knows what holds banks back from being fully transparent is the fact they profit from opacity. He knows there is no legitimate business reason banks cannot be fully transparent and provide valuation transparency.

As part of the game played by the Opacity Protection Team, he pretends there is a mystery about what needs to be done to provide valuation transparency and asks for guidance on what more banks could possibly do so the public understands the risks on and off the bank balance sheets.

The simple reply to Mr. Flint is banks have to follow the lead of J.M. Nichols in the 1930s and provide valuation transparency by disclosing at the end of the business day their current exposure details. Market participants, including their banking competitors, are fully capable of turning this data into useful information for understanding the risk on and off each bank's balance sheets.

Mr. Flint's observation about the need to keep enhancing disclosure suggests valuation transparency occurs on a spectrum and is not as shown by the clear plastic and brown paper bag model either a 1 or 0. By suggesting it is on a spectrum, he creates the opportunity for Wall Street and the City to symbolically move towards the clear plastic bag and being fully transparent. However, this movement is done with the aim of retaining the opacity of a brown paper bag.

Benefits of valuation transparency not lost on Wall Street

Opaque markets breed insider profits and abuse of investors. Sunshine can bring competition and lower costs even if regulators do little beyond letting the sunlight shine.

— *Floyd Norris*[179]

Wall Street fully understands what the presence of valuation transparency would do to their risk taking and ability to sell opaque financial products. It understands providing valuation transparency would subject the banks to market discipline. This market discipline would limit their risk taking and ability to sell opaque financial products.

Wall Street also understands valuation transparency is the key to restoring trust in both the financial system and the banks. It understands so long as there is opacity, market participants will believe the financial system is a game rigged against their interests. When market participants think the game is rigged against them, they don't play. This hurts Wall Street's profitability. As a result, Wall Street has an incentive to try to dispel the notion the game is rigged. It does this by proposing alternatives it claims will deliver the same benefits as valuation transparency while allowing Wall Street to continue to operate in opacity.

Wall Street and faux valuation transparency

One of the best illustrations of this is the September 23, 2011 Bretton Woods Gathering speech on improving the safety and soundness of the financial system given by former Citigroup CEO Vikram Pandit. He frames the issue by observing that relying on regulations is not enough. Instead, he recognizes the need for valuation transparency by making it the centerpiece of his core themes for fixing the global financial system in the wake of our current financial crisis:

> Second, disclosure requirements should be simplified for consumers and strengthened for institutions.
>
> Third, market structures should be reformed to create more transparency and invite more market discipline.
>
> All of these ideas are united by a common principle: the more information that we can make available to a larger number of participants in the system, the more safely and efficiently the financial markets will operate.

179 Norris, Floyd (2009, November 27), Keeping Derivatives in the Dark, NY Times, http://www.nytimes.com/2009/11/27/business/27norris.html?_r=0&pagewanted=all

> Think of these ideas collectively as a version of the "wisdom of crowds" thesis applied to the financial system.[180]

Mr. Pandit effectively dismissed all of the claims made by Wall Street's Opacity Protection Team as the self-serving, misleading statements they are. He dismissed all of these claims with the "wisdom of crowds". Specifically, the wisdom of the crowds comes from its ability to analyze the data disclosed under valuation transparency. With this wisdom, comes the ability of the crowds to exert market discipline.

Without saying so, Mr. Pandit explicitly recognized the existence of opacity across wide areas of the financial system. By calling for more transparency, he is saying the wisdom of the crowd is limited by the lack of information in the opaque corners of the financial system.

Having called for more market discipline, he explains why regulatory restraint on banks alone is not enough to ensure the stability of the financial system.

> The current model tries to manage risk at the institutional level. That is, regulators devise ways to gauge the risk exposure of firms on a bank-by-bank basis and set capital and liquidity requirements to protect those institutions—and by extension the whole system—in the event of some catastrophic event.
>
> There are some limitations to this approach….
>
> [It] presumes a level of clairvoyance that no regulator possesses or could possibly possess….[181]

Under the FDR Framework, the financial system is designed not to be dependent on the clairvoyance of regulators in setting bank capital and liquidity requirements. It is designed to be primarily dependent on market discipline enabled by valuation transparency restraining risk-taking as investors limiting their exposures to what they can afford to lose. Regulatory restraint is a backup in case market discipline fails. Regulatory restraint is there not to protect banks from failure, but rather to protect the deposit insurance fund and ultimately the taxpayers.

---

180 Pandit, Vikram (2011, September 23), Citigroup CEO Vikram Pandit speaks at 2011 Bretton Woods Committee International Council Meeting, Reuters Insider, http://insider.thomsonreuters.com/link.html?cn=share&cid=266045&shareToken=MzplMTE4ZDA1Yy0wM2ZmLTQxMmMtOWJmZi0yMmE5YTc4ODFjYTY%3D, speech transcription verification http://www.citigroup.com/citi/press/executive/110923a.htm

181 ibid

And what is needed so there is more market discipline and less reliance on the clairvoyance of regulators?

> The missing element in Basel, I believe, is transparency. Under the current rules, it's hard to tell whether two banks with a declared 10 percent Tier 1 ratio are equally risky. You don't know how they calibrate risk because you don't know enough about what those underlying assets actually are or how that risk is measured. Basel III and "Stress tests," in which so many put so much faith, are hampered by a similar problem....[182]

Mr. Pandit and I agree the missing element is transparency.

But true to how Wall Street's Opacity Protection Team operates, he inserts a red herring argument to retain opacity. Where Mr. Pandit and I differ is market participants are not primarily interested in transparency to judge how each financial institution calibrates risk. Market participants are primarily interested in valuation transparency so they can independently assess the risk being taken by and the value of each financial institution.

Let's look at how Mr. Pandit's observation would read if the focus was where it belongs on investors understanding the risks and value of each financial institution:

> The missing element in Basel and the "Stress tests", I believe, is valuation transparency. Under the current rules, it's hard to tell whether two banks that passed the "Stress Tests" with a declared 10 percent Tier 1 ratio are equally risky. Without knowing what the banks' underlying assets are (only insiders and select regulators know that), market participants cannot independently value the banks or independently assess how much risk the banks are taking or compare the level of risk between two banks.

This is the way the paragraph needs to be written if the goal is to strengthen the financial system by requiring valuation transparency. Valuation transparency is the obvious solution if market participants don't have the information they need to properly assess how much risk is being taken and therefore do not have the information for properly pricing their exposure to the financial institution.

> For reasons ranging from complexity to competitiveness, financial institutions are not prepared to disclose their entire balance sheets to the world. Thankfully, it's unnecessary.[183]

---

182 ibid

183 ibid

Actually, it is necessary financial institutions do what they have historically done and disclose their entire balance sheets to the world. It is only with this disclosure that market participants can independently assess the risk of and value the financial institutions.

Notice how Mr. Pandit casually throws out a couple of misleading claims as if they were facts for why banks cannot disclose their entire balance sheets to the world. First, he cites complexity. Is his bank so complex that JPMorgan's or Bank of America's analysts wouldn't understand it if they could see the entire balance sheet? If so, this claim suggests his bank should be reduced in size until these analysts can understand it. Second, he cites competitiveness. Disclosure of a bank's entire balance sheet doesn't hurt its competitiveness. It hurts its ability to take risk through proprietary bets.

Notice how Mr. Pandit dismisses the notion of banks being required to provide valuation transparency. He states financial institutions are not prepared to disclose their entire balance sheets to the world. He is asserting financial institutions have the right not to provide valuation transparency and Wall Street's Opacity Protection Team will fight tooth and nail to prevent this from occurring.

Mr. Pandit then offers up an alternative Wall Street would be willing to provide rather than valuation transparency.

> It makes more sense for regulators to create a "benchmark" portfolio and require all financial institutions—not just banks—to measure risk against that. Institutions would be required to produce, on a quarterly basis for that benchmark portfolio, a hypothetical loan-loss reserve level, value-at-risk, stress-test results and risk-weighted assets.
>
> The benchmark portfolio would not actually exist on the balance sheet of any actual institution. Rather, it would be a collection of assets representative of the kinds of assets that most financial institutions actually hold at the time. What's more, the contents would be 100% public.
>
> Right now, loan-loss reserves, value-at-risk, stress-test results and risk-weighted assets are run only against an institution's actual portfolio, whose composition is known only to insiders and select regulators. The results of the tests, therefore, have no common frame of reference. That could be changed simply by requiring financial institutions to run the exact same risk measures against the benchmark portfolio in addition to its own portfolio—and disclose the results of both tests publicly.[184]

The benchmark portfolio is Mr. Pandit's attempt to direct attention to the issue of "how" banks measure risk and away from "what" risk is on their balance sheets. Market participants would know what assets were inside the benchmark

---

[184] ibid

portfolio and they could independently assess the risk of these assets. Then, market participants could compare their independent assessment of risk on the benchmark portfolio to how each bank assesses the risk of these same benchmark assets.

According to Mr. Pandit, the results from the faux transparency provided by the benchmark portfolio would be the same as those expected from valuation transparency.

> Knowing how a given company's risk measurements perform against the benchmark portfolio tells the world how its management thinks about risk, and therefore just how conservative or risky its own portfolio probably is.
>
> An institution that cheerfully reports minimal expected losses from the benchmark portfolio in the event of a one-in-a-thousand market decline might well be understating the risk in its own portfolio. By contrast, one that predicts significant losses from the benchmark portfolio even from a routine decline is very conservative about risk. The benchmark portfolio allows for the kind of "apples to apples" comparison that the current approach does not provide.
>
> The market will be able to reward institutions that take a conservative approach to risk. It will also be able to discount the claims of those whose predictions appear too optimistic. Investors will finally have some basis for judging whether that claimed 10 percent Tier One ratio really is 10 percent—or rather is closer to 8 percent or less.
>
> Even better, the resulting market discipline would strongly encourage financial institutions to take a more conservative approach to risk. Just reporting a capital ratio would no longer be enough. The market would now have a firm basis for evaluating the reality behind the number. And it would reward institutions whose approach to risk and capital holdings seem to be sound and to punish those who appear to get it wrong. In this case, as in so many others, the crowd can be wiser than any individual experts.[185]

While valuation transparency would deliver the results described by Mr. Pandit, there is no reason to believe faux transparency will generate these results. While the assets in the benchmark portfolio are representative of the assets banks hold, there is no reason to believe there is any overlap with the assets the banks are actually holding.

The last time the financial markets relied on a benchmark portfolio was for rating structured finance securities. The rating agencies used a benchmark portfolio of mortgages to rate mortgage-backed securities and a benchmark portfolio of mortgage-backed securities to rate collateralized debt obligations. We know how their reliance on these benchmark portfolios turned out as

185 ibid

investors in mortgage-backed securities and collateralized debt obligations discovered to their dismay, they had bought securities that bore no resemblance to the benchmark portfolio.

Having learned this lesson once, investors understand that they need to have valuation transparency into all of a bank's exposures and not some artificial benchmark portfolio. To do this requires that Citigroup and other financial institutions provide valuation transparency and disclose on an on-going basis their current asset, liability and off-balance sheet exposure details.

As Mr. Pandit acknowledged at the beginning of his speech, to calibrate the risk of a bank the first thing you have to know is what its assets are. Besides, with this data in a standardized form, investors can use this data to create their own apple-to-apple comparisons!

> The goal of reform—creating more systemic safety—is admirable and necessary. The means for achieving it proposed so far can help. But they don't address all the issues. We need to open up new avenues for information to flow where it is needed.
>
> Because the financial system serves the public, more information about it needs to be made public. Armed with more information, the public will be enabled to make better decisions that, in the aggregate, will foster systemic safety—and serve the public interest.[186]

As Mr. Pandit's speech showed, to satisfy the demand for more information being made available to the public, Wall Street is willing to provide faux transparency and claim it is just as good as valuation transparency. However, this faux transparency does not blow away the data fog nor does it deliver the benefits of valuation transparency.

As Mr. Pandit said, Wall Street will fight to maintain the data fog. Wall Street knows opacity provides it with the opportunity to make money based on the mis-assessment of risk/value by other market participants.

In preventing the data fog from being blown away, Wall Street's Opacity Protection Team has an unlikely ally.

---

186 ibid

Chapter 10

SEC BUYS WHAT OPACITY PROTECTION TEAM IS SELLING

The financial sector is deathly afraid that more transparency at this point will only spook investors because it will reveal how bad things really are. They may be right about that, even though restoring long-term investor confidence will require more transparency. In truth, corporations and Wall Street have, through their behavior, consistently opposed transparency, even while giving it lip service in public. All you have to do is read a 10-K report and you realize that the last thing these firms and their lawyers have in mind is giving a true, candid and full assessment of the business to its owners. And a big disappointment to me is that the SEC, through many administrations, has allowed them to get away with this. Frankly, it is an outrage.

—Steven Pearlstein Washington Post blog December 10, 2008[187]

The Opacity Protection Team's ally was and still is the SEC. The SEC was founded in the aftermath of an opacity driven financial crisis, the Great Depression, with the mission to bring valuation transparency to all the opaque corners of the financial system. Valuation transparency so each market participant had a clear plastic bag view of any investment. If the cost of providing valuation transparency made the security unattractive to the issuer to offer, this was intentional.

By the time our current financial crisis arrived over seven decades later, the SEC had abandoned the clear plastic bag standard. It issued regulations for valuation transparency under which different levels of opacity ranging from brown paper bags to black boxes was acceptable and justifiable under a cost/ benefit analysis.

187 Pearlstein, Steven (2008, December 12), response to question on his blog, The Washington Post, http://www.washingtonpost.com/wp-dyn/content/discussion/2008/12/09/DI2008120901766.html

SEC concerned with information overload

Shortly after Mary Jo White became the chairwoman of the SEC, she gave a speech at Fordham Law School on October 3, 2013. In her speech, she talked about how the SEC operates and the SEC's powers of mandatory disclosure.

> In 1996, when he was given the William O. Douglas award, the SEC's highest honor, former Commissioner Sommer captured the essence of the SEC this way:
>
> "The staff of the Commission has never lacked for courage. They have gone to the mat with investment bankers, exchanges, the public utility industry, the accounting profession, the legal profession, and, for that matter, on occasions with the entire world of American industry. In every case there were loud howls, efforts to bring political pressure to bear; unfailingly the Commission stuck to its guns and fought to implement the policies it thought were right. It may rightly be said that the SEC has done more to raise the moral level of the marketplace than any other institution, public or private, in the United States."... [188]

Do you notice how the staff of the SEC has never had to go to the mat with investors? There is a reason the SEC never has to go to the mat with investors. In the absence of the Transparency Label Initiative™, the reason is the SEC is the investors' only advocate for valuation transparency. Every market participant listed by Commissioner Sommer has a vested interest in opacity so naturally they are in opposition to what the SEC staff is proposing. It is the SEC's responsibility to provide the investors with valuation transparency by requiring disclosure despite the objections from these members of Wall Street's Opacity Protection Team.

Commissioner Sommer would like the SEC staff to get credit for raising the moral level of the marketplace. Given the SEC's primary mission is to increase transparency in the marketplace, it could not be otherwise.

Two decades before the SEC's creation, Justice Louis Brandeis explained how transparency raised the moral level of the marketplace.[189] He was prompted to write the article by the excessive commissions bankers were generating through their control over access to investors. To Justice Brandeis, "sunlight is

---

188 White, Mary Jo (2013, October 3), 14th Annual A.A. Sommer, Jr. Corporate Securities and Financial Law Lecture, SEC, http://www.sec.gov/News/Speech/Detail/Speech/1370539864016

189 Brandeis, Justice Louis (1913, December 20), What Publicity Can Do, Harper's Weekly, http://3197d6d14b5f19f2f440-5e13d29c4c016cf96cbbfd197c579b45.r81.cf1.rackcdn.com/collection/papers/1910/1913_12_20_What_Publicity_Ca.pdf, page 12.

said to be the best of disinfectants; electric light the most efficient policeman."[190] He proposed the use of publicity of exactly what the bankers were being paid as the remedy for eliminating excess commissions.

> That is knowledge to which both the existing security holder and the prospective purchaser is fairly entitled. If the bankers' compensation is reasonable, considering the skill and risk involved, there can be no objection to making it known. If it is not reasonable, the investor will "strike."[191]

To Justice Brandeis, full disclosure of the commissions neither fixed the bankers' profits nor prevented investors from making a bad investment, but it helped the investor judge the quality of the investment. The result of full disclosure was market discipline on the bankers and, ultimately, fair and reasonable commissions in response to this discipline.

Continuing with Ms. White's comments,

> Under the law, the SEC is an independent agency ...This independence and the quality of its people allow the agency the freedom to do what it believes is right for investors and our markets, without the interference of politics or outside pressure.
>
> Being independent, of course, does not mean that the SEC does not listen to the ideas and recommendations that come from beyond our building.[192]

Based on my experience with the SEC, they do listen to the ideas and recommendations that come from beyond its building. Specifically, they listen to the ideas and recommendations that come from Wall Street's Opacity Protection Team. The SEC's staff listens as if it were the Opacity Protection Team members who were the SEC's clients rather than investors and other advocates for the buy-side.

The disclosure requirements the SEC adopted for structured finance securities serve as a case study of the Opacity Protection Team's influence over the SEC. These requirements can be found under the Securities and Exchange Commission Regulation AB, 17 C.F.R. §§ 229.1100-1123. Regulation AB was enacted on January 7, 2005. This was well before the financial crisis began.

The best way to summarize Regulation AB is as a result of the lobbying efforts of the Opacity Protection Team this regulation institutionalized the

---

190 ibid, page 10.

191 ibid, page 12

192 White, Mary Jo (2013, October 3), 14th Annual A.A. Sommer, Jr. Corporate Securities and Financial Law Lecture, SEC, http://www.sec.gov/News/Speech/Detail/Speech/1370539864016

information asymmetry between Wall Street with its access to fresh loan performance data and the other market participants who were provided old, stale loan performance data. Wall Street would be valuing the contents of a clear plastic bag and other market participants would be guessing at the value of the contents of a brown paper bag.

What Regulation AB did not do was bring valuation transparency to structured finance securities.

According to former Fed Chair Bernanke in his October 31, 2008 speech on the future of mortgage finance, the structured finance securities at the very heart of the financial crisis failed the test of what is required for a successful securitization.

> The financial crisis that began in August 2007 has entered its second year. Its proximate cause was the end of the U.S. housing boom, which revealed serious deficiencies in the underwriting and credit rating of some mortgages, particularly subprime mortgages with adjustable interest rates. As subsequent events demonstrated, however, the boom in subprime mortgage lending was only a part of a much broader credit boom characterized by an underpricing of risk, excessive leverage, and the creation of complex and opaque financial instruments that proved fragile under stress. ...
>
> Eventually, experience provided three principles for successful mortgage securitization. ... Finally, because mortgage-backed securities are complex amalgamations of underlying mortgages that may themselves be complex to price, transparency about both the underlying assets and the mortgage-backed security itself is essential....
>
> As investors lost confidence, significant flaws in the securitization process, including inadequate risk management and disclosure as well as excessive complexity, became apparent.[193]

The former Fed chairman observed for successful mortgage securitization, "transparency about both the underlying assets and the mortgage-backed security itself is essential". In October 2008, he identified inadequate disclosure as a significant flaw in the current securitization process. This inadequate disclosure just happened to be the disclosure required under the SEC's Regulation AB. This inadequate disclosure just happens to put the SEC at ground zero of the financial crisis and says in bright neon lights the SEC failed to ensure valuation transparency and that investors have access to all the useful, relevant information in an appropriate, timely manner.

---

193 Bernanke, Ben (2008, October 31), The Future of Mortgage Finance in the United States, Federal Reserve, http://www.federalreserve.gov/newsevents/speech/bernanke20081031a.htm

This is a point that needs to be repeated. The failure of the SEC to ensure adequate valuation transparency was the primary cause of the financial crisis.

The failure of the SEC to ensure adequate valuation transparency didn't just occur with structured finance securities. It also occurred with the banks. This point was driven home in 1984 with the run by sophisticated institutional investors on Continental Illinois.

Together, the lack of valuation transparency for structured finance securities and banks created a toxic brew. When the market for opaque structured finance securities collapsed because the lack of valuation transparency made them impossible to assess and value, it triggered a global run on the opaque banking system. Everyone knew the banks had an exposure to these securities, but the lack of valuation transparency made it impossible to assess the impact on the banks.

At the risk of being repetitious, the failure of the SEC to ensure valuation transparency was the necessary and sufficient condition to bring about our current financial crisis.

This inadequate disclosure also just happened to be what Wall Street's Opacity Protection Team sought in its comments and lobbying. After all, you wouldn't expect the Opacity Protection Team to explain to the SEC what was actually needed so there would be valuation transparency. Both the regulations covering bank disclosure and Regulation AB were doomed from the outset. They were based on the use of the intermediary depiction model for disclosure rather than the pure information model. Neither provided the valuation transparency about their underlying assets the former Fed chairman said is necessary for success.

> It also does not mean that we should not welcome the views of investor advocates, companies, Members of Congress, or financial institutions.
>
> Indeed, we depend upon hearing and evaluating the ideas and recommendations of those who will be impacted by our rules, including those required to comply with them. In fact, the laws that govern our "notice and comment" rulemaking process direct us to seek out these views and, more importantly, *consider* them. And, if we do not do so, the courts could potentially strike down the rule and send us back to the drawing board.[194]

The law governing the rulemaking process requires the SEC to seek out and consider the views of Wall Street's Opacity Protection Team. However, the law does not require the SEC to give these views more weight than the views of the investors. After all, without investors, there is no market.

---

[194] White, Mary Jo (2013, October 3), 14th Annual A.A. Sommer, Jr. Corporate Securities and Financial Law Lecture, SEC, http://www.sec.gov/News/Speech/Detail/Speech/1370539864016

So, the question is how to consider the views of Wall Street's Opacity Protection Team. Are the views of each team member considered as separate or are the views considered as part of the team's single voice? If separate, how do the investors' views get equal weight if the ratio of comments during the rulemaking process runs 1 investor response for every 17 Opacity Protection Team responses? How are the views of Opacity Protection Team dominated trade groups considered? The Opacity Protection Team's main lobbying organization formed these trade groups so there is no reason to believe the voices of the investors who belong to these trade groups was given equal or any weight in the trade group's response.

> More importantly, seeking out and considering public comment by all interested and affected parties makes for much better decisions and much better rules.[195]

Even if the rulemaking process did improve Regulation AB, it and the disclosure regulations for banks still failed with catastrophic consequences.

> At the end of the day, however, we make our decisions based on an impartial assessment of the law and the facts and what we believe will further our mission — and never in response to political pressure, lobbying, or even public clamor. All comments and recommendations, from whatever the source, are judged on their merits — and their validity has no greater weight just because more influential or better connected commenters say so, or say so more loudly....[196]

My experience trying to bring valuation transparency to structured finance securities using the clear plastic bag and the brown paper bag model shows Mary Jo White's statement about how the SEC considers each comment and recommendation to have no connection with the reality of how the SEC actually operates.

To its credit, the SEC recognized the catastrophic failure of Regulation AB and tried to revise the regulation. In its attempt to revise the regulation, the SEC began its rulemaking process and solicited input. I responded to their request for comments.

I like to give the staff members at the SEC the benefit of the doubt and think they are smart enough to understand you can value the contents of a clear plastic bag, but you cannot value the contents of a brown paper bag. I want to give the SEC the benefit of the doubt and think its staff members are smart

---

195 ibid

196 ibid

enough to have read my response and understood with observable event based reporting investors would be valuing the contents of a clear plastic bag. I like to think the SEC staff understood with the once per month disclosure provided by opaque subprime mortgage-backed securities investors are being asked to value the contents of a brown paper bag.

The 2014 revision of Regulation AB strongly adhered to the recommendations made by the sell-side dominated industry trade group. One of these recommendations was retaining the same frequency of disclosure provided by the opaque subprime mortgage-backed securities the former Fed chairman said were significantly flawed.

The explanation publicly offered for the failure to adopt my recommendation is the SEC was attempting to minimize the cost of collecting the data. This concern with minimizing the issuer's cost of providing disclosure was specifically excluded from the SEC's mandate to ensure disclosure of all the useful, relevant information in an appropriate, timely manner. It was excluded because the benefit of disclosure was seen as outweighing the cost of disclosure and if the cost of providing disclosure was so high as to make a security unattractive to issue, then the security should not be issued. Later in this book, I present the cost/benefit analysis that accompanied my response to the SEC and demonstrated the benefit of observable event based disclosure outweighed the cost of providing this disclosure by an order of magnitude.

An alternative explanation for the failure to adopt my recommendation could be the fact the SEC does not judge comments and recommendations based on their merits, but rather puts greater weight on the more influential and better connected commenters. If true, this greater weight is so significant the SEC in its revised Regulation AB continued to embrace the notion a brown paper bag is transparent.

By the way, the SEC is not the only financial regulator who appears to be swayed by lobbying and puts greater weight on the responses provided by Wall Street's Opacity Protection Team. Based on my experience dealing with financial regulators on a global basis, there is only one financial regulator who isn't swayed by Wall Street's Opacity Protection Team. Not surprisingly, this one financial regulator is responsible for firms that are on the buy-side.

> Disclosure is indeed a key ingredient in the securities arena. It gives investors the information they need about their investments. It provides them with information about the operations, management and financial condition of the companies they invest in. And, it allows informed investors to participate in a free and fair market.[197]

---

197 ibid

As shown by the freezing of the private label mortgage-backed securities market and the interbank lending market at the beginning of the current financial crisis, when disclosure of all the useful, relevant information in an appropriate, timely manner is not available, investors are not interested and markets effectively freeze and become organized casinos for gamblers only.

> My former colleague Commissioner Troy Paredes, who delivered the Sommer lecture in 2011, put it this way: "[T]he foundational cornerstone of the [SEC's] regulatory regime has remained fixed. It is disclosure. For over 75 years, the SEC's signature mandate has been to use disclosure to promote transparency."
>
> He made the additional unassailable points that there are also costs associated with mandatory disclosure and "too much disclosure can be counterproductive." Commissioner Sommer also frequently expressed concern about the increasing "quantity and complexity" of disclosure.[198]

Commissioner Troy Paredes' point about "too much disclosure can be counterproductive" is not only assailable, but it is flat out wrong.

By mandate and original intention as revealed in FDR's comment, the SEC should error by insisting on more rather than less disclosure. Remember the hurdle to get over for testing the adequacy of disclosure is it provides the most demanding expert with access to what the expert considers all the useful, relevant information in an appropriate, timely manner. To the extent there are several demanding experts, but their informational needs differ, disclosure needs to cover all of their informational needs.

In practice, this has not occurred. Instead, the pursuit of the intermediary depiction model for disclosure has resulted in the SEC buying into the Wall Street's Opacity Protection Team arguments and trying to minimize disclosure requirements. The justification for minimizing disclosure is the Opacity Protection Team's argument for looking at how the unsophisticated investor (pretty much everyone other than professional money managers) would use the data and concern that too much data would overload the unsophisticated investor's ability to analyze it.

Frankly, as shown by the explosive growth of the money management business over the last 3+ decades, the unsophisticated investor doesn't analyze the disclosed data so he/she is never overloaded by too much disclosure. Instead, the unsophisticated investor hires a third party he/she trusts who can analyze the data. For example, the unsophisticated investor invests in mutual funds run by professional portfolio managers who if they cannot assess the disclosed data hire

---

198 ibid

third party experts who can. Or the unsophisticated investor invests in Berkshire Hathaway so that Warren Buffett will read company annual reports and invest on his/her behalf.

The result of the unsophisticated investor's behavior is to confirm the SEC should target its disclosure requirements to the most demanding experts as ultimately this is who the unsophisticated investor relies on to assess the disclosed data.

The fact of the matter is that investors don't say they want less disclosure. Investors know they can chose to use the disclosed information in their own assessment of the risk and value of the investment, hire a third party expert to do the assessment for them or don't do the assessment at all and not buy the security.

The only market participants who argue for less disclosure are Wall Street, the trade groups it controls, its legal representatives, academics hired by Wall Street and the security issuers. Unfortunately, we have our current financial crisis because the SEC listened to Wall Street's Opacity Protection Team arguing for less disclosure.

> Their concerns resonate with me. When disclosure gets to be too much or strays from its core purposes, it can lead to "information overload" — a phenomenon in which ever-increasing amounts of disclosure make it difficult for investors to focus on the information that is material and most relevant to their decision-making as investors in our financial markets.
>
> The Commission also said that disclosure of such non-material information regarding each of the identified matters would render disclosure documents wholly unmanageable and increase costs without corresponding benefits to investors generally.[199]

Consider for a moment just how condescending, demeaning and insulting Ms. White's comments are to investors. She puts forth the idea investors need to have their hand held because they are unable to separate the important from the unimportant when it comes to disclosed information. Actually, the unsophisticated investor is really good at handling increased disclosure. He/she turns to the experts who know how to analyze any information the SEC could see its way to requiring be disclosed.

Ms. White effectively asserts more disclosure actually makes a security more opaque. In her worldview, more disclosure creates opacity because it makes it harder for investors to focus on what is the material and relevant information to make a decision on. Why does the SEC think it has a better handle on what each investor thinks is material or relevant information for making a decision on than

[199] ibid

the investor does? What each investor thinks is material or relevant information for making a decision is their choice and it is the SEC's responsibility to make sure this information is disclosed. FDR called for disclosure of "full information" not for "partial information" based on what some bureaucrat's thoughts about what material and relevant information might be. Ms. White's comment is also fundamentally flawed since there is no evidence to suggest investors are not fully capable of ignoring disclosed information they consider irrelevant.

Her comments reflect the need to justify the SEC's adoption of the intermediary depiction model and not the pure information model for disclosure. If the investors are seen as able to analyze reality, then there is no need for an intermediary to provide a summary depiction. Unfortunately, the SEC's choice of the intermediary depiction model for banks and structured finance securities resulted in our current financial crisis.

> And it noted that "as a practical matter, it is impossible to provide every item of information that might be of interest to some investor in making investment and voting decisions."[200]

Turns out with 21st century information technology it is both practical and very low cost to provide every item of information that might be of interest to some investor in making investment and voting decisions particularly when it comes to structured finance securities and banks.

Shortly after the financial crisis began, I put together and shared with the SEC a cost/benefit analysis showing the cost of pure information disclosure using 21st century information technology (the data warehouse) was a small percentage of the benefit of preventing a financial crisis caused by opacity.

Ms. White followed up with an October 15, 2013 speech to the National Association of Corporate Directors in which she expanded on the SEC's Path forward for disclosure. In this speech, she sets forth as one of her major priorities focusing on reducing disclosure to insure there isn't "too much" disclosure. This is remarkable considering at the very heart of our current financial crisis are the opaque subprime securities and opaque banks that are opaque due to the SEC's failure to require the subprime securities and banks provide valuation transparency. This is remarkable considering this lack of valuation transparency has not been addressed since the beginning of the financial crisis.

This speech also effectively denies what the existence of 21st century information technology means for disclosure, particularly for structured finance securities and banks.

---

200 ibid

> Without proper disclosure, investors would be unable to make informed decisions. They would not know about the financial condition of the company they are investing in.... The core purpose of disclosure, of course, is to provide investors with the information they need to make informed investment and voting decisions. Such information makes it possible for investors to evaluate companies and have the confidence to invest...[201]

Former Fed Chair Bernanke confirmed the absence of proper disclosure leads to a loss in confidence in his October 20, 2008 testimony before Congress.

> The financial turmoil intensified in recent weeks, as investors' confidence in banks and other financial institutions eroded and risk aversion heightened. Conditions in the interbank lending market have worsened, with term funding essentially unavailable.[202]

Why did investor confidence in banks erode? Because the SEC failed to require the banks disclose their current exposure details under the pure information model. Rather banks disclosed under the intermediary depiction model. As a result, banks were black boxes and nobody could determine who was solvent and who was insolvent because of their hidden exposure to the opaque structured finance securities.

> But, I am raising the question here and internally at the SEC as to whether investors need and are optimally served by the detailed and lengthy disclosures about all of the topics that companies currently provide in the reports they are required to prepare and file with us.
>
> When disclosure gets to be "too much" or strays from its core purpose, it could lead to what some have called "information overload" — a phenomenon in which ever-increasing amounts of disclosure make it difficult for an investor to wade through the volume of information she receives to ferret out the information that is most relevant.[203]

How is it that the new chair of the SEC should be so focused on making sure that in the information age investors don't have "information overload"? As the Congressional Oversight Panel noted,

---

201 White, Mary Jo (2013, October 15), The Path Forward on Disclosure, SEC, http://www.sec.gov/News/Speech/Detail/Speech/1370539878806

202 Bernanke, Ben (2008, October 20), testimony before the Committee on the Budget, U.S. House of Representatives, Federal Reserve, http://www.federalreserve.gov/newsevents/testimony/bernanke20081020a.htm

203 White, Mary Jo (2013, October 15), The Path Forward on Disclosure, SEC, http://www.sec.gov/News/Speech/Detail/Speech/1370539878806

> There are of course legitimate questions about how far policymakers should go in requiring disclosure—where the line should be drawn between public and proprietary information. But particularly given the breakdown that has now occurred, it is difficult to escape the conclusion that America's financial markets have veered far from the goal of transparency, fundamentally compromising the health and vitality of the financial sector and, ultimately, the whole economy.
>
> Why our regulatory system failed to expand the zone of transparency in the face of far-reaching financial innovation is a question that merits careful attention.[204]

In her speech, Ms. White provides more insight into why the SEC did not expand the zone of transparency in the face of the collapse of Continental Illinois or the expansion of financial innovation.

> The Supreme Court addressed this overload concern over 35 years ago in *TSC Industries* when it considered, in the context of a proxy statement for a merger, what should constitute a "material" misstatement or omission under the federal securities laws. In reaching its conclusion, it rejected the view that a fact is "material" if an investor "might" find it important. As explained by Justice Marshall, writing for the Court: "[M]anagement's fear of exposing itself to substantial liability may cause it simply to bury the shareholders in an avalanche of trivial information — a result that is hardly conducive to informed decision-making." Instead, the Court held that a fact is "material" if "there is a substantial likelihood that a reasonable shareholder would consider it important in deciding how to vote."[205]

Here is an argument that only a financial regulator run by lawyers who want to deny the impact of the two biggest changes in the investment world could love, but the reasonable shareholder would immediately dismiss as sheer nonsense. According to Ms. White, the Supreme Court addressed the issue of information overload before 21st century information technology became widespread and the SEC would prefer to deny what a profound change using this technology should have on disclosure requirements and practices. The

---

204 Congressional Oversight Panel (2009, January), Special Report on Regulatory Reform, Modernizing the American Financial Regulatory System: Recommendations for Improving Oversight, Protecting Consumers and Ensuring Stability, http://cybercemetery.unt.edu/archive/cop/20110402010517/http://cop.senate.gov/documents/cop-012909-report-regulatoryreform.pdf, page 14.

205 White, Mary Jo (2013, October 15), The Path Forward on Disclosure, SEC, http://www.sec.gov/News/Speech/Detail/Speech/1370539878806

Internet has made it easy for even go it alone retail investors to access experts who are capable of analyzing all of the disclosed information.

Furthermore, the Supreme Court addressed the issue of information overload before the unsophisticated investor's use of professional investment managers took off. It is these professional investment managers, who as part of their pitch to attract assets tout their expertise in analyzing the disclosed information, who vote the vast majority of the stock.

The result of both the movement towards using professional managers and the Internet is the capability of the "reasonable shareholder" to analyze data is now uniformly at the expert level.

Had the SEC retained a goal of transparency, both of these developments along with the run on Continental Illinois would have forced it to adopt the pure information model for, at a minimum, banks and structured finance securities.

As the Congressional Oversight Panel noted,

> The challenge now is to develop a plan not only to bring much-needed sunlight into the most opaque corners of the financial system but to ensure appropriate regulatory adaptation to new financial innovation in the future.[206]

It is clear it is not Ms. White's idea the SEC should develop a plan to bring much-needed sunlight into the most opaque corners of the financial system or to bring sunlight to financial innovations. Her focus is on reducing the already limited disclosure there is.

> Not too long before the *TSC* ruling, the Commission confronted a similar issue and held public hearings on what topics should be required in corporate disclosures. ....
>
> Expressing the view that disclosure should generally be tethered to the concept of materiality, the Commission decided against requiring disclosure of the identified matters, noting that "as a practical matter, it is impossible to provide every item of information that might be of interest to some investor in making investment and voting decisions."
>
> We must continuously consider whether information overload is occurring as rules proliferate and as we contemplate what should and should not be required to be disclosed going forward....[207]

---

206 Congressional Oversight Panel (2009, January), Special Report on Regulatory Reform, Modernizing the American Financial Regulatory System: Recommendations for Improving Oversight, Protecting Consumers and Ensuring Stability, http://cybercemetery.unt.edu/archive/cop/20110402010517/http://cop.senate.gov/documents/cop-012909-report-regulatoryreform.pdf, page 15.

207 White, Mary Jo (2013, October 15), The Path Forward on Disclosure, SEC, http://www.sec.gov/News/Speech/Detail/Speech/1370539878806

By legislative mandate from Congress and charge by FDR, the SEC was not given the responsibility for considering whether information overload is occurring. This made sense in the 1930s and makes sense today. Investors have many ways to avoid information overload including hiring experts who can easily analyze the information.

> After all, the fundamental purpose of disclosure is to provide a reasonable investor with the information that he or she would need to make an informed investment or voting decision.
>
> We need to consider whether the disclosure regime as a whole is generating the information that a reasonable investor would need to make decisions....
>
> After nearly a century in the making, our disclosure regime is not based entirely on line item requirements; rather, it is fundamentally grounded on the standard of "materiality." The staff has typically handled new "disclosure areas" and "hot topics" by starting with the premise that our rules require disclosure of material information. So, our disclosure experts have provided guidance about how to address particular topics within the framework of providing information that is necessary for exercising an investment or voting decision....[208]

Our current financial crisis has shown beyond any doubt in the case of banks and structured finance securities, the disclosure regime is not generating the material information a reasonable investor would need to make decisions. Nor is the SEC ever likely to fix this problem. Its staff starts with the premise that its rules require disclosure of only material information and the assumption as a practical matter it is impossible to provide every item of information that might be of interest to some investor. This starting point denies the impact of 21st century technology on disclosure and the movement to having money managed by experts. This is why the Transparency Label Initiative™ is needed. Unlike the SEC, the Initiative's starting point is looking at what disclosure is actually needed to provide valuation transparency. The Initiative realizes we live in the information age and 21st century information technology gives us the ability to provide valuation transparency.

> Finally, we must ask: Are investors getting the information they need when they need it?[209]

Clearly, in the case of banks or structured finance securities the answer is a resounding **NO**.

---

208 ibid

209 ibid

> And are there ways that our rules can improve investors' access to a company's disclosure?...
>
> The current disclosure requirements for public companies require varying timeframes for disclosure depending on the nature of the information. The shortest is two business days — for disclosing the transactions and holdings of directors, officers, and beneficial owners. Significant corporate events generally must be disclosed within four business days of the event. Companies have more time to disclose quarterly and annual reports. The information is no less important, but companies need more time to compile and prepare the disclosure and financial statements.
>
> But given the ever increasing use of technology by virtually everyone, we need to think about whether the current timeframes in our rules and forms continue to be appropriate. In some cases, investors may benefit from receiving the information sooner than currently required. But we must also consider whether shorter timeframes would impose an undue burden on companies. There also may be concerns that requiring more frequent updates could lead to a decrease in the quality of the information....[210]

In the case of banks and structured finance securities, investors are not getting the information they need when they need it. The former are black boxes and the latter are brown paper bags.

Two decades ago I showed how to use 21st century information technology to provide investors access to the information they needed for both banks and structured finance securities. Since the beginning of our current financial crisis, I have repeatedly explained to the SEC why using 21st century information technology would allow investors to receive the information they need when they need it. This information could be provided without decreasing the quality of the information and without imposing an undue financial burden on the issuer.

As shown in the SEC's most recent reform of the disclosure requirements covering structured finance securities, Regulation AB, the SEC has chosen not to listen to me. In its explanation for why it did not adjust its disclosure requirements so investors could benefit from receiving information sooner, it cited the cost of making this information available. This is a direct rejection of one of the main features of requiring valuation transparency. This feature can be summarized as "if the cost of providing investors with valuation transparency is too high, then the security should not be offered for public sale."

This failure to provide the investors the information they need when they need it demonstrates the fatal flaw in the original FDR Framework and why The Transparency Label Initiative™ is needed. The Initiative ensures the data investors need to assess the risk and value of currently opaque securities, like

[210] ibid

banks and structured finance, is made available or these securities are branded "For Gamblers Only" as they are blind bets. The desire to have a label from the Initiative and not have their securities negatively branded puts pressure on the issuers to provide the valuation transparency the SEC cannot bring itself to requiring.

With this valuation transparency, market participants can once again know what they own, exercise self-discipline and exert market discipline. The Transparency Label Initiative™ returns the financial system to its roots under the FDR Framework. With access to valuation transparency, the market can once again regulate itself while ending its reliance on financial regulators

> Clearly, there is no one system of disclosure that will satisfy everyone. Too much information for some is not enough for others. Too little for some, may be too much for others. And what some investors might want may not be what reasonable investors need.[211]

The goal of disclosure is not to satisfy everyone or to satisfy some mythical reasonable investor, but rather to satisfy the most demanding investor. Every other investor can ignore the parts of the disclosure they are not interested in. The goal of disclosure is to ensure "full information" or as Justice Brandeis said it over 100 years ago to end the "investor's servility … due … to his ignorance of the facts".[212]

Absent from Ms. White's speech or her conclusion is any acknowledgement of the fact the SEC failed to require adequate disclosure from either banks or structured finance securities before, during or after the beginning of our current financial crisis. The result of the SEC's failure was our current global financial crisis. A crisis the SEC could and should have prevented by requiring valuation transparency. By not preventing the crisis, the SEC showed why the buy-side's reliance on financial regulators is the fatal flaw in the original FDR Framework. The crisis showed why we need the Transparency Label Initiative™ to prevent opacity driven financial crises and ensure valuation transparency.

The SEC's failure to require valuation transparency allowed large areas of the global financial system to be hidden behind a veil of opacity. When the financial crisis began, the fog created by this opacity made it difficult to understand the cause of, how to respond to or how to end the financial crisis.

---

211 ibid

212 Brandeis, Justice Louis (1913, December 20), What Publicity Can Do, Harper's Weekly, http://3197d6d14b5f19f2f440-5e13d29c4c016cf96cbbfd197c579b45.r81.cf1.rackcdn.com/collection/papers/1910/1913_12_20_What_Publicity_Ca.pdf, page 11

SECTION 5

ORIGINAL FDR FRAMEWORK FAILURE: EVIDENCE FROM THE FINANCIAL CRISIS

CHAPTER 11

ALL CLUES LEAD TO ONE CONCLUSION: OPACITY

A hefty prospectus veiled in legal jargon should not be considered a transparent tool of disclosure; it is a means of obfuscation. The sheer complexity of repackaging subprime loans to achieve AAA credit-ratings is indicative of efforts to deceive through disguise.

Trust in financial markets vanished when the lack of transparency became apparent; it is only through transparency that investor confidence and public trust can be won back.

— *Huguette LaBelle,*
Chair Transparency International[213]

Wall Street's Opacity Protection Team claims the cause of the global financial crisis and its related panic is not well understood and hence remains a whodunit. They suggest there were multiple causes including complex financial products, the failure of the rating agencies to assign ratings that reflected the true underlying risk of structured finance securities, the failure of the financial regulators to provide adequate supervision or properly regulate the financial system, poor risk management at financial institutions and the actions of the government-sponsored enterprises.

Occam's Razor reveals whodunit

To understand the cause of the global financial crisis and related panic, we need to apply Occam's Razor. Occam's Razor is a principle that says the explanation of an event with the fewest assumptions that is consistent with and doesn't ignore the evidence is likely the best explanation. If we apply Occam's Razor and give each of the suggested causes of the global financial crisis a nice shave, we find the explanation for the global financial crisis that requires the fewest assumptions, that doesn't ignore the evidence and that accounts for what happened is opacity. We also find that each of the suggested causes is actually a symptom of opacity.

213 LaBelle, Huguette, Letter to the editor of The Economist, The Economist http://www.economist.com/node/13272018

This finding is not surprising as credit market bubbles and panics are symptoms of opacity. Where opacity exists it inhibits the ability of markets to discriminate between sound and unsound borrowers because it hides the true fundamentals of each borrower. As a result, market participants make overly optimistic assumptions about weak borrowers during the bubble expansion phase and overly pessimistic assumptions driven by panic about strong borrowers during the bubble contraction phase.

In its January 2009 report, the Congressional Oversight Panel confirmed the whodunit was opacity. Opacity was the necessary and sufficient condition for the global financial panic. The Congressional Oversight Panel described the failure to ensure valuation transparency and the resulting meltdown as it moved from opaque, toxic subprime mortgage-backed securities to the other opaque parts of the global financial system including banks.

> In recent years, however, the regulatory system … failed to require disclosure of risk through sufficient transparency. American financial markets are profoundly dependent upon transparency. After all, the fundamental risk/reward corollary depends on the ability of market participants to have confidence in their ability to accurately judge risk.
>
> Markets have become opaque in multiple ways. Some markets, such as hedge funds and credit default swaps, provide virtually no information. Even so, disclosure alone does not always provide genuine transparency. Market participants must have useful, relevant information delivered in an appropriate, timely manner. Recent market occurrences involving off-balance-sheet entities and complex financial instruments reveal the lack of transparency resulting from the wrong information disclosed at the wrong time and in the wrong manner….[214]

> By the time the crisis struck in 2007-2008, however, one of the most common words used to describe the American financial system was "opaque." …
>
> In addition, the proliferation of off-balance-sheet entities (conduits, structured investment vehicles [SIVs], etc.) and the rapid growth of highly complex financial instruments (such as CDOs) further undermined clarity and understanding in the marketplace….[215]

> The bursting of the housing bubble produced the first true stress test of modern capital markets, their instruments, and their participants. The first

---

214 Congressional Oversight Panel (2009, January), Special Report on Regulatory Reform, Modernizing the American Financial Regulatory System: Recommendations for Improving Oversight, Protecting Consumers and Ensuring Stability, http://cybercemetery.unt.edu/archive/cop/20110402010517/http://cop.senate.gov/documents/cop-012909-report-regulatoryreform.pdf, page 3.

215 ibid, page 14

> cracks were evident in the subprime mortgage market and in the secondary market for mortgage-related securities. From there, the crisis spread to nearly every corner of the financial sector, both at home and abroad, taking down some of the most venerable names in the investment banking and insurance businesses and crippling others, wreaking havoc in the credit markets, and brutalizing equity markets worldwide.[216]

It was opacity that caused the global financial panic. Opacity made it impossible to value structured finance securities. Opacity made it impossible to value banks let alone determine which banks were solvent and which were not.

Opacity provided the feeding ground for fear to sweep the global financial system. Opacity meant that the absence of facts and therefore reason could not check the emotion of fear and hence panic from sweeping the financial system.

It was the brown paper bag of opacity whodunit.

What did the Fed know and when did they know it?

> Mr. Fisher. At the last meeting I asked about commercial paper risk in Europe and got nods of not a great risk. Is there anything that you see or that you can think of that we don't know or that hasn't been in this presentation that would indicate significant potential for risk?
>
> Mr. Dudley. I would hesitate to say that I know with any great clarity that there's nothing else there in Europe. I think we have all been a bit surprised by the size of some of the conduits that some European banks were sponsoring relative to their capital. I would be very hesitant to say that we have transparency regarding that marketplace and know with certainty that there's nothing else there.[217]

By August 7, 2007, the Federal Reserve knew opacity in structured finance securities was causing a problem. Speaking at an FOMC meeting, then manager of the system open market account and now president of the Federal Reserve Bank of New York, Bill Dudley explained the role of opacity and how opacity affected not just the opaque structured finance markets, but transparent markets as well:

> There has been a loss of confidence among investors in their ability to assess the value of and risks associated with structured products, which has led to a sharp drop in demand for such products.

---

216 ibid, page 6

217 Federal Reserve (2007, September 18), *Meeting of the Federal Open Market Committee on September 18, 2007*, Federal Reserve, http://www.federalreserve.gov/monetarypolicy/files/FOMC20070918meeting.pdf, page 12.

> The loss of confidence stems from many sources, including the opacity of such products; the infrequency of trades, which makes it more difficult to judge appropriate valuation; the difficulty in forecasting losses and the correlation of losses in the underlying collateral; the sensitivity of returns to the loss rate and the degree of correlation; and the problem that the credit rating focuses mainly on one risk—that of loss from default.[218]

Wall Street designed structured finance securities to be opaque. As shown by the brown paper bag, it was impossible for market participants to independently assess the risk of and value these securities.

When investors cannot assess the value and risk of an investment due to a lack of valuation transparency, they stop buying or selling said securities. This was reflected in the sharp drop in demand Mr. Dudley mentioned. Investors stop because they have no way of independently determining the value of the securities and comparing this independent valuation to the prices shown by Wall Street to make a buy, hold or sell decision.

On the August 10, 2007, Fed Chair Bernanke observed:

> President Fisher, our goal is to provide liquidity not to support asset prices per se in any way.
>
> My understanding of the market's problem is that price discovery has been inhibited by the illiquidity of the subprime-related assets that are not trading, and nobody knows what they're worth, and so there's a general freeze-up.
>
> The market is not operating in a normal way. The idea of providing liquidity is essentially to give the market some ability to do the appropriate repricing it needs to do and to begin to operate more normally.
>
> So it's a question of market functioning, not a question of bailing anybody out. That's really where we are right now.[219]

Within a span of 3 days following the FOMC meeting in which Bill Dudley said opacity was making it impossible for market participants to value structured finance securities, Fed Chair Bernanke had adopted his solution to addressing opacity in the financial system. His answer to the question "paper or plastic" was paper as he turned on the printing press.

He asserted that the goal was to provide liquidity until the market's problem with price discovery is fixed. And lo and behold, the Fed has been adding

---

218 Dudley, Bill (2007, August 7), FOMC Meeting transcript, Federal Reserve, http://www.federalreserve.gov/monetarypolicy/files/FOMC20070807meeting.pdf, page 8.

219 Bernanke, Ben (2007, August 10), FOMC Conference Call transcript, Federal Reserve, http://www.federalreserve.gov/monetarypolicy/files/FOMC20070810confcall.pdf, page 8.

liquidity through programs like quantitative easing ever since. Unfortunately, monetary policy does not fix a price discovery problem. It only buys time until the financial regulator who can fix the price discovery problems extends valuation transparency to all the opaque corners of the financial system.

Of course, there is no end in sight for these liquidity programs because, as shown by Ms. White's SEC speeches, no one is working to fix the price discovery mechanism by making structured finance securities or the banks provide valuation transparency.

Heading into the financial crisis, the Fed thought the problem of opacity was confined to structured finance securities where through contagion it created minor ripples into the rest of the financial markets. It didn't realize how much more of the financial system was in the grip of opacity and how the freezing of one opaque area of the financial system would quickly spread to other opaque areas of the financial system.

Sir Mervyn King finds more symptoms of opacity's grip

At its core, the financial crisis and the related panic were caused by opacity. Opacity expressed itself in several different ways. Bill Dudley observed it led to the freezing of the market for structured finance securities. Sir Mervyn King discovered other ways opacity expressed itself. He recognized banks had a problem as they were holding structured finance securities that couldn't be sold, couldn't be valued and cast doubt on the solvency of the banks. This doubt had the potential to reignite the rumor driven runs by large, uninsured depositors Continental Illinois experienced.

By March 17, 2008, Sir Mervyn King was telling the global financial regulators they were dealing with a solvency and not a liquidity crisis. His diagnosis was wrong as the global financial regulators were dealing with an opacity crisis of which fears about solvency and the drying up of liquidity were two symptoms.

> Since last summer, the nature of the crisis in financial markets has changed. The problem is now not liquidity in the system but rather a question of systemic solvency, Bank of England (BOE) Governor Mervyn King said at a lunch meeting with Treasury Deputy Secretary Robert Kimmitt and Ambassador Tuttle.
>
> King said there are two imperatives. First to find ways for banks to avoid the stigma of selling unwanted paper at distressed prices or going to a central bank for assistance. Second to ensure there's a coordinated effort to possibly recapitalize the global banking system.[220]

---

[220] WikiLeaks via The Guardian (2010, December 13), The U.S. Embassy cables: the documents, The Guardian, http://www.theguardian.com/world/us-embassy-cables-documents/146196

Eight months into our current financial crisis and the financial regulators were already shaping their response to the financial crisis. They would address a symptom of opacity, in this case concerns over bank solvency, without eliminating the underlying opacity.

The idea a bank could experience stigma can only exist in the presence of opacity. If banks disclosed their current exposure details, market participants would know why they were selling unwanted paper or borrowing from a central bank.

> For the first imperative, King suggested developing a pooling and auction process to unblock the large volume of financial investments for which there is currently no market.[221]

The reason there was no market for these financial investments was opacity. The lack of valuation transparency was not something a pooling and auction process would cure. When investors do not have valuation transparency so they can independently assess the risk and value of an investment, they don't invest. As a result, the market freezes except for gamblers willing to blindly bet on the value of the contents of a brown paper bag.

> For the second imperative, King suggested that the U.S., UK, Switzerland, and perhaps Japan might form a temporary new group to jointly develop an effort to bring together sources of capital to recapitalize all major banks….[222]

But who would invest in a black box bank known to hold losses on structured finance securities that couldn't be valued?

Sir Mervyn King concluded by itself Fed Chair Bernanke's liquidity solution was not going to work. The banks were still threatened with the same type of doubts about their viability that undid Continental Illinois.

> King said that liquidity is necessary but not sufficient in the current market crisis because the global banking system is undercapitalized due to being over leveraged….[223]

In an effort to avoid the Continental Illinois experience, Sir Mervyn King looked for ways to have the banks unload their toxic securities without recognizing their losses.

---

221 ibid

222 ibid

223 ibid

> King said it is also imperative to find a way for banks to sell off unwanted illiquid securities, including mortgage backed securities, without resorting to sales at distressed valuations. He said sales at distressed values only serve to lower the floor to which banks must mark down their assets (mark to market), thereby forcing unwarranted additional write downs….[224]

Again, rather than deal with the underlying opacity, in this case the banks themselves, the choice was made to try to deal with the symptom.

> King noted, though that including the Japanese might force their hand in finally marking to market impaired assets.[225]

Sir Mervyn King's statement about forcing the Japanese banks to recognize their losses on impaired assets almost two decades after the beginning of their financial crisis shows what financial regulators can get away with because of current accounting rules and a lack of valuation transparency.

The canary in the coalmine dies from opacity

His concerns about bank solvency crystallized with the collapse of Lehman Brothers on September 15, 2008. Shortly thereafter, the interbank lending market froze.

The interbank lending market was the canary in the coalmine that passed away in the presence of opacity. The interbank lending market froze because even the banks with deposits to lend could not tell which of the banks looking to borrow was viable and could repay the loan or which bank was so insolvent it was no longer viable.

Opacity prevented the banks with deposits to lend from being able to assess the risk of the banks looking to borrow. The banks with deposits to lend knew the borrowing banks were exposed to structured finance securities that no one could value and no one could sell. However, because of opacity, no one knew the extent of this exposure and whether the banks looking to borrow could repay their debt. Rather than blindly gamble, the banks with deposits to lend simply stopped lending their deposits to other banks and the interbank lending market froze.

At this point, the question became how to handle an opacity crisis that was expressing itself through bank viability concerns.

Former Fed Chair Bernanke's solution reflected his studies of the Great Depression. He flooded the financial markets with liquidity. This solution had

---

224 ibid

225 ibid

been used during the Great Depression when the banks reopened after the bank holiday so depositors who wanted to withdraw their money from a bank could. However, flooding the markets with liquidity was only part of the solution used during the Great Depression. The solution also included the government assessing the viability of each bank it allowed to reopen. Fed Chair Bernanke's Fed did this with Secretary Geithner's stress tests. But again, this was only part of the solution. The solution also included an explicit guarantee of all deposits in the reopened banks. This was done through then Secretary Geithner's pledge of the full faith and credit of the U.S. behind the solvency of the banks subjected to the stress tests.

However, there was one item that was and still is conspicuously absent from the response to the bank viability crisis led by Fed Chair Bernanke. This item was a critically important element in how bank viability was addressed during the Great Depression. This item was and is valuation transparency.

Recall that in the 1930s banks disclosed their current exposure details. Market participants could independently confirm their viability. As a result, facts confirmed the viability crisis was over. In 2008, banks were black boxes. Today, banks are still black boxes. Because they are black boxes, nobody can independently confirm their balance sheets have been cleaned up, their toxic assets disposed of, they are viable and the viability crisis is over. The uncertainty about bank balance sheets still exists. As a result, trust and confidence in the banks hasn't returned.

Anna Schwartz: Hey guys, the problem is opacity

The financial regulators in both the UK and U.S. set off to treat the symptoms of opacity. Was there any reason to believe they should have known they were dealing with an opacity driven financial crisis? Yes.

It is one thing when I used a relationship from my time working at the Federal Reserve to talk with the individual who was then the Vice Chairman and explained using the clear plastic bag and the brown paper bag that we have a financial crisis brought on by opacity. It was entirely another when Anna Schwartz said so.

Who was Anna Schwartz and why was she perceived by the economic policymakers at the Bank of England and the Federal Reserve as more credible when she identified the problem as one of opacity? At the beginning of the financial crisis, Ms. Schwartz was THE global expert on monetary policy with the necessary first hand experience, having lived through the Great Depression, to understand the cause of our current financial crisis.

Among her many credentials was a book she co-authored with Milton Friedman about the role of monetary policy in business cycles. Published in

1963, the book, *A Monetary History of the United States*, examined the role Fed policy played in the Great Depression and concluded if the Federal Reserve had done its job properly, the Great Depression would not have happened.

Ms. Schwartz looked at our current financial crisis and thought the central bank and U.S. Treasury were fighting the last financial crisis and not adopting policies that addressed the underlying cause of this financial crisis. On October 18, 2008, she identified the basic problem in the credit markets:

> Nothing seems to have quieted the fears of either … investors … or … lenders … The basic problem for the markets is … [uncertainty] that the balance sheets of financial firms are credible.[226]

Ms. Schwartz nicely said the cause of the financial crisis is opacity. The reason it is opacity is the uncertainty she identified resulted from opacity. Structured finance securities are the equivalent of brown paper bags and nobody can value the contents of a brown paper bag. Banks are the equivalent of black boxes and nobody can value the contents of a black box. As a result of this opacity, nobody could assess the banks and determine who had the ability to repay them.

Still not seen as opacity driven crisis

The current financial crisis is still not seen as an opacity driven crisis. This is important because until opacity is front and center in the narrative for describing our current financial crisis it limits how the crisis is responded to and prevents us from ending the crisis.

In an October 24, 2013 speech given at an event to celebrate the 125th anniversary of the Financial Times, the Bank of England's Governor, Mark Carney provided the latest financial crisis narrative.

> To strike a balance between making banks safer and maintaining adequate market liquidity, we need to draw lessons from the financial crisis, when contagion from stressed banks spread rapidly through the global financial system via counterparty credit concerns, liquidity hoarding and mass deleveraging. In this environment, core funding and OTC derivative markets seized up and conditions were set for the panic that ensued.
>
> By contrast, markets with greater transparency and more robust trading and settlement infrastructure, such as equity markets and exchange-traded

226 Carney, Brian M. (2008, October 18), Bernanke is Fighting the Last War, Wall Street Journal, http://online.wsj.com/news/articles/SB122428279231046053

> futures and options, performed rather better. Prices were not always to participants' liking, but these markets remained open.[227]

Mr. Carney begins by asserting a false tradeoff between making banks safer and maintaining adequate market liquidity. There is no tradeoff between these two. With valuation transparency, banks can be made safer and market liquidity maintained.

In his discussion of the lessons to draw from the financial crisis, Mr. Carney picks up his narrative of how the financial crisis unfolded after the banks were stressed. Left out of the narrative was why the banks were stressed to begin with. The reason they were stressed was opacity that prevented market participants from being able to assess their creditworthiness and viability. As the Congressional Oversight Panel observed the financial crisis started with opaque, toxic sub-prime mortgage-backed securities and related derivative markets before spreading to equally opaque financial institutions.

Mr. Carney then points out the areas of the financial system that continued functioning throughout the peak periods of financial crisis were the areas of the financial system where there was valuation transparency and where most of the issuers would qualify for a label from the Transparency Label Initiative™. For example, the stock and corporate bond markets continued to function throughout the most hectic early days of the financial crisis. Yes, prices did decline, but there were private buyers who were willing to buy at these prices if the sellers were willing to sell.

Mr. Carney's observation is very important and worth repeating. Financial markets with valuation transparency functioned during times of stress and financial markets characterized by opacity froze. This shows capitalism based on the combination of disclosure and *caveat emptor* works.

It also leads to the conclusion that ultimately we won't end our current financial crisis until there is valuation transparency in all of the opaque corners of the financial system.

As investigations into the financial crisis have shown, the lack of valuation transparency has also undermined the global financial regulatory process.

---

227 Carney, Mark (2013, October 24), The UK at the heart of a renewed globalisation, Bank of England, http://www.bankofengland.co.uk/publications/Documents/speeches/2013/speech690.pdf, page 6.

Chapter 12

THE INVESTIGATIONS INTO AND LESSONS LEARNED FROM THE FINANCIAL CRISIS

The financial crisis is a stark reminder that transparency and disclosure are essential in today's marketplace.

— Senator Jack Reed[228]

In the aftermath of the 1929 stock market crash, the U.S. Senate Committee on Banking and Commerce set up an independent investigation into the causes of the crash and the subsequent bank failures. This investigation was not very productive until Ferdinand Pecora became its leader. From that moment forward, Mr. Pecora set about discovering and exposing how Wall Street misbehaved behind a veil of opacity. Just like our current financial crisis, these schemes included manipulation of prices and deception involving securities being sold.

As Mr. Pecora said in his memoir, *Wall Street Under Oath*,

> Legal chicanery and pitch darkness were the banker's stoutest allies.[229]

Investigations by several countries into the causes of our current financial crisis reveal a common theme: pitch darkness caused by opacity bankers reintroduced into the financial system or financial regulators mistakenly allowed to remain in the financial system was the primary driver of the financial crisis.

In Ireland, the crisis review process culminated in the March 2011 Nyberg Commission Report. Mr. Nyberg and his Commission sought to answer the question:

> Why did so many professionally adept Irish bankers and public servants (as well as politicians, entrepreneurs, experts, media and households) simultaneously

---

228 Reed, Jack (2009, June 16), Floor Statement Introducing the Private Fund Transparency Act, Senator Reed's official website, http://www.reed.senate.gov/news/speech/floor-statement-introducing-the-private-fund-transparency-act-

229 Pecora Commission, Wikipedia, http://en.wikipedia.org/wiki/Pecora_Commission

come to make assessments and decisions that have later proven seriously unsound in a number of ways?[230]

Answering this question resulted in several major findings, including the following:

- It found five factors necessary for a systemic financial crisis to occur. Each of these factors thrives in the presence of opacity. The factors range from banks taking on too much risk to investors not exerting market discipline, to financial regulators unwilling or unable to prevent excessive risk taking.
- It found the intermediary depiction model for disclosure when applied to banks not only doesn't provide an accurate picture of the risks banks are taking, but it also created its own pro-cyclical contribution to the financial crisis.
- It found opacity prevented policymakers from having any insight into the true condition of the banks and this in turn limited the choices available to policymakers to react to the financial crisis. As a result, policymakers allowed the bankers to move from looting the banks to looting the taxpayers.
- It found by themselves financial regulators are not up to the task of protecting the financial system from systemic collapse. The report concluded that industry influence at the peak of politics undermined and would always undermine the regulatory process. When everything appears to be going well, no politician wants to hear from a regulator that a potential problem is brewing. Therefore, regulators are not going to say or do anything that might upset their political masters.

The report also concluded that industry influence with the regulator at the substrata of supervision undermined the supervisory process. Even if the examiners uncover problems at a bank, they have to convince politically appointed superiors who talk to the banks that they are right. As a result, even if a bank examiner's findings are correct, if the findings are politically unpopular they are subject to being suppressed as the regulator speaks with one voice.

---

230 Commission of Investigation in the Banking Sector in Ireland (2011, March), Report: Misjudging Risk: Causes of the Systemic Banking Crisis in Ireland, Commission of Investigation Into the Banking Sector in Ireland, http://www.bankinginquiry.gov.ie/Documents/Misjuding%20Risk%20-%20Causes%20of%20the%20Systemic%20Banking%20Crisis%20in%20Ireland.pdf, page 5.

In the UK, the Financial Services Authority's Report on the failure of RBS made a major contribution by confirming it is a global phenomenon that financial regulators are not up to the task of preventing a financial crisis. The report highlighted how opacity meant the stability of the financial system was dependent on the analytical resources of the regulators. These resources are not up to the task of replacing the analytical resources of all the market's participants.

In the U.S., the Financial Crisis Inquiry Commission nominally investigated the crisis. It was hamstrung by both a lack of budget and a mandate to produce a report in a brief amount of time. Since the report was released after legislation addressing the financial crisis was passed, the findings of the report did not have a significant impact on U.S. financial reform.

Despite these handicaps, the FCIC made two important findings.

- First, it confirmed a lack of valuation transparency in the financial system was the necessary condition for the financial crisis to occur. The reason credit markets like the repo market and interbank loan market froze at the beginning of the crisis was because no market participant could figure out how to value opaque structured finance securities or determine which opaque banks were solvent and which were not solvent.
- Second, it confirmed bank regulators not being able to restrain risk-taking by banks that are reporting high levels of profits is global.

The U.S. Senate's Permanent Subcommittee on Investigations issued its report, *Wall Street and the Financial Crisis: Anatomy of a Financial Collapse,* on April 13, 2011. The principle finding of this report confirmed the central role opacity played in the crisis.

> The investigation found that the crisis was not a natural disaster, but the result of high risk, complex financial products; undisclosed conflicts of interest; and the failure of regulators, the credit rating agencies, and the market itself to rein in the excesses of Wall Street.[231]

231 U.S. Senate Permanent Subcommittee on Investigations (2011, April 13), Wall Street and the Financial Crisis: Anatomy of a Financial Collapse, http://www.hsgac.senate.gov//imo/media/doc/Financial_Crisis/FinancialCrisisReport.pdf?attempt=2, page 1.

The Nyberg Commission Report

I've come to learn there is a virtuous cycle to transparency and a very vicious cycle of obfuscation.

—*Jeff Weiner*[232]

While the Commission of Investigation into the Banking Sector in Ireland focused its investigation on Ireland, its findings are applicable to the EU, UK and US. The Commission was lead by former Finnish senior government official Peter Nyberg.

Report on the causes of the Irish financial crisis

The Nyberg Commission Report, *Misjudging Risk: Causes of the systemic banking crisis in Ireland,* examines what Robert Jenkins, a former member of the Bank of England's Financial Policy Committee, described as "the pervasive beliefs of that day"[233]:

> The theology of the time maintained that: markets were efficient and would provide the necessary discipline to participants; the financial sector could be left largely to police itself; global banking and their host centers were engaged in fierce global competition; regulation should facilitate that competition and not get in its way; and therefore, when it came to regulation, less was more.
>
> This set of beliefs permeated the body politic, shaped the regulatory approach of "light touch" and, believe it or not, established a mindset amongst some supervisors that the regulated banks were to be seen as "clients."[234]

The Nyberg Commission Report begins by looking at the assumption that markets were efficient.

> 1.3.3 Financial market and regulatory policies during the Period were influenced by the efficient market hypothesis. This paradigm was widely accepted, particularly in the U.S. and UK, and provided the intellectual

232 Weiner, Jeff, Business Insider, http://www.businessinsider.com/linkedin-employee-values-2013-2

233 Jenkins, Robert (2012, September 25), Regulators, financial industry and the problem of regulatory capture, published in Making Good Financial Regulations: Towards a Policy Response to Regulatory Capture, Bank of England, http://www.bankofengland.co.uk/publications/Documents/speeches/2012/speech603_foreword.pdf, page 2.

234 ibid, page 2

> underpinning for financial innovation and reduced regulation. One important consequence of the concept was the assumption that self-regulating financial markets tended to remain stable.
>
> If the paradigm was accepted without regard to the simplifying assumptions underlying the original theory (a naïve interpretation), quite radical conclusions for policy could be drawn. For instance, strict or intrusive regulation would generally not be needed and could, instead, reduce financial innovation and efficiency; a light-touch approach to regulation was the obvious recipe.
>
> Furthermore, it could be argued that normal financial activity was benign almost by definition; anything that could attract funding could be seen as acceptable in the absence of specific proof to the contrary. Thus, financial expansion, resulting in increased use of debt and financial innovation, would not necessarily be seen as increasing financial fragility, despite many previous experiences to the contrary.[235]

What were the simplifying assumptions behind the efficient market hypothesis that would justify light touch regulation and thinking of the banks, rather than investors or the taxpayers through their support of the deposit insurance fund, as the "clients"?

The efficient market hypothesis assumes prices reflect the combination of valuation transparency and the principle of *caveat emptor* even in the absence of valuation transparency. It assumes the benefits of this combination, financial stability and market discipline, occur even in the absence of valuation transparency. It assumes away the financial instability and lack of market discipline caused by Wall Street's incentive to re-introduce opacity into the financial system to drive its profits.

By embracing the efficient market hypothesis, financial regulators relieved themselves of the ongoing responsibility under the FDR Framework for ensuring that market participants had access to valuation transparency.

Why would financial regulators want to relieve themselves of the responsibility for ensuring market participants had access to valuation transparency?

It was much easier for the global financial regulators. By adopting the efficient market hypothesis and assuming valuation transparency and all the benefits that flowed from it in terms of financial stability and market discipline existed, the financial regulators didn't have to fight with either Wall Street's Opacity Protection Team or their political masters who had come to think that

---

235 Commission of Investigation into the Banking Sector in Ireland (2011, March), Report: Misjudging Risk: Causes of the Systemic Banking Crisis in Ireland, Commission of Investigation Into the Banking Sector in Ireland, http://www.bankinginquiry.gov.ie/Documents/Misjuding%20Risk%20-%20Causes%20of%20the%20Systemic%20Banking%20Crisis%20in%20Ireland.pdf, page 4.

the banks should be the financial regulators' "client". The very banks that wanted to retain opacity into their current exposure details and avoid market discipline while at the same time introducing opaque financial products like structure finance securities.

What is the efficient market hypothesis?

The efficient market hypothesis asserts that markets are "informationally efficient". In its weakest form, this means market prices reflect all past publicly available information. In its semi-strong form, this means market prices reflect all past publicly available information and change immediately to reflect new public information. In its strongest form, prices change to reflect hidden information too.

For the weak and semi-strong form of the efficient market hypothesis to actually hold true, the financial system must have valuation transparency, the ongoing independent assessment of this information, and the resulting price changes driven by investors responsible for all losses under *caveat emptor*.

When the efficient market hypothesis was first formulated 4+ decades ago, it was tested on U.S. stock prices. Ironically, these stocks are the classic example of a market where, with the exception of financial institutions, the combination of valuation transparency and *caveat emptor* is, for the most part, implemented. In addition, the U.S. stock market has rules to limit if not outright prohibit trading on hidden information.

But what about the strong form of the efficient market hypothesis that hidden information is also reflected in the price? If this is true, then financial regulators do not have to ensure market participants have access to valuation transparency.

Subprime mortgage-backed structured finance securities are a real world example where the government did not fulfill its responsibility for ensuring valuation transparency and the strong form of the efficient market hypothesis does not hold. These securities are intentionally opaque and all useful, relevant information is hidden from investors. The strong form of efficient market hypothesis fails because Wall Street, which has the hidden information, has a financial incentive not to set the price to where the securities are properly valued given their risk, but rather to set the price where it maximizes the profitability of Wall Street.

Unsecured bank debt and bank equity securities are also examples of where the government failed to fulfill its responsibility for ensuring valuation transparency and the strong form of the efficient market hypothesis doesn't hold. Bank managers have all the hidden information, but they have no financial incentive to release this information so the bank's securities are properly valued given their risk. In fact, in their 1993 article, *Looting: The Economic Underworld of Bankruptcy for Profit*, economists George Akerlof and Paul Romer argue bank management can make far more money behind the veil of opacity.[236]

It is opacity that makes it possible for bank management to loot the banks. Opacity prevents market participants from assessing the actual risk level of the banks and exerting discipline in the form of higher cost of funds on the banks to restrain risk taking.

With opacity, market participants are dependent on bank management not to lower its lending standards to stimulate loan growth for the bank. However, bank management has an incentive to lower lending standards to stimulate loan growth as loan growth results in income today and losses realized sometime in the future. As a result, there is a window in time for the bank managers' executive compensation plans to make them very wealthy. Ultimately of course, if the lending standards have been relaxed, the bank will experience losses as the loans turned bad, but by then, senior management has its money. Hence, they effectively looted the bank. This is what occurred in Ireland.

Unlike the efficient market hypothesis, the FDR Framework is explicit in the ongoing need for ensuring that market participants always have access to all the useful, relevant information in an appropriate, timely manner so they can independently assess this information and make a fully informed investment decision. The need for valuation transparency applies to all existing securities and all new financial innovations.

If the government fulfills the responsibility for ensuring valuation transparency under the FDR Framework, markets are both stable and self-regulating. Markets are stable because each investor limits their exposures to what they can afford to lose. Markets are self-regulating because investors exert discipline as they adjust their exposures to reflect changes in the risk of their investments.

However, if the government doesn't fulfill the responsibility for ensuring valuation transparency, history shows that markets are neither stable nor self-regulating.

The Transparency Label Initiative™ is needed so even if governments fail to fulfill the responsibility for ensuring valuation transparency, investors are warned when they are blindly gambling and therefore continue to limit their exposures to what they can afford to lose.

Factors necessary for a systemic financial crisis

Mr. Nyberg and the Commission focused on the symptoms of opacity and how they contributed to a systemic financial crisis.

---

236 Akerlof, George, Romer, Paul (1993), Looting: The Economic Underworld of Bankruptcy for Profit, http://pages.stern.nyu.edu/~promer/Looting.pdf

1.4.2 Systemic financial crises — both in Ireland and elsewhere — are uncommon because they require such a large number of simultaneous institutional and judgmental failures. If even a couple of these failures are absent, the systemic crisis is short-circuited and will morph into a more modest form.

1.4.3 For a systemic financial crisis to occur, at least the following factors must be present (although the last two may not be as essential as the others):

- a sufficiently large number of households and investors who, at some point, start making serious mistakes in judging the value and liquidity of their major assets, holdings and projects;
- banks that provide financing, large in relation to their own capital, for these investments without thoroughly and sufficiently evaluating their prospects and the creditworthiness of borrowers in the longer term;
- providers of funds to such banks (often banks themselves but also depositors) that do not monitor bank soundness with sufficient diligence, in the case of private providers, possibly because of perceived implicit public support for at least important banks;
- a banking regulator that remains unwilling or unable to detect or prevent banks from engaging in excessively risky lending or funding practices;
- a government and a central bank that remains unaware of the mounting problems or is unwilling to do anything to prevent them;
- a parliament that remains unaware of the mounting problems or concentrates its attention on other things perceived to be of greater immediate importance; and
- media that are generally supportive of corporate and bank expansion, profit growth and risk taking while being dismissive of warnings of unsustainable developments.[237]

Each of the first five factors was present in Ireland (as well as the EU, the UK and the US) because of the failure to implement the FDR Framework and provide valuation transparency.

For example, under the FDR Framework, banks that provide funds to support the borrowing bank's lending activities have an incentive to monitor the risk being taken by the borrowing bank. Quite simply, the lending bank wants to be sure the borrowing bank can repay its loan.

With valuation transparency, the lending bank can assess the probability of repayment and exert restraint on the risks the borrowing bank accepts when it

237 Commission of Investigation into the Banking Sector in Ireland (2011, March), Report: Misjudging Risk: Causes of the Systemic Banking Crisis in Ireland, Commission of Investigation Into the Banking Sector in Ireland, http://www.bankinginquiry.gov.ie/Documents/Misjuding%20Risk%20-%20Causes%20of%20the%20Systemic%20Banking%20Crisis%20in%20Ireland.pdf, page 5.

makes a loan. This restraint on the borrowing bank's lending activities results in the borrowing bank lending less and only to borrowers who are capable of repaying their loans.

However, when there is opacity and valuation transparency is not available, this restraint is not applied. As a result, the borrowing bank can engage in higher risk lending and the factors that lead to the systemic financial crisis can take hold.

When there is opacity, everyone is dependent on the bank regulators and central bankers being able to detect excessively risky lending and funding practices and taking action to restrain these risky activities. When there is opacity, everyone is dependent on the bank regulators and central bankers to do a job they are not designed to perform. Due to political pushback, it is also a job they are not particularly well suited to performing. This job happens to be the responsibility of and better performed by the other market participants like investors.

When there is valuation transparency, the financial system works as it is designed. Market participants detect excessively risky lending and funding practices and exert discipline on the banks to restrain these risky activities. The regulators and central bankers get to piggyback on both this market discipline and the market participants' analytical ability to detect excessive risky lending.

Herding and Groupthink

Mr. Nyberg and the Commission introduced two concepts from psychology to explain why people might accept a flawed idea like real estate prices can only go up.

> In explaining the simultaneity of the failures in Irish institutions, the Commission frequently found behaviour exhibiting bandwagon effects both between institutions ("herding") and within them ("groupthink"), reinforced by a widespread international belief in the efficiency of financial markets. ...
>
> As in most manias, those caught up in it could believe and have trust in extraordinary things, such as unlimited real wealth from selling property to each other on credit. Even obvious warning signs went unheeded in the belief that the world had changed and that a stable economy was somehow automatically guaranteed. Traditional values, analysis and rules could be gradually less observed by the banks and authorities because their relevance was seen as lost in the new and different world....[238]

> 1.6.1 It is clear that a widespread consensus formed in Ireland around trends, assessments and policies that participants should have realized to be unsustainable or unsound. This section briefly presents two concepts ("Herding"

[238] ibid, Executive Summary pg i

and "Groupthink") that may help understand why and how so many institutions in Ireland simultaneously made imprudent decisions.[239]

1.6.3 "Herding" refers to the willingness of investors and banks to simultaneously invest in, lend to and own the same type of assets, accompanied by insufficient information gathering and processing. While often superficially resembling the normal process of competition, herding implies lack of rigorous analysis by members of the herd. Some of the participants in a herd have only a partial idea of the economic advantages and disadvantages of a particular course of action — for instance, investing or property lending. However, they assume that others have a clearer view and follow them, thus demonstrating what is commonly referred to as a bandwagon effect.[240]

Banks have a long inglorious history of herding. As previously discussed, banks engaged in herding when they were making loans to less developed countries. With a little information gathering, it would have been apparent countries do go broke.

1.6.4 Herding implies that management groups in different banks implicitly follow each other with little or only modest analysis and discussion. Several possible motives exist. The most obvious … may be the need to achieve similar profitability as competitors, either as a result of shareholder pressure, expected management returns or need for recognition or professional approval. Another reason, valid when there are perceived economies of scale or scope, may be to avoid erosion of profitable market share. Finally, a reason frequently mentioned in economic literature is that there may be a wish, particularly among larger banks, to increase the prospects of rescue in case of insolvency; if several banks follow similar policies and thus are insolvent at the same time they are, for systemic reasons, unlikely to all be closed.[241]

In the U.S., there is a practical reason herding occurs. Banks satisfy the demand for large loans and manage their exposures by using loan syndications. Rather than a single bank funding a loan, many banks fund the loan through a loan syndication. This allows each bank to manage their exposure to the borrower. On the other hand, it spreads the risk of the borrower across the banking system.

1.6.5 Groupthink occurs when people adapt to the beliefs and views of others without real intellectual conviction. A consensus forms without serious consideration of consequences or alternatives, often under overt or imaginary social pressure. Recent studies indicate that tendencies to groupthink may be

239 ibid, page 7

240 ibid, page. 7

241 ibid page 8

both stronger and more common than previously thought. One consequence of groupthink may be herding, if the views in question relate to institutional policies, but this need not be the case.

1.6.6 Within boards, for instance, groupthink would cause alternative solutions to remain insufficiently considered. Broadly speaking, board members would be likely to avoid opposing an already existing preferred strategy (for instance, one proposed by a chairman or managing director, particularly in the case of a dominant personality), where they feel a social bond with the rest of the board (for instance, through long and lucrative membership) and where they do not feel sure of themselves (for instance, in the case of difficult issues of a new financial environment or time pressure). In groups, moreover, views have been shown to converge to the extremes of those expressed rather than to the average private views of its members (implying that few members may actually privately fully support the final public decision). These features may be further strengthened by the presence of external adversarial groups (such as bank competitors, hostile bidders or financial commentators).

1.6.7 Since strategic decisions have to be implemented, for herding to be realised also requires that staff in the participating institutions follow and do not question the decisions made. Even if the decision appears materially questionable, a form of groupthink may still ensure willing staff cooperation. Much more than for board members and managers, staff prospects for advancement and remuneration depend on their perceived standing with their superiors. Superiors often form a view of a staff member from the views and proposals they forward to them. This feeds a tendency among staff to suggest and support proposals that their superiors are known to prefer, hoping to gain a favourable reputation. This results in a bandwagon effect and a tendency to conform to superiors' views as well as those of colleagues. Those challenging their superiors' proposals may risk sanctions and would thus need to feel particularly confident in their preferred alternative.[242]

1.6.9 Some observers see both herding and groupthink as contributing also to the passive role of regulators in their efforts to detect and prevent the global financial crisis. Clearly, groupthink could easily exist in public institutions, with a publicly mandated and thus strongly empowered leader gradually eliminating independent critical analysis among staff.[243]

Opacity contributes to both herding and groupthink. Opacity assures that there is insufficient information available to process and that no one has a clear view of the risks being taken. Opacity hides the facts needed so that a rational discussion can occur on why trends, assessments and policies might be unsustainable or unsound.

---

242 ibid, page 8

243 ibid, page 9

Unlike the five factors the Nyberg Commission identified that must be present for a systemic crisis, the combination of disclosure and *caveat emptor* does not eliminate either herding or groupthink. What the combination of disclosure and *caveat emptor* does do is to moderates the impact of herding or groupthink.

It moderates the impact because investors know they are responsible for all losses on their investment exposures. So even though everyone might be investing in, lending to and owning the same types of assets, each market participant still uses valuation transparency to independently assess the risk and limit their total exposure to what they can afford to lose.

However, when bank balance sheets are opaque, the combination of disclosure and *caveat emptor* doesn't work. As a result, the impact of herding and groupthink is not moderated.

Bank regulators and central bankers buy in too

Mr. Nyberg makes the very important point that for better or worse bank regulators and central bankers are also and always susceptible to herding and groupthink. An example of groupthink among bank regulators was the pre-financial crisis adoption of light touch financial regulation under the efficient market hypothesis.

Equally importantly, bank regulators and central bankers are also and always susceptible to the same type of internal groupthink as the financial institutions. There is an unwillingness of junior staff members to challenge management's views.

> A minority of people indicated that contrarian views were both difficult to maintain during the long boom and unhealthy to present to boards or superiors. A number of people stated that had they implemented or consistently supported contrarian policies they may ultimately have lost their jobs, positions, or reputations.
>
> Other signs were also noted pointing to sanctioning of diverging or contrarian opinions as well as self-censorship because of this. The apparent strength of these expected sanctions is difficult to judge, but the absence of opposition, barring only a handful of identified vociferous contrarians, may have made it easier for institutions to accept toning down the application of vital, tried and traditional prudential practices.
>
> The Commission suspects that this conformity of views and self-limitation of responsibility would have tended to reduce the perceived need for monitoring, checking and thinking about what was really going on. There would have been little appreciation — both domestically and abroad — of the fact that Irish economic growth and welfare increasingly depended on construction and property development for domestic customers, funded by a growing foreign debt.

> The Commission considers that this pervasive pressure for consensus may explain why so many different parties in Ireland simultaneously were willing to adopt specific policies and accepted practices that later proved unsound. At the same time, the apparent consensus of banks and authorities around the view that markets remained sound and prospects remained positive gave further comfort to both. A number of banks essentially appear to have followed the example of peer banks in a "herding" fashion; there is little evidence of original critical analysis of the advantages and risks of the policies. Widespread lack of critical discussion within many banks and authorities indicates a tendency to "groupthink"; serious consideration of alternatives appears to be modest or absent. A tendency to favour silo organisation and submissiveness to superiors strengthened this effect, particularly among the public authorities.
>
> In designing the constraints and rules for banking in the future, full account will need to be taken of the failure of private and public institutions to appreciate the emerging risks and to take action. If responsible authorities are affected by the prevailing paradigms, they cannot be expected to uncover its risks and weak points. Financial systems should, in that case, be designed to be as stable as possible even in the absence of unfailingly vigilant and prescient regulators and central banks....[244]

The FDR Framework is in fact designed to address the difficulty in stating a contrarian view as well as the absence of unfailingly vigilant and prescient regulators and central banks.

Under the FDR Framework, investors are responsible for all losses on their exposures. This gives investors the incentive to independently assess the information disclosed by valuation transparency and use the results of this risk assessment to limit their losses to what they can afford to lose. As a result of limiting their losses to what they can afford to lose, the financial system is stable even without the statement of a contrarian view or vigilant and prescient regulators and central banks.

Of course, in the presence of opacity, the FDR Framework cannot function and the resulting mania that Ireland experienced can occur.

Reliance on wholesale funding makes banks susceptible to a run

The Nyberg Commission observed that a reliance on wholesale funding made the banks susceptible to a run on the banks. Opacity increased the likelihood of a bank run because it meant that nobody could figure out if a bank could repay its liabilities or not.

---

[244] ibid, Executive Summary Pg iii

> 2.8.2 This change in funding structure made banks more vulnerable not only to fluctuations in international interest rates but also to changes in market sentiment and in their own perceived creditworthiness. In benign economic conditions, the wholesale market provides flexible funding in terms of maturity profile, types of structures and instruments as well as pricing. However, this funding can dry up in a very short timeframe if confidence disappears. This is captured in the old adage that "in wholesale funding there is only one depositor" (i.e. when one such depositor leaves, all follow).[245]

Just like Continental Illinois, the investors who engaged in the bank run were the large, uninsured depositors.

Intermediary depiction model for banks made crisis worse

The Nyberg Commission noted how a change in accounting rules for provisioning for loan losses contributed to the crisis. The effect of the accounting change was to make the banks appear to be more profitable while at the same time understating the increase in their risk.

Accounting for loan losses has played a role in previous crises. Recall in the Less Developed Country Debt crisis the accounting rules for provisioning for loan losses were also used to make the banks appear more profitable than they really were. In that case, the banks were not required to reserve for the losses on the loans despite the existence of a market for the loans showing the loans were worth fifty percent of book value.

The accounting rules for loan losses highlight why the intermediary depiction model was and still is inappropriate for use with banks. It is only with a pure information model under which banks report their current asset, liability and off-balance sheet exposure details that market participants can independently assess the true condition of the banks and exert market discipline to restrain risk taking by adjusting their exposures to reflect changes in each bank's risk.

> 2.8.8 A key financial reporting standard change during the Period was the required adoption by all listed EU companies of new IFRS accounting rules applicable, inter alia, to loan loss provisioning for accounting periods beginning in 2005. IFRS was adopted by all of the covered banks at that time.
>
> An objective of IFRS was to reduce subjectivity in financial statements and, in the case of banks, to have a more objective loan-loss provisioning process. Provisions could only be made where objective evidence of impairment existed

245 ibid, page 39

> at the closing balance sheet date i.e. at a historic point in time (the incurred-loss model).[246]
>
> 2.8.9 These new accounting rules proved to be pro-cyclical and had important consequences for the covered banks. In the benign economic environment before 2007, the banks reduced their loan loss provisions, reported higher profits and gained additional lending capacity. The banks could no longer make more prudent through-the-cycle general provisions, or anticipate future losses in their loan books, particularly in relation to (secured) property lending in a rising property market. The higher reported profits also enabled increased dividend and remuneration distributions during the Period.[247]

A quick recap of the negative consequences of the accounting rules is in order. First, in the run-up to the financial crisis, the accounting rules made the crisis worse by artificially inflating the banks' lending capacity. As a result, more risky loans were made. Second, the accounting rules enabled the bankers to pay themselves far more than they should have been given the ultimate profitability of the loans. In fact, the accounting rules facilitated the bankers looting the banks.

> All of this led to reduced provisioning buffers in the covered banks when the financial crisis emerged. Finally, the incurred-loss model also restricted the banks' ability to report early provisions for likely future loan losses as the crisis developed from 2007 onwards.[248]

Loans are risky investments

Mr. Nyberg and the Commission observed everyone appeared to lose sight of the fact loans are investments and each bank was responsible for limiting its total potential losses to its capacity to absorb these losses.

One of the reasons given for banks being comfortable expanding their exposure to real estate was the regulators didn't comment on this exposure. Please recall that bank examiners do not approve or disapprove of any exposure a bank takes. It is the job of the bankers to allocated capital.

Bank examiners are not going to say a bank has too much or too little exposure to real estate or any other type of loan. It is the job of the other market participants, particularly unsecured bank creditors and bank equity investors to express their approval or disapproval of the risks banks are taking by exerting market discipline.

246 ibid, page 42

247 ibid, page 42

248 ibid, page 42

However, in the presence of opacity, the other market participants could not exert market discipline because they did not know and therefore could not assess the risk the banks were taking.

> 2.12.4 It could be argued that bank management in Ireland, like many banks elsewhere in the world, had forgotten the very nature of credit. Providing credit is not a sale of bank services; it is the acquisition of a risky asset. The appropriate prudential focus of such a transaction is therefore limiting and mitigating risk (or, at the very least, understanding the real risk and pricing it accordingly) rather than expanding sales. This apparent inability, some might say unwillingness, of Irish banks to remember this basic principle of banking was a major cause of the banking crisis in Ireland. This problem was further exacerbated as many banks appear to have emphasised and valued loan sales skills above risk and credit analysis skills.[249]

There is a reason loan sale skills are valued at a bank. From the borrower's perspective, money is a commodity. What a borrower is interested in is access to the maximum amount of money at the lowest cost. So, what differentiates two competing banks when they are offering the same amount of money on the same terms? Selling skills.

By design, banks do not rely solely on the risk and credit analysis skills of the banker making the loan. Every loan has to be approved with the larger loans requiring the approval of a credit committee. It is the committee's responsibility to focus on the risk of the loan and to be sure it is priced to reflect this risk.

> 2.12.5 It is not necessarily surprising that banks continued to lend into the property sector considering the fact that the vast majority of academics, independent economists, observers and, indeed, the Irish Government, were strongly supportive of this expansion rather than doubtful. Meanwhile, much of the media enthusiastically supported households' preoccupation with property ownership.
>
> Bank leadership and staff also appear to have taken comfort from the fact that neither the FR (financial regulator) nor the Central Bank, apparently, saw any problem worthy of a policy change with either the very rapid growth of balance sheets or the related concentration of exposure to property.[250]

The experience of the Irish banks repeated the experience of Continental Illinois. Continental Illinois showed when a bank has been successful in the past

---

249 ibid, page 50

250 ibid, page 50

financial regulators are reluctant to criticize either its strategy to grow quickly or the concentration of exposure in one area.

> In addition, there were some indications that prudential concerns voiced within the operational part of certain banks may have been discouraged. Early warning signs generated lower down in the organisation may in some cases not have reached management or the board. If so, the pressure for conformity in the banks has proven to be quite expensive.[251]

Expressing concern about the implementation of the bank's strategy carries career risk for insiders. It is tough to directly challenge the individual with control over your bonus and future earnings.

> The Central Bank (CB) and the FR noted macroeconomic risks and risky bank behaviour but appear to have judged them insufficiently alarming to take major restraining policy measures. Among all the authorities, a very limited number of individuals, either in boards or among staff, saw the risks as significant and actively argued for stronger measures; in all cases they failed to convince their colleagues or superiors. Thus, the authorities largely continued to accept the credit concentration in the property market and avoided forcing action on the failings in the banks.[252]

As former Fed Governor Partee observed, it is hard for financial regulators to tell banks to restrain their lending when the banks are profitable and the losses from the lending activity appear manageable.

Regulators not up to task

The Nyberg Commission looked at how the bank regulators interacted with the banks. Just like the Congressional hearing on Continental Illinois, the Nyberg Commission wondered where were the regulators? Why did regulators trust the bankers knew what they were doing and that opacity would not result in a financial crisis?

Just like Continental Illinois, the Commission noted that the regulators had access to all the information they needed to see what was really going on inside the banks, but the regulators tended to trust bank management and not verify what was actually happening.

The Commission questioned whether the regulators actually understood the risk the banks were taking. The Nyberg Commission offered one potential reason

---

[251] ibid, Executive Summary pg. vii

[252] ibid, Executive Summary Pg vii

regulators did not use this data properly: regulators do not know what to do with the data. This confirmed an observation the Bank of England's Andrew Haldane had previously offered:

> [T]he FSA's practice of dispatching dozens of examiners to banks to collect loads of granular information ... rarely yield much useful information for regulators, who can find themselves overwhelmed by the quantity of data.[253]

A second potential reason for regulators not using this data properly is even if some individuals working for the regulators do know how to use the data and draw the right conclusions, their analysis fails to convince their bosses. As discussed in the report, individuals working for the regulators are forced to convince a bureaucracy they are right. These individuals face an uphill struggle because the bureaucracy is naturally biased towards believing the financial institutions that everything is okay.

A third potential reason regulators do not use this information correctly is related to the process that bank examiners go through when assessing the risk of a bank.

The bank examiners estimate the expected loss from each of the bank's exposures and the probability of this loss occurring. The result is a loss estimate that is then compared to the total of the bank's loan loss reserve and book capital. Since book capital was increasing during the run-up to the financial crisis, the banks appeared to be able to absorb the losses.

The weakness of the bank examination process is the regulator's loss estimate is subject to influence by the bank's management. This influence is not offset by the opinions of independent experts. These experts, including banking competitors and third parties, cannot weigh in because opacity prevents them from assessing a bank's current asset, liability and off-balance sheet exposure details.

The important point is when there is opacity bank examiners are being asked to replace the analytical skill of the market at the same time as they are dealing with internal politics that shapes the conclusion of their analysis.

Regardless of which reason is correct, when banks are black boxes the failure to draw the right conclusions from the data or communicate these conclusions to market participants generates instability in the financial system. It is one thing if the regulators misjudge the solvency of a single financial institution. It

253 Enrich, David, Muñoz, Sara Schaefer (2010, November 17), BOE Wants To Be Less Intrusive, Wall Street Journal, http://online.wsj.com/news/articles/SB20001424052748703628204575618692923523592

is entirely another thing when regulators misjudge the solvency of every financial institution. The latter results in a systemic financial crisis.

> 4.3.2 The particular version of "principles-based regulation" embraced by the FR (and supported by other stakeholders) stressed the importance of sound bank governance and internal bank processes for ensuring appropriate prudential behaviour. This policy was intellectually supported by the efficient market paradigm ... and was consistent with the Government's "Better Regulation" policy. Thus, although the FR did engage with regulated banks and supervised their activities, interactions and communications usually addressed issues of governance or structure.
>
> The FR was unwilling to engage in a process of (what was possibly perceived to be) intrusive verification to establish whether institutions were in fact behaving in a prudent manner and managing risk appropriately. Instead, the FR relied on management and boards to act in the best interests of their respective institutions. Given that the FR did not perform the required detailed scrutiny of lending practices it is very unlikely that it would, at any time, have formed an adequate understanding of bank exposures or the risks arising from the "procedures creep"....[254]

Fear of spooking the market

Mr. Nyberg confirmed the fear of spooking the market silenced any attempt to engage in honest public discussions about what was and is happening with the banks.

When the banks provide valuation transparency, there is no need for the Central Bank or bank regulators to publicly offer their opinion on each bank as market participants have the ability to independently assess this data for themselves or hire third party experts who can. In fact, FDR explicitly told central banks and bank regulators not to publicly offer their opinion on individual banks so as to avoid the appearance of endorsing an investment.

When the banks provide valuation transparency, central banks and bank regulators are permitted to discuss what they see as the risks in the financial system. When there is valuation transparency, there is no reason to believe that this discussion of risk will spook the market. After all, everyone has the same facts. The central bank and bank regulators, like the investors who are expressing

---

[254] Commission of Investigation into the Banking Sector in Ireland (2011, March), Report: Misjudging Risk: Causes of the Systemic Banking Crisis in Ireland, Commission of Investigation Into the Banking Sector in Ireland, http://www.bankinginquiry.gov.ie/Documents/Misjuding%20Risk%20-%20Causes%20of%20the%20Systemic%20Banking%20Crisis%20in%20Ireland.pdf, page 62.

an opinion by buying and selling bank securities, are simply expressing their opinion on how to interpret these facts.

However, when there is opacity like there was in the run-up to the financial crisis and still is today, market participants are dependent on the central bankers and bank regulators to both properly assess the risk of each bank and to communicate this risk to the market. Unfortunately, communication of risk is prevented due to bank examination secrecy requirements and concerns over spooking the market.

> 4.4.6 The CB (Central Bank) appears to have chosen the path of addressing macro-economic risks through carefully formulated "concerns" in its Financial Stability Report (FSR). The FSR was, in theory, a cooperative effort by the CB and the FR but, in practice, it was almost entirely written by CB staff. The text regularly and correctly refers to a great number of uncertainties and potential risks to stability, yet the overall conclusion of these FSRs was consistently a reassuring one; the most likely outcome was a "soft landing" for the property market, and the banking system was considered sound and well placed to deal with any potential shocks. Although the evidence in favour of this view was far from analytically compelling, it was widely accepted by banking circles and among the authorities. This message remained essentially unchanged even as funding and lending risks increased and the property market was beginning to collapse.[255]
>
> 4.4.8 The Commission has also noted evidence of a tendency to ensure that the FSRs should not convey a negative message even when some internal contrarian information, analysis or view argued for a less benign tone. There are clear indications that little attention was paid to such material or that it was only included after toning down in redrafting. This approach risked creating an internal intellectual climate that discouraged less senior staff from offering their best professional assessments. It also encouraged staff to focus their research work in areas with less relevance for financial stability but where publication would not be subject to such pressures. While it is one thing to tone down external messages, the Commission has difficulty in understanding the apparent lack of interest in fostering critical debate within the confidential confines of the CB on stability issues. There are signs that reinforced by the relatively hierarchical structure of the CB, a climate of self-censorship had become prevalent in CB policy work.[256]
>
> 4.4.9 The Commission accepts the view that it may not be in the best interests of financial stability to publish alarmist views in the FSRs. Given the traditionally fine-tuned nature of CB statements, any sudden or major change in the degree of stated optimism could, in principle, be interpreted by markets

[255] ibid, page 67

[256] ibid, page 68

> as a sign of a looming problem. On the other hand, if official publications are seen as not addressing relevant concerns, there is also the risk of reducing public credibility. Nevertheless, if the CB had had greater concerns there was nothing preventing them from confidentially voicing these concerns to the Government while keeping its public messages benign. However, the Commission has found no evidence that this was done.[257]

The issue of spooking the market only exists because of opacity.

Opacity used by bankers to loot both banks and taxpayers

The Nyberg Commission explained the true cumulative contribution of opacity to the Irish financial crisis. As Mr. Nyberg and the Commission phrased it:

> "Authorities should have had a much better understanding of the underlying situation of the banks ... this would have been a precondition for any crisis management approach based on the real underlying situation."[258]

Said less delicately, it was opacity and the lack of understanding into the underlying situation at each bank that allowed bankers to first loot the banks and subsequently to loot the taxpayer through the policies adopted to deal with the financial crisis.

It is only with valuation transparency where banks disclose their current exposure details that the underlying situation at each bank could have been or can be known. It is only when there is a clear plastic bag view into each bank's current exposure details that market participants, including central banks, can assess the risk and solvency of each bank and the banking system.

Without valuation transparency, there is no understanding of the underlying situation. Without valuation transparency at the start of the financial crisis, the bankers who got us into this mess were seen as the "experts" to get us out of this mess.

It was opacity and the lack of understanding into the underlying situation at each bank that allowed the bankers to prey on the fears of politicians, central bankers and financial regulators and drive policy choices that favored the bankers.

> the absence of sufficient information on the underlying quality of the banks' balance sheets is likely to have had a significant impact on the alternatives that were considered reasonable on September 29, 2008. **Proper information is a precondition for any crisis management based on reality.**

[257] ibid, page 68

[258] ibid, page 80

> As it turned out, decisions were made on the erroneous assumption that all banks were and would remain solvent. Only on that assumption could the decision to simply provide a broad guarantee be understood.
>
> Given the information available and the imminent liquidity problem at the time, the Commission understands the pressing need to ensure access to liquidity for the banks the next morning. The broad and legally binding guarantee did, however, represent a considerable risk to the sovereign in the case of any negative surprises. ...
>
> If accurate information on banks' exposures had been available at the time it seems quite likely to the Commission that a more limited guarantee combined with a state take-over of at least one bank might have been more seriously contemplated. Indeed, on the basis that such information had been available, banks could have been directed to raise substantially more private capital well before end-September 2008.[259]

If sufficient information is quite likely to have altered the policymakers' response to the financial crisis, it is also likely to have had a significant impact on investors in the run-up to the crisis. Specifically, knowing they were responsible for losses on their exposures to the banks, investors would have exerted market discipline to restrain the risk taking by the banks. This would have either prevented the crisis entirely or moderated its ultimate impact on the real economy.

> As it turned out, however, the Government was advised that banks' insolvency risks were small relative to liquidity risks and it was eventually decided not to consider nationalisation. This proved to be only a temporary reprieve, however. After a series of insufficient government actions and initiatives, Anglo was nationalised on January 19, 2009 following the disclosure of significant governance failings. Shortly afterwards, the solvency implications of several banks' excessive property exposures started to emerge.[260]
>
> 4.4.11 Although action taken by any authority that dampened down the rapid economic growth would have been seen as "spoiling the party", an independent and effective CB must be willing to take unpopular actions. Even in the unavoidable presence of uncertainty, such actions are essential in order to avoid far greater future costs that might (and, in Ireland's case, did) lie ahead. Of course, a CB must first take the steps necessary to ensure that it has an accurate picture of the financial market. Failure to perform either of these tasks is, in the Commission's view, difficult to reconcile with the responsibilities of an independent CB.[261]

---

259 ibid, executive summary page. ix

260 ibid, Executive Summary page ix

261 ibid, page 68

In theory, the central bank should step in and take away the punch bowl just as the party gets going. In reality, as former Fed Governor Partee pointed out, central bankers or bank regulators would face considerable political backlash if they attempted to take away the punchbowl when there are no visible signs of problems.

Former Fed Chairman Alan Greenspan embraced this notion of political backlash. He combined it with the Nyberg Commission's idea of herding and groupthink in explaining why nobody should blame him or the monetary and regulatory policies he pursued for the financial crisis. Mr. Greenspan further argued it is next to impossible to remove the punchbowl when conventional wisdom says everything is fine.

> To lead markets requires a conviction that is rare among public officials because running ahead of markets, of necessity, implies holding a view contrary to the participants in markets themselves.[262]

The combination of disclosure and *caveat emptor* ends waiting for the problems to emerge. It relieves regulators of having to replace the analytical ability of the market's participants. It relieves regulators of having to exert market discipline when regulators would face a political backlash for taking away the punch bowl when the party is just getting going.

The combination of disclosure and *caveat emptor* puts responsibility for taking away the punch bowl on the investors. It does this through the principle of *caveat emptor* that says you can party today, but you are responsible for the hangover tomorrow. Investors know that they and not the taxpayers will be stuck with the losses from excessive risk taking by the banks. As a result, they have an incentive to restrain this risk taking even if it means taking away the punchbowl.

If this form of market discipline does not get the banks to stop their reckless lending or other risky activity, the articles written by the credit and equity market analysts provide plenty of political cover for the regulators to take away the punch bowl.

However, investors cannot take away the punchbowl and credit and equity market analysts do not write articles on reckless lending if there is opacity.

> 4.7.12 That being said, in the Commission's view there is no question but that the Authorities should have had a much better idea of the underlying situation of the banks for some considerable time prior to September 29. This

262 Lenzner, Robert (2013, October 24), Greenspan Finally Wakes Up To Fear and Eurphoria as Market Forces, Forbes, http://www.forbes.com/sites/robertlenzner/2013/10/24/what-alan-greenspan-learned-from-the-2008-crisis/

> would have been a precondition for any crisis management approach based on the real underlying situation. On this basis, a much more systematic and rigorous assessment of the alternative measures suitable for the Irish situation could have been undertaken, possibly several years before. In particular, banks with impaired assets would probably have been required to raise additional capital prior to any guarantee on their liabilities.[263]

If a better idea of the underlying situation at the banks would have changed how bank regulators managed the banks in the run-up to the crisis, a better idea of the underlying situation also would have changed how the other market participants acted towards the banks.

One reason for requiring banks to disclose their current exposure details is it results in market discipline on the banks to address their impaired assets in a timely manner. Since the losses are not hidden, the bankers have an incentive to deal with the bad assets quickly.

A second reason for requiring banks to disclose their current exposure details is it makes it easier for the banks to raise additional capital. Investors are not being asked to gamble on the contents of a black box.

> However, given the uncertain and unstable environment prevailing at the time, the emphasis on the need to avoid bank closures as well as the increasing amount of property losses, it is difficult to conclude with any certainty that this would have appreciably reduced the ultimate burden to the State of saving the Irish banking system.[264]

The ultimate burden to the State of saving the Irish banking system could have been reduced had there been valuation transparency. For example, rather than the Irish taxpayers paying for the banks' losses, future pre-banker bonus earnings could have been used to pay for the losses. To the extent possible, a claw back of past banker pay could also have been used.

Of all the ways to organize a banking system

Of all the ways to organize a banking system, the way each country's banking system is currently organized is the worst. The reason it is the worst is in the absence of valuation transparency the financial regulators have a monopoly on

---

263 Commission of Investigation into the Banking Sector in Ireland (2011, March), Report: Misjudging Risk: Causes of the Systemic Banking Crisis in Ireland, Commission of Investigation Into the Banking Sector in Ireland, http://www.bankinginquiry.gov.ie/Documents/Misjuding%20Risk%20-%20Causes%20of%20the%20Systemic%20Banking%20Crisis%20in%20Ireland.pdf, page 80.

264 ibid, page 80

all the useful, relevant information on the financial institutions and there is an expectation the regulators will use this information to restrain bank risk taking.

With this monopoly, all other market participants are dependent on the financial regulators to properly assess and communicate the riskiness and viability of the financial institutions.

If the financial regulators do not properly assess and communicate each bank's risk and viability, then market participants cannot restrain bank risk taking. Instead they mis-allocate capital by providing it too cheaply to the banks and taxpayers are left on the hook for bailing out the financial system and addressing issues like contagion.

The Nyberg Commission observed the absence of sufficient information on the underlying quality of loan books at the banks impacted on the options considered by the Government when it decided to introduce the bank guarantee in 2008.

> If accurate information on banks' exposures had been available at the time it seems quite likely to the commission that a more limited guarantee combined with a state take-over of at least one bank might have been more seriously contemplated.[265]

If accurate information on the underlying quality of loan books at the Irish banks would have altered the decision to guarantee all the bank liabilities, it is reasonable to assume that this same information in the hands of other market participants would have altered their behavior too.

If accurate information on bank exposures had been available, the other market participants would not have been dependent on the financial regulators to assess risk and viability. They would have done so for themselves since they expected before the credit crisis that they would have had to absorb any losses on their investments.

Given their incentive to avoid losses, the other market participants would have reacted well before the risk of loss would have wiped out their investments. At a minimum, they would have dramatically raised the cost of funds and reduce the availability of funds to the Irish banks. This action would have significantly reduce the total losses incurred by the Irish banking system and may have completely eliminated the need for any Irish taxpayer involvement.

Finally, please note the report makes a point of saying that modeling exercises like stress tests do not provide sufficient information on the underlying quality of the assets at the banks and in fact placed the Irish taxpayers and the financial system at greater risk.

---

265 ibid, executive summary Pg ix

The story of the Irish banking crisis also applies to EU, UK and US

The Nyberg Commission understood that the Irish financial crisis was not an isolated event, but part of the broader global financial crisis that began on August 9, 2007. As a result, the findings of the Nyberg Commission also apply globally.

The primary findings are the role opacity played and the need for the FDR Framework to be implemented in a dynamic and not static manner. If the FDR Framework had not been static, but instead extended disclosure across financial institutions and structured finance products, the systemic financial crisis would not have been so severe if it occurred at all. The combination of valuation transparency and *caveat emptor* at a minimum would have restrained the property bubble as investors limited their exposure to what they could afford to lose.

> 5.1.2 For instance, Irish banks compared their policies and achievements with peer groups containing well regarded banks in the UK and the EU. Risk management systems and remuneration practices were often adopted from abroad. Judging from results, similar problems, as in Ireland, arose in implementing them in a manner consistent with prudent credit policies. The relatively greater losses seen in Ireland may thus be seen as a consequence of somewhat greater abandon in accessing wholesale funding and in lending to domestic property than in other countries. Thus, there is a difference in degree rather than in concept.[266]

The problems were global because opacity was global. It was no easier for market participants to assess and restrain the risk taking of a black box Irish bank than a black box UK bank than a black box EU bank or a black box U.S. bank.

> 5.1.3 Similarly, central banks and regulators abroad generally were almost as unsuspecting of growing financial fragility as their Irish counterparts. The method of regulation or the number of available macroeconomists does not generally seem to have made a great deal of difference. The same seems true of auditors, rating agencies, analysts and investors, most of whom remained calm and optimistic until the crisis actually broke. Internal investigations in the IMF also indicate a widespread lack of understanding and clear communication of the accumulating risks by that organisation. There were incentives to conform with prevailing views, even in cases where proper analysis would have identified growing risk.[267]

The lack of awareness of the growing risk in the financial system was a direct result of opacity. While investors had primary responsibility for restraining this risk, they couldn't because it was hidden behind a veil of opacity.

---

[266] ibid, page 88

[267] ibid, page 88

> 5.2.13 Banks, clearly somewhat in agreement with the Financial Regulator (FR) itself, believed that they were in a better position than the FR to judge and decide upon what was most prudent in their own operations. This belief was underpinned by the fact that regulation was "light touch" and seemed to stress consumer issues rather than prudential issues. There was almost an element of the FR being "fobbed off" by banks that had particularly full confidence in the quality and sophistication of their models and systems.[268]

Had there been valuation transparency, each of the banks could have assessed its competitors to see if they were acting prudently. This assessment might have revealed the excess risk taking and caused the banks to pull back on their own lending.

> 5.3.2 The Irish authorities had the data required to arouse suspicion about trends in the property and financial markets. The relaxed attitude of the authorities was therefore the result of either a failure to understand the data or not being able to evaluate and analyse the implications correctly.[269]

Political backlash is one of the reasons central bankers and financial regulators cannot take away the punchbowl. The Nyberg Commission offered up another: incompetence. "The failure to understand the data or not being able to evaluate and analyze the implications correctly" both directly point towards incompetence.

The incompetence of the financial regulators contributed to our current financial crisis.

> 5.3.3 Provided the appropriate structures and processes were in place, the FR's approach was to trust bank leadership to make proper and prudent decisions. However, even when problems were identified and remarked upon, the FR did not subsequently ensure that sufficient corrective action was taken. Thus, even insightful and critical investigation reports tended to have little impact on banking practices. Furthermore, readily available information on, for instance, sector or borrower concentrations was not sufficiently critically analysed by the FR. Even if it were accepted that the FR was significantly under-resourced throughout the Period, this would not explain why available information was not acted upon.[270]

As Former Fed Governor Partee observed, it is not acceptable for regulators to rein in the banks when they are making money. It is the responsibility of the investors and they were prevented from doing this by opacity.

---

268 ibid, page 91

269 ibid, page 91

270 ibid, page 91

> 5.3.6 The CB chose to rely on the FR appropriately handling individual bank stability issues, much as the FR in turn chose to trust bank leadership. By implication, unless there were problems in the individual banks, there could not be major stability issues in the system as a whole. The Financial Stability Report (FSR) was constrained to present benign conclusions with a number of almost routine warnings voiced in the text itself. Simultaneously, macro-economic data signalling the emergence of the two key risks — growing dependence on foreign funding and the concentration of bank lending in the property sector — did not appear to have caused acute concern.[271]
>
> 5.3.7 At least at policy level, the CB seems not to have sufficiently appreciated the possibility that, while each bank was following a strategy that made sense, in the aggregate, when followed by all banks, this strategy could have serious consequences for overall financial stability. This was a classic macroeconomic fallacy that must have been recognised in the CB and it remains unclear why it was not appreciated at senior levels there. However, there are signs that a hierarchical culture, with elements of self-censorship at various levels, developed in the CB. Of course, this eventually made it even harder to address the increasing instabilities in the financial market.[272]

The Nyberg Commission is looking for the central bank to take an action it is not designed to do. The central bank is not in the credit allocation business. The central bank is also not in the business of telling banks how to fund themselves.

> 5.3.11 From mid-2007 onwards, cooperation improved between the key institutions involved and some important preparatory crisis management work was undertaken. However, the view that the only relevant problem was a threat to the liquidity position of the banks remained unchallenged throughout. There appears to have been no fears and, at most, a modest discussion on possible underlying acute solvency problems. This is true of the banks themselves as well as of the authorities.[273]

It is not surprising there were no fears about solvency. First, as shown by the testimony of the OCC's Conover who insisted Continental Illinois was solvent, there was probably a bank regulator saying the banks were solvent. Second, banks are designed so they can transition from solvent to insolvent and back to solvent again. They can do this so long as depositors think they will be protected from losses. This would naturally put the focus on guaranteeing the uninsured depositors.

---

271 ibid, page 92
272 ibid, page 92
273 ibid, page 93

However, extending the deposit guarantee only makes sense if the bank is capable of earnings its way back to solvency. This is where the information the Nyberg Commission Report called for is critical.

> 5.3.12 The discussions for alternative measures before and on September 29, 2008, were conducted on the basis of very deficient information. The authorities were apparently convinced that bank solvency issues were not pressing or significant, as were the banks themselves, and that it therefore would be possible to resolve the acute liquidity issue. Furthermore, the liquidity problems appear to have been seen as temporary only and related mainly to international developments. If more relevant information on and analysis of the underlying position of some of the banks had been available, discussions and policy recommendations may have been very different.[274]

In the absence of good information, specifically valuation transparency, nobody makes good decisions.

> 5.3.14 The lack of information on bank exposures among the Authorities over time had profound implications for the decision actually taken. Had better information on exposures and thus the risk of future impairments already been readily available in earlier years, government advisors could have suggested, even much before September 2008, that such banks with reasonably foreseeable problems should be taken into public administration immediately and gradually closed or restructured. Management could have been changed to eliminate further lending and risk-taking. Banks could, alternatively, have been required to raise additional capital from the markets while it could be accessed markets still were open for this. However, authorities continued to believe that banks did not have excessive property exposure and even outside evaluators only gradually came to a different view. As it turned out, no bank restructuring was contemplated until several months after the Guarantee when plans announced by the Government on a piecemeal basis had proved to be insufficient, thus reducing the credibility of the Irish authorities.[275]

The Nyberg Commission concluded better information on bank exposures would have dramatically improved how the Government responded to the banking crisis. By definition, had better information on bank exposures through valuation transparency been available to market participants, it would have dramatically improved how they restrained bank risk taking and moderated the severity of our current financial crisis.

---

274 ibid, page 93

275 ibid, page 94

5.4.1 It has been argued in this Report that during the Period the paradigm of efficient financial markets was widely accepted, particularly among developed nations. Believers in a naïve version of this paradigm would tend to assume that developments in the financial markets, almost by definition, could not be seriously flawed from a systemic point of view. Furthermore, they would also tend to assume that regulation of the financial markets would reduce innovation and efficiency without improving stability; less and lighter regulation was therefore better. Since there was widespread international belief in this paradigm, the international nature of the financial crisis, as well as the general unpreparedness of banks and authorities, is easier to understand.[276]

5.4.2 To the extent that this paradigm, in its naïve version, had become widely trusted among Irish financial professionals in private and public institutions, such an assumption may have been made both across institutions and within institutions (strengthened through groupthink). These assumptions in turn would have led, in the absence of strong and specific proof, to a belief that virtually any market feature or development was benign almost by definition, whether in the property market, the financial market or, indeed, in any individual bank. In effect, if it was financed by somebody, it must almost by definition be sound.[277]

5.4.5 The general acceptance of the paradigm of efficient markets also throws light on why most international institutions, foreign analysts, rating agencies, lenders, authorities and commentators were as relaxed about Irish developments as people in Ireland themselves. It is argued that the long period of benign conditions in Ireland played a substantial role in convincing observers that developments were stable. Furthermore, if large numbers of people also believed in the naïve interpretation of the efficient financial markets paradigm, very few developments in the financial markets would appear unsound or imprudent to them anymore.[278]

In the absence of the strong and specific evidence valuation transparency makes available, it is hard to show conventional wisdom is wrong.

5.4.9 The external watchdogs generally remained inactive as management's new banking model was introduced and implemented. There was no strong external reaction when management prudence eroded within the Irish banking system, as evidenced by the very rapid growth in lending and wholesale funding.[279]

---

276 ibid, page 94

277 ibid, page 94

278 ibid, page 95

279 ibid, page 96

The external watchdogs remained inactive when Continental Illinois did the same thing including rapid growth in lending and wholesale funding.

> 5.5.5 Secondly, there was a conspicuous lack of timely critical debate and analysis by bank analysts within institutions and among the public at large. The complacent views of Government, other authorities, banks and their customers appear to have been very well aligned with each other. Public policy and discourse seems to have almost unanimously accepted and encouraged views and practices that later proved disastrous. Examples are not difficult to find; for instance, the pervasive assumption of continued growth, the failure to see growing indebtedness as a serious policy problem, the "soft landing" scenario and, finally, an unwillingness to recognise the existence of long-standing problems in some banks. When alarms were finally sounded, they were too late for meaningful action; the problem loans were already on the banks' books and were largely illiquid.[280]
>
> 5.5.6 The very limited number of warning voices was largely ignored. Attempts by banking insiders during the Period to send cautionary signals to market participants about escalating property values were dismissed as ill-informed and wrong. Doubters (the few that identified themselves as such to the Commission) in the main grew unsure over the years when nothing seemed to go wrong. It also appears that some stayed silent in part to avoid possible sanctions. The Commission suspects, on the basis of discussions held with a wide number of people, that there may have been a strong belief in Ireland that contrarians, non-team players, fractious observers and whistleblowers would be informally (though sometimes even publicly) sanctioned or ignored, regardless of the quality of their analysis or their place in organisations.[281]

The only doubters who can express their opinion are investors. They can do so by cutting back on their exposure.

> 5.5.13 The Commission therefore has reluctantly come to the conclusion that at least some of the financial market professionals at the time must have entertained private, undisclosed doubts on the sustainability of banks' lending and funding policies. However, for various reasons "the dance had to go on". Similarly, it seems likely that the public and private watchdogs remained less active than required, not only because they did not know, but also because it was not publicly acceptable, legally necessary or prudent to act at the time.[282]
>
> 5.5.14 During much of the Period, Ireland was still seen as a success story that provided a large number of its inhabitants with self-esteem as well as rising

280 ibid, page 97

281 ibid, page 97

282 ibid, page 98

incomes, wealth and welfare. Anybody seriously interfering with this process would expect to be publicly castigated as causing the very distress, loss and crisis that they would have been trying to prevent. Instead, by allowing the party and deal-making to continue, management, investors and public and private watchdogs participated in its positive but temporary gifts.[283]

5.5.15 That said, the Commission is not suggesting that financial professionals in Ireland consciously decided to let banks get into trouble. As indicated earlier, it is much more likely that professional suspicions were explained away or suppressed, in light of the new financial dogma and a long period of good times, in order not to appear fractious, unprofessional or alarmist among colleagues, superiors and others who were believed to possess equal or even superior knowledge.[284]

And the conclusion the Nyberg Commission draws from this is

> 5.6.4 If this hypothesis is accepted, an important implication emerges. Because the real reason for the crisis is the spread of an ultimately irrational point of view, regulations and watchdog institutions cannot be counted on to be efficient preventers of a systemic crisis.[285]

This point is very important and says very clearly what financial reform should not be put in place. The financial reform that should not be put in place is one that relies on more complex regulations and regulators to prevent a systemic crisis.

Unfortunately, the reforms that have been put in place globally since the beginning of the current financial crisis rely on more complex regulations and regulators to prevent the next systemic crisis. Based on the Nyberg Commission Report, there is no reason to believe these financial reforms will work.

> As has been seen in Ireland and other countries, central bankers and regulators embraced much the same paradigm as the market participants and adapted their policies to their convictions. The result, as shown by the crisis itself, was that no effective brake on risk-taking existed for years. It does not appear wholly unfair to propose that this is what may happen also in the future if and when another new financial or banking paradigm appears. Many of the very reforms that recently have been undertaken, at short notice, to shore up the functioning of the present financial system could turn out, once again, to be ineffective.[286]

---

[283] ibid, page 99

[284] ibid, page 99

[285] ibid, page. 100

[286] ibid, page 100

The Nyberg Commission Report wasn't content to say more complex regulations and regulators shouldn't be counted on to prevent the next systemic crisis. It said the reforms being put in place globally with their emphasis on the use of more complex regulations and regulators are likely to be ineffective.

So what does the Nyberg Commission Report recommend should be done?

> 5.6.5 Permanently improving financial stability therefore should perhaps, instead, be done in ways that do not necessarily demand the unfailing attention, prescience or vigilance of ministries, central banks or regulators. Arguably, the most important goal of such a system should be to directly reduce the likelihood of serious disturbances to the real economy.[287]

The Nyberg Commission Report effectively calls for the Transparency Label Initiative™. It addresses the Nyberg Commission's request for a solution that permanently improves financial stability without demanding the unfailing attention, prescience or vigilance of ministries, central banks or regulators. By design, the Transparency Label Initiative™ is dynamic and ensures pressure from the buy-side for valuation transparency is continuously applied across the global financial system. It reduces the likelihood of serious disturbances to the real economy. It does this by effectively constraining risk taking both where there is a valuation transparency label and where there is not as investors know they are responsible for the losses on their investments.

---

[287] ibid, page 100

The FSA Report

The real lesson from these events is that policymakers should never have permitted such a yawning information gap to emerge between bankers and everyone else.[288]

The UK regulator's report on the failure of RBS

The Financial Services Authority's report on the failure of RBS is very important for three reasons. First, the FSA Report confirmed the conclusions of the Nyberg Commission Report on the Irish Financial crisis. Second, it showed the conclusions of the Nyberg Commission Report applied globally. Third, it showed the role opacity played in the failure of RBS and why this failure was preventable if RBS had been required to provide valuation transparency.

A repeat of Continental Illinois

The failure of RBS confirmed for Too Big to Fail banks, history doesn't repeat itself, but it certainly rhymes. Recall that Continental Illinois was a well-regarded bank that adopted an ambitious growth strategy. So too did the Irish banks and RBS. Recall that Continental Illinois funded this growth using short-term uninsured deposits. So too did the Irish banks and RBS. Recall that Continental Illinois did not disclose its current exposure details so market participants could assess its risk. The Irish banks and RBS didn't disclose their current exposure details either. Recall that Continental Illinois was known to have an exposure to bad debt and the lack of valuation transparency prevented market participants from assessing the impact of the bad debt on the bank's long run viability. Also true for the Irish banks and RBS. Recall the financial regulators used a taxpayer-funded bailout to stop the wholesale deposit run on Continental Illinois. Financial regulators used a taxpayer-funded bailout to stop the run on the Irish banks and RBS too.

The FSA Report discussed the role opacity played in the financial crisis and the failure of RBS.

> The system-wide collapse of market confidence which followed [the failure of Lehman Brothers in September 2008] was driven by extreme uncertainty about the creditworthiness of trading and interbank counterparties, and about the potential knock-on consequences of any one failure for others.[289]

---

288 Tett, Gillian (2008, October 1), Insight: Seeds sown in murky finance, Financial Times, http://www.ft.com/cms/s/0/a48af6e2-8fd3-11dd-9890-0000779fd18c.html

289 U.K. Financial Services Authority (2011, December), The failure of the Royal Bank of Scotland, FSA, http://www.fsa.gov.uk/pubs/other/rbs.pdf, page 56

There was uncertainty about counterparty creditworthiness because opacity prevented any market participant other than the primary supervisors from assessing any counterparty's risk and solvency.

> In that environment, banks which were perceived to be (and in many cases actually were) relatively poorly positioned — in capital, liquidity or asset quality — became subject to a self-fulfilling downward spiral of falling confidence, with funding sources closed. RBS, as a result of poor management decisions over the previous several years, was one such bank.[290]

In the absence of facts, fear about just how bad the losses on the banks' exposures could be comes to dominate. This could be seen in the run on RBS triggered by the collapse of Lehman Brothers.

> Over a three-week period following the bankruptcy of Lehman Brothers, during which a number of other financial institutions collapsed or came near to collapse, RBS's gradual liquidity run reached extreme proportions.
>
> On 7 October 2008, RBS's wholesale counterparties, as well as, to a lesser extent, retail depositors, were simply not prepared to meet its funding needs and RBS was left reliant on ELA from the Bank of England.[291]

The FSA Report attempted to identify the precise reason confidence in RBS collapsed and the subsequent run by the wholesale depositors occurred. This attempt highlighted the difference between what regulators think is important and investors think is important.

The regulators viewed RBS's capital position and its reliance on short-term wholesale funding as important. From the regulators' perspective, had RBS had more loss-absorbing capital, market participants wouldn't have been worried about its possible failure. From the regulators' perspective, had RBS had less reliance on wholesale-funding it would have been less prone to a run.

The investors focused on asset quality, asset quality, and asset quality. Why would investors focus on asset quality exclusively and not on a bank's reported capital levels or funding strategy? The quality of a bank's assets is a direct indicator of its long-term viability. Banks with good quality assets survive. Banks with bad quality assets are resolved.

Because of opacity, investors could not assess the quality of any bank's assets. As a result, the

---

290 ibid, page 56

291 ibid, page 56

> losses that RBS incurred in H1 2008 signalled significant asset quality problems in both its trading book and banking book....[292]

When RBS's reported losses were combined with the investors' concern about future losses hidden on and off the bank's balance sheet,

> A reasonable conclusion may therefore be that liquidity problems were driven by underlying solvency concerns.[293]

The FSA Report linked the collapse in market confidence to the extreme uncertainty in the creditworthiness of the banks. This uncertainty was the result of opacity. Without access to each bank's current exposure details, market participants could not tell which banks were solvent and which were insolvent.

As a result, the FSA Report finds banks that were perceived to have asset quality problems became the subject of a self-fulfilling downward spiral in confidence. It was the perception of asset quality problems that drove the downward spiral. In the absence of valuation transparency, there were no facts to show reality was different from this steadily worsening perception.

Perception in the presence of opacity played a major role in how the market interpreted loss recognition by RBS. Market participants knew RBS was exposed to troubled assets. They didn't know the extent of the troubled assets and therefore could not put the limited loss recognition RBS did do in the appropriate context. Instead, the loss was seen as a signal of significant asset quality problems. Of course, in the absence of valuation transparency and disclosure of current exposure details, there was no way to verify if this interpretation was true or not.

Just like Continental Illinois, the large uninsured depositors withdrew their funds as doubts about the solvency of RBS grew. What let these doubts grow and ultimately triggered a bank run was opacity. Large uninsured depositors were unwilling to gamble on the contents of a black box.

As Walter Bagehot observed, a well-run bank needs no capital, no amount of capital will rescue a badly run bank. In the presence of opacity, it was impossible to tell if RBS was a well run or poorly run bank.

> [RBS's capital adequacy] proved inadequate to reassure the market in autumn 2008 that the firm would remain solvent in the face of uncertainty about the scale of losses that banks might face.[294]

---

292 ibid, page 57

293 ibid, page 57

294 ibid, page 120

Subsequent to the collapse of Lehman Brothers, all opaque banks became much more susceptible to bank runs due to the potential for further losses on their exposures ranging from structured finance securities to real estate loans. Since the market did not know the specifics of these exposures, it opted for safety. For wholesale depositors, this meant getting their money back from the banks and finding a lower risk investment.

We know a great deal about how the mix of known facts and market perceptions led to the bank runs on Continental Illinois, RBS and the other banks.

In all cases, market participants knew the banks were exposed to assets that were rapidly losing value as shown by the size of the losses the banks recognized. Market participants also had two more pieces of information. First, due to opacity, market participants knew they did not have the current exposure details they needed to assess the current risk of the banks. Second, market participants knew if RBS or any of the other banks had nothing to hide it would disclose its current exposure details so market participants could independently confirm it could absorb the losses and continue in business. This is what banks did prior to the late 1930s.

The market participants correctly perceived each bank's unwillingness to provide valuation transparency as a sign each bank was hiding the true weakness of its asset quality and the risk implied by banks hiding their asset quality did not justify being an uninsured depositor.

The FSA Report tried to understand the role market perceptions about RBS's asset quality played in its bank run. Market perceptions about asset quality were assessed by reviewing analysts' questions, contemporaneous research reports and by interviews with investors.

Importantly, the investigation of market perceptions found the opacity of the bank's disclosures prevented investors from doing the risk assessment they wanted to do.

> The inherent complexity of RBS's financial reporting from end-2007, following the acquisition of ABN AMRO via a complicated consortium structure, also affected market participants' view of RBS's exposures.
>
> This complexity made it more difficult to communicate with the market about the transaction risks and RBS's underlying position.
>
> The presentation of the acquisition and its impact, involving extensive use of pro forma financial statements alongside statutory reporting formats, had the effect of obscuring the firm's presentation of risks and exposures, as well as its underlying capital position. This occurred at the very point when market participants began to voice concerns about the lack of transparency of banks' exposures.[295]

---

295 ibid, page 135

The FSA found the intermediary depiction model does not work for banks. Instead of helping market participants, the FSA found the current financial reporting had the effect of obscuring the bank's risks, exposures and underlying capital position.

From the end of 2007, FSA also found market participants wanted transparency into the banks' current exposures. They wanted pure information because market participants knew they needed this detailed data if they were going to be able to assess the risk of the banks.

> In summary, it is clear that RBS's involvement in certain asset classes (such as structured credit and commercial real estate) left it vulnerable to a loss of market confidence as concerns about the potential for losses on those assets spread.[296]

What left RBS vulnerable to a loss of market confidence was not its exposure to certain asset classes, but rather it was opaque. Without the current exposure details, market participants estimates of the size of the losses on its exposures was not constrained by the facts.

The failure of RBS was preventable

The failure of RBS was preventable. There were numerous times where adherence to the FDR Framework, specifically, insuring that market participants had access to all the useful, relevant information in an appropriate, timely manner would have prevented the failure of RBS.

The first time the failure of RBS was preventable by valuation transparency was when RBS made the decision in mid-2006 to grow Global Banking & Markets (GBM) and in particular its structured credit business. Valuation transparency combined with market discipline would have restrained RBS's efforts to grow its structured credit business.

Why would valuation transparency and market discipline have restrained RBS?

Market participants know it is important to observe and conservatively enforce the number one rule of all trading businesses: do not take on a greater exposure than you can unwind should the trade move against you. The size of the position that can be unwound is not fixed, but varies. This is important because what appears a reasonable size position given today's market liquidity could be far too large given tomorrow's market liquidity. Simply put, unwinding a too large position in an illiquid market increases the size of the losses. Knowing this,

---

296 ibid, page 135

market participants would have been very sensitive to and exerted discipline on RBS to limit the total size of RBS's exposure to structured credits to what it could afford to lose if it couldn't unwind its positions at all.

However, in the absence of the market discipline made possible by valuation transparency, RBS took on a greater exposure to structured credits than it could afford to lose, hedge or distribute to "often poorly informed end investors".[297]

The irony here was RBS itself was a poorly informed end investor. The structured credits RBS focused on were collateralized debt obligations (CDOs) composed of subprime mortgage-backed bonds. I like to refer to these securities as opacity squared. Not only were the underlying bonds opaque, but so too were the CDOs composed of these bonds. RBS was engaged in creating, buying and selling large brown paper bags, the CDOs, filled with small brown paper bags, the subprime mortgage-backed bonds.

Naturally, no one knew the value of the contents of all these brown paper bags. This however did not stop the rating firms from assigning a rating. For the highest rated "super senior" slice of the brown paper bags, banks were required to hold a minimum amount of capital. As a result, RBS accumulated a sizable position with many "super senior" tranches of brown paper bags. Of course, when the underlying subprime mortgages started defaulting it turned out the rating firms were no better at guessing the value of the contents of a brown paper bag than you or I.

By August 9, 2007 and the start of our current financial crisis, the growth in RBS's structured credit positions had left it with losses. The question then became what to do with these losses.

Like the U.S. bank that bet long 30-year U.S. Treasury bonds, RBS trading business faced three choices: do nothing and pray the market moves in your favor, sell and recognize the loss, or buy a hedge and determine the best strategy for exiting the trade later. There are two problems with do nothing and pray. First, the market can keep moving against your bet and the losses get worse. Second, the quality of the investment itself can deteriorate. This happened to RBS when the underlying subprime mortgages started defaulting. The problem with selling and recognizing the loss is everyone understands just how big a bet you took and lost. The problem with hedging is it costs money if the hedges are available, sometimes they are not, and there is no guarantee when you remove the hedge market conditions will improve to allow the position to be unwound with a smaller loss.

Compounding the problem for RBS was the fact it had taken a position in opaque securities. At the beginning of the financial crisis, readily available market

---

297 ibid, page 52

prices disappeared as any liquidity for these securities effectively went away. RBS was left with the challenge of determining "what were best estimates of losses incurred at any given date."[298]

Naturally, the best estimate of losses had a distinctive rose color.

> [W]hile RBS's approach to the valuation of its CDOs was within the bounds of what could be justified, it displayed a bias to optimism.[299]

The absence of valuation transparency meant this bias towards optimism effected the decision on what to do with the losses. It did this in two ways.

First, using optimistic valuations allowed the bank to minimize the impact of the losses on its financial statements. Bankers prefer this. Recall the bank moved its 30-year U.S. Treasury bond bet into the hold to maturity account so as to minimize the impact of the mark to market losses on its financial statements.

Second, the bias towards optimism made the decision to do nothing easier. The problem seemed much smaller and answering the bank's prayers didn't look like it would take a miracle. However, once the decision is made, to do nothing tends to be very difficult to reverse, as the decision makers fall into the "it is too late now" trap.

Recall how the value of the bank's 30-year bond bet declined over several months. After an initial decline, senior bank management elected to do nothing arguing the market would stabilize and the price would recover. The bonds continued to decline in value and this additional decline sprung the "it is too late now" trap. Senior management expressed how it wished it had a) sold the bonds or b) hedged them earlier to avoid the additional loss. Then, senior management would commit to take some unidentified action if the losses on the bonds reached a target level of $200 million, $300 million, $400 million, or $500 million… As each target level for containing the losses was breached, the cycle would resume with senior management expressing how it wished it had a) sold the bonds or b) hedge them earlier.

RBS had the same experience.

> [O]n a number of occasions, RBS made decisions not to crystallise losses. When interviewed as part of the enforcement investigation into his conduct, the Chairman of Global Markets recalled that 'I became aware of that sort of general feeling that, we always seemed to be thinking, 'Oh, if only we'd hedged last week' was the general sense I was getting. 'It's too late now — if only we'd hedged last week'.'[300]

---

[298] ibid, page 53

[299] ibid, page 142

[300] ibid, page 149

There are two ways to avoid the "it is too late now" trap. First, the bank has an internal discipline that says once losses reach a specific level, the position will be closed and the losses realized. Second, the bank provides valuation transparency and is subject to market discipline. In this case, losses are also realized before they threaten the solvency of the bank.

The second time the failure of RBS was preventable by valuation transparency is when it acquired ABN AMRO. The FSA report argued even if RBS had been provided with valuation transparency into ABN AMRO it is unclear it wouldn't have still gone ahead with the acquisition.

> More due diligence would have provided greater depth of information concerning ABN AMRO's risk profile. It is unclear however whether, even if RBS had had access to a greater level of information, its due diligence would have resulted in estimates of future potential losses anywhere near the losses that actually arose, or even that it would have resulted in estimates of losses to any material degree, particularly given the judgements that RBS was making in relation to its own business.[301]

The FSA Report misses how market discipline would have prevented the merger. If market participants had valuation transparency into both RBS and ABN AMRO, they could have assessed the risk of the combined entity. The result would have been a sharp decline in RBS's stock price and a sharp increase in its cost of funds as it was beginning to pursue the merger. Bank management tends to be particularly responsive to this "no" vote.

Political backlash

The FSA Report confirmed the fear of political backlash prevents financial regulators from leaning against the wind or taking away the punchbowl. The FSA Report also confirmed the Nyberg Commission Report's conclusion so long as financial regulators are answerable to their political masters the fear of political backlash is a permanent reality that will always prevent financial regulators leaning against the wind or taking away the punchbowl.

In the run-up to the financial crisis in the UK, the FSA found its political masters saying an intrusive approach to regulating the banks was unnecessary and would damage London's competitive position.

> For example, in a Treasury press release dated 24 May 2005, at the launch of the Better Regulation Action Plan, Gordon Brown said '…the new model we propose is quite different. In a risk based approach there is no inspection

[301] ibid, page 33

> without justification, no form filling without justification, and no information requirements without justification. Not just a light touch but a limited touch'.[302]

Mr. Brown, as the UK's Prime Minister, called for a new model for supervising the banks that runs exactly contradictory to the FDR Framework based financial system adopted by the UK. His model involved justifying access to information. In an FDR framework based financial system, access to information does not have to be justified. The government is responsible for ensuring market participants have access to the information each market participant sees as useful and relevant in an appropriate, timely manner. Included in the market participants who are suppose to have access to information are the bank regulators.

> In the following year, during a speech on 14 June 2006 at Bloomberg, the then Economic Secretary to the Treasury, Ed Balls MP, said '...we must keep the UK's regulatory system at the cutting edge — the best in the world... at all times we will apply a principled system of risk-based regulation, without unnecessary administration burdens... nothing should be done to put at risk a light-touch, risk-based regulatory regime'.[303]

Mr. Balls, the UK's Economic Secretary to the Treasury, set the hurdle for changing the model for supervising the banks very high. Specifically, nothing should be done to put at risk light-touch. Clearly, having information on the underlying bank exposures would put light-touch at risk.

What was this light-touch regulatory regime?

It was a low-cost replacement for the detailed rules and intrusive compliance reviews then being used by the bank regulators. As described by the FSA, adopting a light-touch regulatory regime meant

- moving away from detailed, prescriptive rules and supervisory actions targeted at how firms should operate their businesses;
- placing greater reliance on principles and outcome-focused, high-level rules as a means to drive regulatory compliance; and
- focusing more on the outcomes that the FSA wanted to achieve, leaving more of the judgement of how to achieve those outcomes to the senior management of firms....[304]

---

302 Ibid, page 262

303 ibid, page 262

304 ibid, page 257

The practical implication of moving from intrusive to light-touch supervision was

> The FSA's overall supervisory approach to RBS (and its peers) prior to the market turmoil in autumn 2007 involved little fundamental assessment of firms' underlying assets, or balance sheet structure.
>
> Instead, the focus was primarily on encouraging the firm to improve its own stress-testing methodologies. This focus on management process for assessing asset quality, rather than on substantive analysis by the FSA of a firm's asset composition and quality or on senior management experience in relation to significant areas of new business, was characteristic of the FSA's pre-crisis supervisory approach.[305]

Of course, the shift from detailed rules and intrusive regulation to principles and light-touch need not have produced a bad outcome. What guaranteed the bad outcome was the lack of valuation transparency. Without valuation transparency, market participants could not exert discipline and restrain bank risk taking. Without market discipline, relying only on principle-based light-touch regulation was guaranteed to result in failure as no one was restraining the risk taking by the banks.

The FSA Report recognized the importance of valuation transparency, particularly the need to assess the underlying exposure details.

> The consequence of the prevailing approach was that the nature of the risks inherent in the assets held by RBS was not fully appreciated by the FSA…[306]
>
> With hindsight, the predominant regulatory approach to trading book risk (i.e. reliance on value-at-risk, or VaR, models) was deficient. In particular, it did not focus on analysing the underlying trading book inventory.[307]

In addition to political support, justification for adopting a light-touch principles-based approach to supervision came from several areas.

First, a global approach to capital adequacy under the leadership of the Basel Committee was adopted. This approach assigned risk-weights to each category of asset and then compared book capital levels to total risk-weighted assets.

Second, the belief financial innovations, like structured finance, reduced the risks to the financial system and to the banks by transferring risk to investors rather than leaving it on bank balance sheets. If the financial innovations had been designed to maintain valuation transparency, this belief would have been

---

305 Ibid, page 135

306 ibid, page 135

307 ibid, page 142

true. However, these financial innovations were designed expressly to create opacity so Wall Street and the City could profit from a proprietary information advantage. Third, support from the academic community.

Like every other financial regulator, political appointees ran the FSA. They reported to politicians. Therefore, they were very sensitive to charges of 'heavy-handed, gold-plating'. The report showed just how much financial regulators feared political backlash and therefore how heavily influenced they are by politicians.

> Within this context, if senior leaders of the FSA had proposed, before the first signs of the crisis (for example, before summer 2007), a supervisory approach which entailed higher capital and liquidity requirements supervisory caps on rapid bank balance sheet growth, or intensive analysis of asset quality, it is almost certain that their proposals would have been met by extensive complaints that the FSA was pursuing a heavy-handed, gold-plating approach which would harm London's competitiveness.[308]

If the FSA's statement sounds familiar, it repeats former Fed Governor Partee's comment it is not acceptable for financial regulators to restrain the banks on a day-to-day basis when they are making money. Nor, by design, is restraining the banks' risk taking on a day-to-day basis the financial regulators' responsibility. By design, it is the other market participants' responsibility to restrain the banks' risk taking. However, the other market participants can only restrain bank risk taking in the presence of valuation transparency.

Requiring valuation transparency effectively ends banks being able to use politicians to avoid restraint on their risk taking. Market participants who are responsible for the losses on their exposures to the banks are going to continue to exert market discipline and don't care what a politician has to say about regulators engaging in "heavy-handed, gold plating".

Slow-motion train wreck

Beginning in 2007, subprime mortgages began experiencing rising delinquencies. As a result, market participants became concerned about the exposure of financial institutions to these mortgages either as loans or through structured finance securities. Market participants thought the banks were sitting on huge losses, but because of opacity, no one knew exactly what was on the banks' books. This concern translated into increasing pressure on the banks to open their books and become more open about declaring their losses.

---

308 ibid, page 262

By the end of the year, as valuation transparency was not forthcoming, the global financial system experienced increasing stress. This was shown in the interbank lending market where the risk premium required by lenders continued to climb.

The global financial system was showing just how harmful opacity is. It was becoming clear to market participants no one, including the financial regulators, knew what was hidden on and off the banks' balance sheets.

The FSA Report provided a timeline for the global financial crisis in 2008 leading up to the failure of RBS. This timeline shows how the global financial system experienced a slow-motion train wreck driven by opacity. Each stop before the wreck featured a loss of confidence, inadequate disclosure to restore this confidence and therefore an increase in market uncertainty that set the stage for a global run on the banks by the sources of wholesale funding.

Table 3: Timeline of financial crisis during 2008[309]

March	Federal Reserve Bank of New York supplied liquidity to Bear Stearns (through JPMorgan Chase) to avert the collapse of the firm.
Mid-July	Evidence of deterioration on available wholesale funding maturities for major UK banks and building societies, including aggregate increase in reliance on very short-term wholesale funding.
8 to 15 July	Fannie Mae and Freddie Mac share prices plunged sharply. Possibility that market participants might refuse credit, making U.S. government support necessary.
8 August	RBS announced its first loss in 40 years, a statutory operating loss before tax of £692m after credit market write-downs of £5.9bn for H1 2008.
7 September	Fannie Mae and Freddie Mac placed in conservatorship.

309 ibid, page 193

15 September	Bankruptcy of Lehman Brothers broke confidence that major institutions were too big to fail. Following collapse of Lehman Brothers, already impaired liquidity in the interbank markets dried up, as banks chose to hoard cash instead of lending it on even short maturities; both secured (repo) and unsecured markets seized up. Firms, including RBS, experienced the most difficult funding conditions since the crisis period started. Major banks significantly reliant on central bank support.
16 September	Federal Reserve Bank of New York announced that it would lend up to US$85bn to AIG to ensure it could meet its obligations as they fell due; in return, the U.S. government took a 79.9% equity interest in AIG.
17 September	Lloyds TSB and HBOS confirmed their intention to merge.
25 September	Collapse of Washington Mutual one of the largest U.S. retail banks.
28 September	Governments of Belgium, the Netherlands and Luxembourg announced their intention to inject €11.2bn to shore up Fortis's position, protect the interests of account holders and help to ensure financial stability.
29 September	Bradford & Bingley transferred into public ownership with the retail deposit book and branch network transferred to Abbey National plc (now Santander). Icelandic government forced to take a 75% stake in the country's third-largest bank, Glitnir, after it experienced liquidity problems.
30 September	The Irish government announced it would guarantee the deposits of Irish banks (this initial announcement did not apply to banks such as RBS's subsidiary Ulster Bank as it was part of a UK group).
7 October	RBS received Emergency Liquidity Assistance from the Bank of England. Landsbanki placed into receivership in Iceland.
8 October	UK government announced its recapitalisation package for banks to increase their tier 1 capital ratios.

Bear Stearns was the first shot across the bow opacity was the problem. It was an investment bank with no insured deposits. It was also a large player in originating, selling and trading subprime mortgage-backed securities. As doubts about the value of these securities grew, so too did doubts about the viability and solvency of Bear Stearns. Without disclosure of its current exposure details and the current performance of the loans backing its security investments, these doubts could not be addressed. Naturally, because their doubts were not addressed, the suppliers of wholesale funding became unwilling to lend to Bear Stearns and a wholesale funding run ensued. To stop this run, the Fed orchestrated a buyout of Bear Stearns by JPMorgan.

Bear Stearns highlighted the fact no one could value either the opaque structured finance securities or the equally opaque global financial institutions. Naturally, market participants asked the banks to provide valuation transparency.

> It should be noted, however, that RBS was not alone in being relatively slow to respond to market participants' requests for greater transparency. For example, the Financial Stability Forum commented in April 2008 that 'weaknesses in public disclosures by financial institutions have damaged market confidence during the turmoil'.[310]

After Bear Stearns collapse, market participants not only were on the lookout for other financial institutions experiencing deteriorating asset quality in their structured finance exposures, but actively reducing their exposure to these firms. The intensity of the reduction in exposure was not at the same intensity as a run on the bank, but rather a jog on the bank.

Market participants had some help in identifying which financial institutions would experience asset quality problems. These institutions originated the troubled structured finance securities and tended to have on their balance sheet some exposure to these securities for trading or investment purposes as well as the underlying assets waiting to be put into new securities. However, even though the financial institutions with trouble had been identified, because of opacity nobody could assess just how much trouble these institutions were in. This inability to assess what was really going on undermined confidence and spurred on the jog on the banks. By mid-July, wholesale funds were only being made available on an overnight or slightly longer basis.

The market for opaque structured finance securities continued to worsen and concerns about the opaque borrowing banks continued to increase. On September 15, 2008, another major global financial institution fell when Lehman Brothers filed for bankruptcy. Immediately, the wholesale funding market froze

---

310 ibid, page 90

and in doing so triggered a run on the large, global financial institutions that relied on this market for funding.

As Continental Illinois showed, in the presence of opacity relying on wholesale funding is imprudent. The run on the large, global financial institutions subsequent to the failure of Lehman Brothers confirmed this.

So why didn't the banks rely on the tried and true method of using valuation transparency to head off the run by the wholesale funding market? One explanation was senior bank management had a financial incentive to not provide valuation transparency as it would have triggered recognition of the losses hidden on and off the bank balance sheets.

> One hedge fund described the RBS CEO as taking a dismissive approach to further write-downs on the loan book. A few of the hedge funds remembered that, at that time, they considered that the RBS CEO ran the firm on a profit and loss basis, with a primary focus being to increase returns. These same hedge funds elaborated that, in their view, this approach resulted in poor decision-making at RBS as the risks associated with its expanding balance sheet and asset quality were not adequately considered. Another also noted the emphasis placed on earnings per share based measures in the RBS CEO's remuneration package.[311]

The FSA Report provided another explanation. Banks had difficulty providing the requested data. [One benefit of requiring valuation transparency is a bank cannot take on an exposure unless it is capable of disclosing it.]

> The Review Team learned that significant additional data requests were made to RBS to try to assess its structured credit exposures, its approaches to the valuation of those assets, and the likelihood of further losses, but that RBS had challenges in providing these data.
>
> The FSA also continued to have 'minimal data' on ABN AMRO's structured credit portfolios, which had considerably increased RBS's exposures to these assets. Therefore, the analysis undertaken by the FSA specialist team in relation to RBS was often based upon limited data.
>
> It was not until late September 2008 that a comprehensive and standardized valuation benchmarking exercise was rolled out. This was designed to assess major banks' exposures to troubled asset classes, including structured credit, and to inform the FSA's view on firms' risk profiles and the potential for future losses from these portfolios in the event of continued market dislocation.[312]

---

311 ibid, page 206

312 ibid, page 216

Of course, by late September 2008 it was too late to just be rolling out a method for understanding each bank's risk profile and potential for future losses. The FSA Report shows the policy response by the UK was hampered by the same lack of information found by the Nyberg Commission Report in Ireland.

This point bears repeating: nobody makes a good decision in the absence of all the useful, relevant information in an appropriate, timely manner.

Like Ireland, there is no reason to believe the UK's response to the financial crisis benefitted anyone other than the bankers. This is exemplified by the decision to adopt the policy of Too Big to Fail and bailout out the banks.

> On 8 October 2008, the UK government announced a recapitalisation package, asking banks to increase their tier 1 capital ratios. 'The objective was to ensure that the banks had a level of capital "where people could absolutely clearly and without doubt have confidence in them"'.
>
> Participating banks could either obtain capital through the UK government's recapitalisation scheme or raise capital in the markets.[313]

In 1870, Walter Bagehot said a well-run bank needs no capital and no amount of capital will rescue a badly run bank. In 2008, because of opacity it was impossible to tell which bank was well run or badly run. In the absence of valuation transparency, how could any market participant know if "the banks had a level of capital where people could absolutely clearly and without doubt have confidence in them"?

The only way "where people could absolutely clearly and without doubt have confidence in them" was if the banks provided valuation transparency and disclosed their current exposure details. Market participants could then independently assess each bank and see if there was any reason for confidence in them.

Of course, bailing out the banks did not restore confidence.

But by choosing to focus on bank book capital levels, policymakers adopted a very banker friendly policy as it prevented the banks from recognizing the losses on their exposures to the excess debt in the financial system. Preventing banks from recognizing their losses was good for bankers at it allowed them to keep receiving their bonuses. The alternative of the banks recognizing their losses would have seen the bankers' bonuses instead being used to rebuild bank book capital levels.

---

313 ibid, page 192

The FCIC Report

A bank needs models to measure risk. The problem, however, is that any one bank can measure its risk, but it also has to know what the risk taken by other banks in the system happens to be at any particular moment.
— Myron Scholes[314]

What did the U.S. Financial Crisis Inquiry Commission find?

The Financial Crisis Inquiry Commission found opacity was at the very heart of our current financial crisis. Its findings about opacity confirmed the Nyberg Commission Report and the FSA Report.

The Financial Crisis Inquiry Commission described the critical role the lack of valuation transparency played.

> Furthermore, when the crisis began, ... Investors would realize they did not know as much as they wanted to know about the mortgage assets that banks, investment banks, and other firms held or to which they were exposed.
>
> To an extent not understood by many before the crisis, financial institutions had leveraged themselves with commercial paper, with derivatives, and in the short-term repo markets, in part by using mortgage-backed securities and CDOs as collateral.
>
> Lenders would question the value of the assets that those companies had posted as collateral at the same time that they were questioning the value of those companies' balance sheets.[315]

What the lack of valuation transparency meant was

> "In a context of opacity about where risk resides, . . . a general distrust has contaminated many asset classes. What had once been liquid is now illiquid. Good collateral cannot be sold or financed at anything approaching its true value," Moody's wrote on September.[316]

Ultimately,

314 Solomon, Deborah (2009, May 14), Crash Course: Questions for Myron Scholes, NY Times, http://www.nytimes.com/2009/05/17/magazine/17wwln-q4-t.html

315 Financial Crisis Inquiry Report, Final Report of the National Commission on the Causes of the Financial and Economic Crisis in the United States (2011, January), http://fcic.law.stanford.edu/report, page 228.

316 ibid, page 253

> The key concern for markets and regulators was that they weren't sure they understood the extent of toxic assets on the balance sheets of financial institutions—so they couldn't be sure which banks were really solvent.[317]

The Financial Crisis Inquiry Commission found opacity introduced by the banks into the global financial system was at the heart of the financial crisis because it made it impossible to understand and value the mortgage-backed assets and the financial institutions.

Had valuation transparency been available there would not have been this uncertainty.

Had valuation transparency been available in the run-up to the financial crisis, market participants would have purchased far less "toxic" securities in the first place by limiting their exposure to what they could afford to lose given the risk. They would have seen the deteriorating underwriting standards and that the quality of the mortgages did not match the representations in the prospectus or the ratings by the rating firms.

Had valuation transparency been available, market participants would also have known the extent of each bank's exposure to "toxic" assets and therefore which banks were solvent and which were not.

The issue of "toxic" assets causing solvency concerns would not have occurred because market participants would also have been able to exert discipline on the banks. As the exposure to "toxic" assets went up, the bank's share price would have declined and the bank's cost of funds would have increased to reflect the increase in risk the bank was taking on. A decline in share price and an increase in the cost of doing business is an unambiguous and easily understood message to bank management to cease and desist.

Had the Transparency Label Initiative™ existed, there would have been dramatically less opacity in the global financial system. The absence of a label would have put pressure from the buy-side on both banks and issuers of structured finance securities to provide valuation transparency. This pressure takes two forms. First, there is the red warning flag raised by the absence of a label saying investing in the security is an act of blindly gambling. Second, there is the reduced access to funds as investors limit their exposure to what they can afford to lose while blindly gambling.

However, the Transparency Label Initiative™ did not exist and valuation transparency was not available. Instead a financial crisis occurred.

---

[317] ibid, page 373

FCIC also found regulators aware of pushback

The Financial Crisis Inquiry Commission also confirmed pushback prevents financial regulators from restraining bank risk taking.

> Senior supervisors told the FCIC it was difficult to express their concerns forcefully when financial institutions were generating record-level profits.
>
> The Fed's Roger Cole told the FCIC that supervisors did discuss issues such as whether banks were growing too fast and taking too much risk, but ran into pushback. "Frankly a lot of that pushback was given credence on the part of the firms by the fact that—like a Citigroup was earning $4 to $5 billion a quarter. And that is really hard for a supervisor to successfully challenge. When that kind of money is flowing out quarter after quarter after quarter, and their capital ratios are way above the minimums, it's very hard to challenge."[318]

Mr. Cole's observation shows U.S. bank regulators are not up to the task of restraining bank risk-taking when the banks are making good money. As pointed out by the Nyberg Commission Report, Irish bank regulators were not up to the task of restraining bank risk-taking when the banks are making good money too. Had this failure by bank regulators only occurred in Ireland, it could have been dismissed as unique. As pointed out by the Financial Services Authority Report, UK bank regulators were also not up to the task of restraining bank risk-taking when the banks are making good money. Had this failure by bank regulators only occurred in Ireland and the UK, it could have been dismissed as a coincidence. The fact the U.S. bank regulators also failed shows it is true for bank regulators globally.

This inability of the bank regulators to restrain bank risk-taking when banks are making good money is the reason why the financial system should not be dependent on their doing so in the future. Fortunately, the global financial system is designed so it isn't dependent on bank regulators restraining bank risk-taking. By design, the primary responsibility for restraining bank risk-taking falls on unsecured creditors and shareholders. They exercise this restraint by exerting market discipline. However, they can only exercise market discipline if there is valuation transparency and the banks are required to disclose on an on-going basis their current global asset, liability and off-balance sheet exposure details.

> Supervisors also told the FCIC that they feared aggravating a bank's already-existing problems. For the large banks, the issuance of a formal, public supervisory action taken under the federal banking statutes marked a severe

---

318 ibid, page 307

> regulatory assessment of the bank's risk practices, and it was rarely employed for banks that were determined to be going concerns.[319]

Bank supervisors were scared of taking formal action because of fear of spooking the market. Spooking the markets is only a problem when banks are opaque. It is not a problem when banks provide valuation transparency. With valuation transparency, market participants know what is going on and understand why the regulators took action. In addition,

> Richard Spillenkothen, the Fed's head of supervision until early 2006, attributed supervisory reluctance to "a belief that the traditional, nonpublic (behind-the-scenes) approach to supervision was less confrontational and more likely to induce bank management to cooperate; a desire not to inject an element of contentiousness into what was felt to be a constructive or equable relationship with management; and a fear that financial markets would overreact to public actions, possibly causing a run."...[320]

Valuation transparency enhances the effectiveness of the traditional behind-the-scenes approach to supervision. Bank management has an incentive to cooperate rather than deal with the market discipline it would face should the market find out management was not cooperating with a request from the banking regulators.

> Douglas Roeder, the OCC's senior deputy comptroller for Large Bank Supervision from 2001 to 2010, said that the regulators were hampered by inadequate information from the banks but acknowledged that regulators did not do a good job of intervening at key points in the run-up to the crisis.[321]

Valuation transparency ends regulators being hampered by inadequate information. Valuation transparency provides the data many market participants are able to turn into the information the regulators need. For example, the regulators can use the analytic capabilities of each bank, specifically their assessment of their competitors, to help the regulators assess the banks.

---

319 ibid, page 307

320 ibid, page 307

321 ibid, page 308

The U.S. Senate Report

The IOSCO Code of Conduct to which the rating agencies signed up has been shown to be a toothless wonder. The fact is that despite the checks on compliance with the IOSCO Code, no supervisor appears to have got as much as a sniff of the rot at the heart of the structured finance rating process before it all blew up.

— Charlie McCreevy,
EU Internal Markets Commissioner[322]

Anatomy of a Financial Collapse

After a two-year investigation, the U.S. Senate Permanent Subcommittee on Investigations released its report on the causes of the financial crisis. Like the Nyberg Commission Report, the FSA Report and the Financial Crisis Inquiry Commission Report, this report also showed the central role that opacity played in making the financial crisis possible.

In describing how bankers at the major financial institutions engaged in bad behavior behind a veil of opacity, Senator Carl Levin said,

> The overwhelming evidence is that those institutions deceived their clients and deceived the public, and they were aided and abetted by deferential regulators and credit ratings agencies who had conflicts of interest."[323]

This overwhelming evidence also confirms how much of this behavior would have been prevented if the FDR Framework had been properly enforced and valuation transparency made available. The overwhelming evidence also confirms how much of this behavior would have been prevented if the Transparency Label Initiative™ existed and the banks' attempts to sell opaque financial products were identified with a warning that purchasing this product could be bad for your financial health.

Enforcement would have greatly restricted the ability of financial institutions like Washington Mutual to underwrite risky loans. If investors had been able to do their homework on the mortgage-backed deals its loans went into, investors would have been properly able to assess the risk and would have purchased far fewer deals at a much lower price.

---

322 McCreevy, Charlie (2008, June 16), Regulating in a Global Market, press release by the European Commissioner for Internal Market and Services, European Commission, http://europa.eu/rapid/press-release_SPEECH-08-334_de.htm?locale=de%20/

323 Morgenson, Gretchen, Story, Louise (2011, April 13), Naming Culprits in the Financial Crisis, NY Times, http://www.nytimes.com/2011/04/14/business/14crisis.html?ref=business&_r=0

Enforcement would have mitigated the impact of the deferential regulator. To the extent that Washington Mutual was taking more on-balance sheet risk by holding dodgy loans, its cost of funds would have increased and its stock price decreased to reflect this risk.

Enforcement would have ended the gamesmanship by the investment banks. Investors would have a) seen that the investment banks were reducing their net exposure to sub-prime mortgage backed securities and b) been able to do their homework so as to properly price the securities given the risk in the underlying collateral.

Enforcement would have eliminated the problem of conflicted rating agencies. Investors could have either analyzed the data themselves or they could have used independent third parties with no conflict of interest to analyze the data and properly price the risk.

However, there was not enforcement of the FDR Framework and valuation transparency for structured finance securities and banks. Instead, there was opacity.

Reliance on rating firms

It was the spread of this opacity the credit rating firms enabled. Wall Street took advantage of the fact in an opaque global financial system the ratings provided by these firms were seen as a substitute for an investor doing their own homework. Why were these firms' ratings seen as a substitute for an investor doing their own homework?

The rating firms' business model was based on the rating firms having access to material non-public information that by definition was not available to other market participants. For example, businesses would disclose to the rating firms their current financial performance when the most recent data available to other market participants was as of the end of last quarter. The rating firms would use this material non- public information in their corporate bond ratings.

In addition, Wall Street knew the rating firms were paid by the issuers of the securities. This gave the rating firms an incentive to compete for the issuers' business. Who determined where the issuers would go for a rating? Wall Street's investment bankers.

> Wall Street firms helped design RMBS and CDO securities, worked with the credit rating agencies to obtain ratings for the securities, and sold the securities to investors like pension funds, insurance companies, university endowments, municipalities, and hedge funds.
>
> Without investment grade ratings, Wall Street firms would have had a more difficult time selling structured finance products to investors, because

> each investor would have had to perform its own due diligence review of the product.[324]

Wall Street firms would have had a more difficult time selling structured finance products because investors knew they were being asked to blindly gamble on the contents of a brown paper bag. The primary reason the principle of *caveat emptor* exists in the FDR Framework is to provide investors with an incentive to do their own due diligence in order to know what they own. Investors recognized this was not possible with structured finance securities.

So how to get around the issue of investors being unwilling to blindly gamble because they could not do their own due diligence and know what they owned? Wall Street's solution was the credit rating firms.

Having been conditioned by the corporate bond market, market participants assumed the rating firms' access to all the useful, relevant material non-public information also held true for structured finance securities. Market participants also assumed the rating firms' access to the current performance of the underlying collateral would be reflected in timely changes to the ratings on these securities. The financial crisis showed both of these assumptions to be false.

Besides their access to material non-public information, rating firms also occupied a unique position as their ratings were embedded in federal and state regulations.

> Investment grade credit ratings, thus, purported to simplify the investors' due diligence review, ensured some investors could make a purchase, reduced banks' capital calls, and otherwise enhanced the sales of the structured finance products.[325]

From Wall Street's perspective this was a very good thing as the ratings enabled Wall Street to sell an opaque security. Wall Street sold over $2 trillion of opaque mortgage-backed securities alone.

However, it is a recipe for disaster for investors to rely on third parties they do not hire to assess the risk and value of an investment. As the U.S. Senate Subcommittee pointed out, some of the regulations required specific types of institutional investors to only purchase securities with an investment grade rating. These buyers invested based on what they assumed was someone else's analysis of the contents of a brown paper bag. When the financial crisis hit, these

---

324 U.S. Senate Permanent Subcommittee on Investigations (2011, April 13), Wall Street and the Financial Crisis: Anatomy of a Financial Collapse, http://www.hsgac.senate.gov//imo/media/doc/Financial_Crisis/FinancialCrisisReport.pdf?attempt=2, page 29.

325 ibid, page 29

buyers discovered the analysis had not been done. By relying on the rating firms, these buyers lost billions and were literally left holding the bag.

Financial regulators also relied on ratings and included them in the Basel Committee bank capital requirements. As a result, throughout 2007 and 2008 when the banks knew the subprime mortgage-backed securities they held were not investment grade, they only had to hold capital against these securities based on the rating firms' investment grade rating.

But did rating firms actually look at the underlying assets?

Why did investors or financial regulators accept ratings on brown paper bags as an indication of the value of its contents?

> Here's how one federal bank regulator's handbook put it:
>
> "The rating agencies perform a critical role in structured finance — evaluating the credit quality of the transactions. Such agencies are considered credible because they possess the expertise to evaluate various underlying asset types, and because they do not have a financial interest in a security's cost or yield. Ratings are important because investors generally accept ratings by the major public rating agencies in lieu of conducting a due diligence investigation of the underlying assets and the servicer."[326]

The federal bank regulator handbook said rating firms could be trusted because of their expertise and their lack of a financial interest in a security. But this did not mean the rating firms were free of conflicts of interest. Rating firms are paid to rate securities. As a result, they have an incentive to rate securities. The federal bank regulator handbook also implied the belief the rating firms actually conducted due diligence on the assets in the brown paper bags.

The U.S. Senate Subcommittee report explained in fact the rating firms didn't conduct the due diligence and ongoing monitoring of the underlying assets investors and financial regulators expected.

> CRA analysts relied on their firm's quantitative rating models to calculate the probable default and loss rates for particular pools of assets. These models were handicapped, however, by a lack of relevant performance data for the high risk residential mortgages supporting most RMBS and CDO securities, by a lack of mortgage performance data in an era of stagnating or declining housing prices, by the credit rating agencies' unwillingness to devote sufficient resources to update their models, and by the failure of the models to incorporate accurate

326 ibid, page 30

> correlation assumptions predicting how defaulting mortgages might affect other mortgages.[327]

The rating firms didn't conduct the due diligence and ongoing monitoring of the underlying assets investors and financial regulators expected because they couldn't. The rating firms didn't have all the useful, relevant information in an appropriate, timely manner for assessing the risk of these securities. However, the lack of adequate data didn't stop the rating firms from issuing ratings.

Inadequacies in the data

Adequate data was necessary if the ratings were going to be accurate. For structured finance securities, the ratings relied on the performance track record of nearly identical assets in the calculation of probable default and loss rates for the pool of assets used to back a specific security. Of course, this performance track record didn't exist for subprime mortgages.

> From 2004 through 2007, many RMBS and CDO securities were comprised of residential mortgages that were not like those that had been modeled in the past. As one S&P email observed:
>
> "[T]he assumptions and the historical data used [in the models] ... never included the performance of these types of residential mortgage loans .... The data was gathered and computed during a time when loans with over 100% LTV or no stated income were rare."...[328]

The rating firms tried to compensate for the absence of a performance track record for nearly identical assets.

> In fact, Moody's RMBS rating model was not even used to rate subprime mortgages until December 2006; prior to that time, Moody's used a system of "benchmarking" in which it rated a subprime mortgage pool by comparing it to other subprime pools Moody's had already rated.[329]

Another way they compensated for the lack of a performance track record was through the use of HPA. What in the world is HPA? HPA stands for house price appreciation.

House price appreciation is a get out of jail free card for both bankers and rating firms. For bankers, house price appreciation bails them out of poor

---

327 ibid, Page 288

328 ibid, page 288

329 ibid, page 288

underwriting. It bails them out because even though the borrower might default on the mortgage, the value of the house has appreciated by enough so when it is sold the proceeds repay the mortgage, missed interest payments and any delinquency related fees. For rating firms, house price appreciation bails them out because even if there are more defaults than expected, it minimizes losses incurred on the mortgages and justifies the assigned ratings.

I will always remember the first time I came across the term HPA. An investment banker introduced me to HPA. It was memorable because of the word appreciation. I asked why the use of appreciation as opposed to the word change. After all, house prices didn't have to rise and could even fall. The response was the U.S. had never had house prices decline on a national basis. Oops.

House prices not only stagnated in the run-up to the financial crisis, but they began to fall. This exposed the inadequacies of how the rating firms assigned ratings in the absence of all the useful, relevant information.

> As one February 2007 presentation from a Deutsche Bank investment banker explained, the models used to calculate "subprime mortgage lending criteria and bond subordination levels are based largely on performance experience that was mostly accumulated since the mid-1990s, when the nation's housing market has been booming."
>
> A former managing director in Moody's Structured Finance Group put it this way: "[I]t was 'like observing 100 years of weather in Antarctica to forecast the weather in Hawaii.'"[330]

Basing ratings on bad data had the same predictable bad outcome as forecasting the weather in Hawaii based on the weather in Antarctica.

> The absence of relevant data for use in RMBS modeling left the credit rating agencies unable to accurately predict mortgage default and loss rates when housing prices stopped climbing. The absence of relevant performance data for high risk mortgage products in an era of stagnant or declining housing prices impacted the rating of not only RMBS transactions, but also CDOs, which typically included RMBS securities and relied heavily on RMBS credit ratings.[331]

In short, the U.S. Senate Subcommittee found that the absence of relevant data for evaluating RMBS or CDO transactions meant the rating firms couldn't accurately assess the risk of the transactions. A fact the rating firms conveniently failed to mention to the other market participants.

---

330 ibid, page 289

331 ibid, page 289

Limited effort by rating firms to get and use necessary data

Consistent with the notion the other market participants didn't need to know the rating firms were blindly guessing due to inadequate data, the rating firms also showed a remarkably cavalier attitude about getting good data for themselves. Had the firms seriously attempted to get the necessary data, they would have discovered that the data was not just difficult to obtain, but because of how the securities were designed it was impossible to obtain.

At the core of the rating firm business model is the idea of these firms independently assessing the useful, relevant information about a security in an effort to make their ratings as accurate as possible. If the rating firms do not have this information to assess, what exactly is the value they offer to investors or other market participants?

One of the main costs of the rating firm business model is acquiring this useful, relevant information and creating the analytical tools to assess it. As shown by Moody's, rating firms preferred not to spend the money to acquire this information and in fact did so for marketing purposes rather than to improve the quality of their ratings.

Moody's senior managers even expressed skepticism about whether new loan data was needed and, in fact, generally did not purchase new loan data for a four-year period, from 2002 to 2006.

In a 2000 internal email exchange, the head of Moody's Structured Finance Group at the time, Brian Clarkson, wrote the following regarding the purchasing of data for Moody's RMBS model:

> "I have a wild thought also — let[']s not even consider BUYING anymore data, programs, software or companies until we figure out what we have and what we intend to do with what we have.... I suggest we spend less time asking for more data and software (I have not seen anything that sets forth the gains in revenue from such spending[332]

In response to Brian Clarkson's email, a managing director wrote:

> "As you know, I don't think we need to spend a lot of $ or resources to improve the model from an analytic perspective; but I'd need to defer to people more in the loop (looks like you're that person) on whether the marketing component mandates some announcement of model and data improvement. ...[333]

---

332 ibid, page 290

333 ibid, page 290

As everyone knows, bad data going into a model produces bad results coming out of the model. The best analytical model doesn't provide worthwhile results if the data is bad.

> Make sure you talk to Noel and maybe Fons about the decision to buy the data; I was invited to the original meeting so that the powers that be (at the time) could understand the data originally used. I felt that the arguments for buying the data and re-inventing the model were not persuasive .... The most convincing argument for buying the data was that it would be a cornerstone for marketing, that S&P touted the size of their database as a competitive advantage and that this was why they had the market share advantage."[334]

Moody's didn't perceive getting good data as a necessity for producing accurate ratings, but rather simply as a marketing tool. S&P saws acquiring data as a source of competitive advantage. However, having data by itself is not sufficient. It needs to be combined with useful methods of analysis.

> the former head of the S&P RMBS Ratings Group, Frank Raiter, who worked at S&P until 2005, told ... the Subcommittee ... even though S&P revenues had increased dramatically and were generated in large part by the RMBS Group, senior management had no interest in committing the resources needed to update the RMBS model with improved criteria from the new loan data.
>
> Mr. Raiter said that S&P did not spend sufficient money on better analytics, because S&P already dominated the RMBS ratings market: "[T]he RMBS group enjoyed the largest ratings market share among the three major rating agencies (often 92% or better), and improving the model would not add to S&P's revenues."[335]

Like Moody's, S&P didn't see improving the accuracy of its ratings as a competitive priority. After all, so long as house price appreciation continued to occur, any rating mistakes were effectively covered up. Of course, for investors who were dependent on these ratings, this unwillingness to spend money to improve the accuracy of the ratings proved very costly when house prices stagnated and then fell.

> The lack of performance data for high risk residential mortgage products, the lack of mortgage performance data in an era of stagnating or declining housing prices, the failure to expend resources to improve their model analytics, and incorrect correlation assumptions meant that the RMBS and CDO models

334 ibid, page 290

335 ibid, page 292

> used by Moody's and S&P were out of date, technically deficient, and could not provide accurate default and loss predictions to support the credit ratings being issued.
>
> Yet Moody's and S&P analysts told the Subcommittee that their analysts relied heavily on their model outputs to project the default and loss rates for RMBS and CDO pools and rate RMBS and CDO securities….[336]

Despite the known lack of good information going into their models, the rating firms continued to provide ratings.

One of the ways S&P made up for its lack of good information was its use of dummy assets in rating collateralized debt obligations (CDOs). S&P would rate a CDO using assets that were suppose to be similar to the assets that would be in the CDO when it was sold to investors. Of course, if the assets in the final CDO were of lower quality than the assets used in the rating process, the ratings on the CDO would be overstated.

The lesson from the use of dummy assets is you cannot assess the risk of, value or rate a security when you do not even know what is in the security.

Historical data becomes available

One of the issues the rating firms faced was the question of how long to rely on their statistical models for rating a structured finance security and when to use actual performance information on the assets underlying the securities. The argument for using actual performance data is it is a more accurate indicator of future performance than a statistical model. The argument against using actual performance is it does not incorporate expectations of future performance.

If these were the only two choices, the decision of which to use would be difficult. However, there is a third choice. Use the actual performance data in a model that allows the user to incorporate expectations of future performance. The use of actual performance data anchors the analysis to the reality of each security.

Some CRA employees expressed concern about the limitations placed on their ability to alter ratings to reflect expected performance of the rated securities. In a July 2007 email just before the mass ratings downgrades began, for example, an S&P senior executive raised concerns about these limitations to the head of the RMBS Surveillance Group as follows:

> "Overall, our ratings should be based on our *expectations* of performance, not solely the *month to month* performance record, which will only be backward looking. ... Up to this point, Surveillance has been 'limited' in *when* we can

---

336 ibid, page 294

> downgrade a rating (only *after* it has experienced realized losses), how far we can adjust the rating (no more than 3 notches at a time is preferred), and how high up the capital structure we can go (not downgrading higher rated classes, if they 'pass' our stressed cash flow runs)."
>
> In addition, many of the RMBS loans were less than a year old, making any performance data less significant and difficult to analyze. In others words, the loans were too unseasoned or new to offer any real predictive performance value.[337]

As actual performance data becomes available, it also raises the question of should a security be re-rated. The rating firms were responsible for monitoring these securities and market participants assumed they would change the rating on these securities to reflect their actual and expected performance.

From the rating firm perspective, there were several issues with re-rating the securities, particularly if there was a downgrade. First, it required resources to review the ratings. Second, downgrading the securities would have disrupted the market "upsetting investment bankers and investors."[338]

> When asked about the failure of Moody's and S&P to retest existing securities after their model updates in 2006, the global head trader for CDOs from Deutsche Bank told the Subcommittee that he believed the credit rating agencies did not retest them, because to do so would have meant significant downgrades and "they did not want to upset the apple cart."
>
> Instead, the credit rating agencies waited until 2007, when the high risk mortgages underlying the outstanding RMBS and CDO securities incurred record delinquencies and defaults and then, based upon the actual loan performance, instituted mass ratings downgrades....[339]

Ultimately, when market participants were able to get enough data the rating firms were effectively forced to downgrade their ratings.

The lesson here is by requiring valuation transparency, market participants are able to exert discipline on the rating firms to make their initial and ongoing ratings reflect what is actually happening.

By requiring valuation transparency, market participants could also have seen the epidemic of mortgage fraud. Recall the federal bank regulator's handbook assumed as part of its rating process, the rating firms would conduct due

---

337 ibid, page 299

338 ibid, page 300

339 ibid, page 303

diligence into the assets underlying each structured finance deal. This assumption was totally wrong.

> The former head of S&P's RMBS Group, Frank Raiter, stated in his prepared testimony for the Subcommittee hearing that the S&P rating process did not include any "due diligence" review of the loan tape or any requirement for the provider of the loan tape to certify its accuracy. He stated: "We were discouraged from even using the term 'due diligence' as it was believed to expose S&P to liability." Fraud was also not factored into the RMBS or CDO quantitative models.[340]

Having not bothered to do any due diligence on the actual mortgages, the rating firms then used fraud as an excuse for their ratings not being accurate.

> In 2008, Moody's CEO Ray McDaniel told a panel at the World Economic Forum:
>
> "In hindsight, it is pretty clear that there was a failure in some key assumptions that were supporting our analytics and our models. ... [One reason for the failure was that the] 'information quality' [given to Moody's,] both the complete[ness] and veracity, was deteriorating."[341]

The lesson relearned as a result of the rating firms assigning ratings to opaque securities is the need to require every security provide valuation transparency. With valuation transparency, market participants are not reliant on the rating firms or their ratings. Instead, market participants can independently analyze the disclosed information and assess the risk and value of each security. Of course, if every security provided valuation transparency, then the rating firms themselves would become dramatically less important and influential.

With valuation transparency, competition based on the quality/accuracy of the ratings would also be introduced in the ratings world. With a level playing field in terms of access to data, new firms could enter the rating business and focus on their areas of expertise. A premium would be placed on being right with the rating. Issuers would want to go to the firms with the best reputation for accuracy in their ratings.

Each of the investigations into the causes of the financial crisis found opacity was necessary for the financial crisis to have occurred. Had the Transparency Label Initiative™ existed, the opacity necessary for the financial crisis to occur would have either been greatly reduced or entirely eliminated. As a

---

340 ibid, page 311

341 ibid, page 312

result, the financial crisis would not have occurred and, to the extent there was a problem in the financial system, it would not have been so damaging.

But how did we get to the point where Wall Street and the City were able to inject opacity into a global financial system designed to embrace transparency and the benevolent invisible hand in the first place?

The Queen of England turned to the economics profession for an answer.

Chapter 13

WHERE WAS EVERYONE ELSE WHEN OPACITY CREPT IN?

It slightly worries me that when people find a problem, they rush to judgment of what to do.

—*Janet Yellen*[342]

Prior to the Queen of England's intervention, like the bankers, the economics profession appeared to have escaped any responsibility for its actions including promoting the efficient market hypothesis in the run-up to the financial crisis. After the crisis hit, life for the economists was normal except now they were volunteering their solutions to the crisis. Their ideas continued to find a receptive audience. Why? Politicians and financial regulators have an interest in justifying their policy choice by trotting out an economist whose views support the politician's or financial regulator's choice of policy. There is a belief the name of the institution, particularly when the economist works for a prominent university, or the awards the economist has won adds credibility to the policy.

But why did these economists not pause before offering their solutions and listened to the major lesson of the Great Depression that for opacity based financial crises it is valuation transparency that restores confidence, financial markets and the real economy?

They didn't listen because Wall Street's Opacity Protection Team, including politicians and financial regulators, rewards solutions that address the symptoms of opacity without addressing opacity itself. In effect, economics is a "discipline hijacked by banks"[343] to prove that what makes them the most money ought to be government policy.

---

342 Uchitelle, Louis (2002, July 28), Broken System? Tweak It, They Say, NY Times, http://www.nytimes.com/2002/07/28/business/broken-system-tweak-it-they-say.html

343 Essex, Martin (2012, January 20), What Value Economic Research?, Wall Street Journal blogs, http://blogs.wsj.com/source/2012/01/20/what-value-economic-research/?mod=WSJBlog&mod=thesource

The Queen's Question: Why did economists fail to predict the financial crash?

During an official visit to the London School of Economics in November 2008, the Queen held the economics profession accountable and asked a professor why the economics profession had failed to predict our current financial crisis. Her simple question of what went wrong and why did virtually every economist and economic policymaker fail to see the financial crisis coming now haunts the economics profession.

A possible answer to her question can be found by examining the assumptions underlying macro-econometric models. Dating back to when I worked with these models at the Federal Reserve, the models essentially excluded the financial sector. Banks and financial markets could be ignored as they were seen as intermediaries. Savings flowed through them on their way to their most productive uses. Banks and bankers were seen as benign actors.

Of course, it turns out bankers are not benign actors at all. The reason there are regulations is to control the bankers' behavior. By assuming the banker are benign actors and wouldn't manage to make large portions of the global financial system opaque, the models and hence the economics profession were doomed to fail at either predicting the financial crisis or how the economy would respond to the different policies adopted after the crisis.

The economic actors in these models were also assumed to behave rationally. Of course, the dot.com and housing bubbles were testament to the idea these actors do not behave rationally. Therefore, a possible answer for why economists didn't see the financial crisis coming was the absence of a few behavioral economics equations in their models.

The only problem with adding a few behavioral economic equations to the models is these equations don't account for the effects of Wall Street's introduction of opacity into the global financial system. As a result, the models with behavioral economics equations would be as blind towards predicting a financial crisis as the current econometric models without a few behavioral economics equations.

In response to the Queen's Questions, economists could have followed the lead of two members of the IMF Research Department and replied "Ma'am, to see this one coming would have ruined our perfect record of failure to see it coming".[344] They showed for the economics profession "the record of failure to predict recessions is virtually unblemished."[345]

---

344 Ahir, Hites and Loungani, Prakash (2014, March), *Can Economists Forecast Recessions? Some Evidence from the Great Recession*, Forecasters.org, http://forecasters.org/wp/wp-content/uploads/PLoungani_OracleMar2014.pdf, page 1

345 ibid , page 1

Rather than look at the shortcomings of their models, economists answered the Queen's Question by instead blaming "a failure of the collective imagination of many bright people, both in this country and internationally, to understand the risks to the system as a whole".[346]

Of course, there were economists who were exceptions that not only understood the risks to the system as a whole prior to the crash but spoke out about it. This very, very short list of economists includes William White, Claudio Borio, Dean Baker and Raghuram Rajan. At the time they spoke out, each of them had their work dismissed by the profession as it was based on an analysis of objective evidence with no apparent economic theory to support their conclusion. The necessary formalized economic theory did not arrive until I developed the FDR Framework.

Without the FDR Framework, how could economists be expected to have predicted the financial crisis when the need for buyers and sellers to have valuation transparency and access to all the useful, relevant information in an appropriate, timely manner is briefly implied, but not taught at length in Economics 101? In 23 leading principles of economics textbooks, not one discussed opacity or how the presence of opacity in the financial system was the result of a government failure that produced a market failure.[347]

Instead of confessing they forgot or worse didn't understand the role of valuation transparency and opacity in the proper functioning of markets, the economists offered up as an excuse even though we are bright, nobody could possibly expect us to understand all the risks in the modern, complex global financial system. Left unsaid is the fact that nobody asked them to understand all the risks in our modern, complex global financial system. They were asked to understand, advocate for and teach valuation transparency is needed for properly functioning markets and opacity is associated with outcomes like the Great Depression.

They failed to see the financial crisis coming not because of a lack of intelligence or failure of imagination. They failed to see the financial crisis coming because in their first course in economics the professor never said the invisible hand **only** works for markets where there is valuation transparency and buyers and sellers have access to all the useful, relevant information in an appropriate, timely manner.

---

346 Douzinas, Costas (2011, December 15), The IMF must realise that, in Greece, the treatment is worse than the disease, The Guardian, http://www.theguardian.com/commentisfree/2011/dec/15/imf-greece-treatment-worse-disease

347 author updated Gwartney, James, Fike, Rosemarie (2014), Public Choice versus the Benevolent Omniscient Planner Model of Government: Evidence from Principles Textbooks, http://mailer.fsu.edu/~jgwartne/garnet-jgwartne/Documents/Gwartney%20Fike%20Public%20Choice.pdf

The Efficient Market Hypothesis

Andy Haldane, the Bank of England's chief economist and former executive director for financial stability, offered an explanation for why the economic profession did not see the financial crisis coming. In an interview with OurKingdom, the UK arm of openDemocracy, Mr. Haldane said of the economics and finance profession:

> We started to believe that what were assumptions were actually a description of reality, and therefore that the models were a description of reality, and therefore were dependable for policy analysis.
>
> With hindsight, that was a pretty significant error.[348]

In plain English, economists cling with almost religious fervor to the assumptions underlying their models.

Paul Krugman, a Nobel prize winning economics professor, confirmed Mr. Haldane's insight that the economics profession had come to believe the assumptions underlying its economic models were in fact a description of reality. In a speech, Professor Krugman used Mr. Haldane's insight to point out it was the wide-spread belief in the efficient market hypothesis (EMH) and its assumptions that was responsible for the errors in policy analysis and why the economics profession didn't foresee the financial crisis.

> So why were so relatively few economists willing to call the bubble? I suspect that efficient market theory, in a loose sense — the belief that markets couldn't possibly be getting things that wrong — played a major role. And in that sense there was a structural flaw in the profession….[349]

According to Professor Krugman, the economics profession came to believe the efficient market hypothesis' assumption market prices reflected all public and hidden information was in fact reality. In reality, reality was far different. For example, structured finance securities were designed to be opaque so Wall Street and the City could benefit off the mispricing by investors.

Professor Krugman appears to imply in its belief in the efficient market model the economics profession also confused "cause and effect". Under this belief, it was the efficient market hypothesis that was responsible for and guaranteed prices reflected strict adherence to the combination of disclosure and

---

348 Aldrick, Philip (2012, August 1), Bank official admits economists were to blame for recession, The Telegraph, http://www.telegraph.co.uk/finance/economics/9442430/Bank-official-admits-economists-were-to-blame-for-recession.html

349 Krugman, Paul (2011), The Profession and the Crisis, Eastern Economic Journal (2011) 37, 307–312. doi:10.1057/eej.2011.8, http://www.palgrave-journals.com/eej/journal/v37/n3/full/eej20118a.html

caveat emptor. In reality, it is strict adherence under the FDR Framework to the combination of disclosure and *caveat emptor* that is the necessary and sufficient condition for pricing under the efficient market hypothesis to hold true.

> It's quite remarkable how few warnings we had that the system might be dangerously fragile. By all means, let's give credit to people like Rajan who saw some of it; but the very fact that such people were given a hard time for their analysis is telling about the profession.[350]

In the absence of the FDR Framework as an economic model of how the global financial markets are designed to operate, the analysis of the economists providing a warning was easy to dismiss. All the economics profession had to do was say because of the efficient market hypothesis market prices couldn't be that far wrong.

With the FDR Framework, the role of opacity in market's not properly pricing securities is made explicit. The warning from these economists could not have been dismissed without the economics profession showing that valuation transparency actually existed.

Economic profession undone by old evil: opacity

Professor Krugman goes on to say,

> One can make excuses for the failure of the economics profession to foresee that the 2008 financial crisis would happen. It's much harder to make such excuses for much of the profession's failure to realize that such a thing *could* happen….
>
> My best answer is that they were caught up in the spirit of the times, with its faith in the wisdom of markets and of the financial industry….
>
> But to argue, or even to think about, the possibility that the old evils could manifest themselves in new forms would have been to question the whole basis of decades of policy, not to mention the foundations of a very lucrative industry.
>
> You don't have to invoke raw corruption (although there may have been some of that) to see why this was a line of thought few were willing to pursue. And by not pursuing that line of thought, the profession fell down badly on the job.[351]

An economist didn't need to question the whole basis of decades of the FDR Framework as policy, but simply ask how the banking sector was becoming so profitable. An obvious question since history shows banking sector profits and opacity go hand in hand. For example, in the run-up to the Great Depression, bank profitability and opacity in the financial system both peaked.

---

350 ibid

351 ibid

The economics profession fell down on the job because every year it could have asked what are the greatest sources of opacity in the financial system and what can be done to bring valuation transparency to them.

For example, George Akerlof's work on accounting control fraud should have resulted in the economics profession pushing to require banks to provide valuation transparency and disclose on an on-going basis their current asset, liability and off-balance sheet exposure details.

For example, Joseph Stiglitz's work on information asymmetry should have resulted in the economics profession pushing to require that structured finance products report on an observable event basis (where an observable event includes a payment, delinquency, default or modification involving the underlying collateral) with disclosure occurring after the close of business on the day the observable event occurred.

For example, the economic profession could have pointed out having banks with an incentive to manipulate the LIBOR interest rate setting this rate behind closed doors would be inviting problems.

Since the economics profession was not looking at where the financial system was becoming opaque, I wondered what economists who studied the Great Depression looked at if not how the financial system was redesigned to prevent the old evil of opacity from manifesting itself. To find out, I constructed Table 13-1 using Amazon's word search on former Fed Chair Bernanke's book, *Essays on the Great Depression*. Published in 2000, it summarized two decades of his research into the "causes and propagation of the Great Depression"[352]

Table 4: References to Key Concepts in *Essays on the Great Depression*

Word Searched	Number of Results
Banking Panic	46
Monetary Policy	41
Bank Runs	16
Deposit Insurance	4
Fundamental Restructurings (of the banks)	1
Securities Act	0
Disclosure	0
Opacity	0
Transparency	0

352 Bernanke, Ben S. (2000), Essays on the Great Depression, preface page viii. Princeton, New Jersey: Princeton University Press

Not surprisingly, Fed Chair Bernanke paid considerable attention to monetary policy in response to a financial crisis. He also looked at banking panics and bank runs. However, he paid little to no attention to opacity as the source of banking panics or runs. Similarly, he didn't look at the actual reforms of the banking and financial systems during the Great Depression to prevent opacity's return. Had he studied the role of opacity in the run-up to the Great Depression, he would have found it was the necessary condition for a financial crisis generated by the financial system to occur. In addition, he would have seen that monetary policy is capable of buying time until valuation transparency is restored in all the opaque corners of the financial system. But, by itself, monetary policy cannot do much about the problem of opacity that has undermined trust and created uncertainty throughout the financial system.

Economists like Fed Chair Bernanke also studied what he called the "financial accelerator".[353]

> I think the way we got started was that I had done some earlier work with Fed Chair Bernanke, and we were interested in understanding why there was such a sharp contraction in the Great Depression and why it was so persistent. We were drawn to a theory originally put forward by Irving Fisher in 1933, the debt-deflation theory. Fisher argued that the deflation at the time increased the real debt burden of borrowers, and that led to a reduction in their spending, which put downward pressure on the economy, and further deflation, and so on. What we saw in that was a kind of feedback mechanism between the real sector and the balance sheets in the financial sector that amplified the cycle.
>
> That's what we wanted to capture with the financial accelerator, that is, the mutual feedback between the real sector and the financial sector. We also wanted to capture the primary importance of balance sheets—when balance sheets weaken, that causes credit to tighten, leading to downward pressure on the real economy, which further weakens balance sheets. I think that's what one saw in the financial crisis.
>
> So we were inspired by Fisher's debt-deflation theory, and we were trying to formalize that idea using modern methods. Then we found some other implications, like the role of credit spreads: When balance sheets weaken, credit spreads increase, and credit spreads are a natural indicator of financial distress.
>
> And again, you saw something similar in the current crisis — with a weakening of the balance sheets of financial institutions and households, you saw credit spreads going up, and the real economy going down.

---

353 Bernanke, Ben, Gertler, Mark, Gilchrist, Simon (1996, February), The Financial Accelerator and the Flight to Quality, The Review of Economics and Statistics, Vol. 78, No. 1. (Feb, 1996), pp. 1-15 http://www.ssc.wisc.edu/~mchinn/restat_96.pdf The financial accelerator framework attempts to describe the link between the real economy and the financial system.

> I didn't speak to Fed Chair Bernanke a lot during the height of the crisis. But one moment I caught him, asked him how things were going, and he said,
> "Well, on the bright side, we may have some evidence for the financial accelerator."[354]

The financial accelerator ignores how the FDR Administration redesigned the banking system so it could absorb the losses on the excess debt in the financial system while continuing to provide the credit the real economy needs for growth. By concentrating the damage from excess debt on the book equity accounts of the banks, this redesign eliminated the negative feedback mechanism between the real sector and the financial sector. This set in place the mechanism by which the financial sector's balance sheet would save the real sector from the harm caused by the excess debt in the financial system and address the weak household balance sheets caused by this excess debt. Of course, in the presence of opacity, policymakers were able to pursue the Japanese Model. Under the Japanese Model, policymakers bypassed the redesign of the banking system and inflicted on the real economy the excess debt driven negative feedback mechanism captured by the financial accelerator.

The financial accelerator model has some other serious shortcomings. Specifically, the model misses banks are not the only lenders in the global financial system and the other lenders provide much more credit than the banks. When the financial crisis began on August 9, 2007, more credit was being provided by the so-called shadow banking system, approximately $20 trillion globally, than the regulated global banking system, approximately $14 trillion. Much of the credit held by the shadow banking system went to the small businesses and households the financial accelerator model said banks would abandon in a flight to quality when asset values declined. The model also misses that the condition of bank balance sheets only limits the total amount of loans banks can hold and not their ability to originate loans and resell them to other market participants like hedge funds, insurance companies and pension funds. What limits the banks ability to distribute loans to other market participants or to the shadow banking system is the absence of valuation transparency. Without valuation transparency, investors are unwilling to provide credit through the shadow banking system because they cannot assess the risk of and do not know what they are buying.

Instead of promoting valuation transparency where there was opacity in the financial system, the economics profession effectively assumed away the problem under the efficient market hypothesis.

---

354 Gertler, Mark (2013), Interview, Richmond Fed, https://www.richmondfed.org/publications/research/econ_focus/2013/q4/pdf/interview.pdf

Then when the financial crisis hit, the economics profession showed no clue that the financial system was based on the FDR Framework and suddenly started inventing and promoting flawed ideas like the concept of informationally-insensitive debt.

Attempting to explain the financial crisis while ignoring opacity

In a May 9, 2009 paper for the Atlanta Fed, Yale Professor Gary Gorton introduced the concept of "informationally-insensitive debt".[355] He claimed the various types of debt that exist span a range of different information sensitivities from insensitive to sensitive.

Professor Gorton described one end of this range.

> Intuitively, informationally-insensitive debt is debt that no one needs to devote a lot of resources to investigating. It is exactly designed to avoid that.[356]

He provided two examples of informationally-insensitive debt: demand deposits and the senior tranches of securitized debt. He does note a difference between these two types of debt. The senior tranches of securitized debt are not riskless like demand deposits.

Let's begin to untangle the mess this paper makes of the simple concepts that underlie our financial system starting with the notion of informationally-insensitive debt as a descriptor.

Debt that is insensitive to information does not exist.

Even a six-year old opening their first bank account intuitively understands investments, including demand deposits, are sensitive to information and that it makes sense to acquire and assess this information before investing. Before opening the bank account, the six-year old learned money is valuable and shouldn't be lost. So a natural question for a six-year old to ask prior to handing their money to a banker they have never met before is "how do I know I am going to get my money back?" The question is a simple request for all the useful, relevant information in an appropriate, timely manner for assessing the risk and valuing an investment.

Under the combination of disclosure and *caveat emptor*, all investments, including both debt and equity, are always sensitive to information. Because of their responsibility for all losses, investors have an incentive to devote all the

355 Gorton, Gary (2009, May 9), Slapped in the Face by the Invisible Hand: Banking and the Panic of 2007, Atlanta Fed, http://www.frbatlanta.org/news/conferen/09fmc/gorton.pdf, page 10

356 ibid, page 10

resources that are necessary to investigate those investments that are of interest to them.

The only question is how much effort is required to process all the useful, relevant information for any specific investment.

Some investments, like demand deposits, require little effort by investors to assess all the useful, relevant information. If the size of the investment in demand deposits is equal to or less than the amount of the government guarantee, as soon as the investor knows the demand deposits are covered by the government guarantee they are done with their initial assessment of loss. Once the investment in demand deposits is made, investors monitor the investment by tracking information on either the government announcing a change in the amount of the guarantee or something happening to the sovereign's creditworthiness.

Other investments, like senior tranches of structured finance securities, require a significant amount of effort by investors to assess initially and on an ongoing basis. To assess the risk and value the senior tranches of a structured finance security, an investor or third party hired by the investor would use a valuation model that combines the structure of the deal, the current performance of the underlying collateral and the projected future performance of the underlying collateral.

Were senior tranches of subprime deals designed for lazy investors?

Professor Gorton argues investors have a need for securities that don't require a lot of resources to assess. This may be true, but this does not mean that investors are too lazy to apply the resources necessary to assess the risk of each security they invest in.

By suggesting that investors are lazy, Professor Gorton ignores the possibility that there might be opacity that prevents investors from devoting the resources that are necessary to analyzing the senior tranches of securitized debt.

From the Commonwealth of Virginia complaint, we had confirmation that investors were not lazy, but were fully capable of and interested in assessing the information if it had been made available. In discussing how the losses on these securities could have been avoided had there been transparency, the complaint observes "This means that misrepresented loans and misrepresented securities experienced delinquency, default, and value loss at a rate that could have been anticipated had they been represented accurately in the first place."[357]

As far as I can tell, structured finance securities were designed to be opaque and prevent investors from being able to perform a resource intensive assessment

[357] Commonwealth of Virginia, Page 305

rather than to tap some unmet investor need to avoid a resource intensive risk assessment.

Furthermore, investors were interested in applying the necessary resources to assess the risk of the senior tranches of securitized debt, but the banks prevented them from accessing this information. This featured prominently in the statement of facts and press release announcing JPMorgan's November 19, 2013 $13 billion settlement for misleading investors about securities containing toxic mortgages.

> On some occasions, prospective investors in mortgage-backed securities marketed by JPMorgan requested specific data on the underlying loan pools, including information on due diligence results and loan characteristics, such as combined-loan-to-value ratios. JPMorgan employees sometimes declined to provide information to such investors concerning such loan data, including combined loan-to-value ratio data. In some instances, JPMorgan employees also provided data on the percentage of defective loans identified in its own due diligence process as a percentage of the pool that was acquired rather than as a percentage of the diligence sample, without disclosing the basis of their calculation.[358]
>
> The settlement includes a statement of facts, in which JPMorgan acknowledges that it regularly represented to RMBS investors that the mortgage loans in various securities complied with underwriting guidelines. Contrary to those representations, as the statement of facts explains, on a number of different occasions, JPMorgan employees knew that the loans in question did not comply with those guidelines and were not otherwise appropriate for securitization, but they allowed the loans to be securitized — and those securities to be sold — without disclosing this information to investors. This conduct, along with similar conduct by other banks that bundled toxic loans into securities and misled investors who purchased those securities, contributed to the financial crisis.[359]

In the run-up to the financial crisis, investors knew they did not have access to all useful, relevant information in an appropriate, timely manner. Without this information, it was not a question of did investors need to do the assessment or not. Investors were prevented by opacity from spending the considerable amount of time and effort needed to analyze the senior tranches of securitized debt.

---

358 U.S. Department of Justice (2013, November 19), Statement of Facts on JPMorgan's mortgage-backed securities settlement, U.S. Department of Justice, http://www.justice.gov/iso/opa/resources/94320131119151031990622.pdf, page 6.

359 U.S. Department of Justice (2013, November 19), Press Release announcing JPMorgan's mortgage-backed securities settlement, U.S. Department of Justice, http://www.justice.gov/opa/pr/2013/November/13-ag-1237.html

Clearly, investors thought there was a need for this type of analysis and they solved this problem with the regulators' stamp of approval by turning to the rating firms.

Investors assumed that the rating firms had all the useful, relevant information because a significant part of the rating firms' business model is having access to material non-public information. In the case of structured finance securities, it was assumed that this material non-public information was the current asset performance information investors wanted but could not access. In addition, investors assumed the rating firms were devoting a lot of resources to investigating this debt.

Based on all these assumptions investors felt they could piggyback off of the rating firms' efforts and trust their risk assessment as revealed in their ratings.

It came as a surprise to investors who had effectively outsourced the risk analysis to the rating firms when in September 2007 the rating firms provided testimony to the U.S. Congress that they did not have any material non-public information on structured finance deals and therefore they were not doing the assessment that investors assumed they were doing.[360]

The result was completely predictable. Upon hearing that the rating firms weren't doing the resource intensive analysis, the investors tried once again to do it themselves. Unlike the database Pershing Capital constructed in early 2008 showing which bond insurers were exposed to which CDOs, investors went looking for the current performance of the individual mortgages backing each deal. When the investors realized that the banks would not make all the useful, relevant data available and therefore they couldn't go through the investment process, the investors stopped buying or selling the senior tranches of private label mortgage-backed securities, and the market froze.

According to Professor Gorton,

> a "banking panic" occurs when "informationally-insensitive" debt becomes "informationally-sensitive" due to a shock, in this case the shock to subprime mortgage values due to house prices falling.[361]

---

360 Testimony of Vickie A. Tillman, Executive Vice President, Standard & Poor's Credit Market Services, Before the Committee on Banking, Housing and Urban Affairs, United States Senate (2007, September 26), http://www.banking.senate.gov/public/index.cfm?FuseAction=Files.View&FileStore_id=e8329689-cdca-4a9e-b927-bb744f58792f

361 Gorton, Gary (2009, May 9), Slapped in the Face by the Invisible Hand: Banking and the Panic of 2007, Atlanta Fed, http://www.frbatlanta.org/news/conferen/09fmc/gorton.pdf, page 5.

If a "shock" like a drop in house prices can cause debt that was previously informationally-insensitive to become informationally-sensitive, this debt was always sensitive to information and the need for investors to dedicate the necessary resources to assessing. This is just as one would expect under the combination of disclosure and *caveat emptor*. After all, a decline in house prices is information.

The passage of time has also put to rest the idea investors are lazy and have a huge need for debt that doesn't take many resources to analyze. If investors were lazy and had this huge need, the private label mortgage market would not be a fraction of its pre-crisis size as Wall Street would be happy to create these securities and the rating firms would be happy to rate them.

What triggered the financial crisis?

Finally, it might be useful to see how Professor Gorton's informationally-insensitive debt model and the FDR Framework describe the events of August 2007 and therefore how the entire subsequent financial crisis should be interpreted and responded to. This comparison is necessary for several reasons including Fed Chair Bernanke adopted the idea of informationally-insensitive debt and used it when he explained why the financial crisis occurred.

According to the November 9, 2010 version of Professors' Gary Gorton and Andrew Metrick's *Securitized Banking and Run on the Repo* paper,

> The banking system has changed, with "securitized banking" playing an increasing role alongside traditional banking. One large area of securitized banking — the securitization of subprime home mortgages — began to weaken in early 2007, and continued to decline throughout 2007 and 2008. But, the weakening of subprime per se was not the shock that caused systemic problems.
>
> The first systemic event occurs in August 2007, with a shock to the repo market that we demonstrate using the "LIB-OIS," the spread between the LIBOR and the OIS, as a proxy.
>
> The reason that this shock occurred in August 2007 — as opposed to any other month of 2007 — is perhaps unknowable.
>
> We hypothesize that the market slowly became aware of the risks associated with the subprime market, which then led to doubts about repo collateral and bank solvency.
>
> At some point — August 2007 in this telling — a critical mass of such fears led to the first run on repo, with lenders no longer willing to provide short-term finance at historical spreads and haircuts.[362]

[362] Gorton, Gary, Metrick, Andrew (2010, November 9), Securitized Banking and Run on the Repo, NBER Working Paper No. 15223, http://www.nber.org/papers/w15223, page 29.

According to Professors Gorton and Metrick's informationally-insensitive debt model, what happened in August 2007 is an unknowable mystery that resulted in the first repo run. With the informationally-insensitive debt model, we are left without an explanation of the cause of the financial markets freezing in August 2007, what to do to unfreeze the markets or what to do to prevent the markets from freezing again.

So how does the FDR Framework compare in explaining why the financial markets froze in August 2007, what to do to unfreeze the markets and what to do to prevent the markets from freezing again?

In searching for an explanation, I'll start with the Libor-OIS spread. According to the St. Louis Fed,

> The term Libor-OIS spread is assumed to be a measure of the health of banks because it reflects what banks believe is the risk of default associated with lending to other banks.
>
> Indeed, former Fed Chairman Alan Greenspan stated recently that the "Libor-OIS remains a barometer of fears of bank insolvency."[363]

So, what happened to the Libor-OIS spread in August 2007?

> Figure 1 shows the daily term Libor-OIS spreads for terms of 1, 3, and 6 months: There was a sharp rise in the term spreads on August 9, 2007, after a lengthy period of being small and relatively constant. Indeed, there was little difference in the spreads across terms of the assets.[364]

So, what happened on August 9, 2007?

> According to the BBC News,
>
> Investment bank BNP Paribas tells investors they will not be able to take money out of two of its funds because it cannot value the assets in them.[365]

Specifically, it could not value the subprime mortgage backed securities in these funds.

Why could it not value these securities?

BNP Paribas could not independently value these securities because they were opaque.

---

363 Thornton, Daniel L. (2009), What the Libor-OIS Spread Says, Economic Synopses, Number 24, Federal Reserve Bank of St. Louis, http://research.stlouisfed.org/publications/es/09/ES0924.pdf, page 1.

364 ibid, page 1

365 BBC News (2009, August 7), Timeline: Credit crunch to downturn, BBC, http://news.bbc.co.uk/2/hi/7521250.stm

The impact of this announcement was as memorable for the financial markets as August 4, 1914 and the start of World War I.

> It marks the cut-off point between "an Edwardian summer" of prosperity and tranquility and the trench warfare of the credit crunch — the failed banks, the petrified markets, the property markets blown to pieces by a shortage of credit.[366]

Under the FDR Framework, what happened in August 2007 is not a mystery. On August 9th, BNP Paribas announced to the world that the useful, relevant information about the subprime mortgage-backed securities was not available in an appropriate, timely manner and therefore the securities could not be independently valued.

Once this announcement by a Too Big to Fail bank had been made it was obvious why lenders would not be willing to accept the senior tranches of subprime mortgage-backed securities as collateral for a repo. To know that they will be repaid, lenders want to know that the value of the collateral they receive is greater than the amount of money they lend out. Since the collateral could not be valued, lenders could not receive this assurance.

Once this announcement had been made it was obvious why the interbank lending market would freeze. Just like the lenders in repo transactions, the lending banks want to know that they would be repaid. However, when the lending banks looked at the borrowing banks what they saw were opaque institutions with an unknown amount of exposure to securities that couldn't be valued.

Once this announcement had been made, both the cause (opacity) and how to stop the global financial crisis (provide valuation transparency) were easy to identify.

What we found when we asked the economics profession to explain how we got to the point where there was opacity in a global financial system designed to embrace valuation transparency was it wasn't their job to monitor or prevent the buildup of opacity. Instead, they believed the efficient market hypothesis' assumption valuation transparency was always reflected in market prices made it a reality.

In addition, the economics profession was very willing to offer up ideas on why the financial crisis occurred. Of course, these ideas could be easily dismissed if one understood our financial system was based on the combination of disclosure and *caveat emptor*.

---

366 Elliott, Larry (2008, August 5), Credit crisis — how it all began, The Guardian, http://www.theguardian.com/business/2008/aug/05/northernrock.banking

Unfortunately, because of the economics profession's willingness to offer up explanations and solutions, it effectively crowded out the voices of those who had seen the crisis coming.

Crowding Out

Recall that, including myself, there were only a small handful of economists and other individuals who could say they actually warned about the financial crisis and therefore had an insight into why the crisis occurred. Based on this insight, these individuals offered up solutions on how to moderate and end the financial crisis.

However, these solutions were crowded out by the army of economists who didn't predict the financial crisis, but were only too willing to offer up their insights about the financial crisis. Without attaching a warning saying their understanding of the causes of the financial crisis might be suspect due to their failure to predict the crisis, this army of economists provided their solutions for either ending the crisis or their opinions for how the financial system should be reformed as a result of the crisis.

Nowhere was this crowding out better exemplified than when six Nobel-prize winning economists endorsed the retention of opacity in the financial system. The Nobel-prize winning economists included Harry Markowitz, Robert Merton and Myron Scholes. Alan Greenspan credited the work of this trio as the genesis for the risk-management paradigm that failed at the beginning of the financial crisis. The other Nobel-prize winning economists who endorsed retention of opacity in the financial system were Robert F. Engle III, William F. Sharp and Vernon Smith.

They endorsed the retention of opacity in the financial system by signing a letter from the Committee to Establish the National Institute of Finance calling for a government agency to see into all the opaque corners of the financial system.

> The recent financial crisis has revealed fundamental gaps in our understanding of financial markets and how they affect the broader economy. These gaps were evident in the inability of regulators and policy makers to see the buildup of systemic risks that led to the recent crisis and to understand the potential impact of their decisions at the most critical times of the crisis.
>
> Going forward, a significant regulatory weakness is the absence of a sustained effort to gain a deep understanding of risks to the financial system, including the lack of essential data and the analytical capacity to turn that data into useful information to enable regulators to better safeguard our financial system...

> There has been far too little attention devoted to strengthening the research efforts and fixing the inadequate data and analytical capability on which sound regulatory decisions must be based.
>
> In his opening comments to the Senate Banking Committee, on June 18, 2009 Secretary Geithner commented, "We must be able to look in every corner and across the horizon for dangers and our system was not able to do that." In spite of this observation, the bill that recently passed the U.S. House of Representatives does nothing to provide authority to collect system-wide data or to provide the permanent staff and resources needed to develop these critical capacities.
>
> To be successful, legislation intended to equip the government to understand and monitor systemic risk and be able to reduce the risks of major financial crises in the future must include provisions to strengthen research efforts and provide the government with previously unavailable data and analytical capabilities.
>
> Over the past year a large group of academic scholars, regulators, and financial sector experts, calling themselves the Committee to Establish the National Institute of Finance (CE-NIF), came together in a volunteer effort to develop a proposal for how to enable the government to develop the research capacity and acquire the data and analytical capability to remedy this glaring regulatory weakness.
>
> We strongly urge you to include in the U.S. Senate's financial regulatory reform legislation the authorities and resources needed to assure that the U.S. government will have the understanding, data and analytical capabilities proposed by the CE-NIF that are necessary if government regulators are to have the tools needed to safeguard the U.S. financial system.[367]

With their endorsement, the agency for monitoring systemic risk was created as part of the Dodd-Frank Act. It is publicly known as the Office of Financial Research. To the Wall Street's lobbyists who drafted this part of the Act and myself, it is referred to as the agency where the economics profession sent the philosophy of disclosure and valuation transparency to die.

Compare and contrast how our financial system based on the combination of disclosure and *caveat emptor* operates with what the six economic Nobel laureates requested in their letter to fix what the letter acknowledges is a problem of opacity in the financial system.

They requested that the Office of Financial Research be set up specifically so the government has access to the information necessary for assessing risk in

---

[367] Committee to Establish the National Institute of Finance (2010, February 11), Letter to the Honorable Christopher J. Dodd, Chairman Committee on Banking, Housing and Urban Affairs, http://www.ce-nif.org/images/docs/nif_ltr_to_sen_dodd.pdf

the global financial system. It is the government regulators who are suppose to then assess this risk. It is the government regulators who are suppose to then take steps to address the risk so another systemic financial crisis is avoided.

The Nobel laureates embraced the idea the financial regulators should take over the process by which the collective assessment of risk by all market participants is reflected in their exercise of self-discipline and the enforcement of market discipline. Going forward, it is the financial regulators' responsibility to assess risk and enforce self-discipline.

Think for a second just how complicated it would be to assess the risk of financial contagion in the financial system and then manage each market participant so financial contagion doesn't occur.

By definition, the idea of financial contagion is one market participant fails and their failure triggers a domino-style cascade of failures throughout the financial system. To properly assess the risk of financial contagion quite literally requires understanding every market participant's current direct and indirect exposures to every other market participant and being able to assess which market participants have a greater level of total exposure to another market participant than they can afford to lose. To eliminate financial contagion would require that the regulators step in every time a market participant has a greater level of total exposure to another market participant than they can afford to lose.

These six prominent economists recommended putting this complex burden on financial regulators as a substitute for simply making valuation transparency available to all market participants in what are all the currently opaque corners of the financial system and letting the financial system operate as designed under the FDR Framework.

Investors, knowing they are responsible for all losses on their investment positions, have an incentive to limit the size of these positions to what they can afford to lose. However, investors can only do this when they have valuation transparency and can independently assess the risk of each of their investments. By bringing valuation transparency to all the currently opaque corners of the financial system, investors can perform their risk assessment and then adjust the amount of their exposure. This ends the risk of financial contagion.

If there is anything the economics profession should understand and be able to provide useful advice on, it is the importance of valuation transparency as the necessary condition for the invisible hand of the market to operate properly and set prices that efficiently allocate resources.

If there is anything the economics profession should understand and be able to provide useful advice on, it is the importance of valuation transparency to the investment process so that there is both market discipline and the elimination of financial contagion.

So what did six of the most highly acclaimed living economists do when they were effectively speaking for the entire economics profession and stepped up to address the problem of opacity in the financial system?

Collectively they failed to recognize the need to bring valuation transparency to all market participants and not just regulators. Together they effectively recommended retaining opacity in the financial markets and making it the regulators' responsibility to ensure all the benefits the combination of valuation transparency and *caveat emptor* deliver like eliminating financial contagion and market discipline.

By failing to recognize the response to opacity is valuation transparency, the six Nobel-prize winning economists' recommendation crowded out the voices calling for valuation transparency.

I know this crowding out occurred because for several months before the passage of the Dodd-Frank Act, I talked with both Congressional staffers and the leadership of the Committee to Establish the National Institute of Finance.

I used the clear plastic and brown paper bags to explain why valuation transparency was necessary and the Office of Financial Research was the wrong solution. Of course, the leadership of the Committee rejected my argument. Congressional staffers pushed back against the clear plastic bag and valuation transparency by pointing to the Nobel-prize winning economists and the large group of academics, regulators and financial sector experts calling for the Office of Financial Research.

When I pointed out to the Congressional staffers the Office of Financial Research does not provide valuation transparency so market participants can know what they own, the staffers pushed back using the Wall Street's Opacity Protection Team's claim that disclosing this data would create information overload for investors.

When I pointed out that investors didn't have to analyze the data themselves, but could use third party experts who could analyze the data, the Congressional staffers pushed back with if investors having valuation transparency was important, six Nobel-prize winning economists and the Committee would have pushed this idea instead.

In 2012, I met with one of the individual who led the Committee to Establish the National Institute of Finance. Having seen how the Wall Street Opacity Protection Team used the Office of Financial Research to cement opacity into the financial system, he apologized for not listening to me.

Perhaps investors who are dependent on valuation transparency will be better able to answer how we ended up with opacity in a global financial system designed to embrace valuation transparency.

Chapter 14

WHAT HAPPENED TO INVESTORS EXERCISING SELF-DISCIPLINE?

If you're an intelligent investor, you invest in things where there is truth and transparency.
— Paul O'Neill, Former U.S. Treasury Secretary[368]

Please note that as designed in the 1930s,

- Disclosure was based on the idea of providing investors with access to all the useful, relevant information they needed at the time of their investment to make a fully informed investment decision.
- Of equal importance, no specific burden was placed on an investor to use this disclosure!

How does the market work if investors are not required to use the disclosed information?

How does the market for an individual security (stock, bond, structured finance product) work if investors are not required to look at the information disclosed?

The fact all investors are not required to look at the disclosed information does not mean some investors will not look at the disclosed information. It is the investors and the third party experts who look at the information who are likely to understand how to use the disclosed information in the analytic and valuation models of their choice to independently assess the risk of and value the security.

The investors who don't look at the disclosed information can piggyback off of these investors and third party experts. For example, the investors who did their homework or hired trusted third party experts to do their homework for them add stability to the price of the security by being buyers when the price is below their valuation and sellers when the price is above their valuation.

368 O'Neill, Paul (2009, March 16), Banks must show U.S. the money, CNN, http://www.cnn.com/2009/US/03/16/oneill.qanda/index.html?iref=nextin

In the absence of valuation transparency, investors who use the disclosed information to provide price stability are absent. As a result, prices for securities make movements similar to what occurred for structured finance securities in 2008 — one day the price is par and the next it is 20% of par.

One reason for providing loan-level disclosure on an observable event basis for structured finance securities or current exposure details for banks is to eliminate these severe price swings by making it possible for investors to assess the risk of and value these securities. With the ability to make this assessment, investors can know what they own or know what they are buying.

The bank/sell-side dominated lobby, part of Wall Street's Opacity Protection Team, has pushed back strongly against this type of disclosure. One of their leading arguments against providing disclosure, on an observable event basis or a current exposure detail basis, has been that providing this much data would confuse investors.

Frankly, the unsophisticated investor[369] cannot analyze or value banks or structured finance securities, he/she has enough trouble with stocks and plain vanilla bonds. However, the unsophisticated investor is not likely to buy these securities directly. He/She is likely to invest through a mutual fund or hedge fund with a professional portfolio manager.

The professional portfolio manager can choose to use the loan-level disclosure to value structured finance securities and the exposure detail disclosure to value banks or they can hire an independent pricing service that is capable of valuing the securities using this disclosure.

Let me repeat that, the unsophisticated investor cannot analyze or value structured finance securities or banks. So, he/she hires a professional portfolio manager. He/She hires a manager assuming either the manager or their firm have the ability to analyze and value the structured finance securities using loan-level data and the banks using current exposure details or that the manager or the manager's firm will hire an independent third party service to do so.

Asset allocation fallacy

> As a fiduciary, having a clear understanding of the limits of your own knowledge is essential, but perhaps not as common as one would hope. A combination of hubris and over-confidence can lead to poor decision-making as

369 To me, unsophisticated investors are basically everyone other than professional money managers. This definition differs from the SEC's definition of a sophisticated investor based on net worth or the last three year's net income.

> admitting 'I don't understand' is difficult when you have been hired on the basis of your experience and expertise.[370]

On the surface, it is reasonable for the unsophisticated investor to turn to a professional investment manager to do what the unsophisticated investor cannot do and that is assess the risk of and value securities. Unfortunately, where this reasonable strategy by the unsophisticated investor breaks down is the "asset allocation fallacy".

First, the unsophisticated investor assumes that because an investment manager will take his/her money to invest in a specific type of asset this means the manager thinks investing in assets of this type is a good idea from a risk/reward perspective. This could not be further from the truth as a willingness to accept money to invest in a specific type of asset doesn't say anything about whether an investment manager thinks these assets are undervalued or represent a good idea from a risk/reward perspective. Instead, it might reflect an investment manager might be constrained in what assets the manager can invest in by his charter.

Second, the investment manager assumes the unsophisticated investor's investment reflects the unsophisticated investor's fully informed asset allocation decision and therefore his/her desire for exposure to the assets the manager invests in. The manager assumes the unsophisticated investor understands the risk of these investments as outlined in a prospectus or in the investment manager's presentation of their expertise. It is this assumption that the unsophisticated investor understands the risk that is flawed.

The unsophisticated investor knows he/she cannot assess the securities' risk and value. What he/she doesn't know is that in the case of opaque banks or opaque structured finance securities neither can the investment manager.

Why don't the investment managers disclose in plain English opacity prevents them from assessing the risk of or value of banks and structured finance securities?

It would make them unemployed. How much money do you think an investment manager would manage if he said to investors that he was going to blindly gamble with their money?

So, rather than disclose that he is blindly gambling with the investors' money, the investment manager justifies blindly gambling by saying he is simply following the investors' asset allocation decision. A decision that most likely wouldn't have been made if the investment manager had to disclose he was investing in assets that didn't have a Transparency Label Initiative™ label saying

---

370 Lady FOHF (2014, August 3), *On Embracing Stupid*, Notes from the Hedge, http://ladyfohf.tumblr.com/post/93685456346/on-embracing-stupid

the assets provided the valuation transparency necessary so the risk and value of the assets could be assessed.

This exercise in not telling the truth to the unsophisticated investor has significant implications for the investment manager's ability to demand valuation transparency.

Buy-side has no leverage to force valuation transparency

The way the buy-side can apply pressure for valuation transparency is to refuse to buy opaque securities. This is known as the Wall Street Walk: as in, walk by the opaque securities and buy the securities offering valuation transparency.

However, the Wall Street Walk is not possible for investment managers who manage funds that are limited by charter to investing in the opaque securities. They have to buy these securities.

Because they have to buy these securities and they are unwilling to disclose they are blindly gambling to investors who hired them on the basis of their claimed expertise in the unknowable, these investment managers not only have no leverage to force the provision of valuation transparency, but they act as a barrier to bringing valuation transparency to the securities they invest in.

These portfolio managers are also unwilling to disclose to the press they are blindly gambling. As a result, when asked by the press if they need valuation transparency to assess the risk and value of the black-box banks or the brown paper bag subprime mortgage-backed securities, the portfolio managers respond "no". They assert they have proprietary ways including sophisticated computer models for valuing the contents of a black box or brown paper bag.

By looking at unsophisticated investors, we discovered their use of the professional investment management industry means not only do they end up unknowingly blindly gambling with investments where there is not the valuation transparency they deserve, but their ability to demand valuation transparency is also severely restricted. Simply put, there are charter constrained portfolio managers whose job depends on their not admitting the securities they invest in are opaque. Naturally, to avoid admitting they are blindly betting with the investors' money, they do not push for valuation transparency. Instead, they become cheerleaders for the current inadequate disclosure practices. As a result, even though the unsophisticated investors are responsible for all losses on their investments, they don't have a strong voice for preventing opacity taking over a financial system based on valuation transparency.

This is where the Transparency Label Initiative™ comes in. Unsophisticated investors can use the labels to prevent opacity taking over a financial system based on valuation transparency. For example, unsophisticated investors can prevent portfolio managers from blindly gambling with their money by restricting their investments to funds where the portfolio manager can only invest in securities that have a label.

What about large investors?

Without the Transparency Label Initiative™, the unsophisticated investor might not be able to demand valuation transparency, but what about institutional investors like hedge funds and Warren Buffett?

Warren Buffett would be happy to point out, disclosure of each position in the banks' trading and investment portfolios at the end of each business day would dramatically squash the potential profitability of this business model.

A number of years ago, he negotiated with the SEC and received permission to delay disclosure of his investment positions.

Why would he have wanted to delay disclosure?

As Mr. Buffett said,

> How would you feel if you had to announce every story idea you had?[371]

If he was buying, he wanted to delay disclosure to minimize the price he paid for his entire position. By not filing, he does not have to compete with investors who piggyback on his reputation and ideas. These investors would have increased the cost of his position by driving up the price of stock with their buying.

If he was selling, he wanted to delay disclosure to maximize the price he received for his entire position. By not filing, he does not have to compete with investors who piggyback on his reputation. These investors would have decreased his sale proceeds by driving the price of the stock down with their selling.

Clearly, there are advantages to having opacity when it comes to buying and selling securities.

Mr. Buffett shows why certain large investors do not push for valuation transparency. They are worried they will have to provide transparency too. By showing a clear preference for having opacity on their own actions, these large investors undermine their call for better valuation transparency.

However, there are a number of other large investors who don't have the same concern about providing transparency into their positions. These investors include endowments, foundations, pension funds, central banks and sovereign wealth funds. They benefit from requiring valuation transparency because there is

---

371 Sorkin, Andrew Ross (2011, November 14), One Secret Buffett Gets to Keep, NY Times Dealbook, http://dealbook.nytimes.com/2011/11/14/one-secret-buffett-gets-to-keep/?ref=business

no reason these investors should engage in blindly gambling. For these investors, the Transparency Label Initiative™ is a necessity as it both identifies investible securities and puts pressure on issuers to provide valuation transparency.

In the absence of the Transparency Label Initiative™, regulators are the only market participants who can prevent opacity from taking over a financial system based on valuation transparency. In Wall Street, they are up against a formidable foe.

CHAPTER 15

WALL STREET'S MASTERY IN PREVENTING VALUATION TRANSPARENCY

We could talk about a lot of ways the system is rigged—lobbyists, campaign finance, the court system. But I want to raise a very specific issue that we need to spotlight: how much powerful interests benefit from a system that is complicated and opaque.
— Senator Elizabeth Warren[372]

Our system is mirrors and smoke
Our new regulations...a joke!
Our banks are opaque
A massive mistake
Our structures of finance are broke

Our banks have become a concern
Our system is starting to burn
New regulations
Are bank fabrications
Transparency needs to return![373]

Lobbyists are an important part of Wall Street's Opacity Protection Team. Through their efforts, they help to create opacity in the global financial system. In addition, once there is opacity in part of the global financial system, they employ a number of tactics to defend the status quo and neuter any legislation or regulation that would restore valuation transparency.

372 Warren, Elizabeth (2013, November 7), Remarks by Senator Elizabeth Warren, National Consumer Law Center, Consumer Rights Litigation Conference, http://www.masslive.com/politics/index.ssf/2013/11/sen_elizabeth_warren_addresses.html

373 The Limerick King (2014, July 30), email

Lessons in Lobbying

The lobbyists' choice of tactics is based on the fact the process of moving a restraint on the banks from idea to law to a regulation to enforcement is a series of negotiations. Negotiating just happens to be one of Wall Street's strengths. How Wall Street's Opacity Protection Team operated in neutering the Volcker Rule provides insights into how it negotiates to prevent valuation transparency.

The Volcker Rule began with Paul Volcker's simple idea banks should not be allowed to gamble with insured deposits and gambling through proprietary trading is an activity that you know when you see it. Mr. Volcker's idea was included in the Dodd-Frank Act and regulators were given the charge to draft the related regulation and enforcement.

As simple as Mr. Volcker's statement is, it is loaded with opportunity for the members of the Opacity Protection Team.

The first opportunity comes in setting the terms of the negotiation. The Opacity Protection Team did this by focusing the bank regulators on defining gambling. The Volcker Rule bans gambling so the opening gambit from the Opacity Protection Team is to ask the bank regulators to define when is a trader gambling. If the trader is gambling, it is banned under the rule. If not, then the activity is permitted.

This opening gambit is very clever. Knowing the bank regulators are never going to admit they are not the equal of the bankers, the Opacity Protection Team presents the bank regulators with a choice: rise to the challenge, define what gambling is and then use regulatory oversight to enforce the Volcker Rule or don't define what gambling is, but require valuation transparency and rely on market discipline to enforce the Volcker Rule. The decision to define what gambling is and then use regulatory oversight to enforce the Volcker Rule assures the Opacity Protection Team of victory even before the regulation has been drafted. Victory is assured because banks don't have to provide valuation transparency.

In the U.S., UK and EU, the process by which regulations are written offers many more opportunities as it invites the interested public to comment on a proposed regulation. Who do you think provides most of the long, detailed comments? Wall Street and its lobbyists.

The U.S. financial regulators asked for public comments on the implementation of the Volcker Rule and

> By [Better Market CEO] Mr. Kelleher's count, of the substantive responses, 13 were pro-reform, compared with 300 from the industry.[374]

---

[374] Eisinger, Jesse (2012, February 22), The Volcker Rule, Made Bloated and Weak, NY Times Dealbook, http://dealbook.nytimes.com/2012/02/22/the-volcker-rule-made-bloated-and-weak/

It was 23:1 against reform and we are not even counting the number of times members of the Opacity Protection Team met with the financial regulators to lobby against the Volcker Rule. Between July 2010 and October 2011, Duke University law professor Kimberly Krawiec documented the Opacity Protection Team had

> 419 meetings with federal regulators to dicker over the rule. In the same period, public advocacy groups such as the AFL-CIO and Public Citizen got 19 meetings. Paul Volcker himself got only one.[375]

In person meetings were only 21:1 against reform.

As Robert Jenkins, a former lobbyist and former member of the Bank of England's Financial Policy Committee observed,

> At the moment, you might say our priority is to protect the banks from the financial system, and the financial system from the banks....
>
> And for this, we need look no farther than the lobbying efforts of the banking industry in general and their campaign against banking reform in particular....
>
> Ladies and gentlemen, up to a point, it has been amusing to watch big banking's fight against financial reform.[376]

Actually, the banks fighting reform has proved extraordinarily expensive to the nations that host them. By blocking valuation transparency, the banks have significantly increased the cost to taxpayers of the financial crisis.

For example, imagine how much more efficient it would have been to recapitalize the banking system if no bonuses were paid to bankers until such time as the market value of each bank's assets exceeded the book value of its liabilities.

> Remember their first response to the crisis? It was to deny the very need for reform. How dumb was that? They quickly regrouped.
>
> The next phase was to acknowledge that reform was necessary — but only if the rules could be agreed to globally. "Level playing field" was the rallying cry. "We will if they will." ... The lobby reasoned that global standards would

---

375 Hiltzik, Michael (2013, September 13), Big U.S. banks keeping door open to another financial crisis, Los Angeles Times, http://www.latimes.com/business/la-fi-hiltzik-20130915-column.html#ixzz2qmDTlMqn&page=1

376 Jenkins, Robert (2011, November 22), Lessons in lobbying, Bank of England, http://www.bankofengland.co.uk/publications/Documents/speeches/2011/speech533.pdf, page 2.

> be difficult to achieve and if achieved, would be set to the lowest common denominator of international consensus.[377]

Unlike the other regulations for restraining the banks, valuation transparency is not set by the lowest common denominator. Countries that require their banks to provide valuation transparency have tilted the playing field to their advantage. It is a fundamental principle of finance the more accurately investors can assess the risk of an investment, the less they require as a return. Those banks that don't provide valuation transparency by definition are hiding something that makes them riskier than the banks that do provide valuation transparency. Hence, the playing field is tilted towards providing valuation transparency and away from opacity.

The strategy of framing the terms of bank reform to exclude banks having to provide valuation transparency was very successful. Think of all the complex regulations that have resulted as a substitute for valuation transparency and market discipline. For example, there are the Basel III capital regulations under which millions of assumptions are used in the 100s of different internal models run by the banks.

> Best of all, the deadline for implementation was set for 2019 — a date so distant as to be irrelevant to any banker's career and so extended as to be vulnerable to lots more lobbying.[378]

This strategy of playing for time and hoping the pressure for real reform of the banks and the financial system will dissipate has been very successful.

For example, by passing the almost totally worthless Dodd-Frank Act, the Obama Administration can claim they passed the most extensive piece of financial reform legislation since the 1930s. The claim is true, but the bar isn't very high as there hasn't been any other substantial financial reform legislation since the 1930s. However, having made the claim, the Obama Administration is highly unlikely to pass additional legislation. Instead, it has said and will continue to say give the Dodd-Frank Act a chance. Give the Dodd-Frank Act a chance even though the Nyberg Commission Report flatly stated that complex regulations and regulatory oversight are not up to the task of preventing the next financial crisis.

Fortunately, the legislation to require banks and other issuers of securities to provide valuation transparency has already been passed. What it takes is enforcement!

---

377 ibid, page 2

378 ibid, page 2

However, to make sure that existing law isn't enforced too strictly,

> the latest lobby tactic is to convince pundits, public and politicians that encouraging prudence too soon will hit the economy too hard. This is no longer amusing. This strategy is intellectually dishonest and potentially damaging.[379]

It is dishonest because it is untrue....

> And it is potentially damaging because it promotes fear for an economy which the banks are there to serve and from which they draw their livelihood.[380]

The fact is banks could provide valuation transparency without triggering a financial collapse. Since the beginning of the financial crisis, governments have put the banking sector on life support through actions like extending the deposit guarantee to cover all deposits. As a result, wholesale bank runs have been stopped.

If the banks were required to provide valuation transparency, everyone could see the losses currently hidden on and off their balance sheets. Once these losses become visible, market discipline would force the banks to recognize them.

While this would greatly reduce bank capital, this is a good outcome for the real economy. Once the losses have been recognized, the excess debt in the financial system can be restructured to what borrowers can afford to pay. This takes the burden of the excess debt off the real economy and allows the real economy to resume growing.

Of course, this is a fair outcome for the bankers. They were responsible for the bad loans and excess debt in the first place. So, it is only fair that this outcome would end their bonuses until such time as the banks had rebuilt their book capital levels.

However, Wall Street's Opacity Protection Team is not interested in an outcome that would be good for the real economy and fair for bankers. They are out to protect the bankers' profits and bonuses from opacity. Perhaps their crowning achievement in this regard is the Dodd-Frank Act.

The Dodd-Frank Act was effectively written by and for the financial industry with the exception of the Volcker Rule and the Consumer Financial Protection Bureau. The Act is 2,000+ pages calling for an enormous expansion in complex regulation and regulatory supervision of the financial sector. However, if the current financial crisis has shown anything, it has shown a financial system that is dependent on complex regulations and regulatory supervision

---

379 ibid, page 3

380 ibid, page 3

has the illusion of safety but is an inherently unstable financial system prone to collapsing.

The reason for this instability is the combination of complex regulations and regulatory supervision create opacity. Where there is opacity, market participants cannot properly assess risk. When risk is priced improperly and the price is too low, too much risk is created.

The Basel capital requirements are a prime example of complex regulations and regulatory oversight creating both the illusion of safety and opacity. As the Nyberg Commission Report showed, regulators thought these regulations would restrain bank risk taking and prevent the bankers from blowing up the global financial system. Clearly, this did not happen. In fact, the Basel capital requirements are designed to hide the leverage and true level of risk the banks are taking. I know this because I worked on Basel I.

One of the Opacity Protection Team's favorite tactics for preventing enforcement of valuation transparency is to argue there is no evidence it is necessary and, even if there were evidence, the cost of valuation transparency exceeds the benefit.

When it comes to bringing valuation transparency to banks and structured finance securities, it is very well documented, see Financial Crisis Inquiry Commission for example, that market participants did not have adequate valuation transparency to be able to value either banks or structured finance securities.

The question is does the benefit of valuation transparency justify its cost?

Cost/benefit analysis in the regulatory process

The price of light is less than the cost of darkness.
—*Arthur C. Nielsen*[381]

Both Democrats and Republicans agree on the essential need for cost/benefit analysis in the regulatory process. The positive aspect of cost/benefit analysis is it prevents hugely expensive regulations that have minimal benefits. However, there is a critical weakness to cost/benefit analysis. It is difficult to do. On the one hand, industry exaggerates the true cost of compliance with a regulation. On the other hand, the benefits of a regulation are sometimes hard to quantify. This is particularly true for valuation transparency.

The one good thing to come from our current financial crisis is that we can now do the definitive cost/benefit analysis for valuation transparency. Valuation

381 Nielsen, Arthur C., quote, http://spinnakr.com/blog/data-2/2013/03/44-more-of-the-best-data-quotes/

transparency lies at the very heart of the financial system. It is the focus of the philosophy of disclosure that was adopted during the Great Depression to restore trust and confidence in the financial system. It was the absence of valuation transparency that characterized the areas of the financial system like the interbank lending market and structured finance that have stopped functioning during our current financial crisis.

I say this is the definitive cost/benefit analysis for valuation transparency because it uses hard numbers for both the costs and benefits. It ignores qualitative benefits like reducing the issuer's or the borrower's costs because of the elimination of the illiquidity premium.

This definitive cost/benefit analysis only applies to valuation transparency and not price transparency. This is intentional. The way the investment process works, the important form of transparency is valuation transparency. Valuation transparency is important because it allows market participants to independently assess the risk of and value a security. It is only with the independent valuation of a security that an investor can tell if they want to buy, hold or sell the security at the price being shown by Wall Street.

In doing this cost/benefit analysis for valuation transparency, the intent is to cover all currently opaque areas of the global financial system and any that might be developed in the future. Without a one-time cost/benefit analysis that forever covers all valuation transparency regulations, Wall Street will argue that each area of finance needs its own cost/benefit analysis.

The danger of doing a cost/benefit analysis on each financial product is Wall Street's lobbyists will claim for a small financial product the cost of valuation transparency exceeds the benefit and the financial regulators will be unable to refute this claim. As a result, a regulation requiring valuation transparency will be defeated and in its place, a regulation permitting opacity will be passed. Subsequently, this opaque area of finance will grow so large that when it fails because of a lack of valuation transparency it brings down the entire global financial system.

This just happens to be the story for structured finance and its disclosure regulation, Regulation AB. This story was related to me by one of the lead architects of the SEC disclosure rules for structured finance. When the SEC originally tried in the early 2000s to bring valuation transparency to structured finance, Wall Street's Opacity Protection Team effectively argued the benefits to investors from having all of the useful, relevant information in an appropriate, timely manner did not outweigh the cost of providing this information. The SEC was unable to internally generate a cost/benefit analysis that justified requiring valuation transparency. The individual told me the SEC knew I was right about the need for observable event based reporting, but their economists did not see the benefit of valuation transparency exceeding the costs to provide valuation transparency. As a result, the SEC backed off from requiring valuation transparency and instead issued a rule leaving investors to value the contents of a brown paper bag.

Oops.

So, using what we know about the cost of bringing valuation transparency to structured finance securities and the benefit it would generate, what would the definitive cost/benefit analysis look like?

The benefit of valuation transparency is the significant amount of losses that could have been avoided if investors had access to loan-level deal specific data on an observable event basis so they could have accurately assessed the risk in each securitization deal.

According to the Securities Industry and Financial Market Association, over $1.75 trillion in non-agency mortgage backed securities, home equity loan-backed securities and CDOs were issued globally between the time securities firms like HSBC, Goldman Sachs and Morgan Stanley with access to observable event based data through their subprime mortgage billing and collecting subsidiaries decided to stop buying such securities and the beginning of the credit crisis in 2007. Had investors had accessed to the same data and reached the same conclusion, several hundred billion dollars of losses analysts and traders estimated occurred on these thinly traded securities could have been avoided.

In addition, there were other avoidable losses in the financial system as there were loans made during this time period that ended up on the balance sheets of financial institutions both to replace the loans sold into the capital markets and to grow the financial institutions' internal loan portfolios. If market discipline had been exerted on the financial institutions in late 2006, these loans might not have been made. These loans also incurred a significant amount of losses. At a minimum, the benefit to the global financial system from providing loan-level deal specific data on an observable event basis would have been several hundred billion dollars of losses avoided.

The annual cost of providing loan-level deal specific data on an observable event basis for securitization transactions is much less than the losses described above. In order to provide this data, a data-handling infrastructure is needed to collect, store and distribute this information. Based on the cost for comparable information services for securitizations, the on-going annual cost of the proposed infrastructure for loan-level deal specific performance data daily would be 5 basis points (0.05%) or less of the principal amount of the loans that are supporting a particular securitization. The annual cost to bring valuation transparency to the $2 trillion market for non-agency mortgage backed securities would be $1 billion or less.

By spending $1 billion per year, the securitization market can have valuation transparency and avoid repeating the several hundreds of billions of losses from not being able to accurately assess and price the risk of securitizations. Clearly, the benefit is multiples of the cost.

So, what would the cost/benefit analysis look like for the entire financial system including opaque areas like banks and structured finance securities?

The benefit of bringing valuation transparency to all the currently opaque corners of the financial system is substantial. At a minimum, it is a majority of the losses on the opaque securities that would have been avoided if there were valuation transparency. Alternatively, it is a substantial portion of the broader cost to the global economy from the current financial crisis that could have been avoided if there were valuation transparency.

According to the Bank of England's June 2009 Financial Stability Report, mark to market losses on opaque structured finance securities reach $2.6 trillion by mid-March 2009.[382]

According to economist Dean Baker at CEPR, the cost of our current financial crisis is $7.6 trillion.[383] Interthinx's Ann Fulmer put the cost of the current financial crisis even higher at $13 trillion.[384]

The Bank of England's Andy Haldane put the benefit of preventing another opacity driven global financial crisis substantially higher.

> [T]hese direct fiscal costs are almost certainly an underestimate of the damage to the wider economy which has resulted from the crisis — the true social costs of crisis. World output in 2009 is expected to have been around 6.5% lower than its counterfactual path in the absence of crisis.... In money terms, that translates into output losses of $4 trillion...
>
> Moreover, some of these GDP losses are expected to persist. Evidence from past crises suggests that crisis-induced output losses are permanent, or at least persistent, in their impact on the level of output if not its growth rate. If GDP losses are permanent, the present value cost of crisis will exceed significantly today's cost....
>
> Put in money terms, that is an output loss equivalent to between $60 trillion and $200 trillion for the world economy.[385]

---

382 Bank of England (2009, June), Financial Stability Report, Bank of England, http://www.bankofengland.co.uk/publications/Documents/fsr/2009/fsr25sec1.pdf, page 15.

383 Baker, Dean (2014, January 21), The Damage From the Housing Bubble: How Much Did the Greenspan-Rubin Gang Cost Us?, Center for Economic and Policy Research, http://www.cepr.net/index.php/blogs/beat-the-press/the-damage-from-the-housing-bubble-how-much-did-the-greenspan-rubin-gang-cost-us

384 Panchuk, Kerri Ann (2012, September 11), Cost of housing meltdown rivals GDP: MBA conference, HousingWire, http://www.housingwire.com/articles/cost-housing-meltdown-rivals-gdp-mba-conference

385 The Economist (2010, March 31), Crisis Costs: Big Numbers, The Economist, http://www.economist.com/blogs/freeexchange/2010/03/crisis_costs

So, what is the cost of providing valuation transparency across the global financial system? At $50 billion or less annually, it is orders of magnitudes less than the losses sustained on opaque structured finance securities or the cost of our current financial crisis. This cost figure reflects detailed conversations with individuals at the leading global information technology firms for what it would take to implement my patented information technology to deliver valuation transparency.

Clearly, the benefits of providing valuation transparency to all the opaque corners of the financial system are orders of magnitude greater than the cost of providing valuation transparency. As a result, the SEC, CFTC and the bank regulators should be publishing regulations requiring disclosure of all the useful, relevant information in an appropriate, timely manner.

Brain-washed

But will the financial regulators use existing authorization to require and force valuation transparency into all the opaque corners of the global financial system? Doing so would require the financial regulators break free of the Opacity Protection Team's embrace.

> Driven by hubris, greed and stupidity bankers led the charge off the cliff. But where were the regulators? Why did they not see it coming? Why did they not prevent it? Why did they trust bankers to know what was best for banking? In short, how could regulators have been so dumb as to believe that bankers were so smart? ....[386]

Excellent questions.

> Industry influence operates at all levels of the rule making ranks — from the peak of politics to the substrata of supervision .[387]

The Opacity Protection Team's influence at the peak of politics was confirmed in the Nyberg Commission Report and the FSA Report. It was also confirmed by former Fed governor Charles Partee and former Fed chairman Alan Greenspan.

Each concluded the banking industry influence at the peak of politics undermined and would always undermine the regulatory process. When

386 Jenkins, Robert (2012, September 25), Regulators, financial industry and the problem of regulatory capture, http://www.bankofengland.co.uk/publications/Documents/speeches/2012/speech603_foreword.pdf, page 2.

387 ibid, page 2

everything appears to be going well, no politician wants to hear from a financial regulator that a potential problem is brewing.

Each also concluded banking industry influence with the regulator at the substrata of supervision undermined the supervisory process. Even if the examiners uncover problems at a bank, they have to convince politically appointed superiors who talk to the bank's management they are right.

The only way around this industry influence is the Transparency Label Initiative™. The banks need the buy-side to invest in their securities and hence they have a strong incentive to qualify for a label by providing valuation transparency and disclosing on an ongoing basis all of their current global asset, liability and off-balance sheet exposure details. With this information, market participants can independently assess each bank. With this assessment, market participants can act as the primary restraint on bank risk taking and exert discipline on the banks. With this assessment, market participants are not reliant on bank regulators.

> It need not be unhealthy. Indeed, interaction between regulators and the regulated is natural and normal. Yes, industry seeks to shape the rules under which it will operate. But rule-makers need industry input in order to craft sensible policy. Some degree of influence is therefore inevitable.[388]

One of the reasons the financial system is designed so bank regulators are not the primary restraint on bank risk taking is it is inevitable the banks will exert some degree of influence over the regulators. This is not true of the other market participants. For example, investors know they are responsible for any losses on their exposures to the banks and therefore they have an incentive to restrain risk-taking by adjusting the amount of their exposure to what they can afford to lose.

> Unfortunately, there are times and industries where special interest groups are able to bring disproportionate influence to bear — a condition called "regulatory capture." The financial sector is one such industry and the run-up to the crisis one such time. The obvious question which arises: is such influence still excessive and thus unduly shaping the needed regulatory response?
>
> Yes.
>
> My first encounter with "capture" came at a moment of meltdown in 2008. At the time I chaired both a London-based investment firm and the trade association representing the UK investment industry.

388 ibid, page 2

> As financial panic spread I watched in disbelief as bankers trooped through the doors of Downing Street to advise Government on how best to address a problem which bankers themselves had largely created.[389]

I also shared this disbelief when watching the bankers who created our current mess advising governments on how they should respond.

> Far from being discredited, the guidance of these "experts" was eagerly sought — and with virtually no counterbalancing input from other stakeholder groups. ... But at that key moment in time — capture was complete.
>
> "Political capture" can be fueled by campaign contributions but in the case above, it resulted from the pervasive beliefs of the day....
>
> The technical term here is "cognitive or intellectual" capture. The non-technical term is brainwashed.[390]

My disbelief has only grown over time as I have watched other members of the Opacity Protection Team, like academic economists, also offering their advice to governments on how they should respond to our current financial crisis.

It is not surprising that neither the bankers nor the economists have managed to end the financial crisis. It is not surprising as none of them called for bringing valuation transparency to all the opaque corners of the global financial system.

> [O]ne might imagine that bankers' ability to bewitch and bamboozle would have ebbed. Alas not.
>
> Their formidable lobby has led and continues to lead an effective campaign to persuade pundits, public and politicians that calls for [valuation transparency] are impeding the economic recovery.
>
> It is an argument framed so as to force the gullible and well intentioned to choose between public safety and economic growth. It is a false argument and a false choice....[391]

In fact, it appears the Opacity Protection Team has become an even more formidable lobby. For example, the Federal Reserve joined the team when it fought tooth and nail to resist Freedom of Information Act requests by Bloomberg News for disclosures relating to its emergency lending during and soon after the crisis began. When disclosure was finally forced, the information proved very embarrassing for the Fed.

---

389 ibid, page 2
390 ibid, page 2
391 ibid, page 3

Had the Fed's actions been known during the passage of the Dodd-Frank Act, different policy choices might well have been made regarding both enforcement of valuation transparency and the powers of the Federal Reserve.

Are the Regulators up to the task?

The U.S. Congress and the EU and UK Parliaments pass laws, but it is the regulators in these countries who are responsible for turning these laws into regulations and then enforcing these regulations. As confirmed by the different investigations into the cause of the financial crisis, it is in turning these laws into regulations and then enforcing these regulations where the regulators fail.

This failure can be best illustrated by looking at two laws that were passed in response to our current financial crisis: Article 122a of the European Capital Requirements Directive and the Dodd-Frank Act's Volcker Rule.

In May 2009, despite intense opposition from the banks and their sell-side lobbyists, the European Parliament passed Article 122a as an amendment to the European Capital Requirements Directive. It applies to European credit institutions that are broadly defined to include commercial and investment banks.

In response to the losses incurred by European credit institutions as a result of buying opaque, toxic subprime mortgage-backed securities, Article 122a embodied the sensible notion that if these institutions invest in structured finance securities they should "know what they own". If they do not know what they own, Article 122a required that they not be able to use any leverage to support their purchases of these securities. This too is sensible as it prevents the credit institution from losing more than its equity capital on investments where it is effectively blindly betting.

Under Article 122a, the bank regulators, specifically the Committee of European Banking Supervisors, were left to define what "know what you own" means and then to enforce this definition.

Wall Street and the City agree with my definition of "know what you own"

Article 122a represented an opportunity for European regulators to shine. It was a chance for these regulators to show that they could develop regulations that would restart a deep, liquid structured finance market.

Why was this an opportunity for European regulators to shine? Under Article 122a, they are left to define what "know what you own" means for the purposes of enforcing Article 122a.

That should not have been difficult. How many definitions of "know what you own" could there possibly be?

There are two: one as practiced by Wall Street and the City and one that Wall Street and the City along with the industry trade groups and lobbyists they control advocate.

What is the definition of "know what you own" Wall Street and the City actually uses?

The definition can be uncovered by looking at the actions of Wall Street and the City. According to a December 6, 2010 Reuters article discussing Goldman and Litton Loan Servicing, a subprime billing and collecting firm,

> Banks often bought these kinds of businesses … because they could give an informational edge for mortgage bond trading, according to bankers that helped their institutions evaluate these deals.[392]

What informational advantage could Goldman's mortgage bond trading receive from purchasing loan servicing companies like Litton?

This informational advantage takes two forms.

First, there is 'when' information is disclosed.

Wall Street and the City receive observable event based information on the performance of the loans underlying structured finance securities. Through ownership of the billing and collecting firms, they see all payments, delinquencies, defaults, and insolvency filings before the beginning of the next business day. This information results in Wall Street and the City valuing the contents of a clear plastic bag.

Contrast this to investors who are trying to value the contents of a brown paper bag. They receive information on a once per month or less frequent basis and have to guess what the current performance of the underlying loans is.

Wall Street and the City enjoy a significant informational advantage for trading structured finance securities as they effectively have inside information without any legal restrictions on how they can use the information. There are a number of ways they can capitalize on this information. Remember the Abacus CDO transaction under which Goldman Sachs sought to benefit from a collapse of the subprime mortgage market was a deal put together by traders.

Second, there is 'what' information is available.

Wall Street and the City would have access to all the information experts thought necessary to monitor and value the underlying loans. By definition, since

392 Bansal, Paritosh, Wilchins, Dan (2010, December 6), Goldman Sachs could find Litton sale tough, London South East, http://www.lse.co.uk/FinanceNews.asp?ArticleCode=ubzptvc5r50htzi&ArticleHeadline=DEALTALKGoldman_Sachs_could_find_Litton_sale_tough

it is in the business, a firm like Litton tracks all the information its experts thinks is necessary to monitor and value the loans.

Compare this to the disclosure templates adopted by the SEC and other regulators. These disclosure templates include a subset of the information tracked by firms like Litton.

The definition of "know what you own" as **practiced** by Wall Street and the City is a three-step process:

- Have access to valuation transparency in the form of loan-level disclosure on an observable event basis;
- Combine this valuation transparency with the terms of the deal;
- Use the analytic and cash flow models of choice to value the security.

What is the definition of "know what you own" Wall Street, the City, their lobbyists, and the industry trade groups they control advocate? The definition of "know what you own" as **lobbied for** is a three-step process:

- Have access to loan-level disclosure on a once-per-month basis where the information reported for each loan is a subset of the information available and needed to value and monitor the loan;
- Combine the restricted loan-level disclosure on the underlying collateral with the terms of the deal;
- Use the analytic and cash flow models of choice to value the security.

Not surprisingly, there is nothing in the lobbied for definition of "know what you own" that would eliminate the informational advantage enjoyed by Wall Street and the City. There is also nothing in the lobbied for definition of "know what you own" that would restart the structured finance market as investors are aware of the informational advantage the sell-side enjoys.

The question is would the European regulators take the opportunity to shine and adopt how Wall Street and the City practice "know what you own" as the definition of "know what you own" they would enforce under Article 122a?

Regulators warned about Wall Street and the City

Paul Volcker, Mervyn King, Jean-Claude Trichet and the Group of Thirty, in a January 2009 report, "Financial Reform: A Framework for Financial Stability", offered a relevant recommendation to regulators tasked with defining what "know what you own" means:

> The appropriate national regulator should, in conjunction with investors, determine what information is material to investors in these products and should consider enhancing existing rules or adopt new rules that ensure disclosure of that information, for both asset-backed and synthetic structured products.[393]

Why did leading central bankers feel the need to stress regulators should listen primarily to the investors when it comes to know what you own?

Because under the FDR Framework, the primary role of regulators in the global financial system is to ensure that investors have access to what they consider to be all the useful, relevant information in an appropriate, timely manner so that investors can independently assess this information and make a fully informed investment decision.

It is the investors, particularly the experts, who know what needs to be disclosed and when it needs to be disclosed for them to know what they own when it comes to structured finance securities.

The Group of Thirty also recognized both Wall Street and the City would fight tooth-and-nail against valuation transparency. This fight against valuation transparency was confirmed when the European Commission was considering Article 122a as an amendment to the Capital Requirements Directive. The amount of lobbying against the principle of 'know what you own' was the most that Brussels had ever seen.

Mr. Pecora recounted in his memoir, *Wall Street Under Oath*, passing the securities legislation with the philosophy of disclosure resulted in the same response by Wall Street,

> Bitterly hostile was Wall Street to the enactment of the regulatory legislation....[394]

In a June 2009 speech in Cambridge, then EU Commissioner for Internal Markets, Charlie McCreevy, who was the driving force behind the adoption of Article 122a, reminded regulators they are suppose to, if not completely ignore Wall Street and the City, not give Wall Street and the City more weight than investors:

> It is readily apparent that the Brussels financial services lobby is dominated by the sell side of the market.

---

393 Group of Thirty (2009, January), Financial Reform: A Framework for Financial Stability, Group of Thirty, http://www.group30.org/rpt_03.shtml, page 67.

394 Pecora Commission, Wikipedia, http://en.wikipedia.org/wiki/Pecora_Commission

> As regulators, we need to be conscious of this and do everything possible to ensure that the buy side's views are adequately and well represented.
>
> When I talk about the buy side, I am not so much talking about the retail consumer — who is generally well represented by consumer organizations. I am talking about the professional "buy side" of the market in areas like, for example, structured products.
>
> We have become more conscious of this in recent times. That's why I have indicated to the Commission Services that equal weight be given to the views of the buy side and to the representation of the buy side in expert and consultative groups in the future — because by definition the buy side of the market is as important a player as the sell side.[395]

So, did the Committee of European Banking Supervisors give at least equal weight to the buy-side in determining what "know what you own" means?

Bank regulators buy Wall Street and the City's bogus "know what you own" definition

The answer to this question is revealed in the summary of responses to the Committee of European Banking Supervisors consultation paper on Article 122a of the Capital Requirements Directive (Consultation CP40). In this public consultation, CEBS asked how it should interpret "know what you own".

There were 18 responses to this public consultation of which 17 came from the Wall Street, the City, their lobbyists, their legal advisors and the industry trade groups they control, i.e., Wall Street's Opacity Protection Team.[396] Not surprisingly, each of the team member's responses asserted the same disclosure practices that were the standard for disclosure used by opaque, toxic sub-prime mortgage-backed securities were adequate to 'know what you own'.

The Committee of European Banking Supervisors summary of responses reflected its acceptance of the sell-side's position. For example, on whether Article 122a required disclosure of the individual underlying exposures that backed a structured finance security (clause 103) the sell-side argued:

---

395 McCreevy, Charlie (2009, June), Future industry landscape, lessons from the market crisis, press release by European Commissioner for Internal Market and Services, http://europa.eu/rapid/press-release_SPEECH-09-323_en.htm?locale=en

396 Committee of European Bank Supervisors (2010, July 1), responses to consultation paper on guidelines on Article 122a of the Capital Requirements Directive (CP40), https://www.eba.europa.eu/regulation-and-policy/securitisation-and-covered-bonds/cebs-guidelines-on-the-application-of-article-122a-of-the-crd/-/regulatory-activity/consultation-paper/106834

> Although the guidance interprets "individual underlying exposures" as meaning loan-level data, it is argued by respondents that Paragraph 7 does not require originators to publish loan-level data, and should not bring in a requirement for loan-level data "through the back door" via Article 122a.[397]

And how did the Committee of European Banking Supervisors respond to the sell-side's response given the whole purpose of passing Article 122a was to put the buy-side in a position where it could know what it owns as a result of having access to the underlying loan level data?

> The guidance has been amended to outline that loan-level information is in principle required; however, CEBS recognises that in certain circumstances (e.g. for granular portfolios) stratification tables of loan-level information may be more appropriate to satisfy the requirement. This distinction should be equally valid for the information that credit institutions, as originators and sponsors, need to provide (under Paragraph 7), and for the due diligence that credit institutions as investors (or otherwise assuming exposure) would expect to receive and analyze (under Paragraphs 4-5).[398]

In plain English, the Committee of European Banking Supervisors agreed with Wall Street's Opacity Protection Team that opaque toxic subprime mortgage-backed securities provide adequate disclosure so investors could know what they own. The regulators agreed there was no need for loan-level data, let alone loan-level data that was kept current through the disclosure of all observable events involving the loans.

It was the purchase of these opaque securities that prompted the EU Parliament to pass Article 122a. Yet, here are the regulators effectively gutting Article 122a by listening to the 17 sell-side respondents.

Unfortunately, as the Committee of European Banking Supervisors showed, regulators don't break down the responses by "buy-side" versus "sell-side" or "for" versus "against" reform. Rather, regulators favor the sheer number of responses even when the responses were created using the same Word document and are printed on different letterhead.

By favoring the quantity of responses, the regulators ignore the admonition of the EU's Charlie McCreevy that the buy-side is equally important to the sell-side. By favoring the quantity of responses, the regulators ignore the admonition

---

397 Committee of European Banking Supervisors (2010, December 31), Feedback to the public consultation on Guidelines to Article 122a of the Capital Requirements Directive, https://www.eba.europa.eu/documents/10180/16094/Feedback-document.pdf, page 25.

398 ibid, page 25

of the Group of Thirty central bankers that when it comes to matters of disclosure, it is only the buy-side that can tell you if disclosure is adequate.

By the way, let me share with you the identity of the 18th respondent, me. And yes, I used the clear plastic and brown paper bags to explain "what" needed to be disclosed and "when" disclosure needed to take place so that investors could "know what they own".

ECB also buys bogus definition of "know what you own"

On December 16, 2010, the European Central Bank as part of its ABS loan-level initiative proposed its definition of "know what you own".

> The Governing Council of the European Central Bank (ECB) has decided to establish loan-by-loan information requirements for asset-backed securities (ABSs) in the Eurosystem collateral framework. The Governing Council intends to introduce the loan-by-loan information requirements approximately within the next 18 months, first for retail mortgage-backed securities (RMBSs) and thereafter gradually for other ABSs.
>
> Loan-level data will be provided in accordance with the template which is available on the ECB's website, at least on a quarterly basis on, or within one month of, the interest payment date of the instrument in question.
>
> To allow the processing, verification and transmission of the data, the Eurosystem will encourage market participants to establish the necessary data-handling infrastructure. This is expected to facilitate the application of the loan-by-loan information requirements and contribute to further developing transparency in the ABS market.
>
> When the necessary data-handling infrastructure has been established, the provision of loan-by-loan information will become an eligibility requirement for the instruments concerned. The Eurosystem will continue to accept securities not meeting the new information criteria until the obligation to submit loan-level data comes into force.[399]

Why would the ECB adopt the current once-per-month or less frequent disclosure practices? After all, the European Parliament was aware of these disclosure practices and specifically did not include them as part of Article 122a.

Perhaps the answer lies in the composition of the ABS Technical Working Group[400] that drafted the ECB's position.

---

399 ECB ABS Loan-Level Initiative, http://www.ecb.europa.eu/mopo/assets/loanlevel/html/index.en.html

400 ECB ABS Technical Working Group, http://www.ecb.europa.eu/mopo/assets/loanlevel/twg/html/index.en.html. The composition of the group has changed as members of the group have gone to work for the entity the

Did the ECB follow the recommendation of the Group of Thirty and include only investors on the ABS Technical Working Group or any of its subcommittees? No!

Did the ECB follow the recommendation of Commissioner McCreevy and include an equal number of investors and sell-side participants (lobbyists, investment banking, issuers and rating services)? No!

A brief look at the composition of the ABS Technical Working Group shows that with a couple of exception, the members of the working group are from the sell-side.[401] As noted by Commissioner McCreevy, these sell-side participants have a significant vested interest in retaining opacity.

Did the ECB realize with its adoption of current once per month or less frequent disclosure the ECB is saying the disclosure practices that made it impossible to value opaque, toxic subprime mortgage-backed securities satisfies the "know what you own requirement" of Article 122a?

Probably not!

I suspect that the sell-side used its position on the ABS Technical Working Group to effectively end the "know what you own requirement" of Article 122a and the ECB representatives, who are not experts in disclosure or did not understand the implications for Article 122a, went along with it.

What we do know is, despite championing a firm primarily owned by the sell-side to provide valuation transparency for structured finance securities, the ECB in a May 2014 discussion paper is still wondering how to bring valuation transparency to EU structured finance securities.[402]

Will bogus definition of "know what you own" restart structured finance?

Why should the level of disclosure the global financial regulators adopted end the buyers' strike in structured finance? After all, investors have plenty of investment opportunities other than structured finance securities where they do have access for free to all the useful, relevant information in an appropriate, timely manner.

ECB is sponsoring to handle this disclosure initiative, the European Data Warehouse. For example, one individual worked for the sell-side lobbying group while on the technical working group and then joined the European Data Warehouse.

401 European Central Bank (2010, December 17), ABS Technical Working Group, https://www.ecb.europa.eu/paym/coll/loanlevel/twg/html/index.en.html

402 Bank of England, European Central Bank (2014, May), The case for a better functioning securitisation market in the European Union, https://www.ecb.europa.eu/pub/pdf/other/ecb-boe_case_better_functioning_securitisation_marketen.pdf

Why invest in securities that have a track record of Wall Street and the City showing they are willing to use their information advantage for their benefit and to the detriment of investors [think shorting sub-prime mortgage backed securities]?

Ultimately, the regulators' definition of "know what you own" doesn't protect money managers from having to disclose the following to a perspective investor:

> Due to a lack of current information on the underlying collateral performance, investing with me in structured finance securities is asking me to blindly bet on your behalf as there is no way for me to actually know what I am buying or selling. Without actually knowing what I am buying, I do not know how to tell if the price Wall Street shows represents the bigger fool as a buyer or seller. Therefore, I cannot make informed investment management decisions.

So long as money managers are investing their clients' money without this disclosure, they are guaranteeing their investors that the investors will not lose money. How could it be otherwise?

The money managers know the disclosure adopted by the European bank regulators and the ECB is the same level of disclosure that was not adequate for BNP Paribas to value sub-prime mortgage backed securities in August 2007.

The money managers know under Article 122a of the European Capital Requirements Directive they have an obligation to know what they own. No amount of lobbying by the sell-side or regulatory incompetence changes the legislative intent. The European Commission and European Parliament knew what level of disclosure was inadequate for BNP Paribas and they did not intend to set this level of disclosure as adequate for knowing what you own.

Common sense tells money managers that if the level of disclosure was not adequate for BNP Paribas to value securities, it is not adequate for knowing what they own.

It is simply not a defense for a money manager to argue, "well other money managers were buying these securities". Money managers have a fiduciary duty.

The Volcker Rule

The Volcker Rule shows that financial regulators in the U.S. are not immune to lobbying by Wall Street.

Just like Article 122a of the European Capital Requirements Directive left the definition and enforcement of 'know what you own' to the regulators, the Dodd-Frank Act left the definition of proprietary trading and the enforcement of the ban on proprietary trading to the regulators.

In the same way that the European regulators screwed up defining and enforcing the simple concept of 'know what you own', the U.S. regulators have screwed up defining and enforcing the ban on proprietary trading by banks.

There are two parts to each regulation: what the regulation covers and how it is enforced. The Volcker Rule could be written in two short paragraphs.

Paragraph one would be what the Volcker Rule covers and simply says banks are not allowed to engage in proprietary trading. Paragraph two would describe how the regulation is enforced and says banks must disclose on an ongoing basis their current global asset, liability and off-balance sheet exposure details. With this data, market participants, including the global regulators, could assess whether the banks are complying and not engaging in proprietary trading. Disclosure allows for enforcement of market discipline to prevent proprietary trading and regulatory sanctions if proprietary trading does occur.

However, the regulators haven't pursued simple broad rules that are confirmed using valuation transparency. Instead, the regulators have pursued complex regulations combined with regulatory oversight.

As shown by the Volcker Rule, regulators prefer substituting complex regulations and regulatory oversight for valuation transparency and market discipline.

Chapter 16

FINANCIAL REGULATORS WANT ONE MORE CHANCE

I don't know a single time when federal regulators—primarily the FDIC—actually identified a significant bank failure in advance. Regulators are always the last ones to the party after everyone in the market (the other bankers) know something is going on. Thus, in that context, regulators have a 100 percent failure rate.
John Allison, former chairman and CEO of BB&T[403]

That loyal retainer of the Chase Manhattan Bank, the American president.
— Gore Vidal[404]

The global bank regulators' preference for complex regulations and regulatory oversight is best illustrated with bank capital regulations. Regulators adopted the complex Basel III capital regulations despite the failure at the beginning of the financial crisis of the complex Basel II bank capital regulations.

The Basel capital regulations attempt to link the amount of capital banks have to the risks they take. But is there any reason to think the new capital regulations will result in banks holding the right amount of capital? After all, the reason cited for bailing out the banks at the beginning of the financial crisis was the interconnectedness of the financial system. Increasing bank capital to 20% of risk-adjusted assets does not guarantee the financial system will not collapse from contagion. Without this guarantee, no government will gamble on the system not collapsing.

---

403 Dowd, Kevin (September 3, 2014), *Math Gone Mad: Regulatory Risk Modeling by the Federal Reserve*, Cato Institute, http://object.cato.org/sites/cato.org/files/pubs/pdf/pa754.pdf, page 2.

404 The Economist (2012, August 3), in comments to A dying breed: remembering Gore Vidal, http://www.economist.com/blogs/prospero/2012/08/remembering-gore-vidal

What is the right amount of capital for a bank to have?

Walter Bagehot's observation that a well-run bank needs no capital and no amount of capital is enough to save a poorly run bank raises two interesting questions:

- How much is enough capital; and
- How could you prove a bank has enough capital?

Valuation transparency indirectly answers the first question and directly answers the second question.

With valuation transparency, market participants can independently assess the risk of each bank and adjust the price it pays for funds so that the price is related to the risk of the financial institution. This linkage between the cost of a bank's funding and its risk drives a bank's funding structure and how much capital is in this structure.

When there is valuation transparency, market participants determine how much capital is enough based on their willingness to invest in the bank's capital instruments that would absorb losses. The proof a bank is seen as having enough capital comes when the bank is able to take on additional risk without increasing its cost of funds or decreasing its stock price.

In the absence of valuation transparency, financial regulators are left to guess how much is enough capital and what is the best way to measure this capital to prove it.

The problem regulators face in answering these questions can be illustrated by looking at the interbank lending market. Despite bankers and regulators claiming the black box banks are adequately capitalized because they have passed capital adequacy stress tests, the interbank lending market that froze in late 2008 remains frozen. So clearly, financial regulators have not convince banks with deposits to lend that the banks looking to borrow have adequate capital.

Regulators adopt reliance on own judgment

The bank regulators preference for regulatory oversight is best illustrated by the regulators' decision to replace the failure of "light-touch" regulation with a "judgment-based" approach. Rather than relying on bank management to say everything is okay, the regulators will now analyze each bank and draw their own conclusions about its safety and soundness.

There are two problems with this approach. First, it substitutes the judgment of the regulators for the judgment of the market. No one believes the regulators can do a better job of assessing and restraining the risk of each bank than the market. Second, bank regulators are unable to restrain bank risk taking because of political pressure. When everything seems to be going well, politicians will push back against regulators trying to restrain risk taking.

The common sense test for understanding why, in the absence of valuation transparency, regulators relying on their own judgment will fail is asking two questions:

- Who do you think would do a better job of assessing the risk of Citi — a competitor like JPMorgan or the bank regulators?
- Who do you think would do a better job of restraining the risk-taking by Citi — a competitor like JPMorgan who would be responsible for all losses on its exposures to Citi or the bank regulators who would have to explain their actions to politicians?

Who Guards the Guardians?

Why are regulators pursuing regulatory micro-management based on complex regulations and regulatory oversight over the simpler, more effective combination of valuation transparency and market discipline?

A cynic might say that the pursuit of complex regulations and regulatory oversight is the result of financial regulators trying to enhance their power and prestige as it makes the financial system more dependent on them.

Alternatively, a cynic might say the pursuit of complex regulations and regulatory oversight is a way to mask the failure of the financial regulators to prevent our current financial crisis.

Finally, a cynic might point out all this complex regulation simply reflects regulatory capture as it is designed to give the appearance of lots of activity while at the same time fundamentally not changing anything of significance in how banks operate.

What gives each of these cynical views of the regulators and their complex regulations credibility is the failure of the regulators to rely on or ensure market participants have access to valuation transparency even when they know it is the solution.

The FDR Framework is designed so that market participants can Trust, but Verify not only the investments they make but also that the financial regulators are doing what they are suppose to do. Valuation transparency allows the market participants to exert discipline on the financial regulators too.

Under the FDR Framework, the answer to the question of who guards the guardians is the market participants. And when the financial regulators don't ensure access to valuation transparency, market participants don't trust what the regulators are doing.

After all, why would market participants want to trust the regulators and give them a second chance when their safety net failed to prevent the current financial crisis and the result of their failure in the future would be another financial crisis?

This is particularly true when the future financial crisis is likely to involve policymakers making a choice between a regulator recommended bank bailout or requiring the banks to absorb their losses.

SECTION 6

OPACITY MADE POLICY RESPONSE TO 2007 FINANCIAL CRISIS POSSIBLE

It is odd, as well as infuriating, that ... bankers managed to take the public for ... an expensive ride again... with governments... opting to rescue banks rather than risk economic disaster.

—*John Gapper*[405]

---

405 Gapper, John (2008, October 1), The Fatal Banker's Fall, Financial Times, http://www.ft.com/intl/cms/s/0/ccc6d456-8fd7-11dd-9890-0000779fd18c.html#axzz2vs2uiyup

Chapter 17

WHAT ARE THE CHOICES IN HOW TO RESPOND TO A FINANCIAL CRISIS?

Every day since September 23, 2008 when the global financial system was placed on taxpayer backed life support, global policymakers and financial regulators have had to make a series of choices about how to handle the opacity driven crisis. As Sir Mervyn King observed,

> Right through this crisis, from the very beginning when we were concerned about financial institutions, right up to now when we're more concerned with sovereigns, an awful lot of people wanted to believe that it was a crisis of liquidity. It wasn't; it isn't; and until we accept that, we'll never find an answer to it.
>
> It was a crisis based on solvency or, to be more precise, the build up of very large amounts of debt where concerns crept in about the ability of the borrowers to repay that debt — initially financial institutions, and now sovereigns. So whatever is the answer, provisional liquidity can buy only time. That time has to be used, it has to be used to go right to the heart of the underlying problems...
>
> The reason why it is difficult to handle the crisis in practice is not so much because of a failure of crisis management, but because the different actors involved have different views about the right long-run solution.
>
> But that's the challenge — to come to a view about what is the right long-run solution and to put in place a transition to it which will give confidence to markets that ultimately this problem will indeed be tackled.[406]

Because of the opacity of the banks, from the beginning of the financial crisis on August 9, 2007 to September 23, 2008, the policymakers and financial regulators were limited in how they could respond to the financial crisis to the Japanese Model. After September 23, 2008, they have had to make a daily choice

[406] Bank of England (2011, June 24), Financial Stability Report Q&A, Bank of England, http://www.bankofengland.co.uk/publications/Documents/fsr/2011/conf110624.pdf, page 8.

between two different policy models for handling the excess debt in the global financial system: the Japanese Model and the Swedish Model.

Who bears the pain?

First, there is the financial regulator preferred Japanese Model that protects bank capital levels and banker bonuses at all cost while placing the burden of the excess debt in the financial system on the real economy. Bank capital levels and banker bonuses are protected under a "budget" for recognizing the losses on the excess debt that exists on and off the banks' balance sheets. The budget for recognizing losses reflects how quickly banks can generate earnings in excess of what is needed to pay banker bonuses and shareholder dividends as well as grow book capital levels. This is good for bankers as it guarantees their bonus payments.

The Japanese Model involves hiding the banks' true condition and pursuing policies designed to boost bank earnings. The policies for hiding the true condition of the banks include bailouts, suspension of mark-to-market accounting and regulatory forbearance. These policies also include financial regulator sponsored stress tests. In theory, these tests are designed to identify weak banks, but in practice these tests appear to cover up problem banks that subsequently are nationalized. The policies for boosting bank earnings include zero interest rates and quantitative easing.

Under the Japanese Model, policymakers and financial regulators also go into prevent the next financial crisis mode while the problems associated with the excess debt in the financial system from the current financial crisis are not addressed. This undermines confidence. Financial market participants know the losses on the excess debt exist. What they don't know because of opacity is how quickly, if ever, the banks' "budget" for recognizing the losses on this excess debt will eliminate the problem.

The same policies that are good for bankers and their bonuses are bad for the real economy because they distort asset prices and access to capital. For proof that the Japanese Model is bad for the real economy, look at Japan's economic malaise since its bank solvency crisis began in the late 1980s.

Ultimately, the reason the Japanese Model is bad is it doesn't address the impact of the excess debt in the financial system on the real economy. The effect on the economy of this excess debt is three-fold. First, debtors go into pay down the debt mode. The interest they avoid paying provides a higher return than investing in alternative "risk-free" assets like government bonds. Second, lending ceases to be about allocating capital between creditworthy borrowers, but rather is focused on hiding insolvent borrowers. Not allocating credit to its best use hurts the real economy as legitimate growth opportunities aren't realized due to an inability to get funding. Third, the excess debt diverts capital needed for reinvestment, growth and social programs to debt service. This diversion of capital acts like a tax and lowers spending by households and businesses. The greater the amount of excess debt, the higher the tax and the more spending is lowered.

At best, the resulting lower spending triggers an economic malaise and a stagnant economy operating at less then full employment. At worse, the resulting lower spending triggers a great recession. In either case, due to the lack of demand, the private sector doesn't perceive there are enough good investment opportunities to enable full employment. As a result, the economy tends to one of two extremes: inadequate, slow growth or monetary policy driven unsustainable bubbles.

Since the start of our current financial crisis on August 9, 2007, on the advice of the bankers, policymakers in the EU, UK and U.S. have adopted and pursued the Japanese Model with its focus on identification, treatment and management of the symptoms of the financial crisis. However, suppression of the symptoms doesn't address or fix the root cause of the financial crisis.

Second, there is the Swedish Model that our financial system was designed to support. It directly addresses the root causes of the financial crisis. So, what is the Swedish Model? Facing an insolvent banking system in 1992,

> Sweden did not just bail out its financial institutions by having the government take over the bad debts. ... Banks had to write down losses and issue warrants to the government.[407]

By telling its banks to write down their losses promptly before coming to the state for recapitalization, banks and the bankers were held responsible for the losses. In addition, Sweden avoided the costs of a long foreclosure and liquidation process for the loans borrowers couldn't repay. Loans were written down to reflect the borrower's capacity to repay and then restructured to become performing assets again.

> Sweden did more than this.
>
> The government issued blanket insurance for a period of four years to creditors in all the country's 114 banks.[408]

---

407 Dougherty, Carter (2008, September 22), Stopping a Financial Crisis, the Swedish Way, The New York Times, http://www.nytimes.com/2008/09/23/business/worldbusiness/23krona.html?_r=1&&gwh=B0F623A6211845CA59FEB404E27877C5&gwt=pay,

408 Purvis, Andrew (2008, September 24), Sweden's Model Approach to Financial Disaster, Time Magazine, http://content.time.com/time/business/article/0,8599,1843659,00.html

This prevented a run on the Swedish banks by uninsured depositors and unsecured creditors.

Finally, according to Occasional Paper 79 by the Group of Thirty (otherwise known as Lessons Learned from Previous Banking Crisis: Sweden, Japan, Spain and Mexico), Sweden combined all of the above with transparency.

> Both the banks and the authorities had to disclose the extent of the problems and the methods for solving them in some detail and based on realistic, even conservative, assessments.[409]

In summary, the Swedish Model has four main elements.

- Any funds invested by the government should receive a return that reflects the true risk being taken on.
- Banks write-down their bad on and off-balance sheet exposures today and rebuild book capital through retention of future earnings and equity issuance.
- Governments guarantee both depositors and unsecured debt holders for several years while the banks rebuild their book capital.
- Banks provide transparency.

The Swedish Model is bad for book capital levels and banker bonuses, but good for the real economy. It is bad for book capital levels because the banks are required to recognize the losses on the excess debt in the financial system today and these losses flow through the book capital accounts. Fortunately, banks, as redesigned by the FDR Administration and shown by the U.S. in the 1930s and Sweden in the 1990s, can recognize these losses and continue to operate and support the real economy. Banks can do this because of the combination of deposit insurance and access to central bank funding. With deposit insurance, the taxpayers become the banks silent equity partner when banks have low or negative book capital levels.

It is worse for banker bonuses because 100% of pre-banker bonus earnings are retained to rebuild the bank's book capital level. Rebuilding a bank's book capital level is a process that could take several years.

It is good for the real economy because it avoids the distortion in asset prices and access to funding associated with hiding the losses under the Japanese Model. The performance of the U.S. economy in the first year of the FDR

---

409 Group of Thirty Occasional Paper 79 (2009, April), Lessons Learned from Previous Banking Crisis: Sweden, Japan, Spain and Mexico, http://www.group30.org/images/PDF/OP79.pdf, page 21.

Administration, Sweden's economy following its bank solvency crisis in the 1990s and Iceland's economy following its bank solvency crisis in 2008 is proof the Swedish Model is good for the real economy.

It is not as if the bank regulators don't know they should adopt the Swedish Model. As the NY Fed observed,

> BOX: A Good Example: Lessons from the Resolution of the Swedish Financial Crisis
>
> Sweden experienced a twin crisis in the early 1990s, which marked the first systemic crisis in industrialized countries since the 1930s. It is usually argued that this episode can be regarded as a good example of a swift, effective and low cost resolution of banking crisis. However, the Swedish experience has some unique features that may be difficult to replicate in all crises.
>
> **Crisis and intervention:** ... Overall, to resolve the crisis, Swedish authorities forced banks to write-down their losses, used methods such as capital injections (both private and public), and separated troubled institutions into "good banks" and "bad banks", employing AMCs to restructure and divest the assets of the bad banks. Banks were told to write down heir losses promptly. Bank owners were invited to inject capital, or let the Swedish authorities intervene, which implied wiping out shareholders.
>
> **Exit:** Exit from the guarantees and the divesting of assets has been smooth with low cost. In 1996, Sweden rescinded the guarantees, replacing them with a bank-financed depositor-protection scheme. ...
>
> Sweden shelled out 4 percent of its GDP to rescue its financial system. After the recovery from asset sales, the cost ended up being less than 2 percent. It is argued that factors such as political consensus, decisiveness and transparency surrounding the management of the crisis contributed to restoring confidence and to the eventual success of the resolution.[410]

And why wasn't the Swedish Model adopted given the bank regulators knew it worked?

> **Complexity of financial instruments:** The assets that were resolved mostly involved those related to real estate and were not very complex, a factor that made the resolution easier and less costly. However, over time the financial industry and financial contracts became much more complex. An important feature of the recent crisis was the difficulty to assess complex financial instruments and structures, as well as off-balance sheet commitments and bank related vehicles such as SIVs and conduits. These complex instruments,

---

410 White, Phoebe, Yorulmazer, Tanju (2014, April 21), Bank Resolution Concepts, Trade-offs, and Changes in Practices, page 22. FRBNY Economic Policy Review, http://www.ny.frb.org/research/epr/2014/1403whit.html

> valuation issues, and institutional arrangements make it more difficult for analysts and counterparties to understand a bank's financial position adding to the difficulties of the resolution.[411]

One reason the regulators didn't use the Swedish Model was the very opacity that was the necessary condition for our current financial crisis. According to the NY Fed, the Swedish Model would have been pursued if there had been transparency into banks and structured finance securities. The only problem with this excuse is it is and was no longer valid after September 23, 2008 when the global financial system was put on taxpayer backed life support. At that point, there was no reason transparency could not have been provided and the banks required to pursue the Swedish Model.

> **Macroeconomic factors helped recovery in Sweden:** Sweden had a fixed exchange rate before the crisis. Once the krona peg had been abandoned and the currency depreciated, Swedish goods regained competitiveness in export markets. Furthermore, a quick rebound in the Swedish economy stemmed from an increase in economic growth in Europe. The strong international recovery helped push up real estate values in Sweden and improved the balance sheet of banks, which played an important role in the recovery process. While Sweden is a small economy compared to the rest of the world, the slow-down in big industrial countries such as the United States and those in Europe can drag the global economy down and such an export-led recovery may not be feasible especially when countries are in a currency union, such as in Europe.[412]

Another reason the regulators used to justify not pursuing the Swedish Model was the "our country is not Sweden" excuse. Given the Swedish Model was originally used successfully by the FDR Administration to end the worst of the Great Depression, we know it works in the U.S. As a result, the NY Fed is left to argue our economic circumstances were different than Sweden's and therefore it won't work.

The IMF debunked this excuse in arguing that the lesson from history is the way to deal with and end an opacity driven crisis with minimum damage to the real economy or the social contract is to adopt the Swedish Model and require the banks to absorb upfront their losses on the excess public and private debt in the financial system. As the IMF observed,

> Based on case studies, we find that government policies can help prevent prolonged contractions in economic activity by addressing the problem of

411 ibid, page 23

412 ibid, page 23

> excessive household debt. In particular, bold household debt restructuring programs such as those implemented in the United States in the 1930s and in Iceland today can significantly reduce debt repayment burdens and the number of household defaults and foreclosures. Such policies can therefore help avert self-reinforcing cycles of household defaults, further house price declines, and additional contractions in output.[413]

The choice between the Japanese and the Swedish Models is really a choice between pretending the excess debt doesn't exist and a debt deal. It is a choice between a rational resolution of the excess debt in the global financial system or preserving the capital structure of the banks and banker bonus payments. Under the Japanese Model, banks are allowed to pretend the excess debt borrowers have no ability to repay is worth book value. Rather than work with the borrowers and restructured the debt to something affordable, the banks engage in activities that make the situation worse and hurt the real economy. Under the Swedish Model, banks are forced to recognize their mistakes and write-down their debt and investments. As a result, the banks can work with the borrowers to restructure the debt to something that is affordable and helps the real economy.

The reason global policymakers have to make a choice every day is their initial choice to listen to bankers and the financial regulators and pursue the Japanese Model does not mean after the global financial system was put on taxpayer backed life support that they couldn't change their mind today and instead pursue the Swedish Model.

A financial crisis needn't do significant harm to the real economy

It is how policymakers respond to a financial crisis that dictates the amount of damage to the real economy. It is the choice between the Japanese and Swedish models for handling an opacity driven financial crisis that dictates how much damage is done to the real economy.

Unfortunately, by choosing and staying with the Japanese Model, the global policymakers have chosen to turn our current financial crisis into a disaster for their economies. The moment when these policymakers made this choice is when they decided that despite the global financial system being on taxpayer backed life support banks should not absorb the losses on the financial excesses they created. Instead of having banks and their book capital accounts operate as a safety valve between the financial excesses and the real economy,

---

413 Leigh, Daniel, Igan, Deniz, Simon, John, Topalova, Petia (2012, April), World Economic Outlook: Growth Resuming, Dangers Remain, Chapter 3, http://www.imf.org/external/pubs/ft/weo/2012/01/pdf/c3.pdf, page 89.

global policymakers decided to put the burden of the financial excess on the real economy.

This decision hurts the real economy in multiple ways.

- It hurts demand. Debtors focus on, if at all possible, repaying their debt. One way to do this is by reducing their discretionary spending.
- It diverts capital the real economy needs for reinvestment, growth and paying for social programs to supporting the excess debt. Troubled borrowers face both an increase in the interest on their debt as well as a significant leap in fees. This higher cost of debt service for both individuals and firms effectively sucks out of the borrowers any cash they might generate to invest and grow. Think of this as vampire banks preying on the real economy by sucking the capital out of zombie firms that in turn engage in competition in such a way as to suck capital out of successful firms.

The result of the decision to pursue the Japanese Model has been to effectively condemn the global economy to follow Japan's lead into economic malaise and the promise of multiple lost decades.

A more subtle way the decision to pursue the Japanese Model hurts the real economy is it prevents adoption of a system for restructuring the excess debt in the global financial system including the excess sovereign debt. It prevents this by pretending the sovereign debt doesn't have to be restructured even when there is no possibility of the debt of countries like Greece or Japan ever being repaid in the traditional sense.

It is still not too late to change course and put the losses where they belong — on the banks. Having the banks recognize the losses makes sense. First, the bankers are experts in assessing credit risk and it was their responsibility to ensure they didn't lend too much. Second, bankers know some of their loans will default and their business model is based on absorbing these losses.

Forcing the banks to write their assets down to a realistic value has many benefits. Among the benefits are it stops the distortion in pricing of assets that is currently going on — think commercial real estate prices being influenced by extend and pretend or residential real estate prices being influenced by artificially low interest rates. When asset prices are being distorted, it is very difficult for market participants to make investments. Writing down the debt to a realistic value also allows debts to be restructured consistent with the borrower's ability to pay.

Chapter 18

WHY REGULATORS PREFER THE JAPANESE MODEL

When a big bank fails, bail in is never a soft option...the temptation is always there for governments to reach for the check book ... [it's] irresistible."
--- *Andy Haldane, Bank of England*[414]

I think the problem that we are facing is probably insufficient transparency regarding the balance sheets of the European banks.
— *Danièle Nouy, the ECB's chief banking regulator and the person in charge of the EU regulators' 2014 bank asset quality review and stress test process.*[415]

The Bank of England's Andy Haldane acknowledged the elephant in the room when he observed financial regulators have an "irresistible"[416] urge to bailout banks using taxpayer funds rather than bail-in banks using future bank earnings or stockholder and unsecured debt holder funds.

The "irresistible" urge to bailout banks

Mr. Haldane called for a set of binding rules on authorities to "tie their hands"[417] and force them to bail-in rather than bailout the banks. In addition, he wanted higher levels of capital to make it more likely that at a time of crisis the

414 Buell, Todd (2013, May 28), *BOE's Haldane: Worried Bail in Rules Won't Be Enough*, The Wall Street Journal, http://online.wsj.com/article/BT-CO-20130528-703047.html?mod=dist_smartbrief

415 Nouy, Danièle (2014, February 9), transcript of interview, Financial Times, http://www.ft.com/intl/cms/s/0/3e0420e2-91a8-11e3-adde-00144feab7de.html#axzz2tmCPwihU

416 Buell, Todd (2013, May 28), *BOE's Haldane: Worried Bail in Rules Won't Be Enough*, The Wall Street Journal, http://online.wsj.com/article/BT-CO-20130528-703047.html?mod=dist_smartbrief

417 ibid

authorities would not ask that the rules be taken off and that the capital on bank balance sheets actually be used.

History has already shown that Mr. Haldane's proposed solutions to stop the irresistible urge have proven to be ineffective.

In an ironic twist, one of Mr. Haldane's fellow members on the Bank of England's Financial Policy Committee, Donald Kohn, gave a speech in which he showed why in the presence of opacity regulators always have this irresistible urge. In his speech, Mr. Kohn talked about how the committee, set up as a result of our current financial crisis as a prudential regulator with a mandate to promote financial stability by removing or reducing systemic risk, thought about using bank capital. Mr. Kohn dismissed banks using their capital to absorb losses and pursuing the Swedish Model by observing,

> When the economy is weakening and bad debts are building, easing [capital and liquidity] requirements may reduce the effect of financial sector problems on the real economy.[418]

There is no 'may' in the effect of these policy actions on the real economy. It has been well known since the Great Depression that implementing the Swedish Model and making banks absorb the losses today on the existing excesses in the financial system, which is the equivalent of easing capital requirements, does reduce the effect of financial sector problems on the real economy.

NY Fed documents Swedish Model works

The NY Fed documented the Swedish Model with banks acting as a safety valve between the excesses in the financial system and the real economy worked as far back as the Great Depression.

> Contemporary observers consider the [US] Bank Holiday and [FDR's] Fireside Chat [discussed previously in which he introduced a deposit guarantee] a one-two punch that broke the back of the Great Depression....[419]

Breaking the back of the Great Depression sure sounds like making banks absorb the losses on the financial excesses unambiguously works.

---

418 Kohn, Donald (2011, December 2), Speech: The Financial Policy Committee at the Bank of England, Bank of England, http://www.bankofengland.co.uk/publications/Documents/speeches/2011/speech536.pdf, page 7.

419 Silber, William L. (2009, July), Why Did FDR's Bank Holiday Succeed, Federal Reserve Bank of New York Economic Policy Review, Volume 15, Number 1, pages 19-30, http://www.newyorkfed.org/research/epr/2009/EPRvol15n1.pdf, page 20.

In fairness, the NY Fed article refers to an implied 100% deposit guarantee but does not mention banks taking losses. Literally true, but once there is an implied 100% deposit guarantee in place, there was no reason that a bank could not recognize all of its losses. It does not have to fear a run as no one is looking at its financial statements.

As a practical matter, once the government formally began guaranteeing deposits, bank regulators had an incentive because banks were disclosing their current exposure details to make sure the banks cleaned up their bad assets as quickly as possible. To help the banks do this, in April 1933 the FDR Administration set up the Home Owners' Loan Corporation.

The Home Owners' Loan Corporation bought mortgages that were at-risk or already in default from the banks. The HOLC bought the mortgages from the banks at a price reflecting what the borrower could afford to repay on a restructured loan with a fixed rate of interest and a longer term to maturity. As a result, the banks were still held responsible for their losses.

In addition, by restructuring the mortgages to what the borrowers could afford to repay, HOLC stimulated the economy.

> A key feature of HOLC was the effective transfer of funds to credit-constrained households with distressed balance sheets and a high marginal propensity to consume, which mitigated the negative effects on aggregate demand ... The objective, emphasized by President Roosevelt in a message to Congress, was to relieve "the small home owner ... of the burden of excessive interest and principal payments incurred during the period of higher values and higher earning power"[420]

Mr. Kohn continued and presented the regulators' case for protecting bank capital levels by pursuing the Japanese Model.

> But how do you know the problems won't get much worse, perhaps for reasons entirely external to the economy in question and out of control of the authorities.
>
> If conditions do continue to deteriorate substantially, releasing capital and liquidity buffers — lowering requirements — could come back to haunt the economy and the authorities if it results in widespread failures, unemployment as credit tightens, and if it comes to require fiscal action to stem the downward slide.[421]

---

420 Leigh, Daniel, Igan, Deniz, Simon, John, Topalova, Petia (2012, April), World Economic Outlook: Growth Resuming, Dangers Remain, Chapter 3, http://www.imf.org/external/pubs/ft/weo/2012/01/pdf/c3.pdf, page 106.

421 Kohn, Donald (2011, December 2), Speech: The Financial Policy Committee at the Bank of England, Bank of England, http://www.bankofengland.co.uk/publications/

Now there is a prescription for financial regulators always supporting the Japanese Model and never requiring the banks to recognize the losses on the excess debt in the financial system. After all, it is always possible that the economic situation will get worse.

> The FPC has faced just such an issue as the situation in the euro area worsened last summer and fall, and its discussion of the conflicting pressures is reflected in the record of our September meeting, already published.
>
> The committee concluded that lowering buffers would not be appropriate at that time, out of concern about what might be coming next.[422]

Mr. Kohn confirmed why regulators in the presence of opacity are incapable of requiring banks to recognize their losses. Recognizing losses would use the capital buffer that regulators think is so important to maintain if the situation were to get worse.

There is another reason why regulators will never be able to require banks to recognize their losses: regulators place an artificial constraint on the ability of banks to absorb losses by requiring banks always have a positive book capital level.

Bank book capital is an accounting construct and by definition can have a positive or negative value. It is the account through which losses taken by the bank ultimately flows.

Since it is an accounting construct, it is easy to manipulate. For example, regulators can manipulate it by engaging in regulatory forbearance and letting banks practice 'extend and pretend' to turn non-performing loans into zombie loans. This results in no losses flowing through the banks' book capital accounts and the real economy suffering as it has to deal with the zombie borrowers and the resulting misallocation of resources.

The fact that the losses are not flowing through each bank's book capital account does not mean that the losses do not exist. The fact that existing losses are not flowing through the bank's book capital account also does not mean that market participants are completely unaware of these losses.

The losses on loans to less developed countries is a classic example where investors knew losses existed and regulators worked with the bankers to keep the losses from flowing through the banks' book capital accounts. The activity by regulators was unnecessary. Market participants simply adjusted each bank's reported book capital level for an estimate of the bank's losses on its loans to less developed countries. This adjustment showed a number of large banks had very low or, in Security Pacific's case, negative book capital levels.

Documents/speeches/2011/speech536.pdf, page 7.

422 ibid, page 7

> The cost of leaning unnecessarily hard against expanding credit and rising asset prices would be growth and innovation foregone — very hard to see.
>
> The cost of inadequate capital and liquidity is large and visible — a loss of confidence and an unstable financial system.[423]

The loss of confidence is not a result of inadequate capital and liquidity, but rather from opacity. When market participants cannot Trust, but Verify, financial systems are unstable as there is no basis other than wishful thinking for confidence.

A direct link between a stable financial system in the presence of opacity and high levels of capital and liquidity in the banks has never been shown to exist. For example, there were bank runs on well-capitalized, liquid banks before the creation of a lender of last resort. A direct link between opacity and an unstable financial system has been shown to exist. Examples of this financial instability include both the Great Depression and our current financial crisis. A direct link between valuation transparency and a stable financial system has been shown to exist. The period of financial stability in the U.S. after the adoption of the philosophy of disclosure is an example.

As Donald Kohn explained, bank regulators will never require banks to use their book capital to absorb losses during a financial crisis. Bank regulators see a decline in book capital levels as sending the wrong signals about the safety and soundness of the financial system and fear the situation could get worse. The bank regulators would rather engage in regulatory forbearance and let banks practice 'extend and pretend' to turn non-performing loans into 'zombie' loans than see book capital levels decline.

Also, bank regulators will never give up using taxpayer funds to bailout the banks in a time of financial crisis. Even if a law is passed today, everyone knows the law is likely to be repealed if the bank regulators think that the failure to repeal the law will make the financial crisis worse.

It is opacity that allows banking regulators to pursue their "irresistible" urge to bailout the banks using taxpayer funds. Hence, there is only one simple solution to take this option off of the table. Require the banks to provide valuation transparency and disclose on an ongoing basis their current global asset, liability and off-balance sheet exposure details.

With this information, market participants can independently assess the risk of each bank. Then, they can adjust their exposure before a crisis to what they can afford to lose given the risk of each bank. This eliminates the fear banks' recognizing their losses will make the situation worse. Valuation transparency eliminates the risk of financial contagion as all market participants have

423 ibid, page 7

adjusted their exposure to what they can afford to lose. With financial contagion eliminated and investors expecting to absorb losses, there is no reason for bank regulators to continue to support the Japanese Model and have an irresistible urge to bailout the banks.

This is the way our financial system is designed to operate under the FDR Framework.

Unfortunately, at the start of the financial crisis on August 9, 2007, our financial system was not operating the way it was suppose to under the FDR Framework. Large areas of the financial system were opaque including structured finance securities and the banks. As a result, policymakers and financial regulators did not have a choice, but rather were forced to pursue the Japanese Model.

This changed on September 23, 2008. After the U.S. Congress had been asked to put the financial system on taxpayer-backed life support, the choice to pursue the Swedish Model became an option.

In the remainder of this chapter, I am going to focus on two significant speeches given by individuals who were at the very center of the choice to continue pursuit of the Japanese Model after the Swedish Model became an option. These individuals used these speeches to describe how they saw the financial crisis, why they succumbed to the irresistible urge to use taxpayer funds to bailout the banks and the policy response to all the new problems this created. Both individuals were fully aware of the role opacity was playing in the financial crisis, but neither suggests ending it and adopting the Swedish Model.

Sir Mervyn King defends choosing the Japanese Model

In his 2012 BBC lecture, former Bank of England governor Mervyn King expressed his view of the financial crisis and the subsequent regulatory reforms.

> So tonight I want to try to answer three questions. First, what went wrong? Second, what are the lessons? Third, what needs to change?...
>
> So what was the problem? In a nutshell, our banking and financial system overextended itself. That left it fragile and vulnerable to a sudden loss of confidence.
>
> The most obvious symptom was that banks were lending too much. Strikingly, most of that increase in lending wasn't to families or businesses, but to other parts of the financial system.
>
> To finance this, banks were borrowing large amounts themselves. And this was their Achilles' heel. By the end of 2006, some banks had borrowed as much as £50 for every pound provided by their own shareholders. So even a small

> piece of bad news about the value of its assets would wipe out much of a bank's capital, and leave depositors scurrying for the door.[424]

There is plenty of evidence with a deposit guarantee in place retail and business depositors don't scurry for the door. This has held true in countries like Ireland, Portugal, Spain and Cyprus even when it was clear that banks were insolvent. Core depositors have stayed.

The depositors who run are the hot money wholesale depositors.

> What made the situation worse was that the fortunes of banks had become closely tied together through transactions in complex and obscure financial instruments. So, it was difficult to know which banks were safe and which weren't....[425]

Mervyn King identifies the risk of financial contagion that resulted from opaque financial institutions investing in opaque securities. The inability to determine which banks were solvent and which were insolvent is exactly the same conclusion that the U.S. Financial Crisis Inquiry Commission reached. This is not surprising as banks are black boxes everywhere.

> So how did banks find themselves in such a precarious position?[426]

Banks found themselves in this precarious position because management has a financial incentive to take on risk and opacity prevented market discipline from restraining this risk taking.

> Banks are a vital part of our economy. They run the payment system, allowing us to pay our bills and receive our wages. They finance businesses investing in new ventures and families buying a new home. Without a banking system, our economy would grind to a halt.
>
> Because of that, markets correctly believed that no government could let a bank fail since that would cause immense disruption to the economy....[427]

In a modern banking system, bank failure only occurs when the regulators step in and shutdown a bank and not at the moment in time a bank becomes

---

424 BBC Lecture (2012), The Today Lecture 2012: Sir Mervyn King", http://bufvc.ac.uk/dvdfind/index.php/title/av74060 audio, http://news.bbc.co.uk/today/hi/today/newsid_9718000/9718062.stm transcript accessed 26 December 2013

425 ibid

426 ibid

427 ibid

insolvent. Between deposit guarantees and access to central bank funding, an insolvent bank can continue to operate for years.

This fact is well known to U.S. bank regulators and was demonstrated in their handling of the Less Developed Country Debt crisis and the Savings and Loan crisis. This fact would have been well known by the global financial regulatory community in the run-up to our current financial crisis.

As shown by the freezing of bank funding markets like the interbank lending market and the decline in bank share prices during the acute phase of our current financial crisis, markets believed banks, and by extension their investors, would be responsible for absorbing the losses the banks were exposed to. Markets didn't believe that governments wouldn't allow a bank to fail.

Bankers correctly believed bank regulators would succumb to the irresistible urge to have taxpayers cover the banking industry's losses and bank regulators would lobby policymakers to adopt the Japanese Model. The story about banks running the payment system is true, but it is used as political cover to justify the use of taxpayer funds.

> But there are only so many good loans and investments to be made. In order to expand, banks made increasingly risky investments.[428]

Sir Mervyn King understands that the bankers engaged in looting. Their risky investments were hidden by the opacity of current disclosure practices.

Compounding the opacity problem, the financial regulators, who had access to the data to see just how risky these investments were, told the market that risk had been moved out of the banking system.

The combination of opacity and the failure of the regulators to properly convey the true level of risk in the banking system resulted in investors providing additional funding to the banks at prices that did not reflect the true risk of the banks rather than exerting market discipline.

> To make matters worse, they started making huge bets with each other on whether loans that had already been made would be repaid. The seeds of the eventual downfall of the financial system had been sown. As loans and investments went bad, those seeds started to sprout.[429]

The seeds for the eventual downfall of the financial system had been sown decades before when the SEC adopted the intermediary depiction model rather than the pure information model for disclosure for banks. The SEC compounded

---

428 ibid

429 ibid

this mistake by then applying the intermediary depiction model to structured finance securities.

The seeds for the eventual downfall of the financial system had been sown when professional money managers failed to include in their disclosure to investors that due to the opacity of both banks and structured finance securities by purchasing either they were blindly gambling with the investors' money.

The seeds for the eventual downfall of the financial system had been sown when financial regulators failed to ensure valuation transparency across the global financial system. This failure is readily apparent as Wall Street and the City manipulated every opaque price including benchmark prices on interest rates (Libor), commodities and foreign exchange.

> In August 2007 came the moment when financial markets began to realise that the emperor had no clothes. The announcement by the French bank BNP Paribas that it would suspend repayments from two of its investment funds triggered a loss of confidence and a freezing of some capital markets.[430]

Unlike Yale professors Gary Gorton and Andrew Metrick, Sir Mervyn King knows exactly when and what event triggered the financial crisis, a loss of confidence and a run on the wholesale funding markets.

> BNP Paribas announced that it could not value the opaque, toxic structured finance securities in its two funds. At that moment, market participants began to look around for who else might be holding these securities.
>
> A month later, the crisis claimed its first victim when Northern Rock failed. In the months that followed, there was a steady procession of banking failures culminating in the collapse of the American bank Lehman Brothers in September 2008.
>
> Financial waters, already extremely chilly, then froze solid. Banks found it almost impossible to finance themselves because no-one knew which banks were safe and which weren't.[431]

Without valuation transparency, it is impossible for market participants to know which banks are safe and which are not.

> From the start of the crisis, central banks provided emergency loans but these amounted to little more than holding a sheet in front of the emperor to conceal the nakedness of the banks.

---

430 ibid

431 ibid

> They didn't solve the underlying problem — banks needed not loans but injections of shareholders' capital in order to be able to absorb losses from the risky investments they had made.
>
> From the beginning of 2008, we at the Bank of England began to argue that UK banks needed extra capital — a lot of extra capital, possibly £100 billion or more.[432]

At the beginning of 2008, opacity forced the Bank of England to adopt the Japanese Model. First, it attempted to conceal the nakedness of the banks using emergency loans. Second, it protected bank book capital levels. It argued rather than use the existing capital to absorb the losses on the risky investments there was a need for banks to raise more capital to absorb the losses already on and off their balance sheet. But why would anyone invest capital in an opaque bank when even the Bank of England is holding a sheet in front of the emperor to conceal the nakedness of the banks? That is not investing, that is blindly gambling on what is hidden behind the sheet.

> It wasn't a popular message. But nine months later, market pressure forced banks to raise new capital or accept it from the state.
>
> UK tax payers ended up owning large portions of two of our four biggest banks, Royal Bank of Scotland and Lloyds TSB, but almost all banks would have failed had not taxpayer support been extended.[433]

Just like in the US, the UK banks were put on taxpayer-backed life support.

> That bold action in October 2008 could have happened sooner. But the most important thing is that it was done. And the policy of recapitalising the banks was soon copied by other countries.[434]

Bailing out the banks was unnecessary. During the Great Depression, the addition of deposit insurance made taxpayers the banks' silent equity partners when the banks had low or negative book capital levels. This implicit taxpayer support ended the need for any explicit support like bailouts. With the modern financial system that exists in the UK, these banks could have continued to operate and support the real economy as they were rebuilding their book capital levels over the next several years.

More importantly, like the US, once the UK decided to put the banks on taxpayer-backed life support, the UK policymakers and financial regulators were

---

432 ibid

433 ibid

434 ibid

no longer forced to pursue the Japanese Model and bailout the banks, but now could implement the Swedish Model for handling the financial crisis. The fact other countries followed the UK lead does not make bailing out the banks and continuing to pursue the Japanese model the right decision. In fact, Iceland chose the Swedish model and did not bailout its banks. Its economy rebounded.

> Bailing out the banks came too late though to prevent the financial crisis from spilling over into the world economy.[435]

Actually, the decision by policymakers on the recommendation of the financial regulators who listened to the advice of the bankers to bail out the banks rather than have the banks absorb the losses on the excesses in the financial system caused the financial crisis to spill over into the real economy.

This is critically important to understand.

It was the financial regulators recommendation and the global policymakers' decision to protect bank book capital levels and banker bonuses at all costs under the Japanese Model that forced the global economy to deal with the excess debt in the financial system.

Had the financial regulators advised global policymakers not to protect bank book capital levels and banker bonuses, it is the bank book capital levels and banker bonuses that would have been forced to deal with the losses on the excess debt.

> The realisation of the true state of the banking system led to a collapse of confidence around the world and a deep global recession.
>
> Over 25 million jobs disappeared worldwide. And unemployment in Britain rose by over a million. To many of you this will seem deeply unfair, and it is. I can understand why so many people are angry.[436]

In the presence of opacity, nobody knows the true state of the black box banking system. As a result, it was not the realization of the true state of the banking system that led to a collapse of confidence, but rather the realization you could not tell which banks were solvent and which were insolvent. In addition, there was the realization governments would do anything to protect bank book capital levels along with banker bonuses and not the real economy or taxpayers.

This is a very important point.

By pursuing the Japanese Model, policymakers created a number of economic distortions that plunged the real economy into a recession and the potential for multiple Japan style lost economic decades.

---

435 ibid

436 ibid

People are angry because the policies pursued by the government and the financial regulators put protecting the banks and banker bonuses ahead of protecting the country's citizens, the country's social programs and the country's economy. Society had already made the choice to provide help to the poor and designed the financial system not to help the wealthy banker. Yet here was the government and financial regulators reversing this choice.

> It's vital that we learn from the crisis. A good place to start is to ask, as the Queen famously did, "Why did no-one see this coming?"
>
> The answer is extremely simple: no one believed it could happen....[437]

Actually, I did. And I have been talking about what it would take to end the financial crisis and moderate its impact on the real economy since before the global financial regulators and policymakers elected to continue to pursue the Japanese Model rather than the Swedish Model to handle an opacity driven financial crisis.

The "no-one" who believed it could happen was limited to most of the economics profession and particularly central bankers and bank regulators. To everyone else, it was quite easy to believe it could happen considering all of the opacity that the global financial regulators let build up in the global financial system.

> But conquering inflation was not enough to ensure stability.[438]

This is an excuse for not preventing our current financial crisis. If true, this statement reveals a fundamental lack of understanding by economists that financial stability is dependent on the combination of the philosophy of disclosure and *caveat emptor*.

> Although inflation was under control, fragilities were building in the banking system.[439]

Fragilities were building everywhere in the global financial system where the global financial regulators allowed opacity.

> On all sides there was a failure of imagination to appreciate the scale of the fragilities and their potential consequences. No one could quite bring

437 ibid
438 ibid
439 ibid

themselves to believe that in our modern financial system the biggest banks in the world could fall over. But they did.

That isn't to say we were blind to what was going on.[440]

Actually, without the authority to examine the banks and in the absence of the requirement banks provide valuation transparency, the Bank of England was blind to the true extent of what was going on. As the Bank of England's Andy Haldane observed, current disclosure practices leave banks resembling 'black boxes'.

The result of this opacity was, like every other market participant, the Bank of England had no idea of how much risk was actually building up in the financial or banking system.

For the record, the UK banking regulators should have had an idea. However, like their counterparts in the U.S. and elsewhere, they either did not see the risk or for fear of political pushback were incapable of communicating the risk to all market participants including their fellow global banking regulators.

> For several years, central banks, including the Bank of England, had warned that financial markets were underestimating risks....[441]

As the Nyberg Commission Report discussed, these warnings were perfunctory and done in such a way as to minimize the possibility of spooking the market. In addition, without valuation transparency, the Bank of England could not quantify how badly market participants might be underestimating risk. More importantly, without valuation transparency, market participants could not independently confirm the Bank of England's findings.

> Three reforms top my list. The first concerns regulation of banks. Next year, the responsibility for regulating banks will return to the Bank of England.
>
> Next time we find ourselves with steady growth and low inflation, but with risks building in the financial sector, we shall be able to do something about it. The Bank's new Financial Policy Committee will have the power to step in and prevent a hangover by taking away the punchbowl just as the party in the financial system is getting going.[442]

Prior to the financial crisis, in the U.S., the Fed was responsible for regulating the banks and monetary policy. This did not result in the Fed removing the punchbowl just as the party was getting going. In fact, former Fed

---

440 ibid

441 ibid

442 ibid

Chairman Alan Greenspan pointed out that despite the Fed's "independence" it is politically impossible to take away the punchbowl just as the party in the financial system is getting going. This point was confirmed in the UK by the FSA report. There is zero reason to belief the Bank of England will do better.

The reshuffling of regulatory authority highlights the fact: when market participants are denied access to valuation transparency, financial regulators are a single point of weakness in the financial system. They are a single point of weakness because they currently have a monopoly on all the useful, relevant information about the banks. This information monopoly makes other market participants dependent on them to both a) accurately assess this information and b) either communicate this assessment to all market participants or act on this assessment and exert the discipline on banks the market participants would.

If either does not occur, the result is financial instability at a minimum and, more likely, a financial crisis like the one we are experiencing.

> We believe that successful regulation means understanding and guarding against the big risks, not compliance with ever more detailed rules. That means focussing on the wood not the trees, looking not just at individual banks but also at how their fortunes are tied together with other banks and with the rest of the economy....[443]

Just like the Nobel Prize winning economists who supported the creation of the Office of Financial Research in the U.S., Sir Mervyn King wants regulators to take on responsibility for financial contagion and providing the other benefits delivered by the combination of the philosophy of disclosure and *caveat emptor*.

Just like the Nobel Prize winning economists, Sir Mervyn King chooses not to realize that under the FDR Framework, it is the responsibility of each market participant, including each bank, to limit their exposures to what they can afford to lose on any single exposure and in total. However, market participants can only end financial contagion by limiting their exposures if they have valuation transparency.

> In future, to protect the rest of the economy from failures in the banking system, we need to ensure that more of banks' shareholders' own money is on the line, and banks rely correspondingly less on debt.
>
> If banks and their shareholders have more to lose, they will be more careful in choosing to whom they lend. And, when banks make losses, there is more of a cushion before the bank fails, and less chance that the taxpayer will have to foot the bill....[444]

---

443 ibid

444 ibid

While the statement is mathematically correct, in the presence of opacity that makes banks resemble black boxes, there is no reason as Donald Kohn showed to believe bank regulators will actually require the banks to absorb the losses.

In the presence of opacity, why would bankers give up looting their banks? There is no one to see what they are doing who will enforce any discipline on the individual bankers as any fines for misbehavior are paid for by the shareholders and excessive risk taking results in bailouts paid for by the taxpayers.

In the presence of opacity that makes banks resemble black boxes, how are shareholders going to be more careful? For shareholders to be more careful requires that the banks provide valuation transparency and disclose their current exposure details. It is only with this information that shareholders can independently assess what is going on and exert market discipline on the banks by limiting their exposure to what they can afford to lose.

In the presence of opacity, bank regulators will always succumb to the "irresistible" urge to use taxpayer money rather than shareholder money to protect the rest of the economy from failures in the banking system. Protecting the rest of the economy from failures in the banking system does not require money from taxpayers. It requires valuation transparency, and policymakers not overriding how the modern banking system is designed with bank book capital absorbing the losses on excess debt in the financial system.

> *On page 96 of my book it says "when banking troubles…met with fundamental reform…during Depression…performance better."*
>
> *— Ben Bernanke*[445]

Ben Bernanke explains why the Japanese Model was chosen

In his November 8, 2013 speech titled *The Crisis as a Classic Financial Panic*, Fed Chair Bernanke laid out his reasons behind choosing the Japanese Model to handle our current opacity driven financial crisis.

As you are reading his speech, please notice how closely it parallels and appears to accept the findings of the previously discussed academic articles by Professors Gorton and Metrick. As I previously showed, their research could not explain why the financial crisis started when it did, what was needed to unfreeze the capital markets to end the crisis or how to prevent either markets freezing again or another financial crisis.

---

[445] Bernanke, Ben S. (2000), Essays on the Great Depression, Princeton, New Jersey: Princeton University Press, page 96.

As you are reading his speech, also notice how it ignores what economist Anna Schwartz said in her October 2008 Wall Street Journal interview. She was very explicit about the need to properly diagnose the cause of the current financial crisis, opacity, because without the proper diagnosis the policies pursued would be inappropriate for ending the financial crisis.

The reason for highlighting what Fed Chair Bernanke accepts as the story describing the financial crisis is it drives his and the global policymakers' choice of policy to deal with the financial crisis.

> I think the recent global crisis is best understood as a classic financial panic transposed into the novel institutional context of the 21st century financial system. An appreciation of the parallels between recent and historical events greatly influenced how I and many of my colleagues around the world responded to the crisis.
>
> Besides being the fifth anniversary of the most intense phase of the recent crisis, this year also marks the centennial of the founding of the Federal Reserve. It's particularly appropriate to recall, therefore, that the Federal Reserve was itself created in response to a severe financial panic, the Panic of 1907. This panic led to the creation of the National Monetary Commission, whose 1911 report was a major impetus to the Federal Reserve Act, signed into law by President Woodrow Wilson on December 23, 1913. Because the Panic of 1907 fit the archetype of a classic financial panic in many ways, it's worth discussing its similarities and differences with the recent crisis.[446]

Fed Chair Bernanke makes a very important point. There was a lesson learned from the Panic of 1907 and that lesson was the need for a central bank to act as a lender of last resort as initially described by Walter Bagehot.

There was also a lesson learned from the next major financial crisis, also known as the Great Depression, that Fed Chair Bernanke conveniently skips over. That lesson was the need for valuation transparency.

Fed Chair Bernanke then goes on to describe the archetype of a classic financial panic.

> Like many other financial panics, including the most recent one, the Panic of 1907 took place while the economy was weakening; according to the National Bureau of Economic Research, a recession had begun in May 1907. Also, as was characteristic of pre-Federal Reserve panics, money markets were tight when the panic struck in October, reflecting the strong seasonal demand for credit associated with the harvesting and shipment of crops.

---

446 Bernanke, Ben S. (2013, November 8), The Crisis as a Classic Financial Panic, Federal Reserve, http://www.federalreserve.gov/newsevents/speech/bernanke20131108a.htm

> The immediate trigger of the panic was a failed effort by a group of speculators to corner the stock of the United Copper Company. The main perpetrators of the failed scheme, F. Augustus Heinze and C.F. Morse, had extensive connections with a number of leading financial institutions in New York City. When the news of the failed speculation broke, depositor fears about the health of those institutions led to a series of runs on banks, including a bank at which Heinze served as president.[447]

What is a classic financial panic? It is a run on the banks, broadly defined to include commercial and investment banks.

A key characteristic of a classic financial panic is it has an identifiable immediate trigger that calls into question the ability of the financial institution(s) to repay all of the depositors' funds. In the case of the Panic of 1907, the identifiable immediate trigger was the failed effort to corner the stock of the United Copper Company.

> To try to restore confidence, the New York Clearinghouse, a private consortium of banks, reviewed the books of the banks under pressure, declared them solvent, and offered conditional support--one of the conditions being that Heinze and his board step down. These steps were largely successful in stopping runs on the New York banks.
>
> But even as the banks stabilized, concerns intensified about the financial health of a number of so-called trust companies--financial institutions that were less heavily regulated than national or state banks and which were not members of the Clearinghouse.
>
> As the runs on the trust companies worsened, the companies needed cash to meet the demand for withdrawals. In the absence of a central bank, New York's leading financiers, led by J.P. Morgan, considered providing liquidity. However, Morgan and his colleagues decided that they did not have sufficient information to judge the solvency of the affected institutions, so they declined to lend.[448]

In Fed Chair Bernanke's description of the archetype of the classic financial panic, there is one precondition that is necessary for the triggering event to set off the panic. That precondition is opacity.

As described by Fed Chair Bernanke, the Panic of 1907 illustrates the role of opacity as the necessary condition for a classic financial panic and valuation transparency as both a preventative and cure for a classic financial panic.

---

447 ibid

448 ibid

In 1907, the difference between ending a run on the banks and not ending a run on the trust companies was valuation transparency. As a sign they could stand on their own two feet, banks in the early 1900s provided valuation transparency. This valuation transparency limited the 1907 run on the banks in the first place. In addition, as a result of banks providing valuation transparency, the Clearinghouse could restore confidence because market participants could confirm its assessment the banks were solvent after recognizing their losses.

On the other hand, the trust companies did not provide valuation transparency. As a result of opacity, the depositors in the trust companies ran to get their money back because they could not tell if the trust companies were solvent or not. Furthermore, as a result of opacity, the banks were unwilling to lend to the trust companies because the banks didn't have the information they needed to determine if the trust companies would be able to repay the loans.

> Overwhelmed by a run, the Knickerbocker Trust Company failed on October 22, undermining public confidence in the remaining trust companies.
>
> To satisfy their depositors' demands for cash, the trust companies began to sell or liquidate assets, including loans made to finance stock purchases. The selloff of shares and other assets, in what today we would call a fire sale, precipitated a sharp decline in the stock market and widespread disruptions in other financial markets.
>
> Increasingly concerned, Morgan and other financiers (including the future governor of the Federal Reserve Bank of New York, Benjamin Strong) led a coordinated response that included the provision of liquidity through the Clearinghouse and the imposition of temporary limits on depositor withdrawals, including withdrawals by correspondent banks in the interior of the country. These efforts eventually calmed the panic. By then, however, the U.S. financial system had been severely disrupted, and the economy contracted through the middle of 1908.[449]

The response to the trust company solvency led crisis was a combination of liquidity and valuation transparency. The banks through the Clearinghouse stepped in, restricted depositor withdrawals from the trust companies and began to provide limited liquidity. Left unsaid is as a condition of making the loans, the opacity of the trust companies was ended. The banks were given each trust company's exposure details so they could assure themselves they were lending against good collateral. National City VP Frank Vanderlip confirmed this when he observed the NY banks were standing behind trust companies "whose assets have been examined and found good in every way."[450]

---

449 ibid

450 Prins, Nomi (2014), All the Presidents' Bankers: The hidden alliances that drive American power, New York, NY: Nation Books, page 10.

Equally importantly, the response to the trust company solvency led crisis did not include any taxpayer bailouts. Ultimately, it was the investors in the trust company debt, including deposits, and equity that absorbed the losses.

> The recent crisis echoed many aspects of the 1907 panic. Like most crises, the recent episode had an identifiable trigger--in this case, the growing realization by market participants that subprime mortgages and certain other credits were seriously deficient in their underwriting and disclosures.[451]

For the Panic of 1907, Fed Chair Bernanke cites a very specific event as triggering the crisis: the failure to corner the stock of United Copper Company. But when it comes to the Financial Crisis of 2008, Fed Chair Bernanke cites the same unknowable trigger for our current financial crisis as Professors Gorton and Metrick.

However, as I have already shown and the Bank of England's Mervyn King confirmed, the trigger for our current financial crisis was much more identifiable than a nebulous growing realization by market participants that subprime mortgages and certain other credits were seriously deficient in their underwriting and disclosures. On August 9, 2007, BNP Paribas made an announcement that they couldn't value subprime mortgage-backed securities because they lacked valuation transparency. This was the immediate trigger for the crisis.

> As the economy slowed and housing prices declined, diverse financial institutions, including many of the largest and most internationally active firms, suffered credit losses that were clearly large but also hard for outsiders to assess.
>
> Pervasive uncertainty about the size and incidence of losses in turn led to sharp withdrawals of short-term funding from a wide range of institutions; these funding pressures precipitated fire sales, which contributed to sharp declines in asset prices and further losses.[452]

Fed Chair Bernanke describes how opacity, the necessary precondition for a classic financial crisis, existed throughout the financial system. Financial institutions were impossible for outsiders to assess. As a result, even though there was deposit insurance, other investors in these banks could not determine if these opaque financial institutions were capable of repaying their debt. This gave the uninsured wholesale investors an incentive to run on the financial institutions.

---

451 Bernanke, Ben S. (2013, November 8), The Crisis as a Classic Financial Panic, Federal Reserve, http://www.federalreserve.gov/newsevents/speech/bernanke20131108a.htm

452 ibid

> Institutional changes over the past century were reflected in differences in the types of funding that ran: In 1907, in the absence of deposit insurance, retail deposits were much more prone to run, whereas in 2008, most withdrawals were of uninsured wholesale funding, in the form of commercial paper, repurchase agreements, and securities lending.[453]

There was absolutely nothing surprising about uninsured wholesale funding engaging in a bank run. This is exactly what they did when they engaged in a run on Continental Illinois in 1984.

It is not surprising that Fed Chair Bernanke leaves the role of opaque structured finance securities out of his description of our current financial crisis as he described the identifiable trigger to the financial crisis as "the growing realization" of deficient underwriting and disclosure. The actual immediate trigger was the August 9, 2007 BNP Paribas press release saying that subprime structured finance securities could not be valued.

The wholesale run on the banks began with a run on repurchase agreements. This resulted from the use of these structured finance securities as collateral for the repurchase agreements. Once it was publicly announced structured finance securities could not be valued, lenders would no longer accept them as collateral.

> Interestingly, a steep decline in interbank lending, a form of wholesale funding, was important in both episodes.[454]

There should be no surprise that banks with money to lend want to be able to determine if they will be repaid. In both the Panic of 1907 and our current financial crisis, banks with money to lend were prevented by opacity from determining if the borrower, trust companies in 1907 and banks in our current crisis, could repay their loans.

> Also interesting is that the 1907 panic involved institutions--the trust companies--that faced relatively less regulation, which probably contributed to their rapid growth in the years leading up to the panic. In analogous fashion, in the recent crisis, much of the panic occurred outside the perimeter of traditional bank regulation, in the so-called shadow banking sector.[455]

In both episodes, it was not the lack of regulation, but the lack of valuation transparency. It is opacity that is the necessary precondition for a classic financial panic to occur. In 1907, it was the trust companies that were opaque. In 2008,

---

453 ibid
454 ibid
455 ibid

it was the banks, which were inside the perimeter of traditional regulation, and structured finance securities that were opaque.

Fed Chair Bernanke asserts "much of the panic occurred outside the perimeter of traditional bank regulation". This is simply an attempt to justify a response to the financial crisis that ignores banks were opaque and instead adopts regulatory micro-management through the combination of complex regulation and regulatory oversight as a substitute for valuation transparency and market discipline.

> The responses to the panics of 1907 and 2008 also provide instructive comparisons. In both cases, the provision of liquidity in the early stages was crucial.
>
> In 1907 the United States had no central bank, so the availability of liquidity depended on the discretion of firms and private individuals, like Morgan. In the more recent crisis, the Federal Reserve fulfilled the role of liquidity provider, consistent with the classic prescriptions of Walter Bagehot. The Fed lent not only to banks, but, seeking to stem the panic in wholesale funding markets, it also extended its lender-of-last-resort facilities to support nonbank institutions, such as investment banks and money market funds, and key financial markets, such as those for commercial paper and asset-backed securities.
>
> In both episodes, though, liquidity provision was only the first step. Full stabilization requires the restoration of public confidence. Three basic tools for restoring confidence are temporary public or private guarantees, measures to strengthen financial institutions' balance sheets, and public disclosure of the conditions of financial firms.[456]

The Panic of 1907 showed conclusively liquidity from firms and private individuals flows to where there is valuation transparency and away from where there is opacity. Liquidity flowed to the banks because everyone could use valuation transparency to confirm the Clearinghouse statement the banks were solvent. Liquidity flowed from the trust companies until such time as they disclosed their current exposure details and their solvency could be confirmed.

Fed Chair Bernanke mentions three tools for restoring public confidence and none of these tools in the absence of valuation transparency is capable of doing this job. This fact has been well known since the Great Depression and the introduction of the combination of the philosophy of disclosure and *caveat emptor* as the basis for our financial system.

---

[456] ibid

The tool that is closest is "public disclosure of the conditions of financial firms". However, in the presence of opacity, this tool is inadequate to restore public confidence because it does not let the public Trust, but Verify.

Public confidence comes from the ability of the public to Trust, but Verify. If each financial institution is required to provide valuation transparency, market participants can independently assess and verify that the disclosures made about the condition of the financial firms are true. Trust and confidence results from the fact that market participants trust their own independent assessment.

> At least to some extent, Morgan and the New York Clearinghouse used these tools in 1907, giving assistance to troubled firms and providing assurances to the public about the conditions of individual banks.[457]

As Fed Chair Bernanke previously discussed in this speech, the response to the Panic of 1907 was a combination of liquidity and valuation transparency. The assistance given to the troubled trust companies consisted of liquidity given only after the lending banks could verify the value of the collateral they were lending against.

In 1907, banks routinely disclosed their exposure details as a preventative against rumor driven bank runs and as a sign they could stand on their own two feet. As a result, the public could confirm that the assurances given about the conditions of individual banks were true. In fact, JPMorgan and the Clearinghouse made the banks absorb their losses on their exposures to bad debt to show the banks were still viable.

As described by Fed Chair Bernanke, the response to the Panic of 1907 for the trust companies did not have either "temporary public or private guarantees" or "measures to strengthen financial institutions' balance sheets". According to his speech, nobody provided any guarantees of the trust companies. It was only after being able to assess the value of the trust companies' collateral that the banks lent them money so the depositors could be repaid.

What Fed Chair Bernanke's three basic tools do have in common is they are the tools of choice when implementing the Japanese Model and protecting bank book capital and banker bonuses at all costs. These tools were used after September 23, 2008 as part of implementing the Japanese Model.

> All three tools were used extensively in the recent crisis: In the United States, guarantees included the Federal Deposit Insurance Corporation's (FDIC) guarantees of bank debt, the Treasury Department's guarantee of money market funds, and the private guarantees offered by stronger firms that

---

[457] ibid

> acquired weaker ones. Public and private capital injections strengthened bank balance sheets. Finally, the bank stress tests that the Federal Reserve led in the spring of 2009 and the publication of the stress-test findings helped restore confidence in the U.S. banking system.[458]

Left off the Chair's list was Mr. Geithner's guarantee under which he pledged the full faith and credit of the United States to keep the Too Big to Fail banks solvent.

> Collectively, these measures helped end the acute phase of the financial crisis, although, five years later, the economic consequences are still with us....[459]

Yes, these measures which effectively put the financial system on taxpayer-backed life support helped to end the acute phase of the financial crisis by addressing the symptoms, but these measures did not address the underlying cause of the crisis, opacity, or its toxic legacy, too much debt. As a result, our current crisis continues.

In addition, since the banks still do not provide valuation transparency, market participants still have no way to independently assess the banks' true financial condition. As a result, it is impossible to restore trust and confidence in the financial system.

> As we try to make the financial system safer, we must inevitably confront the problem of moral hazard. The actions taken by central banks and other authorities to stabilize a panic in the short run can work against stability in the long run, if investors and firms infer from those actions that they will never bear the full consequences of excessive risk-taking.[460]

Moral hazard is the direct result of the choice to continue pursuing the Japanese Model after September 23, 2008 and subsequently bailing out the banks in order to protect their book capital levels and banker bonuses. This is a very important point. Moral hazard did not occur after the Panic of 1907 or the Great Depression because the banks, the bankers and the bank investors were not bailed out of their losses. Moral hazard has never occurred anywhere in the world where the Swedish Model or its equivalent has been pursued. It was only with Fed Chair Bernanke, Sec. Paulson and the Bank of England's Mervyn King leading the call for pursuing the Japanese Model and bailing out the banks that moral hazard became a global problem.

---

458 ibid

459 ibid

460 ibid

> As Stan Fischer reminded us following the international crises of the late 1990s, the problem of moral hazard has no perfect solution, but steps can be taken to limit it.[461]

Actually, there is a perfect solution. Recognize that banks today are simply black boxes wrapped in moral hazard. Ending moral hazard requires the financial institutions provide valuation transparency. Market participants understand the tradeoff for receiving valuation transparency is they will not be bailed out of any losses. As a result, market participants can and will assess the risk of and value the financial institutions. With this assessment, knowing they are responsible for all losses on their exposures to the banks, market participants can and will adjust their exposure to what they can afford to lose. Moral hazard is ended because with no risk of financial contagion there is no reason for policymakers and financial regulators to pursue their irresistible urge to bailout the banks.

In his speech, Fed Chair Bernanke goes on to discuss regulatory micro-management by providing several examples of complex regulations combined with regulatory oversight that he hopes can achieve the same outcome as the combination of valuation transparency and market discipline.

> First, regulatory and supervisory reforms, such as higher capital and liquidity standards or restriction on certain activities, can directly limit risk-taking.
>
> Second, through the use of appropriate carrots and sticks, regulators can enlist the private sector in monitoring risk-taking. For example, the Federal Reserve's Comprehensive Capital Analysis and Review (CCAR) process, the descendant of the bank stress tests of 2009, requires not only that large financial institutions have sufficient capital to weather extreme shocks, but also that they demonstrate that their internal risk-management systems are effective. In addition, the results of the stress-test portion of CCAR are publicly disclosed, providing investors and analysts information they need to assess banks' financial strength.[462]

The only way to enlist the private sector in monitoring risk-taking is by requiring the banks provide valuation transparency and disclose on an ongoing basis their current exposure details. It is only when the private sector has this information that it can actually monitor risk-taking.

Disclosing the results of the stress tests does not help investors and analysts assess each bank's financial strength. Without each bank's current exposure details, investors and analysts cannot independently confirm the results.

---

461 ibid

462 ibid

Instead, what the stress test exercise does is to reinforce moral hazard by creating an obligation to protect the investors from any bank solvency related losses. Moral hazard and the obligation to bailout investors arises from the fact that it is reasonable for an investor to invest in reliance on the Fed's stress tests and the published results saying a bank is solvent and can "weather extreme shocks". The investor's actions are reasonable because without disclosure of each bank's current exposure details, an investor doesn't have any information with which to show the results are wrong.

Please note FDR was keenly aware of the problem of moral hazard. This is why he said it is the government's responsibility to ensure that market participants have valuation transparency and the government should not appear to endorse an investment. What are the results of a stress test if not a public endorsement of an investment in the tested banks?

> Of course, market discipline can only limit moral hazard to the extent that debt and equity holders believe that, in the event of distress, they will bear costs.[463]

The quid pro quo for investors being responsible for all losses is that they are provided with valuation transparency so they can know what they are buying and know what they own.

When valuation transparency is missing and financial regulators are asking investors to invest in banks by blindly gambling on the contents of a black box the financial regulators stress tested, the government has a moral obligation to protect the investors and limit their losses.

> In the crisis, the absence of an adequate resolution process for dealing with a failing SIFI left policymakers with only the terrible choices of a bailout or allowing a potentially destabilizing collapse.[464]

Here is the reason Fed Chair Bernanke cites for choosing and continuing to pursue the Japanese Model after September 23, 2008. He could only see the terrible choice between a bailout and a potentially destabilizing collapse.

The Panic of 1907 showed there was and still is an alternative to a bailout or allowing a potentially destabilizing collapse. The alternative was the forerunner of the Swedish Model. It combined liquidity and valuation transparency. The Great Depression showed there was and still is an alternative to a bailout or allowing a potentially destabilizing collapse. Like the Panic of 1907, it combined

---

463 ibid

464 ibid

liquidity and valuation transparency. This alternative its the original Swedish Model. It combined liquidity and valuation transparency with the banks, like all other investors, taking their losses upfront. The option to pursue the Swedish Model instead of the Japanese Model was available to Fed Chair Bernanke as soon as he asked Congress to put the banks on taxpayer-backed life support on September 23, 2008.

Asking Congress to put the banks and the rest of the financial system on taxpayer-backed life support was the equivalent of putting a patient needing a heart valve replacement on a heart-lung bypass machine. Once on the machine, the patient continues to survive even if the valve fails prior to its being replaced. Putting the global financial system on the taxpayer-backed life support meant there was plenty of time to do the equivalent of replacing a heart valve by fixing the problem of opacity and its toxic legacy of too much debt in the global financial system.

Unfortunately, as shown in this speech, Fed Chair Bernanke and the other financial regulators did not seize the opportunity provided by having put the global financial system on the equivalent of the heart-lung bypass machine. Rather, they applauded themselves for having alleviated the symptoms caused by the problem of opacity and its toxic legacy, excess debt, in the global financial system. Then they proposed regulatory micro-management to deal with all the new problems, like moral hazard, created from pursuing the Japanese Model. Meanwhile, market participants are still waiting for the part of the surgery where the problem of opacity and its toxic legacy, excess debt, are actually addressed and fixed.

CHAPTER 19

FEAR AND THE CHOICE OF THE JAPANESE MODEL

Back in August 2008, as the credit crunch was really starting to bite, Tim Price, director of investments at PFP Wealth Management in London, had this to say:

A banking specialist Ph.D. who has spent 20 years at Bank College studying nothing but banks, and whose every waking second is committed to understanding banks, would struggle to conduct due diligence upon banks consistent with making an informed assessment of the risks they hold and the risk they represent.

Let's be thankful that six years later, the world has learned its lesson about bank complexity, and regulators are now ensuring that the balance sheets, ownership structures and risk exposures of the finance industry are transparent, intelligible and suitably constrained.

Except, of course, nothing in the above sentence is true.[465]

— *Mark Gilbert*

By choosing to continue to pursue the Japanese Model rather than the Swedish Model after September 23, 2008, financial regulators and global policymakers confirmed the cover-up is worse than the crime.

The facts are bad loans and investments were made. The losses already exist. In principle, under the FDR Framework, all investors who lent and invested in the bad loans and investments should pay the price. In the case of the banks, their losses exceeded their book capital.

In theory, bank regulators were given discretion as to when to step in and close a bank so as to minimize the cost to the deposit insurance fund and taxpayers. In practice as shown by our current financial crisis, this discretion has been undermined by opacity and political protection.

---

465 Gilbert, Mark (2014, August 1), *Portugal should let Espirito Santo fail*, Bloomberg View, http://www.bloombergview.com/articles/2014-08-01/portugal-should-let-espirito-santo-fail

In theory, the decision of when to close a bank is driven by whether the bank's insolvency is considered "temporary" or "permanent".

- The bank's insolvency is temporary if after recognizing its losses the bank can generate earnings and rebuild its book capital level even if this would take several years. Examples of financial institutions operating in insolvency for years include the U.S. Savings & Loans and the large U.S. banks like Security Pacific where the losses on their loans to less developed countries exceeded their book equity.
- The bank's insolvency is permanent if after recognizing its losses it cannot generate earnings to rebuild its book capital level.

In practice, opacity allows a lack of political will to effect the process of deciding whether to close a bank or not. As shown by Continental Illinois and our current financial crisis, it is impossible for bank regulators to justify restraining bank risk-taking to politicians when there are no sign of problems. In the same vein, it is also impossible for bank regulators to explain to politicians why banks should be closed when there are still doubts about whether their insolvency is temporary or permanent. As a result, the bank regulators delay in making a decision as to whether the bank's insolvency is temporary or permanent.

> [T]he issue of disclosure is closely related to that of forbearance. If the purpose of non-disclosure is to facilitate the continued operation of a bank which the market would close if it had the relevant information, then it also implies that the authorities (who have the information) are forbearing to take closure action themselves.[466]

With opacity, bank regulators are not subject to market discipline. This makes it dramatically easier for them to grant regulatory forbearance and not close a bank. If there were valuation transparency and banks had to disclose their current exposure details, bank regulators would be under pressure to close banks the market has determined are permanently insolvent.

> [I]t is widely accepted that forbearance and non-disclosure weaken incentive structures and ease the work of political lobbyists who would seek to restrain regulatory action.[467]

466 Honohan, Patrick (1997, January), Banking System Failures in Developing and Transition Countries: Diagnosis and Prediction, Bank for International Settlements, Working Paper No. 39, http://www.bis.org/publ/work39.pdf, page 29.

467 ibid, page 29

In other words, opacity makes it even easier for the banks to lobby against financial reform and to lobby their problems are temporary and not permanent. After all, the problem of insolvency would truly be temporary if the banks' losses were allocated elsewhere. To date, the response in the EU, UK and U.S. has been to socialize the losses by protecting the banks and bankers who made bad loans or invested imprudently.

To cover-up the insolvency of the banks, the financial regulators took a series of unprecedented and unnecessary steps that turned on its head everything governments are suppose to do to support the FDR Framework based global financial system.

Under the FDR Framework, the role for financial regulators is to ensure valuation transparency and refrain from endorsing an investment. Under the Japanese Model, financial regulators actively support opacity by not requiring financial institutions to provide valuation transparency. In addition, the regulators endorsed investments in specific stress-tested financial institutions.

With the blessing of the global policymakers under the mantra of giving the regulators a second chance, the regulators also took it upon themselves to redesign the financial system in a misguided attempt to create the illusion of safety. As fast as they can, the regulators are generating new complex regulations and increasing regulatory oversight in the hopes of achieving the same results that would have been produced had the financial institutions been required to provide valuation transparency and been subject to market discipline in the first place. However, there is no reason to believe these new regulations micro-managing the global financial system and replacing rather than reinforcing market discipline will succeed. Why? Assuming these untested and unproven micro-management regulations would actually work, success still requires enforcement of the regulations. Unfortunately, financial regulators have a very long history demonstrating this is not guaranteed. Financial regulators will always be fearful of political pushback and susceptible to regulatory capture.

Fear

Why did the regulators choose to protect opacity in the financial system after September 23, 2008 when the regulators' most important task is to ensure valuation transparency?

Fear. The fear of the second Great Depression Fed Chair Bernanke exhibited when he went to testify with Sec. Paulson before Congress.

If the large global financial institutions had to disclose their current exposure details, they would have been shown to be insolvent. Like Jack Nicholson's character in *A Few Good Men*, lead by Fed Chair Bernanke and Sec. Paulson, government officials chose to continue pursuing the Japanese Model after deciding of the market participants "you can't handle the truth".[468] Their fear was if market participants knew the truth about the banks, they would act in such a way as to trigger the second Great Depression.

Avoiding the second Great Depression was the counter-factual used to justify ongoing implementation of the Japanese Model and all of its related policies. The counter-factual went something along the following line: if we don't pursue the Japanese Model and all of its related distasteful policies like protecting bank book capital levels and banker bonuses, then we will end up with something worse, namely the second Great Depression.

Of course, it is impossible to argue we would not have ended up in the second Great Depression because they did pursue the Japanese Model and its related policies. However, this was never the right counter-factual. It was chosen to justify the policies pursued.

The right question is does this policy response make the financial crisis worse for the real economy than it would have been had an available different set of policies been chosen.

Based on the actions of the FDR Administration when confronted with the same problem of bank insolvency including runs on the banks in 1933, it is easy to show in fact the policy response since September 23, 2008, when the global financial system was put on taxpayer-backed life support, has made and continues to make the situation worse for the real economy.

By pursuing the Japanese Model and allowing banks to remain opaque, regulators created numerous additional problems that undermine their credibility as well as trust and confidence in the financial system. An example of this is the conflicting roles played by the financial regulators that make bank capital surreal.

On the one hand, the global financial regulators are calling for banks to recognize all the losses hidden on and off their balance sheets and accurately reflect the value of their exposures.

On the other hand, with the choice of the Japanese Model, the global financial regulators are protecting book capital levels at all costs. They are doing everything they can to not use bank capital to absorb losses. This includes preventing through use of accounting changes and regulatory forbearance the losses on the banks' exposures to toxic assets ranging from mortgage-backed securities to credit derivatives to bad loans from lowering book capital levels.

Their choice of the Japanese Model committed the government to hiding the truth from the market and tailoring its policies to support a narrative where the large global financial institutions were healthy as oppose to insolvent. It also left us with not only are the banks fighting to maintain opacity so they can

---

468 Jessup, Col. Nathan R (1992), A Few Good Men, http://www.imdb.com/title/tt0104257/quotes

continue to gamble and engage in bad behavior like manipulating Libor, but the government has committed itself to helping the banks maintain opacity.

By pursuing the Japanese model, policymakers and financial regulators have gotten comfortable with the idea that it is acceptable for banks to hide losses on and off their balance sheets. This has resulted in significant collateral damage. When actively engaged in a massive cover-up of the banking system, it is hard for them to fight for valuation transparency from other firms.

For example, in a clear win for Wall Street's Opacity Protection Team, Congress passed and President Obama signed into law the "JOBS" Act. This Act effectively repeals disclosure requirements for small businesses. The argument for passage of this Act was based on the following sound bite: regulations requiring small firms provide valuation transparency reduce their access to capital and hold back economic growth. In reality, valuation transparency is the fundamental building block for our financial system and is necessary for attracting investors and capital to our financial markets. Without valuation transparency, only gamblers are attracted to buying or selling the contents of a brown paper bag based on the story told about its contents.

Chapter 20

THE BANK OF ENGLAND TRIES TO ESCAPE JAPANESE MODEL'S GRIP

This problem can be handled, we shouldn't be frightened of it; we should face up to it and do it and then we will take great pride in fact that the UK will have a banking system that is at the start line ready to support our economic recovery, with balance sheets in which people can have confidence because the numbers mean what they say.

—Sir Mervyn King[469]

Once the financial regulators decided market participants could not handle the truth about the actual condition of the banks, they pursued policies to hide this fact. Hiding this fact and pursuing the Japanese Model created a number of significant additional problems besides introducing moral hazard from bailing out the banks.

First, the result of divorcing bank financial statements from their underlying economic reality created what former RBS chief Stephen Hester referred to as 'Alice in Wonderland' accounting.[470]

Second, hiding the losses slowed down the pace at which the losses could be realized. As Mr. Hester observed, RBS, like all the other banks, had a budget for recognizing losses and only recognized these losses as RBS generated the earnings to absorb them.

> Each year we have … a budget for making losses for clean-up – … the better or worse our profits are, the bettor or worse that budget is and the faster or slower that we can go.[471]

469 Bank of England (2012, November 29), Financial Stability Report Q&A, Bank of England, http://www.bankofengland.co.uk/publications/Documents/fsr/2012/conf121129.pdf, page 29

470 Wilson, Harry (2012, February 23), RBS 'deliberately' doubled losses to £2bn in 'Alice in Wonderland' accounting, The Telegraph, http://www.telegraph.co.uk/finance/newsbysector/banksandfinance/9101879/RBS-deliberately-doubled-losses-to-2bn-in-Alice-in-Wonderland-accounting.html

471 ibid

What he didn't say was RBS also had a budget for paying bonuses to bankers and payment of banker bonuses came before recognition of losses. Had RBS recognized all of its losses upfront under the Swedish Model, the budget for paying banker bonuses would have been used to restore book capital levels instead.

Problems number one and two together left market participants wondering: is there any truth to bank earnings presentations?

As Rob Taylor observed:

> the truth is in Lloyd's latest results presentation....somewhere....banks claim improvements ... then turn round and tell us there is still garbage inside their businesses that needs to be written off.[472]

In fact, since the September 23, 2008 choice to continue pursuing the Japanese Model, there has been no truth to reported bank earnings by the global systemically important Too Big to Fail banks. Nor will there be until such time as each bank discloses its current exposure details and shows it has recognized all the losses currently hiding on and off its balance sheet.

Third, hiding the banks' losses also prevented the banks from acting as a safety valve and protecting the real economy from the excesses in the financial system. Mr. Hester said RBS "'never' had sufficient capital to recognize all its losses upfront."[473] This statement is misleading. Capital is an accounting construct and can be positive or negative. What RBS didn't have was enough book capital to absorb all its losses and retain a positive book capital level. By insisting RBS maintain a positive book capital level, the regulators forced the burden of the excess debt on to the real economy.

Having made the decision to continue implementing the Japanese Model and create these problems, global policymakers are now faced with the issue of how to end its policies and fix these problems. The simple solution is to adopt the Swedish Model with valuation transparency. Under this solution, banks would disclose their current exposure details and recognize the losses currently hidden on and off their balance sheets. Once again their financial statements would reflect their underlying economic reality. In addition, market participants

---

472 Taylor, Rob (2012, February 24), The Truth is in Lloyds's latest results presentation ... somewhere, The Guardian, http://www.theguardian.com/business/blog/2012/feb/24/truth-lloyds-results-somewhere

473 Wilson, Harry (2012, February 23), RBS 'deliberately' doubled losses to £2bn in 'Alice in Wonderland' accounting, The Telegraph, http://www.telegraph.co.uk/finance/newsbysector/banksandfinance/9101879/RBS-deliberately-doubled-losses-to-2bn-in-Alice-in-Wonderland-accounting.html

could confirm the banks had been cleaned up, the excess debt purged from the financial system and the financial crisis effectively ended.

Bank of England tried, but failed to restore confidence in banks

However, bank regulators are not yet ready to adopt this solution. They are prepared to try everything else instead in the hopes something other than the Swedish Model with valuation transparency will work. Consider how the Bank of England tried to restore confidence in bank financial statements.

The set-up

After September 23, 2008, each bank had a minimum level of book capital it maintained under the Japanese Model policies. Consistent with maintaining this minimum level, the pace at which losses could be realized was limited to a bank's earnings less the payment of bonuses to the bankers. The pace for recognizing losses was further slowed down when, at the urging of academic economists, bank regulators added increasing current book capital levels to prevent future bailouts. Now, the budget for how earnings would be used also included increasing book capital levels and payment of banker bonuses before recognition of losses.

The BoE, through its Financial Policy Committee (FPC), was among the regulators calling for banks to continue to build their capital levels.

> Over the past year, the FPC has emphasised the need for banks to continue to build and maintain capital buffers against unexpected losses, for example arising from euro-area stresses. And UK banks currently report substantial buffers over the minimum level allowed.[474]

Having further broken the linkage between bank financial statements and their underlying economic reality, the Bank of England now tried to re-establish it.

The Bank of England began by acknowledging there is excess debt borrowers will never be able to repay in the global financial system. It asserted UK banks had an exposure to this debt that had not yet been reflected in their financial statements.

> But, in judging whether banks are adequately capitalised, we need to ensure that reported capital ratios do in fact provide an accurate picture of banks' health. At present there are good reasons to think that they do not.[475]

---

474 Bank of England (2012, November 29), Financial Stability Report Press Conference, Opening Remarks by the Governor, Bank of England, http://www.bankofengland.co.uk/publications/Documents/fsr/2012/fsrspnote121129.pdf, page 1

475 ibid, page 1

With this statement, the BoE confirmed bank financial statements do not reflect their underlying economic reality. It was the first global financial regulator to admit losses are being hidden. In November 2012, it was an unprecedented step to acknowledge the time bombs sitting on bank balance sheets and say it was time the hidden losses were realized.

However, rather than say what the size of the losses being hidden were for each bank, the BoE simply pointed out there were good reasons to know losses were being hidden.

Financial market participants were well aware of these reasons and knew the banks were hiding losses on the bad loans and investments they had made prior to the beginning of the current financial crisis. Just like with the losses on the loans to less developed countries, what the market participants didn't know was the exact amount of the losses at each bank.

> That uncertainty around capital adequacy is in part responsible for low investor confidence in banks, whose equity is valued by the market at on average only two thirds of its book value. Investors need confidence that banks have adequate buffers against stress in order to be willing to fund them at the low rates necessary to support a recovery.[476]

Investor confidence is not a function of bank capital adequacy, but rather a function of the availability of valuation transparency. Investors want to know what they are buying and what they own. Who is confident when betting on the contents of a brown paper bag? Investors need the ability to independently assess the risk and value of each bank in order to be willing to fund them at the low rates necessary to support a recovery. Without this ability, funding the banks is simply blindly betting and hoping to be bailed out if necessary.

> In today's *Report* we draw attention to **three** reasons that lead us to think that UK banks' capital ratios — and hence the buffers available to absorb unexpected losses — are currently overstated. First, expected future credit losses may be understated; second, costs arising from past failures of conduct may not be fully recognised; and third, the risk weights used by banks in calculating their capital ratios may be too optimistic.[477]

Opacity is a factor in each reason bank capital ratios might not reflect reality. Like the U.S., UK banks use an intermediary depiction model for disclosure. Like the U.S., the failure to use a pure information disclosure model meant market participants did not have the information they needed to get an accurate

---

[476] ibid, page 1
[477] ibid, page 1

picture of the banks' book capital levels or for seeing how the banks game their risk-weighted capital ratio calculations. On top of this, the opacity of the banks allowed the bankers to engage in bad behavior. As a result, the banks were facing sizable charges for misconduct including manipulating key financial benchmarks and mis-selling financial products like interest rate swaps.

So the question for the BoE was how to address the three reasons for thinking bank capital ratios were overstated in a credible manner when market participants could not independently confirm the action taken was sufficient to restore credibility to the financial statements.

> The FPC therefore recommends that the FSA takes action to ensure that the capital of UK banks and building societies reflects a proper valuation of their assets, a realistic assessment of future conduct costs, and prudent calculation of risk weights.
>
> Where such action reveals that capital buffers need to be strengthened to absorb losses and sustain credit availability in the event of stress, the FSA should ensure that firms either raise capital or take steps to restructure their business and balance sheets in ways that do not hinder lending to the real economy.[478]

The BoE's solution to restore the credibility of bank capital levels and ratios sounds good, but ultimately it comes down to *Trust Us*. But why would anyone trust the BoE and the FSA when it comes to revealing all the losses currently hidden on the bank balance sheets or providing an estimate of the size of the fines to be imposed as a result of banker misconduct? After all, bank regulators are the ones who insisted banks must have a positive book capital level and as a result helped to hide the losses in the first place.

The BoE's acknowledgement of the losses and its solution was designed to not create great uncertainty in the financial markets. There was no reason for market participants to over react to the BoE's confession about the hidden losses. They already knew the losses existed and the banks needed more capital.

On the other hand, it is a solution that didn't generate confidence in the banks either. The solution immediately waved a giant red flag. It reminded everyone that without valuation transparency under which the banks disclose their current exposure details, there was no way for market participants to independently confirm the adequacy of the banks' capital levels.

Market participants learned from bank stress tests the importance of independently confirming what bank regulators say about the banks' health. These stress tests were designed to show the banks were adequately capitalized

---

478 ibid, page 2

and could absorb the losses on their exposures. Since stress tests were first run in 2009, there have been several banks nationalized shortly after the results of the stress tests were published and showed these soon to be nationalized banks were very well capitalized. In the absence of valuation transparency that allows market participants to Trust, but Verify, why should the BoE's solution produce a better result than the failed stress tests?

Ultimately, calling attention to the banks' fictional financial statements hints at the idea the BoE would like to stop pursuing the Japanese Model and would prefer to adopt the Swedish Model. However, it is powerless to do so. The BoE understands the policies adopted under the Japanese Model are driving the economic malaise with an economy that oscillates between no growth and bubbles. They know investors don't trust the banks because they are hiding substantial amounts of losses. The BoE would like it if the banks were honest about and recognized their losses, but realizes in the absence of market discipline made possible by valuation transparency this is unlikely to happen as a result of regulatory pressure. Finally, the BoE realizes monetary policy and financial reform are held hostage until such time as the banks recognize their losses.

Just the facts

> In the United Kingdom, progress by banks in raising capital has slowed and investor confidence remains low. One indicator of that is the market value of major UK banks' shareholder equity, which has fallen on average to around two thirds of the book value.
>
> Market concerns are likely to reflect in part uncertainty about bank capital adequacy. One factor which may make stated levels of capital misleading is underrecognition of expected future losses on loans. Information from supervisory intelligence and banks' own public disclosures suggest that expected losses on loans, including those subject to forbearance, are in some cases greater than current provisions and regulatory capital deductions for UK banks' expected losses.
>
> In recent years, UK banks have also underestimated and underprovisioned for costs for conduct redress, notably for payment protection insurance mis-selling. In 2012, the number of identified conduct issues has grown and it seems likely that banks could face additional sizable costs.
>
> Banks' capital positions could also be overstated because of aggressive application of risk weights. The current framework for calculating risk weights used in determining regulatory measures of capital adequacy is complex and opaque and that may have undermined investor confidence....
>
> In combination, these factors would imply that UK banks' capital buffers, available to cushion losses and maintain the supply of credit following realisation of a stress scenario, are not as great as headline regulatory capital ratios imply....

> Historical experience suggests that more rapid progress in tackling balance sheet problems would support improved funding conditions and the ability of banks to extend new loans to households and businesses. The FPC's recommendation is aimed at achieving such an outcome.[479]

Given these facts, calling for valuation transparency was and still is the appropriate solution. With the exception of the losses each bank faces for misconduct, valuation transparency directly solves the problems identified by the Bank of England's Financial Policy Committee.

It replaces low confidence in opaque banks with higher confidence in fully transparent banks. It subjects banks to market discipline and as a result, the banks address their balance sheet problems. This includes the absolute level of bank capital adjusting so it much more fully reflects the losses currently hidden on and off the banks' balance sheets. It subjects banks to market discipline and as a result, they stop gaming their capital calculations. Finally, sunlight is the best disinfectant and with it comes a change in the culture that permitted, if not actively encouraged, bad behavior.

Of course, the BoE did not recommend valuation transparency. Instead, the BoE opted for regulatory oversight and *Trust Us*.

The Q&A

The financial press understood the message the UK banks' financial statements have been fictitious since the beginning of the financial crisis. First, the financial press wanted to confirm the BoE had really said the disclosed bank capital levels were inaccurate.

Sir Mervyn King's response was to assure them

> It's capital levels that we're talking about.[480]

Next, the financial journalists wanted to know how much capital was needed so the financial statements would reflect reality.

Sir Mervyn King declined to provide a specific number and insisted it was up to each bank to tell the investment community how much capital it needed for expected losses, conduct losses and more appropriate risk weights. It is

---

479 Bank of England (2012, November), Financial Stability Report: Executive Summary, http://www.bankofengland.co.uk/publications/Documents/fsr/2012/fsrsum1211.pdf, page 6.

480 Bank of England (2012, November 29), Financial Stability Report Q&A, Bank of England, http://www.bankofengland.co.uk/publications/Documents/fsr/2012/conf121129.pdf, page 2.

entirely unclear why breaking down additional capital needed into these three categories conveys the true amount of capital needed. For example, how could anyone independently confirm the additional capital for expected losses covered 100% of the expected losses and not something closer to 10% of the expected losses? Was the BoE hoping having three categories of additional capital needs would lend an artificial precision to the exercise that would mask the fact nobody could confirm if the additional capital was sufficient?

> It feels that the number is going to be material in aggregate, but the key thing is that what we want to do is to give clarity to the investor community by making sure that the banks themselves reveal very clearly the provisions they should be making under the three headings that I've identified today: expected losses, provision against conduct losses and more appropriate risk weights.[481]

The financial journalists realized the logical step after setting aside capital for expected losses is to then realize these losses by writing-down the value of specific loans and investment securities. If banks formally recognized their losses, the journalists wonder if they would continue to be flexible in repayment or would they foreclose on delinquent borrowers and force businesses into insolvency.

> Mervyn King: I think it's making adequate provision for expected losses. And that seems to be the key thing. In other words, to have an honest and open statement of what the balance sheet is. ... But I do think that one of the things that's made confidence less secure than it would otherwise have been is just the sheer uncertainty about knowing how far these reported provisions are accurate or not. Paul....[482]
>
> Paul Tucker: the watchword here is capital adequacy; it's not — there's no magic ratio here. And capital adequacy requires that banks have honest balance sheets. And they shouldn't be constrained by particular accounting policies. They need to look at their assets and say — well what rate of loss do we expect, given plausible macroeconomic and other assumptions? ...
>
> So in some respects this is going back to very old lessons from the past. Some of you here — Larry might remember the risk matrix, provisioning matrix for sovereign debt in the mid-1980s. Now we're not going as far as that; we're not setting out numbers — what the provisioning should be for different parts of the economy. But we are saying this is a major issue for all top bankers; they have to look at their loan books and say — well what actually do we think the rate of recovery is going to be? ...

---

481 ibid, page 4

482 ibid, page 5

> Andrew Bailey: putting in place appropriate capital buffers does not involve writing down individual loans; it involves having an appropriate buffer of capital. And that's the important distinction in your question, because having those buffers then enables those banks to make sensible decisions about their policy towards individual borrowers.
>
> Paul Tucker: That's right. In the old language this could be general provisions rather than specific provisions — a concept which went out of fashion, but which is actually quite useful.[483]

The BoE's leadership response emphasized it was unnecessary for the banks to realize their losses or stop being flexible in repayment. The goal of the capital adequacy initiative was to make bank balance sheets "honest" and improve investor confidence in the banks by eliminating uncertainty and this did not require an end to being flexible in repayment.

This response is a strong "tell" the BoE's leadership had taken a big step towards the Swedish Model as shown by its admission banks are hiding losses, but it was not yet ready to propose ending the Japanese Model and adopting the Swedish Model. Unfortunately, not adopting the Swedish Model creates problems for restoring confidence. If the bank regulators were still following the Japanese Model that embraced hiding the true extent of the losses, why was there any reason to *trust* they would make the bank balance sheets "honest"?

The response also confirmed the reluctance of bank regulators to actually have bank capital absorb losses. In the response, the emphasis is on building a buffer and having the buffer absorb the losses. This means there is a floor on the absolute level of book capital. Of course, this artificially caps how much of the existing losses can be recognized as a result of the BoE's initiative. This cap effectively undermines the credibility of the entire exercise.

The alternative to setting a floor on bank capital levels is to recognize bank capital is an accounting construct that can have positive or negative values. The Swedish Model takes advantage of this and freely uses the capital account to absorb all the losses on and off the bank balance sheet today.

It wasn't lost on the financial journalists that banker bonuses stood in the way of either recognizing the losses on the existing debt or rebuilding book capital levels.

> Andrew Bailey: There really are two important things in the remuneration from our perspective ... which is to ensure that the impact of costs that the banks have incurred is properly reflected into the allocation of post-tax income between building capital, paying dividends and variable remuneration. And that

483 ibid, page 6

> is critical, because obviously that determines one of the elements going back to our main recommendation of capital building.[484]

Mr. Bailey confirmed the bank regulators' on-going support for the "budget" for loss recognition under the Japanese Model. Banks only recognize their losses to the extent the income they generate exceeds what is needed to pay banker bonuses, dividends and build book capital levels. This budget is great for bankers, but bad for the real economy. By not recognizing their losses, banks divert capital that would be used for reinvestment, growth or social programs from the real economy to debt service.

The journalists caught on to the fact bank financial statements under amortized cost accounting do not provide an accurate view of each bank's true financial condition and may in fact not be honest. If they were, then the Bank of England would not need to encourage the banks to increase their capital to reflect reality.

> Mervyn King: No, it's not a question of not being honest. They are constrained by accounting conventions which legally they're obliged to follow....
>
> In terms of accounts on expected losses, banks themselves also publish a number which purports to give the fair value of their loan book as opposed to the accounting value. But we think this does need to be looked at in a clearer way because, 4 again, what maters here is what is likely to be (as Paul said) in an old-fashioned prudent banker sense, what would be a sensible provision to make against losses — even though you can't pin them to individual loans? What is likely to be the cost overall?[485]

Sir Mervyn King tried to explain how even though amortized cost accounting hid the decline in the value of each bank's loan portfolio, a hint of the size of this decline could be found because banks also disclose what they think is the fair value of their loan portfolio. However, in the absence of valuation transparency, there is no way to independently confirm if the bank's estimate of fair value is realistic or not.

Naturally, when the conversation is on banks addressing the issue of their bad loans and either setting up a reserve for or recognizing losses, the issue of forbearance came up.

There are two sources of forbearance. The banks that cut borrowers a break on loan payments because the bankers think the borrowers' set back is temporary. The regulators who cut the banks a break in how the bank handle their borrowers experiencing financial difficulty because the regulators don't want

484 ibid, page 7

485 ibid, page 14

to create a fire sale from having many of the same type of assets up for sale at the same time.

In the context of a financial crisis, forbearance is seen as a way

> to smooth the economy's response to shocks and avoid waves of costly liquidation.[486]

To understand how forbearance works and the impact this has on bank balance sheets requires a little understanding of how banks account for bad loans. When I first started in the banking industry, the accounting regime utilized the expected loss approach. It was commonly understood that despite a bank's best efforts in underwriting its loans, there would be some loans that defaulted. Therefore, based on the bank's historical loan loss experience, when a bank made a loan it would also recognize an expense, called a provision for loan losses, on its income statement. The provision was not against the specific loan that had just been made. After all, if the bank knew this specific loan would default, it wouldn't have made the loan. Rather, it was a "general" provision for the losses the bank expected to experience over time from the whole loan portfolio. The provision increased an account on the bank's balance sheet called the loan loss reserve.

As time passed and the loans matured, some of the loans would start to experience repayment difficulties. Based on whether or not the bankers expected the borrower to recover from temporary difficulties and resume paying under the terms of the loan, the bank had two choices. If it expected the borrower to recover, it could engage in forbearance and reduce the borrower's loan payments until the borrower recovered. While granting forbearance, the bank would take a further provision for loan losses through its income statement. This was a specific provision for this non-performing loan in case the borrower didn't recover. If the bank didn't expect the borrower to recover or the borrower receiving forbearance actually defaulted, the loss on the loan was charged-off against the loan loss reserve.

There are several key takeaways. First, if a bank was properly reserving for bad debt, while it was rapidly growing its loan portfolio it didn't generate a lot of earnings. The earnings were consumed by the provision for loan losses. Second, if banks experienced an unexpectedly high level of bad debt, they had to rebuild their loan loss reserve by taking an additional provision for loan losses. Sometimes, the provision for loan losses expense was greater than the bank's

---

486 Bank of England (2012, November), Financial Stability Report, Short-term risks to financial stability, Bank of England, http://www.bankofengland.co.uk/publications/Documents/fsr/2012/fsr32sec2.pdf, page 31.

income. In this case, the bank's book capital level would decrease. Examples of banks experiencing losses above their historic norm abound and include the loans to less developed countries. Third, the loan loss reserve account and bank capital are directly linked by the provision for loan losses expense in the income statement. This is why past, current and future bank earnings can be used to absorb the losses that exist in the banks' loan portfolios today.

Of course, bankers objected to having to set aside a reserve when they made a loan. It was bad for bonuses as it lowered net income. They argued the time to recognize the expense for bad debt was when a loan actually defaulted. This is known as incurred loss accounting. In some parts of the world, this is the current accounting regime.

The issue of forbearance is particularly important when a loan defaulting is the trigger for recognition of the bad debt expense. So long as there is forbearance and banks engage in activities like 'extend and pretend', the losses on the loans are not triggered and therefore don't flow through the income statement or the capital accounts. The result, of course, is the banks' financial statements are completely divorced from their underlying economic reality.

Most of the time, the issues of forbearance and reserving for loan losses are based on the condition of the borrower. However, when there is a financial crisis and bank regulators adopt the Japanese Model, the issue of forbearance and reserving for loan losses are based on the condition of the bank. If the bank is experiencing difficulties, regulators grant the bank forbearance until it has solved its difficulties. When this occurs, banks engage in exercises like 'extend and pretend' with their non-performing loans regardless of the borrower's capacity to ultimately repay the loan. While engaging in 'extend and pretend' and similar activities, the banks stretch out over several years when they add to their loan loss reserves to cover this bad debt.

In his discussion on loan forbearance, Mr. Haldane addressed the issue policymakers and financial regulators fear most. Having adopted the Japanese Model, have they reproduced the same experience Japan has had including the creation of "zombie" borrowers who only continue to exist because the banks are unwilling to recognize the losses on these loans?

The issue of loan forbearance is only a major issue because the banks are opaque. When banks have to provide valuation transparency, market discipline pushes the banks to adopt the Swedish Model and with it an alternative to forbearance that avoids costly waves of liquidation. The alternative is for banks to write-down the value of their loans to what they would expect to receive if they went through the expensive foreclosure and liquidation process. A good proxy for what the bank would expect to receive is the greater of the amount of a loan the borrower can afford to repay or what an independent third party would pay for the asset that has been pledged as collateral for the loan (for example, a house is the collateral for a mortgage). When a loan is written-down to what the borrower can afford to repay and then restructured to reflect this reality, it becomes a performing asset again while avoiding costly waves of liquidation.

> Andy Haldane: Well as the Governor says, there isn't any hard and fast rule about when and whether forbearance is a good or bad thing we have elements of both. I think the key factor when determining whether this is a good or a bad thing is exactly ... how forward looking a bank is when it's providing for the loans it's making.
>
> I think you know a forward-looking bank that can say — look I have a company or a household that's struggling today, but its prospects over the medium term are good, is doing the right thing by forbearing on that loan ... What it should do in that situation however is still to provide, to provision, for the possibility of that loan going bad.
>
> I think an example of bad forbearance practices would be one in which the bank is not forward looking, it's not looking to the longer term prospects of that household or company, but instead is staving off the day of reckoning so as not to crystallise losses today.... we look at the Japanese experience which is one in which for a lengthy period we had evidence of bad forbearance practices, banks weren't looking forward. They were keeping afloat companies that did not have a future, that clogged up their balance sheet, that made them less willing to make loans available to good businesses, and in turn retarded the recovery.[487]

And where might loan forbearance have been particularly acute?

> Andy Haldane: [T]he area that I'd highlight which we have looked at very closely is not so much on the residential side but rather on the commercial side, where we do have a significant overhang of legacy loans, commercial property loans that account for fully half of all corporate lending by UK banks. A sizable chunk of those loans we know to be subject to forbearance — a third, perhaps more, of those loans are subject to forbearance. And we think in some cases there is evidence of those loans being under provided for....[488]

The UK commercial real estate market provided a classic example of why the Japanese Model reduces the availability of credit to support the real economy. The reason is simple: it was easier for a zombie borrower, in this case the commercial real estate borrower receiving forbearance, to get credit than it was for a creditworthy borrower.

---

487 Bank of England (2012, November 29), Financial Stability Report Q&A, Bank of England, http://www.bankofengland.co.uk/publications/Documents/fsr/2012/conf121129.pdf, page 17.

488 ibid, page 21

The creditworthy borrower was up against a major obstacle. The banks knew how much in the way of similar collateral they had supporting zombie loans. The bankers have to figure out what the likely value for all this commercial real estate collateral is if they are ever required to recognize the losses on the zombie loans and the collateral is sold. The result is a gap between what the creditworthy borrower wants to borrow against their commercial real estate collateral and what the bank is willing to lend based on the bank's estimate of collateral value. Forbearance created uncertainty in the value of the commercial real estate collateral the creditworthy borrower has to pledge for a loan.

Mr. Haldane confirmed this.

> The truth is for a large part of the commercial property market right now the existing prices, the existing valuations are not very firm because there's effectively no liquidity, no transactions in the secondary market, much less the tertiary market for commercial property.[489]

Finally, the focus of the questions and answers shifted to one of the many policies adopted in the UK under the Japanese Model. As Sir Mervyn King observed, the policy, also known as the Funding for Lending scheme, was a subsidy for the banks as it gave them funds at substantially below the market rates investors required because they could not assess the risk of the banks. He wanted to restore confidence in the banks so investors fund the banks and this subsidy could be ended.

> We have put in place the Funding for Lending scheme as a temporary scheme to provide a breathing space. It provides a subsidy to banks that cannot possibly continue indefinitely, and therefore banks have to get themselves into a position where they have sufficient confidence in the investor community for people to be willing to lend to banks and to buy equity in banks at rates which make it possible for our banks to lend to the real economy at normal premia over Bank Rate.
>
> That is not happening at present, and it will need to take place before we get back to a fully-fledged recovery.[490]

As a banker, would you want this subsidy to end? Would you want this subsidy to end if it meant ending your ability to profit on opacity? Would you want this subsidy to end particularly if it meant recognizing the expense of the losses currently hidden on and off your bank's balance sheet?

---

489 ibid, page 21

490 ibid, page 28

No. Providing the valuation transparency necessary to end this and similar subsidies would result in lower net income and a future of greatly diminished banker bonuses.

Did the whole effort by the Bank of England result in the banks acknowledging the true size of the losses hiding on or off their balance sheets? Did the whole effort by the Bank of England to restore trust in bank balance sheets work? No. Supporting evidence comes from the interbank lending market. It still hasn't thawed. Banks with money to lend still do not trust the solvency of the banks looking to borrow.

Chapter 21

FED GIVES BANKS TAXPAYERS' MONEY

And the estimates [of the cost of the bailout of Continental Illinois] may well be only the tip of the iceberg if the FDIC and the Federal Reserve have created—without congressional approval—a brand new entitlement program for money center banks. If Continental is a precedent, the big bank fail-safe security program may, someday, rival defense outlays.

—Rep. St. Germain

Opacity is the reason financial regulators originally adopted and can continue to pursue the Japanese Model. Opacity is also the reason financial regulators can engage in nontransparent acts to save the banks. It is the lack of valuation transparency and the disclosure of each bank's current exposure details that provides room for bank regulators to exercise discretion over what the regulators see as a tradeoff between financial stability and the need for disclosure to other market participants.

However, there is the very real issue of what are the limits to regulatory discretion and the non-transparent acts regulators can engage in.

For example, in our current systemic financial crisis, the regulators granted regulatory forbearance to improve financial stability. On the surface, this simple act to not spook the financial markets and limit the potential for the fire sale of bank assets appears reasonable. All it required the regulators to do was allow banks to value their investment securities using mark-to-model valuation and engage in 'extend and pretend' which changed nonperforming loans into performing loans. This reduced the need for banks to recognize mark-to-market losses on the declining value of their securities portfolio or to reserve for loan losses. Both of these boosted the banks' reported income and equity. As a result, the banks reported financial statements that made them appear healthier than they actually were.

However, this simple act of regulatory discretion creates clear winners and losers. Bankers win. As a result of regulatory discretion, the banks appear healthy and the bankers continue to loot the banks by paying themselves bonuses as if the banks were actually healthy. The real economy loses. It has to deal with the burden of the excess debt and the misallocation of resources caused by zombie borrowers. Investors lose. To investors, the bank regulators' exercise of discretion doesn't appear so reasonable. After all, the result of regulators granting forbearance is to separate bank financial statements from their underlying economic reality. From the investors' perspective, in the name of financial stability, the bank regulators effectively told the banks to lie about their true condition.

Regardless of whether or not the bank regulators actually told the banks to lie to investors, bank regulators in our current crisis have gone beyond simple acts of discretion like regulatory forbearance. They appear to have given into their "irresistible" urge and engaged in nontransparent acts that resulted in taxpayer money going to the banks and subsequently the bankers as bonuses without the approval of Congress.

The opacity of the banks allowed the bank regulators to realize the fears Congress expressed during the Continental Illinois hearing. Specifically, Congress was concerned the bank regulators had created an entitlement program for the banks controlled by the regulators and not by Congress. Congress was concerned bank regulators would exercise their discretion and without Congressional approval or any accountability effectively give taxpayer money to the banks.

And lo and behold, that is exactly what the Federal Reserve did during our current financial crisis.

Secret Fed bank loans

Recall as the lender of last resort, following Walter Bagehot's prescription, the Fed was suppose to lend to solvent banks at high rates of interest. With deposit insurance, this prescription was modified to lend at high rates of interest. However, in the 2008-2009 period, the Fed, exercising its discretion as a bank regulator, secretly abandoned lending at high rates of interest and instead lent at below market rates of interest. The Fed could do this because banks used the intermediary depiction model for disclosure and this hid the loans and the terms on these loans from the other market participants. If banks disclosed under the pure information model, the Fed could still have provided below market rate loans to the banks, but this exercise of regulatory discretion would probably have caught the market's attention and resulted in the Fed being subject to a negative reaction by Congress.

Just how low the interest rates were took a lawsuit pursued by Bloomberg reporter Mark Pittman and financed by Bloomberg News to find out.

Mark was not a random reporter to me. He was someone I had dined with and exchanged ideas with (either by phone or email). Several weeks prior to his death in 2009, we had our last telephone conversation. The focus of the conversation was Wall Street's Opacity Protection Team.

I was pointing out all the different ways Wall Street was preventing valuation transparency from occurring in the structured finance market. Mark pointed out that the Opacity Protection Team extended well beyond Wall Street and included its regulators. He talked about where he was in the pursuit of the Fed's bailout data and how the Fed lent new meaning to the term significant, well-financed resistance to transparency.

He concluded our conversation by observing with only the two of us pursuing transparency Wall Street's Opacity Protection Team would win. I am glad that Bloomberg News carried Mark's quest to the finish line.

What they found was the Fed gave the banks an undisclosed $13 billion boost to income[491]. In addition,

> Bankers didn't mention that they took tens of billions of dollars in emergency loans at the same time they were assuring investors their firms were healthy.[492]

Bankers took the loans at the same time as the government was providing them with money through the Troubled Asset Relief Program's Capital Purchase Program. Under this program, the money from the government supposedly only went into healthy banks. The bankers were happy to repeat that their participation in this program meant they were healthy. But if they were healthy, why did they need billions of dollars of below market interest rate loans?

This point bears repeating, due to opacity, the bankers were able to represent to investors with the bank regulators' blessing their firms were healthy while benefiting to the tune of $13 billion from the Fed's below market rate loans. Was this representation a lie? There is a readily apparent inconsistency between banks being healthy and the Fed seeing a need to exercise regulatory discretion and boost the banks' income by $13 billion. Whether it was or wasn't a lie, by calling themselves healthy, bankers were entitled to bonuses made possible by the Fed's below market rate loans.

Did the markets believe the banks when they said they were healthy? No. Please notice the interbank lending market froze at the beginning of the financial crisis because banks with deposits to lend could not determine which banks were solvent and could repay the loans and which were not.

---

491 Ivry, Bob, Keoun, Bradley, Kuntz, Phil (2011, November 27), Secret Fed Loans Gave Banks $13 Billion Undisclosed to Congress, Bloomberg, http://www.bloomberg.com/news/2011-11-28/secret-fed-loans-undisclosed-to-congress-gave-banks-13-billion-in-income.html

492 ibid

The interbank lending market is still effectively frozen. This is the banks' way of telling the market that they are still concerned with the solvency of other banks because they know that they too are using Alice in Wonderland accounting and hiding losses on and off their balance sheets.

Imagine for a second how different the response to the crisis would have been had the banks been required to provide valuation transparency under the pure information model and market participants had access to their current exposure details. With valuation transparency, market participants would have known if the banks were healthy or needed the loans to survive. With valuation transparency, the Fed would have been unlikely to subsidize the banks with taxpayer money without Congressional approval. With valuation transparency, regulators would have been permanently blocked from inadvertently supporting misrepresentations to the financial markets. With valuation transparency, the bankers' effectiveness at lobbying against new government regulations would have been dramatically decreased.

However, banks don't provide valuation transparency and the Fed argued for opacity so the Fed could continue to engage in nontransparent acts to save the banks. The Fed under Fed Chair Bernanke took the position that market participants should not know the true condition of the banks because if they did it might start a second Great Depression as the market participants properly assess the risk of the banks and adjust the amount and price of their exposure accordingly.

Joseph Stiglitz, a Nobel-prize winning economist, summarized the impact of the Fed's position on disclosure.

> The "fundamental problem" is that capital markets need information to work properly, yet the Fed is saying, "we believe in capital-market discipline without information."[493]

But how does the Fed justify a $13 billion gift from the taxpayers through the Fed to the banks. By arguing that by acting as a lender of last resort, it prevented a collapse of the financial system and kept credit flowing. As Fed Chair Bernanke pointed out in discussing the Panic of 1907, the response to a classic financial panic is liquidity and valuation transparency.

No one has any problem with the fact that the Fed should have provided and did provide liquidity to the banks, securities firms and shadow banking firms like

---

493 Lanman, Scott, Keoun, Bradley (2011, December 11), No One Telling Who Took $586 Billion in Swaps With Fed Condoning Anonymity, Bloomberg, http://www.bloomberg.com/news/2011-12-11/no-one-says-who-took-586-billion-in-fed-swaps-done-in-anonymity.html

money market mutual funds during the financial crisis. To the extent there is a problem with the Fed's extension of liquidity, it is in the pricing of this liquidity. Specifically, the $13 billion banks made from the Fed's liquidity programs.

In the absence of valuation transparency, market participants, including Congress, didn't and still don't know if the banks were healthy and the $13 billion resulted from bankers negotiating favorable terms or the banks were unhealthy and the Fed was trying to restore them to solvency as quickly as possible.

SECTION 7

THE TRANSPARENCY LABEL INITIATIVE™ AND FIXING THE GLOBAL FINANCIAL SYSTEM

The valuation process will take as long as it takes, but it is the primary step toward effectively utilizing the very controversial bailout and avoiding the structural problem of a stagnant economy.

— *Harry Markowitz*[494]

494 Crovitz, L. Gordon (2008, November 3), The Father of Portfolio Theory on the Crisis, The Wall Street Journal, http://online.wsj.com/news/articles/SB122567428153591981

Chapter 22

ENDING THE CURRENT FINANCIAL CRISIS

Moreover, looking at the experiences with debt crises in Scandinavia and Japan in the 1990s, there is much to be said for not putting off the balance sheet repair process.
—*Jens Weidmann*[495]

Despite their irresistible urge to adopt the Japanese Model, financial regulators know the lesson from history for ending an opacity driven financial crisis is to adopt the Swedish Model. The lesson of history is based on two facts: hiding the losses under the Japanese Model doesn't fool the financial markets and it only increases the final cost of the bad debt when the losses are realized.

Financial market participants aren't fooled because they know the banks are hiding their losses on and off their balance sheet. As shown by the loans to less developed countries, they just don't know the exact amount of each bank's losses.

Besides the damage to the real economy from diverting capital to debt service, there are easily quantified direct costs to the policymakers' and bank regulators' effort to try to perpetuate the myth the losses don't exist. For example, take a $100,000 loan at 7% that is worth its collateral value of $50,000. Under the Japanese Model, the regulators grant the bank the flexibility to engage in 'extend and pretend' with the loan and "lend" the borrower the 7% annual interest payment. At the end of the first year, the balance on the loan has increased to $107,000, the collateral value hasn't changed and the loss on the loan has grown from $50,000 to $57,000. If the bank's book capital increased by the $7,000 interest "payment", this increase would offset the increase in the loss on the loan.

Unfortunately, perpetuating the myth the losses don't exist means not all of the $7,000 is retained in equity. Of the several reasons not all of the income is retained, three stand out. First, there is the bank's cost of funds to support the bad debt. In this example, the bank will fund the loan with a combination of

---

495 Weidmann, Jens (2014, April 7), Stable banks for a Stable Europe, speech at the 20th German Banking Congress, Berlin, BIS, http://www.bis.org/review/r140415b.htm?utm_content=buffer8af00&utm_medium=social&utm_source=twitter.com&utm_campaign=buffer

$5,000 of equity and $95,000 of deposits, wholesale funding and unsecured borrowing. If the average cost of the bank's deposits, wholesale funding and unsecured borrowing is 1%, there is an interest expense of $950 to fund this loan for the year. Half of this interest expense, $475, is for the loss on the bad debt that is being hidden. Second, there are banker bonuses under the budget for loss recognition. If these are 15% of net revenue, significantly less than Too Big to Fail banks pay, there is an expense of $907.50 ((income of $7,000 minus interest expense of $950) times percentage paid out as bonuses of 15%). Third, there are dividend payments to shareholders under the budget for loss recognition.

The cost of perpetuating the myth this borrower's problems are temporary is a minimum of $1,382.50 per year, the $475 of interest expense on bad debt portion of the loan plus the $907.50 of banker bonuses. If interest rates were to increase, the cost of hiding the bad debt would go dramatically higher. One of the reasons central banks pursue zero interest rate policies under the Japanese Model is to minimize the cost to the banks of perpetuating the myth the losses don't exist.

Now imagine this $100,000 loan is representative of $100 billion in bad loans and investments a global financial institution has. The annual cost to perpetuating the myth the losses don't exist is now $1.3825 billion. Even for the big banks, that is real money.

RBS is an example of why banks should be required to recognize their losses upfront following the Swedish Model approach rather than increase the final cost of the bad debt when the losses are realized under the budget for losses in the Japanese Model approach.

The UK taxpayers took an 82% stake in the bank with the intention RBS would be restructured, recapitalized quickly and then returned to the private sector. This plan immediately went awry with the adoption of the Japanese Model and the requirement to protect bank capital levels and banker bonuses. Under the Japanese Model, RBS had a "budget" for recognizing losses. This "budget" was the amount of earnings RBS generated over what was needed to pay banker bonuses, pay shareholder dividends and generate additional book capital for the bank. As a result, years later RBS is still in the process of recognizing losses.

Contrast this with what would have happened had the Swedish Model been adopted. RBS would have been required to recognize its losses upfront. As a result, its book capital level would have declined significantly. Then, RBS would have faced the issue of how to recapitalize. While completely unnecessary, one way to quickly recapitalize the bank would have been for the UK taxpayers to buy a stake. A second way would be for RBS to sell equity. A third way to recapitalize the bank would be for RBS to rebuild its book capital through retention of 100% of pre-banker bonus earnings.

As Sir Mervyn King observed about RBS,

> The arguments for a restructuring sooner rather than later are powerful ones.... We shouldn't worry about the consequential impact."[496]

Of course, one of the primary reasons financial regulators cited for adopting the Japanese Model and bailing out the bank was the fear of the consequential impact of requiring the opaque banks to recognize their losses upfront. This fear included fear of financial contagion.

As a result of pursuing the Japanese Model and policies like regulatory forbearance under which banks have a budget for recognizing the losses currently hidden on and off their balance sheets, bank financial statements are completely fictitious. The process of restoring any meaning to the financial statements requires as Sir Mervyn King said accepting

> that whatever we do now will mean recognizing losses relative to where the public accounts currently show them....[497]

If after six years of cleaning up its exposures, RBS has not managed to put its bad debt and pre-crisis investments behind it, there is no reason to believe that any other Too Big to Fail bank has done so.

Sir Mervyn King left no doubt that RBS is hiding so much in the way of bad debt on and off its balance sheet that it is impeding RBS' ability to continue to lend to the real economy.

Clearly, the time has come to have the banks recognize the losses they are hiding.

The question now facing the bank regulators is do they ask for another taxpayer bailout of the banks to cover these losses or do they let the banks operate with low or negative book capital levels as they are designed to do? With the combination of deposit insurance and access to central bank funding, there is no need to make the implicit role of the taxpayer as the banks' silent equity partner explicit through a bailout.

What is needed is that the banks be required to provide valuation transparency and disclose on an ongoing basis their current global asset, liability and off-balance sheet exposure details. With this information, market participants can independently assess whether the banks have recognized all the losses on their bad debt.

---

496 Finch, Gavin, Hamilton, Scott (2013, March 6), BOE's King Says Government Should Split up RBS, Accept Loss, Bloomberg, http://www.bloomberg.com/news/2013-03-06/boe-s-king-calls-on-government-to-decisively-restructure-rbs.html

497 ibid

More importantly, with this information, market participants can exert discipline on the banks so that they restrain their future risk taking and do not gamble on redemption while they are rebuilding their book capital levels through retention of 100% of pre-banker bonus earnings.

With valuation transparency in place and banks recognizing upfront all the losses on the excess public and private debt in the financial system, the real economy is poised to resume growing and the banks are positioned to provide the necessary lending to support this growth.

Japanese Model façade begins to crack

At last, the facade bank regulators have constructed since the beginning of the global financial crisis about the solvency of the large global financial institutions is beginning to crack and with its collapse the Swedish Model is gaining acceptance.

In talking about Europe's entire banking sector, Sir Mervyn King said

> until losses are recognised, and reflected in balance sheets, the current problems will drag on.[498]

This is the same point he made about RBS. Hiding the losses actually makes it difficult for banks to lend and support the real economy.

It is the placement of the financial firewall that is important

Since September 23, 2008 and the choice to pursue the Japanese Model, global policymakers and financial regulators have placed a firewall around protecting the banks' book capital levels.

Examples of actions the regulators have taken to protect book capital levels include, but certainly are not limited to

- Suspension of mark-to-market accounting and the introduction of mark-to-make-believe for opaque, toxic structured finance securities.
- Purchases of bank equity securities by governments.
- Regulatory forbearance on recognition of problem loans.
- Stress tests where the regulators make explicit representations about the each large bank's solvency.

---

498 Halligan, Liam (2012, June 16), Bank 'throws kitchen sink' at credit problem, The Telegraph, http://www.telegraph.co.uk/finance/comment/9336435/Bank-throws-kitchen-sink-at-credit-problem.html

By erecting a firewall around bank book capital levels, global policymakers and financial regulators have linked their sovereign debt to the book capital levels of their banking system.

Clearly, positioning the financial firewall around book capital levels is something that favors the bankers. It allows them to continue to privatize any gains and socialize any losses.

But is erecting the financial firewall around book capital levels the appropriate place to erect the firewall?

No.

By erecting the financial firewall around bank book capital, global policymakers and financial regulators interfere with the ability of the banks to perform one of their core functions: acting as the safety valve between the excesses in the financial system and the real economy. In order for banks to prevent the excesses in the financial system from spilling over into the real economy, they have to be allowed to recognize all of their losses from the financial excesses.

By erecting the firewall around bank capital levels, global policymakers and regulators are preventing banks from recognizing these losses any faster than they have offsetting earnings. This policy has resulted in Japan experiencing two plus decades of economic malaise.

The firewall should be moved. Instead of protecting the banks' book capital levels, it should be moved to protect the real economy. To protect the real economy, the right place to erect the firewall is around the depositors.

So long as deposits are guaranteed and the central bank is willing to lend against a bank's assets, the banks can continue operating indefinitely. With the financial system protected from collapse, banks can recognize all of the losses hidden on and off their balance sheets.

Erecting the firewall around the depositors breaks the linkage between sovereign debt and bank solvency. The sovereign no longer has to put money into the banking system to maintain positive book capital levels. Instead, the banks can rebuild their book capital levels through retention of **future** profits.

With the firewall around deposits, banks should be required to provide valuation transparency and disclose on an on-going basis their current asset, liability and off-balance sheet exposure details. There are many reasons for requiring valuation transparency including:

- Market discipline on the banks stops them from taking unnecessary risks and gambling on redemption while they are retaining earnings to pay for their current losses.
- It restores confidence in the banking system because market participants can assess the risk of the individual banks and see that they are not hiding any losses.

- It frees up the sovereign to issue debt to support economic growth rather than to absorb the losses in bank book capital.

Banking reform fails because focus is not on valuation transparency

> Here, then, is a simple test that people can apply: if a politician or a regulator pushes a structural overhaul of the industry with a view to transforming the incentives of financiers, they can be considered to have understood the lessons of the great financial crash. If, on the other hand, they talk earnestly about curbing bankers' behaviour through complex new rules, but propose to leave the existing industry structure in place, they have, alas, learned nothing.[499]

Since the early 1930s, the financial systems of most western nations have been based on the FDR Framework. Under this framework, reform should have been focused on ending opacity in and restoring valuation transparency to the financial system. Reform should also have focused on ensuring the enforcement of valuation transparency adapts to future innovations by Wall Street and the City.

Instead, banking reform since the beginning of our current financial crisis has focused on curing the symptoms of opacity. In addition, it uses technocratic solutions to constrain Wall Street and the City despite the fact our current financial crisis shows the inherent cleverness of Wall Street and the City will get around both simple and complex regulations. The result of all these technocratic solutions has been a veritable explosion in new regulations and regulatory initiatives, think macro prudential regulation.

The first lesson from our current financial crisis is complex rules and regulatory oversight doesn't work as a preventative for a financial crisis. The Nyberg Commission Report, the FSA report, the FCIC Report, former Fed Governor Partee and former Fed chairman Alan Greenspan described how regulatory oversight is compromised because regulators could never take away the punch bowl before a crisis as this would be unacceptable to politicians. As former Fed Chair Bernanke succinctly put it: Congress is our boss.[500]

---

499 Chu, Ben (2014, July 31), *Only structural reform will clean up our unsound banking system*, The Independent, http://www.independent.co.uk/news/business/comment/ben-chu-only-structural-reform-will-clean-up-our-unsound-banking-system-9639052.html

500 Zumbrun, Joshua, Kearns, Jeff (2014, January 7), Yellen's Record-low Senate Support Reflects Fed's Politicalization, Bloomberg, http://www.bloomberg.com/news/2014-01-07/yellen-s-record-low-senate-support-reflects-fed-s-politicization.html

In addition, regulators are subject to being captured by the banks. They rely on the banks for access to their exposure details and help in interpreting this information. Regulators also have political masters who are easily captured by the banking lobby. Because the financial regulators are subject to capture by the banks, regulators are the very last market participants to be able to exert strict discipline on the banks.

In fact, a case could be made that regulatory micro-management is simply gold plating bank regulation in an effort to appease an angry public. Most of the banking regulations passed since the beginning of our opacity driven crisis in 2007 are essentially worthless because they try to solve in a one-off manner something valuation transparency addresses directly.

The Dodd-Frank Act in the U.S., the Vickers Commission in the UK and most recently the Liikanen Commission in the EU, have focused on substituting the combination of complex regulations with regulatory oversight for the combination of valuation transparency and market disciplines. This substitution is seen in regulatory micro-management.

An example of regulatory micro-management is the Basel III capital requirements. U.S. banks are losing the battle over the adoption of the complex Basel III capital requirements including the requirement for larger banks to hold additional capital. However, this 'loss' allows them to continue to win the war to retain opacity.

The banks perceive they benefit because with Basel III they can continue to take excessive amounts of risk that market participants cannot see. Even better, they get to represent themselves as being less risky so that they can access funds for rates far below what a fully informed market would charge for their risk.

Requiring valuation transparency allows market participants to calculate bank capital ratios however they would like. More importantly, it allows market participants to assess the actual risk of the bank and adjust both the amount and price of their exposure based on this assessment.

With valuation transparency, market discipline will drive banks to reduce their risk relative to their capital. Banks with high risk and low capital will pay a premium to attract funds. Banks with low risk and high capital will be able to access funds at a much lower cost.

Even when a new regulation could have had a positive impact, like the Volcker Rule, it is mind-numbingly complex and so full of loopholes as to effectively neuter the regulation. The Volcker Rule has 71 pages of regulations and 800 plus pages of explanation. The Volcker Rule based on valuation transparency can be done in 3 pages or less.

Valuation transparency accomplishes what Mr. Volcker initially set out to achieve. It forces the banks to announce every story idea they have. Once a proprietary trade is exposed, it subjects the bank to having its bet traded against by other market participants. This minimizes the opportunity for the bank to profit and maximizes its opportunity to lose money. This form of market discipline works to limit proprietary trading.

Finally, all these new regulations are expensive for the banks to comply with. The cost estimate for ring-fencing alone runs 7 billion pounds a year. By comparison, valuation transparency is very, very low cost. It can be done in the UK for every bank for a fraction of the annual cost of the UK's ring-fencing alone.

Unlike all the proposed new regulations, valuation transparency is simple, inexpensive and proven over decades to be very effective. What is there for market participants other than banks not to like?

Chapter 23

REGULATORY REFORM LITMUS TEST: WOULD IT BE USED DURING A FINANCIAL CRISIS

Officials doubt politicians have the courage to pull the trigger

— Philip Aldrick[501]

The Bank of England's Andy Haldane expressed concern about the various post crisis reforms to the financial system. He noted about bail-in debt

> Having debtors assume pain is fine on paper. But crisis wars are not waged on paper.[502]

His concern about any regulatory reform leads directly to a litmus test. The litmus test for any regulatory reform is not does it look fine on paper, but rather would regulators actually use it to fight a financial crisis.

To see how this litmus test works, let's apply it to bank capital. The theory behind bank capital is that it is there to absorb losses. As a result, a significant amount of regulatory time and energy since the beginning of the opacity driven financial crisis has gone into crafting the Basel III capital rules including the requirement that systemically important financial institutions carry an additional capital buffer. As Mr. Haldane would say, all of that is fine on paper. The litmus test is would financial regulators actually use bank capital to fight a financial crisis.

Unfortunately, history shows using bank capital to absorb losses was abandoned in the teeth of our current financial crisis. With the choice on September 23, 2008 to continue pursuing the Japanese Model, financial

---

501 Aldrick, Philip (2012, February 19), Bank of England fears bail-out protection won't be used, The Telegraph, http://www.telegraph.co.uk/finance/newsbysector/banksandfinance/9091887/Bank-of-England-fears-bail-out-protection-wont-be-used.html

502 ibid

regulators chose to protect bank book capital levels at all costs rather than to use it to absorb losses. The choice to protect bank book capital levels reflected the fear if these capital levels declined it would scare market participants and trigger the second Great Depression.

Bank capital is not the only area where regulatory reform fails this litmus test. Virtually all of the Dodd-Frank Act, Vickers Commission recommendations and Liikanen Commission recommendations are fair game. It looks fine on paper, but it will do nothing to help in the battle against the next financial crisis.

In fact, the only reform that would be used and wouldn't be subject to being abandoned is requiring valuation transparency. Please note, the financial regulators didn't abandon requiring valuation transparency at the start of our current financial crisis. It had been abandoned by the financial regulators years before the financial crisis began.

How would you change the financial system?

> Some regulators and banks say that disclosure … risks undermining market confidence and accelerating a lender's losses. The argument doesn't fit with the experiences in Denmark… Disclosure increases transparency and increasing transparency increases market discipline…. That's the way it works.
>
> Kristian Vie Madsen, deputy director of the FSA in Copenhagen[503]

Imagine you were given the opportunity to enact one reform to make the financial system safer. What would this one reform be?

Would you increase bank capital requirements? Would you enhance bank liquidity requirements? Would you ring-fence proprietary trading from bank deposit taking? Would it be any of the reforms included in the Dodd-Frank Act? Would you require banks to be subject to margin requirements and have to post collateral to support their derivative book?

Or would this reform reflect the primary lesson from our current opacity driven financial crisis?

The primary lesson is what investors and other market participants don't know is what hurts them. Opacity prevents market discipline, obscures risks and results in nasty surprises.

Furthermore, when banks hide their current exposures, it is impossible to determine how risky they are or if they are solvent or insolvent. If we are ever to restore confidence in the global financial system, banks must not be left with the choice between transparency and opacity. Under the FDR Framework, banks do

---

503 Schwartzkopff, Frances (2014, August 8), *Bank Capital Race Not Enough for Basel as Nordics Break Away*, Bloomberg, http://www.bloomberg.com/news/2014-08-08/banks-hoarding-capital-not-enough-for-basel-as-nordics-raise-bar.html

not have this choice. Banks are required to provide valuation transparency and disclose their current asset, liability and off-balance sheet exposure details.

Given that we have effectively reached the limits of fiscal and monetary policy, it is time to adopt a new approach to ending the opacity driven crisis. This approach is the Transparency Label Initiative™ and with it restoring valuation transparency to all the opaque corners of the financial system.

The following three case studies clearly demonstrate the positive impact bringing valuation transparency to all the opaque corners of the financial system would have. I chose these cases not just because of how clearly they highlighted the need for valuation transparency, but because I tried and failed to find a case study that demonstrates a compelling need for retaining opacity in some corner of the financial system.

Chapter 24

CASE STUDIES

Case study I: Anglo Irish Bank: Bankers cynically bankrupting Ireland

Investment bankers, as a class, are the Earnest Hemingways of bullshit.
—*Jay Jordan*[504]

Anglo Irish Bank provided a vivid illustration of why complex regulation and regulatory oversight is an inadequate substitute for the combination of valuation transparency and market discipline.

Anglo Irish did this by over-extending itself in risky property loans.

Background on Anglo Irish Bank

In the years preceding the global financial crisis, Ireland based Anglo Irish Bank grew rapidly by lending against real estate development projects and commercial buildings. A primary source of funding for these loans was uninsured wholesale deposits.

By late 2007, the real estate bubble in Ireland had peaked and financial market participants sensed that Anglo Irish, among other Irish banks, had overextended itself and was facing significant losses on its loans. Concerned about this potential for losses, wholesale depositors began to withdraw their money.

On September 15, 2008, Lehman Brothers declared bankruptcy. One of the consequences of this action was to accelerate the wholesale depositors withdrawal of their money and to trigger a wholesale bank run on Anglo Irish and the other Irish banks.

By the end of the month, to stop the bank run on the Irish financial system, Ireland had offered a blanket guaranteed on all insured and uninsured deposits.

504 Moore, Heidi (2014), pic.twitter.com/BuaRId4G80

When Anglo Irish Bank was closed in 2009, as a result of this guarantee, Irish taxpayers would incur 30 billion euros in losses.

Was it a liquidity or solvency crisis?

The Irish experience, which paralleled the EU, UK and U.S. experience with their banks, can be boiled down to a simple question: in September 2008, did the policymakers and financial regulators know what they were dealing with.

Kevin Cardiff, a senior level official at the Irish Finance Ministry, testifying on the decision to offer the blanket guarantee:

> We based "our" guarantee — I am not supposed to comment on the decisions of Ministers — on the basis of the situation as it presented itself, including the mix of risks, the mix of potential options, and how those two interacted.
>
> I do not think it would be accurate to say that we were totally oblivious to solvency issues, or that we had a fine picture of how the solvency would come undone over time and that we therefore had perfect knowledge. We were somewhere in between those two extremes.[505]

Confirming the findings of the Nyberg Commission Report, Mr. Cardiff's comment highlights the lack of information on which the policy response to the financial crisis was made. The lack of information meant that policymakers and financial regulators couldn't determine if they were dealing with a rumor driven or bank solvency driven liquidity crisis. They were aware that there was a bank run going on, but they had no idea of the size of the losses on the bad debt the banks were holding.

One potential source of information for answering the question of was it a rumor driven or bank solvency driven liquidity crisis was the banking regulators. Their bank examination process concluded that under the Basel II capital requirements the banks were both adequately capitalized and solvent. Therefore, the bank regulators' answer was it was a rumor driven liquidity crisis. A second potential source of information was the bankers. As the following tapes from internal Anglo Irish conversations show, the bankers said it was a liquidity crisis and they were adequately capitalized. A third potential source of information was the investors. They were not only saying the banks were sitting on large losses that made them all insolvent, but taking action and running down to the bank to get their money.

---

505 Cardiff, Kevin (2010, July 22), testimony, http://debates.oireachtas.ie/DDebate... Node=H3&Page=9

Of the three potential sources of information, the least credible was the investors. They lacked credibility because they did not have access to each bank's current exposure details. The banks were black boxes to them.

Clearly, policymakers recognized there was a large gap between what the banks and their regulators were saying and what the investors were saying. To find out who was right, consultants were sent into the banks to examine the loan exposures. As described by a U.S. Embassy wikileaks cable,

> Econoff spoke with Kevin Cardiff, Second Secretary General at the Department of Finance, who has been deeply involved in putting together the guarantee package.
>
> Cardiff echoed the regulator and pointed out that auditors contracted by his Department to look at the books of at least two of the institutions under pressure came away with "a favorable impression of the loan books."[506]

In the Panic of 1907, as described by Fed Chair Bernanke, JPMorgan and his fellow bankers did not send in auditors to look at each bank's loan book. The bankers sat down themselves and went through each bank's loan book. It was the bankers who forced each bank to write down their bad debt.

The bankers could do this because the bankers knew the borrowers at the other banks. Why? Borrowers don't just look for a loan from one bank, but rather apply at multiple banks seeking the cheapest loan. In addition, bankers know how their own borrowers in similar situations are performing.

There was no reason to believe that auditors who didn't have the same access to information as the bankers could accurately assess each bank's loan book. In fact, the Irish government would hire consultants on three more occasions over the next couple of years to get to the bottom of the banks' bad loans. These three efforts were also unable to determine the bottom for the banks' bad loans.

> While he admitted that the amount of "speculative loans, or those that are not currently productive, is not insignificant," he stressed that all involved in putting together the package were confident that the government would not be forced to bail out the banks.[507]

By design, banks should never be bailed out.

With the introduction of deposit guarantees to the banking system, the predictable result was insolvency was no longer a trigger for a run on the bank's liquidity that forced a bank into closing. Instead, a bank could continue to

---

506 WikiLeaks cable (2009, October 9), The Bank Guarantee: An Irish Solution to an Irish Problem, http://www.cablegatesearch.net/cable.php?id=08DUBLIN556&q=kevin-cardiff

507 ibid

operate and make loans to support the real economy even if recognition of all its losses would leave the bank with negative book capital levels. Taxpayers through the deposit guarantee implicitly cover the negative capital levels and central banks provide liquidity to meet any withdrawals.

By introducing deposit insurance, banks are able to go from solvent to insolvent and back to solvent again. It is the bank's future earnings and not a taxpayer bailout that pay for the bank's losses.

The only time a bank cannot go from insolvent back to solvent again is if it is unable to generate any pre-banker bonus earnings. A bank that is unable to generate any pre-banker bonus earnings is a bank that should be closed. It is only when a bank is closed that taxpayers put up money to cover the bank's losses in excess of its book capital and unsecured debt.

> Cardiff said that credit to the Irish banks "virtually dried up" on September 29 and that the government had to step in to salvage the Irish financial sector. The genesis of this was classic "herd mentality" based mostly on rumor and innuendo about Irish banks rather than any hard facts. However, fighting the herd became impossible, he added....[508]

The reason that there were no hard facts was the banks did not disclose their current exposure details. In the absence of hard facts, it was predictable that there would be a classic financial panic and a run on the banks. It was predictable that this run on the banks would occur in the uninsured wholesale deposits as these investors understood they were exposed to losses and had no way of assessing how likely they were to lose money.

As Fed Chair Bernanke discussed with the Panic of 1907, the two elements to fight the herd mentality of a classic financial panic and end a rumor driven bank run are liquidity and valuation transparency. The Irish government, like the governments throughout the EU and in the UK and U.S., responded to the wholesale deposit bank run by focusing on the issue of liquidity and ignoring the need for disclosing the hard facts through valuation transparency.

Anglo Irish Bank tapes

Beginning in late 2007, the Anglo Irish bank tapes are interesting because they provide an inside look at how the bank's management thought about and dealt with the regulators, investors and rating agencies.

The tapes reveal a culture of deception. This culture is the direct result of the veil of opacity that surrounds banks because they do not have to disclose on an

---

[508] ibid

ongoing basis their current global asset, liability and off-balance sheet exposure details.

For example, the tapes reveal how the bankers attempted to manipulate the Irish government and central bank.

There are four speakers on the tapes of interest:

- John Bowe — the Acting Director of Treasury and Director of Capital Markets
- Peter Fitzgerald — the Director of Retail Banking
- David Drumm — Anglo Irish bank's CEO
- Matt Pass — a senior executive at Merrill Lynch

The tapes cover the time period from when Anglo Irish bank approached the central bank for liquidity assistance to after the Irish government had provided the guarantee.

During the first conversation on September 18th, 2008, John Bowe describes a meeting with the Irish Financial Services Regulatory Authority (IFSRA) during which Anglo Irish bank requests a bridge loan collateralized by loans on its balance sheet. The IFSRA was the single regulator for all Irish financial institutions and was responsible for prudential supervision of the individual firms. It was also part of the Central Bank of Ireland.

> Peter Fitzgerald: Look c'mere, what's going on?
>
> John Bowe: Ah Jesus…
>
> Peter Fitzgerald: Tell me the…
>
> John Bowe: Fun and games. yeah. We went down to the, we went down to the regulator. Did I tell you that we went down to the regulator yesterday?
>
> Peter Fitzgerald: Yesterday? Yesterday, yeah, yesterday was fine. Yeah, I got yesterday, yeah.
>
> John Bowe: And we basically…did I tell you we went down in the evening?
>
> Peter Fitzgerald: No, no you didn't.
>
> John Bowe: Went into IFSRA and basically kind of gave it to them between the eyes and there were sort of pointing in different directions.
>
> Not us, not us but Jeez, you would want to get on that, that sounds… hmm…hmm.
>
> So we went down… and we basically said…
>
> Peter Fitzgerald: In Central?
>
> John Bowe: In Central yeah. And I mean to cut a long story short we sort of said look, what we need is €7 billion and we're going to give you, what we're going to give you is our loan collateral so we're not giving you ECB, we're actually giving you the loan clause.

> We gave him a term sheet and we put a pro note facility together and we said that's what we need. And that kind of sobered up everybody pretty quickly, you know.[509]

The first thing to notice is Mr. Bowe suggests by the response of the regulator's representatives they were surprised by both the request and its size.

One of the myths destroyed by the financial crisis is the bank regulators know the current condition of each bank ranging from its solvency to its access to wholesale deposits.

Even though the regulators have examiners embedded inside a bank of Anglo Irish's size, they don't know its current financial condition. The regulators are better informed than investors, but this is a low hurdle given that the investors have absolutely no current information on the black box banks.

In response to a question from Senator Elizabeth Warren on whether the Fed had enough resources reviewing the Too Big to Fail banks' books to prevent another financial crisis, Fed chair Janet Yellen implied it did when she said "the Fed has approximately 215 staff members at the six largest bank-holding companies, including JPMorgan Chase & Co. and Goldman Sachs Group Inc."[510]

Let me assure you that each of the six largest bank-holding companies has more than 215 of its own highly trained staff members involved in just monitoring itself. There is no reason to believe the 36 examiners at each bank can have the same depth of knowledge about everything that is going on in an organization the size of JPMorgan or Goldman Sachs as the bank itself. This fact is shown in the next case study as the examiners failed to detect JPMorgan's "London Whale" trade.

As previously discussed, examiners were not intended to be a replacement for the market and its vastly superior analytical capabilities. Examiners are there to try to protect the taxpayer from losses under the deposit guarantee and not to prevent the banks from taking on specific individual exposures.

One of the advantages of banks providing valuation transparency is it allows the examiners to do a better job of monitoring the risk at each bank and protecting the taxpayer. Examiners can piggyback off of the analytical resources

---

509 Williams, Paul (2013, June 24), Inside Anglo: the secret recordings, http://www.independent.ie/business/irish/inside-anglo-the-secret-recordings-29366837.html, Transcripts of Anglo Irish Bank tapes (2013, September 22), http://www.passionforliberty.com/2013/09/22/anglo-irish-bank-tapes-the-transcripts/

510 Zumbrun, Joshua, Hopkins, Cheyenne (2013, November 19), Yellen Defends QE as Economic Benefit in Letter to Senator, Bloomberg, http://www.bloomberg.com/news/print/2013-11-19/fed-s-yellen-defends-qe-as-economic-benefit-in-letter-to-senator.html

at the competing banks. With valuation transparency, the examiners can ask the staff members at JPMorgan for insights into Goldman Sachs and visa versa. These staff members are likely to have these insights because they are likely to be responsible for helping their own bank assess the risk of their competition so their own bank doesn't have a greater exposure than it can afford to lose.

> Peter Fitzgerald: Yeah.
>
> John Bowe: And why do you need that and what's happening…and Jesus oh…oh…you have certainly focused our minds. So I think.
>
> Peter Fitzgerald: And is that €7bn a term?
>
> John Bowe: This is €7bn bridging.
>
> Peter Fitzgerald: Yeah.
>
> John Bowe: So… so it is bridged until we can pay you back…which is never.
>
> Peter Fitzgerald: Yeah, yeah, and that's in the pro note, that's in the terms and conditions?
>
> John Bowe: (Laughing) That's right. So under the terms that say repayment, we say: no.[511]

While the Anglo Irish bankers called the loan a bridge loan, they know they are facing a solvency problem and there is a high likelihood the bank will never be able to repay the loan.

Mr. Bowe then recounted the regulators' response to being asked for what is a de facto equity injection.

> Peter Fitzgerald: None…just none. Not applicable. Okay and what did he say? "I need a change of underwear?"
>
> John Bowe: (Laughing) There was a bit of that…
>
> [relating regulators response]. Jesus that's a lot of dosh. Jesus fucking hell and God. Well, do you know the Central Bank only has €14 billion of total investments so that would be going up to 20. Gee, that would be seen. And how would we do that? Gee, we would need to give you. We need to. Jesus, you're kind of asking us to play ducks and drakes with the regulations and we said yeah.[512]

The regulator's first response is it would have to disclose the loan amount and the market would notice that something was going on. By implication,

---

511 Williams, Paul (2013, June 24), Inside Anglo: the secret recordings, http://www.independent.ie/business/irish/inside-anglo-the-secret-recordings-29366837.html, Transcripts of Anglo Irish Bank tapes (2013, September 22), http://www.passionforliberty.com/2013/09/22/anglo-irish-bank-tapes-the-transcripts/

512 ibid

if the market noticed, the central bank would need a story to explain what was happening.

If banks provided valuation transparency, there would be no need to have a story to explain what was happening. Market participants would know which bank was borrowing money from the central bank and, much more importantly, why the bank was borrowing money.

The regulator's second response is it is going to have to bend the regulations to accommodate the Anglo Irish bank request. While central banks are lenders of last resort in a liquidity crisis, under EU rules, it is suppose to be the ECB that lends the money. However, Anglo Irish didn't have enough collateral that would be acceptable to the ECB. That is why it was pledging its loans.

In theory, the Irish Central Bank should have some idea about the value of these loans because it had inspectors, the equivalent of examiners in the U.S., looking at Anglo Irish's loan portfolio. In practice, as the Nyberg Commission Report documented, due to political pressure the inspectors weren't going to find trouble with the individual loans even though the loan portfolio was heavily concentrated in real estate loans.

To motivate the regulator to provide the requested loan, Mr. Bowe described to the regulator how financial contagion would occur and the calamity that awaited the Irish financial system if the Anglo Irish loan request wasn't met.

> John Bowe: We said, look what we are telling you is that if we get into difficulties we have 100,000 plus lump sum depositors in Ireland, all of whom would be very vocal.
>
> And I said, "take it that the other Irish banks will not be able to raise any wholesale funding for, for how long you want. So I said, "Bank of Ireland, their balance sheet is €200 billion and 45 per cent of that is wholesale, so let's call that €90bn. And let's say that 60 per cent of that is rolling in the next 12 months, so that's €54 billion — take it that that won't roll…okay. And I said you can also do a similar sum for Allied [Allied Irish Bank] and Irish Permanent. So I said that's what is at stake because these guys, even though they're big in our world, are minnows in the outside world.
>
> Peter Fitzgerald: Yeah.
>
> John Bowe: So I said that's what you're protecting. And I said you have got to.[513]

So the bankers' explicit threat to the regulator was if you don't bail us out, the financial system will collapse. Is there any reason to believe that this same threat wasn't used elsewhere like Washington D.C., London or Berlin?

---

[513] ibid

What makes this threat credible is opacity. The policymakers and financial regulators in Ireland, like their counterparts in the EU, UK and U.S., did not have the hard facts. Like the investors and every other market participant, they did not have the hard facts to tell which banks were solvent and which were insolvent.

What the policymakers and financial regulators could see is that in the absence of valuation transparency, wholesale depositors, including banks making unsecured interbank loans, were unwilling to invest where they could not assess the risk of loss.

The question was how would the policymakers and financial regulators interpret the resulting withdrawal of wholesale deposits and the freezing of the unsecured interbank lending market.

Naturally, the bankers stepped up to help the policymakers and financial regulators by framing the crisis. In what can only be described as entirely self-serving, the banks and their lobbyists insisted it was a classic rumor driven run on solvent banks. Nothing better exemplifies this framing of the crisis as a classic rumor driven bank run than Anglo Irish asking for a bridge loan.

The conversation turned to the mechanics of making the loan. Specifically, the regulators wanted to know if Anglo Irish had any good collateral to pledge as security for the loan. In asking this question, the regulator is expressing a legitimate concern about getting its money back. If banks were required to provide valuation transparency, the regulator could confirm the quality of the assets pledged as collateral with independent third parties. However, because Anglo Irish's disclosure left it resembling a black box, this was not possible. The regulator was now reliant on its inspectors and the bank to assess if the collateral was good or not.

The regulator also asked for an assurance that if it made the loan, Anglo Irish wouldn't be back with a request for more money. In seeking this assurance, the regulator confirmed it was aware it would be asked for additional loans if it turned out the situation were worse than represented.

> John Bowe: So anyway, that sort of got everybody's attention and then we had Pat Neary [the head of IFSRA]. Pat Neary coming in and saying (mimicking), "C'mere lads, I just want to have a word with ya...yeah Jesus...so look c'mere, have you actually got assets, decent assets, that you can put in play? Is there stuff in there, like, that has value, you know?'
>
> Peter Fitzgerald: Yeah, yeah.
>
> John Bowe: "And look lads you know, if you're going for this now make sure whatever you get sorts it out. Okay? You know?"
>
> Peter Fitzgerald: What do you mean whatever you get sorts it out?
>
> John Bowe: In other words, whatever you get from the Regulator sorts out the issue.
>
> Peter Fitzgerald: Oh yeah, yeah...just makes it fuckin' happen

John Bowe: Don't...
Peter Fitzgerald: Don't fuck it up.
John Bowe: Don't be coming back....[514]

Mr. Fitzgerald then asked if the regulator is having similar conversations with the other large Irish banks. This question confirms that every bank would assess its competitors if they were required to provide valuation transparency. They would like to know how the other banks are doing.

> Peter Fitzgerald: Is anyone else having these meetings with them?
>
> John Bowe: What do you mean?
>
> Peter Fitzgerald: Well I mean, have they had the same conversations with Permo (Irish Permanent) or have they told Permo that they're f**ked like?
>
> John Bowe: No, I wouldn't say so...
>
> Peter Fitzgerald: Okay and what about the Irish Nationwide?
>
> John Bowe: I think they've had discussions with them going back weeks, you know.
>
> Peter Fitzgerald: They took their hands off the steering wheel over there and said we're doing this now.
>
> John Bowe: Yeah.[515]

Mr. Fitzgerald than asked if the regulator will extend the loan. Mr. Bowe responds by explaining how long the regulator has to decide to make a loan given Anglo Irish's financial condition.

The run on the banks put the policymakers and financial regulators under tremendous time pressure. They have to do their own due diligence on the banks to assess exactly how bad the situation is and they have to consider what are their options before the threat of the collapse of the banking system is realized. This works to the bankers' advantage.

> Peter Fitzgerald: Okay, okay...will it happen?
>
> John Bowe: Well it has to happen. It has to happen, because if it doesn't happen we're going to hit a wall in the next week.
>
> Peter Fitzgerald: Yeah, yeah.
>
> John Bowe: So you tell me what's going to happen.
>
> Peter Fitzgerald: Yeah, and what em...
>
> John Bowe: We're already in breach, you know.[516]

---

514 ibid

515 ibid

516 ibid

Mr. Bowe then explained what he saw as the options the regulator faces. He thought the most likely outcome would be the regulators would try to stabilize the financial system and then sort it out. Mr. Bowe was right about Ireland.

In the EU, UK and U.S., regulators chose to stabilize the financial system and then ignored sorting it out. Rather, the regulators tried to restore, with the exception of banks that had gotten larger due to crisis related mergers, the financial system to what it was before the financial crisis.

> Peter Fitzgerald: I know yeah, but how does this play out? What's the playbook like? What does it look like?
>
> John Bowe: Well, I think there's different playbooks. I thought one playbook is that they, they decide they're willing to put their hands in their pockets and support the financial sector, or at least support the weakest elements of the financial sector.
>
> Peter Fitzgerald: Yeah.
>
> John Bowe: I think another, and I think what comes out of that is that ultimately that gets, that will become apparent, you know what I mean? So either in your accounts or whatever, it will become apparent at some level, it will become apparent that somebody somewhere has borrowed a lot of money, you know. And there will be explanations for that or speculation, so I think what it does is it buys us time. And I would say it buys us up to our year-end results, max.
>
> Peter Fitzgerald: Yeah. And what then?
>
> John Bowe: Well, I think it's what can we do before that, you know, so can we do a deal before that?
>
> Peter Fitzgerald: Yeah. Would it not be easier for them to stuff us into Allied?
>
> John Bowe: Well I think, I think how this works, I think their playbook is stabilise it and then try and sort it out. And I think sort it out means sooner rather than later. So my guess is that within a few weeks they will be asking Allied to get involved or Bank.
>
> Peter Fitzgerald: Yeah, but do they have the capacity to get involved?
>
> John Bowe: I don't think so.
>
> Peter Fitzgerald: That's the problem.
>
> John Bowe: I don't think so. I don't think they have the financial muscle themselves. They don't have the standing in the markets themselves to get involved.
>
> Peter Fitzgerald: True. Well they don't now. Do you know what I mean? They might have had earlier but they don't now. The perception of, like Bank is all over the UK press today, Bank of Ireland you know.
>
> John Bowe: Over what?
>
> Peter Fitzgerald: Just I mean, their, their, their interim statements, their, their..ah, just about everything. I read three or four articles about them online today in the UK.
>
> John Bowe: Yeah.

Peter Fitzgerald: Yeah, I have been hearing like f**kin'. I got a text to say that Allied and Bank f**kin' play on.

John Bowe: I know yeah, yeah. I know and I know rumor, I think you were there that Bank and Permo (Irish Permanent) had done a deal, you know what I mean. The market is just rife at the moment, you know. I think the reality is that there is certainly a lot more happening than nothing at all. You know what I mean?

Peter Fitzgerald: Yeah, oh yeah, yeah.

John Bowe: You know what I mean. You can take it that in every bank there is boardroom discussions on where to next, you know....[517]

Mr. Fitzgerald asked how was the size of the loan request arrived at. Mr. Bowe's response appears to show the Anglo Irish bankers were trying to manipulate the regulator and the Irish government by using the opacity of the bank's current performance to their advantage.

He explained how he chose the figure so that it would be big enough to get the regulator's attention and could be plausibly explained as Anglo Irish having a liquidity problem that could be fixed in a few months time.

Peter Fitzgerald: Ah we are, yeah, and what, who did you arrive at the seven?

John Bowe: Just, as Drummer would say, picked it out of my arse, you know. Em...I mean, look, what we did was we basically said: what is the amount we can securitize over the next six months? And basically say to them: look, our problem is time; it's not our ability to create the liquidity, the enemy is time here.

Peter Fitzgerald: Yeah.

John Bowe: So we can rebuild, in other words, we can rebuild the liquidity off our loan book, but what we can't do is, we can't do it now and the balance sheet's leaking now.

Peter Fitzgerald: Yeah, yeah unless the balance sheet stabilises, then you can buy some time.[518]

Mr. Bowe then explained Anglo Irish needed much more money than it asked for or had assured the regulator would be sufficient. He explained the strategy was to get the regulator to make a small loan and then use this loan as leverage to extract the money that was really needed to address the solvency crisis occurring at Anglo Irish.

John Bowe: Yeah and that number is seven. But the reality is that actually we need more than that.

---

517 ibid

518 ibid

> But you know the strategy here is you pull them in, you get them to write a big check and they have to keep, they have to support their money, you know.
>
> Peter Fitzgerald: Yeah, yeah, yeah, yeah, yeah. They've got skin in the game and that's the key.[519]

Mr. Bowe explained why deception was necessary as the alternative of telling the regulator the truth about Anglo Irish's current financial condition would most likely not result in a bailout.

> John Bowe: They have and they have invested a lot. If they saw, if they saw the enormity of it upfront they might decide, they might decide they have a choice. You know what I mean? They might say the cost to the tax payer is too high. But em…if it doesn't look too big at the outset…if it looks big, big enough to be important but not too big that it kind of spoils everything.
>
> Peter Fitzgerald: Yeah, yeah.
>
> John Bowe: Then, then I think you have a chance. So I think it can creep up.
>
> Peter Fitzgerald: Yeah, yeah, yeah. They'll give you a bit of drip….[520]

This whole gambit by Anglo Irish bank is based on the simple fact the true condition of the bank is hidden behind a shroud of opacity. The bankers know this. Even with inspectors in place, the bankers know the regulator doesn't have the information needed to know the proposed loan total has no basis in reality.

As a result of opacity, in as self-serving a way as is possible, the bankers were able to frame the problem as a rumor-driven bank run and the solutions considered to address it. By framing it as a liquidity crisis, the bankers took off the table consideration of solvency solutions where the bank and the bankers would be held responsible for the cost of the bad debt.

Mr. Bowe revealed just how self-serving the request for a loan was when he explained how the loan from the regulator would let the bankers keep their jobs as the bank was cleaned up for sale.

> Peter Fitzgerald: What do you think will happen?
>
> John Bowe: What do I think will happen? I don't know. I really don't know. I mean I don't think we're an easy sell to anyone.
>
> Peter Fitzgerald: No.
>
> John Bowe: And the home interest should be, should be there, except that they don't have the financial standings themselves. So do I think it's going to be possible to offload it? No I don't. What will it end up being? It could be breaking it up and selling individual books; it could be nationalization, you know.

---

519 ibid

520 ibid

Peter Fitzgerald: Yeah.

John Bowe: That would be fantastic. If it was nationalization we'd all keep our jobs.

Peter Fitzgerald: It would be fantastic, wouldn't it?

John Bowe: Yeah, civil servants...[521]

The second phone conversation took place on September 19, 2008. John Rowe and David Drumm discuss their plans for a follow up meeting with the regulator. Their message to the regulators was there is a run on Anglo Irish bank and either you give us the loan or we give you the keys to the bank and let you deal with the resulting collapse of the Irish financial system.

John Bowe: But anyway I think we should, now, either we do it tomorrow morning or we do it this evening but we should sit down and go through all the, map out how this is going to play out, as well, in terms of tomorrow.

David Drumm: Em, You can do. I told _ we would meet in here at half ten. But ah, but em, being honest there's not a lot to map out. There are three strands here that are alive at the minute. Two of them concern the Central Bank and one doesn't. The other one is: 'Can I have the loan please?'

John Bowe: Yeah, that to me, that's the first order and then I'll be saying: 'Ok, thanks very much, can we leave now?' And I'll want them to be saying: 'No, no, come here, we've got something else for you to do.'

David Drumm: Yeah.

John Bowe: You know

David Drumm: No, well, we've already talking about the loans, what do we need to think about? We need the f**king loans because we're running out of money. We gave you the term sheet. Can we have the money?

John Bowe: Yeah, ok.

David Drumm: Do ya know? Just keep it simple.

John Bowe: Yeah I know. I don't know how simple it's going to be though.

David Drumm: It'll be stupid simple 'cause that's where I'm going to take it.

John Bowe: Yeah.

David Drumm: I'm going to keep asking the thick question. 'When? When is the cheque arriving?'

John Bowe: Well Jesus, you know, you definitely need the donkey in the room. You know.

David Drumm: Well, it's worked so far. Because if we stay in their language, nothing happens.

John Bowe: Yeah.

David Drumm: Get into the f**king simple speak: 'We need the moolah, you have it, so you're going to give it to us and when would that be?' We'll start there.

---

521 ibid

John Bowe: Yeah.

David Drumm: And by the way the game has changed because really the problem now is at their door.

John Bowe: It is yeah, yeah.

David Drumm: Because if they don't, don't give it to us on Monday they have a bank collapse, potentially, if the f**king money keeps running out the door the way it has been running out the door.

John Bowe: That's it.

David Drumm: Really we'll be sitting there kind of going we'll be kind of a little looking a bit somber looking, sort of look, d'ya know, 'What do you want? How are you getting on with that loan lads?'

John Bowe: Yeah.

David Drumm: Or do you want the f**king keys now. I can given them to you. So I'm relaxed about it John.[522]

The third phone conversation occurred ten days later on September 19, 2008. Mr. Drumm and Mr. Bowe discuss how the wholesale deposits continue to leave the bank and how to keep the pressure on the regulators to lend Anglo Irish money.

David Drumm: J.B.

John Bowe: Hiya doing.

David Drumm: How're ya.

John Bowe: Grand

David Drumm: Another day, another billion.

(Snicker)

John Bowe: Yeah, yeah, yeah. I'd like to say if your friend _ was talking, he'd say: 'A great day. A great buzz in the dealing room. Everybody's tail was up. Fantastic'.

David Drumm: Oh yeah, did I lose him a billion?

(Laughs)

John Bowe: A great day but we lost a bill. Yeah, the money, I mean, it was another bad day but, but perversely it actually felt like it was a much better day than it turned out to be.

David Drumm: Going to prove that everything is in the head. We're on the front foot today. That's the difference, the mood is better and view towards us is better, so we just want to keep that momentum.

John Bowe: We do, yeah. We do.

David Drumm: What, what just in terms of gameplan for tomorrow, are we going to sit down and go through what the, what's on the table.

John Bowe: Now I sent you the document. But that just says what we are going to be discussion. Is it us we're going to be talking about or is it…?

---

522 ibid

David Drumm: Well now, well now. We don't know. We're going down to meet the whole f**king shooting gallery of them.

John Bowe: Yeah.

David Drumm: I do know this. There's a big meeting in the Department of Finance tonight, which I am told is a kind of a pow-wow. I assume they're going to make up their minds what the f**k they're doing on the basis that they can't spend another week, next week, flapping around. So I'm making the, jumping to the mad conclusion that the meeting of tomorrow is about discussing bringing that to fruition.

John Bowe: Yeah.

David Drumm: But I could be bitterly disappointed. It could be another bureaucratic go nowhere meeting. But having said that, I won't, I won't put up with that.

John Bowe: Yeah.

David Drumm: I'll be forcing the agenda. Really, we'll be going down there with our arms swinging. I'm very clear on the proposal and what we can and can't do.

John Bowe: I think, I think the first order of business is sorting ourselves out.

David Drumm: No, no, that goes without saying. Do you have the cheque here now for the loan. That will be the first thing I'll ask. Ehm, have we got the collateral ready or do we need to have it ready?

John Bowe: Well, we don't have it ready in the sense that, eh, we, we've never, we've never got into a discussion about what is it you will be giving us exactly. You know what I mean? What we've got is we've got collateral that we can put our hands on, and you can describe it so in other words we can identify the loans pretty quickly, we can identify the amounts of loans outstanding, we can put any covered bonds, non-eligible, and anything into it. We can put two and a half billion of non ECB eligible stuff into it so.

David Drumm: I think it would be very helpful if you had a schedule of available collateral...

John Bowe: Ok, ya.

David Drumm: ...including all those bits and bobs, such that if we get into it tomorrow, we're not embarrassed, kind of, you known trying to explain it. Just shove the pages, bring a few copies, shove the pages there and say: 'Look, this is by way of tidying up, this is the collateral that's available to you and you have your auditors in confirming you are in rude financial health and this is obviously a liquidity issue, so, em, can we have the money on Monday 'cause we may need it.

John Bowe: Yeah, yeah.

David Drumm: That's the line. Well we do need it on Monday.

John Bowe: Well, I think things are, things are, we're, we're deteriorating more slowly than our worst case scenario, which only means, it doesn't mean, it means that instead of the two weeks that we are going to be, or the, the week that we are going to be dead, it's still a week, but it will be a week tomorrow, as well, or a week the next day, you know what I mean.

David Drumm: Yeah, the retail will recover slightly. We've got momentum on that.

John Bowe: And the corporate will continue to go out but.

David Drumm: But there's a bottom to that.

John Bowe: Yeah, there is, yeah. So what will happen is that the amounts will get smaller, which means that your time from death extends out, but, you know, you are still two weeks away, you're not, it's not disappearing. It's only when we can actually start attracting net funding in that you can start talking about, you know, life.[523]

For a bank to continue in operation, at a minimum, it needs to be able to hold onto its core funding from retail depositors and businesses who use the bank to run their payments like payroll through. Attracting additional funding simply allows the bank to fund more loans with its balance sheet.

Regardless of whether a bank is just holding onto its funding or is attracting more funding, a bank is able to continue to originate loans and support the real economy. A bank can originate loans because origination of the loan and funding of the loan are separate. The loan can be funded on the bank's balance sheet or sold to another bank or an investor like an insurance company, a pension fund or a hedge fund.

After the Irish government has agreed to the blanket guarantee of all insured and uninsured deposits, Mr. Bowe and Mr. Drumm have another conversation on October 2, 2008. This conversation focuses on using the guarantee to attract deposits as quickly as possible despite pushback from Germany and the UK. It is an example of how bankers, the Irish just like the U.S. Saving & Loan bankers before them, hiding behind a veil of opacity will gamble on redemption. In this case, the bankers are using the guarantee to buy time by attracting deposits with a long maturity.

David Drumm: What's up today?

John Bowe: En, ah no, making, em, nice progress.

David Drumm: Ah, you're abusing that guarantee. Paying too much in Germany I hear now as well. Fucking ridiculous, John.

John Bowe: (Singing) Deutschland, Deutschland, Ubber Alles.

(Both laughing)

David Drumm: I had _ on this morning. I just should be recording these calls for the f**king crack — or at least making notes.

John Bowe: He was on to me as well.

David Drumm: (Mimicking) 'It's f**king awful what's going on out there. I mean the f**king Germans are on to us now, David, you know.'

---

523 ibid

He's saying: 'Look eh, have you seen any, eh, kind of strange money market money coming through on term?'

And I said: "I'm not sure what you mean.'

He says: 'Ya know, two year money.' (Laughs)

And I said: 'Eh..'.

He says: 'ya know, ya have to be careful here because there's people setting us up.'

And I said: 'Is it a bit of eh, beware of strangers bearing gifts, _.

'Exactly, exactly.'

Setting us up by giving us money. I don't mind being set up that way.

John Bowe: Well, what he's suggesting is that UK banks are setting us up by pointing money in our direction and then saying: 'There ya go. That's something that was ours that they've got.'

David Drumm: So f**king what? Just take it anyway.

John Bowe: Yeah.

David Drumm: Stick fingers up. I had a pop at him this morning about Northern Rock. I said: 'Look, they went around with the f**king Union Jack wrapped tightly around them like a jumpsuit and grabbed all the deposits and where was our f**king Minister of Finance then?

(Mimicking) 'I know, I know, I'm getting it from all sides here David.'

(Laughs) So I'm playing a little bit of a game of 'oh Jesus_, look we don't want you to be under pressure, we're going to do the best we can. We won't do anything blantant, but _, we have to get the money in'.

Well we'll have to fucking tiddly-winkle for it.

John Bowe: So I'm just saying to the guys 'look, just be smart, don't be stupid, get it in, don't be overtly pumping it so that somebody can quote you but we want to get the liquidity ratios up.

David Drumm: Correct.

John Bowe: You know?

David Drumm: Correct and right. So ok so just keep nursing along.

John Bowe: We will. Now I have… Sorry go on.

David Drumm: Jack the rates up. That's what I really meant, get the f**king money in. Get it in.

John Bowe: That's right, just do it.[524]

Animal House

Perhaps the movie Animal House best illustrated the relationship between the banks and the politicians and regulators. The bankers, quoting the character Otter, say,

524 ibid

Flounder, you can't spend your whole life worrying about your mistakes! You fucked up... you trusted us! Hey, make the best of it! Maybe we can help.[525]

A phone conversation between John Bowe and Matt Pass captures the essence of this quote.

Matt Pass: I can tell you, right, again in presenting all this stuff to, you know there's an issue here, we are retained by the Ministry of Finance.[526]

Mr. Pass works for Merrill Lynch. Merrill needed to be rescued and was purchased by Bank of America which was in turn bailed out by the U.S. taxpayer.

There's the NTMA in there. There's the Central Bank in there and there's IFSRA and as you can imagine there are various people within that group who think other people within that group haven't really done a great job etc so you can imagine there is a bit of tension there.

But in some of the meeting I have been in Cardiff in particular has been f**king outstanding.

John Bowe: Sorry, who is that?

Matt Pass: Kevin Cardiff

John Bowe: Oh yeah.

Matt Pass: In, not necessarily his decision-making but his ability to deal with the s**t which comes his way. The fact his head doesn't explode and he gets sent off to a mental asylum, because this is just one like I said he has loads of s**t he is dealing with.

And, he's, he is presented with the meltdown of his own banking system within the meltdown of the global banking system, y'know?

And it is like I felt quite guilty actually and I have said this to a lot of people, I said y'know I think our industry has totally f**king let the world down, y'know, and it has been handed to people like him and your prime minister and our prime minister and they are going to pay for it.

John Bowe: Yeah, yeah.

Matt Pass: These are the guys, they are going to lose their jobs. Gordon Brown, it doesn't matter what the f**k he does he is going to lose his job.

John Bowe: Yeah.

Matt Pass: His only recourse would have been in more recent years would have been to go to the banks and tell them they shouldn't have been doing the type of lending they were doing.

---

525 Animal House (1978), http://www.imdb.com/title/tt0077975/quotes

526 Lyons, Paul, Sheridan, Gavin (2013, September 15), New Anglo Tapes: 'We've F**King let the world down', Independent.IE, http://www.independent.ie/business/world/new-anglo-tapes-weve-fking-let-the-world-down-29580091.html as transcribed by this book's author

> There would have been an almighty stink.[527]

This almighty stink is why politicians and bank regulators who report to them will never be able to prevent the next financial crisis. The Nyberg Commission Report, the FSA Report and former Fed chairman Alan Greenspan confirmed this is true globally.

Fortunately, the design of our financial system does not require that the politicians tell the banks they shouldn't be doing the type of lending they are doing.

Our financial system is designed so that banks provide valuation transparency and disclose on an ongoing basis their current exposure details. This data can then be independently assessed and market discipline can be exerted on the banks to restrain their lending.

Unfortunately, our financial system is not operating as it is designed and the banks do not provide valuation transparency. The result is our current financial crisis.

> John Bowe: Yeah, but you know the other thing is, if he didn't have the banks handing out credit during the Labour years, people wouldn't have spent money, the economy wouldn't have been as prosperous. ...[528]

One of the reasons politicians will never discipline bank lending is it contributes to economic growth which in turn contributes rising tax payments the politicians can spend.

> John Bowe: In a way, there is a certain amount of you pay the piper, what is the expression, you pay the piper you call the tune? So...
>
> Matt Pass: No, look y'know again it has now gotten to the point where y'know everybody's going to pay for it now.
>
> John Bowe: Yeah, I think that is right.
>
> Matt Pass: There is no point pointing fingers at anybody quite frankly because we are all in the s**t.[529]

Perhaps the bankers' greatest sale was getting the policymakers and financial regulators to buy into the notion that everybody is going to have to pay. In the introduction to this book, I described how Sec. Paulson pulled this off in the U.S. with assistance from Fed Chair Bernanke.

---

527 ibid

528 ibid

529 ibid

Just like Flounder, the taxpayer screwed up because they trusted the financial regulators to prevent a financial crisis. Just like Flounder, the financial regulators screwed up because they trusted the banks to prevent a financial crisis.

And how did the bankers respond to the financial crisis they created? Just like the Animal House movie character Otter, they offered to help the financial regulators and taxpayer make the best of it.

Naturally, this involved the taxpayer paying for the financial crisis and not the banks and the bankers.

Trust and complex bank capital regulations

In examining Anglo Irish Bank, the bank regulators placed their trust in the complex Basel II capital regulations. Specifically, the regulators trusted the capital regulations as a "state-of-the-art approach to assessing risk and ensuring efficient use of capital in financial institutions."

— Nick Dunbar[530]

The Irish bank regulators trusted the Basel II capital regulations to show if a bank was solvent or not. The Irish bank regulators were not alone.

Globally, bank regulators see bank capital as the most important element in prudential financial regulation and in signaling to market participants the safety and soundness of a bank.

Unfortunately, as the global financial crisis has shown, bank capital as a measure of the safety and soundness of a bank is fundamentally flawed.

As shown by Ireland's experience, bank capital is not immune to what George Akerlof described as accounting control fraud. For banks, this takes the form of management making loans to riskier borrowers and, knowing that there is inadequate disclosure to investors of the increase in riskiness, under-reserving for losses. By under-reserving for losses, accounting control fraud directly boosts common equity through higher net income. Assuming that the bank substituted the riskier loan for a less risky loan, accounting control fraud also produces an improvement in capital ratios. In this case, higher capital ratios are not an indicator of less risk, but rather mask the increase in the bank's risk profile.

In addition, there are problems with risk-adjusted capital ratios. Not only can banks manipulate with accounting control fraud the book capital in the numerator, but they can also manipulate the level of risk-adjusted assets in the denominator.

---

530 Dunbar, Nick (2013, July 5), Basel, Bayes and Anglo's Arse-Picking, NickDunbar.net, http://www.nickdunbar.net/articles/basel-bayes-and-anglos-arse-picking/

The idea behind a risk-weighted capital ratio is to recognize there are different level of risks a bank faces from holding sovereign debt like U.S. treasuries as oppose to holding a loan from a subprime borrower. Each asset class is assigned a risk weight. U.S. Treasury securities are seen as virtually risk free, so its risk weight is zero. The loan to the subprime borrower is seen as risky, so its risk rate is 100 percent.

For purposes of calculating total risk-weighted assets, a bank multiplies the total amount of assets in each class by the risk weight for that asset class and then sums the results. For example, a bank that only invests in U.S. Treasury securities would show total risk-weighted assets equal to zero. A bank that only invests in loans to subprime borrowers would show risk-weighted assets equal to the assets reported in their financial statement.

Banks are responsible for calculating their own capital ratio. As a result, the opportunities for the banks to game the risk-weighted capital regulations were and are endless. In fact, there are so many opportunities to game the risk-weighted capital regulations that the banks have a name for this activity: risk-weighted asset optimization.

As Adrian Blundell-Wignall, deputy director of the Organization for Economic Cooperation and Development's financial and enterprise affairs division in Paris, observed, "we are allowing the poacher to participate in being the game-keeper." [531] As a result, risk-weighted capital ratios are a

> ratio of two meaningless numbers, which itself is a meaningless number because banks can alter the ratio themselves.[532]

In the run-up to the financial crisis, the Irish regulators put their trust in a meaningless number. As a result, in September 2008 they, like their fellow global bank regulators, did not know the banks were facing a solvency crisis for which the liquidity crisis was merely a symptom. As a result, they, like their fellow global bank regulators, were especially vulnerable to the bankers' hard sale on the need for a "bridge" loan to buy time to address a liquidity problem. As the Nyberg Commission Report pointed out, this lack of understanding negatively influenced how the regulators responded to the crisis and greatly increased the cost of the crisis to the Irish taxpayers.

With the absence of valuation transparency, market participants could not do their own independent assessment and verify the bank capital ratios actually

---

531 Vaughan, Liam (2011, November 9), Financial Alchemy Foils Capital Rules as Banks Redefine Risk, Bloomberg, http://www.bloomberg.com/news/2011-11-09/financial-alchemy-undercuts-capital-regime-as-european-banks-redefine-risk.html

532 ibid

showed what the bankers represented they showed and the regulators trusted they showed. The solution to restoring meaning to the bank capital ratios and preventing bankers from misrepresenting the financial condition of their banks in the future is requiring the banks to provide valuation transparency. With this information, all market participants can trust, but verify both the capital ratios and the financial condition of the banks. Knowing the actual financial condition of the banks also assures that in the future, the banks won't be bailed out with taxpayer funds when they encounter solvency problems.

Case Study II: JPMorgan and the "London Whale": 12 lessons why complex regulations and regulatory oversight fail

Let's embrace productive capitalism, not casino capitalism, by restoring transparency.
Senator Maria Cantwell[533]

JPMorgan showed why in practice the combination of complex regulation and regulatory oversight is and always will be an inadequate substitute for the combination of valuation transparency and market discipline.

It did this by "losing" several billion dollars gambling on corporate defaults. JPMorgan placed its bets through its Chief Investment Office's London location. Bets were made by a group of traders, including one the market referred to as the "London Whale", by buying and selling credit derivatives. A credit derivative is a security that allows the buyer or seller to gamble on whether a specific company or a specific group of companies will experience a negative event like bankruptcy during a specified time period.

The U.S. Senate investigation into this credit derivatives gamble revealed the enormous gap between the regulators' lofty speeches saying it is their job to restrain bank risk taking and the reality for any bank larger than a community bank. The investigation confirmed it is market discipline that restrains bank risk taking and bank supervision is a complement to and not a substitute for market discipline. Despite this investigation and its findings, in a speech celebrating the 150th anniversary of the founding of the U.S. Comptroller of the Currency, Comptroller Thomas Curry observed:

533 Cantwell, Senator Maria (2009, October 30), Wall Street Has a Gambling Problem, Huffington Post, http://www.huffingtonpost.com/sen-maria-cantwell/wall-street-has-a-gamblin_b_340252.html

> In the worst days of the crisis, everyone understood the need for strong supervision. If anything, the question asked was why we didn't get tougher sooner. But in good times, when loan losses are low and capital appears strong, pressure will mount to relax standards and go easy as emerging weaknesses are discovered. When the party is going full roar, it's easy to believe it will go on forever, and nobody understands why supervisors might be eyeing the punch bowl.
>
> But it's our job as supervisors to lean against the wind. It's our job to identify the soft spots that will turn into losses when the economy changes direction. And it's our job to direct corrective actions in advance, when it is most easy for banks to adjust.[534]

JPMorgan's credit derivative trades were also an example of the larger problem of opacity that caused our current financial crisis. To paraphrase the Senate Subcommittee report on these trades,

> Because banks provided limited information about their exposures as a result of the SEC's use of the intermediary depiction model for disclosure, market participants, including the bank regulators, remained in the dark about the size and risks of their exposures for years. When losses began rolling in, policymakers and bank regulators had to exercise oversight on the basis of incomplete, inaccurate, and misleading information. The Nyberg Commission Report confirmed this was true in Ireland. The FSA Report confirmed this was true in the UK. The Senate Investigation into the losses on JPMorgan's trading confirmed this was still true in the US.
>
> Furthermore, the banks' practices, to create opacity and led by the Opacity Protection Team to prevent valuation transparency from returning, impeded market participants' ability to detect and exercise discipline to stop unsafe and unsound lending and trading practices.

JPMorgan's credit derivative trades highlighted the fact that the dangers for the financial system lie not in what we know and is disclosed through valuation transparency, but in what we don't know because it is hidden behind a veil of opacity. The goal of the FDR Framework is to minimize what we don't know.

Jamie Dimon: 'I want to see the positions'

As JPMorgan's credit derivative trade was unraveling on its way to posting a loss of $6.2 billion, the bank's CEO Jamie Dimon met with associates on April 30, 2012. He was presented with:

---

534 Curry, Thomas (2014), Building on 150 Years: The Future of Nation Banking, Office of the Comptroller of the Currency, http://www.occ.gov/news-issuances/speeches/2014/pub-speech-2014-47.pdf, page 6.

> summaries and analyses of the losses. But there were no details about the trades themselves.
>
> "I want to see the positions!" he barked, throwing down the papers, according to attendees. "Now! I want to see everything!"[535]

By demanding to see the credit derivative trade details behind the Synthetic Credit Portfolio (SCP), Mr. Dimon confirmed for all time why banks must provide valuation transparency and disclose on an ongoing basis their current asset, liability and off-balance sheet exposure details. He showed that it is only with the current exposure details that market participants can know what they own. Jamie Dimon also showed it is only with the current exposure details market participants are able to assess a bank's risk.

By his actions and his words, Mr. Dimon

- Ended reliance by market participants on summaries, like financial statements, as they are a form of opacity and hide what is really going on;
- Established looking at a bank's current exposure details at the granular level is the gold standard for knowing what is going on within a bank;
- Demonstrated bank information systems have current data as nobody thinks that the attendees went off to get position data as of the end of last year or last quarter or even last week; and
- Confirmed the market, which is full of individuals with similar training to Mr. Dimon, can make sense of the exposure details and do their own independent analysis.

In short, Jamie Dimon said the only way to know what is going on in a bank is to look at its current exposure details.

The only way for market participants to do this is if banks provide valuation transparency and disclose on an on-going basis their current asset, liability and off-balance sheet exposure details.

Absent valuation transparency and the disclosure of the current exposure details, banks are black boxes even to management.

---

535 Langley, Monica (2012, May 18), Inside J.P. Morgan's Blunder, The Wall Street Journal, http://online.wsj.com/news/articles/SB10001424052702303448404577410341236847980?mod=WSJ_hp_MIDDLENexttoWhatsNewsSecond&mg=reno64-wsj&url=http%3A%2F%2Fonline.wsj.com%2Farticle%2FSB10001424052702303448404577410341236847980.html%3Fmod%3DWSJ_hp_MIDDLENexttoWhatsNewsSecond

Bank lobbyist confirms need for valuation transparency

Naturally, one would expect there would be an impact of JPMorgan's trading loss on the on-going global effort to re-regulate the banks through regulations like the Volcker Rule, swap rules, and TBTF living wills. To minimize this impact, Timothy Ryan, then the chief executive of the Securities Industry and Financial Markets Association and now global head of regulatory policy and strategy at JPMorgan, observed

> Everybody needs to take a breath. Very few people have the facts. We don't have them, and the regulators don't have them...[536]

Here is the head of Wall Street's leading lobbying firm pointing out the elephant in the room. Very few people have the facts when it comes to any bank and its trades. The list of market participants who don't have the facts includes bank regulators and investors.

Mr. Ryan's observation suggests the proper impact on regulatory reform should have been the enforcement of valuation transparency. Then everyone would have access to the facts.

A Dozen Lessons from JPMorgan's bet

The U.S. Senate Permanent Subcommittee on Investigations looked into the JPMorgan credit derivative trade. This investigation uncovered a number of important lessons. It confirmed why the combination of complex regulations and regulatory oversight sounds good in theory, but doesn't work in practice. It confirmed the importance of bringing valuation transparency to the global banking system and restoring market discipline on banks.

Lesson 1: In the presence of opacity, no restraint on bankers gambling

The first thing you notice looking at the entire story of JPMorgan's credit derivative bet is how in the presence of opacity, JPMorgan was too big and complex to be controlled by senior management or supervised by the global bank examiners.

---

536 McGrane, Victoria, Trindle, Jamila (2012, May 21), Trading Misstep For Bank Opens Door to New Rules, The Wall Street Journal, http://online.wsj.com/news/articles/SB10001424052702304791704577418610977819788?mod=dist_smartbrief&mg=reno64-wsj&url=http%3A%2F%2Fonline.wsj.com%2Farticle%2FSB10001424052702304791704577418610977819788.html%3Fmod%3Ddist_smartbrief

> The JPMorgan Chase whale trades … demonstrate how inadequate derivative valuation practices enabled traders to hide substantial losses for months at a time; lax hedging practices obscured whether derivatives were being used to offset risk or take risk; risk limit breaches were routinely disregarded; risk evaluation models were manipulated to downplay risk; inadequate regulatory oversight was too easily dodged or stonewalled; and derivative trading and financial results were misrepresented to investors, regulators, policymakers, and the taxpaying public who, when banks lose big, may be required to finance multi-billion-dollar bailouts.[537]

It is only when banks are required to provide valuation transparency that constraints are put on the banks and each of these issues goes away.

Lesson 2: Disclosure of trades ends proprietary betting

In his emails and testimony, the London Whale explained why requiring banks to disclose on an ongoing basis their current exposure details would effectively end proprietary trading.

> Mr. Iksil later explained to the JPMorgan Chase Task Force investigation that he had switched from the IG9 index to the more recent series to be "less noticeable" to the rest of the market.
>
> He explained that he had sold so much protection in the IG9 index that he believed the other credit traders "knew" his position, and were taking advantage.[538]

If banks provided valuation transparency, credit traders would know each bank's position with certainty. This would make it much easier for the credit traders to take advantage of each bank. By definition, market making does not provide credit traders with either the size or the length of time the position is held to make it attractive for taking advantage of a bank. Instead, credit traders would focus on the proprietary trades. As shown by JPMorgan's credit derivatives bet, proprietary trades are both sizeable and held for a long enough period so the credit traders can actually trade against the position. Traders would prefer not to be taken advantage of and therefore they would restrict themselves to market making and not taking proprietary bets.

537 United States Senate Permanent Subcommittee on Investigations (2013, March 15), JPMorgan Chase Whale Trades: A Case History of Derivatives Risks and Abuses, http://www.hsgac.senate.gov/subcommittees/investigations/hearings/chase-whale-trades-a-case-history-of-derivatives-risks-and-abuses, page 1.

538 ibid, page 83.

In fact, on March 19, 2012, Mr. Iksil warned his supervisor that the SCP was a very visible player in a small market: "[T]here is a trap that is building: if we limit the Mark-to-Market we risk increasing the notionals further and weaken our position versus the rest of the market." Later, Mr. Iksil wrote to a colleague:

> "[I]t had to happen. [I]t started back in 2008 you see. [I] survived pretty well until [I] was alone to be the target. [Y]es [I] mean the guys know my position because [I] am too big for the market. ... [B]ut here is the loss and it becomes too large and this is it. [W]e realize that [I] am too visible."[539]

While Warren Buffett wanted to hide his trades so others could not piggyback on his ideas, the London Whale wanted to hide his trades so others would not target and trade against him. Both Warren Buffett and the London Whale recognize disclosure makes their positions less profitable.

As the London Whale observed, he became too big for the market.

> An additional consequence of the size of the positions was that the CIO's positions became visible to the rest of the market.[540]

As a result, hedge funds and other asset managers tried to figure out both the specifics of JPMorgan's synthetic credit position and how they could profit by trading against JPMorgan. In attempting to profit at JPMorgan's expense, these market participants confirmed the most direct and effective method for enforcing the Volcker Rule and eliminating proprietary trading is to require banks to disclose on an on-going basis their current asset, liability and off-balance sheet exposure details. It is precisely this information market participants needed to successfully trade against JPMorgan. If banks knew they had to provide valuation transparency, they would not take proprietary positions because they know the market would profit at their expense.

> Mr. Iksil had expressed for some time a concern that the traders on the opposite side were moving against him. In January, he had predicted a fight in March.[541]
>
> See, e.g.,1/30/2012 email from Bruno Iksil, CIO, to Javier Martin-Artajo, CIO, "there is more loss coming in the core credit book," JPM-CIO-PSI 0001225 ("The guys have a huge skew trade on and they will defend it as much as we do .... It is pointless to go for a fight."); 1/30/2012 email from Bruno

539 ibid, page 83

540 ibid, page 91

541 ibid, page 90

Iksil, CIO, to Javier Martin-Artajo, CIO, "core credit," JPM-CIO-PSI 0001226 ("they really push against our positions here everywhere. there is more pain to come in HY too.").[542]

In an April 10, 2012 email sent by Ina Drew at the end of the day to Jamie Dimon, Douglas Braunstein, John Wilmot, and others, she attributed the $400 million loss to the market moving against the CIO's positions in anticipation of its liquidating the SCP book:

> "[T]he mtm [marked-to-market] loss is [$]412 mil today, an 8 standard deviation event mostly from the steep[en]ing of the [IG]9 curve. SPECIFIC to our position. No other high grade or high yield index moved much clearly anticipating our liquidation."

Her email notified the most senior officials in the bank about an "8 standard deviation event," meaning a wholly unexpected and unpredictable loss; however, bank officials told the Subcommittee that, at the time, they were expecting large losses as a result of the media attention.[543]

JPMorgan and its traders were keenly aware the market, primarily hedge funds in this case, would trade against its proprietary bets. Forcing the banks to disclose their current exposure details effectively draws a bulls-eye target around these proprietary bets. Something the bank and its traders want to avoid as it makes the proprietary bets too painful to hold.

This pain and therefore reluctance to take proprietary bets is not a bug, but rather a feature of valuation transparency. A feature that was intended in the redesign of the banking system in the 1930s.

Requiring the banks to provide valuation transparency also removes the issue of whether the traders adequately understand or have the ability to properly manage a trading portfolio. It is far better to eliminate proprietary bets upfront by having the discipline of the market trading against a bank position than it is to have the banks lose money because their traders do not adequately understand or have the ability to properly manage a trading portfolio.

Compare and contrast how valuation transparency ends proprietary trading with how the Volcker Rule attempts to achieve the same outcome while the banks are still hiding behind a veil of opacity.

Bank regulators argue had the Volcker Rule been in existence it would have prevented JPMorgan from entering into the money losing trades. The regulators' argue JPMorgan would have had to provide regulators with documentation

---

542 ibid, page. 90

543 ibid, page 134

showing the trades were actually a hedge and not simply a banned proprietary bet. To demonstrate it is a hedge, the documentation has to include a discussion of what the hedging strategy is and how well correlated the hedge is to the position being hedged.

At the inception of this trade, JPMorgan would have handed the regulators a sheet of paper which showed their current outstanding corporate loan balance and the credit default swaps they were going to buy to hedge this portfolio against losses. It would show the efficacy of the trade and how JPMorgan's exposures were changing and becoming less risky.

The regulators would have said thank you very much and put the piece of paper in a file. Challenging the trade would violate rule number one of not approving or disapproving individual positions. After all, if the regulator challenges the hedge and then says go ahead, there is no doubt that constitutes approval.

Now we move on to the second part of the trade where rather than close out the position by selling the credit default swaps, the credit default swaps themselves were hedged.

It would replicate what happened when the trade was initially put on: the trade would have been put down on a sheet of paper and handed to the regulators and the regulators would put the piece of paper into a file.

Hopefully, I have made the point that the entire activity between JPMorgan and the primary bank regulator would not have prevented the trade or protected the regulators from the theatrical kicking they received from members of Congress in an election year.

If you want to stop JPMorgan from engaging in these types of trades in the future you simply require that JPMorgan provide valuation transparency and disclose on an on-going basis its current asset, liability and off balance sheet exposure details.

Fear of market discipline from being trading against would eliminate the gambling behavior.

Lesson 3: Bankers push back on findings of examiners

The reason market discipline is the primary means of restraining bank risk taking is, unlike the bank regulators, the market cannot be bullied. The bankers know the bank regulators can be bullied and as shown by JPMorgan, they bully the examiners.

> On December 8, 2010, after concluding its examination of the CIO's investment activities, the OCC sent a Supervisory Letter to CIO head Ina Drew with its findings, requirements, and recommendations. The Supervisory Letter included a Matter Requiring Attention (MRA) — meaning a matter that required corrective action by the bank — stating that CIO management

> needed to "document investment policies and portfolio decisions." The Supervisory Letter also found that the "risk management framework for the investment portfolios (Strategic Asset Allocation and Tactical Asset Allocation)" lacked "a documented methodology," "clear records of decisions," and other features to ensure that the CIO was making investments and controlling associated risks in line with the expectations of senior management and the appropriate Board of Directors committee.[544]
>
> Prior to the OCC's issuance of a Supervisory Letter, it is standard practice for the OCC to hold a close-out meeting with the bank to discuss the examination findings, requirements, and recommendations, and receive bank management's response. The OCC's head capital markets examiner at JPMorgan Chase held that meeting with CIO head Ina Drew, whom he said did not react well to the examination's criticisms.
>
> According to a later email by his supervisor, the OCC Examiner-In-Charge, Ms. Drew "'sternly' discussed [the OCC's] conclusions with him for 45 minutes." The OCC told the Subcommittee that, among other objections, she complained that the regulator was trying to "destroy" JPMorgan Chase's business, and that its requirements would take away necessary flexibility from the CIO.[545]

In trying to bully the regulator, Ms. Drew tries to make the case prudential restraint will "destroy" the bank's business. This claim plays to the simple fact it is unacceptable for bank regulators to exert prudential restraint on banks when they are profitable. The unacceptability of prudential restraint on profitable, politically connected large banks was spelled out in 1987 by former Federal Reserve governor Partee and confirmed during our current financial crisis by the Nyberg Commission Report, the FSA report and the FCIC Report.

> Moreover, according to the Examiner- In-Charge's email, Ms. Drew informed the OCC "that investment decisions are made with the full understanding of executive management including Jamie Dimon. She said that everyone knows what is going on and there is little need for more limits, controls, or reports."[546]
>
> The OCC Examiner-In-Charge characterized Ms. Drew's response as an attempt to invoke Mr. Dimon's authority and reputation in order to try to avoid implementing formal documentation requirements.[547]

544 ibid, page 222
545 ibid, page 223
546 ibid, page 223
547 ibid, page 223

In pushing back against the OCC's findings, Ms. Drew highlighted how JPMorgan could effectively access the head of any of the bank regulatory agencies and their political overseers. In order for a Supervisory Letter to be signed off on by the regulatory agency, it needs the approval of its regulatory bureaucracy including the political appointee at the top. Ms. Drew's remarks were designed to, if not stop the Supervisory Letter from being issued, at least tone down its conclusions.

> When asked if the CIO's aggressive reaction to the 2010 examination of the CIO was unique, the OCC indicated that it was not. In fact, the OCC Examiner-In-Charge at JPMorgan Chase told the Subcommittee that it was "very common" for the bank to push back on examiner findings and recommendations. He recalled one instance in which bank executives even yelled at OCC examiners and called them "stupid".[548]

JPMorgan's bankers know they can get away with bullying the bank regulators. Bank regulators need valuation transparency so the market, which is bigger than the individual banks, will stand up to the bankers with them. By design, with valuation transparency, bank regulators are reinforcing market discipline.

Lesson 4: Current SEC disclosure requirements allow banks to hide risk

The SEC's use of the intermediary depiction model as the basis for banks making disclosures hides more than it illuminates. As shown by the whale trades, the risk of the trades and the losses incurred were hidden without violating generally accepted accounting practices.

> The bank told the Subcommittee that, despite the favorable pricing practices noted in the May memorandum, it did not view the CIO as having engaged in mismarking until June 2012, when its internal investigation began reviewing CIO recorded telephone calls and heard CIO personnel disparaging the marks they were reporting.
>
> On July 13, 2012, the bank restated its first quarter earnings, reporting additional SCP losses of $660 million. JPMorgan Chase told the Subcommittee that the decision to restate its financial results was a difficult one, since $660 million was not clearly a "material" amount for the bank, and the valuations used by the CIO did not clearly violate bank policy or generally accepted accounting principles.[549]

548 ibid, page 224

549 ibid, page 6

The intermediary depiction model introduces the concept of "material" into disclosure. As JPMorgan pointed out, the losses being hidden by the CIO were, at the time, not material to the bank's financial results. This lack of materiality is another example of how the intermediary depiction model for disclosure hides the true risk of the banks. There is no way of knowing how many not material positions like the CIO's are lurking on a bank's balance sheet. When added up, all these hidden not material positions could in fact be very material.

> The bank told the Subcommittee that the key consideration leading to the restatement of the bank's losses was its determination that the London CIO personnel had not acted in "good faith" when marking the SCP book, which meant the SCP valuations had to be revised....[550]
>
> The ability of CIO personnel to hide hundreds of millions of dollars of additional losses over the span of three months, and yet survive internal valuation reviews, shows how imprecise, undisciplined, and open to manipulation the current process is for valuing credit derivatives....
>
> The whale trades' bad faith valuations exposed not only misconduct by the CIO and the bank's violation of the derivative valuation process mandated in generally accepted accounting principles, but also a systemic weakness in the valuation process for all credit derivatives.[551]

When the SEC's required disclosure allows risk to be hidden, it is impossible for market participants to accurately assess the risk of or value each bank and exert discipline. The only way market participants could have accurately assessed the risk of JPMorgan was if it provided valuation transparency and disclosed its current exposure details. With this information, market participants could have seen the whale trades and adjusted their exposure and JPMorgan's cost of funds accordingly.

Lesson 5: Banks use opacity to escape any restraints on risk-taking

The Federal Reserve's general counsel, Scott Alvarez, observed

> We have to rely on the information that we get from the management of the organization.[552]

The Comptroller of the Currency Thomas Curry added

---

550 ibid, page 6

551 ibid, page 7

552 Zibel, Alan, Holzer, Jessica (2012, June 19), Dimon Takes Heat on Hill. The Wall Street Journal, http://online.wsj.com/news/articles/SB10001424052702303703004577476483221472646?mod=WSJ_hp_LEFTWhatsNewsCollection&mg=reno64-wsj&url=http%3A%2F%2Fonline.wsj.com%

> In hindsight, if the reporting were more robust or granular, we believe we may have had an inkling of the size, the potential complexity, the risk of the position.[553]

With the whale trades, JPMorgan showed how far banks go to operate behind a veil of opacity by withholding data even when asked by the bank regulators.

> The OCC said that, in August 2011, the daily Investment Bank P&L report stopped arriving in OCC electronic inboxes. The OCC explained that when it brought up what it thought was simply a glitch in JPMorgan Chase's email delivery, the bank responded that the bank would no longer be providing the Investment Bank's daily P&L reports, because it was too much information to provide to the OCC.
>
> The OCC said that the bank explained further that it had experienced a series of unauthorized data disclosures and the bank, not knowing who was leaking the data, sought to limit the information it provided to the OCC, even though OCC had not been responsible for the leaks.[554]

There are two very important facts revealed by the bank's actions.

First, as discussed in Lesson 2, there is a reason that a bank is afraid of leaks. If the market knows what your positions are, it will trade against you to minimize the profitability and maximize the loss of the proprietary bet. Equally importantly, if the market knows what your positions are, it can see how risky your bank really is. As a result, investors will charge more to provide funds. This further minimizes the profitability and maximizes the loss from taking a proprietary bet. The reason a bank is afraid of leaks of its proprietary bets is precisely the reason requiring banks to provide valuation transparency ends the banks taking proprietary bets.

Second, bank management knew it could control the amount of information provided to the regulators. Controlling the information shared with the bank regulators allowed bank management to prevent the bank regulators from taking any action if the bank regulators were so inclined.

2Farticle%2FSB10001424052702303703004577476483221472646.html%3Fmod%3DWSJ_hp_LEFTWhatsNewsCollection

553 ibid

554 United States Senate Permanent Subcommittee on Investigations (2013, March 15), JPMorgan Chase Whale Trades: A Case History of Derivatives Risks and Abuses, http://www.hsgac.senate.gov/subcommittees/investigations/hearings/chase-whale-trades-a-case-history-of-derivatives-risks-and-abuses, page 224.

> According to the OCC, when it requested resumption of the daily Investment Bank P&L reports, Douglas Braunstein, JPMorgan Chase's Chief Financial Officer, agreed to the request, but had apparently not informed Mr. Dimon.
>
> At a meeting shortly thereafter, attended by Mr. Braunstein, Mr. Dimon, and OCC Examiner-in-Charge Scott Waterhouse, according to Mr. Waterhouse, when Mr. Braunstein stated that he had ordered resumption of the reports, Mr. Dimon reportedly raised his voice in anger at Mr. Braunstein.
>
> Mr. Waterhouse said that Mr. Dimon then disclosed that he was the one who had ordered a halt to the reports and expressed the opinion that the OCC did not need the daily P&L figures for the Investment Bank.[555]

Here is Jamie Dimon telling his subordinate in no uncertain terms what information the bank regulator does and does not need to do its job. This is very important as Mr. Dimon's actions and statement confirm for all time why banks must be required to provide valuation transparency. It simply is not an option to let bankers only disclose the information they want when they want.

The global financial system is based on the FDR Framework that combines the philosophy of disclosure and *caveat emptor*. Under this framework, governments are responsible for ensuring market participants, including bank regulators, have all the useful, relevant information in an appropriate, timely manner so they can independently assess this information and make a fully informed decision.

Under the FDR Framework, it is not the firm making the disclosure that gets to determine what is adequate disclosure and when it should be made. Rather, it is the other market participants who get to determine what they consider adequate disclosure and when disclosure should be made. The FDR Framework recognizes Jamie Dimon, his firm and other banks would rather provide less disclosure. Hence, it says his and their opinion about the adequacy of disclosure is of no consequence.

> The bottom line is that the OCC's quarterly meeting with the CIO took place at a critical time. Had the CIO disclosed the size, risk profile, losses, and plans for the SCP to its regulator during the January 2012 meeting — rather than downplayed the portfolio by saying the CIO planned to reduce it — the OCC could have evaluated the trading strategy and raised questions about the rapid expansion in size and risk that took place over the next two months and later led to multi-billion-dollar losses.[556]

555 ibid, page 225

556 ibid, page 229

By not having access to the portfolio, the OCC could not Trust, but Verify what management told it about the portfolio.

Of equal importance, the Senate Subcommittee also explained the limit to what the OCC could have done had it had access to the information. It could have raised questions about the trading strategy, but because it does not approve or disapprove of any exposure the bank takes on it could not have prevented implementation of the trading strategy.

Because banks are not required to provide valuation transparency, the bank regulators are the only market participants who are in a position where they can analyze the exposure details. The question is "can they get the exposure details to analyze when Jamie Dimon and other bankers wants to limit the information they can have?"

> Despite that $2 billion disclosure, the spotlight of public attention, and repeated examiner requests, the OCC told the Subcommittee that obtaining the necessary information from the bank was not easy; the bank resisted and delayed responding to SCP requests and sometimes provided incorrect information.[557]
>
> The next day, April 10th, in response to a request from the OCC and Federal Reserve for more information about the whale trades, the bank provided a table entitled, "Summary of Positions," identifying an incomplete group of CIO positions in various credit indices and tranches by notional amount. The table did not provide basic P&L data for the positions or other risk information, leading OCC examiners to describe the table in an internal email as "useless" and in a Subcommittee interview as "absolutely unhelpful" and seemingly designed to make regulators "go away."[558]
>
> [L]ater in May 2012, the OCC asked for a comprehensive set of SCP positions, instead of the scant summary table provided in April. The OCC told the Subcommittee that the bank responded by providing a long list of 60,000 positions in a format useless for data analysis purposes, frustrating the OCC's efforts to understand the portfolio.
>
> Ultimately, after repeated requests, the OCC told the Subcommittee it believed it received the necessary information. While the OCC's difficulty in obtaining information offers additional proof of the bank's unacceptable conduct.[559]

The Senate Investigation found JPMorgan erected a veil of opacity to hide its activities when it gave the "stupid" examiners the run-around and stonewalled their request for information on the portfolio.

---

557 ibid, page 236

558 ibid, page 236

559 ibid, page 243

But this stonewalling did not stop with the bank regulators.

> Since JPMorgan Chase transferred many SCP index positions to its Investment Bank on July 2, 2012, the total amount of losses associated with the Synthetic Credit Portfolio will likely never be known.[560]

It also extended to Congress. By transferring the position, JPMorgan intended to prevent the Senate Investigation from knowing what the true losses were. To get the Senate to belief this, JPMorgan needed the Senate to believe

> The differing figures over the SCP's holdings are an indicator of not only how poor the SCP recordkeeping was, but also how quickly the portfolio was changing and how imprecise existing systems are for valuing derivative positions.[561]

In reality, transferring the positions did not in fact hide the losses to bank insiders. Bank information systems are fully capable of tracking a position whether it is in the CIO's synthetic credit portfolio or the investment banking portfolio. JPMorgan was and still is fully capable of tracking every trade it makes. If it were not, how could its auditors sign-off on JPMorgan's financial statements?

The intent of dismantling the portfolio and moving it to different parts of the bank was to hide what was going on. This action alone should compel Congress, the SEC and the bank regulators to push through the requirement that banks provide valuation transparency. Without valuation transparency, neither the regulators nor the market know what the true level of risk is at the banks.

When there is no valuation transparency, the market cannot exert discipline. When the regulators are stonewalled in their request for information, the regulators cannot exert restraint. The lack of valuation transparency to other market participants, including limiting the regulators access to information, means 100% of the time JPMorgan and other banks are not subject to any restraint on their activities.

Lesson 6: Market discipline never takes a day off

The reason market discipline is the primary method for restraining risk taking by the banks is the markets never sleep and bank regulators do. Market participants were not misled by JPMorgan's assurances to its regulators about the portfolio.

---

560 ibid, page 87

561 ibid, page 85

> On April 6, 2012, when media reports unmasked the role of JPMorgan Chase in the whale trades, the OCC told the Subcommittee that it was surprised to read about the trades and immediately directed inquiries to the bank for more information. The OCC indicated that it initially received such limited data about the trades and such blanket reassurances from the bank about them that, by the end of April, the OCC considered the matter closed.[562]

JPMorgan effectively stonewalled and dodged any regulatory oversight of the synthetic credit portfolio.

> The JPMorgan Chase whale trades demonstrate how much more difficult effective regulatory oversight is when a bank fails to provide routine, transparent performance data about the operation of a large derivatives portfolio, its related trades, and its daily booked values.....[563]

The JPMorgan whale trades demonstrate it is impossible to assert market or regulatory discipline on a bank when it fails to provide routine, transparent performance data about its derivatives portfolio and its related trades.

> JPMorgan Chase's ability to dodge effective OCC oversight of the multi-billion-dollar Synthetic Credit Portfolio until massive trades, mounting losses, and media reports exposed its activities, demonstrates that bank regulators need to conduct more aggressive oversight with their existing tools and develop more effective tools to detect and stop unsafe and unsound derivatives trading.[564]

The Senate Subcommittee highlighted the need for banks to provide valuation transparency not just to the regulators, but so all market participants have the information they need to detect and stop risky trading. In the presence of opacity, the Senate Subcommittee urges the bank regulators to try to perform the task of market discipline. This will never happen because the regulators don't approve or disapprove of individual positions. That is the role of market discipline.

Bank regulators focus on the question of does the bank have enough book capital to absorb the 'expected' losses on its exposures. Bank regulators step in to stop unsafe and unsound practices only when the losses threaten the ability of the bank to continue as a going concern.

---

[562] ibid, page 9

[563] ibid, page 10

[564] ibid, page 10

Market discipline works to prevent the accumulation of positions and too much risk. Bank regulators work by trying to minimize the losses after the positions have been taken.

The Senate Subcommittee confirmed how bank regulators operate even though it wished the regulators could exert market discipline.

> The OCC's primary examination role is to ensure that banks operate in a safe and sound manner, including by assessing and monitoring the risks that a bank poses to the FDIC's Deposit Insurance Fund.[565]

Examiners practice Trust, but Verify.

> The lack of bank disclosures essentially made it more difficult for OCC to effectively oversee this high risk portfolio in its early years.[566]

The lack of disclosures made it impossible for the examiners to verify what management told them about the portfolio.

> In 2006, JPMorgan Chase approved a request by the CIO to create a new credit derivatives trading portfolio as part of an internal "New Business Initiative Approval" (NBIA). Typically, the bank does not share NBIAs with the OCC, and the OCC told the Subcommittee that it was unaware of whether it received a copy of the 2006 NBIA that gave rise to the CIO's Synthetic Credit Portfolio.
>
> The OCC also told the Subcommittee that, even if it had known at the time, it would have had no role in approving and could not have prohibited establishment of the new Synthetic Credit Portfolio as proposed in 2006, although it could have monitored its activities and development.[567]

Bank examiners are not in business of approving or disapproving of any exposure taken by the banks. That is the role of market discipline. As the OCC pointed out, it views its role as monitoring what is happening. The goal is to protect the deposit insurance fund and this requires stepping in before losses get out of hand.

Having described how difficult a process the banks make it to obtain information, bank examiners must then use the information so they can Trust, but Verify.

---

565 ibid, page 218

566 ibid, page 219

567 ibid, page 220

> The initial reactions of Ms. Williams and Mr. Brosnan, two of the OCC's then-most senior officials, were to view JPMorgan Chase as an effective risk manager and to view the Synthetic Credit Portfolio as a hedge that would lower bank risk. The skepticism and demand for hard evidence that might be expected of bank regulators were absent.
>
> Also, the OCC did not question JPMorgan Chase's resistance to providing critical information needed for effective bank oversight.[568]

When JPMorgan resists providing the information needed for effective bank oversight, it is a safe bet all large banks resist providing the information needed for effective bank oversight. This is by choice. The banks know if they do not provide this information to the bank regulators, due to the lack of valuation transparency to the other market participants, there will be no restraint on their risk-taking.

Like the Bank of Italy with the Monte dei Paschi derivative scandal, the OCC was in position, but failed to take action. It is not surprising the OCC did nothing. Financial regulators do not see it as their role to question individual positions as this gets them into allocating capital across the economy. Instead, the regulators focus on whether the bank has the ability to absorb the 'expected' losses on the position.

Rather than change the regulatory focus to allocating capital across the economy, banks must be required to provide valuation transparency. With this data, the markets can exert discipline on the banks by questioning individual positions.

Lesson 7: Opacity allows bank management to spin the facts

By adopting the intermediary depiction model for bank disclosure, the SEC set up the situation where there is a gap between management's knowledge of the facts and the other market participants' knowledge. In theory, this gap only applies to non-material information. In practice, the gap between management's and the other market participants' knowledge also exists when it comes to material information too.

One of the weaknesses of the intermediary depiction disclosure model is this gap allows bank management to spin the facts. Two of the leading ways to spin the facts are to use models to hide the underlying reality and to use conference calls so management can frame how the facts should be assessed. With its whale trades, JPMorgan did both.

First, JPMorgan used models to hide the underlying reality.

568 ibid, page 247

> JPMorgan Chase, like all major financial institutions today, uses various risk metrics and mathematical models to measure, track, and evaluate the risks presented by its trading activities. Those activities typically involve numerous, complex financial instruments around the globe, with different time horizons, risk characteristics, and potential interactions. They also often feature daily trading and quick asset turnovers. The models needed to track and analyze the risks posed by those trading activities and the resulting financial instruments are usually designed by quantitative analysts with doctorates in mathematics, finance, or even physics.[569]
>
> Increasingly, for regulators to evaluate the risks and quality of risk management at a financial institution, they have to understand the institution's risk metrics and models. Regulators also rely on mathematical models to help determine, among other matters, how much capital a financial institution must hold to mitigate its risks. Regulators' duties today include determining whether proposed models meet detailed regulatory requirements, overseeing model changes and variations, examining model implementation which can raise complex operational issues, and overseeing back-testing of the models to evaluate their accuracy. These complex tasks are made more difficult if banks' quantitative experts are developing new or revised models to artificially lower the bank's risk ratings and capital requirements.[570]

The sheer complexity of the models suggests the bank regulators need significant help to understand the models and see how each bank is gaming the models to look better.

One of the benefits of requiring banks to provide valuation transparency and disclose on an ongoing basis their current global asset, liability and off-balance sheet exposure details is that it taps the quantitative analysts at the competitor banks for help in flagging for the regulators the risks that each bank is taking.

By requiring all the banks to provide valuation transparency, each bank's quantitative analysts can model both their bank and its competitors. From the bank regulators' perspective, they can then ask why different quantitative analysts produced different results for the same bank. It is a lot easier for a regulator to figure out that there is a problem if a bank says a trade is risk-less and its competitors see it as being risky.

In the case of the whale trades, JPMorgan hid the underlying reality in its Value at Risk model (VaR). The Value at Risk model is suppose to measure the risk the bank is taking and describe for investors how much money the bank could lose 19 out of 20 trading days.

---

569 ibid, page 164

570 ibid, page 165

"The Firm calculates VaR to estimate possible economic outcomes for its current positions using historical simulation, which measures risk across instruments and portfolios in a consistent, comparable way. The simulation is based on data for the previous 12 months. This approach assumes that historical changes in market values are representative of the distribution of potential outcomes in the immediate future.

VaR is calculated using a one day time horizon and an expected tail-loss methodology, and approximates a 95% confidence level. This means that, assuming current changes in the market are consistent with the historical changes used in the simulation, the Firm would expect to incur losses greater than that predicted by VaR estimates five times in every 100 trading days, or about 12 to 13 times a year. However, differences between current and historical market price volatility may result in fewer or greater VaR exceptions than the number indicated by the historical simulation. The firm's VaR calculation is highly granular and incorporates numerous risk factors, which are selected based on the risk profile of each portfolio.

According to the OCC's Examiner-in-Charge at JPMorgan Chase, the bank's 10-Q VaR estimated the potential loss to the bank's portfolio over the course of a day by looking at the previous 264 trading days and taking the average loss of the worst 33 days.[571]

How did JPMorgan hide the risk of the whale trades in its VaR model?

Another problem involves modern reliance by both banks and regulators on mathematical metrics and models to measure risk, especially with respect to synthetic derivatives, which are inherently hard to value, have no underlying assets to stem losses, offer unreliable past performance data, and often undergo split-second trading and price changes.

Risk metrics and models with complex variations can proliferate at a financial institution with the size and variety of JPMorgan Chase, and the pressure on analysts to reconfigure those metrics and models to produce lower risk results is difficult to counteract.

OCC regulations already contain numerous safeguards against manipulation, requiring risk models to be developed by independent experts, tested to see if they detect specific risk problems, and backtested for accuracy. Proliferation of models and metrics, however, make meaningful oversight and enforcement difficult.[572]

---

571 ibid, page 167

572 ibid, page 214

In short, the bad faith valuations provided by the traders undermined the VaR model with the result being the model didn't accurately reflect the risk JPMorgan actually had.

Second, JPMorgan's management spun how the whale trades should be looked at on a conference call.

> To ensure fair, open and efficient markets for investors, federal securities laws impose specific disclosure obligations on market participants. Public statements and SEC filings made by JPMorgan Chase in April and May 2012 raise questions about the timeliness, completeness, and accuracy of information presented about the CIO whale trades….[573]
>
> At the end of the week, on April 13, 2012, JPMorgan Chase filed an 8-K report with the SEC with information about the bank's first quarter financial results and hosted an earnings call. On that call, JPMorgan Chase Chief Financial Officer Douglas Braunstein reassured investors, analysts, and the public that the SCP's trading activities were made on a long-term basis, were transparent to regulators, had been approved by the bank's risk managers, and served a hedging function that lowered risk and would ultimately be permitted under the Volcker Rule whose regulations were still being developed. CEO Jamie Dimon dismissed the media reports about the SCP as a "complete tempest in a teapot."[574]
>
> Given the information that bank executives possessed in advance of the bank's public communications on April 10, April 13, and May 10, the written and verbal representations made by the bank were incomplete, contained numerous inaccuracies, and misinformed investors, regulators, and the public about the CIO's Synthetic Credit Portfolio.[575]

This summary of how JPMorgan spun the facts to investors about the whale trades needs to be flushed out.

Market participants know that opacity prevents them from being able to see each bank's current exposures. They also know bank regulators have the authority to see each bank's current exposures. This allows bankers to engage in the exercise of implying the bank regulators approve of these exposures.

JPMorgan engaged in this activity at the same time as it was denying the bank regulators access to the information on the whale trades.

> In the bank's April 13 earnings call, Mr. Braunstein said that the SCP positions were "fully transparent to the regulators," who "get information

573 ibid, page 10
574 ibid, page 11
575 ibid, page 11

> on those positions on a regular and recurring basis as part of our normalized reporting."
>
> In fact, the SCP positions had never been disclosed to the OCC in any regular bank report. The bank had described the SCP's positions to the OCC for the first time, in a general way, only a few days earlier and failed to provide more detailed information for more than a month. Mr. Braunstein's statement also omitted the fact that JPMorgan Chase had dodged OCC oversight of the SCP for years by failing to alert the agency to the establishment of the portfolio and failing to provide any portfolio-specific information in CIO reports.
>
> During the April 13 call, the bank led investors to believe that the SCP operated under close OCC supervision and oversight, when the truth was that the bank had provided barely any SCP data for the OCC to review.[576]

Whether investors believed it or not, they should have known the bank regulators would never approve or disapprove of any exposure the bank takes on. Bank regulators know they are not in the capital allocation business and therefore they would not approve or disapprove of any exposure.

That JPMorgan intended to convey the message the whale trades were transparent to the bank regulators is clear.

> The Evangelisti email and talking points indicate that, from the beginning of the bank's public discussion of the SCP in April 2012, JPMorgan Chase planned to describe the portfolio as a risk-reducing hedge that was transparent to the bank's regulators, even though neither characterization was accurate. Furthermore, by tempering the points about hedging and transparency to regulators, the revision shows that bank was aware that its initial characterizations were not entirely true.[577]

The Senate investigation speculates the goal of saying the positions are transparent to bank regulators is to reassure investors the risk of these positions is manageable as otherwise the bank regulators would have stepped in.

This is most definitely not true. Bank regulators have a history of failing to step in while the risk of a position is still manageable. For example, bank regulators were aware that Continental Illinois was buying loans from Penn Square. They failed to step in before Continental Illinois blew itself up.

> On the call, Mr. Braunstein stated that he wanted to "talk about the topics in the news around CIO, and just sort of take a step back and remind our investors about that activity and performance." In his remarks, Mr. Braunstein described the CIO and its excess deposits portfolio. He then went on to state:

---

576 ibid, page. 252

577 ibid, page 255

> "... I would add that all of those positions are fully transparent to the regulators. They review them, have access to them at any point in time, get the information on those positions on a regular and recurring basis as part of our normalized reporting."[578]

This statement by Mr. Braunstein had no basis in fact.[579]

> By telling investors that the Synthetic Credit Portfolio positions were "fully transparent" to regulators, the bank likely sought to reassure investors about the risky whale trades that the media had characterized as large enough to "driv[e] prices in the $10 trillion market."
>
> It would be reasonable for investors to want to know if such large positions were known to the bank's regulators. Investors might have reasoned that such trades, if known to regulators, could not have been overly risky; but if hidden, investors might have worried they were high risk transactions that regulators might otherwise have challenged.[580]

Regulators do not challenge individual transactions because they might be high risk. Individual transactions are capital allocation decisions. It is market discipline's role to restrain the risk taking and effectively approve or disapprove of individual transactions.

Perhaps no statement in the earnings conference call summed up the degree to which JPMorgan was spinning the facts to investors as well as a statement made by Mr. Dimon.

> In the April 13 earnings call, in response to a question, Mr. Dimon dismissed media reports about the SCP as a "complete tempest in a teapot." While he later apologized for that comment, his judgment likely was of importance to investors in the immediate aftermath of those media reports. The evidence also indicates that, when he made that statement, Mr. Dimon was already in possession of information about the SCP's complex and sizeable portfolio, its sustained losses for three straight months, the exponential increase in those losses during March, and the difficulty of exiting the SCP's positions.[581]

If banks provided valuation transparency, management's incentive to spin the facts would be greatly reduced as market participants could easily verify if what management was saying was accurate or not.

---

578 ibid, page 258

579 ibid, page 268

580 ibid, page 269

581 ibid, page 11

Lesson 8: Opacity allows banks to game valuation of their exposures

Originally, JPMorgan's Synthetic Credit Portfolio was set up as a hedge against the risk of the bank's loan portfolio (a "portfolio hedge"). In this case, the change in value of SCP was intended to offset any credit quality driven change in value of the bank's loan portfolio. If the SCP were a perfect hedge, its value would increase or decrease by exactly the same amount as the credit quality driven value of the bank's loan portfolio decreased or increased.

By definition, hedging is not a profit making opportunity, but rather focused on locking in the economic value of the financial instrument being hedged, in this case, the value of JPMorgan's loan portfolio. When the SCP shows a profit, the bank's loan book should be experiencing a credit quality driven decrease in value of approximately the same amount. When the SCP shows a loss, the bank's loan book should be experiencing a credit quality driven increase in value.

If it were one side of a hedge, the question is why would JPMorgan have wanted to hide the SCP's losses? It would not have.

The first indication the SCP might have been used to place bets came when the pricing of the underlying derivatives was changed to minimize losses.

> To minimize its reported losses, the CIO began to deviate from the valuation practices it had used in the past to price credit derivatives. In early January, the CIO had typically established the daily value of a credit derivative by marking it at or near the midpoint price in the daily range of prices (bid-ask spread) offered in the marketplace. Using midpoint prices had enabled the CIO to comply with the requirement that it value its derivatives using prices that were the "most representative of fair value."
>
> But later in the first quarter of 2012, instead of marking near the midpoint, the CIO began to assign more favorable prices within the daily price range (bid-ask spread) to its credit derivatives. The more favorable prices enabled the CIO to report smaller losses in the daily profit/loss (P&L) reports that the SCP filed internally within the bank.[582]

How JPMorgan valued these derivatives calls attention to the larger issue of asset valuation. How are assets where the bank's trading influences market prices valued? How are assets that don't trade very much valued?

Behind the veil of opacity about their individual exposure details, banks have significant discretion in asset valuation. For example, assets the bank determines are without a reliable market price fall into the Level 3 category. Banks are entitled to value these assets using their own models.

---

582 ibid, page 5

At the beginning of the financial crisis, this discretion in asset valuation played into the fears about the banks in two ways. First, there were the banks' exposures to opaque, hard to value assets. Second, there were the opaque bank balance sheets that prevented market participants from knowing what was on them.

These same fears resurfaced when the media reported on JPMorgan's "Whale trades".

With valuation transparency, these fears would be ended. Market participants could independently estimate the value of the bank's assets. The result of the market participants' estimates would reveal whether the bank was conservative or aggressive in its valuations.

Furthermore, sunlight is the best disinfectant. Requiring banks to disclose on an ongoing basis their current global asset, liability and off-balance sheet exposure details discourages trying to hide trading losses by assigning favorable prices. With this level of disclosure, market participants can see, track and price every position. Trying to hide trading losses using favorable prices will attract the market's attention. Attention a bank would rather not have as it results in the bank being seen as riskier and increases its cost of funds.

Lesson 9: Opacity renders bank risk management unenforceable

In theory, bank risk management acts as a brake to limit the risk a bank takes on. In practice, bank risk management simply documents the risk a bank takes on so bank regulators have something to put into their files.

What separates theory from practice is opacity. The whale trades highlight why without valuation transparency, bank risk management is effectively a meaningless exercise in creating documents. Traders and bankers did what they wanted. After all, they were the ones who contributed to the bank's bottom line.

> This case study elucidates the tension between traders and risk managers. Traders are incentivized to be aggressive and take on significant risk. Risk managers are supposed to be a voice of caution, limiting and reigning in that risk.[583]

If the synthetic credit portfolio was in fact a portfolio hedge, the tension between risk managers and traders doesn't exist. The trading strategies being pursued are designed to lock in the value of a loan portfolio of known size. The gains or losses on the credit derivative trades simply reflect the change in value of the loan portfolio.

---

583 ibid, page. 156

If JPMorgan were using the synthetic credit portfolio to gamble on corporate credits, the tension between risk managers and traders would exist.

> Just because trading strategies sometimes succeed does not mean they are prudent. Bad bets sometimes pay off, and it is easy to confound profits with successful trading strategies. At the CIO, initial success in high risk credit derivative trading contributed to complacent risk management, followed by massive losses.[584]

While bad bets sometimes pay off, one of the major issues with hedging is do you lift the hedge when the side purchased to hedge the bank's position shows a gain. Recognizing the gain increases the risk of the bank as the bank still has its position. Another problem with lifting the hedge is the traders think they should be compensated for the "gain" even though in theory there is an offsetting economic "loss" elsewhere in the bank.

The decision on whether or not to lift the hedge shows another shortcoming of the intermediate depiction model for disclosure. Due to inadequate disclosure, investors are blind to the increase in the bank's risk profile when the hedge is lifted.

> In contrast to JPMorgan Chase's reputation for best-in-class risk management, the whale trades exposed a bank culture in which risk limit breaches were routinely disregarded, risk metrics were frequently criticized or downplayed, and risk evaluation models were targeted by bank personnel seeking to produce artificially lower capital requirements.[585]

Effective best-in-class risk management and opacity cannot exist together. Where there is opacity, the traders are far more influential than the risk managers. Our current financial crisis illustrated this point. At the start of the crisis, it appeared JPMorgan was the only large global bank to have its risk under control and not become insolvent. JPMorgan's management was happy to pat itself on the back and claim it was a result of their risk management prowess. As shown by the whale trade, it was simply luck the government stepped in before it became apparent JPMorgan had failed too.

> The CIO used five key metrics and limits to gauge and control the risks associated with its trading activities, including the Value-at-Risk (VaR) limit, Credit Spread Widening 01 (CS01) limit, Credit Spread Widening 10% (CSW10%) limit, stress loss limits, and stop loss advisories. During the first

---

584 ibid, page 156
585 ibid, page 7

> three months of 2012, as the CIO traders added billions of dollars in complex credit derivatives to the Synthetic Credit Portfolio, the SCP trades breached the limits on all five risk metrics. In fact, from January 1 through April 30, 2012, CIO risk limits and advisories were breached more than 330 times.[586]

It was okay to breach the internal risk management limits, because

> In practice, the bank told the Subcommittee that its risk metrics were intended to act, not as ironclad limits, but as guidelines and red flags. Mr. Dimon told the Subcommittee that a breach in a risk "limit" was intended to lead to a conversation about the situation, not to an automatic freeze or unwinding of positions. The CIO used the same approach. If a risk limit were breached, CIO traders were expected to express a view about the risk in the portfolio and what should be done, but not to immediately reduce the portfolio's holdings to end the breach.[587]

Just like the bank with its gamble on the 30-year U.S. Treasury Bonds, breaching JPMorgan's risk management limits doesn't lead to any action. Instead, JPMorgan is left with three choices: 1) do nothing and pray the market moves in its favor; 2) sell the position and recognize the losses; or 3) hedge the position and hope it can be unwound with smaller losses in the future.

And what was the view of the CIO traders?

> CIO traders, risk personnel, and quantitative analysts frequently attacked the accuracy of the risk metrics, downplaying the riskiness of credit derivatives and proposing risk measurement and model changes to lower risk results for the Synthetic Credit Portfolio.
>
> In the case of the CIO VaR, after analysts concluded the existing model was too conservative and overstated risk, an alternative CIO model was hurriedly adopted in late January 2012, while the CIO was in breach of its own and the bankwide VaR limit. The bank did not obtain OCC approval as it should have to use the model for the SCP. The CIO's new model immediately lowered the SCP's VaR by 50%, enabling the CIO not only to end its breach, but to engage in substantially more risky derivatives trading. Months later, the bank determined that the model was improperly implemented, requiring error-prone manual data entry and incorporating formula and calculation errors. On May 10, the bank backtracked, revoking the new VaR model due to its inaccuracy in portraying risk, and reinstating the prior model.[588]

586 ibid, page 7

587 ibid, page 158

588 ibid, page 8

Apparently, the conversation was on how to change the risk metrics so the bank would be in compliance.

> The head of the CIO's London office, Achilles Macris, once compared managing the Synthetic Credit Portfolio, with its massive, complex, moving parts, to flying an airplane. The OCC Examiner-in-Charge at JPMorgan Chase told the Subcommittee that if the Synthetic Credit Portfolio were an airplane, then the risk metrics were the flight instruments. In the first quarter of 2012, those flight instruments began flashing red and sounding alarms, but rather than change course, JPMorgan Chase personnel disregarded, discounted, or questioned the accuracy of the instruments instead. The bank's actions not only exposed the many risk management deficiencies at JPMorgan Chase, but also raise systemic concerns about how many other financial institutions may be disregarding risk indicators and manipulating models to artificially lower risk results and capital requirements.[589]

How many other financial institutions disregard risk limits? How many other financial institutions manipulate models to artificially lower risk results and capital requirements? All of them do this. I say this based on personal experience. Please recall the bank that purchased the 30-year U.S. Treasury bonds. There is simply no way this position complied with prudent risk management.

The only way to enforce the discipline of risk management is by requiring the banks to provide valuation transparency. With this level of disclosure, market participants can exert discipline on the banks so that they do not exceed their own risk limits or manipulate risk models. Market participants enforce risk management by holding the banks accountable. A bank that violates its risk limits is seen as riskier and the market reflects this in the bank's higher cost of funds.

Lesson 10: Opacity is the necessary condition for a financial crisis

The whale trades highlights the failure of the SEC's intermediary depiction model for disclosure and the corresponding lack of discipline on the banks.

> The whale trades provide a striking case history of how a major bank, with 65 bank examiners on site, can keep a multi-billion-dollar derivatives portfolio off the radar screen of its regulator for years, at least until it begins to lose money.[590]

The whale trades confirmed Congressman St. Germain's concern that a handful of bank examiners, 65 in this case, are not up to the task of

---

589 ibid, page 8

590 ibid, page 250

understanding all the positions on and off a global financial institution's balance sheet. The only way to understand all of these positions is to harness the analytical horsepower of the market, including each bank's competitors. This can only be done if the banks provide valuation transparency.

> For nearly six years, JPMorgan Chase failed to disclose key information to its primary regulator about the CIO's Synthetic Credit Portfolio, even though the bank claimed it played an important role in hedging the bank's credit risk.[591]

JPMorgan's intentional failure to disclose key information prevented the bank regulators from exerting any restraint as the result of monitoring the SCP or asking any questions.

> The bank failed to report the existence of the portfolio to the OCC when it was created, during a 2010 examination of CIO investment portfolios, when it expanded in size by tenfold in 2011, and when it produced approximately $400 million in 2011 profits.
>
> Along the way, at times, bank personnel lectured OCC examiners about being overly intrusive.[592]

Given the existence of a taxpayer backed deposit guarantee, banks should be held to a higher level of disclosure. With valuation transparency, examiners don't have to worry about being lectured about being overly intrusive.

> The bank first reported the SCP to the OCC in January 2012, when it began breaching the bank's VaR limit and incurring losses, but even then the bank misinformed the OCC about its significance by describing plans to reduce its size.
>
> As SCP losses mounted during the first few months of 2012, the bank failed to include information about the SCP in routine reports to the OCC. When the CIO repeatedly breached internal risk and stress limits, the bank downplayed their significance and allowed the breaches to continue.
>
> After the whale trades attracted media attention, the bank still resisted providing detailed SCP information to the OCC, disclosing the extent of the SCP losses only when it was legally compelled to disclose its financial results in an SEC filing. The OCC's repeated requests were often ignored and not adequately enforced.
>
> The questionable bank practices that came to light when the whale trades were disclosed includes the CIO's creation of a high risk trading portfolio using bank deposits, using valuation practices to hide losses, disregarding breaches

591 ibid, page 250

592 ibid, page 250

> of risk limits, manipulating risk and capital models to artificially lower the portfolio's risk profile, and dodging OCC oversight.
>
> Because JPMorgan Chase provided such limited information about the SCP, the OCC remained in the dark about the size and risks of the portfolio for years. When losses began rolling in, it had to exercise oversight on the basis of incomplete, inaccurate, and misleading information. The bank's practices impeded the OCC's ability to detect and stop unsafe and unsound derivatives trading practices.[593]

JPMorgan's whale trades were an example of the larger problem of opacity that caused our current financial crisis. Our financial system only works properly when all market participants are fully informed. The only way to insure all market participants are fully informed about the banks is to require valuation transparency with ongoing disclosure of each bank's current exposure details.

Mr. Dimon should not object to providing this disclosure. After all, he wanted to look at the exposure details so he could understand what was happening with the whale trades.

In addition, the original J.P. Morgan had his bank provide valuation transparency. During the Panic of 1907, this was useful as it was the sign of a bank that could stand on its own two feet. Can the same be said of Mr. Dimon's JPMorgan?

Lesson 11: Get the data

Given the prominent role of opacity in the JPMorgan whale trades, it is not surprising to see the prominence disclosure is given in preventing any recurrence.

> Based upon the Subcommittee's investigation and findings of fact, the Report makes the following recommendations.
>
> **(1) Require Derivatives Performance Data.** Federal regulators should require banks to identify all internal investment portfolios containing derivatives over a specified notional size, and require periodic reports with detailed performance data for those portfolios.[594]

The Subcommittee makes getting the data its number one recommendation.

The whale trades also showed the Dodd-Frank derivative rules are inadequate for helping regulators catch the existing JPMorgan "Whale" trade or any other similar position. This is not surprising because Dodd-Frank was

593 ibid, page 250
594 ibid, page 16

effectively written by and for Wall Street. The derivative rules are an example of this as rather than use a simple direct solution they rely on the combination of complex rules and regulatory oversight.

The simple, direct solution is to have each financial institution disclose to all market participants on an ongoing basis its current global derivative exposure details. This makes it easy for the regulators to find risky positions (at a minimum, the regulators tap the analytical expertise of the market for help in finding and analyzing these positions).

Instead, Dodd-Frank proposed an indirect solution where the authors knew they were creating a data nightmare. Remember, Wall Street wants to protect opacity and the ability to gamble behind the veil of opacity. Wall Street knew what it allowed to be written into Dodd-Frank and the subsequent rules would protect opacity by creating this data nightmare.

Speaking about the swap-trade data collected as a result of the Dodd-Frank Act, Scott O'Malia, a former Commodity Futures Trading Commission member said,

> The data "is not usable in its current form … The problem is so bad that staff have indicated that they currently cannot find the London Whale in the current data files."…[595]

By making getting the data its number one recommendation, the Senate Subcommittee also focused attention on the fact our current opacity driven financial crisis has been going on for several years, yet market participants still don't know what each bank's current on and off balance sheet exposures are.

Why do market participants still know so little about the risks of the banks and what losses might be hidden on and off their balance sheets? Without current exposure details, how are market participants suppose to be able to assess the risk of the banks and enforce market discipline?

The whale trades showed more disclosure is needed. Specifically, what is needed is valuation transparency under which the banks disclose their current exposure details. Then, even if the regulators do not monitor the trades or take any action, market participants can and will.

Our financial system is built on valuation transparency. Its absence is a systemic risk issue as shown by both the whale trades and our current financial crisis.

---

595 Brush, Silla (2013, March 19), Dodd-Frank Swap Data Fails to Catch JPMorgan Whale, O'Malia Says, Bloomberg, http://www.bloomberg.com/news/2013-03-19/dodd-frank-swap-data-fails-to-catch-jpmorgan-whale-o-malia-says.html

Lesson 12: Valuation transparency works

The JPMorgan London Whale trading scandal showed how important it is that all market participants, not just management and regulators, have access to each bank's current global exposure details. For example, when everyone can see a bank's proprietary trades, banks don't make these bets. JPMorgan demonstrated this fact by closing its position as quickly as possible after the position had been "leaked" to the marketplace.

The trading scandal demonstrated JPMorgan is too big to manage and too big for regulators to oversee. If it is too big to manage or regulate, the logical conclusion is that it should be shrunk.

But how do you effectively shrink JPMorgan or other similar Too Big to Fail banks and exert restraint on them so they doesn't become a problem in the future?

By requiring each bank to provide valuation transparency into its current global asset, liability and off-balance sheet exposure details and letting the market exert discipline. With valuation transparency, the first thing to go are each bank's proprietary bets, as oppose to the market making positions, as each bank doesn't want the market to trade against its bets. Hence, we get compliance with the Volcker Rule without 71+ pages of regulations and 800+ pages explaining the regulations.

With valuation transparency, the second thing to go are each bank's thousands of subsidiaries that exist for regulatory or tax arbitrage.

In short, with valuation transparency, market discipline gives each bank the incentive to reduce its risk profile and organizational complexity as the failure to do so results in a lower stock price and higher cost of funds.

Case Study III: Libor interest rate: Regulators watching bankers manipulating the price of money for personal gain

MR STEPHEN DAVIES: on Friday 31 August 2007, Mr del Missier sends an email to Mr Diamond and to Mr Ricci, and he said:

"The whole LIBOR curve is rubbish. The real story is that these are all fantasy rates."

That's an email between board members. The real story is that these are all fantasy rates. This has been pored over by at least four regulatory authorities in conjunction with Barclays. I am entitled, I think, to say that it is obvious that very crafted plea bargains have been negotiated and agreed.

MR JUSTICE FLAUX: Yes.

MR DAVIES: Barclays has agreed that this sentence, this admission in relation to the so-called occasional sterling submissions, is not just appearing in the American documents, the statement of facts annexed to the non-prosecution agreement, it appears in all of the documents. The FSA have relied on it as well.

MR JUSTICE FLAUX: The FSA don't seek to distinguish between sterling and dollar, do they?

MR DAVIES: No, but the gist --

MR JUSTICE FLAUX: At paragraph 12 of the final notice:

"Barclays acted inappropriately in breach of principle 5 on numerous occasions between September 2007 and May 2009, by making LIBOR submissions which took into account concerns over the negative media perception for Barclays LIBOR submissions."

It doesn't identify whether it's sterling or dollar.

MR DAVIES: Any more than --

MR JUSTICE FLAUX: So it encompasses really, does it not, 5(c) and probably goes further?

MR DAVIES: Yes, and when Mr del Missier says, you know, "The LIBOR rates are fantasy" and so forth, he doesn't say that the dollar LIBOR rates are fantasy, he can't do, because everyone knew that they were all fantasy. Because Barclays' case is this: Barclays say, and we see this time and time again in the contemporaneous documents, "All the other banks, or at least many of them, were being dishonest in their submissions", dishonest, and that Barclays' case before your Lordship is that Barclays were being honest, and when they talk about having their heads above the parapet, it's because they were out of the dishonest pack and they wanted to come back into the dishonest pack so as not to be conspicuous. It's an extraordinary case to run. So they themselves then brought their LIBORs down even further away from the true position.

MR JUSTICE FLAUX: Yes.

MR DAVIES: Now, it simply doesn't run for Barclays to say, and they don't yet say it at all in any evidence that I've read, "We have no idea which of these sterling submissions were improper in this 20-month period, it just went into the statement". It's just not in the real world. We said in correspondence "Then you had better give us a statement", because somebody solemnly has to go on oath and say that is the position, because it beggars belief.[596]

The bankers' manipulation of benchmark interest rates and prices provides a vivid illustration of why complex regulation and regulatory oversight is an

596 Graiseley Properties Limited & Others v. Barclays Bank PLC (2014, March 21), Day 1 court transcript, page 17

inadequate substitute for the combination of valuation transparency and market discipline.

I'll focus on Libor, the London Interbank Offered Rate, which is used to price global financial products ranging from home mortgages to commercial and consumer loans to interest rate swaps to futures contracts.

The interest rate is intended to reflect what creditworthy banks would pay to borrow in London on an unsecured basis from other banks. We know from Barclays that this is not true. Banks manipulated Libor to benefit their trading positions tied to the benchmark rates or to hide their difficulty raising funds.

In addition to Libor, the bankers also manipulated its equivalent benchmark interest rates in Europe (Euribor or the Euro Interbank Offered Rate) and Japan (Tibor or the Tokyo Interbank Offered Rate). But the bankers did not stop with only manipulating benchmark interest rates. They also manipulated other markets where the benchmark price is not based off of actual trades including commodities and foreign exchange.

As Joaquín Almunia, EU Commission Vice-President in charge of competition policy, said:

> What is shocking about the LIBOR and EURIBOR scandals is not only the manipulation of benchmarks, ... but also the collusion between banks who are supposed to be competing with each other.
>
> Today's decision sends a clear message that the Commission is determined to fight and sanction these cartels in the financial sector.
>
> Healthy competition and transparency are crucial for financial markets to work properly, at the service of the real economy rather than the interests of a few.[597]

How is Libor set?

While Libor was marketed as reflecting the average cost for creditworthy banks to borrow in the unsecured interbank lending market, it is not based off of or compared to actual transaction data. Rather, the banking industry's lobbying group calculates Libor based on each of the panel banks' estimate of what it would cost it to borrow money. As described by the CFTC, the mechanics for setting Libor are:

---

597 European Commission press release (2013, December 4), Antitrust: Commission fines banks € 1.71 billion for participating in cartels in the interest rate derivatives industry, http://europa.eu/rapid/press-release_IP-13-1208_en.htm

> Daily LIBORs are issued for ten currencies with fifteen tenors ranging from overnight through twelve months. According to the [British Bankers' Association ("BBA")], LIBOR "is based on offered interbank deposit rates contributed in accordance with the Instructions to BBA LIBOR Contributor banks." The BBA requires that "[a]n individual BBA LIBOR Contributor Panel Bank will contribute the rate at which it could borrow funds, were it to do so by asking for and then accepting interbank offers in reasonable market size just prior to [11 :00 a.m. London time]. By its definition, LIBOR requires the submitting panel banks to determine the rates at which they can obtain funds in the London interbank market. The definition of LIBOR does not permit consideration of factors unrelated to the costs of borrowing unsecured funds.
>
> Every business day shortly before 11 :00 a.m. London time, the banks on the LIBOR panels submit their rates to Thomson Reuters. On behalf of the BBA, Thomson Reuters compiles a day's LIBOR for each currency and tenor by excluding the top and bottom quartile of rates and averaging the remaining eight rates. That average rate becomes the official BBA daily LIBOR (the "LIBOR fixing"). The BBA then makes public the daily LIBOR fixing for each currency and tenor, as well as the daily submissions of each panel bank, through Thomson Reuters and the other data vendors licensed by the BBA. This information is made available and relied upon throughout the world, including in the United States.[598]

As a result of these mechanics, Libor is prone to manipulation because market participants could not verify what the banks said about their cost to raise funds in the unsecured interbank lending market is true.

Given banks had little chance of being caught, it was predictable the banks would rig the Libor interest rates. It was easy. All it required was the banks to lie about their cost to raise funds in the unsecured interbank lending market.

Unfortunately, similar mechanics are used for setting the other benchmark interest rates and prices. A confidential discussion paper by the International Organization of Securities Commissions found more than half of the benchmark interest rates used globally are subject to Libor-like manipulation because these rates were

> [C]alculated by methodologies that were unclear, not transparent and only rarely subject to specific regulatory standards or obligations.... Even in

598 Commodity Futures Trading Commission legal pleading (2012, June 27), Barclays PLC, Barclays Bank PLC and Barclays Capital Inc., http://www.cftc.gov/ucm/groups/public/@lrenforcementactions/documents/legalpleading/enfbarclaysorder062712.pdf, page 6.

> benchmarks ... based on actual transaction data ... compiling bodies retain discretion in producing the actual rates or prices.[599]

David Zervos at Jeffries & Co described how with the Libor rate setting process Wall Street intentionally erected a veil of opacity so that it could manipulate the financial system for its benefit.

> It should come as no surprise to anyone that major commercial banks manipulate Libor submissions for their own benefit.
>
> The OTC derivatives markets was designed by the big banks, for the big banks, to ensure that as they set up their own private securities exchanges — away from regulatory scrutiny — they could control the interest rate settings.
>
> Money center commercial banks did not want the "truth" of market prices to determine their loan rates. Rather, they wanted an oligopolistically controlled subjective survey rate to be the basis for their lending businesses.[600]

Bankers understood how they would benefit and had an incentive to introduce opaque benchmarks that they could easily manipulate. Naturally, they created a structure that would both allow them to manipulate the benchmarks and minimize being subject to regulation.

They did this through associations, like the British Bankers' Association, or private entities they controlled. By using third parties, the bankers placed the construction of and the manipulation of the benchmarks outside the regulators' authority to take enforcement actions.

How widely used is Libor in the financial system?

As described by the CFTC in its settlement with Barclays over manipulating the Libor interest rates,

> LIBOR is intended to be a barometer to measure strain in money markets, that it often is a gauge of the market's expectation of future central bank interest rates, and that approximately $350 trillion of notional swaps and $10 trillion of loans are indexed to LIBOR.
>
> LIBOR also is the basis for settlement of interest rate futures and options contracts on many of the world's major futures and options exchanges, including the three-month and one-month Eurodollar contracts on the Chicago

[599] Gallu, Joshua (2012, September 20), Libor-Like Manipulation Possible in Other Benchmarks, Iosco Says, Bloomberg, http://www.bloomberg.com/news/2012-09-19/libor-like-manipulation-possible-in-other-benchmarks-iosco-says.html

[600] Whalen, Christopher (2012, July 12), The Institutional Risk Analyst, http://us1.institutionalriskanalytics.com/pub/IRAMain.asp

> Mercantile Exchange ("CME"). Measured by the notional value of open interest, the CME Eurodollar contract is the most liquid and largest notional futures contract traded on the CME and in the world. The total traded volume of the CME Eurodollar contract had a notional value of over $437 trillion in 2009 and $564 trillion in 2011. It settles based on the three-month U.S. Dollar LIBOR published on the Monday before the last trading day of the contract month.
>
> Moreover, LIBOR is fundamentally critical to financial markets and has an enormously widespread impact on global markets and consumers. LIBOR also affects businesses seeking credit, consumers obtaining mortgages or personal loans, and market participants transacting in numerous other financial contracts in the U.S. and abroad that are based on the benchmark interest rates.[601]

Libor is the base off of which credit in the global financial system is priced. Over $500 trillion of financial products reference it.

$500+ trillion is a big number. To put this number into perspective, everyone who borrowed or saved money was affected by the banks rigging the Libor interest rates. The Libor interest rates are at the very core of our global financial system.

With $500+ trillion of financial products tied to Libor, there is a tremendous incentive to manipulate the rate. The value of artificially manipulating Libor can be calculated. For example, imagine that the banks were paying Libor interest rates on $10 trillion of interest rate swaps. Assuming the Libor, interest rates were manipulated downward by on average 3% from when Lehman Brothers' collapsed on September 15, 2008 to September 15, 2009, the value of the savings to the banks of this manipulation equals $300 billion (3% * $10 trillion).

Adrian Blundell-Wignall, a special adviser to the secretary general of the OECD, observed,

> We will never know the amounts of money involved, but it has to be the biggest financial fraud of all time. Libor is the basis for calculating practically every derivative known to man."...[602]

601 Commodity Futures Trading Commission legal pleading (2012, June 27), Barclays PLC, Barclays Bank PLC and Barclays Capital Inc., http://www.cftc.gov/ucm/groups/public/@lrenforcementactions/documents/legalpleading/enfbarclaysorder062712.pdf, page 6.

602 Vaughan, Liam, Finch, Gavin (2012, December 13), Secret Libor Transcripts Expose Trader Rate-Manipulation, Bloomberg, http://www.bloomberg.com/news/2012-12-13/rigged-libor-with-police-nearby-shows-flaw-of-light-touch.html

Code of conduct

Minos Zombanakis, a Greek banker credited with inventing the Libor interest rate, said the mechanism for ensuring Libor was not manipulated was the unwritten code of conduct under which

> "You always worked in the market with the assumption that you were dealing with gentlemen, and you assumed that people acted honourably because they couldn't afford to act otherwise."[603]
>
> Minos Zombanakis, a Greek banker

This unwritten code of conduct allows market participants to trust each other. However, trust does not relieved market participants of the need to also verify. The enforcement mechanism to ensure everyone acts honestly and follows the unwritten code of conduct is valuation transparency.

Libor and the other benchmark prices were deliberately set in an opaque manner that prevented market participants from verifying them.

An industry-wide culture of acceptance of breaking the rules

> Through all of my experience, what I never contemplated was that there were bankers who would purposely misrepresent facts to banking authorities. You were honor-bound to report accurately, and it never entered my mind that, aside from a fringe element, it would be otherwise. I was wrong.
>
> Alan Greenspan, former chairman of the Federal Reserve[604]

> When a bank can benefit financially from doing the wrong thing, it generally will.
>
> Sheila Bair, former chairman of the FDIC[605]

The Libor scandal highlights the shift inside the banks from old school banking focused institutions with the unwritten code of conduct that kept bankers honest to capital markets focused institutions where honesty was enforced by valuation transparency and the ability to Trust, but Verify.

---

603 Smith, Helena (2012, December 17), Libor founder Minos Zombanakis condemns rate manipulators, The Guardian, http://www.theguardian.com/business/2012/dec/17/libor-minos-zombanakis

604 Vaughan, Liam, Finch, Gavin (2012, December 13), *Secret Libor Transcripts Expose Trader Rate Manipulation*, Bloomberg, http://www.bloomberg.com/news/2012-12-13/rigged-libor-with-police-nearby-shows-flaw-of-light-touch.html

605 ibid

One place this shift showed up was when the banks passed their corporate clients from the lending side of the institution to the capital markets side of the institution. In the lending side, the old school unwritten code of conduct resulted in the client being viewed as a party in which the bank had an interest in their future success. In the capital markets side, the corporate client is viewed as a counter-party in a zero-sum trading game where either the buyer or seller profits as a result of the trade.

As a former Barclays Capital trader's observed about selling derivatives, a capital market's product, to benefit at the expense of the bank's corporate clients:

> We all talked about it like it was lambs to the slaughter.... because corporate clients perceived the bank to be looking out for their interests and not as an adversary.[606]

Imagine the culture that supports taking advantage of a client because the client thinks their interests are being looked out for.

It is this type of culture that deliberately puts the interests of the traders and bankers ahead of the bank's and the bank's interest ahead of the clients.

It is this type of culture that deliberately creates opaque products to take advantage of clients who see banks as business partners and not as counter-parties trying to maximize their profits at the client's expense.

It is this type of culture that deliberately creates opaque sub-prime mortgage backed securities to take advantage of investors who do not have access to current information and therefore don't know what they are buying.

It is this type of culture that deliberately breaks the law to transfer cash for criminals and rogue states because it is profitable and doesn't think twice about doing so.

It is this type of culture that deliberately manipulates Libor interest rates to take advantage of market participants on the other side of derivative contracts the bank has sold.

It is this type of culture that permeates all of the large universal banks that combine commercial and investment banking.

This culture explains why each scandal is not the result of a few rogue traders, but is the personal responsibility of every senior employee of the banks.

---

606 Ebrahimi, Helia (2012, July 21), 'BarCap was the Wild Wild West — that's what we called it', The Telegraph, http://www.telegraph.co.uk/finance/newsbysector/banksandfinance/9417801/BarCap-was-the-Wild-Wild-West-thats-what-we-called-it.html

In the presence of opacity, financial institutions don't naturally engage in ethical conduct. This observation has been confirmed by two different industry studies.

The CFA Institute and the Economist Intelligent Unit conducted a survey of the financial services industry in September 2013. It found ethical conduct in the financial services industry was seen as a barrier to both advancement and competitiveness.

> 53% say … career progression would be tricky without being "flexible" over ethical standards; … rises to 71% of investment bankers taking … survey.
>
> Rigid adherence to ethical standards would also damage the firm's competitiveness, say 53%.[607]

Labaton Sucharow LLP also confirmed the industry-wide culture of acceptance of bending if not breaking the unwritten code of conduct. Its July 2013 survey covering Wall Street executives on corporate ethics, wrongdoing in the workplace and the role of financial regulators in policing the marketplace found:

- 29% believed that the rules might have to be broken in order to be successful.
- 24% admitted they would engage in insider trading to make $10 million if they could get away with it.
- 23% have personally observed or have first hand knowledge of wrongdoing in the workplace.
- 17% felt that leaders in their firm were likely to look the other way if they suspected a top performer had engaged in insider trading.
- 15% doubted these leaders would report actual insider trading violations to law enforcement authorities if a top performer was involved.[608]

Since there was a lot of money to be made from manipulating benchmark prices like Libor and bosses were known for looking the other way rather than examining how a top performer was producing their results, it is not surprising that Libor and other benchmark prices would be openly manipulated.

---

607 A report from the Economist Intelligence Unit and CFA Institute (2013), A Crisis of Culture: Valuing Ethics and Knowledge in Financial Services, CFA Institute, http://www.cfainstitute.org/about/research/surveys/Documents/crisis_of_culture_report.pdf, page 9.

608 Labaton Sucharow LLP (2013, July 16), Wall Street In Crisis: A Perfect Storm Looming, Labaton Sucharow LLP, http://www.labaton.com/en/about/press/Wall-Street-Professional-Survey-Reveals-Widespread-Misconduct.cfm

While some individuals raised concerns about breaking the unwritten code of conduct and submitting false rates to hide their bank's difficulty in raising funds in the interbank lending market, they were in the minority. One insider discussed how breaking the unwritten code of conduct was viewed as acceptable by the vast majority of individuals working at the banks.

> Trader said … general acceptance that you lowered the price … "everyone was doing it"…. openness alone suggested no collusion or secrecy. Management had been in the meeting … clearly no surprise or secret.[609]

As shown in the trial of a Jefferies mortgage-backed securities trader, in the absence of valuation transparency, traders engaging in a game of lies, fraud and misinformation is considered acceptable. One portfolio manager observed about the game traders play:

> it is appropriate to use skepticism." The perception that the other side either withholds information or tells falsehoods "is exactly why I don't say, 'How high?' when they tell me to jump,[610]

The acceptance of bankers engaging in scandalous behavior is the result of opacity. Because of opacity, other market participants cannot see the bad behavior and exert discipline to restrain this behavior. In the presence of opacity, it seems perfectly acceptable to manipulate Libor or other benchmark interest rates because telling the truth might jeopardize one's job and all the other banks are doing it.

RBS traders boasted of Libor 'cartel'

Just like the senior executives at Anglo Irish Bank, the traders who manipulated Libor were not at all reluctant to discuss what they were doing.

> August 19, 2007, Mr. Tan Chi Min: "It's just amazing how Libor fixing can make you that much money or lose if opposite. It's a cartel now in London."[611]

---

609 Anonymous insider letter to The Telegraph, Libor scandal: How I manipulated the bank borrowing rate, The Telegraph, http://www.telegraph.co.uk/finance/newsbysector/banksandfinance/9368430/Libor-scandal-How-I-manipulated-the-bank-borrowing-rate.html

610 Dillon, John, Dolmetsch, Chris (2014, February 25), Ex-Jefferies Trader's Customers Say Lies Part of the Job, Bloomberg, http://www.bloomberg.com/news/2014-02-25/ex-jefferies-trader-s-customers-say-lies-are-common-tactic-1-.html

611 Swinford, Steven, Wilson, Harry (2012, September 26), RBS traders boasted of Libor 'cartel', The Telegraph, http://www.telegraph.co.uk/finance/newsbysector/

Several methods of manipulating the benchmark interest rates were freely talked about. The CFTC report on Barclays provided examples of manipulation.

Barclays manipulated Libor from at least 2005 to benefit the bank's derivative positions. When the bank bet with derivatives, the Barclays employees who submitted data for calculating the Libor interest rates would send in numbers that guaranteed the Barclays traders won their bet.

> Senior traders on the NY Swaps Desk instructed several other swaps traders to make the requests of the LIBOR submitters on Barclays' London Money Market Desk for certain LIBOR submissions in order to move their LIBOR submissions in a direction to benefit the desk's derivatives trading positions.
>
> The traders' conduct was common and pervasive, and known by other traders and trading desk managers located near the interest rate swaps desk, both in New York and London. None of the traders attempted to conceal the requests from supervisors at Barclays during the entire period that the activity occurred. In fact, on occasion, the traders discussed their requests with trading desk managers....[612]
>
> 1) "WE HAVE TO GET KICKED OUT OF THE FIXINGS TOMORROW!! We need a 4.17 fix in 1m (low fix) We need a 4.41 fix in 3m (high fix)" (November 22, 2005, Senior Trader in New York to Trader in London);
>
> 2) "You need to take a close look at the reset ladder. We need 3M to stay low for the next 3 sets and then I think that we will be completely out of our 3M position. Then it's on. [Submitter] has to go crazy with raising 3M Libor." (February 1,2006, Trader in New York to Trader in London);
>
> 3) "Your annoying colleague again...Would love to get a high 1m Also if poss a low 3m ... if poss... thanks" (February 3, 2006, Trader in London to Submitter);
>
> 4) "This is the [book's] risk. We need low 1M and 3M libor. PIs ask [submitter] to get 1M set to 82. That would help a lot" (March 27,2006, Trader in New York to Trader in London)...[613]
>
> The LIBOR submitters regularly considered the swaps traders' requests when determining and making Barclays' U.S. Dollar LIBOR submissions.

---

banksandfinance/9568087/RBS-traders-boasted-of-Libor-cartel.html

612 Commodity Futures Trading Commission legal pleading (2012, June 27), Barclays PLC, Barclays Bank PLC and Barclays Capital Inc., http://www.cftc.gov/ucm/groups/public/@lrenforcementactions/documents/legalpleading/enfbarclaysorder062712.pdf, page 8

613 ibid, page 9

> To accommodate the swaps traders, the submitters moved Barclays' U.S. Dollar LIBOR submissions by one or more basis points in the direction requested by swaps traders, or submitted a specific rate depending on the particulars of the swaps traders' requests....
>
> 4) "For you ... anything. I am going to go 78 and 92.5. It is difficult to go lower than that in threes. looking at where cash is trading. In fact, if you did not want a low one I would have gone 93 at least." (March 16, 2006, Submitter's response to swaps trader's request for a high one-month and low three-month U.S. Dollar LIBOR);
>
> 5) "Always happy to help, leave it with me, Sir." (March 20,2006, Submitter's response to a request);
>
> 6) "Done ... for you big boy..." (April 7, 2006, Submitter's response to swaps trader requests for low one-month and three-month U.S. Dollar LIBOR)...[614]

Barclays also manipulated Euribor in a similar fashion to benefit the bets the bank took with its derivative positions.

> Just as the NY Swaps Desk openly discussed requests to LIBOR submitters, Barclays' Euro swaps traders' requests to Barclays' Euribor submitters to change their submissions to benefit the traders' derivatives trading positions were an open, common and pervasive practice on the desk.
>
> Multiple traders engaged in this conduct, and no attempt was made by any of the traders to conceal the requests from supervisors at Barclays during the more than four-year period in which the activity occurred. In fact, traders would often shout across the desk to fellow traders to confirm there were no conflicting requests before they sent their requests to the Euribor submitters, and, on occasion, the traders discussed their requests with trading desk managers....[615]
>
> 1) June 1,2006:
>
> - Senior Euro Swaps Trader: "Hi [Euribor Submitter], is it too late to ask for a low 3m?"
> - Euribor Submitter: "Just about to put them in.....so no."
>
> 2) September 7, 2006:
>
> - Senior Euro Swaps Trader: "i have a huge 1m fixing today and it would really help to have a low 1m tx a lot."

614 ibid, page 10

615 ibid, page 13

- Euribor Submitter: "I'll do my best."
- Senior Euro Swaps Trader: "because I am aware some other bank need a very high one .... if you could push it very low it would help. Ihave50bnfixing."...[616]

Barclays was not alone in rigging Euribor. It coordinated with other banks to manipulate Euribor to benefit each of the bank's derivative positions.

> During the period from at least mid-2005 through mid-2008, certain Barclays Euro swaps traders, led by the same former Barclays' senior Euro swaps trader, coordinated with traders at certain other panel banks to have their respective Euribor submitters make certain Euribor submissions in order to affect the official EBF Euribor fixing. These requests to and among the traders were made to benefit the traders' respective derivatives trading positions and either maximize their profits or minimize their losses....[617]
>
> December 5, 2006:
>
> - Barclays' Senior Euro Swaps Trader requested that traders at Banks A, Band C have their Euribor submitters make a high six-month Euribor submission.
> - When the trader at Bank C stated that he needed the same submission, Barclays' Senior Euro Swaps Trader agreed to make the request of the Barclays Euribor submitters.
> - Barclays' Senior Euro Swaps Trader emailed the Barclays Senior Euribor Submitter: "hi [Senior Euribor Submitter] is it possible to have a high 6m fixing [sic]? Where do you think it will fix?"
> - Barclays' Senior Euribor Submitter responded: "Hi [Senior Euro Swaps Trader]. We have posted 3.73, hope that helps..can put in higher if you like?"
> - Barclays' Senior Euro Swaps Trader replied: "that's fine tx a lot for your help."...[618]

Barclays and the other banks also manipulated Libor to hide the stress they were experiencing in funding their bank with unsecured loans. The interbank lending market on which Libor is based froze. The banks with deposits to lend could not assess the risk or solvency of the banks looking to borrow. As a

---

616 ibid, page 14

617 ibid, page 15

618 ibid, page 17

result, they stopped lending and the market froze. Barclays and the other banks made up the rates they submitted hoping these rates would convince market participants the banks were stronger than they really were. These rates were intended to deceive.

> During the financial crisis period, Barclays directed its U.S. Dollar LIBOR submitters to lower their daily U.S. Dollar LIBOR submissions in order to protect Barclays' reputation against what it believed were negative and unfair media and market perceptions that Barclays had a liquidity problem based in part on its high LIBOR submissions…[619]
>
> For example, on November 28,2007, Barclays' senior U.S. Dollar LIBOR submitter emailed a large group of Barclays' employees, including the senior Barclays Treasury managers, stating "LIBORs are not reflecting the true cost of money. I am going to set ..., probably at the top of the range of rates set by libor contributors ... [T]he true cost of money is anything from 5- 15 basis points higher." A senior Barclays Treasury manager endorsed the submissions, replying "[f]ine on LIBOR settings — thanks for remaining pragmatic but at the upper end."[620]

Manipulating Libor breaks bank solvency measure

Recall that Libor is intended to reflect the rate that creditworthy banks pay to borrow on an unsecured basis from other banks. But what happens if doubt is cast about just how creditworthy these banks really are? As doubt rises about the ability of the banks to repay their unsecured borrowing, the cost of this borrowing as reflected by Libor should increase relative to other interest rates.

And there was plenty of reason to doubt the banks' ability to repay. Beginning on August 9, 2007, doubts began to grow when BNP Paribas said it couldn't value sub-prime mortgage-backed securities. Market participants knew these banks were exposed to subprime mortgage-backed securities and related derivatives. However, because of a lack of valuation transparency, market participants could not determine the extent of this exposure and which of the banks were solvent and which banks were not.

Doubts grew stronger with the failure of first, Bear Stearns and then Lehman Brothers. Ultimately, these doubts and the inability to assess the borrowing banks' ability to repay resulted in the interbank lending market freezing. The banks with deposits to lend simply didn't want to take the gamble on the opaque borrowing banks.

---

619 ibid, page 19

620 ibid, page 21

The change in Libor interest rates did not show this inability to assess who was solvent. By manipulating the rates, banks effectively broke this measure of bank solvency.

Knowing that their submissions would be disclosed, the banks knew that telling the truth would be to admit how precarious their financial situation was. Instead, the banks gamed the Libor interest rate submission process.

Barclays was not alone in manipulating Libor to hide its financial condition and what it would actually have paid to borrow on an unsecured basis. As reported by the CFTC in discussing the manipulation of Libor by Lloyds:

> On April 16, 2008, the *Wall Street Journal* published an article questioning whether LIBOR panel banks were making LIBOR submissions lower than what they were actually paying for funds in the money markets to prevent the market from concluding that the banks were desperate for cash. The BBA, in response to this article, began an inquiry into the integrity of the LIBOR fixing. On May 6, 2008, an HBOS senior manager in an email to two other HBOS senior managers and other HBOS personnel, including the senior manager of the LIBOR submitters, reported that "it will be readily apparent that in the current environment no bank can be seen to be an outlier. The submissions of all banks are published and we could not afford to be significantly away from the pack." Later, on August 8, 2008, the same HBOS Senior Manager circulated to HBOS managers and senior managers a presentation in which he stated, *inter alia,* that:
>
>> As a bank we are extremely careful about the rates we pay in different markets for different types of funds as paying too much risks not only causing a re-pricing of all short term borrowing but, more importantly in this climate, **may give the impression of HBOS being a desperate borrower and so lead to a general withdrawal of wholesale lines.** (emphasis added)
>
> The HBOS LIBOR submitters' supervisor ("HBOS LIBOR Supervisor") understood the importance of not being an outlier in LIBOR submissions. He noted in an August 29, 2008 email to several HBOS LIBOR submitters that HBOS should not be a "material outlier," at least with respect to its Sterling and Euro LIBOR submissions.[621]
>
> On September 26, 2008, after discussing the HBOS LIBOR submissions with more senior HBOS managers, the HBOS LIBOR Supervisor told the U.S. Dollar LIBOR Submitter that the U.S. Dollar LIBOR submissions should be

621 Commodity Futures Trading Commission Order (2014, July 28), *Lloyds Banking Group PLC,* http://www.cftc.gov/ucm/groups/public/@lrenforcementactions/documents/legalpleading/enflloydsorderdf072814.pdf, page 14.

> lower relative to the other panel members and directed him to reduce the spread between the HBOS U.S. Dollar LIBOR submissions and the submissions of the other panel members.
>
> That same day, the HBOS U.S. Dollar LIBOR Submitter, in a chat with an employee of another financial institution, stated, "youll like this ive been pressured by senior management to bring my rates down into line with everyone else."[622]

As reported by the NY Fed in its April 11, 2008 MarketSource: Weekly Market Review,

> On the margins, some have suggested that the relatively high stop out rate at this week's $50 billion TAF [Term Auction Facility] auction was indicative of the ongoing strains in the interbank market. The TAF auction stopped out at 2.82 percent, or 71 basis points over the minimum bid rate, which is the highest spread since the inception of the TAF program. The stop out rate of 2.82 percent also exceeded the British Bankers' Association (BBA) LIBOR fixing rate on that day of 2.72 percent....
>
> Further, the fact that the TAF stopped out above LIBOR has also triggered a significant amount of questions over the accuracy of the BBA's LIBOR fixing rate. Over the past few weeks, the 1-month term dollar deposit rate and the 1-month LIBOR fixing have diverged by as much as 30 basis points. The divergence between the two rates is similar to that observed during prior periods of heightened market stress, most notably in August and early December 2007.
>
> Our contacts at LIBOR contributing banks have indicated a tendency to under-report actual borrowing costs when reporting to the BBA in order to limit the potential for speculation about the institutions' liquidity problems....
>
> Though a different set of contributors than the LIBOR panel, data collected by the Federal Reserve Bank of New York on actual brokered fed funds trades may provide a more complete picture of the dispersion of rates paid for dollar funding. This data shows that over recent sessions some banks have paid as much as 10 percent for overnight funds.[623]

By breaking the bank solvency measure, banks hid the fact the banks with deposits to lend were losing and eventually lost trust in the ability of the banks looking to borrow to repay their loans.

---

622 ibid, page 15

623 Miu, Jason (2008, April 11), NY Fed MarketSource Weekly Market Review, Federal Reserve Bank of New York, http://www.newyorkfed.org/newsevents/news/markets/2012/libor/April_11_2008_Internal_FRBNY_Weekly_Market_Review.pdf, page 2.

The question is where were the financial regulators when the banks manipulated Libor and presented a false picture of their financial health to other market participants? Did the financial regulators permit this activity as part of preventing a meltdown of the financial system?

What did the financial regulators know and when did they know it?

It turns out that the global financial regulators knew the banks were gaming their Libor submissions to present a favorable financial picture. The New York Fed released a transcript of an April 11, 2008 call between an employee, Fabiola Ravazzolo, and a trader at an unidentified bank. They discussed the trader's bank, along with the other banks, was falsifying its Libor submissions.

> : [The Libor submission rules] actually say that it is where we could um borrow money.
>
> FR: You could
>
> : So where, um…
>
> FR: Borrow, so not necessary where you are borrowing?
>
> : Yeah, because the-the panel is supposed to be, a, um, a panel of prime banks
>
> FR: Yeah.
>
> : And so it's where those banks, um, decide they, they could actually borrow cash in the interbank market….Now, um, you know, obviously there has been a lot of speculation about LIBORs and, you know…I've read some really interesting articles about them….Um, and uh, w-, you know we, w-we, we strongly feel it's true to say that…Dollar, Dollar LIBORs do not reflect where the market is trading which is you know the same as a lot of other people have said….Um, wha-, it depends on which part of the curve you're looking at….Um, currently, we would say that in the three months, um, if we as a prime bank had to go in the interbank market and borrow cash, it's probably eight to ten basis points above where LIBOR is fixing.
>
> FR: So you're above ten to fifteen?
>
> : About eight or ten above. If, if, if we had to go in the market and
>
> FR: Yeah.
>
> : Properly borrow money, it would be
>
> FR: Yeah.
>
> : About eight to ten above and in the one year
>
> FR: Okay.
>
> : It would probably be about twenty basis points in the market.
>
> FR: And, and why do you think that there is this, this discrepancy? Is it because banks maybe they are not reporting what they should or is it um…
>
> : Well, let's, let's put it like this and I'm gonna be really frank and honest with you.

FR: No that's why I am asking you [laugher] you know, yeah [inaudible] [laughter]

: You know, you know we, we went through a period where...We were putting in where we really thought we would be able to borrow cash in the interbank market and it was...Above where everyone else was publishing rates...And the next thing we knew, there was um, an article in the Financial Times, charting our LIBOR contributions and comparing it with other banks and inferring that this meant that we had a problem raising cash in the interbank market.

FR: Yeah.

: And um, our share price went down.

FR: Yes.

: So it's never supposed to be the prerogative of a, a money market dealer to affect their company share value.

FR: Okay.

: And so we just fit in with the rest of the crowd, if you like.

FR: Okay.

: So, we know that we're not posting um, an honest LIBOR.

FR: Okay.

: And yet and yet we are doing it, because, um, if we didn't do it...It draws, um, unwanted attention on ourselves.

FR: Okay, I got you then.

: And at a time when the market is so um, gossipy, and...Prone to... Speculate about other names...In the market...It's um...Not a useful thing for us as an organization...To do. And in fact, wha-what we've noticed is almost like um, a um, um perverse thing where people that we know that are paying for money actually put in the lowest LIBOR rates.

FR: Okay.

: So it, it's almost to um, you know the ones that need cash the most put in the lowest, lowest rates.[624]

The unidentified trader tells the NY Fed the bank the trader works for is knowingly falsifying its Libor submissions to avoid calling attention to itself and having it stock price drop as a result of faulty conclusions. These conclusions were particularly faulty according to the trader because the banks paying the highest price to access money in the unsecured interbank market are submitting the lowest rates.

---

624 Federal Reserve Bank of New York (2012, July 13), April 11, 2008: transcript of phone call between Barclays employee and analyst in the Markets Group of the New York Fed, Federal Reserve Bank of New York, http://www.newyorkfed.org/newsevents/news/markets/2012/libor/April_11_2008_transcript.pdf, page 7.

In the 1930s, banks believed their best protection against rumors was for banks to provide valuation transparency. With valuation transparency, banks wouldn't lie about their Libor submissions because market participants could verify these submissions against actual trades made by the banks. With valuation transparency, the media would not have singled out the bank to infer it was having trouble raising cash in the interbank market as it would have seen all the banks were having trouble accessing the interbank market.

As the result of opacity, by 2008, banks perceived their best protection against rumors was to lie. In the presence of opacity, banks needed to create a story to justify lying to market participants. When it came to manipulating Libor, banks justified providing false submissions and hiding useful, relevant information by pointing out that truthful disclosure would hurt their share price.

The conversation then moves on to discuss how Libor doesn't represent reality. Banks engage in a game of providing submissions that won't call attention to themselves. Finally, the conversation focuses on what it will take to fix Libor. The trader offers up a suggestion: transparency.

> : And we need to kind of clear the table with ea- with each other, you know. We need to um make this uh, I know people use all these words like transparency and that they're all very easy to, to say but fundamentally at the bottom of this for instance at Barclays Bank, what is stopping him lending three month Euros to
>
> FR: Y up.
>
> : Uh, BNP Paribas Paris at four seventy, instead of lending him some overnight money at three ninety?
>
> FR: Okay. Mm hmm.
>
> : You know there's eighty basis points there. Um, I, I need to be able to start trading back for interest rate views and compelling interest rate views and yield and carry rather than just on the liquidity side, you know, and I need to sort of start feeling to myself, um, I don't need to be scared of all my interbank counterparties. I don't need to fear that if I lend them some three month money that during those three months they might go broke and not be able to pay me back, you know?
>
> FR: Mm hmm. Mm hmm.
>
> : Um, so I-I kind of need to um, kind of educ-educate myself a little bit you know, I need to get, get my own confidence levels up as well, Fa-Fabiola.[625]

The banks know opacity prevents market participants from knowing who is telling the truth and who is lying about their financial condition in their Libor submission. As predicted by game theory, the banks experiencing difficulties are

[625] ibid, page 29

lying about their current condition. The banks experiencing difficulties think they are better off lying because they won't be the subject of a Financial Times article and its unflattering inferences.

This leaves the banks that would otherwise not lie in an interesting position: tell the truth or lie too. To avoid being the subject of a Financial Times article and its unflattering inferences, these banks also have an incentive to lie and submit lower rates.

> FR: I understand. No, no and I completely understand the, the point is that ah you know, you, you, you always try to, to try and help for everybody you know, and this is so bizarre what is going on in the market
>
> : It is bizarre. Yeah
>
> FR: Because this is creating
>
> : We felt very un-, very
>
> FR: Uncertainties.
>
> : I mean we, it- it's true words to…Say we feel very…Very uncomfortable with it.
>
> FR: I understand now.
>
> : But, the-the position we find ourselves in, is one where we can't really fight it.
>
> FR: I know, I know…You have to accept it. I understand
>
> : Yeah.
>
> FR: Despite it's against what you would like to do.
>
> : Yes.
>
> FR: I understand completely
>
> : Yeah.[626]

The trader confirms the results predicted by game theory.

The way to get a transparent fixing is to require the banks to provide valuation transparency. Then, Libor can be based off of all the actual interbank deals.

How did the NY Fed respond to hearing Libor was being manipulated?

The NY Fed claimed its response to hearing Libor was being manipulated was to call attention to the problem and press for reform. According to the NY Fed,

> An important and longstanding role of the New York Fed Markets Group is to monitor a wide range of markets for the purpose of understanding and reporting on market conditions and market functioning….[627]

---

626 ibid page 14

627 Federal Reserve Bank of New York (2012, July 13), New York Fed Responds to Congressional Request for Information on Barclays — LIBOR Matter, Federal

The Federal Reserve has two responsibilities: conducting monetary policy and supervising and regulating the banks. The New York Fed Markets Group is in the area concerned with conducting monetary policy and not in the supervision and regulation of the banks.

This is a very important point because it factors into how the New York Fed responds to an admission of rigging Libor and the price of credit.

> Following the onset of the financial crisis in 2007, markets monitoring played a critical role by identifying the nature and location of rapidly mutating financial stress. Markets Group analysts engaged with market participants — including staff at Barclays — to better understand the nature of market stress. In the course of these exchanges, market participants reported dysfunction in the form of illiquidity and anomalous pricing across many different markets.[628]

Dysfunction is a nice way of saying that every market where there was opacity effectively froze.

> Among the information gathered through markets monitoring in the fall of 2007 and early 2008, were indications of problems with the accuracy of LIBOR reporting. LIBOR is a benchmark interest rate set in London by the British Bankers' Association ("BBA") under the broad jurisdiction of the UK authorities, based on submissions by a panel of mostly non-US banks.
>
> The LIBOR panel banks self-report the rate at which they would be able to borrow funds in the interbank money market for various periods of time. As the interbank lending markets dried up these estimates became increasingly hypothetical.[629]

The reason the interbank lending market dried up was the banks with deposits to lend could not assess the risk or solvency of the banks looking to borrow because these banks were black boxes. Rather than gamble on the contents of these black boxes, the banks with deposits to lend simply stopped lending and the interbank lending market froze.

Unfreezing and keeping unfrozen the interbank lending market requires the banks to provide valuation transparency. With this information, bank with deposits to lend can assess the risk and solvency of the banks looking to borrow. The banks with deposits to lend can use this assessment to adjust both the amount and price of their exposure to each of the banks looking to borrow.

Reserve Bank of New York, http://www.newyorkfed.org/newsevents/news/markets/2012/Barclays_LIBOR_Matter.html

628 ibid

629 ibid

> Suggestions that some banks could be underreporting their LIBOR in order to avoid appearing weak were present in anecdotal reports and mass-distribution emails, including from Barclays, as well as in a December 2007 phone call with Barclays noting that reported "Libors" appeared unrealistically low.
>
> As market strains intensified in early 2008, to better understand the nature and extent of the potential problems with LIBOR, analysts in the Markets Group gathered additional and more in-depth information.
>
> As part of this broad effort, on April 11, an analyst from the Markets Group queried a Barclays employee in detail as to the extent of problems with LIBOR reporting.
>
> The Barclays employee explained that Barclays was underreporting its rate to avoid the stigma associated with being an outlier with respect to its LIBOR submissions, relative to other participating banks. The Barclays employee also stated that in his opinion other participating banks were also under-reporting their LIBOR submissions. The Barclays employee did not state that his bank had been involved in manipulating the rate for its own trading advantage.[630]

There was no reason for the Barclays employee to report the bank was manipulating the rate for its own trading advantage. By definition, it was manipulating the rate for its own trading advantage. Do you think Barclays took on positions where it would lose money knowing Libor was being artificially suppressed?

> Immediately following this call, the analyst notified senior management in the Markets Group that a contact at Barclays had stated that underreporting of LIBOR was prevalent in the market, and had occurred at Barclays.
>
> That same day — April 11, 2008 — analysts in the Markets Group reported on the questions surrounding the accuracy of the BBA's LIBOR fixing rate in their regular weekly briefing note. The briefing note cited reports from contacts at LIBOR submitting banks that banks were underreporting borrowing rates to avoid signaling weakness.
>
> In accordance with standard practice for briefing notes produced by the Markets Group, this report was circulated to senior officials at the New York Fed, the Federal Reserve Board of Governors, other Federal Reserve Banks, and U.S. Department of Treasury....[631]

So following protocol, the Federal Reserve and U.S. Treasury knew the Libor interest rates and the global credit markets was being manipulated.

---

630 ibid

631 ibid

> Five days later, the first media report on problems with LIBOR emerged. From this point onwards the notion that banks were underreporting LIBOR in order to avoid signaling weakness was widely discussed in the press and in market commentary.[632]

While banks underreporting Libor was discussed, in the absence of valuation transparency and disclosure of each bank's interbank borrowing details, there was no way for market participants to know which banks were underreporting. There was also no way for market participants to know whether Libor interest rates were being manipulated by 1/100th of 1%, 1/10th of 1% or even 1%.

The fact underreporting of Libor was being discussed also didn't mean that market participants condoned it.

> In late April and into May 2008, New York Fed officials met to determine what steps might be taken to address the problems with LIBOR.
>
> The New York Fed also acted to brief other U.S. agencies. On May 1 Tim Geithner, then President of the New York Fed, raised the subject at a meeting of the President's Working Group on Financial Markets ("PWG"), a body that comprised the heads of the principal regulatory agencies in the U.S., chaired by Treasury. On May 6 New York Fed staff briefed senior officials from the U.S Treasury in detail.
>
> On May 20 the Markets Group sent a further report on problems with LIBOR to the broad set of senior officials who receive its regular analysis.... On June 5, New York Fed officials also briefed an interagency working group comprised of staff from the PWG...[633]
>
> New York Fed officials also met with representatives from the British Bankers' Association to express their concerns and establish in greater depth the flaws in the LIBOR-setting process. The New York Fed analysis culminated in a set of recommendations to reform LIBOR, which was finalized in late May.[634]

New York Fed officials met with the British Bankers' Association as it was in charge of putting together Libor, to "express their concerns and establish in greater depth the flaws in the Libor-setting process". The result was a set of recommendation to reform Libor.

All of this seems perfectly reasonable until you take a step back and realize the banks manipulating the Libor interest rates control the British Bankers' Association. Is there any reason to believe that the banks will recommend changes to Libor-setting process that will prevent them from continuing to

632 ibid

633 ibid

634 ibid

manipulate Libor interest rates, particularly because the banks do not want to disclose their difficulty raising funds on an unsecured basis?

> On June 1, 2008, Mr. Geithner emailed Mervyn King, the Governor of the Bank of England, a report, entitled "Recommendations for Enhancing the Credibility of LIBOR."
>
> Among the recommendations were specific proposals to improve the integrity and transparency of the rate-setting process, including the suggestion that LIBOR submissions should be subject to internal and external audit of the accuracy of the reporting by banks....
>
> Shortly afterwards, Mr. King confirmed to Mr. Geithner that he had transmitted the New York Fed recommendations to the British Bankers' Association soon afterwards. After putting forward recommendations for LIBOR reform to the UK authorities, the New York Fed continued to monitor for problems related to LIBOR.[635]

Based on the response by the NY Fed, you would never have guessed it had been told by Barclays that it and the other banks were manipulating for their own benefit the interest rate on hundreds of trillions of dollars of financial products.

Based on the response by the NY Fed, you would never have guessed it had any idea that artificially holding down Libor saved the banks money.

Based on the response by the NY Fed, you would never have guessed it had any problem with the integrity of the global credit markets being compromised.

Based on the response by the NY Fed, you would never have guess it thought manipulating the Libor interest rates may in fact be illegal.

The Geithner e-mail

So, what did Mr. Geithner say in his June 1, 2008 e-mail to Sir Mervyn King? Did he say a trader from Barclays had told the NY Fed Barclays was systematically under-reporting through its Libor submissions it true cost of funds in the unsecured interbank loan market? Did he say the same trader said banks paying the most for funds were reporting the lowest rates?

What he said was:

> Mervyn:
>
> We spoke briefly in Basel about the BBAs LIBOR regime, and you said you would welcome some suggestions.

[635] ibid

> I have attached a list of recommendations prepared by my staff. We would welcome a chance to discuss these and would be grateful if you would give us some sense of what changes are possible.
>
> With best wishes,
> Tim[636]

Nowhere in this email or the 80 pages of emails[637] the Bank of England released showing its communications with the Fed and the British Bankers' Association does the Fed or anyone else tell the Bank of England a Barclays' trader has said Barclays is submitting manipulated rates.

On the other hand, on May 22, 2008 there is an internal Bank of England document that suggests the Bank of England has some idea that Libor was being manipulated.

> There is a long standing perception that Libor by virtue of the manner in which it is set is open to distortions: panel banks have no obligations to trade or to have traded at the rates that they submit, so it is at least *plausible* that these are influenced by commercial incentives….[638]
>
> And in the extreme conditions of the last eight months banks have been subject to the more powerful incentive of avoiding **stigma** from being seen to submit high rates reflective of what they are actually paying[639]

However, in defending the Bank of England's failure to understand that the Libor interest rate was being fiddled with, Mervyn King said

> We had no evidence of wrongdoing (in that respect), none was supplied to us and the evidence that you cite here, there were plenty of academic

---

636 Federal Reserve Bank of New York (2012, July 13), Tim Geithner e-mail to Mervyn King with recommendations to fix Libor, Federal Reserve Bank of New York, http://www.newyorkfed.org/newsevents/news/markets/2012/libor/June_1_2008_LIBOR_recommendations.pdf

637 Bank of England releases Libor correspondence: the emails (2012, July 20), The Telegraph, http://www.telegraph.co.uk/finance/newsbysector/banksandfinance/9415004/Bank-of-England-releases-Libor-correspondence-the-emails.html

638 Bank of England (2012, July 20), Libor: Further information and correspondence in relation to the email chain, Bank of England, http://www.bankofengland.co.uk/publications/Documents/other/treasurycommittee/financialstability/emailchain.pdf, page 22.

639 ibid, page 23

> articles that looked into it and said we cannot see in the data any evidence of manipulation.[640]

The way Libor interest rates were calculated using self-certified submissions created the veil behind which Libor could be manipulated. Without disclosure of actual trades, how could anyone know if the submissions were fiddled with or not? The NY Fed stumbled upon this fact when it tried to confirm the confession by the Barclays trader that Barclays was manipulating its submissions.

While Mr. Geithner's email isn't very exciting, maybe this is what constitutes a call between regulators to take immediate action. If so, maybe the list of recommendation prepared by the NY Fed staff will address the issue of how to end manipulation of the Libor interest rates and incorporate the trader's recommendation of a transparent fixing.

The recommendations for fixing Libor from the NY Fed's staff

Attached to Mr. Geithner's email to Sir Mervyn King were the following recommendations:

> Recommendations for Enhancing the Credibility of LIBOR
> FRBNY Markets and Research and Statistics Groups
>
> 1) Strengthen governance and establish a credible reporting procedure
>
> To improve the integrity and transparency of the rate-setting process, we recommend the BBA work with LIBOR panel banks to establish and publish best practices for calculating and reporting rates, including procedures designed to prevent accidental or deliberate misreporting. The BBA could require that a reporting bank's internal and external auditors confirm adherence to these best practices and attest to the accuracy of banks' LIBOR rates.
>
> To further enhance perceptions of the BBA as au objective intermediary in the rate-setting process, we recommend greater transparency with respect to the financial relationships between the BBA and the panel banks, and around the BBA's financial interests in LIBOR.[641]

640 Bank of England and FSA before MPs: quotes (2012, July 17), The Telegraph, http://www.telegraph.co.uk/finance/financialcrisis/9405522/Bank-of-England-and-FSA-before-MPs-quotes.html

641 Federal Reserve Bank of New York (2012, July 13), NY Fed's recommendations to fix Libor, Federal Reserve Bank of New York, http://www.newyorkfed.org/newsevents/news/markets/2012/libor/June_1_2008_LIBOR_recommendations.pdf

So the NY Fed would like to see the banks document their procedure for making up their Libor submissions and have each bank's auditors confirm the bank faithfully submitted completely made up numbers.

> 2) Increase the size and broaden the composition of the USD panel…
> 3) Add a second USD LIBOR fixing for the U.S. market…
> 4) Specify transaction size
>
> Banks currently quote the rate at which they could borrow in "reasonable market size." To eliminate some of the ambiguity that comes with this definition, we recommend that the BBA provide more specific guidance as to the size of the transaction being referenced in the reported quoted rates….
>
> 5) Only report the LIBOR maturities for which there is a net benefit…
>
> We recommend that, in consultation with panel banks, the BBA adopt guidance on consistent methods for determining quotes across the range of maturities of LIBOR. In addition, we recommend that the BBA consider reducing the number of maturities for which it solicits quotes and publishes rates. For tenors such as the 3-month tenor, LIBOR quotes provide valuable information to the public because of the volume of activity occurring at that tenor, while quotes for tenors at which little or no trading occurs, such as the 11-month, are less indicative and therefore less valuable……
>
> 6) Eliminate incentive to misreport
>
> If the combination of best practices and audit recommendations in (1) above seems unlikely to be sufficiently effective in ensuring accurate reporting, a complimentary approach might be to adopt the following process for collecting, calculating, and publishing LIBOR rates. The BBA could collect quotes from all members of the expanded panel, and then randomly select a subset of 16 banks from which the trimmed mean would be calculated. The names and quotes for the 8 banks whose rates are averaged to calculate the LIBOR fixing would be published. The banks' whose reports fall above or below the midrange would not be publicly identified, nor would the level of their outlying rates. This random sampling from an expanded panel would lessen the likelihood that the market would draw a negative inference regarding a particular bank's continued absence from the list of published quotes.[642]

Absent from these recommendation is any change to the process that would actually end manipulation of the Libor interest rates and result in a transparent fixing. Nowhere does the NY Fed say each bank should disclose on an ongoing basis all of its transactions in the unsecured interbank lending market and Libor should be based off of these transactions.

---

642 ibid

So where did these recommendations come from?

Banks frame discussion of Libor reform and resulting recommendations

To its credit, the NY Fed investigated the credibility of Libor and how to fix it. In a May 20, 2008 internal memo, the NY Fed indicated it talked to market participants about what is the problem with and how to restore the credibility of Libor.

> Most of the recent concern regarding LIBOR has focused on U.S. dollar LIBOR panel, and in particular on what might be called its "credibility" or "accuracy" the question of whether panel banks accurately report the rates at which they could actually borrow unsecured dollars. Several features of the LIBOR process and definition contribute to these concerns:
>
> - Banks quote the rate at which they "could borrow funds" and these rates are published. This may lead to some deliberate misreporting designed to avoid the stigma of revealing high funding costs.
> - The panel is asked to provide quotes that are subject to ambiguity along at least two dimensions. First, the transaction size is not clearly specified. Second, quotes are often given for maturities (e.g., 7-month LIBOR) or in market conditions (e.g., now) in which there is little or no actual interbank term activity. The lack of clarity results in panel members using dissimilar methods for determining quotes.
>
> Many market participants feel the BBA does not currently have sufficient monitoring mechanisms in place to ensure the quality or validity of the quotes.
>
> Note: although some analysts point out that the panel banks may have incentives to misreport in order to manipulate the level of the LIBOR fixing, and thereby influence their funding or derivative positions, this is not the primary driver of recent alleged misquotes.[643]

The primary driver of the alleged misquotes is in fact to influence the bank's funding. If a bank were to accurately quote where it was borrowing, there is the fear that it would attach a stigma to the bank and this stigma would result in the bank having to pay even more for its funding.

Is there any evidence that banks were misreporting?

643 Cheun, Samuel, Raskin, Matt (2008, May 20), NY Fed's MarketSource, Federal Reserve Bank of New York, http://www.newyorkfed.org/newsevents/news/markets/2012/libor/MarketSource_Report_May202008.pdf, page 2.

> Around the time the WSJ article first reported on this matter in mid-April, we heard from several Eurodollars brokers and bank funding desks that many LIBOR banks were bidding for funds up to 25 basis points above their LIBOR quotes in the same maturity on the same day.
>
> The BBA also received a number of formal complaints along these lines.
>
> Several of these market participants suggested that discrepancies between funding rates and LIBOR quotes had existed since at least last August, but had gotten marginally worse since mid-March.[644]

The NY Fed found that manipulation of the Libor interest rates by banks to avoid any stigma was notable since August 2007. What happened in August 2007 that would have called into question the ability of the banks to repay unsecured debt? The financial crisis started with BNP Paribas' announcement it could not value subprime mortgage-backed securities.

The manipulation of Libor to hide the difference between what banks were actually paying for funds and the rates they submitted increased in mid-March 2008 at approximately the time that Bear Stearns faced bankruptcy and was taken over by JPMorgan.

The size of the gap between reality and Libor was already 25 basis points and this was several months before Lehman Brothers failed.

> Additionally, around days on which the BBA's efforts to address LIBOR have received media attention, there have been fairly dramatic increases in the LIBOR fixings.
>
> For example, in the two days surrounding the WSJ's April 16 article, 3-month LIBOR increased 17 bps, which was the largest two-day increase in the rate since August 9.
>
> Earlier this week, as the integrity of LIBOR again received attention, 1-year LIBOR increased 21 bps, and OIS and fed funds-LIBOR basis swaps suggest that a large portion of this rise was not due to a re-pricing of policy expectations.[645]

So, every time the media started poking around into the possibility that Libor interest rates were being manipulated, the rates increased so it was closer to reflecting the banks' actual cost of borrowing in the unsecured interbank lending market.

> Beyond the anecdotal evidence and LIBOR re-sets, it is difficult to find convincing evidence of actual misreporting.

---

644 ibid, page 2

645 ibid, page 2

> Few public sources of data on actual Eurodollar transaction rates exist, and again, the extent of credit tiering makes it difficult to extrapolate from what data there is.[646]

The NY Fed staff discovered that in the absence of valuation transparency under which the banks disclose their actual transaction data it is impossible to see or confirm the banks actually manipulating the Libor interest rates.

The NY Fed already has a confession by the trader at Barclays, but it does not have the data it needs to confirm this confession.

Having uncovered the need for banks to report their actual transaction data, do the NY Fed recommendations for fixing Libor include basing Libor on actual disclosed transactions or at least the disclosure of actual transaction data? As shown by the list of recommendations sent to Sir Mervyn King, the answer is a definitive no!

So, who are these market participants that suggested what changes should be made to how Libor interest rates are calculated?

> A variety of changes aimed at enhancing LIBOR's credibility has been proposed by market participants, and seem to be under consideration by the BBA.[647]

While we don't know the specific market participants who suggested changes, we do know that their suggested changes are under consideration by the BBA. The BBA is the British Bankers' Association. It oversees the calculation of the Libor interest rates. It is also a lobbying organization controlled by and run for the benefit of the banks that just happen to be manipulating Libor.

Here is the NY Fed effectively asking the banks that are manipulating the Libor interest rates what should be done to prevent banks from rigging these rates in the future. The NY Fed acts like it expects the very banks making money on a risk-free basis by betting on derivatives and rigging the Libor interest rates so they win to actually tell them how to prevent the banks from manipulating Libor. The NY Fed acts like it expects the very banks hiding their true financial condition by rigging the Libor interest rates to actually tell them how to prevent the banks manipulating Libor.

The NY Fed should know the banks and the associations they control have every incentive to protect the status quo and not bring about changes that will lower the banks' profitability or expose the true financial condition of the banks.

646 ibid, page 3

647 ibid, page 3

How credible can the banks' recommendations for fixing the Libor-setting process be when they have just told you they are lying about what might be the most important interest rates in the global financial system? The banks, led by Barclays, have confessed that they will lie to enhance their profitability and avoid any stigma in the market place. Yet, the NY Fed treats the recommendations made by these banks as credible.

At a minimum, the banks are able to use the BBA to frame the discussion about how to reform Libor. After all, the BBA runs Libor. By having the BBA propose changes, the bankers are able to further their agenda of retaining opacity in the Libor rate-setting process.

These proposed changes include, but are not limited to:

- Changing the definition of the quoted rate, so that it no longer references the banks' own borrowing costs. For example, Euribor asks its panel banks for the rate at which one "prime bank" could obtain funds from another. Interestingly, this was the definition used by LIBOR until 1998.
- Making some or all of the individual quotes anonymous, so that even if the quotes refer to own-borrowing rates, banks at the high-end of the rate spectrum won't fear reporting accurately.
- Specifying transaction size, which could adjust flexibly to market conditions.
- Reducing the number of maturities quoted. The high number of maturities may lead to formulaic responses, and it is not clear that the market highly values, for example, a 7-month LIBOR quote. A key issue here may be the existence of derivatives contracts that reference all existing maturities.
- Increasing the size of the panel and including more U.S. institutions, so that the resulting rate is more representative of the global demand for unsecured interbank dollar funding, and less susceptible to issues concentrated within any particular region's banking sector.
- Changing the time of the fixing, or adding a second fixing that occurs when US-based sources of dollar funding are active.
- Implementing an audit process designed to ensure that reporting procedures and quotes adhere to an agreed and published set of best practices.
- Using a different measure of central tendency to calculate the LIBOR fixings from the individual quotes — e.g., the median instead of trimmed mean — with the goal of further reducing incentives to misreport in order to manipulate the level of the fixing.[648]

---

648 ibid, page 3

Every recommendation for fixing Libor sent by Mr. Geithner to Sir Mervyn King was based on a recommendation from market participants that had been filtered through the banks' lobbying group. The lobbying group representing banks who were engaged in manipulating Libor for profit and to avoid market stigma. The lobbying group representing banks that wanted to protect the opacity of the Libor interest rate setting process and therefore would never suggest using the actual transactions as disclosed through valuation transparency.

Regulators consider overhaul of Libor rate-setting process

To no one's surprise, the opacity surrounding the setting of the Libor interest rates allowed the big banks to manipulate these rates and make untold billions of dollars. When it finally came out that the banks were manipulating Libor, the global financial regulators sprang to action to reform the Libor interest rate setting process.

Leading the charge in the UK was Martin Wheatley. His commission asked for recommendations on how to fix the Libor interest rate setting process. I responded to the request for comment calling for Libor to be based on actual trades that were disclosed as part of the banks' disclosure under valuation transparency.

There were others who also called for basing Libor on actual trades. Daniel Sheard, chief investment officer at $60 billion asset manager GAM U.K. Ltd. observed there is no:

> [V]alid argument for why it can't be based on actual trades.[649]

Rosa Abrantes-Metz, an associate professor with New York University's Stern School of Business and author of a 2008 paper entitled "Libor Manipulation?" observed:

> [B]asing it on actual transactions ... would only be disruptive if current quotes are inaccurate ... resistance is suspicious.[650]

My comment was not published as part of the public record nor did my comment or these other calls for basing Libor interest rates off of actual transactions appear to factor into the commission's decision. Instead, it adopted the banks' recommendations on how to overhaul the setting of the Libor interest rates.

---

649 Vaughan, Liam, Finch, Gavin (2012, June 28), Libor Guardians Said to Resist Changes to Broken Rate, Bloomberg, http://www.bloomberg.com/news/2012-06-25/libor-guardians-said-to-resist-changes-to-broken-benchmark-rate.html

650 ibid

First, my cover letter:

Dear Mr. Wheatley,

I have attached my comments to your initial discussion paper on LIBOR. The comments focus on the simple solution for fixing LIBOR and restoring market confidence. This solution is to require the banks to provide what I call ultra transparency.

In the 1930s, ultra transparency, [which is another way of referring to valuation transparency], was routinely provided by banks as they published all their accounts fit to print. It was the standard for a bank looking to demonstrate that it could stand on its own two feet.

Since the advent of deposit insurance, ultra transparency has been the level of disclosure provided to bank regulators. It is seen as necessary in order to protect the taxpayer guarantee.

However, banks abandoned the practice of publishing all their accounts fit to print because they had the regulators already looking at their accounts. As a result, market participants no longer had the information they need to independently assess the risk of the banks.

The interbank lending market froze in 2007 when banks with funds to lend realized that they could not independently assess the risk of the banks looking to borrow. As a result, they stopped lending. It has remained frozen since, with a few exceptions like when the governments guaranteed interbank loans.

The way to unfreeze the interbank lending market is to require the banks to provide ultra transparency and disclose on an ongoing basis all the accounts fit to print. In addition to unfreezing the interbank lending market, this disclosure will also provide the actual trade data that can be used as the basis for calculating LIBOR.

I look forward to talking with you and answering any questions you might have.

Second, my response to the Wheatley Commission Review:

August 27, 2012
Sent via e-mail: wheatleyreview@hmtreasury.gsi.gov.uk
The Wheatley Review
HM Treasury
1 Horse Guards Road
London
SW1A 2HQ
The Wheatley Review of Libor

Dear Mr. Wheatley:

TYI, LLC appreciates the opportunity to submit this letter in response to your request for comments on how to reform LIBOR in a way that restores market confidence.

This letter will focus on two consultation questions: can LIBOR be strengthened in such a way that it will remain a credible benchmark and are there credible alternative benchmarks that could replace LIBOR in the financial markets.

Conclusion

Banks should be required to provide ultra transparency and disclose on an on-going basis their current global asset, liability and off-balance sheet exposure details.

These details would be collected, standardized and disseminated for free to all market participants by a conflict of interest free data warehouse.

With this disclosure, the interbank lending market would resume functioning as banks with deposits to lend could assess the risk of banks looking to borrow. With this assessment, banks with deposits to lend could determine who much they are willing to lend on an unsecured basis at different interest rates to the borrowing banks.

As a result, the interbank lending market would unfreeze and remain unfrozen. There would be no need for an alternative benchmark and LIBOR could be based on all or a subset of the actual trades.

Frozen interbank lending market drives search for alternative benchmarks

As the initial discussion paper pointed out, "LIBOR is intended to be a representation of unsecured interbank term borrowing costs." This definition assumes that there is a functioning interbank lending market.

However, since the beginning of the financial crisis, the interbank lending market has been frozen.

To get around the frozen interbank lending market, in his Wall Street Journal column, Daniel Doctoroff, CEO and president of Bloomberg, LP offered a complicated one-off solution.

One potential solution to this problem is to combine two types of inputs to compensate for the diminished volume in loans available for bank reference.

The first input would follow the current Libor approach. The interbank borrowing rate—the numbers they submit—will be transparent. That is, if bank X says it borrowed at rate Y, that submission to Bloomberg would be public.

The second, supplemental inputs would consist of market-based quotes for credit default swap transactions, corporate bonds, commercial paper and other sources of credit information. Analysis of these sources of information would yield an "indicative" Blibor index.

Another way to get around the frozen interbank lending market would be to adopt an alternative benchmark as the basis for the LIBOR interest rate.

As describe in a Bloomberg editorial, the two leading contenders are overnight index swaps and the general collateral repo index. Both of these contenders are flawed.

Overnight index swaps are contracts based on the so-called federal funds effective rate, which is the interest U.S. banks charge one another on overnight loans. The underlying loans are observable: The Fed records them and publishes a weighted average interest rate every day.

Problem is, banks tend to pull out of the market during times of stress, leaving it too small and too easily skewed to provide a true picture of borrowing costs....

In short, overnight index swaps suffer from the same problems as the interbank lending market.

The general collateral repo index looks like a better option. It tracks the very large market for repurchase agreements, known as repos, typically overnight loans made against good collateral such as U.S. Treasuries.

The Depository Trust & Clearing Corp. publishes a daily weighted average of the actual interest rates paid on these loans. Aside from being secured by collateral, a large portion of the loans are processed through a central counterparty that protects the system against default by any one participant. These features make the repo market, and especially the part that uses Treasuries as collateral, relatively resilient in times of crisis.

However, this index also has problems. For starters, it does not represent the interest rate that banks can borrow on an unsecured basis.

Keep in mind that most banks these days tend to package their loans into securities. They then pledge the bundled loans as collateral when they borrow in the repo market.

The index also has similar problems to the freezing of the interbank lending market. At the beginning of the financial crisis, it was exactly these loan-backed securities that could not be used in the repo market as no one could value the securities.

The initial discussion paper offers several other potential benchmarks and why their flaws make them inappropriate for use as a replacement benchmark for LIBOR.

For example, treasury bills and the central bank policy rate have nothing to do with the rate on unsecured bank lending and rather are rates that are highly manipulated by monetary policymakers.

Bottom line: the search for an alternative benchmark to base LIBOR off of reveals that the best solution is to unfreeze and keep unfrozen the interbank lending market.

Unfreezing the interbank lending market

Why go for the complex or substitute a flawed alternative benchmark for LIBOR when there is a simple solution for unfreezing the interbank lending market?

The interbank lending market has frozen repeatedly since the beginning of the financial crisis because lending banks do not have the information they need to assess the risk of the borrowing bank.

Banks are, in the words of the Bank of England's Andy Haldane, 'black boxes'.

But don't take Mr. Haldane's or my word that banks do not disclose enough information so that they can be independently assessed. The U.S. Financial Crisis Inquiry Commission (FCIC) reached the same conclusion. The FCIC observed that the interbank lending market froze because banks could not tell which banks were solvent and which were not.

The result of the lack of disclosure is that banks with deposits to lend do not lend to banks looking to borrow because they cannot independently assess the risk of the borrowing banks and determine the proper amount or price for their unsecured exposure.

The reason for requiring banks to provide ultra transparency and disclose all of their exposure details and not just their funding details is that ultra transparency provides the data that each bank needs in order to independently assess the risk of every other bank and determine the amount and price they are willing to lend to each of the other banks.

This point needs to be repeated: it is only with ultra transparency that banks have all the useful, relevant information in an appropriate, timely manner to independently assess the risk of lending to the other banks and that market confidence is restored.

With ultra transparency, banks disclose on an ongoing basis their current global asset, liability and off-balance sheet exposure details.

With this information, banks with funds to lend can independently assess the risk of the banks looking to borrow. With this information, transactions that are priced to reflect the true risk of each bank can take place.

As a result, Libor can be based on what it truly costs banks to borrow on an unsecured basis. This is what Libor was intended to represent under the definition provided in the initial discussion paper.

Basing LIBOR off of actual trades requires that the interbank lending market be unfrozen and can be credibly kept unfrozen in the future. Ultra transparency is the key to unfreezing the interbank lending market and to preventing it from freezing again.

Basing LIBOR off of actual trades

Once the interbank lending market is functioning again, then the liability data provided under ultra transparency can be used in the calculation of LIBOR.

Specifically, market participants will have access to all the interbank trades and can use all or a subset of these trades as the basis for determining the LIBOR interest rates.

In your initial discussion paper, you presented an analysis by Oliver Wyman of 2011 interbank trading data. Since the beginning of the financial crisis in 2007, the interbank lending market has been essentially frozen. The 2011 data confirms this by highlighting the lack of trades.

At a minimum, this analysis shows why ultra transparency is needed to restore a functioning interbank lending market.

Without ultra transparency and a functioning interbank lending market, the analysis shows that the LIBOR interest rate across a range of currencies and maturities would be based off of a limited number of transactions in small, illiquid, easily manipulated markets.

With ultra transparency and a functioning interbank lending market, there are a number of ways to determine a Libor interest rate across all the currencies and maturities that take advantage of the most liquid interbank lending markets.

For example, if there are trades available to calculate a Libor interest rate for both a shorter and longer maturity than the illiquid maturity, it is easy to mathematically determine an interest rate for the illiquid maturity.

For purpose of restoring credibility to LIBOR, regulators should be agnostic to which of these solutions is adopted. What is important is that regulators focus on ensuring that there is ultra transparency so that the interbank lending markets function and do not freeze in the future.

Cost of data warehouse to support ultra transparency

One of the issues with basing LIBOR off of actual transactions and requiring ultra transparency from the banks is the issue of cost and complexity of the supporting data warehouse and information infrastructure.

My firm has done a considerable amount of work in this area and the bottom line is that neither cost nor complexity is a barrier to requiring ultra transparency and basing LIBOR off of actual trades.

Let me deal with cost first. Specifically, there is the issue of who pays for the data warehouse and the information infrastructure.

The banks should pay. The banks are major beneficiaries from providing ultra transparency and basing LIBOR off of actual trades.

Banks benefit from providing ultra transparency because market participants can independently assess their risk and are therefore willing to lend them money on an unsecured basis.

Without ultra transparency, the interbank lending market is effectively closed. This implies an infinite cost of funds.

I realize that banks are currently relying on inexpensive funding from the central banks, but eventually central banks will enforce Walter Bagehot's advice of lending at high rates against good collateral. At this point, banks are going to realize the 'savings' from providing ultra transparency and having access to the interbank market.

Now let me turn to the issue of complexity.

My firm patented an information infrastructure that uses a data warehouse to provide observable event based reporting on a borrower privacy protected basis for the collateral supporting structured finance securities to all market participants. It would be simple to modify this infrastructure to support ultra transparency and basing LIBOR off of actual transactions.

Based on my firm's expertise, setting up and operating the data warehouse and information infrastructure to support ultra transparency and LIBOR can be easily done.

I look forward to talking with you about how this can be accomplished and restoring market confidence in LIBOR.

Chapter 25

WHAT NEEDS TO BE DONE TO FIX THE GLOBAL FINANCIAL SYSTEM?

"So what is to be done? ... That can best be achieved by ... ensuring maximum transparency of balance sheets. This is even more vital if the aim is to safeguard the economy and the solvency of governments.

— Martin Wolf[651]

The Libor scandal effectively destroyed the global financial regulators' credibility. At the heart of their loss of credibility are two interesting questions:

1. Why did the regulators not put an end to the manipulation of the Libor interest rates when they found out in April 2008?
2. Why did the Federal Reserve and U.S. Treasury not disclose to everyone in 2008 a bank had confessed to manipulating the Libor interest rates or at least disclose this manipulation in 2010 when the Dodd-Frank Act was being debated?

We will never know why the global financial regulators didn't and still haven't put an end to the manipulation of benchmark rates and prices. We do know the global financial regulators pushed for adoption of the Japanese Model for handling an opacity driven bank solvency led financial crisis. Under the Japanese Model, preservation of the myth that the banks have positive book capital levels necessitated deception. A prime example of deception is regulatory forbearance that blesses the banks keeping zombie borrowers alive using 'extend and pretend' techniques. Looking the other way as banks manipulated Libor interest rates would just be another example of deception.

651 Wolf, Martin (2013, September 15), 'Too big to fail' is still a threat to the financial system, Financial Times, http://www.ft.com/intl/cms/s/0/f755c450-c3c2-11e3-870b-00144feabdc0.html?ftcamp=published_links%2Frss%2Fcomment_columnists_martin-wolf%2Ffeed%2F%2Fproduct&siteedition=intl#axzz2yygKrjAT

We will never know why the Federal Reserve and U.S. Treasury did not disclose a bank confessed to manipulating Libor interest rates. We do know the failure to disclose the admission banks were manipulating the Libor interest rates dramatically changed the discussion of how to reform the banks.

Libor manipulation undermines whole premise of financial reform

The manipulation of Libor interest rates and the lack of an appropriate response by the global financial regulators undermines the whole premise of the Dodd-Frank Act and the Vickers Recommendations that regulators will use their expanded powers to protect the global financial system.

What we saw with the manipulation of the Libor interest rates were regulators who didn't use their current powers and sat by and watched the banks engage in conduct that was detrimental to the global financial system. At best, their excuse was they were willing to overlook criminal conduct out of concern that exposing this conduct would make the financial crisis worse.

Of course, this defense does not address the question of why the financial regulators did not bring up the manipulation of Libor interest rates prior to the debate over the Dodd-Frank Act or to the UK's Independent Commission on Banking.

It would appear that the financial regulators were covering up for the banks and by doing so dramatically affected how the Dodd-Frank legislation or the Independent Commission on Banking recommendations reshaped the financial system.

After all, look what happened after Barclays publicly confessed to manipulating Libor. The Financial Times' Martin Wolf showed how reshaping the financial system would have been changed had the Libor interest rate manipulation been disclosed. To the list of reforms championed by the Vickers Commission, he added transparency.

Valuation transparency is needed not only to prevent bad behavior by bankers, but to ensure good behavior on the part of the financial regulators too.

Without valuation transparency, the question is why would market participants ever trust the financial regulators again? The old adage goes: fool me once, shame on you; fool me twice, shame on me.

Heading into the financial crisis, market participants substituted trust in the financial regulators for valuation transparency as the financial regulators let large areas of the financial system become opaque.

As highlighted by the Libor scandal, trust in the global financial regulators was misplaced.

Trust in the financial system is a result of valuation transparency. With valuation transparency, market participants can Trust, but Verify.

With valuation transparency, market participants have access to all the useful, relevant information in an appropriate, timely manner so they can independently assess risk. Market participants trust their own assessment.

All trust in banks and financial regulators now gone

The leading casualty of the Libor scandal is trust.

In the aftermath of the Libor scandal, Sandy Chen, a bank analyst at Cenkos Securities, explained why it was pointless for analysts to forecast bank earnings until banks provide valuation transparency

> [P]rice movements in markets track the flow of conversation around one basic question — 'Do I trust them and their promised returns?' Without … trust, nothing stands. ... The trust has been breached.[652]

All trust in either the banks or their regulators is now gone. The banks were willing to rig Libor interest rates to guarantee they couldn't lose on their derivative bets or to mislead on their financial health. The global financial regulators showed they had no problem with bankers rigging markets as the global financial regulators were willing to let this activity continue for four more years **after** they learned the bankers were rigging the financial markets.

Since 2007, there has been a lack of meaningful reform of the global financial system.

Yes, the Dodd-Frank Act was passed, but beyond the Consumer Financial Protection Bureau, its most significant achievement is how precious little it does to restore trust in the financial system.

Trust in the financial markets flows from valuation transparency and the fact that market participants trust their independent assessment of an investment. Trust does not flow from the substitution of the combination of complex regulations and regulatory oversight for valuation transparency.

In fact, the Dodd-Frank Act misses the crucial role valuation transparency has in restoring and maintaining trust in the financial system. The Act so badly misses this role it creates an agency, the Office of Financial Research, where valuation transparency can go to die.

Behind every financial crisis since the Panic of 1907 is a lack of valuation transparency.

---

652 Osborne, Alistair (2012, July 2), Bank forecasts futile now all trust has gone, says analyst, The Telegraph, http://www.telegraph.co.uk/finance/newsbysector/banksandfinance/9371082/Bank-forecasts-futile-now-all-trust-has-gone-says-analyst.html

Yet, regulators have opposed restoring valuation transparency to all the opaque corners of the global financial system. Perhaps they do so because valuation transparency reduces the dependence of the global financial system on them. Perhaps they do so because valuation transparency shines a bright light on their actions and subjects them to market discipline to perform their job.

Opacity is the core problem with our financial system. Fortunately, it is a problem that we learned how to fix in the 1930s. Valuation transparency is an elegant, proven solution.

Libor scandal highlights how banks fight to retain opacity

The Libor scandal provides an excellent example of how banks use opacity for their benefit and then defend their actions. The use of opacity for their benefit and defense of their actions is not limited to manipulating Libor, but extends into all the opaque corners of the financial system like structured finance and the 'black box' banks themselves.

The Libor scandal is significant for a number of reasons, but perhaps the most important one is showing how bankers talk a good game, but they don't practice what they preach. Bankers talk about free markets when it benefits them, but they engage in practices that undermine the proper functioning of these very same markets.

The necessary condition for Adam Smith's invisible hand to work and the proper functioning of any market is buyers and sellers have all the useful, relevant information in an appropriate, timely manner so they can make a fully informed investment decision. However, bankers routinely engage in activities that prevent this from occurring.

For example, given the choice between basing Libor on actual disclosed trades or on make believe, the industry chose make believe. For another example, given the choice between having structured finance securities provide observable event based reporting so investors could value the contents of a clear plastic bag, bankers chose once per month or less frequent disclosure so investors would be valuing the contents of a brown paper bag.

When the bankers' use of opacity to line their pockets becomes known, one line of defense is to dismiss the bad behavior saying that it was the work of a few now fired rogue employees. Banks did this after the fines for the Libor scandal were announced.

This response clearly misses the gravity of what has occurred. What occurred is the banks have admitted to lying when they submitted interest rates to be used in calculating the Libor benchmark interest rates and the banks intended to profit from these lies.

The most valuable commodity a bank has to offer is trust. The global banks have just admitted they cannot be trusted. At the end of the day, firing a few sacrificial lambs does nothing to provide the market with a reason to trust these banks.

Remember, banks needs the market to trust them, the market does not need this set of dishonest banks.

Given the banks need to earn back the market's trust, banks needs to take a step that will in fact signal to the market that they can be trusted now and going into the future. The only step the banks can take that does this is to voluntarily begin providing valuation transparency and disclosing on an on-going basis their asset, liability and off-balance sheet exposure details.

Any other step is just confirmation these banks are not to be trusted and they are trying to preserve using opacity for their benefit.

Another line of defense used by the banks is to attack the individual who says there is a problem created by opacity. This attack takes many forms, but ultimately the script for the attack boils down to the real problem is not opacity or the bankers hiding behind the veil of opacity and engaging in activities like rigging the financial markets, but rather the problem is the individual who suggested opacity and the bankers' behavior is a problem.

The banks' attack is an attempt to shift the focus from looking at how the bankers used opacity to their benefit to looking at the individual. The Opacity Protection Team claims in the appendix of this book are the result of first hand experience with the industry attacks.

Of course my Fortune article on how Goldman exploited its informational advantage when it came to shorting subprime mortgage-backed securities elicited a response from the Wall Street Opacity Protection Team. Shortly thereafter, a less than flattering editorial attempted to discredit both me and my observation Goldman received significant insight into the current condition of the subprime mortgage market from its investment in Senderra that informed its decision to short the market in December 2006. The U.S. government in the *Federal Housing Finance Agency v Goldman, Sachs & Co.* not only agreed with my observation, but it found the smoking guns to show this observation was 100% correct. Specifically, it cited emails sent by the senior management of Senderra in the days leading up to the December 2006 decision by Goldman's management to short the subprime securities. These emails described what was happening with existing subprime mortgages defaulting at a higher rate than expected, and what was happening with new subprime mortgages, fraud was increasing and quality was rapidly deteriorating. Senderra's management's conclusion was the subprime mortgage market was experiencing a "perfect storm, the wrong way".[653] Goldman's traders understood this and they understood it would take several months before the market had the information they currently possessed. That made it easy for them to sell their subprime mortgage exposures and short the market.

I was not surprised by the editorial with its personal attacks or the attempt to discredit what I was saying. As a senior executive of a foreign Too Big to Fail bank put it to me, pushing back against valuation transparency is simply a game for Wall Street. It will push back through editorials or speeches or responses to proposed regulation or in meetings with politicians and regulators. What makes it a game is Wall Street knows it ultimately will have to provide valuation transparency. It is just trying to see how long it can postpone providing valuation transparency.

Why would Wall Street want to postpone providing valuation transparency? Two reasons. First, Wall Street knows it makes money from selling transparent or opaque securities. It knows it makes far less money per transaction selling transparent securities than it makes selling opaque securities. What Wall Street doesn't know is how much harder it is going to have to work to make more money in total selling transparent securities than selling opaque securities. Second, Wall Street knows it will be subject to market discipline when it too is forced to provide valuation transparency. This will limit, if not eliminate, Wall Street's ability to take bets.

To date, Wall Street's Opacity Protection Team has been very effective at preventing the return of valuation transparency in all the opaque corners of the global financial system. They have prevented it from returning in the legislation passed in Europe and the U.S. in response to the financial crisis. They have prevented it from returning in the disclosure regulations passed in Europe and the U.S. in response to the financial crisis. They have prevented it from returning in the firms set up in Europe and the U.S. to make asset level performance data for structured finance securities available to market participants. They have prevented it from returning in the reform of the global financial benchmarks.

Just like the winner of a fight between a shark and bear depends upon the terrain, rather than fight the Opacity Protection Team on its turf, it is time to change where the fight takes place. Unlike legislation, regulation, data warehouses and global financial benchmarks, the Transparency Label Initiative™ operates on a terrain where it isn't subject to capture by Wall Street and the Opacity Protection Team. As a result, the Transparency Label Initiative™ is in the unique position of being able to apply the necessary pressure to bring

653 *Federal Housing Finance Agency v Goldman, Sachs & Co.*, page 37

valuation transparency to all the currently opaque corners of the global financial system.

Updating the original FDR Framework for the 21st century and beyond

It is clear from the Libor scandal and the JPMorgan whale trade that there is a need for financial reform.

What is equally clear is that the 2,000+ page Dodd-Frank Act and all of its thousands of pages of regulations to implement the Act would not have prevented either the Libor scandal or the whale trade (remember, the stated intent of the trade was to hedge a risk in the commercial bank).

Dodd-Frank was written and passed before there was an exhaustive examination, like the Pecora Commission, of what caused the crisis. Dodd-Frank was written and passed before the Financial Crisis Inquiry Commission could make its report. Dodd-Frank was written and passed before the NY Fed let anyone know that Libor was being manipulated.

Given these facts, other than luck, why would anyone think that Dodd-Frank would have any positive impact?

Fortunately, the Libor scandal and the JPMorgan "Whale" trade reopen the discussion of exactly what financial reform is needed.

The critical question that financial reform has to answer is would having the reform in place have prevented the Libor scandal or the JPMorgan "Whale" trade or (fill in the blank with another banking scandal) from happening.

Fortunately, there is one reform that can answer yes to these critical questions. That reform is restoring valuation transparency to the financial system through an investor lead Transparency Labeling Initiative™. This reform doesn't require the approval of either the global policymakers or the financial regulators. This reform simply requires investors to assert their right to all the useful, relevant information in an appropriate, timely manner so they can know what they own rather than have to gamble on the contents of a brown paper bag.

Conclusion

"Anything that is measured and watched improves."
— Bob Parsons[654]

Global policymakers have had to make a choice everyday since September 23, 2008 in how they address the financial crisis. Every day, they have to choose between continuing with the failed Japanese model (only absorb losses as quickly as the banking system generates earnings) or adopting the Swedish model (banks absorb all the losses today). Every day during the crisis, policymakers have chosen the failed Japanese model despite the obvious damage to society (it does raise an interesting question: are banker bonuses really more important than a productively employed younger generation).

Implementing the Transparency Label Initiative™ and ending our current crisis

Clearly the policies that have been pursued since the opacity driven financial crisis began on August 9, 2007 have not stopped the crisis, but rather have seen the crisis morph from a subprime security crisis to a bank "solvency" crisis to a sovereign debt and bank solvency crisis to a lower the living standards of a younger generation through a stagnation without end crisis.

The fact is there is significantly more debt outstanding globally than the borrowers can afford to pay. Until this fact is addressed, the global financial crisis in the form of economic malaise punctuated by occasional monetary policy driven financial asset bubbles will continue.

Sir Mervyn King observed governments and banks need to stop pretending the banks' bad loans and investments will be repaid.

> He compared the situation to the "pretence that debts could be repaid" in the 1930s and added: "We must not repeat that mistake."[655]

---

654 Parsons, Bob, http://spinnakr.com/blog/data-2/2013/03/44-more-of-the-best-data-quotes/

655 Aldrick, Philip (2012, October 23), Sir Mervyn King: no recovery until banks recapitalise, The Telegraph, http://www.telegraph.co.uk/finance/newsbysector/banksandfinance/9628997/Sir-Mervyn-King-no-recovery-until-banks-recapitalise.html

He expressed concern over how hard it is to stop using the Japanese Model and unwind the policies adopted under it. As Japan has shown after 2+ decades, the next generation has to live with the excess debt the current generation was unwilling to acknowledge would not be repaid.

The time has come to finally stop the financial crisis.

Today, we need to adopt policies that put Main Street before Wall Street. Today, we need to put the economic well being of younger generations ahead of paying banker bonuses. Both of these can be accomplished by applying the well-known Swedish model playbook.

Today, we need an investor lead Transparency Label Initiative™ to insure that valuation transparency is restored to all the opaque corners of the global financial system. This helps to end today's financial crisis. This also prevents future opacity driven financial crises.

Today, we need an investor lead Transparency Label Initiative™ to insure valuation transparency so both banks and financial regulators are subjected to market discipline. Subjecting banks to market discipline restrains their risk taking to what is needed to support the real economy. Subjecting financial regulators to market discipline eliminates the need to use taxpayer funding to bailout the banks.

Today, we need an investor lead Transparency Label Initiative™ to insure transparency that prevents banks from rigging financial markets.

Today, we need an investor lead Transparency Label Initiative™ to bypass Wall Street's Opacity Protection Team and insure that the financial markets have the valuation transparency they need in order to deliver the benefits they are suppose to in terms of the efficient allocation of resources across our global economy.

Today, perhaps most importantly, we need an investor lead Transparency Label Initiative™ to restore trust and confidence in the global financial system and the real economy.

Appendix

DEBUNKING WALL STREET'S MYTHS AND MISREPRESENTATIONS ABOUT VALUATION TRANSPARENCY

Don't need valuation transparency

- *Claim 1: Market participants do not need observable event based reporting for structured finance securities to know what they own; or market participants do not need ongoing disclosure of the current global asset, liability and off-balance sheet exposure details of a financial institution to know what they own.*

  This claim is the equivalent of saying that investors blindly gambling results in the same positive outcomes as investors making fully informed decisions while exerting self-discipline and market discipline. The basis for the proper functioning of the invisible hand and all of economics is this statement is not true.

  When market participants have disclosure on an observable event basis for structured finance securities and on a current exposure details basis for financial institutions, it is the equivalent to valuing the contents of a clear plastic bag. Investors can know what they own, exercise self-discipline to limit their exposures to what they can afford to lose and exert market discipline to restrain risk taking.

  Without observable event based reporting for structured finance securities, market participants are being asked to value the contents of a brown paper bag. This was confirmed by international financial regulators when they provided fourteen criteria[656] securitization transactions must have so investors could know what they own. Of these criteria, five focused on transparency as it applied to the risk of the underlying pool of assets (nature of assets, asset performance history, payment status, asset selection

[656] Basel Committee on Banking Supervision and the Board of the International Organization of Securities Commissions (2014, December 11), *Consultative Document: Criteria for identifying simple, transparent and comparable securitizations*, https://www.bis.org/bcbs/publ/d304.pdf, page 9

and transfer, and initial and ongoing data). Only observable event based reporting meets all of these criteria.

Without current exposure details for financial institutions, market participants are being asked to value the contents of a black box. When investors are trying to value an opaque security, they are simply guessing. This makes it impossible for the investor to know what they own if they buy the opaque security or to exert market discipline. Investors still can exert self-discipline when it comes to opaque securities. Investors can simply refuse to buy these securities or restrict their purchases to amounts they can afford to lose.

- *Claim 2: Requiring banks to disclose their current exposure details is unnecessary as financial regulators are now looking more closely at each bank.*

  Market discipline and financial stability are the result of market participants adjusting the size of their investments to what they can afford to lose given their independent assessment of the risk of each investment.

  In the run-up to the financial crisis that began in 2007, market participants were prevented from independently assessing the risk of each bank because the banks did not disclose their current exposure details. Instead, market participants relied on the financial regulators to both properly assess this risk and communicate this risk to the market participants. This created a single point of failure in the financial system and made it prone to a systemic financial crisis.

  Clearly, the systemic financial crisis occurred because the financial regulators either failed to accurately assess the risk of each bank or they failed to communicate this assessment accurately to the market.

  The only way to guarantee that we will not repeat this failure in the future is to either require or force banks to disclose their current exposure details and ensure that all market participants can independently assess the risk of each bank. Since regulators don't appear to be interested in requiring this disclosure from the banks, the Transparency Label Initiative™ is needed to force this disclosure.

- *Claim 3: The combination of bank capital, liquidity and exposure regulations means risk is contained and therefore there is no need for banks to disclose their current exposure details.*

  The primary lesson from the financial crisis is the combination of complex regulations and regulatory oversight is not an effective substitute for valuation transparency and market discipline.

  The restraint put on bank risk taking by complex regulations and regulatory oversight can weaken over time as a result of financial innovations and bank lobbying.

The restraint put on bank risk taking by valuation transparency and market discipline doesn't weaken over time. Investors remain responsible for their losses and thus have an ongoing incentive to respond to increases in risk at the bank by changing the amount and cost of their investment.

- *Claim 4: Existing reporting is sufficient. Investors could have done their homework with once-per-month or less frequent data and seen the problems with subprime mortgage-backed securities.*

  This objection substitutes the ability to recognize a trend for the ability to value a specific security. Clearly, the stale data disclosed in once-per-month reporting allows investors to see trends in the performance of the assets underlying a specific type of asset-backed security. A few investors made a substantial amount of money from recognizing the downward performance trend of subprime mortgages.

  However, as demonstrated by a brown paper bag, once-per-month reporting does not provide investors with the current detailed information that is necessary to value a specific structured finance security. The gap between the ability to recognize a trend and the ability to value individual structured finance securities cost investors several hundred billion dollars during the financial crisis.

- *Claim 5: The information has already been disclosed to third parties conducting due diligence on the structured finance security or financial institution and therefore the investors do not need to see the data.*

  This objection is another way of saying that investors should rely on the rating firms. However, reliance by investors on rating firms who implied they had access to loan-level performance information for structured finance securities or current exposure details for financial institutions was one of the primary contributors to the credit crisis.

  In Europe, under Article 122a, there is a mandate that investors do their own homework so they know what they own. In the U.S., the President's Working Group on Financial Markets' March 2008 Policy Statement on Financial Market Developments[657] also stressed the importance of investors doing their own homework.

  Global investors in securitizations need to have access to collateral-level observable event data so they can do their own homework regardless of

[657] President's Working Group on Financial Markets (2008, March 13), *Policy Statement on Financial Market Developments*, http://www.treasury.gov/resource-center/fin-mkts/Documents/pwgpolicystatemktturmoil_03122008.pdf, page 2

whether or not third parties have conducted due diligence on the underlying loans or receivables.

Global investors in financial institutions need to have access to each firm's current exposure details so they can do their own homework or hire third party experts they trust to do their homework for them.

- *Claim 6: The financial institutions have been talking with investors and the financial institutions know what information investors need to invest in financial institutions or structured finance securities.*

  It may be true that the sell-side believes it understands what investors in financial institutions and structured finance securities need, however, it is equally clear that under current reporting standards financial institution investors are not receiving the information necessary to analyze individual financial institutions and structured finance securities investors are not receiving the information necessary to analyze individual securities.

  For example, it takes approximately 300 data fields to run all the standard analyses for commercial mortgage-backed deals. However, fewer than 200 data fields are included in the sell-side dominated trade association template. With observable event based reporting, we would expect this type of problem not to occur. Subject to protecting borrower privacy, all of the data fields that are used by originating, billing and collecting entities would be provided to structured finance securities investors.

- *Claim 7: Asset classes other than RMBS, CMBS and CDO have not experienced significant credit problems, so loan-level disclosure would be inappropriate for such other asset classes.*

  The fact that some structured finance security investors have bought the contents of a brown paper bag in the past without losing their investment does not mean that structured finance security investors should continue to blindly place bets or that they will not experience credit problems in the future. Observable event based reporting would allow structured finance security investors to evaluate these deals and select those deals which meet their investment criteria.

- *Claim 8: Some assets are not in the ABS pool for very long and therefore, it is not worthwhile to provide loan-level disclosure and instead only summary data is needed.*

  The fact that the pool of assets is not static is even more reason that structured finance security investors should know what is in the securitization pool. AIG discovered this when the managers of AIG insured CDOs replaced lower risk securities with higher risk securities.

- *Claim 9: Securitizations were opaque because they were a response to a need for burying bad information and requiring observable event based reporting will end investor demand for these securities.*

  Securitization did indeed use opacity to hide bad information. It was this opacity that made these securities toxic. Investors didn't understand just how much risk they were taking on. Opacity also allowed Wall Street to profit from the investors' inability to accurately assess the risk of these securities.

  However, it doesn't appear that there is any significant demand for opaque securities. If there were, the primary market for private label mortgage-backed securities market would not be a small fraction of its pre-crisis size.

  The lack of demand for opaque securities is not surprising as the amount of capital that gamblers have to commit to blindly betting is a fraction of the amount of capital that investors have to invest in investments that provide valuation transparency.

- *Claim 10: Banks' asset portfolios are not just larger and more complex than for non-financial companies. The business of banking is predicated on banks' capacity to screen and monitor these assets more accurately than capital markets. Banks serve as a "delegated monitor" for investors....*[658]

  Investors in banks don't fully delegate the responsibility for monitoring a bank's exposures to the bank's management. Investors in a bank's stock or unsecured debt know they are responsible for the bank's losses. Therefore, they have an incentive to monitor and assess the bank's exposures for themselves. Investors exert market discipline on the banks based on this independent assessment.

- *Claim 11: Disclosure of each bank's current exposure details is not a panacea for all the ills of banking.*

  True. Valuation transparency will not address all of the ills of banking, but it will help address many of the ills and it does so in a way that positively reinforces the other proposed cures. For example, valuation transparency helps with enforcement of the Volcker Rule as it allows market discipline to restrain banks taking proprietary bets. For example, valuation transparency helps with enforcement of capital regulations as it allows market discipline to restrain banks gaming the regulations.

---

658 Haldane, Andrew (2012, January 19), Accounting for bank uncertainty, Bank of England, http://www.bankofengland.co.uk/publications/Pages/speeches/2012/540.aspx, page 4

Valuation transparency will not address how bankers are compensated. It will however address both the magnitude of these payments and making sure these payments are earned as opposed to the result of looting the bank.

- *Claim 12: Valuation transparency would have done nothing to prevent our current financial crisis.*

  False. Valuation transparency at a minimum would have made the financial crisis less extreme. Market discipline on the banks would have restrained their exposure to toxic mortgage-backed securities and related derivatives. With valuation transparency, the value of the mortgage-backed securities would have reflected their risk. This would have reduced the total amount of these securities that were issued.

  Valuation transparency also would have reduced, if not completely eliminated, the fear of financial contagion. In the run-up to the crisis, market discipline would have restrained banks exposures to each other to what each bank could afford to lose. This would have eliminated the justification for bailing out the banks.

- *Claim 13: We have a system design problem that has resulted in a tightly coupled financial system. Better data through valuation transparency won't help. If you want to reduce the frequency and severity of financial crises, you have to redesign the financial system.*

  Actually, it is a data problem. The global financial system that was designed in the 1930s is based on investors using the data disclosed through valuation transparency to limit their exposures to what they can afford to lose. If there isn't valuation transparency, the global financial system doesn't function properly and there is no market discipline to restrain risk taking.

  The claim confuses a symptom of the problem, tight coupling, with the problem that gives rise to tight coupling, opacity.

  The reason the financial system is tightly coupled is the lack of data. Without granular level data, market participants cannot assess the risk of loss. As a result, market participants have tended to underestimate risk and taken on more exposure than they can afford to lose. When valuation transparency is provided, market participants can use the data provided in their independent risk assessment and in turn reduce the tight coupling in the financial system by reducing their exposures to what they can afford to lose.

  The answer lies in better data as one of the benefits of better data is it is the market, which is bigger than the financial services industry, which then stares down the industry and prevents the next financial crisis.

- *Claim 14: At best valuation transparency gives market participants the raw material to assess risk, but it's left up to them to do so. Market participants may assess risk differently, but they will exhibit pro cyclical behavior. In a bull market, most market participants will underestimate the true level of risk and the probability of something bad happening to them. As a result, market discipline won't be very strong and financial contagion will continue to be a problem as market participants continue to have more exposure than they can afford to lose.*

  If this claim is true, it confirms the FDR Administration was right in setting up bank regulation as a backstop to market discipline. Bank regulation should be counter-cyclical as it becomes binding should a bull market cause market discipline to become too lax.

  If the Opacity Protection Team is right that market discipline in the presence of valuation transparency won't be very strong during a bull market, then regulation to restrain bank risk taking is also necessary to avoid the potential for financial contagion.

  Of course, the bankers have argued for years bank regulation is unnecessary in the presence of market discipline. However, valuation transparency is necessary for market discipline to occur.

- *Claim 15: If market discipline really works, why haven't shareholders forced the Too Big to Fail banks to take less risk?*

  The opacity of the banks dictates the type of shareholders that banks attract.

  Under the FDR Framework, there is a three-step investment process:

  - Investors independently assesses all the useful, relevant information to determine the risk of and value of the investment;
  - Investors solicit bids from Wall Street to buy or sell the investment.
  - Investors compare the price shown by Wall Street to their independent valuation to make buy, hold or sell decisions.

  When there is opacity, as is the case with the black box banks, investors do not have access to all the useful, relevant information and therefore they cannot independently assess the risk or value the investment. As a result, investors cannot go through the investment process.

  This has important implications for the types of shareholders that banks attract. Investors are not attracted to banks because investors cannot go through the investment process. They recognize that buying or selling bank shares is nothing more than gambling on the contents of a black box.

  Naturally, the shareholders who are attracted to the big banks are not investors who would exert discipline on management, but rather gamblers.

By definition, these gamblers want bank management to take on risk because their downside is capped and their upside is unlimited.

Valuation transparency is too hard to use

- *Claim 1: You can trust Wall Street not to take advantage of investors by using its information monopoly in the absence of valuation transparency.*

  The lawsuits against Wall Street by the US government and the states for fraud and misrepresentation when it sold subprime mortgage backed securities forever shows the notion of trusting Wall Street not to take advantage of investors is nonsense.

  A major reason for valuation transparency is to protect the investors from the great salesmen on Wall Street.

- *Claim 2: Most of the market participants cannot analyze this data.*

  The combination of disclosure and *caveat emptor* does not require that every market participant be able to independently assess the disclosed data. Market participants are given an incentive to either analyze the data themselves or hire third party experts they trust to analyze the data because they are responsible for all losses on their investments.

  As a result, the market participants who are not capable of analyzing the data have two choices: do not invest where they are not capable of analyzing the data or hire someone who is capable of analyzing the data. Warren Buffett not buying technology stocks is a classic example of an investor not investing where they are not capable of analyzing the data. Most individuals go the later route and instead hire portfolio managers who can analyze the data. If needed, these managers might in turn hire the relevant expertise.

  Each market participant does not need to be a rocket scientist or have the ability to precisely measure tail risk to benefit from the better data made available under valuation transparency. All each market participant needs to do to benefit from better data is to be able to recognize when the risk of an investment has increased and ask themselves: "am I comfortable with my current level of exposure given the increased risk of loss?"

  For example, you don't need fancy statistical models or the ability to measure tail-risk to see the risk of MF Global was increasing as its bet on sovereign debt increased. All that was necessary was to look at the size of the sovereign debt position and compare it to book capital. Knowing the risk of loss was increasing provides the information necessary for a participant to rethink and adjust the size of their investment.

- *Claim 3: This much data will create information overload and confuse market participants.*

  At a minimum, competitors should be able to use this data to independently assess the risk of each individual financial institution they do business with. If they cannot, this is a clear message the financial institutions are too big and needs to be reduced in size until these sophisticated market participants can assess their risk.

  It is worth repeating the combination of disclosure and *caveat emptor* gives investors an incentive to independently analyze the information disclosed, but it does not require that they do this analysis themselves. Investors can hire trusted third party experts to do this assessment for them. This is well understood by investors.

  According to the Association for Financial Markets in Europe's February 26, 2010 response to the European Central Bank's Public Consultation on Provision of ABS Loan-Level Information,

  > From an investor perspective, loan-level data could provide a number of benefits: ... provision of loan-level data will give investors certain options: either to rely on the level of data that they currently use, or, alternatively, to employ third parties to transform the large amount of data into a more useable and value-added format.[659]

  As discussed in the Association of Mortgage Investors' March 2010 white paper on reforming the ABS market,

  > Arguments that the amount of loan-level information exceeds the capacity of investors to process and analyze – when issuers, underwriters and asset servicers have no problem processing and analyzing the very same data – are absurd on their face.[660]

  It is simply inaccurate to assume that investors are unable to use or to engage third parties to help them to use loan-level information. Investors in structured finance securities and financial institutions have computers to process loan-level or exposure detail data. To the extent investors are unable

---

659 Association for Financial Markets in Europe (2010, February 26), *Comments on the European Central Bank's Public Consultation on the Provision of ABS LoanLevel Information in the Eurosystem Collateral Framework*, http://www.afme.eu/divisions/securitisation.aspx , page 4

660 Association of Mortgage Investors (2010, March), *White Paper: Reforming the Asset-Backed Securities Market*, http://blogs.reuters.com/alison-frankel/files/2014/04/AMI-whitepaper.pdf , page 2

to analyze this data, they have a very long history of relying on trusted third parties with the capabilities to analyze this data for them.

- *Claim 4: Disclosing this much information increases the chances that market participants, including regulators, will incorrectly analyze the data.*

  Common sense suggests the wisdom of the crowd with more market participants, including industry experts, competitors, and regulators analyzing the data the more likely it is some of the participants will do the analysis correctly and by their actions communicate their findings to the market.

  This claim strongly suggests financial institutions should be reduced in size. If the amount of data they are disclosing under valuation transparency increases the chances their competitors cannot correctly analyze the financial institution, the solution is to shrink the financial institutions until the competitors can correctly analyze the data they disclose.

- *Claim 5: If there is too much data, it is hard to make a good risk model.*

  There are other uses for data than in a complex risk model.

  For example, prior to buying the securities from Goldman Sachs that allowed it to short the subprime mortgage market, it might have been useful for potential investors to see that Goldman was reducing its exposure to and taking a proprietary bet against the subprime mortgage market.

- *Claim 6: No one could assess the millions of individual exposures a Too Big to Fail bank has.*

  If true, then the Too Big to Fail banks should be reduced in size until they can be assessed.

  The claim is probably false because of the existence of other Too Big to Fail banks. Each of these banks should have the ability to assess its Too Big to Fail competitors. If they cannot, this is an argument for shrinking these banks.

- *Claim 7: It would take too long to assess the risk of all the Too Big to Fail banks as they have millions of exposures spread out across thousands of subsidiaries around the globe.*

  Even using 21st century information technology, initially it will take a while to identify all of the risks hidden on and off the Too Big to Fail bank balance sheets. Subsequently, information technology can be used to identify when there has been a change in a bank's exposures and what the change implies for the bank's risk profile.

  One of the benefits of having the market assess each bank's risk is it forces these banks to make a decision. Do they want to be easily assessed by the market or do they want to hide the risks they are taking until the investors can discover them.

The reason for a bank making itself easy to assess is it will have a competitive advantage over its peers. This competitive advantage is a much lower cost of funds. After all, the market will assume that any bank that doesn't make itself easy to assess is deliberately hiding something. The risk of whatever is being hidden is reflected in the market's demanding a higher cost to fund the opaque, Too Big to Fail bank.

- *Claim 8: It is unclear if any market participant, including the regulators, has the resources to properly use each bank's current exposure detail data.*

  Presumably, each Too Big to Fail bank has the ability to properly use their competitors' current exposure detail data to assess the risk of each competitor. If not true, then the Too Big to Fail have to be shrunk in size until they can do this assessment.

  In addition, under the principle of *caveat emptor*, investors have a very strong incentive to either use the data themselves or to hire an independent third party expert who can assess the data for them. Fitch's efforts to understand the repo market show that market participants do know how to use the granular level data valuation transparency would provide and turn it into useful information.

It will hurt (fill in the blank)

- *Claim 1: Requiring banks to disclose their current exposure details undermines the safety and soundness of the financial system and financial stability by making bank runs more likely.*

  Requiring banks to disclose their current exposure details improves the safety and soundness of the financial system and financial stability because it subjects the banks to market discipline. As a result, there is a restraint on bank risk taking before the bank faces a solvency problem.

  The likelihood of bank runs is also reduced as market participants have the information they need to assess the risk and the ability of each bank to absorb its losses and continue operating. This reduces the impact of the types of rumors that trigger bank runs.

- *Claim 2: Disclosure of current exposure details increases the chances of a bank run when depositors get nervous about a bank's solvency.*

  Under the FDR Administration's solution for reducing bank runs, small depositors are protected from losses by a deposit guarantee. Hence, they have no reason to engage in a bank run.

The market participants with an incentive to reduce their exposure to a bank based on its solvency are large uninsured depositors and unsecured debt holders. They are the ones who can either independently assess or hire a trusted third party to assess the information disclosed under valuation transparency. Based on this assessment, before solvency becomes an issue, they can exert market discipline on the bank by reducing the amount of their exposure to the bank and increasing the cost of these funds when the bank's risk increases.

- *Claim 3: Requiring banks to disclose their current exposure details would provide an incentive for banks to lend and invest less with the result being harm to the real economy.*

  Under this and similar claims, if Wall Street cannot make money from rigging the financial system, it threatens it will stop engaging in its core activities that benefit society.

  In the U.S. and to a certain extent the EU and UK, bank lending is separate from how the loans are funded. This separation occurs because there are many alternative ways to fund a loan. It can be funded on the originating bank's balance sheet, through a securitization or covered bond, or sold to other market participants including banks, insurance companies, pension funds and hedge funds.

  Regardless of how the loan is funded, disclosure of a bank's current exposure details doesn't affect the bank's incentive to make the loan.

- *Claim 4: Valuation transparency would hurt our banks' ability to compete globally.*

  Valuation transparency would actually improve our banks' ability to compete globally. As shown by the clear plastic bag and brown paper bag, investors would provide funds at a lower cost to a bank that provided valuation transparency than to a bank that was shrouded behind a veil of opacity. Having a lower cost of funds would be a huge advantage when competing globally.

- *Claim 5: Disclosing current exposure details would reduce the ability of banks to make markets and the result would be less efficient capital markets and slower economic growth.*

  Disclosure of current exposure details would reduce the ability of banks to make proprietary bets, but not their ability to make markets.

  This elimination of proprietary betting and not market making can be best illustrated by the JPMorgan "London Whale" trade. This was a proprietary bet that cost the bank $6.2 billion. As soon as the market found out about the bet, JPMorgan unwound it.

Compare and contrast this to market making where the size of the position could never expose a bank to losses of say $200 million let alone $6.2 billion.

- *Claim 6: Disclosure of current exposure details would reduce the ability of banks to generate a high enough return on equity to attract capital.*

  The argument banks need to be able to generate a high return on equity was used as justification to introduce the Basel capital requirements in the 1980s. These capital requirements are based on the simple notion of using risk weighting to hide the leverage and related risk that banks are taking on.

  But do banks actually need a higher return on equity to attract capital? No. There is no reason banks could not be like utility companies with low returns on equity and high dividend payouts. Clearly, equity capital is available to utilities.

- *Claim 7: Disclosure of current exposure details increases the risk of each bank because market participants like hedge funds can trade against the bank's positions.*

  Disclosing current exposure details lowers the risk of the banks. By reducing the profitability of the bank's proprietary bets, it significantly reduces the incentive to take these bets in the first place.

  Disclosing current exposure details reduces the profitability of the bank's proprietary bets by showing hedge funds and other market participants what the bets are. This allows these market participants to then trade against a bank's proprietary bets. There are many ways trading could occur to minimize the profitability of the bets and maximize the likelihood for loss. This includes increasing the cost of the bet by buying when the banks are buying and decreasing the return on the bet by selling when the banks are selling.

- *Claim 8: Disclosing current exposure details will create more illiquid capital markets and make it harder for investors to sell their positions because banks cannot take on these positions.*

  As was shown with the clear plastic bag and the brown paper bag, valuation transparency increases both a security's liquidity and reduces the fluctuation in a security's price. It makes it easier for an investor to sell because there is a buyer for their position. The price the buyer might be willing to pay may not be the price the seller is hoping to achieve, but a transaction can take place as the buyer has access to the information they need to know what they are buying.

  As market makers, banks can continue to buy investors' positions. What disclosure of the current exposure details restrains is the purchase of these positions to make a proprietary bet.

- *Claim 9: Valuation transparency will reduce liquidity in the capital markets and will hurt investors because of the wider spreads when they buy or sell a security.*

  As was shown with the clear plastic bag, valuation transparency improves liquidity where liquidity is measured as narrowing price spreads.

  As was shown with the clear plastic and brown paper bags, valuation transparency improves liquidity when liquidity is measured by number of potential buyers of a security. With valuation transparency, there are more potential buyers than exist for opaque securities that only attract gamblers.

- *Claim 10: Banks disclosing their current exposure details will hurt companies as the companies will not be able to hedge their risks because banks won't be able to act as counter-parties.*

  Disclosing their current exposure details does not prevent banks from acting as counter-parties and taking on risk. Disclosure of their current exposure details simply restrains how much risk banks take on in the aggregate.

  As a result, it puts pressure on banks to engage in more of a matchmaking role and find other counter-parties to take on the risk that companies would like to hedge.

- *Claim 11: Disclosing their current exposure details will cause banks to shrink and this will be bad for the economy.*

  There is no reason banks being smaller would be bad for the economy.

  One of the best ways for banks to shrink is to reduce the size of their loan book using structured finance securities that provide observable event based reporting. This frees up the banks to make new loans and puts the risk of the old loans on to investors who understand the risk and are capable of absorbing any losses.

- *Claim 12: Disclosing current exposure details or providing observable event based reporting will require disclosure of proprietary information that would hurt a financial institution's competitive position.*

  Disclosing current exposure details or observable event based reporting will not require the disclosure of proprietary information like how a financial institution internally calculates credit ratings. Investors do not need this information. Investors do need all of the data fields that went into calculating the internal credit ratings; such as the borrower's credit score and income, in order to analyze the risk of the loans and receivables on a financial institution's balance sheet or supporting a securitization.

  This objection is also presented as a reverse engineering argument. If competitors are given all the information the investor needs to properly analyze the risk of the loans and receivables, competitors can back into how the financial institution or deal sponsor prices its loans relative to the borrower's credit quality.

This argument is misleading as competitors already have multiple sources of this information including professionals who move between competitors and borrowers who disclose competitors' offers in the hopes that someone will offer them a better deal.

- *Claim 13: Disclosing current exposure details will interfere with financial institutions' ability to make markets in different securities and will result in less liquidity in these markets.*

  It is not market making, but proprietary betting that disclosing current exposure details interferes with. Market participants are perceptive enough to distinguish between an exposure a bank holds to make a market and an exposure a bank holds because it is taking a proprietary bet.

  Disclosing current exposure details is the enforcement complement to the Volcker Rule's proprietary trading ban.

- *Claim 14: Requiring valuation transparency will reduce the availability of credit to the economy.*

  Originating and funding loans are separate activities. So long as a bank originates a loan that is properly priced for the risk of the borrower, there is funding for this loan. The funding might be on the originating bank's balance sheet or on another market participant's balance sheet.

  Valuation transparency contributes to making credit available in the economy. Peer to peer lending is an example of market participants using information technology to provide valuation transparency and make credit available.

- *Claim 15: Valuation transparency will force all of the banks to pursue the same business strategy and this increases the likelihood of another financial crisis.*

  Unlike regulations, valuation transparency doesn't force banks to pursue the same business strategy. Each bank can select the business strategy that maximizes the value of its franchise.

  What valuation transparency does is put a premium on reducing the complexity of the business so that market participants can understand it. The easier it is for market participants to assess how the business strategy translates into the overall risk level of the bank the lower the bank's cost of funds for a given level of risk.

- *Claim 16: Valuation transparency will reduce the ability of the financial sector to support the needs of the real economy.*

  Valuation transparency actually enhances the ability of the financial sector to support the needs of the real economy. Banks will be subject to restraint on risk taking that doesn't support the real economy. This frees up balance sheet capacity to support additional lending to the real economy.

- *Claim 17: Valuation transparency will drive up the costs for businesses, investors and bank customers that rely on the banks for capital.*

  There is no reason to think this assumption is true because it implies banks are currently systematically underpricing their loans and as a result of market discipline, this underpricing will go away. If banks were systematically underpricing their loans, banks wouldn't be able to sell their loans to third party buyers today. The third party buyers like insurance companies, pension funds and hedge funds would not be buyers because they understand the need to be properly compensated for the risk they take on.

Valuation transparency will not (fill in the blank)

- *Claim 1: Requiring banks to disclose their current exposure details won't make them safe. Therefore, valuation transparency is useless.*

  Claims like this are true to the extent that valuation transparency by itself won't produce any number of outcomes. However, our financial system is not design to rely solely on valuation transparency. Rather, it combines valuation transparency with *caveat emptor*. It is this combination that produces the positive outcomes.

  For example, banking can be a very risky business. The question is how to reduce the chances a bank will fail.

  Requiring banks to disclose their current exposure details subjects them to market discipline as investors assess on an ongoing basis the risk of the bank and adjust the amount and pricing of their exposure based on this assessment. This gives bank management an incentive to reduce the bank's risk to a point where it won't fail and also optimize net income given the cost of its funds.

- *Claim 2: More data will not make investors do their due diligence so they know what they own.*

  You cannot make investors use the data and do their own due diligence. The best you can do is give investors an incentive to use the data and do their own due diligence so they know what they own by making them responsible for all losses on their investment exposures.

- *Claim 3: If investors don't use the data, more data will not increase the stability of the financial system.*

  The stability of the financial system comes from every investor knowing they are responsible for losses on their investment exposures. This gives every investor an incentive to limit their losses by adjusting the amount of each exposure to what they can afford to lose given the risk of the exposure. This is true whether the investment is one where they know what they own or they are blindly gambling.

  What makes enforcement of the principle of investors being responsible for their losses credible is the presence of the valuation transparency. Even if investors blindly gambled, they cannot expect to be bailed out of their losses by claiming they did not understand the risk of the investment when they do not use the data provide to assess the risk.

- *Claim 4: Disclosure of each bank's current exposure details will not allow market participants to mathematically solve for financial contagion.*

  If the problem you are trying to solve is financial contagion and who will ultimately hold the losses should a Too Big to Fail bank fail, I agree this is a horribly complex undertaking and unlikely to be solved mathematically.

  As a first approximation, no one would debate that if everyone had to disclose their exposure to a Too Big to Fail bank, we would know who was holding the losses.

  However, the financial system is more complicated than that. Market participants can both be holding an exposure to the Too Big to Fail bank and also have purchased insurance against a default. In this case, we would also like disclosure of who sold the insurance and would incur the loss. This too is mathematically straightforward to solve.

  However, the financial system is more complicated than that. Once we know who is holding the losses, the natural question to be asking is "can they afford the losses?"

  This is an important question that serves to highlight the ripple in the pond effect losses produce. As the next natural question to ask is "if they cannot afford the losses, then are the market participants with exposure to them able to afford the losses on their exposure?"

  By the time we get to looking at the impact on market participants that are two, three, four steps removed, while it may be theoretically possible to mathematically solve for the impact of the failure of a Too Big to Fail bank, frankly, I would not want to bet the stability of the financial system on this solution.

  Fortunately, with the combination of disclosure and *caveat emptor*, we do not have to bet the stability of the financial system on a complex mathematical solution to financial contagion. The financial system is anti-fragile because all market participants know they are responsible for their losses. As result, the mathematical problem each investor has an incentive to solve is to limit their exposure to losses on a specific investment to what the investor can afford to lose on that investment. In addition, each investor has an incentive to limit their exposure to losses on all their investments to what the investor can afford to lose in total.

The important point here is that by design we don't have to solve the complex mathematical problem of financial contagion as the financial system stops the ripple effect from the losses on the failure of the Too Big to Fail bank before it gets three or four steps removed.

Why? Because when the losses actually occur, each market participant is able to afford their share of the losses and the ripple effect, also known as financial contagion, doesn't get started.

With the combination of disclosure and *caveat emptor*, our financial system is designed to eliminate a fear of financial contagion or the reliance on complex mathematical solutions. However, this works in practice only if each market participant has access to the information necessary to independently assess the risk of their investments and as a result can manage their exposure to losses to a level they can absorb.

Sir Mervyn King uses direct and indirect bank exposures to Greek debt to illustrate the point complex mathematical solutions don't work and what is needed is disclosure of each bank's current exposure details.

> The main problem is that, even if you could calculate some mechanical exposure in this way, at present they can change very rapidly.
>
> This matrix changes from week to week. And that at any given point there is always uncertainty about the scale of exposures and which counterparties out there are the ones which are heavily exposed.
>
> And that uncertainty can lead, at various points, for the funders of banks — people who are willing to think of funding banks — to draw back. And there can be a crisis of confidence and sentiment in which people just say — I simply don't understand the complexity of the interconnectiveness of these exposures, and just won't take the risk of lending.
>
> That is the bigger risk I think. It's not — the direct links you have to monitor very carefully, and there's no reason at all for us to be concerned about the exposures of our banks directly to those countries that could be in serious difficulty. However, it's the indirect exposures

> and the generalized loss of confidence that could result if there were serious problems.
>
> There is no way in which you can do a mechanical calculation to work that out. What you have to do is to keep suggesting and probing, not only our banks, but try to encourage those responsible for dealing with this problem, to go to the heart of the problem, to resolve the underlying tensions in the area that are creating the concerns in the first place.[661]

Of course, there is a data fog and today's financial system does not disclose the data that needs to be disclosed. As a result, we have the problem of contagion in the financial system as it is too tightly coupled — where tight coupling means that market participants have more exposure to each other than they can afford to lose.

- *Claim 5: Valuation transparency will be no more effective than the regulators at stopping bankers from taking bets that put their firms at risk.*

  It is not the job of regulators to allocate capital across the economy by preventing bankers from taking on the exposures they want. It is the job of the investors in the financial institution to use valuation transparency to restrain risk taking through market discipline.

  For example, had MF Global been required to disclose the details of its bet on short-dated Italian government debt from day one, every market participant dealing with MF Global would have been in a position to assess the risk of this bet and adjust their exposure accordingly.

  As MF Global's cost of funds was exploding northward and its stock price plunging, even a banker like Mr. Corzine would have gotten the hint to reduce the size of his bet. This is why market discipline works to restrain risk taking.

Valuation transparency costs too much

- *Claim 1: Implementing valuation transparency or observable event based reporting would require significant changes to computer systems.*

  Actually, it would not require significant changes to computer systems. Existing databases used by financial institutions or servicers do exactly what is needed. They only update when an observable event like the purchase of a

661 Bank of England (2011, June 24), Financial Stability Report Q&A, Bank of England, http://www.bankofengland.co.uk/publications/Documents/fsr/2011/conf110624.pdf, page 3

security or a payment on a loan occurs. As a result, this data can and should be disclosed by the beginning of the next business day.

Consider an observable event-based report that can be accessed today by any person who holds a credit card. The individual credit cardholder can, using existing technology, access a web site of the credit card issuer on any day of the month and review all charges and payments that have been made on the credit card on each day during the month.

Similarly, the credit card issuer can, using existing technology, on any day of the month review all the charges and payments that have been made on each day during the month on i) all of its credit cards, ii) a subset of credit cards which are collateral for a securitization or iii) an individual credit card.

Credit institutions have considerable expertise in observable event-based reporting. This same expertise and the same information systems could be used to support observable event-based reporting for securitizations and current exposure detail disclosure for financial institutions.

- *Claim 2: It is too hard to report this data.*

  It will not be difficult to report this data because this is how the information is already tracked. If this were not the case, how would anyone know if a financial institution's financial statements were accurate or that payments received went to the right structured finance deal?

- *Claim 3: The cost of observable event based reporting or disclosing a bank's current exposure details outweighs the benefits.*

  At the time that the philosophy of disclosure was adopted, it was recognized that the benefit of avoiding a financial crisis far outweighed the cost of providing valuation transparency.

  As a result, the SEC was given the mandate to ensure that market participants have access to all useful, relevant information in an appropriate, timely manner. Equally importantly, the SEC was not required to do a cost/benefit analysis when it set a disclosure requirement.

  If the cost of providing valuation transparency is so high as to render a security uneconomic, it was intended that this security should not be offered to investors.

  Despite the fact that the SEC doesn't have to perform a cost/benefit analysis, in the TYI, LLC response to the FDIC Safe Harbor Proposal[662] a

662 TYI, LLC response to the FDIC Safe Harbor Proposal (2010, February), *Treatment by the Federal Deposit Insurance Corporation as Conservator or Receiver of Financial Assets Transferred by an Insured Depository Institution in Connection*

discussion of the costs and benefits of observable event based reporting for structured finance securities was presented.

The response noted investors such as Goldman Sachs and Morgan Stanley had access to loan-level observable event based data through their investment in or ownership of firms handling the daily billing and collecting of the underlying loans and receivables. By late 2006, Goldman Sachs and Morgan Stanley had concluded the risk in subprime mortgage backed securities was mispriced. As a result, they not only reduced their exposure to these securities but also shorted these securities.

What would have happened if investors had access to the same loan-level observable event based data as the Wall Street firms? Would they have also concluded the securities were mispriced? If so, they would have avoided several hundred billion dollars in losses by not buying subprime mortgage backed securities originated in the years leading up to the financial crisis.

Based on the cost of comparable information services for securitizations, the cost of a data system to collect, standardize and disseminate observable event based data on a borrower privacy protected loan-level basis to all securitization market participants would be in the single digit billions of dollars per year.

The bottom line to the cost/benefit analysis is that the benefit of not losing several hundred billion dollars far outweighs the cost of providing observable event based loan-level data.

The same type of cost/benefit analysis could be extended to banks disclosing their current exposure details. In this case, the benefit of having disclosure is measured in the trillions of dollars. This is the cost of having the financial crisis and the damage to the real economy.

The cost of banks providing valuation transparency is similar to the cost for securitization transactions providing observable event based reporting. The cost is measured in the low tens of billions of dollars per year.

Again, the benefit of requiring valuation transparency is far greater than the cost.

- *Claim 4: The cost of compliance is too high. It will adversely affect the economic attractiveness of financial institutions or securitization and will reduce the amount of credit available to the economy. The related objection is that after a certain period, say twelve (12) months, investors no longer need disclosure and when this happens, to save costs, disclosure should be discontinued.*

---

with a Securitization or Participation After March 31, 2010 (RIN # 3064 – AD55), https://docs.google.com/viewer?a=v&pid=sites&srcid=dHlpbGxjLmNvbXx3d3d8Z3g6MzY3ODRkNWViMzFjNjU4NQ, page 14

As noted above, the cost of observable event based reporting will be minimal. At five basis points (0.05%) or less, the cost of observable event based reporting is significantly less than the illiquidity premium currently built into the securitization market.

The "illiquidity premium" refers to the fact that buyers in the primary securitization market know without effective disclosure they will have to hold the security to maturity, as it is unlikely that they will find buyers in the secondary market for the contents of a brown paper bag.

As a result, investors in the current once-per-month disclosure environment require a higher yield in the primary securitization market than they would if observable event based reporting were available.

It can be expected that observable event based reporting would reduce the illiquidity premium charged by structured finance security investors and that such reduction in the illiquidity premium would more than offset the 5 basis points (0.05%) cost of observable event based reporting. In order to reduce the illiquidity premium over the life of the transaction, observable event based reporting should be required so long as the transaction is outstanding.

- *Claim 5: If only some of the data disclosed as a result of valuation transparency is used, disclosure of the unused data just creates an unnecessary expense for the banks. This unused data also creates potential political and legal risk if it is ignored and turns out to be important.*

  In the run-up to our current financial crisis, the data needed for valuation transparency was effectively kept under lock and key. Only the financial regulators could access it. With valuation transparency, all market participants can access this data. Our financial system is based on the notion that markets work best when all participants, including regulators, investors and third party experts, can access the useful, relevant information in an appropriate, timely manner. The data will be assessed from multiple different perspectives and questions the regulators never would have thought to ask will not only be asked but also answered.

  In practice, the market participants who know how to assess the data and turn it into useful information will use the data. There is no reason to believe these market participants will restrict themselves to the same subset of the disclosed data fields, but rather that each market participant will use the data fields they think are important. Market participants who cannot assess the data will piggyback off these market participants' expertise.

  Under the FDR Framework, it is intentional that the data doesn't have to be used. Therefore, it is highly likely not all information disclosed is going to be used all the time. However, whether the data is used or not is not an excuse for not making it available as market participants are given the incentive to use the data because they are responsible for their losses.

Valuation transparency makes it harder to recover from a financial crisis

- *Claim 1: By requiring banks to disclose their current exposure details, bank regulators won't have the flexibility to engage in regulatory forbearance that allows banks to exercise 'extend and pretend' with bad debt during times of financial crisis.*

  True. By design, market discipline and bank regulations were suppose to prevent a financial crisis from occurring in the first place. In the event a financial crisis occurred, banks were designed not to engage in 'extend and pretend', but rather to write-down the debt to the greater of the amount the borrower could afford to repay or an independent third party would be willing to pay for the collateral. This debt write-down and subsequent restructuring protects the real economy from the negative effects of excess debt in the financial system. Even though recognizing the losses on the excess debt would reduce the banks' book value, they could continue to operate and support the real economy because of the combination of deposit insurance and access to central bank funding.

- *Claim 2: There are times when it is necessary for government officials and bank regulators to make false claims about the solvency of the banking system.*

  There are never times when government officials and bank regulators should be making false claims about the solvency of the banking system. Doing so creates moral hazard and the need for taxpayers to bailout the banking system.

  With disclosure of each bank's current exposure details, market participants are fully aware of the solvency of the banking system. They know they are responsible for losses on their exposures to any bank that is closed as a result of its becoming insolvent, so they have an incentive to exert discipline on bank management not to take on so much risk that the bank becomes insolvent.

- *Claim 3: Disclosing current exposure details makes banks recognize losses upfront and this puts the sovereign credit at risk of default because banks must be recapitalized quickly.*

  Banks do not need to be recapitalized quickly. Because of deposit insurance and access to central bank funding, viable banks are designed to continue to support the real economy even when they have low or negative book capital levels. Banks can do this because the taxpayers effectively become the banks' silent equity partner.

Examples of when bank regulators have taken advantage of this feature include the 1980s Less Developed Country Debt crisis, the U.S. Savings & Loan crisis, and our current global financial crisis.

The sovereign credit is only put at risk of default when the sovereign borrows to recapitalize the banks. This does not have to be done for any bank that is capable of generating earnings and rebuilding its book capital over several years. For banks that are not capable of generating earnings, these banks should be resolved and not recapitalized. Again, this doesn't require much in the way of any issuance of sovereign debt.

- *Claim 4: How to create a sovereign default in one quick lesson: make banks take losses in excess of sovereign's capacity to borrow.*

  This claim assumes that the bank must be recapitalized immediately. However, modern banks are designed to operate and support the real economy even when they have low or negative book capital levels. As a result, future bank earnings can be used to absorb the losses that the banks take today.

- *Claim 5: Disclosure of each bank's current exposure details dangerously restricts how a government can respond to bank solvency issues and excess debt in the financial system.*

  The danger disclosure of each bank's current exposure details represents is to banker bonuses. With this disclosure, governments can now use past, present and future pre-banker bonus earnings as the primary source for absorbing the losses on the excess debt in the financial system.

That's proprietary information you are talking about

- *Claim 1: Disclosing current exposure details results in disclosing proprietary information about how the bank conducts its business.*

  One of the great myths of banking is that there is anything proprietary about it.

  For example, banks would like to say they have a proprietary formula for pricing their loans. However, every bank knows how every other bank prices its loans.

  There are several ways banks get this information. They get this information because they hire each other's employees. They get this information because borrowers share the pricing they are being offered by competitors in the hopes of securing a better deal. They get this information because banks sell their loans.

  What disclosing current exposure details reveals is the risk being taken by the banks. Understanding the risk being taken by the banks is what investors need if they are going to limit their exposure to what they can afford to lose and exert market discipline on the banks.

This claim is part of the broader set of claims that pit confidential information and/or trade secrets against disclosure. By definition, the banks would like to say everything is either confidential information or a trade secret and therefore not subject to disclosure. The securities laws address this series of claims by focusing on the information that needs to be disclosed so that investors have all the useful, relevant information in an appropriate, timely manner. Then, it is up to the banks to make a decision on whether or not they want to sell a publicly traded security. If they don't want to meet the disclosure requirements, then they cannot sell a publicly traded security. After all, nobody forces them to sell a publicly traded security.

- *Claim 2: Transparency would hinder financial innovation because it requires disclosure of proprietary information.*

  The fact valuation transparency would hinder financial innovation is a feature and not a bug. After all, the purpose of most of Wall Street's financial innovation is to create opacity in the financial system so Wall Street can realize higher profits.

  The claim is misleading because it equates valuation transparency with a requirement to disclose proprietary information. A Venn Diagram with valuation transparency in one circle and proprietary information in the second circle would show limited, if any, overlap for the transparent financial innovations investors would want to buy. The Venn Diagram would show substantial overlap for the opaque financial products Wall Street would like to sell.

Borrower privacy objections

- *Claim 1: The risk of compromising borrowers' personal information outweighs the benefit of providing detailed loan-level information.*

  The data fields needed to assess the risk of a bank's loan portfolio or a structured finance security does not overlap with the data fields that identify who the borrowers are. I showed this when I designed an information system to deliver valuation transparency for structured finance securities. The system maintained borrower privacy to the gold standard for privacy set by Congress in the Health Insurance Portability and Accountability Act of 1996 (HIPAA).

  However, to the extent that a borrower is willing to share their confidential information, they should be able to borrow at lower cost relative to a borrower with similar risk who is unwilling to share their confidential information. The reason they should be able to borrow at lower cost is it eliminates an element of uncertainty. Regardless of the risk of the borrower, the less uncertainty about the borrower, the less it costs on a risk-adjusted basis to borrow.

- *Claim 2: Protecting borrower privacy requires disclosure of only a fraction of the data fields that are tracked.*

  I would expect reporting rules would require borrower privacy to be protected in a manner similar to the protections under HIPAA or the most conservative European borrower privacy rules. If borrower privacy is protected in this manner, there are very few data fields that could not be disclosed to investors.

Generic objections to valuation transparency

- *Claim 1: In order for us to compete on a global basis, we need a level playing field. If valuation transparency isn't required in other countries it shouldn't be required here.*

  As can be shown by the clear plastic bag and the brown paper bag, investors are willing to spend more to buy the known contents of the clear plastic bag than the unknown contents of the brown paper bag.

  So it really does tilt the playing field by introducing valuation transparency. It tilts the playing field in the favor of the country that requires valuation transparency and against the country that allows opacity. For example, the U.S. once had a competitive advantage because it had the most transparent, liquid capital markets.

  Requiring valuation transparency also deals with the banks' strategy of avoiding regulations they don't like by engaging in regulatory arbitrage and using "substituted compliance". The idea behind substituted compliance is banks are deemed to be in compliance with U.S. rules if their subsidiaries are in compliance with similar, but not identical, host country rules. Valuation transparency is immune to this activity as banks that try to hide their offshore exposures are immediately seen as riskier as they are sending a clear message they have something to hide.

- *Claim 2: Requiring banks to provide valuation transparency will push activities into the unregulated shadow banking system.*

  So long as there is valuation transparency in all the corners of the global financial system, market participants, like investors, are indifferent to whether the activities occur in the highly regulated banking system or the unregulated shadow banking system. With valuation transparency, market participants can assess the risk of these activities and continue to exert discipline on these activities.

- *Claim 3: This much data creates greater opacity than already exists.*

  This is the equivalent of saying moving the contents from a brown paper bag to a black box makes them harder to value. It ignores the fact that it is impossible to value the contents in either case.

  The market participants who will use the data are the market participants who are capable of analyzing it. The rest of the market participants will either not invest where they are not capable of analyzing the data or they will hire a trusted, independent third party who can analyze the data.

- *Claim 4: More is not the same as better.*

  True. More disclosure simply for the sake of more disclosure does not necessarily result in valuation transparency. The yardstick by which valuation transparency is measured is what information would the experts want so they feel they have access to all the useful, relevant information in an appropriate, timely manner for assessing the risk and value of a security.

- *Claim 5: There is a big difference between the data disclosed under observable event based reporting or current exposure details and useful information.*

  No, there isn't.

  The data disclosed under observable event based reporting comes from the information systems of the originators and servicers who bill and collect the underlying assets for structured finance securities. These firms are experts and have a financial incentive to track only those data fields that are useful for monitoring and valuing the underlying asset. Therefore, these data fields are useful and relevant for all structured finance market participants because other experts, including the experts who work for the competition, can use them.

  The same holds true for the data that banks disclose when they provide their current exposure details. It comes from their information systems and can be used by other banks to assess their riskiness. For example, JPMorgan could use the data to assess Bank of America.

- *Claim 6: Know what you own in Article 122a of the European Capital Requirement Directive is a backhanded way of requiring valuation transparency for structured finance securities through disclosure on an observable event basis.*

  There is nothing backhanded about reminding investors that they are responsible for all losses on their investments and therefore they should know what they own and not invest in opaque, financial products.

  Clearly, the EU Parliament felt that sophisticated investors, like commercial and investment banks, needed to be reminded valuation transparency requires the contents of a structured finance security be disclosed in the equivalent of a clear plastic bag.

- *Claim 7: Investors might have access to observable event based data for structured finance securities or current exposure details for banks and the incentive to use this data, but they are too lazy to do so.*

  Investors might be too lazy to analyze the data for themselves.

  However, this is not an excuse for the lack of valuation transparency for banks or structured finance securities. The current lack of valuation transparency is the fault of the regulators. Under the FDR Framework, regulators are responsible for ensuring market participants have access to all the useful, relevant information in an appropriate, timely manner. This applies to all the currently opaque corners of finance including banks and structured finance securities. Going forward, with the Transparency Label Initiative™, the buy-side will be able to exert pressure on both the regulators and the issuers to ensure valuation transparency is brought to all the currently opaque corners of finance.

  Investors might be too lazy to assess the data for themselves. However, this also does not mean there are not other market participants who will use the data and do the assessment with the intent to profit.

  Tim Bray, director of Web technologies at Sun Microsystems, observed

  > There's money in money and substantial personal upside to someone who can mine the data and uncover the truth.[663]

  There are firms investors can hire to make sense out of the data disclosed by valuation transparency. For example, investors could sponsor a Kaggle competition to explore a question they have. The valuation transparency data and the question of interest are given to the 85,000+ data scientists in the Kaggle community who then compete to win the competition. Prizes awarded have been from $3,000 and up.

- *Claim 8: With each bank disclosing its current exposure details, no investors would be interested in buying bank stocks.*

  There is no evidence to support this claim. There is plenty of evidence for investors having an appetite for everything from low risk, high dividend paying utilities to high risk, no dividend paying start-ups. The question is where in this range will banks fall after they begin disclosing their current exposure details.

  Providing valuation transparency does not reduce investor interest in bank stocks by casting the banks in a poor light. Rather, valuation

---

663 Roth, Daniel (2009, February 23), Road Map for Financial Recovery: Radical Transparency Now, Wired Magazine, http://archive.wired.com/techbiz/it/magazine/17-03/wp_reboot?currentPage=all

transparency just shows what the actual condition of the banks is. This makes it easier for investors to make a decision on whether or not to buy bank stocks.

- *Claim 9: Valuation transparency could cause a global financial crisis.*

  Valuation transparency doesn't cause a financial crisis. It is the existence of opacity that is the necessary condition for a financial crisis. Where there is valuation transparency, market participants can assess risk and adjust their exposures to what they can afford to lose. Where there is opacity, market participants are blindly betting and if they underestimate the true level of risk losing more than they can afford to lose.

- *Claim 10: Do market participants really need all of this granular asset, liability and off-balance sheet-level data?*

  Yes!

  For example, each of the Too Big to Fail financial institutions has both the ability and incentive to analyze this data to determine who their "dumbest competitor" is. That way, they can properly manage both the amount and price of their exposure to this competitor.

- *Claim 11: Isn't there a halfway house that does not require disclosing all the granular asset, liability and off-balance sheet-level data, but would still deliver the same results?*

  No! For example, when monitoring a loan portfolio it is important to be able to answer the question when a loan stops performing is the reason unique to the borrower or is it reflective of a systematic problem. The only way to answer this question is with granular level data.

  Ultimately, the search for a halfway house is an effort to maintain opacity.

- *Claim 12: Valuation transparency is helpful, but ….*

  This claim is best illustrated by the June 2011 Bank of England Financial Stability Report question and answer exchange between the press and Sir Mervyn King.

> Trond Sundnes, Norwegian Business Daily:
>
> A question about transparency, it seems to be important in several of your recommendations here. Would transparency, greater transparency in the financial markets, could that avoid, or at least minimize consequences, the effects of future crises?

Mervyn King:

Well, greater transparency will help.

And I think one of the problems that arose in the financial crisis, both with individual institutions and now with sovereign debt, is that the risk that people will suddenly withdraw funding is increased if there is rather little transparency about the exposures or the assets on the balance sheets of the people to whom they've lent or were used to funding.

I think it would be naive to think that there is a magic answer here, because one of the things that occurs in financial crises is that people's beliefs about the underlying values of the asset can change very radically. And that means that your perception of the solvency, or the risk of levels of indebtedness can change from being one in which you are rather sanguine about the levels of indebtedness to one in which you suddenly become very concerned. In addition, if that is a common change of perception in the minds of investors then you will simply see a run-out of the flow of debt finance to the indebted institutions.

So I think we feel that transparency will help, but in the end there is always going to be a risk if you have fairly high levels of indebtedness, and there always needs to be a recognition that if you are justifying high levels of indebtedness on the basis of current asset values, just be very aware of the fact that current asset values can go down as well as up.[664]

Sir Mervyn King acknowledges transparency will help to avoid or at least minimize the consequences of future financial crises. Specifically, valuation transparency deals with the problem of investors suddenly withdrawing funding for opaque assets. It was the assets without valuation transparency like structured finance securities and bank securities (think unsecured interbank loans) that experienced the greatest change in perceived value at the beginning of the financial crisis. The markets for these assets froze. The markets for assets that provided valuation transparency, like most stocks and corporate bonds, functioned throughout the peak of the crisis without government intervention. There were buyers even if the price was not what the seller wanted.

664 Bank of England (2011, June 24), Financial Stability Report Q&A, Bank of England, http://www.bankofengland.co.uk/publications/Documents/fsr/2011/conf110624.pdf, page 20

However, in his reply, Sir Mervyn King worries transparency doesn't address radical changes in people's beliefs about the value of assets. Valuation transparency directly addresses minimizing radical changes in the value of assets. Let's go back to my example using the clear plastic and brown paper bags. Since you can see the clear plastic bag contains $60 dollars, there just isn't a lot of room for a change in belief about the value of the contents of the bag. With the brown paper bag containing an unknown quantity of money, there is a lot of room for a change in belief about the value of the contents of the bag.

Next, Sir Mervyn King worries transparency won't stop a bank run. Valuation transparency is all about stopping bank runs before they occur and ending rumors before they can become a bank run. As a result of valuation transparency, banks are subject to market discipline and restraint on their risk taking. As a result of valuation transparency, market participants can make their decisions based on facts about the financial institutions rather than rumors.

The argument for valuation transparency is not that by itself it is the magic answer for avoiding or minimizing the consequences of our current or future financial crises. It is in combination with *caveat emptor* that valuation transparency is the answer for avoiding or minimizing the consequences of financial crises. The combination of valuation transparency and *caveat emptor* is an eloquent and far more powerful solution for avoiding or minimizing the consequences of financial crises than any other available solution.

- *Claim 13: We are experts at risk management. The new risk measures we disclose, including stress test results, provide market participants with all the information they need to assess our risk.*

Wall Street's instincts to create, protect and retain opacity even get in the way of its having the data it needs to claim it is prudently managing its own risks.

At the beginning of our current financial crisis, the regulators discovered the opacity of the banks prevented them from having accurate information on the true extent of their exposure to their counterparties, including the other banks, for their derivative trades. Without this information, it was impossible to assess the risk of financial contagion because nobody knew if the banks had a greater exposure to their counterparties than they could afford to lose. After more than 5 years of trying to assemble the necessary information, the banks still have been unable to pierce the opacity they have created.

The January 15, 2014 Senior Supervisory Group's Progress Report on Counterparty Data discussed the opacity surrounding counterparty exposures.

> The early stages of the financial crisis were marked by shortcomings in data aggregation and in timely reporting of counterparty risk—both to firms' own management and to supervisors. Incomplete and delayed risk capture combined with sharply moving markets to create confusion about levels, sensitivities, and, in some cases, direction of counterparty exposure. Those problems constrained the ability of firms' management to execute appropriate risk mitigation and capital conservation transactions and deprived supervisors of critical information needed to understand the true scale of interconnected exposures.[665]

In short, throughout the financial crisis nobody knew what was going on in the opaque derivative market or its impact on the equally opaque banks. In response to this lack of critical information, the regulators began to collect, but not make available to the other market participants,

> daily, global counterparty credit data for reporting firms' largest twenty exposures to each of three distinct types of counterparties: banks, nonbank financial institutions, and nonbank corporate counterparties. Data requested included not only counterparty credit risk exposure to derivatives and securities financing transactions but also exposure to traditional lending, short-term money placements, and issuer risk.[666]

This data is now sent to the International Data Hub at the Bank for International Settlements. As for how good this data is, according to the regulators

> Five years after the financial crisis, firms' progress toward consistent, timely, and accurate reporting of top counterparty exposures fails to meet both supervisory expectations and industry self-identified best practices. The area of greatest concern remains firms' inability to consistently produce high-quality data.[667]

Why are the banks unable to get over the low standards they set for themselves and consistently producing high-quality data?

> Challenges understanding exposures can arise when a firm operates through many of its own legal vehicles, which in turn conduct

665 Senior Supervisors Group (2014, January 15), Progress Report on Counterparty Data, New York Fed, http://www.newyorkfed.org/newsevents/news/banking/2014/SSG_Progress_Report_on_Counterparty_January2014.pdf, page 2

666 ibid, page 2

667 ibid, page 1

> business with many external entities, including some that may ultimately be owned by or affiliated with the same counterparty.[668]

Translation, by operating literally thousands of subsidiaries, banks are able to hide what they are doing. But in hiding what they are doing, they also make it impossible for their counterparties to assemble the data so the counterparties know the true extent of their exposure to each bank.

Fortunately, this is a problem valuation transparency solves. With valuation transparency, banks are required to disclose their current exposure details on a global basis not just for the parent company, but also for all its subsidiaries. With valuation transparency, not only can the banks and regulators see each bank's counterparty exposures, but so too can all the other market participants.

668 ibid, page 1

Glossary

Alice in Wonderland Accounting: Under the Japanese Model for handling a financial crisis, banks have a budget for recognizing losses on the bad debt hidden on and off their balance sheet. As a result of this budget, bank financial statements are completely fictitious and do not reflect the economic reality the banks face. (see Japanese Model)

Amortized cost accounting: Under amortized cost accounting, a bank's assets reflect their historical purchase price and liabilities reflect their historical issuance value. Assets are adjusted for any principal repayments and for any premium paid or discount received when the asset is acquired. Liabilities are adjusted for any principal repayment and for any premium received or discount provided when the liability was sold. (see fair value accounting)

Anti-fragile: A financial system is anti-fragile if it is not prone to crashes. A financial system combining the philosophy of disclosure and *caveat emptor* is anti-fragile. Investors limit their exposures to what they can afford to lose and are able to recognize their losses without causing the financial system to collapse. A financial system with opacity is not anti-fragile as it is prone to systemic collapse because investors unknowingly undertake too much risk.

Article 122a: This is the section of the European Capital Directive says that commercial and investment banks must "know what they own" if they buy a structured finance security.

Asset Allocation Fallacy: This fallacy is the way portfolio managers justify blindly gambling with the investors' money. Under this fallacy, the portfolio managers assume that because an investor has given them money the investor understands all of the risks of the securities the portfolio managers are buying and wants an exposure to these securities. This assumption is flawed because the investor doesn't understand what risks there are in investing in these securities from either reading the prospectus if it fails to disclose the lack of valuation transparency for the securities or listening to the independent manager who represents he has expertise in valuing these securities. Simply put, the investor doesn't know the portfolio managers are blindly gambling with their money when they buy bank or structured finance securities.

Asset-backed security: An asset-backed security is a bond whose payments of interest and principal come from the cash flow generated by a specific group of assets. The assets are put in a trust for the benefit of the investors in the security. Examples of assets used to back these securities range from credit cards to auto loans to mortgages and even other asset backed securities. Asset backed securities are named after the assets used to back them. For example, residential mortgage-backed securities or commercial mortgage-backed securities are securities backed by residential mortgages and commercial mortgages respectively.

Bailout: A modern banking system is designed so there is never a need to explicitly use taxpayer funds to boost an insolvent bank's book capital level. Because of deposit insurance and access to central bank funding, an insolvent bank that generates more in interest income and fees than it spends on interest expense and pre-banker bonus operating costs can retain enough future earnings to restore its solvency. If an insolvent bank cannot generate earnings to restore its solvency, then it should be closed. As a result, a bailout is nothing more than policymakers transferring losses from the banks to the taxpayers.

Bank risk management: In theory, risk management at a bank limits both the size of the individual bets the bank takes and the total risk taken by the bank. In reality, risk management is an exercise for the bank regulators' benefit. When banks are opaque, the individuals responsible for taking risk are the one's who contribute to the bank's bottom line. They are not constrained by risk managers when there is a conflict between risk management limits and profits.

Basel Capital Requirements: International bank supervisors have agreed to a framework for matching the risk of a bank's exposures to the amount of book capital. This framework is called the Basel Capital requirements. (see risk-adjusted capital ratios)

Black Box: A term used by the Bank of England's Andy Haldane to describe the opacity of banks after they have complied with current disclosure regulations. Because banks are opaque, they are not an investible proposition. Rather, buying their securities at a reasonable cost is for gamblers. As Warren Buffett explained of his decision to invest in Goldman Sachs, it is a bet that the government will protect the bank.

Book Capital: Purely an accounting construct comprised of the total amount of money the bank has received from selling its shares plus all of its earnings over time minus the total of the dividends it has paid out. As an accounting construct, both bank management and bank regulators easily manipulate it.

Buy-side: The side of the market that includes institutions such as pension funds, insurance companies and money managers who buy securities. Generally, the buy-side excludes the wholly owned investment management subsidiaries of the sell-side firms. See sell-side.

Buyers' Strike: A buyers' strike occurs when investors refuse to buy a particular type of security. For example, there has been a buyers' strike going on in the private label residential mortgage backed securities market since the beginning of the financial crisis that has seen the volume of new issuance decrease from hundreds of billions to the tens of billions. Ending this strike requires new issuers of such securities to provide valuation transparency.

CAMELS rating: Each year, bank regulators prepare a Report of Examination to tell the bank's board of directors what the examiners found. The centerpiece of this report is the bank's CAMELS rating. The rating is a summary of the bank's overall capital adequacy (C), asset quality (A), management (M), earnings (E), liquidity (L) and sensitivity to market risk (S). The rating scale runs from 1, a good score, to 5, a bad score.

Capital Allocation Business or Business of allocating credit: By design, bankers are in the business of allocating credit as they are responsible both for all decisions to extend credit to borrowers and for any gains or losses on the extended credit. Bank regulators do not make the decision to extend credit to any specific borrower, but they do influence the types of borrowers who have easier access to credit. This influence is exerted through the Basel risk-based capital requirements. Under Basel I and II, banks did not have to hold capital against their sovereign debt. Reality changed this practice.

Capital Buffer: Bank regulators divide bank capital into two pieces: capital below a minimum level and capital above this minimum level. Capital above the minimum level is known as the capital buffer. In normal times, it can be used to absorb losses on the bank's exposures. However, when bank regulators pursue the Japanese Model during a crisis, it is not available to absorb losses. It is not available because a reduction in total book capital levels is perceived by the regulators as sending the wrong message about the safety and soundness of the opaque banks.

Capitalism's inherent instability: There are two primary sources of instability in capitalism: instability caused by creative destruction and instability caused by opacity. Creative destruction is at the heart of a dynamic, adaptive economy and is encouraged as new products or services replace existing products or services. For example, the invention of hand held calculators created significant instability in the market for slide rules. As a result of creative destruction, investors know there are no guarantees in investing. On the other hand, opacity is injected into capitalism solely for greedy bankers to gain an advantage over investors. When markets become more opaque, they become unstable and prone to crashes. This is why there are regulations to require disclosure and prevent opacity driven instability.

Career Risk: Acting in a way that is adversarial to Wall Street's interests places a regulator's career in jeopardy. There is risk of political pushback and there is risk to future job prospects especially given the "revolving door" opportunities regulators find in the private sector

Caveat emptor: *Caveat emptor* is Latin and means "buyer beware". Financial markets are based on the principle of buyer beware because investors are responsible for all losses on their investments.

Classic financial panic: A classic financial panic is a run on the banks by uninsured depositors. The cause of the run is an immediate, readily identifiable trigger that calls into question the ability of the bank(s) to repay all the uninsured depositors' funds. The necessary condition for a classic financial panic is opacity that prevents market participants from assessing if they will be repaid.

Code of conduct: There was once an unwritten code of conduct among bankers that they act honestly. This code of conduct was enforced by valuation transparency that let everyone see if a banker didn't act honestly.

Collateral: For some loans, a borrower must pledge an asset that is worth more than the loan amount. The asset is collateral for the loan and will be forfeited if the loan is not repaid. An example of this is the pledge of the house as collateral for a mortgage loan.

Collateralized debt obligations (CDOs): A CDO is a bond backed by some combination of assets like mortgages as well as multiple asset-backed securities and even other CDOs.

Cost/benefit analysis: A cost/benefit analysis is an analysis applied to regulations to ensure the benefit to society from a regulation does not exceed its cost of compliance. In the case of disclosure, the cost/benefit analysis was done at the time of the Great Depression and it was determined the benefit to society from not having another opacity driven financial crisis was far greater than the cost of requiring disclosure for all securities then in existence or that Wall Street might subsequently create. Our current opacity driven financial crisis confirms the cost/benefit analysis supports disclosure that results in valuation transparency in all parts of the financial system. The concept of a cost/benefit analysis for disclosure for each type of security is an unwarranted extension of the principle and allows the regulated banks to frustrate, delay and diminish the information flow to investors.

Counter-party: A trade involves a minimum of two participants, a buyer and a seller. A counter-party is a participant who is on the opposite side of the trade. If you are a buyer, the counter-party is the seller and visa versa. What is important about the notion of a counter-party is everyone is looking out for their own self-interest. (see zero-sum trading)

Covered Bond: One of the original forms of an asset-backed security was the covered bond. In issuing a covered bond, a bank segregates specific assets on its balance sheet for the benefit of the investors. This effectively pledges the bank to make up any shortfall in the cash flow from the assets in satisfying interest and principal payments on the bond. The security for this bond may potentially be problematic if the asset valuations are substantially overstated and the bank is experiencing financial difficulties.

Credit cycle: The credit cycle can be thought of as a pendulum that swings back and forth between easy and hard credit conditions. A cycle occurs when the pendulum swings from credit being easy to access to very hard to access and back to easy to access.

Credit derivative: A credit derivative is a security that allows the buyer or seller to bet on whether a specific company or group of companies will experience a negative financial event like a bankruptcy during a specified period of time.

Current exposure details disclosure: The gold standard for banks providing valuation transparency is their reporting on an ongoing basis their current asset, liability and off-balance sheet exposure details.

Data Warehouse: A data warehouse is a simply a very large database.

Debt Write-Down: The action taken by a bank to recognize the loss on the difference between the current outstanding balance of the loan and the greater of the amount of the loan the borrower can actually repay or the value of the collateral to an independent third party.

Delay and Pray: A strategy used by bank regulators to postpone recognition of losses by banks until the banks have been able to retain sufficient earnings so they can absorb the losses without their book capital level dropping below zero. This strategy is only possible because of opacity. If the banks provided valuation transparency, market participants would exert discipline on the banks to recognize the losses upfront.

Derivatives: A financial instrument that allows for a bet to be placed on the future value of real assets like stocks, bonds or commodities. These financial instruments can take many forms including swaps, options and futures.

Due diligence: The act of verifying what has been represented about an investment is actually true.

Efficient Market Hypothesis: In its weakest form, this hypothesis asserts market prices reflect all past publicly available information. In its semi-strong form, this hypothesis asserts market prices reflect all past publicly available information and change immediately to reflect new public information. In its strongest form, this hypothesis asserts market prices change to reflect hidden information too. Effectively, the hypothesis assumes valuation transparency and all of its benefits even in the absence of valuation transparency. It also assumes away Wall Street's interest in reintroducing and profiting from opacity.

Euribor: Euribor is the European Interbank Offered Rate. (see Libor and Tibor)

Expected Loss Approach: Despite a bank's best efforts in underwriting its loans, there will be some loans that default. Under the Expected Loss Approach, based on the bank's historical loan loss experience, when a bank makes a loan it also recognizes an expense, called a provision for loan losses, on its income statement. The total provision for loan losses reflects the losses the bank expected to experience over time from its whole loan portfolio. The provision increases an account on the bank's balance sheet called the loan loss reserve. As time passes and the loans matured, some of the loans will start to experience repayment difficulties. Based on whether or not the bankers expected the borrower to recover from temporary difficulties and resume paying under the terms of the loan, the bank has two choices. If it expects the borrower to recover, it can engage in forbearance and reduce the borrower's loan payments until the borrower recovers. While granting forbearance, the bank would take a further provision for loan losses through its income statement. If the bank doesn't expect the borrower to recover or the borrower receiving forbearance actually defaults, the loss on the loan is charged-off against the loan loss reserve. (see Incurred Loss Accounting)

Extend and Pretend: The practice by banks of extending additional credit to borrowers who are unable to repay their loan and claiming the loan is still performing.

Fair value accounting: Under fair value accounting, a bank's assets are valued at the price they would receive if they were sold in the market and the bank's liabilities are value at what the bank would pay to be rid of the liability. (see amortized cost accounting)

FDR Framework: The FDR Framework is the combination of the philosophy of disclosure and the principle of *caveat emptor* plus an institutional infrastructure to enforce this combination. Enforcement was intended to be dynamic and adapt to ensure there was valuation transparency for all of the financial innovations created by Wall Street. The Transparency Label Initiative™ is needed to fix this problem (see Transparency Label Initiative™).

Financial contagion: Financial contagion occurs when the loss on a single investment can trigger a domino effect that drags down other investments too. For example, at the beginning of our financial crisis, bank regulators feared there would be financial contagion and that if one global financial institution failed it would cause the failure of other global financial institutions. Financial contagion is an opacity driven problem as opacity prevents the market discipline necessary to ensure banks do not have more exposure to each other than they can afford to lose. The cure for ending financial contagion is requiring valuation transparency. Then, each financial institution can limit its exposure to other financial institutions to what it can afford to lose.

Financial innovation: Financial innovation is a Wall Street euphemism for the creation of another opaque product to sell to investors. The opacity of the product hides its risk and lets Wall Street profit when investors underestimate the risk and overpay for the product.

Financial market stability: A financial market is stable if it can continue to operate and convert savings into funding and manage risk in the face of economic stress without government intervention. Financial markets combining the philosophy of disclosure and *caveat emptor* are stable because there are willing buyers for each seller even if the price isn't what the seller wants. Furthermore, financial market are stable because investors can assess the risk of their investments and limit the size of their investments to what they can afford to lose. As a result, the financial system is not prone to crashes and the fire sale of assets when losses have to be realized.

FOMC: Federal Open Market Committee consisting of the governors of the Federal Reserve and the presidents of the regional Federal Reserve banks.

Forbearance: There are two types. Banks that cut borrowers a break on loan payments because the bankers think the borrowers' set back is temporary. Regulators who cut banks a break in how the banks handle their borrowers experiencing financial difficulty in order to avoid a fire-sale from the banks foreclosing on the loan collateral and then trying to sell this collateral.

Full information: Full information is the standard for disclosure embodied in the securities laws put in place by the FDR Administration. A security's disclosure can be said to provide full information when the experts in the buying public have access to what they consider all the essentially important information about the security in a timely manner.

Funding for Lending scheme: A program run by the Bank of England to subsidize UK banks by providing them with below market rate funding in an effort to promote more lending.

Gambling on Redemption: When an opaque bank is insolvent, management has an incentive to take greater risks in the hopes it will payoff and restore solvency. During the savings and loan crisis, many of these insolvent institutions bet heavily on commercial real estate development. The result was a glut of office space and more losses.

Gambling: Gambling in the world of investments is simply buying a security based on its price without going through the investment process.

Geithner Guarantee: A promise made by then Treasury Secretary Timothy Geithner to encourage investment in U.S. banks that had passed the bank regulator run stress tests. The promise was the U.S. taxpayer would protect the investors from all the losses hidden on and off the balance sheets of the tested banks. By pledging the full faith and credit of the U.S. to support the solvency of the banks, Mr. Geithner turned the financial crisis into a sovereign debt crisis.

Going concern: A bank can continue to operate if its income from fees and interest exceed its interest expense plus operating costs.

Groupthink: The desire to minimize conflict within a group and reach a consensus leads to the group not considering alternatives.

Heavy-handed, gold-plating: A charge levied by politicians against financial regulators who create complex regulations that are unlikely to prevent the next financial crisis or deter bad behavior by bankers.

Hedge: In finance, a hedge refers to locking in the current value of a single asset or a portfolio of assets. This requires finding a financial security whose value moves in the opposite direction of the value of the single asset or portfolio of assets. For example, when the single asset or portfolio of assets increases in value, the financial security used as a hedge must decrease in value. A perfect hedge is one where the change in the value of the single asset or portfolio of assets is exactly offset by the change in value of the financial security used as a hedge.

Herding or bandwagon effect: Herding refers to investors, including banks, crowding into the same type of investments without independently assessing the risk of the investments.

HIPAA: The Health Insurance Portability and Accountability Act includes standards for protecting the privacy of patient health care data.

HPA: HPA stands for house price appreciation and is a variable used in the models to value residential mortgage-backed securities. Prior to the financial crisis, it was assumed house prices on a nationwide basis could only appreciate.

Illiquidity: A security is referred to as illiquid if there are no buyers for the security. The primary reason a security is illiquid is it is opaque and does not provide valuation transparency. Without valuation transparency, potential buyers cannot independently assess the value of the security. This limits the potential buyers to investors who want to blindly gamble.

Illiquidity Premium: When a buyer purchases an opaque security, they know it is unlikely they will be able to sell the security before maturity. As a result, the buyer requires extra compensation. (see illiquidity)

Impaired assets: For banks, an asset is impaired if the borrower is not capable of making the contracted payments.

Incurred Loss Accounting: Under incurred loss accounting, the expense for bad debt is recognized when a loan actually defaults. The issue of regulatory forbearance is particularly important when a loan defaulting is the trigger for recognition of the bad debt expense. So long as there is regulatory forbearance and banks engage in activities like 'extend and pretend', the losses on the loans don't flow through the income statement or the capital accounts. The result, of course, is the banks' financial statements are completely divorced from their underlying economic reality. (see Expected Loss Approach)

Information asymmetry: This is a form of opacity and refers to a transaction in which one party to the transaction has information the other party needs if they are both to have full information to use to value the good or service being sold. There is a tendency for the party with the information to take advantage of the party without the information, as any deal tends to favor them.

Information overload or too much disclosure can be counterproductive: This red herring claim goes as follows: if too much information is disclosed to a reasonable investor, the reasonable investor will be overwhelmed and will not be able to assess the disclosed information. This claim is wrong on a number of levels. First, a reasonable investor can ignore the parts of the disclosure they are not interested in. Second, a reasonable investor can hire an expert who can assess all the disclosed information. Third, a reasonable investor can conclude they are unable to analyze the disclosed information and therefore they will not invest because they are unable to know what they owned. What is particularly troubling about this claim is neither legislative mandate nor charge from FDR told the SEC to worry about it.

Informationally-Insensitive debt: A concept developed by Yale Professor Gary Gorton who said some debt is sensitive to information and some debt is insensitive. Under his definition, debt that is insensitive to information doesn't require a lot of resources to investigate. Please note that informationally-insensitive debt doesn't exist. Buyers know they are responsible for all losses on their investments. Therefore, they have an incentive to devote as many resources as are necessary to investigating each investment and adjusting their exposure when new information is available.

Insolvency: A bank is insolvent when the market value of its assets is less than the book value of its liabilities.

Interconnected: One of the reasons given for bailing out the banks was their complex web of inter-linkages made it impossible to predict how the failure of one bank would affect the rest of the global financial system. This problem only occurs in the presence of opacity. In the presence of valuation transparency, market participants engage in self-discipline and limit their exposures to what they can afford to lose. As a result, while the failure of a bank is painful to those exposed to it, the failure does not trigger a financial crisis.

Intermediary depiction model: Under this disclosure model, a summary of all the information seen by the intermediary is provided to investors. This disclosure model works best for manufacturers where a summary can still contain all the useful, relevant information. (see pure information model)

Investment process: The investment process is a cyclical three-step process. The first step is to independently assess the risk and value of an investment using the information disclosed under valuation transparency. The second step is price discovery and soliciting the price Wall Street is willing to buy or sell the investment at. The third step is to compare the independently determined value with the prices from Wall Street to make a buy, hold or sell decision.

Invisible hand of the market: Adam Smith introduced the concept of the invisible hand of the market in 1776 in the *Wealth of Nations*. The invisible hand of the market works through prices to coordinate all the economic decisions made by companies and households, both looking after their own self-interest, so the right amount of goods and services are produced.

It's too late now trap: This trap is sprung when traders decide the best strategy for handling a losing trade is to do nothing and pray the market moves in their favor. Subsequently, when losses on the trade increase, the traders lament how it is too late and they wish they had either recognized the smaller loss or hedged the position. (see Trader's Dilemma)

Japanese Model: This model for handling insolvent banks involves protecting bank capital levels and banker bonuses at all cost while placing the burden of the excess debt in the financial system on the real economy. As part of protecting bank capital levels, regulators use opacity to hide the banks' losses due to their exposure to bad debt. As part of protecting banker bonuses, regulators approve a budget for recognizing losses on the bad debt that includes paying bonuses and building book capital levels. By placing the burden of the excess debt on the real economy, this model triggers a multi-year economic malaise and less than full employment. (see Swedish Model)

Know what you own: Know what you own is what separates investing from blindly gambling. Know what you own goes beyond knowing the name of the security and extends to understanding what drives the expected return from owning the security and what the risks of ownership are.

Lender of last resort: Following Walter Bagehot's dictum, in the event of a bank run, central banks are the lenders of last resort to solvent banks that have no other way to raise funds without engaging in the fire sale of assets. Central banks lend against good collateral so the commercial banks can meet the demand for cash by their depositors.

Level 3 assets: Under accounting rules, bank management gets to assign a value to securities for which there is no readily observable market price or for which bank management thinks that due to illiquidity the price does not reflect the fair value of the asset.

Libor: Libor is the London Interbank Offered Rate. It is the benchmark interest rate off of which over $500 trillion in assets is priced. In theory, Libor is suppose to represent the average cost to the largest banks to borrow money at 11 am London time from other banks in the unsecured interbank lending market. In reality, it is a rate bankers manipulate for their benefit as it is based on the banks' estimate of what it would cost them to borrow and not on actual transactions. (see Euribor and Tibor)

Libor-OIS (Overnight Index Swap) spread: This interest rate spread is a barometer of what banks think is the risk of losing money by lending to other banks on an unsecured basis.

Light touch regulation: In the run-up to the financial crisis, UK bank regulators sought to avoid damaging London's competitive position by engaging in limited supervision. Doing so meant the bank regulators relied on bank management to choose how to identify and control risk in a manner consistent with a set of principles and risk-based regulations laid out by the bank regulators. By definition, light touch meant the bank regulators did not intrude into the business of the banks, but rather checked to see if everything was in compliance.

Liquidity: A financial market is said to have liquidity if there is a willing buyer for every seller. However, this does not mean that the price the buyer is willing to pay is the price the seller wants to sell at. Liquidity also refers to a bank's ability without access to the financial markets to either meet unexpectedly high levels of deposit outflows or meet scheduled deposit and debt maturities over a period of time.

Loan Loss Reserve: A contra-asset account on each bank's balance sheet. (see Expected Loss Approach and Incurred Loss Accounting)

Loan servicing: Billing and collecting a loan.

Mark-to-market: Mark-to-market involves valuing a security at its current market price. (see fair value accounting)

Mark-to-model: Securities are priced not to current market values but rather to financial models run by the banks. This is sometimes referred to as mark-to-myth as the assumptions that go into the models tend to be biased towards a higher price. (see mark-to-market)

Market Discipline: By adjusting both the amount and price of their exposure to what they can afford to lose, investors exert restraint on risk-taking by bank management. Investors enforce market discipline by decreasing the amount of funds they make available as the risk of the bank increases. In addition, investors enforce market discipline by increasing their required return at a faster rate than the bank's level of risk increases. By linking access to and the cost of a bank's funds to the bank's level of risk, investors put a natural restraint on risk taking. Ongoing valuation transparency and the ongoing need for new funds are the necessary conditions for market discipline to occur. It is only when there is ongoing valuation transparency that investors can continually assess the risk of their investments and make adjustments to their exposure to reflect the change in risk. Market discipline also applies to bank regulators. When there is valuation transparency, market participants can see if the bank regulators are doing their job.

Market Making: Banks engage in the activity of quoting a price they are willing to buy a security at and a price they are willing to sell the same security at.

Material non-public information: Material non-public information is information buyers or sellers would like to have as it would effect their investment decision, but that hasn't been disclosed yet.

Moral obligation or moral hazard: The government creates a moral obligation to protect investors from losses when it violates the prohibition on endorsing or promoting a private security. For example, by announcing the results of bank regulator run stress tests, the government creates a moral obligation to protect investors in the banks because it is reasonable to assume the investors relied on the government's "endorsement" in making their investment decision.

Non-transparent activities: Regulators take advantage of the lack of valuation transparency to support the bank. These activities range from temporarily suspending regulations to offering the banks below market rate loans. (see regulatory discretion)

Observable event based reporting: Observable event based reporting involves reporting to investors before the next business day whenever an activity, like a payment or delinquency, occurs involving the assets backing an asset-backed security. Credit cards provide the classic example for showing that the assets backing a security are already tracked on an observable event based reporting basis. Anyone with a credit card can use the Interned to see all the current activity including charges and payments on their card. Observable event based reporting is necessary if asset backed securities are going to have the transparency of a clear plastic bag.

Opacity: Opacity is anything that prevents either the buyer knowing what he is buying or the seller knowing what he owns and is selling. There are many different forms of opacity including a lack of disclosure, complexity and information asymmetry. Opacity is the ultimate market imperfection.

Opacity Protection Team: The team includes Wall Street and the City firms, their lobbyists and industry trade groups they control, their legal advisors, friendly politicians and regulators, think-tanks and economists who rent out the reputation of the university they work for. The mission of the Opacity Protection Team is to protect the profits the banks make from opacity at all costs. By definition, if the Opacity Protection Team is successful, the invisible hand of the market does not work properly as resources are misallocated to the banks and bankers.

Originate to Distribute: Under this business model, banks make loans with the intent to resell the loans to investors rather than hold the loans on their balance sheets.

Paper bag: A brown paper bag is the physical model for opacity. Nobody can see the contents of a closed brown paper bag and therefore they have no idea what is in the bag or what might come out of the bag. (see plastic bag and paper or plastic bag model)

Paper or Plastic bag model: Together, a paper bag and a plastic bag are a model for seeing whether a security is opaque or transparent. Valuation transparency is a 0/1 variable. Either a security's disclosures leave it opaque like the brown paper bag (0) and nobody has any idea of what is in the bag or might come out of the bag or the security is transparent like the clear plastic bag (1) and everyone can see the contents of the bag. (see plastic bag and paper bag)

Paradox of transparency: The more information that is disclosed, the more complexity involved in assessing the information.

Plastic bag: The clear plastic bag is a physical model for valuation transparency. Everyone can see the contents of a clear plastic bag. (see paper bag and paper or plastic bag model)

Policy of Deceit: Bank regulators adopted the policy of making intentionally misleading statements about the financial health of a Too Big to Fail bank with the failure of Continental Illinois. Faced with the prospect of a failure that could disrupt the national and/or global economy, the bank regulators issued a carefully worded statement to convey the impression Continental Illinois was not experiencing severe problems. During our current financial crisis, similar statements about the health of the TBTF banks have been made at the time of their annual stress tests. This policy can only exist so long as the banks are opaque and do not disclose their current exposure details. (see regulatory discretion)

Political pushback or backlash: By design, politicians oversee the bank regulators and are in a position to influence their conduct. Bank regulators fear politicians will view their conduct negatively and take action that reduces the bank regulators' authority. It is this fear of political pushback that acts to restrain the regulators and the level of regulatory discipline exerted on the banks.

Political Will: A measure of politicians enthusiasm for supporting the bank regulators when the regulators exercise regulatory restraint to restrict bank risk taking and close banks that are no longer viable. In the absence of political will, regulatory restraint on banks is effectively non-existent as the rules are not strictly enforced.

Portfolio Hedge: A portfolio hedge involves locking in the value of a portfolio of assets by acquiring a financial security whose value changes so as to offset any losses in the portfolio of assets.

Price Discovery or Price Discovery Mechanism: Reflects the buyer's and seller's view at a moment in time of the price they are willing to engage in a transaction for a specific security at. Price is different than the buyer's and seller's independent valuation of the security. Price is typically below what the buyer thinks the security is worth. Price is typically at or above what the seller thinks the security is worth.

Price transparency: Price transparency refers to disclosure of the last price a security was bought or sold at. This price might represent what the greatest investor or biggest fool paid.

Philosophy of Disclosure: The philosophy of disclosure is a defining feature of our capital markets and draws a line between the state and investors. The state is responsible for disclosure and ensuring all market participants have access to all the useful, relevant information in an appropriate, timely manner so they can independently assess this information prior to making an investment decision. Investors are responsible for risk-taking and the results of this risk-taking and thus have an incentive to use the information disclosed. The state is responsible for disclosure because securities that provide valuation transparency allow the invisible hand of the market to operate properly. With valuation transparency, both buyers and sellers have full information and can know what they are buying and selling and make a fully informed decision.

Prompt Corrective Action: To prevent management of banks with low capital ratios gambling on redemption, Congress passed the Federal Deposit Insurance Corporation Improvement Act of 1991 that mandated the FDIC replace bank management if the bank's tangible equity to asset ratio fell below 2%.

Proprietary Bet: Banks take a position in a financial security with the intention of profiting from a change in the price of the security.

Provision for Loan Losses: An expense account on each bank's income statement through which the bank takes a charge for the cost of its bad loans. (see Expected Loss Approach and Incurred Loss Accounting)

Prudential Supervision: Prudential supervision is another name for bank regulators examining each individual bank to assess their safety and soundness as well as compliance with banking regulations.

Pure information model: Under this disclosure model, investors have access to all the information available about their investment without a third party summarizing this information. This model works best for banks and structured finance securities where the useful, relevant information is the granular level details of the underlying exposures held by the banks and structured finance securities. (see intermediary depiction disclosure model)

Rating Firms: There are a handful of companies the SEC recognizes that assign ratings to issuers and different types of debt securities. These ratings seek to capture the ability of the borrower to repay the debt or alternatively how likely the borrower is to default and not repay their debt.

Regulation AB: This regulation was adopted by the SEC on January 5, 2005 and contains the disclosure requirements for structured finance securities. These requirements did not result in the provision of valuation transparency. In full compliance with this regulation, Wall Street was able to issue opaque, toxic subprime mortgage-backed securities.

Regulatory capture: When the banks get their regulators to advance the banks' agenda and not the public's interest.

Regulatory discipline: Regulators exert discipline to restrain risk taking by banks using two methods: regulations and oversight. Regulations are like debt covenants that place restrictions on the activities banks can engage in. Oversight is the ongoing regulatory presence that checks to see if the banks are complying with the regulations. Regulatory discipline is always weaker than and is intended as a complement to and not a substitute for market discipline. (see market discipline)

Regulatory discretion: By design, bank regulators were left with the authority to determine when a bank is closed. Because of opacity, bank regulators expanded the zone of discretion so the bank regulators could engage in non-transparent acts to help the banks facing financial difficulty. An example of a non-transparent act is to let the banks pretend that a non-performing loan is actually performing.

Regulatory forbearance: Regulators making the decision to refrain from taking an action like closing an insolvent bank or requiring the bank to write-down its assets to market value.

Regulatory Reform Litmus Test: The litmus test asks the simple question of would a post-crisis reform be used by regulators during another financial crisis. If not, then the reform is unlikely to be of any value.

Repo Market or Repurchase Market: One of the ways that banks fund themselves is by selling an asset, typically a security like a government bond, and promising to repurchase the asset at a higher price in the future. This is known as a "repo".

Reputational risk: While intangible, a bank's reputation might be its most valuable asset. Banks with good reputations are able to attract employees, clients and funds at lower cost and have a higher share price. Reputation risk can arise from the act of some employees, like manipulating the Libor interest rate, or from the bank itself, like selling loan payment protection insurance that doesn't ever kick in.

Resolution hierarchy: When the bank regulators step in and close a bank, they distribute the losses on the bank's assets starting with common stock holder equity and working their way up the bank's capital structure until all losses have been absorbed.

Risk Management: Everyone knows the old adage: no risk, no return. Risk management is the art of maximizing return while maintaining a risk profile consistent with not losing more than you can afford to lose. Risk management begins with knowing what you own and understanding what factors are going to drive the investments return. It then asks the question of what could derail this expected return and what would be the losses should this derailment occur. Finally, it looks at what can be done to minimize the losses should the derailment occur and then doing this.

Risk: For participants in the financial markets, this measures both the amount of expected loss on an investment if something goes wrong and the likelihood of something going wrong.

Risk-adjusted Capital Ratios: Under the Basel Capital requirements, each asset on or off a bank's balance sheet is assigned a risk weighting of between 0% for sovereign debt to 100% for loans. Risk-adjusted assets are calculated by multiplying each asset by its risk-weighting and summing the total for all assets. Risk-adjusted capital ratios are then calculated by dividing the bank's capital by the total of risk-adjusted assets. (see Basel Capital Requirements)

Run on the bank: A run on the bank or bank run occurs when uninsured depositors no longer believe the bank can repay all depositors and therefore they race to withdraw their funds before other depositors so as not to suffer losses. Prior to the creation of deposit guarantees, retail depositors were involved in bank runs. After the creation of deposit guarantees, it became wholesale depositors who engaged in bank runs.

Safety and soundness: Safety and soundness are characteristics bank regulators try to achieve in banks. Safety refers to the ability of the banks to take risks and to absorb any losses on their exposures without causing the deposit insurance fund to lose money. Soundness refers to banks being financially stable.

Safety valve: By using their book capital to absorb the losses on and confine the damage from excess debt in the financial system, banks can protect the real economy.

Securitization: Securitization is the process by which Wall Street divides up the cash flow generated by select financial assets to create securities that investor groups with different risk appetites will want to buy.

Self-discipline: The on-going process of investors limiting the size of their individual investment exposures to what they can afford to lose based on their independent assessment of the changing risk and value of each investment.

Sell-side: The side of the market that includes firms like commercial and investment banks that creates and sells securities. See buy-side.

Servicer: The firm doing the billing and collecting on the assets backing a structured finance security. (see loan servicing)

Shadow banking system: There are a number of banking functions, like maturity transformation and credit risk transfer, that occur in unregulated entities outside of and in the shadows of the traditional regulated banking system. This so-called shadow banking system is very large and includes $15+ trillion of structured finance securities and $700+ trillion in derivatives.

Solvency: A bank is solvent when the market value of its assets exceeds the book value of its liabilities.

Spooking the Market: Because of opacity, bank regulators are worried if they say something negative about a bank it will scare depositors and trigger a run on the bank. This creates two interesting challenges: how to let the market know material nonpublic information about the banks and how to convey this information without alarming market participants. The fear of spooking the market is ended if banks provide valuation transparency because then everyone can assess the condition of the banks and what the bank regulators say is their interpretation of the facts.

Stigma: As a result of opacity, bank management worries that market participants might misinterpret why the bank is borrowing from the Federal Reserve. Specifically, market participants might view borrowing from the Fed as a sign the bank is having serious financial problems.

Stress Tests: Stress tests are run by regulators with the stated goal of assessing if an opaque bank is capable of remaining solvent in the face of an economic downturn. The announcement of the results of these tests violates the prohibition against government's endorsing an investment in private securities. The announcement creates moral hazard and the obligation to bailout investors in the bank should the bank subsequently run into solvency problems. After all, it can be reasonably assumed the investors who did not have access to valuation transparency to confirm the results of the government stress test relied on the government's representation.

Structured Bonds: These bonds have two parts: a bond and at least one derivative contract. It is the derivative contract that drives the return to the investor. For example, the derivative contract might be tied to the return on the S&P 500 stocks. If stocks increase in value, the return to the investor increases. If stocks decrease in value, the investor loses money.

Structured finance: Structured finance refers to securities manufactured by Wall Street. Wall Street builds these securities by taking a defined group of assets, mortgage loans for example, and putting them into a trust for the benefit of the investors. Then, Wall Street applies complex mathematical models to divide up the cash flow from the assets into multiple securities where each security appeals to a different category of investor based on the investor's risk tolerance. The securities range from "safe" to "very high risk". Wall Street then sells the securities to investors. At its peak, the structured finance market was almost $20 trillion in size.

Substituted Compliance: A bank's foreign subsidiaries are considered to be in compliance with their home country's regulations if the host country (where the subsidiary is located) has similar, but not identical rules and regulations.

Sunlight is said to be the best of disinfectants: Justice Louis Brandeis used sunlight to explain how transparency ends misbehavior by bankers.

Swedish Model: This model for handling insolvent banks is the series of policy choices our financial system is designed to support and involves having the banks recognize upfront their losses on the excess debt in the financial system. Having bank capital absorb the losses protects the real economy in numerous ways. While banks rebuild their book capital, they provide transparency and the government guarantees their deposits. (see Japanese Model)

Synthetic credit portfolio (SCP): A synthetic credit portfolio is made up of investments in securities that allow the buyer or seller to bet on whether a specific company or group of companies will experience a negative financial event like a bankruptcy during a specified period of time. (see credit derivative)

Tabloid Test: The Tabloid Test asks the simple question of would the bank management be proud to have their business affairs appear in a newspaper. This level of sunshine tends to drive out the bad behavior that creates reputational risk.

Take away the punchbowl: Taking away the punchbowl refers to the role central banks have in stepping in and preventing the economy from expanding too quickly or the banks taking on too much risk when their profits are increasing.

Tangible equity: An accounting construct calculated by subtracting intangibles like goodwill from the book value of common shareholders' equity.

The City: The City of London is the UK's equivalent of Wall Street. It is a geographic location used to refer to all the UK's commercial and investment banks.

Tibor: Tibor is the Tokyo Interbank Offered Rate. (see Euribor and Libor)

Too Big to Fail ("TBTF"): Regulators define a bank as Too Big to Fail if the result of its failing would be greater damage to the financial system and real economy than regulators would care to imagine. This policy began in 1984 with the bailout of Continental Illinois, a bank with $40 billion in pre-bailout assets.

Toxic: When used in reference to an investment security, as in a toxic mortgage-backed security, toxic refers to the impact on investors' portfolios as a result of the security's risk being hidden by opacity. The security wouldn't be toxic if its risk wasn't hidden. Knowing what they were buying, investors would require a higher return to hold the security and would purchase less of the security.

Trader's Dilemma: The question of what to do when either a long or short position begins losing money as the market price changes to reduce the value of the position. There are three choices: do nothing and pray the market price moves in your favor; sell and recognize the loss; or buy a hedge and determine the best strategy for exiting the trade later. (see It's too late now trap)

Transparency: There are two forms of transparency: valuation and price. Valuation transparency is the important form as it is necessary so that buyers can know what they are buying and sellers can know what they own.

Transparency Label Initiative™: The Transparency Label Initiative™ fixes the fatal flaw in the FDR Framework. It is a buy-side sponsored effort that exerts pressure on issuers to provide valuation transparency even when regulators do not require valuation transparency. It does this by using a label to divide the global financial system in two parts. One part consists of securities and benchmark financial prices that offer valuation transparency so investors can know what they own and is unrigged. The second part consists of opaque securities and benchmark financial prices that are rigged by the bankers in their favor. See FDR Framework.

Trust and Confidence: Trust and confidence is one of the benefits of providing valuation transparency. Investors trust their own independent analysis of the information valuation transparency makes available. Investors confidence in the analysis translates into a willingness to make buy, hold, and sell decisions.

Trust, but Verify: As part of independently assessing the risk and value of an investment, investors "trust" the story they have been told about the investment and then use the information disclosed under valuation transparency to "verify" if the story is true or not.

Unsecured interbank loan market: In the unsecured interbank loan market, banks with excess deposits lend these deposits on an unsecured basis for short periods of time to banks looking to borrow deposits.

Valuation transparency: Valuation transparency is defined as both buyer and seller have access to all the useful, relevant information in an appropriate, timely manner so they can independently assess this information and make a fully informed decision. It is the necessary condition for the invisible hand of the market to operate and efficiently allocate resources.

Value at Risk: A simple of way of expressing the confidence bank management has in the maximum amount of money the bank expects to lose on its bets. It is frequently expressed as the maximum expected loss in nineteen out of every twenty trading days. However, one day out of twenty trading days the loss will be equal to or exceed this maximum expected loss.

Volcker Rule: A section of the Dodd-Frank Act that bans banks from engaging in proprietary trading and betting with insured deposits.

Wall Street Walk: The way buyers exert pressure for better disclosure is not to buy opaque securities, but to walk on by and buy securities providing valuation transparency. This gives the issuer of the opaque security an incentive to provide valuation transparency.

Wholesale funding market: The wholesale funding market exists so banks can borrow short-term unsecured funds. Investors in this market range from money market mutual funds to foreign depositors. It is called wholesale because the size of each transaction greatly exceeds the deposit guarantee limits. Because they lend the banks money on an unsecured basis, investors in the wholesale funding market are very sensitive to the borrowing bank's financial condition and are prone to "run" when there is doubt about the bank's financial condition.

Wisdom of Crowds: With valuation transparency, all the useful, relevant information is made available to all market participants. Collectively, the market with all of its experts can do a better job of analyzing this information than the financial regulators by themselves.

Write-down or charge-off: The actual process of reducing the balance on a loan to what the borrower can repay and reflecting this action on the bank balance sheet. (see Expected Loss Approach and Incurred Loss Accounting)

Zero-sum: Trading is viewed as an activity where either the buyer or the seller benefits as a result of the trade and the other party is viewed as suffering a loss equal to the benefit. The phrase zero-sum is based on the observation that adding the benefit and the loss together equals zero.

Zombie bank: A zombie bank is a term Boston College's Ed Kane used to describe an insolvent bank that continues to operate because of government support through both the deposit guarantee and deferral by regulators of the option to close the bank.

Zombie loans: A loan where the borrower is unable to repay the loan, but the bank continues to advance additional credit and pretend the loan is performing.

Zone of Transparency: By design, every publicly traded security should provide valuation transparency. Some do and they are said to fall within the zone of transparency. Some do not and they are said to fall outside the zone of transparency. The Congressional Oversight Panel noted the SEC appeared to have limited transparency to a subset of the securities in the financial markets. Excluded from the zone of transparency were banks, structured finance securities and other financial innovations.

Biography

Abacus: Abacus was a collateralized debt obligation put together by Goldman Sachs so it could bet on the value of subprime mortgage-backed securities falling.

ABN Amro: A bank acquired by RBS that contributed to the problems RBS experienced.

Abrantes-Metz, Rosa: Ms. Abrantez-Metz is an associate professor at New York University's Stern School of Business.

AIG: AIG is a global insurer that needed to be bailed out as a result of its losses on its exposures to subprime mortgages and related securities at the beginning of the financial crisis.

Akerlof, George: Mr. Akerlof is a Nobel-prize winning economics professor at UC Berkeley.

Allied Irish Bank: Allied Irish Bank is one of Ireland's leading banks. It was bailed out at the beginning of the financial crisis.

Almunia, Joaquín: Mr. Almunia is the EU Commission Vice-President in charge of competition policy.

Alvarez, Scott: Mr. Alvarez was the Federal Reserve's general counsel during the time of JPMorgan's London Whale trades

Anatomy of a Financial Collapse: A report by the U.S. Senate's Permanent Subcommittee on Investigations based on its analysis of the causes of the financial crisis.

Anglo Irish Bank: Anglo Irish Bank was one of Ireland's leading banks. It failed at the beginning of the financial crisis.

Annunzio, Frank: Mr. Annunzio was a member of the U.S. House of Representatives' committee that investigated the collapse of Continental Illinois.

Article 122a of European Capital Requirements Directive: This article requires European banks, broadly defined to include both commercial and investment banks, to know what they own when they buy a structured finance security.

Association for Financial Markets in Europe (AFME): AFME is one of several industry trade groups dominated by the sell-side. AFME was originally the European Securitisation Forum. It was founded by the sell-side's lobbying group the Securities Industry and Financial Markets Association (SIFMA).

Association of Mortgage Investors (AMI): AMI was formed in the wake of the financial crisis by the buy-side to protect investors' interest in private label mortgage-backed securities.

Bagehot, Walter: Mr. Bagehot was a British journalist who was the father of modern central banking. In his 1873 classic, *Lombard Street*, he made the case for a central bank to act as a lender of last resort to stop rumor driven bank runs by lending to solvent banks at high rates of interest.

Bailey, Andrew: Mr. Bailey works for the Bank of England in the Prudential Regulation Authority area.

Bailey, George: Mr. Bailey is a fictional character in the 1946 movie *It's a Wonderful Life*. His character runs a community bank called the Bailey Building and Loan Association.

Bair, Sheila: Ms. Bair is the former head of the Federal Deposit Insurance Corporation (FDIC).

Baker, Dean: Mr. Baker is an economist at CEPR who warned about the risk of a housing market bubble bursting prior to our current financial crisis.

Balls, Ed: Mr. Balls was the UK Economic Secretary to the Treasury in the run-up to and the beginning of the financial crisis.

Bank for International Settlements (BIS): The BIS is also known as the central banks' bank. Its economists were among the few that predicted the financial crisis. Besides economic research, the BIS also runs the International Data Hub for collecting counterparty risk information.

Bank of America (BoA): Bank of America is a global financial institution that is considered under the Dodd-Frank Act to be systemically important and therefore Too Big to Fail. Because of its size and opacity, financial regulators will never let it fail and will always turn to the U.S. taxpayers to bail it out. It acquired Merrill Lynch at the beginning of our current financial crisis.

Bank of England (BoE): The BoE is the central bank for the UK. It has three primary responsibilities. First, it conducts monetary policy through its Monetary Policy Committee. Second, it tries to ensure financial stability through its Financial Policy Committee. Third, since the beginning of 2014, it oversees the UK's banks through its Prudential Regulation Authority.

Bank of Italy: The Bank of Italy is the Italian central bank. It is responsible for supervision of Italy's banks.

Barclays: Barclays is a global financial institution. Because of its size and opacity, financial regulators will never let it fail and will always turn to the UK taxpayers to bail it out.

Barnard, Doug: Mr. Barnard was a member of the U.S. House of Representatives' committee that investigated the collapse of Continental Illinois.

Basel Committee on Banking Supervision (Basel Committee): The Basel Committee is part of the BIS and provides a forum for bank supervisors to talk about how to oversee the banks. As a result of these discussions, the regulators have proposed a series of bank capital requirements that relate the amount of book capital a bank has to the riskiness of the assets the bank has. These rules are known as the Basel I, Basel II and Basel III.

Bear Stearns: Bear Stearns was a large U.S. investment bank that failed in March 2008 and was merged into JPMorgan.

Bernanke, Ben: Mr. Bernanke was the chairman of the U.S. central bank, the Board of Governors of the Federal Reserve System or simply the Federal Reserve, at the beginning of the financial crisis and for the next six years. Previously, he was an economics professor at Princeton. He developed a reputation as an expert in the Great Depression and offered advice to Japan on how to end their financial crisis. Upon rejecting his advice to require the Japanese banks to recognize their losses on the excess debt in the financial system, the Japanese officials observed it was a lot easier to do what he was recommending when you are an academic than to implement the same policies during a financial crisis.

Blankfein, Lloyd: Mr. Blankfein was the chief executive of Goldman Sachs, a global financial institution, from the beginning of the financial crisis through publication of this book.

Blundell-Wignall, Adrian: Mr. Blundell-Wignall is a special advisor to the secretary general of the Organization for Economic Cooperation and Development (OECD).

Borio, Claudio: Mr. Borio worked with Mr. White at the BIS and warned about the risks to the global financial system.

Bowe, John: Mr. Bowe was the Acting Director of Treasury and Director of Capital Markets at Anglo Irish Bank when the bank approached the Irish government for help.

Brandeis, Justice Louis: Justice Louis Brandeis proposed the use of sunlight as the best disinfectant for bad behavior by Wall Street.

Bray, Tim: Mr. Bray was the director of Web technologies at Sun Microsystems.

British Bankers' Association (BBA): The British Bankers' Association is a lobbying organization for UK banks. It was responsible for overseeing construction and reporting of the London Interbank Offered Rate (Libor) prior to the revelation that the banks were manipulating this rate for their benefit.

Brown, Gordon: Mr. Brown was the UK prime minister in the run-up to and the beginning of the financial crisis.

Buffett, Warren: Mr. Buffett is the head of Berkshire Hathaway and is acknowledged as one of the greatest investors of all time.

Cardiff, Kevin: Mr. Cardiff was the Second Secretary General at the Department of Finance in the Irish finance ministry.

Carney, Mark: Mr. Carney succeeded Sir Mervyn King as governor of the Bank of England. Previously, after a stint at Goldman Sachs, he ran the Canadian central bank.

Central Bank of Ireland: The Central Bank of Ireland was responsible for supervision of the Irish banks through the Irish Financial Services Regulatory Authority (IFSRA).

Chen, Sandy: Mr. Chen is a bank analyst at Cenkos Securities.

Citicorp (now known as Citigroup): Citigroup is a global financial institution that is considered under the Dodd-Frank Act to be systemically important and therefore Too Big to Fail. Because of its size and opacity, financial regulators will never let it fail and will always turn to the U.S. taxpayers to bail it out.

Cole, Roger: Mr. Cole was a senior official in the Federal Reserve's supervision area

Commission of Investigation into the Banking Sector: The commission was led by Mr. Nyberg and investigated the causes of the Irish financial crisis. The commission produced a report of its findings that I refer to as the Nyberg Commission Report.

Committee of European Banking Supervisors (CEBS): The Committee of European Banking Supervisors was the predecessor to the European Banking Authority (EBA). Its role was to coordinate and standardize bank regulations and supervision across the European Union.

Committee to Establish the National Institute of Finance: The Committee to Establish the National Institute of Finance was a group of academics, regulators and Wall Street that championed the idea of creating an agency like the weather service to collect and analyze financial market data. Their efforts led to the creation of the Office of Financial Research.

Congressional Oversight Panel: As part of agreeing to the Emergency Economic Stabilization Act and the $700 billion Troubled Asset Relief Program, Congress set-up the COP as an independent panel chaired by Elizabeth Warren. The COP was charged with examining the current state of financial markets and the regulatory system.

Conover, C. Todd: Mr. Conover was the U.S. Comptroller of the Currency at the time Continental Illinois collapsed. He testified on the collapse of Continental Illinois.

Consumer Financial Protection Bureau (CFPB): The CFPB is the result of Sen. Elizabeth Warren's insight that nobody makes good financial decisions when they do not have access to all the useful, relevant information in an appropriate, timely manner. The CFPB focuses on ensuring that all financial products offered to consumers provide disclosure that allows the consumer to know what they are buying.

Continental Illinois National Bank and Trust (Continental Illinois): Continental Illinois was the original Too Big to Fail bank. Its collapse as a result of a rumor driven run by wholesale depositors in 1984 triggered a congressional hearing on the role of bank regulators and the policy of Too Big to Fail.

Cox, Christopher: Mr. Cox was the chairman of the U.S. Securities and Exchange Commission at the beginning of the financial crisis on August 9, 2007.

Curry, Thomas: Mr. Curry was the Comptroller of the Currency during the time of JPMorgan's London Whale trades.

Delano, Preston: Mr. Delano was the U.S. Comptroller of the Currency in 1938. Historically, the Office of the Comptroller of the Currency (OCC) has had a role in examining the nation's banks.

Dimon, Jamie: Mr. Dimon is the head of JPMorgan.

Dodd-Frank Act: Technically known as 2010 Dodd-Frank Wall Street Reform and Consumer Protection Act, the Act was the U.S. legislative response to our current financial crisis. In its 2,000+ pages, the Act focuses on preventing future financial crises by introducing a massive number of complex technocratic solutions.

Drew, Ina: Ms. Drew ran the Chief Investment Office of JPMorgan where Bruno Iksil, the London Whale, worked and where the credit derivative trades took place.

Drumm, David: Mr. Drumm was the CEO of Anglo Irish Bank when it approached the Irish government for help.

Dudley, Bill: Mr. Dudley is the president of the Federal Reserve Bank of New York. Previously, he worked for Goldman Sachs.

Engle III, Robert F.: Mr. Engle is a Nobel-prize winning economist who contributed significantly to understanding how to analyze unpredictable movements in financial market prices.

Enhanced Disclosure Task Force: This committee was set up by the Financial Stability Board and consisted of representatives from banking, credit rating firms, auditing firms and asset management companies. It focused on developing fundamental principles for enhanced risk disclosures given existing accounting and regulatory disclosure requirements.

European Central Bank (ECB): The ECB is the central bank for the European Union (EU). It is responsible for monetary policy and, as of 2014, oversight of the largest banks in the EU. Since the financial crisis began, the ECB has attempted to bring transparency to structured finance securities. As part of this effort, it assembled the ABS Technical Working Group.

Evans, Charles: Mr. Evans is the president of the Federal Reserve Bank of Chicago. Previously, he led the Chicago bank's research on monetary policy.

FCIC Report: In the U.S., the Financial Crisis Inquiry Commission investigated the causes of the financial crisis and released a report with their findings.

Federal Deposit Insurance Corporation (FDIC): Created by the Banking Act of 1933, the FDIC is charged with maintaining stability and public confidence in the U.S. banking system. It does this in two ways. First, it provides deposit insurance to banks so banks can say the full faith and credit of the U.S. guarantees the safety of the deposits. Second, it has the authority to close banks it determines are no longer capable of operating as a going concern.

Federal Reserve: The Federal Reserve is the central bank of the US. It has two primary responsibilities: monetary policy and oversight of the large banks. By design, monetary policy is conduced by the Board of Governors of the Federal Reserve System in Washington, DC. Oversight of the banks is divided between Washington and the regional Fed banks. The most important regional Fed bank is the Federal Reserve Bank of New York, also known as the NY Fed. Not only does it oversee many of the largest banks in the country, it is also responsible for the day-to-day implementation of monetary policy. For example, it is the NY Fed that buys securities under quantitative easing.

Financial Crisis Inquiry Commission: A bi-partisan commission set up by the U.S. Congress to investigate the causes of the August 9, 2007 financial crisis in the US.

Financial Reform Party: A term coined by Columbia professor John Coffey to describe the members of the U.S. Congress who wanted to reform the financial system so as to eliminate bad practices by Wall Street that contributed to the financial crisis.

Financial Services Authority (FSA): In the run-up to the financial crisis and through the end of 2013, UK banks were overseen by the Financial Services Authority. FSA examined its role in the financial crisis and published a report.

Financial Services Party: A term coined by Columbia professor John Coffey to describe the members of the U.S. Congress who aligned themselves with Wall Street and resisted reforming the financial system in the wake of our current financial crisis.

Financial Stability Board: Its mission is to coordinate the regulation and supervision of the global financial system.

Fitch: Fitch is one of the leading credit rating firms in the world.

Fitzgerald, Peter: Mr. Fitzgerald was the Director of Retail Banking at Anglo Irish Bank when the bank approached the Irish government for help.

Flint, Douglas: Mr. Flint is the chairman of HSBC Holdings Plc.

FSA Report: In the UK, the Financial Services Authority investigated the failure and subsequent nationalization of RBS and released a report with its findings.

Fulmer, Ann: Ms. Fulmer works for Interthinx.

Geithner, Tim: Geithner was the president of the Federal Reserve Bank of New York when the crisis began and subsequently became the U.S. Treasury Secretary. He championed the notion of "foaming the runway" so banks could spread out the time over which they recognized their losses on bad loans and investments. He also championed the notion of giving financial regulators a second chance.

Gensler, Gary: Mr. Gensler is the former chairman of the U.S. Commodity Futures Trading Commission. Previously, he worked for Goldman Sachs.

Gorton, Gary: Mr. Gorton is a professor at Yale.

Greenspan, Alan: Mr. Greenspan is the former chairman of the Federal Reserve. As a follower of Ayn Rand, he reduced regulatory discipline on the assumption that banks were subjected to market discipline.

Group of Thirty: The Group of Thirty is a consultative group on international economic and monetary affairs. Included in its membership are current and former heads of the global central banks.

Haldane, Andy: Mr. Haldane is the chief economist at the Bank of England. Previously, he was the Executive Director for Financial Stability at the Bank of England.

Hester, Stephen: Mr. Hester is the former head of RBS. He was brought in shortly after the UK taxpayers bailed out the bank.

Home Owners' Loan Corporation (HOLC): The Home Owners' Loan Corporation was set up in 1933 to deal with the troubled mortgages on bank balance sheets. By restructuring the terms on these mortgages based on the borrowers' ability to pay, it was able to minimize the losses taken by the bank on selling the mortgages to the HOLC. This also made it possible for borrowers to stay in their houses.

HPA: HPA stands for house price appreciation. HPA is an assumption put into the models to value mortgage-backed securities. In the run-up to the financial crisis, HPA was assumed to be a positive because there had never been a time when house prices declined in the US.

HSBC Holdings Plc.: HSBC is a global financial institution. Because of its size and opacity, financial regulators will never let it fail and will always turn to the UK taxpayers to bail it out.

Hubbard, Carroll: Mr. Hubbard was a member of the U.S. House of Representatives' committee that investigated the collapse of Continental Illinois.

International Monetary Fund (IMF): The IMF works to foster global economic growth and financial stability by assisting countries with their economic policies and providing financial resources when necessary.

International Organization of Securities Commissions (IOSCO): IOSCO is composed of the SEC and its equivalent in different countries.

Jenkins, Robert: Mr. Jenkins is a former member of the Bank of England's Financial Policy Committee. Prior to that, he worked as a lobbyist and on the buy-side.

Kaufman, Henry: Mr. Kaufman is a Wall Street economic and financial consultant.

Kidney, Jim: Mr. Kidney is a former trial attorney at the U.S. Securities and Exchange Commission.

King, Sir Mervyn: Mr. King is the former governor of the Bank of England. He led the BoE from 2003 to 2013.

Kohn, Donald: Mr. Kohn currently works at the Brookings Institute and is a member of the Bank of England's Financial Policy Committee. Previously, he worked for almost four decades at the Federal Reserve where he was the Vice Chairman during our current financial crisis.

Krawiec Kimberly: Ms. Krawiec is a law professor at Duke University who documented the number of times different market participants met with financial regulators to lobby on the Volcker Rule.

Krugman, Paul: Mr. Krugman is a Nobel-prize winning economist.

Lehman Brothers: Lehman Brothers was a large, global financial institution that filed for bankruptcy on September 15, 2008. It failed as a result of a liquidity run when investors realized they could not determine if the firm was solvent or not.

Levin, Sen. Carl: Sen. Levin was the head of the U.S. Senate Permanent Subcommittee on Investigations.

Levitt, Arthur: Mr. Levitt is the former chairman of the SEC.

Litton Loan Servicing: Litton Loan Servicing was a subprime mortgage billing and collecting firm that was acquired by Goldman Sachs in the run-up to the financial crisis. Firms like Litton were valuable to Wall Street because they could give an informational edge for use in trading subprime mortgage-backed bonds and related derivative securities.

London Whale: The nickname given to a JPMorgan trader, Bruno Iksil, who placed a proprietary bet in the credit markets that lost $6.2 billion.

Markowitz, Harry: Mr. Markowitz is a Nobel-prize winning economist who contributed significantly to the development of modern portfolio theory.

McCreevy, Charlie: Mr. McCreevy was the EU Commissioner for Internal Markets who oversaw the passage of the "know what you own" requirements in Article 122a of the European Capital Requirements Directive.

McKinney, Stewart: Mr. McKinney was a member of the U.S. House of Representatives' committee that investigated the collapse of Continental Illinois and it was he who used the expression "too big to fail".

Merton, Robert: Mr. Merton is a Nobel-prize winning economist who contributed significantly to the development of option pricing models.

Metrick, Andrew: Mr. Metrick is a professor at Yale.

MF Global: Mr. Jon Corzine led a small investment bank with aspirations to become much larger. It blew itself up by taking an outsized bet on EU sovereign debt.

Monte dei Paschi: Monte dei Paschi is one of the world's oldest banks. It is embroiled in a scandal from derivative contracts it entered into that hid its financial condition.

Moody's: Moody's is one of the largest credit rating firms.

Morgan Stanley: Morgan Stanley is a global financial institution that is considered under the Dodd-Frank Act to be systemically important and therefore Too Big to Fail. Because of its size and opacity, financial regulators will never let it fail and will always turn to the U.S. taxpayers to bail it out.

Morgan, JP: JPMorgan is a global financial institution that is considered under the Dodd-Frank Act to be systemically important and therefore Too Big to Fail. Because of its size and opacity, financial regulators will never let it fail and will always turn to the U.S. taxpayers to bail it out.

Nichols, J.M.: Mr. Nichols was the president of the First National Bank of Englewood during the Great Depression.

Nyberg Commission Report: In Ireland, a commission led by Peter Nyberg investigated the causes of the Irish financial crisis. This report includes their findings.

Nyberg, Peter: Mr. Nyberg was a former Finnish senior government official who led the investigation into the causes of the Irish financial crisis.

O'Malia, Scott: Mr. O'Malia was a member of the Commodity Futures Trading Commission (CFTC). He is currently working as a lobbyist for Wall Street.

Office of Financial Research (OFR): A federal agency created by the Dodd-Frank Act in response to the lobbying efforts of the Committee to Establish a National Institute of Finance. The agency's mission is to analyze the global financial system and warn about risk. By law, it can collect and analyze data, but it cannot share the data it collects with any other market participant. This effectively makes OFR a black hole and limits its effectiveness as no other market participant can confirm its findings or recommendations. OFR could be salvaged and made an important part of the 21st century FDR Framework. Specifically, OFR should fund a valuation transparency data warehouse that collects the current exposure level information from banks, brokerages and structured finance securities, standardizes this data and then disseminates this data for free to all market participants.

Osborne, George: Mr. Osborne became the Chancellor of the Exchequer and Second Lord of the Treasury of the UK in May 2010.

Pandit Vikram: Mr. Pandit is the former chairman of Citigroup.

Paredes, Troy: Mr. Paredes is a former SEC commissioner.

Paribas BNP: BNP Paribas is a large French bank. On August 9, 2007, it announced that it was unable to value the assets in three funds that invested in subprime mortgage-backed securities. This announcement triggered our current financial crisis.

Partee, J. Charles: Mr. Partee was a member of the Board of Governors of the Federal Reserve System from 1976 to 1986. He was heavily involved in bank supervision and regulation and was the Board's representative on the Federal Financial Institutions Examination Council.

Pass, Matt: Mr. Pass was a senior executive at Merrill Lynch

Patman, Bill: Mr. Patman was a member of the U.S. House of Representatives' committee that investigated the collapse of Continental Illinois.

Paulson, Hank: Mr. Paulson was the U.S. Treasury Secretary at the beginning of the financial crisis in 2007. Previously, he served as the head of one of the world's largest investment banks, Goldman Sachs.

Pecora Commission: Set up to by the U.S. Senate, the commission, led by Ferdinand Pecora, investigated the causes of the Great Depression including the collapse of the stock market.

Pecora, Ferdinand: Mr. Pecora was a prosecutor who was brought in to run the Senate commission investigating the causes of the Great Depression and the collapse of the stock market.

Penn Square: Penn Square was a small bank located in Oklahoma that sold high-risk, poorly underwritten energy loans to Continental Illinois.

Pittman, Mark: Mr. Pittman was a reporter at Bloomberg who initiated a lawsuit to require the Federal Reserve to disclose both the amount and the rate on the loans it provided to the banks at the beginning of the financial crisis. As a result of this lawsuit, it was revealed the Fed provided the banks with a $13 billion income boost.

Rajan, Raghuam: Mr. Rajan is now the head of India's central bank. While a professor at the University of Chicago, he warned about risks to the global financial system at the Fed's annual Jackson Hole get together.

Ravazzolo, Fabiola: Ms. Ravazzolo worked in the NY Fed's Markets Group and was told by a trader at Barclays that the Libor interest rate was being manipulated.

RBS (Royal Bank of Scotland): RBS is a global financial institution. Because of its size and opacity, financial regulators will never let it fail and will always turn to the UK taxpayers to bail it out like they did at the beginning of our current financial crisis.

Reed, John: Mr. Reed was the former chairman and CEO of Citicorp who led the recognition of losses on the loans made to Less Developed Countries.

Roeder, Douglas: Mr. Roeder was the OCC's senior deputy comptroller for Large Bank Supervision from 2001 until 2010.

Romer, Paul: Mr. Romer is a professor at New York University's Stern School of Business.

Roosevelt, Franklin Delano (FDR): Mr. Roosevelt was the 32nd president of the United States. His term began on March 4, 1933 during the worst moments of the Great Depression. At the time of his inauguration, there was a nationwide run on the banks. In response, his administration redesigned the banking system including the introduction of deposit insurance. His administration also redesigned the financial markets with the introduction of the philosophy of disclosure.

Ryan, Timothy: Mr. Ryan is the global head of regulatory policy and strategy at JPMorgan. Previously, he was the head of the sell-side lobbying organization SIFMA.

S&P: S&P is one of the largest rating firms.

Sachs, Goldman: Goldman Sachs is a global financial institution that is considered under the Dodd-Frank Act to be systemically important and therefore Too Big to Fail. Because of its size and opacity, financial regulators will never let it fail and will always turn to the U.S. taxpayers to bail it out.

Scholes, Myron: Mr. Scholes is a Nobel-prize winning economist who contributed significantly to the development of option pricing models.

Schumer, Sen. Charles: During our current financial crisis he was a Senator. Sen. Schumer was a member of the U.S. House of Representatives' committee that investigated the collapse of Continental Illinois.

Schwartz, Anna: Ms. Schwartz co-authored **the** book on monetary policy and was **the** expert in the Great Depression prior to her death. She observed in October 2008 the financial crisis was being driven by opacity that made it impossible to determine who was solvent and who was insolvent. As a result, she was critical of the policy response that treated the financial crisis as being a liquidity driven crisis.

Securities and Exchange Commission (SEC): The SEC is the federal agency responsible for regulating the securities industry and enforcing the federal securities laws. Among its responsibilities is ensuring market participants have access to all the useful, relevant information in a timely manner so it can be independently assessed and used to make fully informed investment decisions.

Securities Industry and Financial Markets Association (SIFMA): SIFMA is global sell-side lobbying organization. It uses affiliated lobbying organizations that focus on specific financial markets to enhance its clout. For example, it established the American Securitization Forum (ASF) and the European Securitisation Forum (ESF) to lobby on rules covering the structured finance markets.

Security Pacific: Security Pacific was a large US bank that overextended itself with loans to Less Developed Countries. It operated for several years while it was insolvent as a result of the losses on these loans.

Senior Supervisory Group: The Senior Supervisory Group is an international group of bank regulators.

Sharp, William F.: Mr. Sharp is a Nobel-prize winning economist who contributed significantly to the development of the capital asset pricing model.

Sheard, Daniel: Mr. Sheard is the chief investment officer at $60 billion asset manager GAM U.K. Ltd.

Smith, Adam: In his 1776 classic, *Wealth of Nations*, Mr. Smith introduced the concept of the invisible hand of the market.

Smith, Vernon: Mr. Smith is a Nobel-prize winning economist who contributed significantly to the development of experimental economics.

Spillenkothen, Richard: Mr. Spillenkothen was the head of supervision at the Federal Reserve until 2006.

St. Germain, Fernand J.: Rep. St. Germain was the Chairman of the U.S. House of Representative's Committee on Banking, Finance and Urban Affairs that in the fall of 1984 investigated the collapse of Continental Illinois.

Stiglitz, Joseph: Mr. Stiglitz is a Nobel-prize winning economist who teaches at Columbia. He has done considerable work in the area of information asymmetry.

Sundness, Trond: Mr. Sundness was a reporter for the Norwegian Business Daily.

Taylor, Rob: Mr. Taylor authored a column in the Guardian newspaper examining the question of is there any truth to bank financial reporting.

Trichet, Jean-Claude: Mr. Trichet is the former president of the European Central Bank. He led the ECB from 2003 to 2011.

Tucker, Paul: Mr. Tucker is a former member of the Bank of England's Financial Policy Committee.

US Financial Crisis Inquiry Commission (FCIC): The FCIC was a bipartisan commission set up to investigate the causes of the financial crisis.

US President's Working Group on Financial Markets: Also known as the Plunge Protection Team, the President's Working Group on Financial Markets is a task force that provides Wall Street's views on how to support the financial markets.

US Senate Permanent Subcommittee on Investigations: This subcommittee looked into both the causes of the financial crisis and JPMorgan's London Whale trade.

Volcker Rule: Named after Paul Volcker, the rule is supposed to ban banks from taking proprietary bets and putting taxpayer money at risk.

Volcker, Paul: Mr. Volcker is a former chairman of the Federal Reserve. He is credited with following monetary policies in the early 1980s that ended the cycle of inflation in the US. He was involved in the policy response to the collapse of Continental Illinois, the Less Developed Country Loan crisis and the U.S. Savings and Loan crisis.

Washington Mutual: Washington Mutual was a bank that grew rapidly from making subprime mortgage loans and ultimately failed when these loans started to go bad. JPMorgan acquired it.

Weidmann, Jens: Mr. Weidmann is the President of the Deutsche Bundesbank (Germany's central bank).

Wheatley, Martin: Mr. Wheatley ran a UK commission charged with figuring out how to fix the Libor interest rate setting process so the rates could not be manipulated in the future.

White, Mary Jo: Ms. White is the chairwoman of the SEC.

White, William: While at the BIS, Mr. White and his team of economists spoke out about the risks to the financial system. His warnings were dismissed.

Wolf, Martin: Mr. Wolf is the senior economics writer for the Financial Times and was a member of the Vickers Commission that recommended how to reform the UK financial system to avoid another financial crisis.

Wriston, Walter: Mr. Wriston was the former chairman and CEO of Citicorp who observed that people go bankrupt, but countries do not.

Wylie, Chalmers: Mr. Wylie was a member of the U.S. House of Representatives' committee that investigated the collapse of Continental Illinois.

Yellen, Janet: Ms. Yellen is the current chair of the Federal Reserve.

Zervos, David: Mr. Zervos is an analyst at Jeffries & Co.

Zombanakis Minos: Mr. Zombanakis is a Greek banker who is credited with inventing the Libor interest rate.

Bibliography

Ahir, Hites and Loungani, Prakash (2014, March), *Can Economists Forecast Recessions? Some Evidence from the Great Recession*, Forecasters.org, http://forecasters.org/wp/wp-content/uploads/PLoungani_OracleMar2014.pdf

Ahmed, Kamal (2011, October 8), Greg Hands levies 'swizz' jibe at Barclays, Telegraph, http://www.telegraph.co.uk/finance/newsbysector/banksandfinance/8815439/Greg-Hands-levies-swizz-jibe-at-Barclays.html

Akerlof, George, Romer, Paul (1993), Looting: The Economic Underworld of Bankruptcy for Profit, http://pages.stern.nyu.edu/~promer/Looting.pdf

Aldrick, Philip (2012, August 1), Bank official admits economists were to blame for recession, The Telegraph, http://www.telegraph.co.uk/finance/economics/9442430/Bank-official-admits-economists-were-to-blame-for-recession.html

Aldrick, Philip (2012, February 19), Bank of England fears bail-out protection won't be used, The Telegraph, http://www.telegraph.co.uk/finance/newsbysector/banksandfinance/9091887/Bank-of-England-fears-bail-out-protection-wont-be-used.html

Aldrick, Philip (2012, October 23), Sir Mervyn King: no recovery until banks recapitalise, The Telegraph, http://www.telegraph.co.uk/finance/newsbysector/banksandfinance/9628997/Sir-Mervyn-King-no-recovery-until-banks-recapitalise.html

American Banker (1931, February), Bank Sets Precedent by Detailing Every Asset, http://www.americanbanker.com/175/index.html?page=28

Anderson, Sarah (2014, March 12), Wall Street Bonuses and the Minimum Wage, Institute for Policy Studies, http://www.ips-dc.org/reports/wall_street_bonuses_and_the_minimum_wage

Animal House (1978), http://www.imdb.com/title/tt0077975/quotes

Anonymous insider letter to The Telegraph (2012, July 1), Libor scandal: How I manipulated the bank borrowing rate, The Telegraph, http://www.telegraph.co.uk/finance/newsbysector/banksandfinance/9368430/Libor-scandal-How-I-manipulated-the-bank-borrowing-rate.html

Antill, Samuel, Hou, David, Sarkar, Asani (2014, March), The Growth of Murky Finance, Liberty Street Economics, http://libertystreeteconomics.newyorkfed.org/2014/03/the-growth-of-murky-finance.html#.U0lYWFe73jc

Armitage, Jim (2014, July 17), *How London bankers at Goldman Sachs and Nomura made millions from taxpayers*, The Independent, http://www.independent.co.uk/news/business/analysis-and-features/

exclusive-blinded-by-science-the-goldman-deal-that-went-off-the-rails-9613719.html

Association for Financial Markets in Europe (2010, February 26), *Comments on the European Central Bank's Public Consultation on the Provision of ABS Loan-Level Information in the Eurosystem Collateral Framework*, http://www.afme.eu/divisions/securitisation.aspx, page 4

Association of Mortgage Investors (2010, March), *White Paper: Reforming the Asset-Backed Securities Market*, http://blogs.reuters.com/alison-frankel/files/2014/04/AMI-whitepaper.pdf, page 2

Bailey, George (1946), It's a Wonderful Life, http://thepioneerwoman.com/entertainment/2011/11/the-five-things-i-learned-from-george-bailey/

Baker, Dean (2014, January 21), The Damage From the Housing Bubble: How Much Did the Greenspan-Rubin Gang Cost Us?, Center for Economic and Policy Research, http://www.cepr.net/index.php/blogs/beat-the-press/the-damage-from-the-housing-bubble-how-much-did-the-greenspan-rubin-gang-cost-us

Bank of America press release (2014, April 28), Bank of America Announces Adjustment to Estimated Regulatory Capital Ratios, http://newsroom.bankofamerica.com/press-releases/corporate-and-financial-news/bank-america-announces-adjustment-estimated-regulatory-c

Bank of England and FSA before MPs: quotes (2012, July 17), The Telegraph, http://www.telegraph.co.uk/finance/financialcrisis/9405522/Bank-of-England-and-FSA-before-MPs-quotes.html

Bank of England (2009, June), Financial Stability Report, Bank of England, http://www.bankofengland.co.uk/publications/Documents/fsr/2009/fsr25sec1.pdf

Bank of England (2012, November), Financial Stability Report Executive Summary, Bank of England, http://www.bankofengland.co.uk/publications/Documents/fsr/2012/fsrsum1211.pdf

Bank of England (2012, November), Financial Stability Report: Short-term risks to financial stability, Bank of England, http://www.bankofengland.co.uk/publications/Documents/fsr/2012/fsr32sec2.pdf

Bank of England (2012, November 29), Financial Stability Report Press Conference: Opening Remarks by the Governor, Bank of England, http://www.bankofengland.co.uk/publications/Documents/fsr/2012/fsrspnote121129.pdf

Bank of England (2011, June 24), Financial Stability Report Q&A, Bank of England, http://www.bankofengland.co.uk/publications/Documents/fsr/2011/conf110624.pdf

Bank of England (2012, November 29), Financial Stability Report Q&A, Bank of England, http://www.bankofengland.co.uk/publications/Documents/fsr/2012/conf121129.pdf

Bank of England (2011, June), Financial Stability Report: Press Conference Transcript, Bank of England, http://www.bankofengland.co.uk/publications/Pages/fsr/2011/fsr29.aspx

Bank of England (2012, July 20), Libor: Further information and correspondence in relation to the email chain, Bank of England, http://www.bankofengland.co.uk/publications/Documents/other/treasurycommittee/financialstability/emailchain.pdf

Bank of England releases Libor correspondence: the emails (2012, July 20), The Telegraph, http://www.telegraph.co.uk/finance/newsbysector/banksandfinance/9415004/Bank-of-England-releases-Libor-correspondence-the-emails.html

Bank of England, European Central Bank (2014, May), The case for a better functioning securitisation market in the European Union, https://www.ecb.europa.eu/pub/pdf/other/ecb-boe_case_better_functioning_securitisation_marketen.pdf

Bank of England (2011, June), Financial Stability Report, Bank of England, http://www.bankofengland.co.uk/publications/Pages/fsr/2011/fsr29.aspx

Bansal, Paritosh, Wilchins, Dan (2010, December 6), Goldman Sachs could find Litton sale tough, London South East, http://www.lse.co.uk/FinanceNews.asp?ArticleCode=ubzptvc5r50htzi&ArticleHeadline=DEALTALKGoldman_Sachs_could_find_Litton_sale_tough

Basel Committee on Banking Supervision and the Board of the International Organization of Securities Commissions (2014, December 11), *Consultative Document: Criteria for identifying simple, transparent and comparable securitizations*, https://www.bis.org/bcbs/publ/d304.pdf,

BBC Lecture (2012), The Today Lecture 2012: Sir Mervyn King", http://bufvc.ac.uk/dvdfind/index.php/title/av74060 audio, http://news.bbc.co.uk/today/hi/today/newsid_9718000/9718062.stm transcript

BBC News (2009, August 7), Timeline: Credit crunch to downturn, BBC, http://news.bbc.co.uk/2/hi/7521250.stm

Bech, Morten L., Gambacorta, Leonardo, Kharroubil, Enisse (2014), Monetary Policy in a Downturn: Are Financial Crises Special? In International Finance, Volume 17, Issue 1, pages 99-119, DOI: 10.1111/infi.12040 http://onlinelibrary.wiley.com/doi/10.1111/infi.12040/abstract

Beim, David (2009, August 18), *Report on Systemic Risk and Bank Supervision*, Prepared for the NY Federal Reserve, http://s3.documentcloud.org/documents/1303305/2009-08-18-frbny-report-on-systemic-risk-and.pdf

Bernanke, Ben (2007, August 10), FOMC Conference Call transcript, Federal Reserve, http://www.federalreserve.gov/monetarypolicy/files/FOMC20070810confcall.pdf

Bernanke, Ben (2008, October 20), testimony before the Committee on the Budget, U.S. House of Representatives, Federal Reserve, http://www.federalreserve.gov/newsevents/testimony/bernanke20081020a.htm

Bernanke, Ben (2008, October 31), The Future of Mortgage Finance in the United States, Federal Reserve, http://www.federalreserve.gov/newsevents/speech/bernanke20081031a.htm

Bernanke, Ben S. (2000), Essays on the Great Depression, Princeton, New Jersey: Princeton University Press.

Bernanke, Ben S. (2013, November 8), The Crisis as a Classic Financial Panic, Federal Reserve, http://www.federalreserve.gov/newsevents/speech/bernanke20131108a.htm

Bernanke, Ben S. (2013, April 8), Stress Testing Banks: What Have We Learned, Federal Reserve, http://www.federalreserve.gov/newsevents/speech/bernanke20130408a.htm

Bernanke, Ben S. (2009, May 7), Statement Regarding the Supervisory Capital Assessment Program, Federal Reserve, http://www.federalreserve.gov/newsevents/press/bcreg/bernankescap20090507.htm

Bernanke, Ben, Gertler, Mark, Gilchrist, Simon (1996, February), The Financial Accelerator and the Flight to Quality, The Review of Economics and Statistics, Vol. 78, No. 1. (Feb, 1996), pp. 1-15 http://www.ssc.wisc.edu/~mchinn/restat_96.pdf

Bessembinder, Hendrik, Maxwell, William, Venkataraman, Kumar (2005, October), Market Transparency, Liquidity Externalities, and Institutional Trading Costs in Corporate Bonds, Journal of Financial Economics, forthcoming, http://finance.eller.arizona.edu/documents/facultypublications/wmaxwell.jfe_transparency.pdf

Blankfein, Lloyd (2009, October 12), To avoid crises, we need more transparency, Financial Times editorial, http://www.ft.com/intl/cms/s/0/94c6ab6c-b763-11de-9812-00144feab49a.html#axzz2pdbqQ2K2

Brandeis, Justice Louis (1913, December 20), What Publicity Can Do, Harper's Weekly, http://3197d6d14b5f19f2f440-5e13d29c4c016cf96cbbfd197c579b45.r81.cf1.rackcdn.com/collection/papers/1910/1913_12_20_What_Publicity_Ca.pdf

Brown, Sherrod, Warren, Elizabeth (2014, April 16), Brown, Warren urge Fed to address risks associated with bank ownership of physical commodities, http://www.brown.senate.gov/newsroom/press/release/brown-warren-urge-fed-to-address-risks-associated-with-bank-ownership-of-physical-commodities

Brush, Silla (2013, March 19), Dodd-Frank Swap Data Fails to Catch JPMorgan Whale, O'Malia Says, Bloomberg, http://www.bloomberg.com/

news/2013-03-19/dodd-frank-swap-data-fails-to-catch-jpmorgan-whale-o-malia-says.html

Buell, Todd (2013, May 28), BOE's Haldane: Worried Bail in Rules Won't Be Enough, The Wall Street Journal, http://online.wsj.com/article/BT-CO-20130528-703047.html?mod=dist_smartbrief

Federal Reserve Bank of New York (2012, July 13), April 11, 2008: transcript of phone call between Barclays employee and analyst in the Markets Group of the New York Fed, Federal Reserve Bank of New York, http://www.newyorkfed.org/newsevents/news/markets/2012/libor/April_11_2008_transcript.pdf

Cantwell, Senator Maria (2009, October 30), Wall Street Has a Gambling Problem, Huffington Post, http://www.huffingtonpost.com/sen-maria-cantwell/wall-street-has-a-gamblin_b_340252.html

Cardiff, Kevin (2010, July 22), testimony, http://debates.oireachtas.ie/DDebate... Node=H3&Page=9

Carney, Brian M. (2008, October 18), Bernanke is Fighting the Last War, Wall Street Journal, http://online.wsj.com/news/articles/SB122428279231046053

Carney, Mark (2013, October 24), The UK at the heart of a renewed globalisation, Bank of England, http://www.bankofengland.co.uk/publications/Documents/speeches/2013/speech690.pdf

Carney, Mark (2014, November 7), Financial Reforms: Completing the Job and Looking Ahead, Financial Stability Board, http://www.financialstabilityboard.org/wp-content/uploads/FSB-Chair's-Letter-to-G20-Leaders-on-Financial-Reforms-Completing-the-Job-and-Looking-Ahead.pdf

Chellel, Kit (2014, March 21), Del Missier Called Libor Rates a 'Fantasy' in E-Mail to Diamond, Bloomberg, http://www.bloomberg.com/news/print/2014-03-21/del-missier-called-libor-rates-a-fantasy-in-e-mail-to-diamond.html

Cheun, Samuel, Raskin, Matt (2008, May 20), NY Fed's MarketSource, http://www.newyorkfed.org/newsevents/news/markets/2012/libor/MarketSource_Report_May202008.pdf

Chu, Ben (2014, July 31), *Only structural reform will clean up our unsound banking system*, The Independent, http://www.independent.co.uk/news/business/comment/ben-chu-only-structural-reform-will-clean-up-our-unsound-banking-system-9639052.html

Committee of European Banking Supervisors (2010, December 31), Feedback to the public consultation on Guidelines to Article 122a of the Capital Requirements Directive, https://www.eba.europa.eu/documents/10180/16094/Feedback-document.pdf

Committee to Establish the National Institute of Finance (2010, February 11), Letter to the Honorable Christopher J. Dodd, Chairman Committee on Banking, Housing and Urban Affairs, http://www.ce-nif.org/images/docs/nif_ltr_to_sen_dodd.pdf

Commodity Futures Trading Commission legal pleading (2012, June 27), Barclays PLC, Barclays Bank PLC and Barclays Capital Inc., http://www.cftc.gov/ucm/groups/public/@lrenforcementactions/documents/legalpleading/enfbarclaysorder062712.pdf

Commodity Futures Trading Commission Order (2014, July 28), *Lloyds Banking Group PLC,* http://www.cftc.gov/ucm/groups/public/@lrenforcementactions/documents/legalpleading/enflloydsorderdf072814.pdf

Commonwealth of Virginia's Complaint-In-Intervention Case No. CL14-399 (2014, September 16), http://www.oag.state.va.us/Media%20and%20News%20Releases/News_Releases/Herring/Complaint%20-%20FINAL%20(9.16.14).pdf

Congressional Oversight Panel (2009, January), Special Report on Regulatory Reform, Modernizing the American Financial Regulatory System: Recommendations for Improving Oversight, Protecting Consumers and Ensuring Stability, http://cybercemetery.unt.edu/archive/cop/20110402010517/http://cop.senate.gov/documents/cop-012909-report-regulatoryreform.pdf

Cox, Christopher (2008, December 4), Address to Joint Meeting of the Exchequer Club and Women in Housing and Finance, SEC, http://www.sec.gov/news/speech/2008/spch120408cc.htm

Crovitz, Gordon L, October 28, 2008, Credit Panic: Stages of Grief, http://online.wsj.com/news/articles/SB122506810764970701

Crovitz, L. Gordon (2008, November 3), The Father of Portfolio Theory on the Crisis, The Wall Street Journal, http://online.wsj.com/news/articles/SB122567428153591981

Curry, Thomas (2014), Building on 150 Years: The Future of Nation Banking, Office of the Comptroller of the Currency, http://www.occ.gov/news-issuances/speeches/2014/pub-speech-2014-47.pdf

DeLong, Brad (2014, May 15), From Tim Geithner: Stress Test: Thursday Focus: May 15, 2014, Equitable Growth. Org, http://equitablegrowth.org/2014/05/15/tim-geithner-stress-test-thursday-focus-may-15-2014/

Dillon, John, Dolmetsch, Chris (2014, February 25), Ex-Jefferies Trader's Customers Say Lies Part of the Job, Bloomberg, http://www.bloomberg.com/news/2014-02-25/ex-jefferies-trader-s-customers-say-lies-are-common-tactic-1-.html

Doctoroff, Daniel L. (2012, August 2), A Market Alternative to Libor, The Wall Street Journal, http://online.wsj.com/news/articles/SB1000

087239639044368750457756339105785 3800?mod=WSJ_Opinion_LEFTTopOpinion&mg=reno64-wsj&url=http%3A%2F%2Fonline.wsj.com%2Farticle%2FSB10000872396390443687504577563391057853800.html%3Fmod%3DWSJ_Opinion_LEFTTopOpinion

Dombret, Andreas (2014, April 15), Speech to the Federal Reserve Bank of Dallas, The State of Europe: End of the Crisis or Crisis without End?, BIS, http://www.bis.org/review/r140417c.htm

Dougherty, Carter (2008, September 22), Stopping a Financial Crisis, the Swedish Way, The New York Times, http://www.nytimes.com/2008/09/23/business/worldbusiness/23krona.html?_r=1&&gwh=B0F623A6211845CA59FEB404E27877C5&gwt=pay

Douzinas, Costas (2011, December 15), The IMF must realize that, in Greece, the treatment is worse than the disease, The Guardian, http://www.theguardian.com/commentisfree/2011/dec/15/imf-greece-treatment-worse-disease

Dowd, Kevin (September 3, 2014), *Math Gone Mad: Regulatory Risk Modeling by the Federal Reserve*, Cato Institute, http://object.cato.org/sites/cato.org/files/pubs/pdf/pa754.pdf

Dr. Seuss (1960), Oh, the Places You'll Go!, New York, NY: Random House Children's Books

Dudley, Bill (2007, August 7), FOMC Meeting transcript, Federal Reserve, http://www.federalreserve.gov/monetarypolicy/files/FOMC20070807meeting.pdf

Dunbar, Nick (2013, July 5), Basel, Bayes and Anglo's Arse-Picking, NickDunbar.net, http://www.nickdunbar.net/articles/basel-bayes-and-anglos-arse-picking/

Durbin, Dick (2009, April), The Banks own the place, interview on WJJG 1530 AM's "Mornings with Ray Hanania. https://www.youtube.com/watch?v=CZbC_IqWEJY

Ebrahimi, Helia (2012, July 21), 'BarCap was the Wild Wild West — that's what we called it', The Telegraph, http://www.telegraph.co.uk/finance/newsbysector/banksandfinance/9417801/BarCap-was-the-Wild-Wild-West-thats-what-we-called-it.html

Eisinger, Jesse (2012, February 22), The Volcker Rule, Made Bloated and Weak, NY Times Dealbook, http://dealbook.nytimes.com/2012/02/22/the-volcker-rule-made-bloated-and-weak/

Eisinger, Jesse, Partnoy, Frank (2013, January/February), What's Inside America's Banks?, The Atlantic, http://www.theatlantic.com/magazine/archive/2013/01/whats-inside-americas-banks/309196/

Elliott, Larry (2008, August 5), Credit crisis — how it all began, The Guardian, http://www.theguardian.com/business/2008/aug/05/northernrock.banking

Ely, Bert (2008), Savings and Loan Crisis, The Concise Encyclopedia of Economics, http://www.econlib.org/library/Enc/SavingsandLoanCrisis.html

Enrich, David, Muñoz, Sara Schaefer (2010, November 17), BOE Wants To Be Less Intrusive, Wall Street Journal, http://online.wsj.com/news/articles/SB20001424052748703628204575618692923523592

Essex, Martin (2012, January 20), What Value Economic Research?, Wall Street Journal blogs, http://blogs.wsj.com/source/2012/01/20/what-value-economic-research/?mod=WSJBlog&mod=thesource

European Central Bank (2010, December 16), ECB introduces ABS loan-by-loan information requirements in the Eurosystem collateral framework, https://www.ecb.europa.eu/press/pr/date/2010/html/pr101216.en.html

European Central Bank (2010, December 17), ABS Technical Working Group, https://www.ecb.europa.eu/paym/coll/loanlevel/twg/html/index.en.html

European Commission (2014, April), Banking Union: restoring financial stability in the Eurozone, http://europa.eu/rapid/press-release_MEMO-14-294_en.htm

European Commission press release (2013, December 4), Antitrust: Commission fines banks € 1.71 billion for participating in cartels in the interest rate derivatives industry, http://europa.eu/rapid/press-release_IP-13-1208_en.htm

Federal Housing Finance Agency v Goldman, Sachs & Co. (2014, July 8), Plantiff's memorandum of law in support of its motion for partial summary judgment on Defendents' due diligence and reasonable care defenses, Case 1:11-cv-06198-DLC, Document 769

Federal Reserve Board (2007, September 18), *Meeting of the Federal Open Market Committee on September 18, 2007*, Federal Reserve Board, http://www.federalreserve.gov/monetarypolicy/files/FOMC20070918meeting.pdf

Field, Richard (2010, April 19), *How Goldman Exploited the Information Gap*, Fortune.com, http://money.cnn.com/2010/04/19/news/companies/goldman_sachs_gap.fortune/?postversion=2010041914

Financial Crisis Inquiry Report (2011, January), Final Report of the National Commission on the Causes of the Financial and Economic Crisis in the United States, http://fcic.law.stanford.edu/report

Finch, Gavin, Hamilton, Scott (2013, March 6), BOE's King Says Government Should Split up RBS, Accept Loss, Bloomberg, http://www.bloomberg.com/news/2013-03-06/boe-s-king-calls-on-government-to-decisively-restructure-rbs.html

First National Bank of Englewood (1931), South Town Economist of Chicago, http://www.newspapers.com/newspage/3955863/

Flint, Douglas (2014), Are Markets Safer Now, Davos 2014, http://www.weforum.org/sessions/summary/forum-debate-are-markets-safer-now

FOMC (2008, March 10), Transcripts and Other Historical Materials: March 10, 2008 FOMC conference call, Federal Reserve, http://www.federalreserve.gov/monetarypolicy/fomchistorical2008.htm

FOMC (2008, March 18), Transcripts and Other Historical Materials: March 18, 2008 FOMC meeting, Federal Reserve, http://www.federalreserve.gov/monetarypolicy/fomchistorical2008.htm

Gallu, Joshua (2012, September 20), Libor-Like Manipulation Possible in Other Benchmarks, Iosco Says, Bloomberg, http://www.bloomberg.com/news/2012-09-19/libor-like-manipulation-possible-in-other-benchmarks-iosco-says.html

Gapper, John (2008, October 1), The Fatal Banker's Fall, http://www.ft.com/intl/cms/s/0/ccc6d456-8fd7-11dd-9890-0000779fd18c.html#axzz2vs2uiyup

Geithner, Timothy F. (2014), Stress Test: Reflections on Financial Crises, New York, NY: Crown Publishers

Gekko, Gordon (1987), Wall Street, http://spinnakr.com/blog/data-2/2013/03/44-more-of-the-best-data-quotes/

Gensler, Gary (2013, November), Quote, ZeroHedge.com, http://www.zerohedge.com/news/2013-11-14/quote-day-gary-batman-gensler

Gertler, Mark (2013), Interview, Richmond Fed, https://www.richmondfed.org/publications/research/econ_focus/2013/q4/pdf/interview.pdf

Gilbert, Mark (2014, August 1), *Portugal should let Espirito Santo fail*, Bloomberg View, http://www.bloombergview.com/articles/2014-08-01/portugal-should-let-espirito-santo-fail

U.S. Department of Justice (2014, July 14), Global Settlement with Citigroup for Misleading Investors about Securities Containing Toxic Mortgages: *Statement of Facts*, U.S. Department of Justice, http://www.justice.gov/iso/opa/resources/558201471413645397758.pdf

Goldman Sachs Global Investment Research (2014, November 13), Top of Mind, Goldman Sachs, https://360.gs.com/research/portal//?st=1&action=action.binary&d=18294469&fn=/document.pdf&a=ed623b89e3bd44e9a68a532d060125b2

Goldstein, Alexis (2013, June), The 'Intimidate the CTFC Act', Washington Post opinion column, http://www.washingtonpost.com/opinions/alexis-goldstein-the-intimidate-the-ctfc-act/2013/06/12/18451f48-d374-11e2-a73e-826d299ff459_story.html

Gorton, Gary (2009, May 9), Slapped in the Face by the Invisible Hand: Banking and the Panic of 2007, Atlanta Fed, http://www.frbatlanta.org/news/conferen/09fmc/gorton.pdf

Gorton, Gary, Metrick, Andrew (2010, November 9), Securitized Banking and Run on the Repo, NBER Working Paper No. 15223, http://www.nber.org/papers/w15223

Graiseley Properties Limited & Others v. Barclays Bank PLC (2014, March 21), Day 1 court transcript

Greenspan, Alan (2005, May 5), *Risk transfer and financial stability*, Federal Reserve Board, http://www.federalreserve.gov/Boarddocs/Speeches/2005/20050505/

Grieder, William (1987), Secrets of the Temple: How the Federal Reserve Runs the Country, New York, NY: Simon & Schuster, Inc.

Group of Thirty (2009, January), Financial Reform: A Framework for Financial Stability, Group of Thirty, http://www.group30.org/rpt_03.shtml

Group of Thirty Occasional Paper 79 (2009, April), Lessons Learned from Previous Banking Crisis: Sweden, Japan, Spain and Mexico, http://www.group30.org/images/PDF/OP79.pdf

Gwartney, James, Fike, Rosemarie (2014), Public Choice versus the Benevolent Omniscient Planner Model of Government: Evidence from Principles Textbooks, http://mailer.fsu.edu/~jgwartne/garnet-jgwartne/Documents/Gwartney%20Fike%20Public%20Choice.pdf

Haldane, Andrew (2012), Accounting for bank uncertainty, Bank of England speech, http://www.bankofengland.co.uk/publications/Pages/speeches/2012/540.aspx

Haldane, Andrew G. (2010, March), Fair value in foul weather, Bank of England speech http://www.bankofengland.co.uk/archive/Documents/historicpubs/speeches/2010/speech427.pdf

Halligan, Liam (2012, June 16), Bank 'throws kitchen sink' at credit problem, The Telegraph, http://www.telegraph.co.uk/finance/comment/9336435/Bank-throws-kitchen-sink-at-credit-problem.html

Harrington, Shannon D. (2014, August 5), *Banco Espirito Santo loan mystery confronts derivatives buyers*, Bloomberg, http://www.bloomberg.com/news/2014-08-05/banco-espirito-santo-loan-mystery-confronts-derivatives-buyers.html

Herring, Richard J. (1993), The Collapse of Continental Illinois National Bank and Trust Company: The Implications for Risk Management and Regulation, University of Pennsylvania, The Wharton School Financial Institutions Center, http://fic.wharton.upenn.edu/fic/case%20studies/continental%20full.pdf

Herz, Robert H. (2009, December 8), Remarks of Robert H. Herz, Chairman, Financial Accounting Standards Board, AICPA National Conference on Current SEC and PCAOB Developments, FASB, http://www.fasb.org/cs/BlobServer?blobkey=id&blobnocache=true&blobwhere=1175827024680&blobheader=application%2Fpdf&blobcol=urldata&blobtable=MungoBlobs

Hiltzik, Michael (2013, September 13), Big U.S. banks keeping door open to another financial crisis, Los Angeles Times, http://www.latimes.com/business/la-fi-hiltzik-20130915-column.html#ixzz2qmDTlMqn&page=1

Honohan, Patrick (1997, January), Banking System Failures in Developing and Transition Countries: Diagnosis and Prediction, Bank for International Settlements, Working Paper No. 39, http://www.bis.org/publ/work39.pdf

Pandit, Vikram (2011, September 23), Citigroup CEO Vikram Pandit speaks at 2011 Bretton Woods Committee International Council Meeting, Reuters Insider, http://insider.thomsonreuters.com/link.html?cn=share&cid=266045&shareToken=MzplMTE4ZDA1Yy0wM2ZmLTQxMmMtOWJmZi0yMmE5YTc4ODFjYTY%3D, speech transcription verification http://www.citigroup.com/citi/press/executive/110923a.htm

Hu, Henry (2012, May 30), Too Complex to Depict? Innovation, 'Pure Information,' and the SEC Disclosure Paradigm, Texas Law Review, Volume 90, Number 7, 2012, http://papers.ssrn.com/sol3/papers.cfm?abstract_id=2083708

IBM (2014), Watson Solutions, http://www-03.ibm.com/innovation/us/watson/watson_in_finance.shtml

Inquiry into Continental Illinois Corp. and Continental Illinois National Bank, Hearings before the Subcommittee on Financial Institution Supervision, Regulation and Insurance of the Committee on Banking, Finance and Urban Affairs, House of Representatives, Ninety-eighth Congress, September 18, 19 and October 4, 1984, Washington, DC: U.S. Government Printing Office, http://fraser.stlouisfed.org/docs/historical/house/house_cinb1984.pdf

Ivry, Bob, Keoun, Bradley, Kuntz, Phil (2011, November 27), Secret Fed Loans Gave Banks $13 Billion Undisclosed to Congress, Bloomberg, http://www.bloomberg.com/news/2011-11-28/secret-fed-loans-undisclosed-to-congress-gave-banks-13-billion-in-income.html

Jacobs, Jane (1969), *The Economy of Cities*, Random House: New York

Jenkins, Robert (2011, November 22), Lessons in lobbying, Bank of England, http://www.bankofengland.co.uk/publications/Documents/speeches/2011/speech533.pdf

Jenkins, Robert (2012, September 25), Regulators, financial industry and the problem of regulatory capture, published in Making Good Financial Regulations: Towards a Policy Response to Regulatory Capture, Bank of England, http://www.bankofengland.co.uk/publications/Documents/speeches/2012/speech603_foreword.pdf

Jessup, Col. Nathan R (1992), A Few Good Men, http://www.imdb.com/title/tt0104257/quotes

Kennedy, Simon, Benjamin, Matthew (2009, January 26), Darkness at Davos might hide Secrecy from Transparency Spotlight, http://www.bloomberg.com/apps/news?pid=newsarchive&sid=aawQ9NWNUsQw

Kidney, Jim (2014, March), Retirement Remarks, http://www.secunion.org/files/RetirementRemarks.pdf

Kix, Paul (2008, February), The Man Who Would Save the Economy, Boston Magazine, http://www.bostonmagazine.com/2008/01/the-man-who-would-save-the-economy

Kohn, Donald (2011, December 2), Speech: The Financial Policy Committee at the Bank of England, Bank of England, http://www.bankofengland.co.uk/publications/Documents/speeches/2011/speech536.pdf

Krastev, Ivan (2013, February), The Transparency Delusion, Eurozine, http://www.eurozine.com/articles/2013-02-01-krastev-en.html

Kroft, Steve (2014, March 30), Is the U.S. Stock Market Rigged?, CBS News, http://www.cbsnews.com/news/is-the-us-stock-market-rigged/

Krugman, Paul (2011), The Profession and the Crisis, Eastern Economic Journal (2011) 37, 307–312. doi:10.1057/eej.2011.8, http://www.palgrave-journals.com/eej/journal/v37/n3/full/eej20118a.html

Labaton Sucharow LLP (2013, July 16), Wall Street In Crisis: A Perfect Storm Looming, Labaton Sucharow LLP, http://www.labaton.com/en/about/press/Wall-Street-Professional-Survey-Reveals-Widespread-Misconduct.cfm

LaBelle, Huguette, Letter to the editor of The Economist, The Economist, http://www.economist.com/node/13272018

Lady FOHF (2014, August 3), *On Embracing Stupid*, Notes from the Hedge, http://ladyfohf.tumblr.com/post/93685456346/on-embracing-stupid

Langley, Monica (2012, May 18), Inside J.P. Morgan's Blunder, The Wall Street Journal, http://online.wsj.com/news/articles/SB10001424052702303448404577410341236847980?mod=WSJ_hp_MIDDLENexttoWhatsNewsSecond&mg=reno64-wsj&url=http%3A%2F%2Fonline.wsj.com%2Farticle%2FSB10001424052702303448404577410341236847980.html%3Fmod%3DWSJ_hp_MIDDLENexttoWhatsNewsSecond

Lanman, Scott, Keoun, Bradley (2011, December 11), No One Telling Who Took $586 Billion in Swaps With Fed Condoning Anonymity, Bloomberg, http://www.bloomberg.com/news/2011-12-11/no-one-says-who-took-586-billion-in-fed-swaps-done-in-anonymity.html

Leigh, Daniel, Igan, Deniz, Simon, John, Topalova, Petia (2012, April), World Economic Outlook: Growth Resuming, Dangers Remain, Chapter 3: Dealing with Household Debt, IMF, http://www.imf.org/external/pubs/ft/weo/2012/01/pdf/c3.pdf

Leighton-Jones, Phillipa (2014, November 21), RBS on what went wrong in the European Stress Tests, Wall Street Journal, http://blogs.wsj.com/moneybeat/2014/11/21/rbs-admits-mistake-in-european-stress-tests/

Lenzner, Robert (2013, October 24), Greenspan Finally Wakes Up To Fear and Eurphoria as Market Forces, Forbes, http://www.forbes.com/sites/robertlenzner/2013/10/24/what-alan-greenspan-learned-from-the-2008-crisis/

Levin, Carl (2014, November 20), Wall Street Bank Involvement with Physical Commodities, Opening Statement for Permanent Subcommittee on Investigations, http://www.levin.senate.gov/newsroom/speeches/speech/levin-opening-statement-permanent-subcommittee-on-investigations-hearing-wall-street-bank-involvement-with-physical-commodities

Lucchetti, Aaron (2010, January 21), Goldman Subprime Fallout hits Home in South Carolina, Wall Street Journal, http://online.wsj.com/news/articles/SB10001424052748703405704575015482366919468

Lyons, Paul, Sheridan, Gavin (2013, September 15), New Anglo Tapes: 'We've F**King let the world down', Independent.IE, http://www.independent.ie/business/world/new-anglo-tapes-weve-fking-let-the-world-down-29580091.html

MacLellan, Kylie (2011, November 14), Bank's Haldane says banks still too much of a black box, Reuters, http://uk.reuters.com/article/2011/11/14/uk-banks-haldane-idUKTRE7AD29D20111114

McCreevy, Charlie (2008, June 16), Regulating in a Global Market, press release by the European Commissioner for Internal Market and Services, European Commission, http://europa.eu/rapid/press-release_SPEECH-08-334_de.htm?locale=de%20/

McCreevy, Charlie (2009, June), Future industry landscape, lessons from the market crisis, press release by European Commissioner for Internal Market and Services, European Commission, http://europa.eu/rapid/press-release_SPEECH-09-323_en.htm?locale=en

McGrane, Victoria, Trindle, Jamila (2012, May 21), Trading Misstep For Bank Opens Door to New Rules, The Wall Street Journal, http://online.wsj.com/news/articles/SB10001424052702304791704577418610977819788?mod=dist_smartbrief&mg=reno64-wsj&url=http%3A%2F%2Fonline.wsj.com%2Farticle%2FSB10001424052702304791704577418610977819788.html%3Fmod%3Ddist_smartbrief

McGrane, Victoria (2014, November 21), N.Y. Fed President Dudley: I'm More of a Fire Warden, Not a Cop on the Beat, Wall Street Journal, http://blogs.wsj.com/economics/2014/11/21/n-y-fed-president-dudley-im-more-of-a-fire-warden-not-a-cop-on-the-beat/

McLeay, Michael, Radia, Amar, Thomas, Ryland (2014), *Money Creation in the Modern Economy*, Bank of England Quarterly Bulletin 2014 Q1, Bank of England, http://www.bankofengland.co.uk/publications/documents/quarterlybulletin/2014/qb14q1prereleasemoneycreation.pdf

Merrill Lynch (2008, November18), Presentation to the Irish Department of Finance Discussion Materials, Merrill Lynch, https://docs.google.com/file/d/0B_p5wXj7Q88MZnpSUG1pQy1lR28/edit

Miles, David, Scott, Andrew (2012), Macroeconomics: Understanding the Wealth of Nations, London, England: Wiley

Commission of Investigation into the Banking Sector in Ireland (2011, March), Report: Misjudging Risk: Causes of the Systemic Banking Crisis in Ireland, Commission of Investigation into the Banking Sector in Ireland, http://www.bankinginquiry.gov.ie/Documents/Misjuding%20Risk%20-%20Causes%20of%20the%20Systemic%20Banking%20Crisis%20in%20Ireland.pdf

Mitchell, Russ (2012, Fall), A Force at the Fed, BerkeleyHass, http://www.haas.berkeley.edu/groups/pubs/berkeleyhaas/fall2012/feature01.html

Miu, Jason (2008, April 11), NY Fed MarketSource Weekly Market Review, NY Fed, http://www.newyorkfed.org/newsevents/news/markets/2012/libor/April_11_2008_Internal_FRBNY_Weekly_Market_Review.pdf

Moore, Heidi (2014), pic.twitter.com/BuaRId4G80

Morgenson, Gretchen, Story, Louise (2011, April 13), Naming Culprits in the Financial Crisis, NY Times, http://www.nytimes.com/2011/04/14/business/14crisis.html?ref=business&_r=0

Federal Reserve Bank of New York (2012, July 13), New York Fed Responds to Congressional Request for Information on Barclays — LIBOR Matter, Federal Reserve Bank of New York, http://www.newyorkfed.org/newsevents/news/markets/2012/Barclays_LIBOR_Matter.html

Nielsen, Arthur C., quote, http://spinnakr.com/blog/data-2/2013/03/44-more-of-the-best-data-quotes/

Norris, Floyd (2009, November 27), Keeping Derivatives in the Dark, NY Times, http://www.nytimes.com/2009/11/27/business/27norris.html?_r=0&pagewanted=all

Nouy, Danièle (2014, February 9), transcript of interview, Financial Times, http://www.ft.com/intl/cms/s/0/3e0420e2-91a8-11e3-adde-00144feab7de.html#axzz2tmCPwihU

Federal Reserve Bank of New York (2012, July 13), NY Fed's recommendations to fix Libor, Federal Reserve Bank of New York, http://www.newyorkfed.org/newsevents/news/markets/2012/libor/June_1_2008_LIBOR_recommendations.pdf

O'Donnell, Paul (2014, January 28), How Wall Street Is Redefining Bipartisanship, Washingtonian Capital Comment, http://www.washingtonian.com/blogs/capitalcomment/the-hill/how-wall-street-is-redefining-bipartisanship.php#.UufnF_PF0L4.twitter

O'Neill, Paul (2009, March 16), Banks must show U.S. the money, CNN, http://www.cnn.com/2009/US/03/16/oneill.qanda/index.html?iref=nextin

Osborne, Alistair (2012, July 2), Bank forecasts futile now all trust has gone, says analyst, The Telegraph, http://www.telegraph.co.uk/finance/newsbysector/banksandfinance/9371082/Bank-forecasts-futile-now-all-trust-has-gone-says-analyst.html

Panchuk, Kerri Ann (2012, September 11), Cost of housing meltdown rivals GDP: MBA conference, HousingWire, http://www.housingwire.com/articles/cost-housing-meltdown-rivals-gdp-mba-conference

Parsons, Bob, http://spinnakr.com/blog/data-2/2013/03/44-more-of-the-best-data-quotes/

Pearlstein, Steven (2008, December 12), response to question on his blog, The Washington Post, http://www.washingtonpost.com/wp-dyn/content/discussion/2008/12/09/DI2008120901766.html

Pecora Commission, Wikipedia, http://en.wikipedia.org/wiki/Pecora_Commission

Post-Crash Economics Society at the University of Manchester (2014), Economics, Education and Unlearning, http://www.scribd.com/doc/220136144/Economics-Education-and-Unlearning

President's Working Group on Financial Markets (2008, March 13), *Policy Statement on Financial Market Developments*, US Treasury, http://www.treasury.gov/resource-center/fin-mkts/Documents/pwgpolicystatemktturmoil_03122008.pdf

Prins, Nomi (2014), All the Presidents' Bankers: The hidden alliances that drive American power, New York, NY: Nation Books

Protess, Ben (2011, May 24), Warren and Republicans Spar Over Bureau's Power, NY Times Dealbook, http://dealbook.nytimes.com/2011/05/24/warren-and-g-o-p-lawmakers-spar-over-bureaus-power/?_php=true&_type=blogs&_r=0

Purvis, Andrew (2008, September 24), Sweden's Model Approach to Financial Disaster, Time Magazine, http://content.time.com/time/business/article/0,8599,1843659,00.html

Puzzanghera, Jim (2010, October 26), Q&A with Elizabeth Warren: 'the changes are starting now', Los Angeles Times, http://articles.latimes.com/2010/oct/26/business/la-fi-elizabeth-warren-20101027

Reed, Jack (2009, June 16), Floor Statement Introducing the Private Fund Transparency Act, Senator Reed's official website, http://www.reed.senate.gov/news/speech/floor-statement-introducing-the-private-fund-transparency-act-

Report from the Economist Intelligence Unit and CFA Institute (2013), A Crisis of Culture: Valuing Ethics and Knowledge in Financial Services, CFA Institute, http://www.cfainstitute.org/about/research/surveys/Documents/crisis_of_culture_report.pdf

Report of the Financial Stability Board Enhanced Disclosure Task Force (2012, October 29), Enhancing the Risk Disclosures of Banks: http://www.financialstabilityboard.org/publications/r_121029.pdf

Roosevelt, Franklin D. (1933, March 12), First Fireside Chat, http://www.berfrois.com/2012/11/fireside/

Roth, Daniel (2009, February 23), Road Map for Financial Recovery: Radical Transparency Now, Wired Magazine, http://archive.wired.com/techbiz/it/magazine/17-03/wp_reboot?currentPage=all

Salas, Caroline (2007, December 4), Subprime Seizure Solution May Be in Hospital Bills, Bloomberg, http://www.bloomberg.com/apps/news?pid=newsarchive&sid=a_gBF9OjtfQI

Schwabel, Dan (2013, April 16), John Gersema: How Women Will Rule the Future of Work, Forbes, http://www.forbes.com/sites/danschawbel/2013/04/16/john-gerzema-how-women-will-rule-the-future-of-work/

Schwartzkopff, Frances (2014, July 30), *Bank risks hidden from investors to be disclosed in Sweden*, Bloomberg, http://www.bloomberg.com/news/2014-07-30/sweden-set-to-disclose-bank-risks-most-investors-can-t-discern.html

Schwartzkopff, Frances (2014, August 8), *Bank Capital Race Not Enough for Basel as Nordics Break Away*, Bloomberg, http://www.bloomberg.com/news/2014-08-08/banks-hoarding-capital-not-enough-for-basel-as-nordics-raise-bar.html

SEC Administrative Proceeding File No. 3-15982 (2014, July 24), *SEC v Morgan Stanley and Co., LLC*, SEC, http://www.sec.gov/litigation/admin/2014/33-9617.pdf

SEC press release (2014, July 24), *Morgan Stanley to Pay $275 Million for Misleading Investors in Subprime RMBS Offerings*, SEC, http://www.sec.gov/News/PressRelease/Detail/PressRelease/1370542355594#.U9E6K2NgC7Z

Sender, Henry (2010, March 18), HSBC drew up exit plans amid liquidity fears, Financial Times, http://www.ft.com/intl/cms/s/0/572c9c3a-32ba-11df-a767-00144feabdc0.html#axzz2n1XHTzHB

Senior Supervisors Group (2014, January 15), Progress Report on Counterparty Data, New York Fed, http://www.newyorkfed.org/newsevents/news/banking/2014/SSG_Progress_Report_on_Counterparty_January2014.pdf

Shirakawa, Masaaki, My Intellectual Journey in Central Banking, BIS Papers No. 77, https://www.bis.org/publ/bppdf/bispap77e.pdf

Silber, William L. (2009, July), Why Did FDR's Bank Holiday Succeed, Federal Reserve Bank of New York Economic Policy Review, Volume 15, Number 1, pages 19-30, Federal Reserve Bank of New York, http://www.newyorkfed.org/research/epr/2009/EPRvol15n1.pdf

Smith, Helena (2012, December 17), Libor founder Minos Zombanakis condemns rate manipulators, The Guardian, http://www.theguardian.com/business/2012/dec/17/libor-minos-zombanakis

Smith, Randall (2007, November 9), How a Good Subprime Call Came to Hurt Morgan Stanley, Wall Street Journal, http://online.wsj.com/news/articles/SB119456736420887284

Solomon, Deborah (2009, May 14), Crash Course: Questions for Myron Scholes, NY Times, http://www.nytimes.com/2009/05/17/magazine/17wwln-q4-t.html

Sorkin, Andrew Ross (2011, November 14), One Secret Buffett Gets to Keep, NY Times Dealbook, http://dealbook.nytimes.com/2011/11/14/one-secret-buffett-gets-to-keep/?ref=business

Spiegel, Peter, March 25, 2015 Financial Times article, Cyprus rescue signals new line on bailouts, http://www.ft.com/intl/cms/s/0/68c9c18e-955e-11e2-a151-00144feabdc0.html?siteedition=intl#axzz35anudA8Y

St. Anthony, Neal (2014, April 13), "Bair says bailouts saved banks, not the economy", StarTribune, http://www.startribune.com/business/254991831.html

Swinford, Steven, Wilson, Harry (2012, September 26), RBS traders boasted of Libor 'cartel', The Telegraph, http://www.telegraph.co.uk/finance/newsbysector/banksandfinance/9568087/RBS-traders-boasted-of-Libor-cartel.html

Taylor, Rob (2012, February 24), The Truth is in Lloyds's latest results presentation … somewhere, The Guardian, http://www.theguardian.com/business/blog/2012/feb/24/truth-lloyds-results-somewhere

Testimony of Vickie A. Tillman, Executive Vice President, Standard & Poor's Credit Market Services, Before the Committee on Banking, Housing and Urban Affairs, United States Senate (2007, September 26), http://www.banking.senate.gov/public/index.cfm?FuseAction=Files.View&FileStore_id=e8329689-cdca-4a9e-b927-bb744f58792f

Tett, Gillian (2008, October 1), Insight: Seeds sown in murky finance, Financial Times, http://www.ft.com/cms/s/0/a48af6e2-8fd3-11dd-9890-0000779fd18c.html

Tett, Gillian (2012, March 8), Guiding light need to cut through data fog, Financial Times, http://www.ft.com/intl/cms/s/0/31f4e2e6-692d-11e1-956a-00144feabdc0.html

The Economist (2010, March 31), Crisis Costs: Big Numbers, The Economist, http://www.economist.com/blogs/freeexchange/2010/03/crisis_costs

The Economist (2012, August 3), in comments to A dying breed: remembering Gore Vidal, http://www.economist.com/blogs/prospero/2012/08/remembering-gore-vidal

The Editors (2012, July 23), Saying Goodbye to Libor Won't Be Easy, but It's Necessary, Bloomberg View, http://www.bloombergview.com/articles/2012-07-23/saying-goodbye-to-libor-won-t-be-easy-but-it-s-necessary

The Limerick King (2014, July 30), email

Thornton, Daniel L. (2009), What the Libor-OIS Spread Says, Economic Synopses, Number 24, Federal Reserve Bank of St. Louis, http://research.stlouisfed.org/publications/es/09/ES0924.pdf

Federal Reserve Bank of New York (2012, July 13), Tim Geithner e-mail to Mervyn King with recommendations to fix Libor, Federal Reserve Bank of New York, http://www.newyorkfed.org/newsevents/news/markets/2012/libor/June_1_2008_LIBOR_recommendations.pdf

TYI, LLC response to the FDIC Safe Harbor Proposal (2010, February), *Treatment by the Federal Deposit Insurance Corporation as Conservator or Receiver of Financial Assets Transferred by an Insured Depository Institution in Connection with a Securitization or Participation After March 31, 2010 (RIN # 3064 – AD55)*, https://docs.google.com/viewer?a=v&pid=sites&srcid=dHlpbGxjLmNvbXx3d3d8Z3g6MzY3ODRkNWViMzFjNjU4NQ, page 14

U.K. Financial Services Authority (2011, December), The failure of the Royal Bank of Scotland, FSA, http://www.fsa.gov.uk/pubs/other/rbs.pdf

U.S. Department of Justice (2013, November 19), Press Release announcing JPMorgan's mortgage-backed securities settlement, U.S. Department of Justice, http://www.justice.gov/opa/pr/2013/November/13-ag-1237.html

U.S. Department of Justice (2013, November 19), Statement of Facts on JPMorgan's mortgage-backed securities settlement, U.S. Department of Justice, http://www.justice.gov/iso/opa/resources/94320131119151031990622.pdf

U.S. Senate Permanent Subcommittee on Investigations (2011, April 13), Wall Street and the Financial Crisis: Anatomy of a Financial Collapse, http://www.hsgac.senate.gov//imo/media/doc/Financial_Crisis/FinancialCrisisReport.pdf?attempt=2

Uchitelle, Louis (2002, July 28), Broken System? Tweak It, They Say, NY Times, http://www.nytimes.com/2002/07/28/business/broken-system-tweak-it-they-say.html

U.S. Senate Permanent Subcommittee on Investigations (2013, March 15), JPMorgan Chase Whale Trades: A Case History of Derivatives Risks and Abuses, http://www.hsgac.senate.gov/subcommittees/investigations/hearings/chase-whale-trades-a-case-history-of-derivatives-risks-and-abuses

US Treasury, May 7, 2009 Statement from Treasury Secretary Tim Geithner Regarding the Treasury Capital Assistance Program and the Supervisory

Capital Assessment Program, US Treasury, http://www.treasury.gov/press-center/press-releases/Pages/tg123.aspx

Vaughan, Liam (2011, November 9), Financial Alchemy Foils Capital Rules as Banks Redefine Risk, Bloomberg, http://www.bloomberg.com/news/2011-11-09/financial-alchemy-undercuts-capital-regime-as-european-banks-redefine-risk.html

Vaughan, Liam, Finch, Gavin (2012, December 13), Secret Libor Transcripts Expose Trader Rate-Manipulation, Bloomberg, http://www.bloomberg.com/news/2012-12-13/rigged-libor-with-police-nearby-shows-flaw-of-light-touch.html

Vaughan, Liam, Finch, Gavin (2012, June 28), Libor Guardians Said to Resist Changes to Broken Rate, Bloomberg, http://www.bloomberg.com/news/2012-06-25/libor-guardians-said-to-resist-changes-to-broken-benchmark-rate.html

Wagner, Daniel, Fitzgerald, Alison (2014), The Center for Public Integrity Meet the Banking Caucus, Wall Street's Secret Weapon in Washington, Public Integrity.Org, http://www.publicintegrity.org/2014/04/24/14595/meet-banking-caucus-wall-streets-secret-weapon-washington?utm_source=email&utm_campaign=watchdog&utm_medium=publici-email

Warren, Elizabeth (2013, November 7), Remarks by Senator Elizabeth Warren, National Consumer Law Center, Consumer Rights Litigation Conference, http://www.masslive.com/politics/index.ssf/2013/11/sen_elizabeth_warren_addresses.html

Weidmann, Jens (2014, April 7), Stable banks for a Stable Europe, speech at the 20th German Banking Congress, Berlin, BIS, http://www.bis.org/review/r140415b.htm?utm_content=buffer8af00&utm_medium=social&utm_source=twitter.com&utm_campaign=buffer

Weil, Jonathan (2013, January 17), Jamie Dimon offers the illusion of transparency, BloombergView, http://www.bloombergview.com/articles/2013-01-17/jpmorgan-s-jamie-dimon-offers-illusion-of-transparency

Weiner, Jeff, Business Insider, http://www.businessinsider.com/linkedin-employee-values-2013-2

Whalen, Christopher (2012, July 12), The Institutional Risk Analyst, http://us1.institutionalriskanalytics.com/pub/IRAMain.asp

White, Mary Jo (2013, October 15), The Path Forward on Disclosure, SEC, http://www.sec.gov/News/Speech/Detail/Speech/1370539878806

White, Mary Jo (2013, October 3), 14th Annual A.A. Sommer, Jr. Corporate Securities and Financial Law Lecture, SEC, http://www.sec.gov/News/Speech/Detail/Speech/1370539864016

White, Phoebe, Yorulmazer, Tanju (2014, April 21), Bank Resolution Concepts, Trade-offs, and Changes in Practices, FRBNY Economic Policy Review, http://www.ny.frb.org/research/epr/2014/1403whit.html

WikiLeaks cable (2009, October 9), The Bank Guarantee: An Irish Solution to an Irish Problem, http://www.cablegatesearch.net/cable.php?id=08DUBLIN556&q=kevin-cardiff

WikiLeaks via The Guardian (2010, December 13), The U.S. Embassy cables: the documents, The Guardian, http://www.theguardian.com/world/us-embassy-cables-documents/146196

Williams, Paul (2013, June 24), Inside Anglo: the secret recordings, http://www.independent.ie/business/irish/inside-anglo-the-secret-recordings-29366837.html, Transcripts of Anglo Irish Bank tapes (2013, September 22), http://www.passionforliberty.com/2013/09/22/anglo-irish-bank-tapes-the-transcripts/

Wilson, Harry (2012, February 23), RBS 'deliberately' doubled losses to £2bn in 'Alice in Wonderland' accounting, The Telegraph, http://www.telegraph.co.uk/finance/newsbysector/banksandfinance/9101879/RBS-deliberately-doubled-losses-to-2bn-in-Alice-in-Wonderland-accounting.html

Wolf, Martin (2013, September 15), 'Too big to fail' is still a threat to the financial system, Financial Times, http://www.ft.com/intl/cms/s/0/f755c450-c3c2-11e3-870b-00144feabdc0.html?ftcamp=published_links%2Frss%2Fcomment_columnists_martin-wolf%2Ffeed%2F%2Fproduct&siteedition=intl#axzz2yygKrjAT

Woodson, Carter Godwin (2000), The Mis-education of the Negro, pages 83-84, USA: African American Images.

Zibel, Alan, Holzer, Jessica (2012, June 19), Dimon Takes Heat on Hill. The Wall Street Journal, http://online.wsj.com/news/articles/SB10001424052702303703004577476483221472646?mod=WSJ_hp_LEFTWhatsNewsCollection&mg=reno64-wsj&url=http%3A%2F%2Fonline.wsj.com%2Farticle%2FSB10001424052702303703004577476483221472646.html%3Fmod%3DWSJ_hp_LEFTWhatsNewsCollection

Zumbrun, Joshua, Hopkins, Cheyenne (2013, November 19), Yellen Defends QE as Economic Benefit in Letter to Senator, Bloomberg, http://www.bloomberg.com/news/print/2013-11-19/fed-s-yellen-defends-qe-as-economic-benefit-in-letter-to-senator.html

Zumbrun, Joshua, Kearns, Jeff (2014, January 7), Yellen's Record-low Senate Support Reflects Fed's Politicalization, Bloomberg, http://www.bloomberg.com/news/2014-01-07/yellen-s-record-low-senate-support-reflects-fed-s-politicization.html

About the Author

Mr. Field is the Director of the Institute for Financial Transparency, an organization focused on bringing valuation transparency to all the opaque corners of the financial system and the sponsor of the Transparency Label Initiative™.

Since the mid-90s, he has been a leader in defining and implementing transparency in the structured finance industry. Mr. Field designed, developed and patented a low cost information system to handle all of the complexity involved in bringing transparency about the performance of the collateral underlying each structured finance deal to all market participants. The transparency solution involves providing easily accessible, standardized loan level collateral data on an observable event basis over the life of each deal. The solution can be provided for each individual asset type that has been used to support an ABS security.

In April 2008, Mr. Field wrote a Learning Curve column for Total Securitization that described the gold standard for transparency for structured finance securities.

Subsequently, Mr. Field consulted with the National Association of Insurance Commissioners on their July 2012 white paper on financing home ownership. In this paper he discussed the need for a data warehouse. Fannie Mae and Freddie Mac are in the process of building this data warehouse. It is called the Common Securitization Solutions LLC [As the beaver said to the rabbit looking down on the Hoover Dam, "I didn't build it all by myself, but it is based on an idea of mine."].

Earlier in his career, he worked as an Assistant Vice President for First Bank System and as a Research Assistant at the Federal Reserve Board. Mr. Field has an MBA from the J.L. Kellogg Graduate School of Management at Northwestern University and a B.A. in Economics and Political Science from Yale University.

Index

C

D

E

F

G

M

N

O

P

R

S

T

U

V

W

Y

Z

Made in the USA
Columbia, SC
07 July 2020

13405258R00346